Gays and Lesbians
in Mainstream Cinema

ALSO BY
JAMES ROBERT PARISH

The Fox Girls (1972)
The RKO Gals (1972)
Good Dames (1973)
The Slapstick Queens (1974)
The Elvis Presley Scrapbook (1976)
The Jeanette MacDonald Story (1976)
The Tough Guys (1976)
The Hollywood Beauties (1978)
The Great Combat Pictures (1990)
The Great Cop Pictures (1990)
Prison Pictures from Hollywood (McFarland, 1991)
The Hollywood Death Book (1992)
Black Action Pictures from Hollywood (McFarland, 1992)
Prostitution in Hollywood Films (McFarland, 1992)
Let's Talk! America's Favorite Talk Show Hosts (1993)
The New Country Music Stars (1993)
— and others —

Gays and Lesbians in Mainstream Cinema

*Plots, Critiques, Casts and
Credits for 272 Theatrical and
Made-for-Television Hollywood Releases*

by JAMES ROBERT PARISH

McFarland & Company, Inc., Publishers
Jefferson, North Carolina, and London

British Library Cataloguing-in-Publication data are available

Library of Congress Cataloguing-in-Publication Data

Parish, James Robert.
    Gays and lesbians in mainstream cinema : plots, critiques, casts
and credits for 272 theatrical and made-for-television Hollywood
releases / by James Robert Parish.
      p. cm.
    Includes index.
    ISBN 0-89950-791-3 (lib. bdg. : 50# alk. paper) ∞
    1. Homosexuality in motion pictures. 2. Motion pictures—United
States—Catalogs. 3. Motion pictures—United States—Plots, themes,
etc. I. Title.
PN1995.9.H55P37   1993
791.43′653—dc20
                                        92-56678
                                          CIP

Manufactured in the United States of America

McFarland & Company, Inc., Publishers
  Box 611, Jefferson, North Carolina 28640

For Elizabeth Taylor,
who has done so much
to bring people together with understanding,
and to advance the cause of AIDS research

Acknowledgments

I gratefully acknowledge the Academy of Motion Picture Arts & Sciences: Center for Motion Picture Study; Beverly Hills Public Library; Kathy Bartels; George Baxt; Jeffrey L. Carrier; John Cocchi; Steve Eberly; Eddie Brandt's Saturday Matinee (Donovan Brandt); Film Favorites (Karen Martin); Alex Gildzen; Steve Grossman; Ken Hanke; Kim Holston; Jane Klain; Larry Edmunds Book Store (Peter Bateman); Alvin H. Marill; Lee Mattson; Doug McClelland; Jim Meyer; Michael R. Pitts; Howard H. Prouty; Margie Schultz; Arleen Schwartz; Les Spindle; Don Stanke; Kevin Sweeney; Vincent Terrace; Video West.

Special appreciation goes to the late Lee Beaupre, Stuart Byron and Addison Verrill for long-ago discussions which provided the genesis for this book.

And finally to my editorial consultant, Allan Taylor.

Contents

Chronology

1961
The Children's Hour
The Roman Spring of Mrs. Stone

1962
Advise and Consent
Billy Budd
No Exit
A View from the Bridge
Walk on the Wild Side

1963
The Balcony
The Haunting

1964
Becket
The Best Man
Lilith
The Night of the Iguana

1965
Bus Riley's Back in Town
Inside Daisy Clover
The Loved One
The Pawnbroker
Sylvia
Who Killed Teddy Bear?

1966
The Chelsea Girls
Deathwatch
The Group
Seven Women

1967
Caprice
The Incident
Reflections in a Golden Eye
Tony Rome
Valley of the Dolls
Wild in the Streets

1968
The Boston Strangler
The Detective
Flesh
The Fox
The Killing of Sister George
The Legend of Lylah Clare
Lonesome Cowboys
No Way to Treat a Lady
P.J.
Petulia
The Producers
Rachel, Rachel
The Sergeant

1969
Chastity
The Gay Deceivers
Justine
Midnight Cowboy
Riot
Uptight

1970
The Adventurers
Beyond the Valley of the Dolls
The Boys in the Band
Cover Me Babe
Five Easy Pieces
The Grasshopper
Guess What We Learned in School
    Today?
The Kremlin Letter
Little Big Man
Myra Breckinridge
The Private Life of Sherlock Holmes
Puzzle of a Downfall Child
Something for Everyone
Tell Me That You Love Me, Junie
    Moon
There Was a Crooked Man
Trash
Where's Poppa?

1971
The Anderson Tapes
The Big Doll House
Doctors' Wives
Fortune and Men's Eyes
Some of My Best Friends Are...

10

1980
American Gigolo
Cruising
Fame
Happy Birthday, Gemini
The Last Married Couple in America
Marilyn: The Untold Story
The Shadow Box
Stir Crazy
Windows

1981
By Design
The Fan
Inmates: A Love Story
Knightriders
Only When I Laugh
Sidney Shorr: A Girl's Best Friend
Zorro, the Gay Blade

1982
Deathtrap
Forty Deuce
Love Child
Making Love
Partners
Personal Best
Victor/Victoria

1983
The Hunger
Lianna
Silkwood
Streamers
To Be or Not to Be
Trackdown: Finding the Goodbar
    Killer
Without a Trace

1984
Angel
The Bostonians
Garbo Talks
The Glitter Dome
The Hotel New Hampshire
Mass Appeal

Meatballs: Part II
Mike's Murder
Protocol

1985
After Hours
Avenging Angel
Buddies
A Chorus Line
Consenting Adult
Desert Hearts
An Early Frost
Kiss of the Spider Woman
The Naked Cage
Once Bitten
Rustlers' Rhapsody
To Live and Die in L.A.

1986
As Is
The Boys Next Door
The Hitcher
My Two Loves
Parting Glances
Reform School Girls
Vendetta

1987
Beyond Therapy
Black Widow
Distortions
Mannequin
Slammer Girls
Too Outrageous

1988
Angel III: The Final Chapter
Haunted Summer
Liberace
Liberace: Behind the Music
Lust for Freedom
Penitentiary III
Torch Song Trilogy

1989
Biloxi Blues

Introduction

By its very definition, a minority group is not part of the "norm" and, as such, is generally subject to the whims of the ruling majority. Such minorities (whether based on race, religion, sex, creed, lifestyle, etc.) have often been the victims of discrimination, bred from centuries-old prejudices, and have been treated poorly by both the law and its enforcers and the public at large. In the twentieth century, such oppressed minorities have included homosexuals, blacks, women, Jews, and various political groups and parties. Regarding homosexuality, ironically just as the gay lifestyle was coming out of the cultural closet in the 1960s and 1970s and finding greater acceptance from mainstream society, along came AIDS. Because this global disaster was labeled a "gay" disease, the repercussions of AIDS had a tremendous and distinctive backlash on the advances made by the gay cause both in real life and on screen. As a result, this epidemic has forced many homosexuals back into the closet or into a posture of never coming out, as well as reinstituting and or reinforcing the heterosexual world's negative images of homosexuality. This fluctuating social history is reflected in how homosexuals and the gay lifestyle have been depicted — whether reviled, exploited or celebrated — in the creative arts in America and elsewhere.

As noted, because the gay lifestyle is a minority one, its presentation on screen has been subject to the politics of majority versus minority rule. Along with denying or ignoring the group's existence, one major element of antiminority discrimination is the fostering of negative stereotypes. One assumption in this discrimination is that the eccentric attitudes, appearance and behavior of a few within the minority represent the whole minority. As such, it is reasoned, these "outlandish" people with a different sexual orientation are safe to hold up to ridicule and scorn and to brand with a variety of epithets (faggot, swish, dyke, fairy, queen, queer, etc.). Such ridicule helps to justify the fears of the majority that they could be tainted, harmed or diluted by the underdogs. The behavior of scornful majorities can be seen as relevant when one examines the flow of twentieth century films and, in particular, those that have dared or bothered to deal with homosexuality.

One can observe an almost consistently steady stream of nonrepresentational homosexual characters who are extremely effeminate (e.g., the characters played by Franklin Pangborn, Edward Everett Horton, Eric Blore and Grady Sutton in the 1930s, right up to main characters in *Norman... Is That You?*, 1976; *To Be or Not to Be*, 1983; *Torch Song Trilogy*, 1988 and *Mannequin Two: On the Move*, 1991). Because these gay characters are so easy to identify and are so obviously unconventional, they are the targets of insensitive jokes and titillation. This on-screen attitude would continue well into the 1970s, especially in police/detective dramas (e.g., *P.J.*, 1968; *The Laughing Policeman*, 1973; *Busting*, 1974; *Freebie and the Bean*, 1974, and *Partners*, 1982). Sometimes, such persons were offered as comic relief in the form of the heroine's best (girl)friend (e.g., *Inside Daisy Clover*, 1965; *Funny Lady*, 1974; *Only When I Laugh*, 1981, and *Frankie & Johnny*, 1991) or as a way of making clear to the viewer that the leading character was indeed very straight (e.g., *Scarecrow*, 1973; *Sheila Levine Is Dead and Living in New York*, 1975 and *Girlfriends*, 1978).

A contrasting trend in the presentation of homosexuals on camera can be found in the many American-made features in which on-screen corruptors and (serial) murderers happen to be gay. Such repeated appearances of homicidal homosexuals helped moviegoers to assume that homosexuality itself leads to deadly antisocial behavior or vice versa (e.g., *Rope*, 1948; *Strangers on a Train*, 1951; *Compulsion*, 1959; *The Detective*, 1968; *Looking for Mr. Goodbar*, 1977; *Cruising*, 1980; *Windows*; 1980; *The Fan*, 1981; *A Bump in the Night*, 1991; *Basic Instinct*, 1992; *The Living End*, 1992; *Swoon*, 1992).

On screen, in between these stereotypical poles of buffoons and vicious villains are the ineffectual gays and lesbians, who either abandon their misguided practices or are depicted as pathetic, repressed figures. Often they are blackmailed or commit suicide, but at the least they suffer angst because they are so "abnormal" in their corrupting of "decent" human beings. (Note *Camille*, 1936; *Tea and Sympathy*, 1956; *The Children's Hour,* 1961; *Advise and Consent*, 1962; *Bus Riley's Back in Town*, 1965; *7 Women*, 1965; *The Incident*, 1967; *Rachel, Rachel*, 1968; *The Sergeant*, 1968; *The Last of Sheila*, 1973; *Ode to Billy Joe*, 1976; *A Different Story*, 1978; *Silkwood*, 1983; *Consenting Adult*, 1985; *Liberace*, 1988 and *My Own Private Idaho*, 1991.)

Portraying a major character in a film as gay or bisexual was thought to lend an exploitative plot twist to a standard story or at least provide a titillating, sophisticated and often voyeuristic tone to the proceedings (e.g., *Spartacus,* 1960; *The Group,* 1966; *Petulia,* 1968; *The Adventurers,* 1970; *Something for Everyone,* 1970; *Doctors' Wives,* 1971; *Cabaret,* 1972; *They Only Kill Their Master,* 1972; *Jacqueline Susann's Once Is Not Enough,* 1975, *California Suite,* 1978; *Deathtrap,* 1982; *Rock Hudson,* 1990; *Poison Ivy,* 1992). This category also includes exposés of the well known (real or literary) who had spent much or all of their existences hiding the truth of their homosexuality or bisexuality (e.g., *Flesh Gordon,* 1974; *James Dean,* 1976; *Valentino,* 1977; *The Private Files of J. Edgar Hoover,* 1978; *Sergeant Matlovich Vs. the U.S. Air Force,* 1978; *Marilyn: The Untold Story,* 1980; *The Private Life of Sherlock Holmes,* 1980, *Zorro, the Gay Blade,* 1981; *Haunted Summer,* 1988; *Liberace,* 1988; *Liberace: Behind the Music,* 1988; and *Rock Hudson,* 1990).

All these negative examples stand in large contrast to the relatively few features which have presented gays as multidimensional characters or role models (e.g., *A Very Natural Thing,* 1973; *Outrageous!,* 1977; *Lianna,* 1983; *An Early Frost,* 1985; Parting Glances, 1986; *Internal Affairs,* 1990; *Long Time Companion,* 1990; *Queens Logic,* 1991; *Fried Green Tomatoes,* 1991 and *Doing Time on Maple Drive,* 1992).

Over time, as Hollywood sought to a degree to liberalize its depiction of gays and lesbians, there were many intertwining influences at work. Through the years, the impact of more free-thinking moviemakers abroad (especially in Germany, France, and England) was a strong factor. Foreign films have long dealt with homosexuality far more candidly and casually than American pictures, and the distribution of these imports in the United States has had an important effect in introducing domestic filmgoers to a broader tolerance of the subject. This, in turn, has induced United States filmmakers to become more sophisticated and open in their handling of the subject.

Landmark foreign productions have included *Pandora's Box* (1929); *Mädchen in Uniform* (1931); *Zero de Conduite* (1933); *Un Chant d'Amour* (1947); *Oscar Wilde* (1960); *A Taste of Honey* (1961); *Victim* (1961); *The Servant* (1963); *Darling* (1965); *The Leather Boys* (1964); *Persona* (1966); *If* (1968); *Teorema* (1968); *Death in Venice* (1971); *Sunday, Bloody Sunday* (1971); *X, Y & Zee* (1971); *Die Bitteren Tränen der Petra von Kant* (1972); *Butley* (1974); *Faustrecht der Freiheit* (1975); *The Consequence* (1977); *La Cage aux Folles* (1978); *Taxi Zum Klo* (1980); *Querelle* (1982); *A Woman Like Eve* (1982); *The Fourth Man* (1983); *Another Country* (1984); *A Man Like Eva* (1985); *My Beautiful Laundrette* (1986); *Maurice* (1987); *Whitnail & I* (1988); *Macho Dancer* (1989); *Last Exit in Brooklyn* (1991); *The Lost Language of*

Cranes (1991); *The Garden* (1991) and *Edward II* (1992).

An equally important influence on how Hollywood has treated the subject of homosexuality was the Production Code, an American industry self-governing regulatory body which, beginning in the early 1930s, sought to "reflect" the "norms" of "decent" society. Because of the existence of the Production Code, hardly any direct mention or illustrations of homosexuality appeared in American cinema from the 1930s to the 1950s. For example, when a Broadway play which dealt directly with homosexual characters was transferred to the screen, the focal topic would be transmuted into a study of heterosexuals or muffled or disguised (e.g., *These Three*, 1936; *Tea and Sympathy*, 1956; *The Strange One*, 1957; *Cat on a Hot Tin Roof*, 1958 and *Suddenly, Last Summer*, 1959).

Up until sometime in the 1960s, by which time the Production Code had lost its power and effectiveness, Hollywood thus mostly chose to ignore homosexual themes or, when such themes did occur, they were handled by vague indirection, a wisp of a suggestion apparent only to the more sophisticated or through symbolic sublimated activity (e.g. *The Maltese Falcon*, 1941; *Gilda*, 1946; *Rebel Without a Cause*, 1955; *Tea and Sympathy, 1956; Cat on a Hot Tin Roof*, 1958; *The Left-Handed Gun*, 1958; *Suddenly, Last Summer*, 1959). This practice continued through-

out much of the 1960s (e.g. *7 Women*, 1965; *Reflections in a Golden Eye*, 1967 and *The Sergeant*, 1968) by which time the Production Code had been dropped in favor of the industry's Rating Administration. The change of attitude represented by the Administration led to an onslaught of gay-themed pictures in the late 1960s and early 1970s, all geared to gain box office attention by their treatment of a daring subject (e.g., *The Fox*, 1968; *The Gay Deceivers*, 1969; *The Boys in the Band*, 1970; *Fortune and Men's Eyes*, 1971 and *Some of My Best Friends Are. . .*, 1973.) When it was discovered that the gimmick did not lead to automatic commercial success, Hollywood turned its attention to (with, e.g., the black action pictures of the 1970s) exploiting other newly-liberated minorities.

Paralleling the constraining effects of the Production Code and the later Motion Picture Association Rating Administration was the matter of film reviewers (ranging from trade paper journalists to critics writing for major consumer publications), who had a far more subtle effect in shaping public interest and reaction to movies dealing with homosexual subjects. Their attitudes affected what gay-themed pictures were produced or released to the general public. Through homophobic negativism, downplaying or ignoring a film's stated gay theme or homosexual characters, or by refusing to review movies with such thematic subjects, critics consciously and subconsciously helped to reinforce and perpetuate stereotypes about these minorities held by the viewing public.

Another complex sidelight of the history of gay feature films is the fact that because the motion picture industry has so long been male-dominated, most homosexual genre pictures until recent years have dealt with male-male love. For many years, whenever a lesbian was presented on camera, it would only be as a very tough and scornful stereotype, such as the harsh females populating many prison dramas (e.g., *Caged*, 1950; *Women's Prison*, 1955; *Born Innocent*, 1974; *Inmates: A Love Story*, 1981 and *Lust for Freedom*, 1988), fighting females in lowbrow barroom scenes (e.g., *Tony Rome*, 1967 and *The Killing of Sister George*, 1968) or caricatures in action features (e.g., *Cleopatra Jones*, 1973; *Black Eye,* 1974 and *Cleopatra Jones and the Casino of Gold*, 1975). Hollywood's inept *The Children's Hour* (1962) and the overly-symbolic *The Fox* (1968) to one side, it was not until the late 1970s that United States filmmakers offered sensitive studies of gay females (e.g., *A Question of Love*, 1978; *The Rose,* 1979; *Lianna*, 1983; *Silkwood*, 1983; *Desert Hearts*, 1985 and *Fried Green Tomatoes*, 1991).

Interestingly enough, the television medium, which has generally followed at a safe distance the changing trends in viewers' inter-est, has proven to be more forthright in the presentation of homosexual subject matter. Following such relatively early, pathfinding television movies as *The Glass House* (1972), *That Certain Summer* (1972), *Born Innocent* (1974), *Dawn: Portrait of a Teenage Runaway* (1976) and *Alexander: The Other Side of Dawn* (1977) came several pathfinding network television series. Shows such as "Hot l Baltimore" (1975), "Mary Hartman, Mary Hartman" (1976–1977) and "Soap" (1977–1981) contained recurring gay characters. In turn, they led to such later series entries as "Love, Sidney" (1981–1983), "Dynasty" (1981–1989), "Brothers" (1984–1989), and "L.A. Law" (1986–   ), all of which have spotlighted substantial and ongoing homosexual characters. There have also been such television miniseries as "Scruples" (1980), "Sophisticated Gents" (1981), "Chiefs" (1983), "Dress Gray" (1986), and "An Inconvenient Woman" (1991), and a host of educational television documentaries and "After School Specials" dealing with homosexuality, AIDS, etc.

This reference book reveals how, over the decades, the makers of mainstream Hollywood product — in contrast to hardcore pornography — have dealt with the subject of homosexuality on screen in theatrical and television feature films. (The book does not cover documentary or short subject releases.)

Contrary to still popular notions, transvestism or transsexualism does not automatically indicate homosexuality. Thus, films which feature characters in drag are not included herein. Also not included is the on-screen portrayal of female impersonators. For similar reasons, features in which characters have undergone sex changes are not part of this book, as their characters are not generally gay-oriented. Also not dealt with are those action buddy films (e.g., *Too Hot to Handle*, 1938; *Test Pilot*, 1938; *Desert Fury*, 1947 and *The Outsider*, 1961) in which, by a liberal stretch of the imagination, one could "read in" a gay sexual undertone to the motivations between the very masculine best friends.

It is only by keeping fully in mind the changing social history of both Hollywood and the United States at large, and the various other subtle and overt influences at work, that one can fully appreciate the ways in which Hollywood has dealt actively and passively in presenting gay characters and themes on screen.

As always, I would be grateful for suggestions, additions or corrections that readers may care to provide. You may write to me in care of the publisher.

A Brief History of Regulatory Codes in the American Film Industry

Pre-Motion Picture Production Code Years (1900–1930)

In 1908, the National Board of Censorship was established by major figures in the Amcrican film industry to counter growing criticism regarding immorality in motion pictures.

In the early 1920s, a series of scandals involving Hollywood personalities (e.g., Olive Thomas, Fatty Arbuckle, William Desmond Taylor, and Wallace Reid) caused the "immoral" motion picture industry to come under increasing attack from a variety of civic and religious pressure groups. As a result, the film industry, fearful that federal and state governmental authorities might step in, hired U.S. Postmaster General Will Hays in 1922 to become president of the Motion Picture Producers and Distributors of America, Inc. (MPPDA). Hays resigned his cabinet post to accept this new position.

In Hays's capacity as "Czar of Hollywood," it was his professed duty to monitor motion picture studios (and their moguls) regarding their supervision of players' social lives to insure that their behavior was, at least publicly, circumspect. He also strove to instruct producers on using discretion in the choice of titles for motion picture; avoiding double entendres; avoiding the (over)use of scanty costumes in films; and submitting synopses and or scripts of planned films in advance for approval/suggestions.

Hays attempted to enforce the above goals through The Formula (1924), which asked MPPDA members to submit summaries of novels and plays which it intended to adapt into motion pictures for advice as to tastefulness. The Formula proved of limited usefulness because it only suggested, but could not enforce its guidelines and it dealt only with adapted material and did not include original screenplays.

The Don'ts and Be Carefuls (1927) covered 11 subjects that should not appear in motion pictures and 25 themes that should be handled with care and discretion, including "any inference of sex perversion." It also proved of limited usefulness because it could not be enforced legally.

The Motion Picture Production Code (1930–1956)

Because American filmmakers of the 1920s had generally provided only lip service to the strictures imposed or suggested by the "Hays Office," it was determined to create a formalized code with which to "govern" the film industry.

Industry trade publisher Martin Quigley and the Reverend Martin Daniel Lord (a Jesuit priest from St. Louis who had served as advisor on many motion pictures), drafted the Motion Picture Production Code under Hays's direction. In February 1930 the Association of Motion Picture Producers, Inc., adopted the Motion Picture Production Code. In March 1930 the Motion Picture Producers and Distributors of America adopted the Motion Picture Production Code.

In 1931, the Resolution for Uniform Interpretation was adjusted to direct the submission of scripts by its members.

In 1934, the Hays Office eliminated the Production Committee in Hollywood which permitted "appeals" from decisions made by the Association board. It also added explanatory/philosophical sections to the Code (Reasons Supporting Preamble of Code, Reasons Underlying the General Principles, and Reasons Underlying Particular Applications). By 1934, a nationwide upsurge in criticism of "immoral" films being turned out by Hollywood filmmakers led to the Catholic clergy's forming its own Legion of Decency and caused Hays to inaugurate new strictures for the already existant Production Code.

As of July 15, 1934, all members had to submit their motion pictures to the Hays Office for a Purity Seal, which would be shown on the screen directly after the main title. It would signify that the film complied with high moral standards and had made all efforts possible to comply with the Production Code. If a film was denied a seal, it would have to be altered before it could be shown. Joseph Breen, whom Hays had hired to enforce the Code, was placed in charge of granting the seal of approval.

Through its existence, the Code was amended by the Association to deal with other specific topics: crime (1938), costumes (1939), profanity (1939) and cruelty to animals (1940).

Under the section entitled Particular Applications, the Code contained 12 subsections. Subsection II

("Sex") in subparagraph 4 instructed that "Sex perversion or any inference to it is forbidden."

The Motion Picture Production Code (1956–1968)

In 1943, Howard Hughes released *The Outlaw*, starring Jane Russell, without Code Approval. It was subsequently withdrawn, but redistributed in 1946. In 1945, Warner Bros., in a dispute with the Production Code Administration, temporarily withdrew from the producer's association. These events demonstrated the growing ineffectiveness of the film industry's self-regulating body.

In 1945, Will Hays retired as president of the MPPDA and Eric Johnston was appointed as his successor. Soon thereafter, the association changed its name to the Motion Picture Association of America (MPAA).

By the 1950s, the Code was facing new challenges. Otto Preminger had defied the authority of the Code twice by refusing to submit either *The Moon Is Blue* (1953) or *The Man with the Golden Arm* (1955)—both major motion pictures—for Code seal approval. The advent of popularized commercial television led to nationwide civic and religious debates as to who was to "control" the motion picture product televised directly into homes. In 1955, Pope Pius XII made a major speech on the power of motion pictures, urging the "banning of corrupt movies wherever they were shown."

Later in 1955, the U.S. Senate Subcommittee on Juvenile Delinquency, headed by Senator Estes Kefauver, issued a report which stated, "the predominance of brutality in both movies and TV is making our nation's youth insensitive to human suffering." It also noted that "the film code seems to have been administered with fartoo much laxity in the last few years." The motion picture and television industries were advised to "police themselves" and "not force the federal government to intervene."

On December 12, 1956, a revised Motion Picture Production Code was issued by Eric Johnston for the MPAA. The revised 1956 Code now only prohibited two main subjects for depiction on screen: venereal disease and sexual perversion.

In 1959, the California State Supreme Court, in dealing with a case concerning a public screening of Kenneth Anger's *Fireworks* (1947) determined that "homosexuality is older than Sodom and Gomorrah" and thus was to be considered a legitimate subject for screen presentation, if handled with proper decorum. This reflected a changing United States legal interpretation of homosexuality. It was no longer necessarily being considered unnatural and against the laws of decency.

An October 1961 amendment to the Production Code altered Section II-4 dealing with sex to permit "sex aberration" when dealt with "care, discretion, and restraint." (One of the last Hollywood films — before the new amendment — to be censored for depiction of a "sex aberration" was *Spartacus*, 1960.)

The Code and Rating Administration (1968-1977)

By the late 1950s and early 1960s, even the revised Motion Picture Production Code was becoming outmoded. Several concurrent factors brought about yet another revamping of the industry's self-censorship regulations. Movies made in Hollywood could not compete in the marketplace with non–censorship-controlled foreign films, which were becoming increasingly popular in distribution.

One of the prime theories in creating the Production Code had been that because the motion picture industry was one of the United States's largest entertainment mediums, it had to be regulated carefully.

This situation was no longer true, since television had eroded much of the film's mass audience. (Filmmakers contended that motion pictures should be granted the "freedoms" long since allowed to such other art forms as novels and plays.)

Two United States Supreme Court decisions were handed down on April 22, 1968: *Ginsberg v. New York* ruled that subject material which was not obscene for adults

could be declared obscene for children. *Interstate Circuit v. Dallas* suggested that a classification system for motion pictures could be ruled as constitutional if the guidelines for such a system were defined clearly.

On November 1, 1968, a new self-regulatory code went into effect, under the guidance of Jack Valenti who had succeeded Eric Johnston as the president of the MPAA in 1966.

The new system did not eliminate the former Production Code completely; it retained a Standards for Productions. A vaguely phrased subsection noted: "Restraint and care shall be exercised in presentations dealing with sex aberrations." Another section noted: "Illicit sex relationships shall not be justified. Intimate sex scenes violating common standards of decency shall not be portrayed."

Under the new regime, any film — regardless of theme or treatment — could be produced. It would be subject, however, to one of four ratings (see below) provided by the now ruling Code and Rating Administration (CARA) of the MPAA. The Board would still examine both film scripts and final cuts of motion pictures, granting all approved films a seal of approval. X-rated films were to be denied a seal, but were still permitted to be shown. Any nonmember company of the MPAA could use the CARA.

The CARA rating system's initial delineations were: G = general audiences (all ages admitted); M = suggested for mature audiences (adults and mature young children); R = restricted (children under sixteen required an accompanying parent or adult); and X = no one under sixteen admitted.

In March 1970, the R and X categories raised their age limits to 17, and the M category became GP = all ages admitted (parental guidance suggested). In 1972, the GP category was redesignated PG (for "parental guidance") to avoid the public's confusion that the GP rating signified "General Public."

The Classification and Rating Administration (1977 to Date)

On August 1, 1977, the MPAA revised its voluntary rating system. Under the new system, the Code concept was eliminated. The administration was renamed the Classification and Rating Administration.

No substantive action was taken to correct the limitations of the system, which saw sex treated restrictively while crime and violence were treated far more leniently; studios re-editing a film to alter a film's rating, leading to increasing complaints that such code-induced editing/censorship was harming the artistry of a film; groups such as the National Catholic Office for Motion Pictures and the National Council of Churches' Broadcasting and Film Commission not supporting the MPAA because they

thought its system was "clearly unrealistic"; and the U.S. Supreme Court's ruling in 1973 that the questions of offensiveness could be judged against "local, not national community standards" which meant that local groups could apply their own standards.

Changes were made to the then existing rating structure. In 1984, the PG-13 category was introduced: "Parents strongly cautioned — some material may be inappropriate for children under 13."

In 1990, to overcome the long-time practice of filmmakers' self-applying an "X" rating to garner publicity for their films, the CARA adopted the NC-17 rating (no children under 17 admitted — age varies in some jurisdictions). Because this was a registered trademark, it could not be self-applied.

Thus the rating classification since 1991 is as follows: G = general audiences (all ages admitted); PG = parental guidance suggested (some material may not be suitable for children); PG-13 = parents strongly cautioned (some material may be inappropriate for children under 13); R = restricted (under 17 requires accompanying parent or adult guardian — age varies in some jurisdictions); NC-17 = no children under 17 admitted (age varies in some jurisdictions).

Note: Motion Picture Association of America (MPAA) ratings listed for the theatrical features detailed in this book are those given at the time of initial release. Many theatrical features when re-issued undergo an initial or new rating procedure and, at that time, are either re-rated or receive their first rating. Television features, when first aired, are not rated by the MPAA. However, many television movies, as well as theatrical releases, receive a first time or new rating or different ratings for different versions, when released in a home video/laser format.

The Films

1. The Adventurers (Paramount, 1970), color, 171 min. R-rated.

Presenter, Joseph E. Levine; producer/director, Lewis Gilbert; based on the novel by Harold Robbins; screenplay, Michael Hastings, Gilbert; production designer, Tony Masters, art directors, John Hoesli, Aurelio Crugnola, Jack Maxsted, Harry Pottle; set decorators, Vernon Dixon, Franco Fumagalli, Colin Grimes; costumes, Ronald Paterson; makeup, Stuart Freeborn; music, Antonio Carlos Jobim; music director/additional music, Eumir Deodato; assistant directors, Bill Cartlidge, Terence Churcher; sound, Vernon Harris; Peter Davies, Bob Jones; special effects, Cliff Richardson; camera, Claude Renoir; second unit camera, Skeets Kelly; editor, Anne V. Coates.

Cast: Bekim Fehmiu (Dax Xenos); Charles Aznavour (Marcel Campion); Alan Badel (Rojo); Candice Bergen (Sue Ann Daley); Ernest Borgnine (Fat Cat); Leigh Taylor-Young (Amparo); Fernando Rey (Jaime Xenos); Thommy Berggren (Sergei Nikovitch); Olivia de Havilland (Deborah Hadley); John Ireland (Mr. Hadley); Delia Boccardo (Caroline de Coyne); Sydney Tafler (Colonel Gutierrez); Rossano Brazzi (Baron de Coyne); Anna Moffo (Dania Leonardi); Christian Roberts (Robert); Yorgo Voyagis (El Lobo); Jorge Martinez de Hoyos (El Condor); Angela Scoular (Denisonde); Yolanda Donlan (Mrs. Erickson); Milena Vukotic (April); Ferdy Mayne (Sergei's Father); Jaclyn Smith (Belinda); Katherine Balfour (Robert's Mother); Roberta Donatelli (Ampara, as a Child); Peter Graves (Trustee Banker); John Frederick (Mr. Erickson); Allan Cuthbetson (Hugh); Zenia Merton (Dax's Sister); Roberta Haynes (Dax's Mother); Lois Maxwell (Woman at Fashion Show); Loris Loddi (Dax, as a Child); Vanessa Lee (Trustee Banker's Wife); Michael Balfour (Detective); Katia Christina (Natalia); Katiushka Lanvin (Marita); Nadia Scarpitia (Giulia); Helen Ronee (Lexie); Linda Towne (Michelle); Joal Carlo (Jose); Gisela Kopel (Maid); David Canon (Hadley's Secretary); Jose Luis Ospira (Roberto); Manuelo Serrano (Sergeant); Rey Vasquez (Manuelo); Juan Esterlich (Radio Announcer); Kiki Gonclaves (General); Anthony Hickox (Robert, as a Child); Carl Ecklund (Sergei, as a Child); Christine Delit (Brunette Girl Friend); Randi Lind (Blonde Girl Friend); Marcus Beck (Philippe).

"There was not one moment in *The Adventurers* when I felt that anyone in it was trying to do a single honest thing. . . . I've seen a lot of rotten movies, but this is the most disgusting of them all, because there's so much of it and it's on such a spectacular scale. . . ." (Pauline Kael, *The New Yorker*)

If ever there was a screen project built on excesses it was *The Adventurers*, derived from Harold Robbins's best-selling *roman a clef* (1966). Producer Joseph E. Levine's worst choice in the international array of personalities assembled for this project was uncharismatic Yugoslavian actor Bekim Fehmiu in the pivotal role. Levine's most specious decision was assigning (then dilettante) actress Candice Bergen to play a lesbian, trading strongly on the publicity surrounding her screen debut in a similar role in *The Group* (1966), q.v.

In the turbulent South American country of Corteguay, ten-year old Dax Xenos

[1]

Ernest Borgnine, Charles Aznavour and Bekim Fehmiu in *The Adventurers* **(1970).**

(Loris Loddi) witnesses the rape and murder of his mother (Roberta Haynes) by government troops. Thereafter, Dax's revolutionist father, Jaime (Fernando Rey) and his men capture the murderers and place Dax in charge of the culprits' executions. In the mountain hideaway of revolutionary leader Rojo (Alan Badel), Dax is attracted to the latter's young daughter Amparo (Roberta Donatelli). Once the government is overthrown and Rojo is in power, Jaime is sent to Rome as an ambassador and Dax accompanies him. Years later, Jaime returns to Corteguay where Rojo has become a dictator and the latter has Jaime killed. Playboy Dax returns to his homeland for his father's funeral where he is tricked by Rojo into causing El Condor (Jorge Martinez de Hoyos) to surrender, which leads to the man's death. Dax, who has by now renewed his ac-

quaintanceship with the adult Amparo (Leigh Taylor-Young) returns to Rome where he becomes a gigolo.

One of Dax's Roman conquests is wealthy married matron, Deborah Hadley (Olivia de Havilland). Later, he marries multi-millionairess American Sue Ann Daley (Candice Bergen). She becomes pregnant but loses their baby in a swing accident, causing her to become barren, sullen and eventually to prefer sexual liaisons with women. As a consequence, Dax divorces her—and marries other heiresses—and, eventually, returns once more to Corteguay. He finds a new revolution brewing under the leadership of El Lobo (Yorgo Voyagis) and learns that Amparo has given birth to Dax's son. After Dax murders Rojo, the uprising succeeds. Dax sends Amparo and their child to Rome, planning to join them there. However, before he can leave Corteguay, Dax is murdered by José (Joal Carlo), the revengeful son of El Condor.

Vincent Canby (*New York Times*) was intrigued but numbed by this gaudy production. "No expense seems to have been spared . . . giving the film a kind of garish physical reality. . . ." *Variety* was more direct: "*The Adventurers* is a classic monument to bad taste. . . . film is marked by profligate and squandered production opulence; inferior, imitative and curiously old-hat direction . . . indulgent, gratuitous and boring violence; and luridly non-erotic sex." The British *Monthly Film Bulletin* concluded, "This might well be described as the film with everything; trouble is, it is difficult to imagine anybody wanting any of it."

With the film's assorted peeping-Tom scenes of carnage, material indulgence, free and bought love, sado-masochism, the sequences spotlighting Sue Ann Daley—the Barbara Hutton-like character—were remarkably chaste by comparison. The storyline rationalizes that Sue Ann Daley's "unnatural" attraction to women was based in tragedy (losing her child and her inability to have other offspring). Amazingly, of all the cast, Bergen—then very much in her apprenticeship period—received the best notices. Canby of the *New York Times* noted: "Candice Bergen . . . is so beautiful and so incapable of masking the amusement she seems to feel at finding herself an actress, that one can forgive her those few dreadful moments when she is required to register either hysteria or a sense of loss. Miss Bergen survives the film with her radiance intact."

Made at a cost of over $10 million and shot in Rome, with location work in the United States, Colombia and Italy, *The Adventurers* grossed only $7,750,000 in distributors' domestic film rentals. Today the film remains a landmark in tacky bad taste; its pseduo psychological explanation of Sue Ann's bisexuality is an example of the films of 1970s which aimed to be daring, but really were very hesitant in explaining non-traditional behavior.

2. **Advise and Consent** (Columbia, 1962), 140 min. Not rated.

Presenter/producer/director, Otto Preminger; based on the novel by Allen Drury; screenplay, Wendell Mayes; production designer, Lyle Wheeler; set decorator, Eli Benneche; wardrobe, Joe King, Adele Parmenter, Michael Harte; makeup, Del Armstrong, Robert Jiras; music, Jerry Fielding; song, Fielding and Ned Washington; assistant directors, L. V. McCardle Jr., Don Kranze, Larry Powell, Charles Bohart; sound, Harold Lewis, William Hamilton; Leon Birnbaum; camera, Sam Leavitt; editor, Louis R. Loefler.

Cast: Henry Fonda (Robert A. Leffingwell); Charles Laughton (Senator Seabright Cooley); Don Murray (Senator Brigham Anderson); Walter Pidgeon (Senator Bob Munson); Peter Lawford (Senator Lafe Smith); Gene Tierney (Dolly Harrison); Franchot Tone (The President); Lew Ayres (Vice President Harley Hudson); Burgess Meredith (Herbert Gelman); Eddie Hodges (Johnny Leffingwell); Paul Ford (Senator Stanley Danta); George Grizzard (Senator Fred Van Ackerman); Inga Swenson (Ellen Anderson); Paul McGrath (Hardiman Fletcher); Will Geer (The Senate Minority Leader); Edward Andrews (Senator Orrin Knox); Betty White (Senator Bessie Adams); Malcolm Atterbury (Senator Tom August); J. Edward McKinley (Senator Powell Hanson); William Quinn (Senator Paul Hendershot); Tiki Santos (Senator Kanaho); Raoul DeLeon (Senator Velez); Tom Helmore (British Ambassador); Hilary Eaves (Lady Maudulayne); Rene Paul (French Ambassador); Michaele Montau (Celestine Barre); Raj Mallick (Indian Ambassador); Russ Brown (Night Watchman); Paul Stevens (Louis Newborn); Janet Jane Carty (Pidge Anderson); Chet Stratton (Reverend Carney Birch); Larry Tucker (Manuel); John Granger (Ray Shaff); Sid Gould (Bartender); Bettie Johnson (Lafe's Girl); Cay Forester (President's Secretary); William H. Y. Knighton Jr. (President of White House Correspondents Association); Henry F. Ashurst (Senator McCafferty); Guy M. Gillette (Senator Harper); Irv Kupcinet, Robert C. Wilson, Alan Emory, Jessie Stearns Buscher, Milton Berliner, Allan W. Cromley, Bruce Zortmann, Wayne Tucker (Journalists); Al McGranary, Joe Baird, Harry Denny, Leon Alton, George Denormand, Ed

Inga Swenson and Don Murray in *Advise and Consent* (1962).

Haskett, Virgil Johannsen, Paul Power, Maxwell Reed, Mario Cimino, Edwin K. Baker, Clive L. Halliday, Roger Clark, Robert Malcolm, Dick Ryan, Gene Matthews, Leoda Richards, Bernard Sell, Brandon Beach, Hal Taggart (Senators).

In the 1950s and 1960s, director Otto Preminger (1906–1986) displayed a knack for generating tremendous publicity for his movie projects. One of his recurrent gambits was to ignore the censorship tenets of the faltering U.S. motion picture industry code administration, a feat he did gleefully with *The Moon Is Blue* (1953), a risque sex comedy, and *The Man with the Golden Arm* (1955), a graphic depiction of drug addiction. By 1961, Hollywood filmmakers, pressured the Motion Picture Association of America (MPAA) to revise its strictures in accordance with the more "liberal" times. In October 1961, the MPAA announced that "In keeping with the culture, the mores and the values of our time, homosexuality and other sexual aberrations may now be treated with care,

discretion and restraints." However, by the time of this enunciation, two genre trendsetting films, *Advise and Consent* and *The Children's Hour* (1962), q.v., were *already* in production by major Hollywood studios. If industry observers noted that the MPAA's belated gesture was to save its crumbling authority, little was made of the Code's amended wording, which labeled homosexuality a "sexual aberration." At this juncture, medical evidence to the contrary, homosexuality was still regarded as a mental disease.

Allen Drury's Pulitzer Prize–winning novel, *Advise and Consent* was published in 1959 and, in the following year the best-seller was adapted for Broadway by Loring Mandel. A focal point of this behind-locked-doors look at Washington politics was the insidious nature of so many national leaders. Included in this tapestry of political intrigue was the seemingly virtuous young Senator from Utah, who has a dark secret—he had a brief episode of homosexuality in his past. (This plot angle became a highly explosive ingredient of the movie's publicity campaign.)

The U.S. President (Franchot Tone), secretly dying of cancer, requests the Senate to "advise and consent" to the selection of Robert A. Leffingwell (Henry Fonda) as the nation's new Secretary of State. In the ensuing partisan uproar over the projected appointment, Senate Majority Leader Bob Munson (Walter Pidgeon), who enjoys a warm relationship with glamorous Washington hostess Dolly Harrison (Gene Tierney), supports the chief executive's choice; the major opposition comes from elderly southern Senator Seab Cooley (Charles Laughton). The latter, with a grudge against Leffingwell, arranges for the mentally-unhinged Herbert Gelman (Burgess Meredith) to testify before a Senate Committee that Leffingwell had belonged once to a Communist cell in Chicago. The very candid Leffingwell, a widower with a young son (Eddie Hodges), admits the truth of the accusation to the President, but insists it was merely a youthful folly.

At the President's bidding, Leffingwell denies the charge under oath in front of the Senate subcommittee, headed by Senator Brigham Anderson (Don Murray) of Utah. Later, Cooley makes sure that Anderson learns the truth, leading the young politician to demand that Leffingwell's nomination be withdrawn. When the President declines to do so, Anderson insists the truth must be made known. At this juncture, Anderson is blackmailed by peacemonger senator Fred Van Ackerman (George Grizzard) who warns Anderson that if he fails to approve the nomination, Anderson's wartime homosexual experience in Hawaii will be revealed. Unable to deal with his past and afraid to tell his wife (Inga Swenson), the distraught Anderson slashes his throat. The grieving widow refuses to reveal the reason that led Brigham to kill himself.

Advised of Anderson's death, the Senate votes on Leffingwell. The matter ends in a deadlock. Vice President Harley Hudson (Lew Ayres) must cast the deciding vote. As he debates his choice, news comes that the President has died. Inspired by the responsibility suddenly thrust on him, the Vice President announces he will select his own candidate for the Secretary of State vacancy. Meanwhile, the Senate privately blackballs Van Ackerman for having gone too far, and he leaves the chambers a politically ruined man.

Bosley Crowther (*New York Times*) rated *Advise and Consent* "sassy, stinging" but emphasized strongly that the movie's great flaw is not "giving the appearance of trying to be accurate and fair about the existence of a reasonable balance of good men and rogues in government." As to the plotline aspect dealing with homosexuality, Crowther complained, "It is in this latter complication that the nature of the drama is finally exposed for the deliberately scandalous, sensational and caustic thing it is. Mr. Preminger has his character go through a lurid and seamy encounter . . . before cutting his throat, an act that seems unrealistic, except as a splashy high point for the film."

While mainstream reviewers pondered how the movie's distribution might sully America's image overseas, critics had little to say about the controversial scene in which a distraught Brigham Anderson flies to New York to talk with Ray Shaff (John Granger), the man with whom he shared a liaison in World War II Hawaii. In Manhattan, Anderson learns that Shaff is at the 602 Club located in a back street of Greenwich Village. Arriving there, the repressed Anderson hardly enters the dimly-lit, crowded bar—where a Frank Sinatra recording is blaring on the juke box and men sit at candle-lit tables—before he panics and rushes outside. However, Shaff spots his one-time friend and follows him into the street. Traumatized by having *even* gone into the bar, the politician hails a taxi. As he jumps into the cab, Anderson shoves the perplexed, pleading Shaff ("I was drunk," Shaff explains, "I needed money. . . . You wouldn't see me, I kept calling!") into a muddy gutter.

For most viewers in 1962, the relatively brief bar scene in *Advise and Consent* was their first sight of what a gay bar was supposed to be like. (It should be pointed out that even trend-breaking Otto Preminger never used the word "homosexual" in this movie.) At the time, the sequence was considered to be so daring, that hardly anyone pondered why such a highly visible public figure as Anderson would chance being seen at a such a public gay establishment. However, there was little confusion about the film's subtext which suggested that the only way out for a remorseful—here passive and seemingly reformed—homosexual was suicide. Another message of *Advise and Consent* was that aggressive gays (such as Shaff) are blackmailers and end in the gutter. As to Don Murray's performance as the nervous homosexual, given the illogical nature of his melodramatic role, he played it with a mixture of his usual square-jaw righteousness and underlying angst.

To be noted in the large cast of *Advise and Consent* are Betty White as a senator from Kansas and Peter Lawford—then in real life the brother-in-law of President John F. Kennedy—as an amiable playboy bachelor Congressman. One personality who refused an *Advise and Consent* cameo role as a senator (at a time when there were no black U.S. senators) was Dr. Martin Luther King Jr., fearful that if he should appear in the movie, it might do more damage than good to the Civil Rights cause. Despite all the sure-fire ingredients to make *Advise and Consent* a blockbuster, it was not; it grossed less than $4 million in distributors' domestic film rentals.

3. After Dark, My Sweet (Avenue Pictures, 1990), color, 114 min. R-rated.

Executive producer, Cary Brokow; producers, Ric Kidney, Robert Redlin; director, James Foley; based on the novel by Jim Thompson; screenplay, Foley, Redlin; art director, Kenneth A. Hardy; set decorator, Margaret Goldsmith; costumes, Hope Hanafin; makeup, Felicity Bowring; music/music director, Maurice Jarre; assistant directors, David B. Householter, Chris Stoia, George C. Bosley; stunt coordinator, A. J. Nay; sound, David Brownlow, Shawn Murphy; special effects, Ken Diaz; camera, Mark Plummer; editor, Howard Smith.

Cast: Jason Patric (Kevin "Collie" Collins); Rachel Ward (Fay Anderson); Bruce Dern (Uncle Bud [Eric Stoker]); George Dickerson (Doc Goldman); James Cotton (Charlie Vanderventer); Corey Carrier (Jack); Ricky Giordani (Bert); Jeanie Moore (Nanny); Tom Wagner (Counterman); Burke Byrnes (Cop); Michael G. Hagerty, James E. Bowen Jr. (Truck Drivers); Vincent Joseph Mazzella Jr. (Flashback Fighter); Napoleon Walls (Boxing Referee).

Based on a 1955 book by prolific pulp novelist Jim Thompson, *After Dark, My Sweet* appeared in the same year as another film (*The Grifters*) based on a different Thompson work. As a requisite of a *film noir*, the "hero" of *After Dark, My Sweet* is a perplexed victim caught in a whirlpool of bad circumstances, and is pulled to his ruin by a femme fatale. In *After Dark, My Sweet*, Kevin "Collie" Collins is an apparently brain-damaged ex-boxer, a paranoid soul whose hunky physical presence makes him a quick sexual target of both sexes.

Within *After Dark, My Sweet*, the problems of Kevin "Collie" Collins (Jason Patric), the 27-year-old drifter, mushroomed years ago when he killed an opponent in the boxing ring. Since then he has been in and out of mental asylums. Now on the run, he wanders into a seedy bar somewhere in the desert country of southern California. There he meets the semi-alcoholic Fay Anderson (Rachel Ward), a fading but still youngish widow who hires him as a live-in gardener. Before long, Uncle Bud (Bruce Dern), a former cop and long-time associate of Fay's, wants to make the newcomer part of a kidnapping scheme he has been hatching. Finding that she cares too much for Collie and not wanting the drifter involved in their criminal plan, she forces him to leave.

On the road again, Collie meets middle-aged Doc Goldman (George Dickerson), a local doctor who takes a great interest in the virile young man. Goldman invites him to stay at his home and gives him a handyman's job. A few days later, the restless Collie returns to Fay who reluctantly makes him part of Uncle Bud's plot to kidnap a millionaire's son. After Fay learns of Collie's dangerous background from Doc, she tries unsuccessfully to break with the love-smitten Collins. Meanwhile, her contradictory actions convinces the young man that neither she nor Doc can be trusted. Nevertheless, dressed as a chauffeur, Collie kidnaps the boy from his school playground. Later, when the victim falls ill, the trio discover he is diabetic. Uncle Bud is willing to let the boy die, while Collie steals insulin from Doc's office. When Fay takes pity on the child and leaves him in the woods to escape, Collie misunderstands her motive.

Doc arrives on the scene and, in an argument, Collie accidentally kills him. Later, after collecting the ransom, Uncle Bud is killed by Bert (Rocky Giordani) to whom he owes money, and the latter, in turn, is shot by the pursuing police. Fay drives into the desert with Charlie. Testing her again, Collie pretends he is going to murder the boy. She shoots Collie. He dies glad in the knowledge that Fay and the boy are safe—she can now tell the law that she was forced to help Collie and that she killed him to save the boy and herself.

Sheila Benson (*Los Angeles Times*) enthused, "For a look at how eerily well Jim Thompson's spare, brackish stories of lovers, losers and sociopathic double-crossers update to today's straightened moral climate, try the stunning surprise of *After Dark, My Sweet*. . . . It's Patric . . . who dominates the screen. . . . He is controlled, subtle, many-layered, physical in ways that tell us everything about the character and intuitively right." *Variety* rated this film a "near-perfect adaptation" and a "small-scale jewel." The trade paper judged, "Ward is at her direct and provocative best as the lonely widow who can

never give a straight answer, and Patric is enigmatic and affecting as the bruised drifter. . . .George Dickerson as Goldman, a doctor who takes rather too personal an interest in Collie's well-being, adds elusively creepy undertones to the role." On the other hand, Philip Strick (British *Monthly Film Bulletin*) observed, "what sabotages *After Dark, My Sweet* . . . is the casting: granted that Thompson's characters are bewilderingly devious, they are not best served by Jason Patric's unvarying croak, somnambulistic shamble, and leaden scowl, or by Rachel Ward's languidly British tones, graceless body language, and clumsy outbursts of perplexity. While Bruce Dern and George Dickerson are closer in their ingratiating unreliability to the Thompson mark, the lack of chemistry at the film's centre leaves an exasperating void, despite all the visual appeal."

In traditional *film noir* style, a good deal of this picture's plotline and motivation is deliberately ambivalent. However, there is much less doubt in the scenario as to Doc Goldman's motivation when he meets the muscular, brooding Collie at the all-night diner. The closeted gay man immediately sizes up the vacant-eyed drifter as a lost soul in need of a stabilizing force. Before long he has taken Collie into his house, with more than a parental good-will attitude in mind. Whether Collie intuitively senses what his benefactor has in mind for the future or just feels trapped again by routine, he takes off. However, Doc is emotionally drawn to the ex-boxer and cannot stay out of Collie's life. He tracks him down, which leads to his "accidental" death when Collie loses control during a confrontation.

A few weeks before the movie's August 1990 release, a *Village Voice* article by writer Gary Indiana insisted that the film pandered to gay bashing. Indiana focused on a sequence in which Doc Goldman is "predictably rewarded by a fatal beating." Filmmaker James Foley countered Indiana's contention that the physician character was not in the original novel; it was. Foley added that the doctor's motives toward the ex-boxer were intentionally ambiguous: "The whole film questions motivations—and everyone's relationship to one another." Insisting that "90% of every word of dialogue is right from the book, verbatim," Foley concluded, "If someone senses any homoerotic yearnings on the part of the doctor for Collie, they should attribute them to [Jim] Thompson."

Despite its virtues, *After Dark, My Sweet* was too downbeat and suffered from the lack of then box-office names. As such, the movie, made at a cost of $1 million, grossed only a minor $1.3 million in distributors' domestic film rentals.

4. After Hours (Warner Bros., 1985), color, 97 min. R-rated.

Producers, Amy Robinson, Griffin Dunne, Robert F. Colesberry; associate producer, Deborah Schindler; director, Martin Scorsese; screenplay, Joseph Minion; production designer, Jeffrey Townsend; art director, Stephen J. Lineweaver; set decorator, Leslie Popel; costumes, Rita Ryack; makeup, Valli; music, Howard Shore; assistant directors, Stephen J. Lim, Christopher Griffin; stunt coordinator, Harry Madsen; sound, Chat Gunter; camera, Michael Balhaus; editor, Thelma Schoonmaker.

Cast: Griffin Dunne (Paul Hackett); Rosanna Arquette (Marcy Franklin); Verna Bloom (June); Thomas Chong (Pepe); Linda Fiorentino (Kiki Bridges); Teri Garr (Julie); John Heard (Tom, the Bartender); Cheech Marin (Neil); Catherine O'Hara (Gail); Dick Miller (Waiter); Will Patton (Horst); Robert Plunket (Mark); Bronson Pinchot (Lloyd); Rocco Sisto (Coffee Shop Cashier); Larry Block (Taxi Driver); Victor Argo (Diner Cashier); Murray Moston (Subway Attendant); John Codiglia (Transit Cop); Clarke Evans, Victor Bumbalo, Bill Elverman (Neighbors); Joel Jason, Rand Carr (Bikers); Clarence Felder (Bouncer); Henry Baker (Jett); Margo Winkler (Woman with Gun); Victor Magnotta (Dead Man); Robi Johnson (Punk Girl); Stephen J. Lim (Club Berlin Bartender); Frank Aquilino, Maree Catalano, Paula Raflo, Rockets Redglare (Angry Mob).

Many of director Martin Scorsese's movies, including *Mean Streets* (1973)

and *New York, New York* (1977), examine the bizarre range of individuals who make up the Big Apple's diverse population. His dark comedy, *After Hours*, is a creative offshoot—more awkwardly minor than major—which continues the director's thesis of man at odds with his environment and himself. As Vincent Canby (*New York Times*) perceived, "*After Hours* is not an easy comedy to get the hang of, that is, until you realize that it's as much about emotional disorientation as it is disorienting." Among the locals, the uptowner hero meets in downtown New York is a lonely gay man on the prowl for company.

In New York City, word process operator Paul Hackett (Griffin Dunne), a Yuppie dullard, works in an office. One rainy night after work he chats with the offbeat Marcy Franklin (Rosanna Arquette) at a coffee shop. She tells him she is going to see her sculptress friend, Kiki Bridges (Linda Fiorentino), who lives in a SoHo loft. Later that evening, on an impulse, he decides to visit her there. In the course of the wild taxi ride there, his $20 bill, the only cash he is carrying, blows out the window. Escaping from the cab, he reaches Kiki only to find that Marcy is out shopping. Meanwhile, kinky Kiki asks him to assist with her papier mache sculpturing. While doing so, he spots a $20 bill among the pile of newspapers she is using, but fails to take it. Marcy returns, but Paul discovers that she is far too neurotic for him and he leaves. Not having even enough money for the subway, he stops at an all-night bar. There, the bartender, Tom (John Heard), agrees to provide him with the fare in exchange for Hackett going to Tom's apartment to retrieve the cash register keys. As security, Paul leaves his own keys with Tom. En route back to the bar, he spots two men carting off Kiki's art project. He grabs it from them and takes the sculpture back to her loft. She and her boyfriend (Will Patton) persuade him to apologize to Marcy. Going into her room, he discovers Marcy dead, she having over-

dosed on sleeping pills. After calling the police, he again leaves.

Returning to the bar, he finds it closed temporarily. When the bar reopens finally, the bartender Tom is greatly upset when he learns that his girlfriend, Marcy, has killed herself. Fearing that Julie might follow suit, Paul rushes back to her place. Finding her okay, he returns to the bar. However, it is now closed. Hurrying to Tom's building, he is chased from the premises by neighbors who think he is the burglar who has been tormenting the neighborhood. While escaping, he meets Mark (Robert Plunket), a lonely gay man cruising the darkened streets. After warning the perplexed Hackett ("There are certain things I will not do, I'm telling you in advance") he timidly invites Paul to his apartment. However, when the heterosexual Paul is non-responsive to the nervous homosexual, Hackett is told to leave. Back at Kiki's, Paul grabs the $20 bill from her sculpture, hails an already occupied taxi, but the cabbie drives off with the money. Gail (Catherine O'Hara), who had been in the cab, offers him a ride home in her ice cream truck. However, she is frightened to discover street posters identifying Hackett as the burglar.

Punk vigilantes from the neighborhood pursue Tom and he hides out at the Club Berlin where he encounters June (Verna Bloom), another sculptress. She hides him in his studio, disguising him as part of her plaster of paris sculpture. Actual burglars—Neil (Cheech Marin) and Pepe (Thomas Chong)—break into her studio and cart the sculpture away. In their pell mell escape, Paul is thrown off their truck. He finds himself back in front of his office building. It is now morning and he gratefully returns to his dull office routine.

For David Denby (*New York* magazine), "Martin Scorsese's fascinating new movie . . . can be seen at the simplest level as a comedy about a terrible date. . . . Paul's evening downtown becomes a forced initiation into the ridiculous, the perverse, and the bizarre. . . . Rather than social

reporting heighte
Scorsese gives us
nival. . . ." To Re
"*After Hours . .*
York nightmare o
could call it a bla
than it should be,
could be. . . . Th
series of class exer
acting school that
ism for fun and pr

Made on a tight
location in New
grossed $4.4 milli
mestic film rentals

5. Alexander:
Dawn (NBC-TV,
min. Not rated.

Executive produce
ducer, Wilford Lloy
Erman; based on cha
Young; story, Walter
play, Dallenbach; art
set decorator, Rick
Verhille; makeup, Ala
Karlin; assistant direc
Lloyd; sound, Patrick
Rescher; editor, Neil

Cast: Leigh J. McC
Duncan); Eve Plumb
Mills (Myra); Jean H
Chapman (Eddie Dun
Church); Alan Fein:
Selby); Asher Brauner
(Clara Duncan); Franc
der (Jack); Claudia Br
Campbell (Bernard);
Dorice Cook (Della);
Shop Owner); Robert
Galardo (Linda); Co
Wayne Heffley (Posseł
(Jeff); Damu King (R
(Michael); Larry Ros
Sanders (Travis); Joe
Bergman (Sam Weis
(Coley); and: Mark Ba
Bennett, John Devlin,
Ben Marley, Fred Sad
Whiteman.

Usually when the
try develops a growi
daring topics it depic

TV media inevitably follows suit— ~~~it at a slower pace and in more diluted ~~~sentations. On September 27, 1976, ~~~C-TV telecast *Dawn: Portrait of a ~~~nage Runaway*, q.v., an uncompromis- ~~~ (for its time and especially for TV) ~~~dy of the fate of teenage runaways in ~~~ Angeles who turn to prostitution for ~~~vival. The TV movie achieved so high ~~~audience rating, that producer Douglas ~~~Cramer immediately packaged a sequel. ~~~e resultant *Alexander: The Other Side ~~~Dawn* focused on Alexander "Alex" ~~~ncan (Leigh J. McCloskey), the teen- ~~~d love interest of Dawn (Eve Plumb) in ~~~ earlier narrative. This time, the tele- ~~~n's primary shock value was its "provoc- ~~~ve" presentation of the bisexual (mis)ad- ~~~tures of its young hero. Not since ~~~ theatrical feature *Midnight Cowboy* ~~~969), q.v., had mainstream Hollywood ~~~let alone network television!—dared to ~~~al so openly with such taboo subject ~~~tter.

~~~One evening, on the lurid streets of ~~~Hollywood, California, earnest Alex- ~~~der is stabbed by Swan (Bo Hopkins), ~~~wn's sometime pimp. As the young ~~~n recuperates at a local hospital, the ~~~e film flashes back to several months ~~~lier in Oklahoma. There, farmer Eddie ~~~ncan (Lonny Chapman) is disgusted ~~~th his moody son Alexander, who would ~~~ her sketch pictures than do farmyard ~~~ores. Alex's mother (Diane Douglas) is ~~~wed by her husband who insists that, ~~~th six other offspring to feed, they can- ~~~t keep Alexander on the farm anymore. ~~~ex head westward, intending to enroll in ~~~ art school.

~~~Fresh off the bus in Hollywood, Alex ~~~counters street-smart Buddy (Asher ~~~Brauner), who advises the newcomer: ~~~Good lookin' guy like you. You'll make ~~~t like a champ." The wily but lonely ~~~ddy lets Alex stay at his apartment. ~~~hen Alex cannot find regular work, he ~~~lows Buddy to arrange a "date" for Alex ~~~ith a wealthy older woman for a $50 fee. ~~~n another occasion, Buddy, whose job

skills includes hustling sex with men and dealing drugs, fixes him up with Myra (Juliet Mills). The ingenuous Alex thinks that middle-aged Myra likes him for his personality. However, the next morning she tips him for his services and brushes him off. Soon, Alex becomes cynical and like the older Buddy, is hustling tricks of either sex.

The scene flashes back to the present, with Alex convincing Dawn to return home to Tucson so each can straighten out his/her life. However, Alex's attempts to lead a legitimate life turn sour. He is fired from his stock boy's job in a clothing store because the police show up to interrogate him about the earlier street stabbing. Disgusted, he returns to the Hollywood streets, surviving by picking up homosexual customers. However, this is short-lived when he is entrapped by undercover vice cops. At the precinct, he is rescued by a psychologist, Ray Church (Earl Holliman), employed at the Gay Community Center. Church urges Alex to attend rap sessions there. Alex protests he is not gay, but cannot deal with his confused feelings about his sexuality and his career path.

One day, as a break from his rough life, Alex stops off at an art gallery, where he encounters professional football star Charles "Snake" Selby (Alan Feinstein). The rich, gay 33-year old celebrity invites Alex to stay at his Malibu surfside home. Soon officially, Alex becomes Selby's "houseboy." Meanwhile, Alex keeps in touch with Dawn, who is not adjusting well to "civilian" life in Arizona.

One evening, fickle Snake, whose infatuation with Alex has waned and who has found a fresh playmate, has Alex pick up some recreational drugs in West Hollywood. However, the police arrest Alex in a drug bust. Because of his prior arrests for male prostitution, the judge is inclined to give him a severe sentence. However, at his sentencing, Alex makes a cogent mercy plea: "What it comes down to is I haven't done a very good job of growing up. I'd just like to do what I want to do for

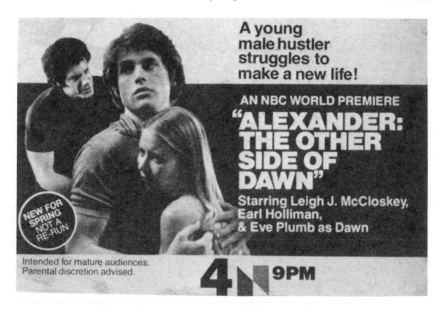

A young
male hustler
struggles to
make a new life!

AN NBC WORLD PREMIERE

"ALEXANDER:
THE OTHER
SIDE OF
DAWN"

Starring Leigh J. McCloskey,
Earl Holliman,
& Eve Plumb as Dawn

NEW FOR
SPRING
NOT A
RE-RUN

Intended for mature audiences.
Parental discretion advised.

4N 9PM

Advertisement for *Alexander: The Other Side of Dawn* **(1977).**

once." He insists he wants to be reunited with his girlfriend and to leave Los Angeles forever. The judge dismisses the case, on condition that he live up to his plans.

Just as Alex steps onto a bus bound for Tucson to be reunited with his girlfriend, he spots Dawn walking down a Hollywood street. (She has given up on her frustrating home life, because no one—including herself—will let her forget her sordid past.) As the two lovers greet one another and decide to relocate to Mendocino, five hundred miles to the north, they observe a teenaged boy arriving on an incoming bus. Much like Alexander, this starry-eyed young newcomer to Hollywood, with all his possessions in a knapsack, seems destined for a troubled life ahead. The cycle continues.

TV Guide magazine felt that this followup telefeature explored its sensational subject "with the same lip-smacking moral prurience that marked the first film." In contrast, John O'Connor (*New York*

Times) thought that *Alexander: The Other Side of Dawn* "turns out to be well worth watching, primarily because of several exceptionally good performances." Regarding its daring subject matter, O'Connor judged, "Much of the betrayal of the hustling scene is unusually convincing." However, O'Connor warned, "The producers want to have their sexual dabbling and, at the same time, retain their innocence. The character of Alexander is conceived as something of a socio-cultural zombie. . . . He is forced to walk through his bisexual adventures in a state of boyish confusion. That's possible after one liaison, but after several, Alexander's character begins to raise questions in the viewer's mind about his mental competence." For Morna Murphy (*Hollywood Reporter*), "Walter Dallenbach has written a tasteful, if rather tedious script that never really comes to grips with the actuality of the hustler's life."

As in *Midnight Cowboy* and the later *American Gigolo* (1980), qq.v., the hero here is presented as a bisexual hustler, primarily to sugarcoat the subject matter for mainstream America. Because Alexander returns to a heterosexual lifestyle at story's end, the typical viewer, it was assumed, could more easily empathize with young Alexander. While the makers of this telefeature, rightly wary of network censorship, compromised the production's validity to a great extent, they did take a giant step forward in presenting for mass market consumption a subject matter that was still "off limits" to most filmgoers.

6. American Gigolo (Paramount,

1980), color, 117 min. R-rated.

Executive producer, Freddie Fields; producer, Jerry Bruckheimer; director/screenplay, Paul Schrader; art director, Ed Richardson; set designer, Mark Fabus; set decorators, George Gaines, Mike Grover; costume co-ordinator, Alice Rush; makeup, Dan Striepeke; music, Giorgio Moroder; songs: Moroder and Schrader; Moroder and Deborah Harry; assistant directors, Peter Bogart, Bill Beasley; stunt coordinator, Jeoffrey Brown; sound, Barry Thomas; camera, John Bailey; editor, Richard Halsey.

Cast: Richard Gere (Julian Kay); Lauren Hutton (Michelle Stratton); Hector Elizondo (Detective Sunday); Nina Van Pallandt (Anne); Bill Duke (Leon Jaimes); Brian Davies (Senator Charles Stratton); K. Callan (Lisa Williams); Tom Stewart (Mr. Rheiman); Patti Carr (Judy Rheiman); David Cryer (Lieutenant Dan Curtis); Carole Cook (Mrs. Sloan); Frances Bergen (Mrs. Laudner); MacDonald Carey (Hollywood Actor); William Dozier (Michelle's Lawyer); Peter Turgeon (Julian's Lawyer); Robert Wightman (Floyd Wicker); Richard Derr (Mr. Williams); Jessica Potter (Jill); Gordon Haight (Blond Boy); Carlo Alonso (Salesman); Michael Goyak (Jason); Frank Pesce (4th Suspect); Judith Ransdell (Cloak Room Girl); John Hammerton (Perino's Maitre d'); Michele Drake (1st Girl at Beach); Linda Horn (2nd Girl at Beach); Faye Michael Nuell (Woman at Juschi's); Eugene Jackson (Bootblack); Roma Alvarez (Maid); Dawn Adams (Co-ed); Bob Jardine (College Professor); Harry Davis (Parke Bernet Gallery Representative); Nanette Tarpey (Waitress); Maggie Jean Smith, Pamela Fong (Girls at Daisy); Randy Stokey (Boy at Sorel); Harris Weingart (Cocktail Lounge Maitre d');

James Currie (Cocktail Lounge Bartender); Norman Stevens (Cocktail Lounge Waiter); Betty Canter, Laura Gile (Women at Political Dinner); Brent Dunsford (Man at Political Dinner); Barry Scatterfield (Street Hustler); Sam L. Nickens (Country Club Waiter); William Valdez (Prison Guard); Mary Helen Barro, John H. Lowe, Kopi Sotiropulos, Gordon W. Grant, Ron Cummins (Reporters).

"The main character of *American Gigolo* is a shallow, materialistic parasite. This poses certain problems for the movie since audiences don't generally 'identify' with shallow, materialistic parasites— even handsome, affluent ones. . . . But we aren't supposed to identify with *American Gigolo*. Rather, we are supposed to keep our distance—to think about the story, not be seduced by it." (David Sterritt, *Christian Science Monitor*)

In Los Angeles, narcissistic, facile Julian Kay (Richard Gere) is a handsome, young male prostitute with a certain talent for linguistics. He serves as "guide and interpreter" to wealthy women of several nationalities visiting the city of Angels. In establishing his career, he was once involved professionally with a homosexual black pimp, Leon Jaimes (Bill Duke), a time of life he tries hard to forget. More recently, Julian has business ties with refined pimp Anne (Nina van Pallandt). Nevertheless, he intends to delete this middle person and work on his own. From surface appearances, he enjoys a flashy lifestyle. However, years of sex-for-money have made him jaded, cold, unhappy and too much a loner. At a bar, Julian meets seductive Michelle Stratton (Lauren Hutton). In their first encounter, he mistakes her for a French visitor to town seeking male company. However, she has few illusions about this stranger.

As a favor to Jaimes, whom he despises for being what he fears he could become, Julian accepts a Palm Springs trick. As it develops, the assignment involves two occupational activities he dislikes: kinky sex and a *menage à trois*. However, greedy for the hefty fee, he follows through with the sado-masochism session with Mr. and Mrs. Rheiman (Tom Stewart, Patti Carr). Back in L.A., Michelle appears at his swank apartment and they make love. Later, Julian finds out that Mrs. Rheiman has been murdered, some time after he was there. Homicide Detective Sunday (Hector Elizondo), helping with the case, informs Julian that Rheiman has an alibi for the evening in question and that he, Julian, has been implicated in the homicide.

While attending a political fundraiser, Julian discovers that Senator Charles Stratton (Brian Davies) is Michelle's husband. Kay realizes his plight when a female client (K. Callan)—with whom he was with at the time of the killing—refuses to corroborate his alibi, fearing public exposure of her tryst. When Julian strengthens his relationship with Michelle, her politically powerful spouse demands that Kay not involve either he or his wife in this homicide investigation. Now frightened, Julian begs his pimp Anne for help. However, she refuses, mad that he has been disloyal to their working agreement. Jaimes agrees to provide an alibi for Julian, but it soon becomes clear that it was Jaimes who had framed him. (The pimp is protecting his own boyfriend who had replaced Julian in servicing the Rheimans and who had gone murderously berserk during one session.) Kay challenges Jaimes and, in a tussle, the latter falls to his death accidentally. Julian is arrested for the Rheiman murder. Thereafter, Michelle disobeys her husband, providing an alibi for Julian. She tells the amazed hustler that she is determined to defend him.

Critical response to *American Gigolo* was mixed at best. Charles Champlin (*Los Angeles Times*) reported, "His [Schrader] account of the life and hard times of a high-priced Southern California male hooker is such an improbable tissue of fantasies and dime-novel borrowings that from moment to moment it seems to be making fun of itself. . . ." Joseph Gelmis

(*Newsday*) reasoned, "But what is surprising about *American Gigolo* is that the dialogue and the performances are no more meaningful than the scenery. . . ." Richard Schickel (*Time* magazine) decided, "Schrader's development of the frame-up story is mechanically melodramatic, and Gere, essentially a boring actor, doesn't help much either. . . . But what finally betrays the film is a redemptive ending." Despite the critical stand-off, the highly-promoted *American Gigolo* grossed a solid $11,500,000 in distributors' domestic film rentals.

Not since the big screen feature *Midnight Cowboy* (1969) and the TV movie *Alexander: The Other Side of Dawn* (1977), qq.v., had mainstream Hollywood dealt so frankly with the world of (heterosexual) male prostitution. (To be noted, there are several indications throughout *American Gigolo* that Julian Kay had turned tricks in the homosexual scene.) As to the despicable Jaimes, a prime people user, he is presented in one-dimensional terms, a close replica of the Brock Peters gay black pimp character in *The Pawnbroker* (1965), q.v. Like his on-screen predecessor, the very ethnic Jaimes is attracted to handsome white dudes, whom he craves homosexually but whom he exploits in bisexual scenes. The masochistic implications of such situations has yet to be explored in dimension on the Hollywood screen.

Originally, John Travolta was to play Julian Kay in *American Gigolo*. Richard Gere and Hector Elizondo of *American Gigolo* would be reunited on camera in *Pretty Woman* (1990).

7. **The Anderson Tapes** (Columbia, 1971), color, 98 min. GP-rated.

Producer, Robert M. Weitman; associate producer, George Justin; director, Sidney Lumet; based on the novel by Lawrence Sanders; screenplay, Frank R. Pierson; production designer, Benjamin J. Kasazkow; art director, Philip Rosenberg; set decorator, Alan Hicks; costumes, Gene Coffin; music/music director, Quincy Jones; assistant director, Alan Hopkins;

sound, Al Gramaglia, Dennis Maitland; camera, Arthur Ornitz; editor, Joanne Burke.

Cast: Sean Connery (Duke Anderson); Dyan Cannon (Ingrid Everleigh); Martin Balsam (Tommy Haskins); Ralph Meeker (Captain Delaney); Alan King (Pat Angelo); Christopher Walken (The Kid); Val Avery ("Socks" Parelli); Dick Williams (Edward Spencer); Garrett Morris (Everson); Stan Gottlieb (Pop); Paul Benjamin (Jimmy); Anthony Holland (Psychologist); Richard B. Schull (Werner); Conrad Bain (Dr. Rubicoff); Margaret Hamilton (Miss Kaler); Judith Lowry (Mrs. Hathaway); Max Showalter (Bingham); Janet Ward (Mrs. Bingham); Scott Jacoby (Jerry Bingham); Norman Rose (Mr. Longene); Meg Miles (Mrs. Longene); John Call (O'Leary); Ralph Stanley (D'Medico, the Attorney); John Braden (Vanessi); Paula Trueman (Nurse); Michael Miller (1st Agent); Michael Prince (Johnson); Frank Macetta (Papa Angelo); Jack Doroshow (Eric); Michael Clary (Eric's Friend); Hildy Brooks (Receptionist); Robert Dagny (Doctor); Bradford English (TV Watcher); Reid Cruckshanks (Judge); Tom Signorelli (Sync Man); Carmine Caridi, George Patelis, William Da Prato (Detectives); Michael Fairman (Sergeant Claire); Sam Coppola (Private Detective); and: Joseph Leon, Helen Martin, George Strus.

The chief gimmick of *The Anderson Tapes*, based on Lawrence Sanders's novel (1970), is the advancing of the plot through characters employing assorted surveillance devices to learn about others' activities. This gambit quickly becomes tiresome, as much a detriment to this thriller as are the quick-and-dirty character stereotypes, especially the swishy homosexual overplayed by Martin Balsam.

Now freed after ten years in prison, Duke Anderson (Sean Connery) calls on his former lover, Ingrid Everleigh (Dyan Cannon), who resides in a chic Manhattan apartment. Neither knows that the residence has been bugged by her jealous lover, Werner (Richard B. Schull). The enterprising Duke decides to rob the luxury building. He organizes his crew: Tommy Haskins (Martin Balsam) an aging gay antique dealer whose phone line is tapped by a federal agency convinced he is selling fakes; the Kid (Christopher

Walken), a former prison-mate pal of Anderson who is being tracked by the Narcotics Squad, and Edward Spencer (Dick Williams), a black truck driver whom law enforcers are tracking as a potentially dangerous activist. (Ironically, none of the assorted policing agencies are after Anderson nor are they aware of one another's overlapping activities.) Anderson obtains backing for his caper from Mafioso Pat Angelo (Alan King), who is being wiretapped by the Internal Revenue Service. As part of the deal with Angelo, Anderson must make one of Pat's expendable underlings (Val Avery) part of the heist and then eliminate him during the burglary.

Selecting the Labor Day weekend for their crime, the gang successfully occupy the apartment building, capturing the tenants and robbing their apartments. Good-naturedly, they permit young Gerry Bingham (Scott Jacoby), a paraplegic, to remain in bed. However, the youth, who is an electronics hobbyist, manages to reach a hidden transmitter in his room and alert the law. Soon the building is surrounded by the police. As the lawbreakers are forced out into the open, the gang members are captured or killed. As for Anderson, who has shot Parelli, he is gunned down by the lawmen, led by Captain Delaney (Ralph Meeker).

Because of the highly-publicized robbery attempt, each of the surveillance agencies quickly erase all their tapes that in any way reference to Duke Anderson.

Pauline Kael (*The New Yorker*) complained, "*The Anderson Tapes* is a broadly played, slovenly crime-caper melodrama with enough crude energy to satisfy people who are looking for a dumb summer show. . . . Sean Connery manages to rise above the material, but he succeeds only in making the rest of the cast look as bad as it is. I've rarely seen so many small, sleazy performances in one movie." Addison Verrill (*Variety*), more tolerant of the feature, noted that the picture "comes at a moment when legal wiretapping and its illegal counterparts are prominent in

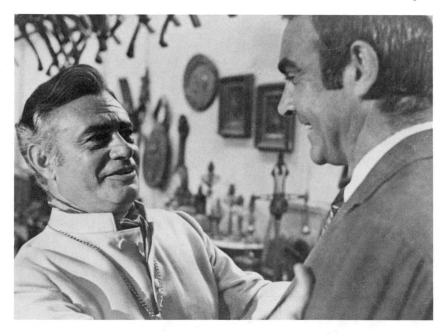

Martin Balsam and Sean Connery in *The Anderson Tapes* **(1971).**

the news. . . ." Richard Combs (British *Monthly Film Bulletin*) pointed out, "The one major issue that the film might be raising—the abuse of electronic surveillance devices by private and government agencies—never materialises as such, but remains as much of a red herring as it was, for different reasons, in Lawrence Sanders' original novel."

Many of the film's characters—immoral in their own ways—are quite homophobic, ranging from the very heterosexual ex-convict Anderson, to the flippant high-price mistress Ingrid who refers to the "fag hairdresser" who lives upstairs in her building, to the assorted sleuthing agencies illegally eavesdropping on the caper-in-the-making. At the opposite end of the pole is the very effeminate Tommy Haskins, complete with pompadour hairstyle and limp wrists. Who better in this gang of misfits and minorities to case the establishment than Haskins who poses as an interior deco-

rator? He is the "queenie" old maid who archly asks Duke, "How was prison? Meet anyone interesting in your cell?" In assessing Balsam's characterization in *The Anderson Tapes*, Verrill of *Variety* noted, "With the flashiest role and most of the laughs, Martin Balsam swishes off with the honors, although gay activists will take umbrage at the abundance of conventional fag jokes, and the general picture of homosexuals as either aging queens with false eyelashes or willowy transvestites who live like Maria Montez."

With location filming in New York City, *The Anderson Tapes* was a box-office hit grossing $5 million in distributors' domestic film rentals. Director Sidney Lumet would deal frequently with gay themes and characters in his movies: *A View from the Bridge* (1961), *The Pawnbroker* (1965), *The Group* (1966), *Dog Day Afternoon* (1975), *Deathtrap* (1982), *Garbo Talks* (1984) and *Q & A* (1990), qq.v.

8. Angel (New World Pictures, 1984), color, 93 min. R-rated.

Executive producers, Mel Pearl, Don Levin; producers, Roy Watts, Don Borchers; director, Robert Vincent O'Neil; screenplay, O'Neil, Joseph M. Cala; art director, Stephen Marsh; set decorator, Chris Amy; costumes, Kathy Clark, Jill Ohanneson; makeup, Kathy Shorkey, Joanne Kozloff; music, Craig Saffin; assisitant directors, Betty Pollock, Jeannine Lucchesi; stunt coordinator, Richard Warlock; sound, Craig Felburg; special effects, Roger George; camera, Andy Davis; editors, Charles Bornstein, Will Henderson.

Cast: Cliff Gorman (Lieutenant Andrews); Donna Wilkes (Angel [Molly Stewart]); Susan Tyrrell (Solly Mosler); Dick Shawn (Mae); Rory Calhoun (Kit Carson); John Diehl (Billy Boy); Elaine Giftos (Patricia Allen); Donna McDaniel (Crystal); Graem McGavin (Lana); Mel Carter (Collins); Steven M. Porter (Yo-Yo Charlie); David Underwood (Ric Sawyer); David Anthony (Howie); Josh Cadman (Spike); Greg Lewis (Themopolis); Karyn Parker (Diane); Dennis Kort (Wayne); Ken Olfson (Mr. Saunders); Peter Jason (The John); Gene Ross (Vice Cop); Jackie De Rouen (Tanya); Laura Sorenson (Roxie); Joseph Michael Cala (Usher); Donna Fuller (Jesus Peddler); Rosso Hagen (Urban Cowboy); Robert Acey (Driver); Dick Valentine (Older Cop); Marc Hayashi (Young Cop); Bob Gorman (Zigmand); Todd Hoffman (Punker); Christian Dante (Police Sketch Artist).

"God knows, if one wants an extreme sense of the American 'now' one need hardly look further than . . . *Angel*, where a pumping-iron, mother-obsessed necrophiliac knife-wilder is slashing to bits hookers accosted on LA's all-human-dregs-are-here Hollywood Boulevard." (John Coleman, *New Statesman*)

In the daytime, attractive fifteen-year old Molly Stewart (Donna Wilkes) is an honor student at an exclusive Los Angeles school, virtuously repulsing the advances of obnoxious school jocks. At nighttime, however, she is a feisty Hollywood Boulevard hooker, using the working name of "Angel." She began in this trade three years earlier after being abandoned by her mother who left town with her latest lover. (Molly's father disappeared when she was six years old.) Molly's income pays the rent on the sparse apartment she and her mother once shared, and her school tuition. Although Angel is street-wise, she relies on the protection/kindness of two Boulevard pals: Kit Carson (Rory Calhoun) a has-been cowboy movie actor/stuntman and Mae (Dick Shawn), a burly transvestite. The latter functions as a surrogate mother for Molly. At home, she shares confidences with her cigar-smoking, lesbian Jewish landlady, the foul-mouthed, raspy-voiced Solly Mosler (Susan Tyrrell).

Meanwhile, psychopathic killer Billy Boy (John Diehl), unhinged by a strong hatred of his mother, occupies a seedy L.A. hotel room. He channels his energies into slashing/killing Hollywood Boulevard hookers and then having sex with the corpses. One night, Molly observes Billy Boy picking up a hooker pal of hers, who soon becomes the mad man's latest victim. Later, homicide detective Lieutenant Andrews (Cliff Gorman) arrests Billy Boy as a suspect in the case. Molly identifies him as the culprit because of distinguishing spurs on his cowboy boots. However, enterprising Billy Boy grabs a gun and makes a bloodbath exit from the police station. Still later, school jock Ric Sawyer (David Underwood) and his cohorts are cruising Hollywood Boulevard one night and spot Molly. She fends off his crude advances with the gun she bought to protect herself against Billy Boy. The rejected Sawyer makes sure everyone at school, including the administration, knows of Molly's dual lifestyle.

By now, Billy Boy is pursuing Molly. He becomes involved in a street tussle with Mae which ends in the latter's death. The angered Molly chases the killer through the streets. As the cornered Billy Boy is about to kill Molly, Kit Carson appears in time to shoot the psychopath.

Kevin Thomas (*Los Angeles Times*) admitted of *Angel*, "The result is pure fantasy, even if there's supposed to be a real Angel out there, that is alternately lurid

Donna Wilkes and Susan Tyrrell in *Angel* (1984).

and sentimental." He also noted, "All but devoid of sex and surprisingly restrained in its depiction of violence, it is simply a routine exploitation picture, and utterly unconvincing at that." Vincent Canby (*New York Times*) rated it "one of the top sleazemobiles 1984." Stanley Crouch (*Village Voice*) was surprised to find that within *Angel* "there is a morality at work which separates this movie from the immoral trash of a *Porky's.* . . ." Crouch pointed out, "Its characters are eccentric and gargoyle variations on situations as old as those in *The Wizard of Oz*, and it is perhaps a comment on our era that the tin man, the scarecrow, and the cowardly lion have been replaced for our young heroine by old movie cowboys, transvestites, prostitutes, and a butched-up lady who would herself be a lady killer."

As with everything else in this quickie picture, the people depicted are caricatures, even those played by such veteran players as Dick Shawn and Susan Tyrrell. In *The Celluloid Closet* (1987), Vito

Russo emphasizes, "The prostitute . . . has two friends—Mae, the pathetic old drag queen played by Dick Shawn as though he were Jack Lemmon in *Some Like It Hot* and Susan Tyrrell as your basic alcoholic crazy lesbian landlady. This film feeds the traditional vision of gays as outcasts who inhabit only the nether world of illicit sexuality. . . ."

With much of its footage shot on the streets of Hollywood, *Angel* grossed an impressive $7,912,740 in distributors' domestic film rentals). It led to two sequels: *Avenging Angel* (1985) and *Angel III: The Final Chapter* (1988), qq.v., neither of which headlined Donna Wilkes in the title role, nor were either as successful financially as the crude but striking original.

9. Angel III: The Final Chapter
(New World Pictures, 1988), color, 99 min. R-rated.

Executive producers, Mel Pearl, Don Levin; producer, Arnold Orgolini; director, Tom De-Simone; based on characters created by Robert Vincent O'Neil, Joseph Michael Cala;

screenplay, DeSimone; art director, Alexandra Kicenik; set decorator, Monette Goldman; costumes, Kristine Chadwick; makeup, Elaine Offers; assistant directors, Michelle Solotar, Mike Johnson; stunt coordinator, John Branagan; special effects, Alan Hall; camera, Howard Wexler; editor, Warren Chadwick.

Cast: Maud Adams (Nadine); Mitzi Kapture (Angel [Molly Stewart]); Mark Blankfield (Spanky); Kim Shriner (Neal); Emile Beaucard (Shahid); Richard Roundtree (Lieutenant Doniger); Tawny Fere (Michelle); Anna Navarro (Gloria); Susan Moore (Pam); Barbara Treutelaar (Shirley); Floyd Levine (Lieutenant Mallin); Kyle Heffner (Tom Santangelo); Dick Miller (Nick Pellegrini); Toni Basil (Hillary); Steven Basil (Porn Assistant Director); S. A. Griffin (Roger); Cynthia Hoppenfeld (Marie); Bob DeSimone (Porn Director); Julie Kristen Smith (Darlene); Kendall Carly Browne (Gallery Woman); Ted Faye (Companion); Paunita Nichols (Black Hooker); Roxanne Kernohan (White Hooker); Laura Albert (Nude Dancer); Tyrone Granderson Jones (Los Angeles Pimp); Kim McKamy, Barbara Hammond, Cheryl Starbuck (Video Girls); Rick Paap (Gallery Officer); Roxanna Hernandez (Girl at Mansion); Michael Bandoni (Mr. Fabazion); Hugh Karraker (Groupie); Phillip Day (Calros); Behop Bedlam (Rap Group).

In the three years since the box-office hit, *Angel*, q.v., New World Pictures had capitalized on the property by releasing *Avenging Angel* (1985), q.v., with Betsy Russell taking over the title assignment from Donna Wilkes. The follow-up was not the lucrative sequel the studio wanted, but was profitable enough to lead to a third entry. *Angel III: The Final Chapter* recycled the formula of its predecessors to minimal effect. While the initial two installments were (relatively) tame in their sexploitation angles, the newest episode changed that. As *The Motion Picture Guide Annual* (1989) noted: "The opening scene in *Angel 3* has more nudity than the first two films put together, and [director Tom] DeSimone tosses naked women into nearly every subsequent scene. . . . DeSimone parades everything from streetwalking to porno filmmaking before the camera with drooling zeal."

Avenging Angel ended with its California-based heroine finishing law school. However, in *Angel III*, Molly Stewart (Mitzi Kapture), a.k.a. Angel, is a 26-year old Manhattan photographer. While on assignment at the Blue Sage Art Gallery, she notices her mother Gloria (Anna Navarro). Before Molly can stop her, the latter vanishes. The street-smart Molly follows her to the West Coast where the two have a reunion in Los Angeles.

Catching up on their years apart, Gloria admits that Molly has a fourteen-year old half-sister, Michelle (Tawny Fere), who is in some sort of trouble. Soon thereafter, Gloria dies in a car bombing. Vengeful Molly decides to rescue Michelle and get her mother's killers. As in years past, Molly returns to the streets in the guise of a prostitute to pick up clues on the homicide. She saunters around Venice Beach where she comes across Spanky (Mark Blankfield), a former drag queen/male prostitute pal who is now a street performer. He explains the drastically changing scene in L.A. due to AIDS, etc.: "Got too weird out there. People dying all around me. So I traded in my mattress for a career in show business." He invites her to stay at his pad and gives her some of his old drag outfits to use in her hooker disguise.

Through Spanky's filmmaker friend, Neal (Kim Shriner), Molly's sleuthing leads to porno moviemaker Tom Santangelo (Kyle Heffner), who auditions Molly for his next picture. On the film set, she hears about Nadine (Maud Adams), who had ordered Gloria's murder and who runs an expensive brothel where Michelle is working. Nadine is also engaged in the white slave trade with drug pusher Shadid (Emile Beaucard). Typically one big step ahead of the law (Richard Roundtree, Floyd Levine), Molly rescues Michelle from Nadine. At the warehouse showdown, Shadid meets a grisly end, Nadine is apprehended, Spanky is wounded (but survives) and Michelle is spared. By now, Molly, fed up with street life of any sort, intends to settle down.

Variety considered this minor effort a "tired-blood melodrama" cluttered with "chintzy" production values. The trade paper forecasted: "[Box-office] Prospects are extremely weak, even among devotees of the first two sexploitationers. . . . Padded film wallows (with too many in-jokes) in the world of porn filmmaking. . . ."

As the resourceful Molly, Mitzi Kapture was more credible than Donna Wilkes or Betsy Russell had been in the focal role in the previous entries. However, she was defeated by the picture's anemic dialogue, careless plot and sloppy direction. One interesting aspect of this sad finale to the saga of Molly "Angel" Stewart was the topical injection of the ramifications of AIDS and how it was changing the street scene, making it deadly and unappealing.

10. As Is (Showtime-Cable, July 27, 1986), color, 90 min. Not rated.

Executive producer, Michael Brandman; producer, Iris Merlis; co-producer, Patrick Whitley; director, Michael Lindsay-Hogg; based on the play by William M. Hoffman; teleplay, Hoffman; art director, Jacques Bradette; set decorator, Angus McCallum; costumes, Julie Ganton; makeup, Jane Meade; music, Peter Matz; assistant directors, Daniel McAree, Ron French; sound, Tom Mather; camera, Rene Ohashi; editor, Ruth Foster.

Cast: Robert Carradine (Rich Farrell); Jonathan Hadary (Saul); Joanna Miles (Lily); Allan Scarfe (Brother); Colleen Dewhurst (Hospice Worker); Julie Ganton (Brother's Wife); Doug Annear (Chet); Samantha Langevin (Partner); Reg Dreger, Gerald Lenton (Doctors); Tonya Williams (TV Commentator); Jeremy Ratchford, Chris Owens (Pickups); Andrew Lewarne, Ted Dillon (Clonea); Robbie Haas (Bartender); Stuart Arnot (1st Man); Linda Kash, Margaret Bard (Women); Brian Young, Paddy Campanaro, Leonard Chow (Persons with AIDS); Elizabeth Rukavina (Nurse); Jason Blicker (Hospital Worker); Robert Morelli, Billie Newton-Davis (Dealers).

By the early 1980s, Acquired Immune Deficiency Syndrome (AIDS) had escalated from a generally unknown disease to a frightening reality; by the mid-1980s, the "gay plague" had reached epic and devastating proportions among both the homosexual and heterosexual population. William M. Hoffman's pathfinding drama, chronicling the mushrooming effects AIDS was having on the gay and straight communities, debuted at New York City's Circle Repertory Theatre on March 10, 1985. It played 62 performances and was given a Drama Desk Award as the Outstanding Play of the season. On May 1, 1985, the production transferred to Broadway's Lyceum Theatre where Jonathan Hadary, Claris Erickson and Jonathan Hogan repeated their leading roles. With the participation of Hadary, an expanded supporting cast and Robert Carradine and Colleen Dewhurst (respectively replacing Jonathan Hogan and Claris Erickson), the pivotal drama was later converted into a made-for-cable film special, airing on July 27, 1986.

The compelling drama avoids moralizing and, instead, focuses on emotions and bonds between people.

Several months ago New Yorker Rich Farrell (Robert Carradine), who has published one volume of short stories, left his loyal if prissy lover Saul (Jonathan Hadary), a photographer, to begin a relationship with handsome, younger Chet (Doug Annear). Now Rich, long an advocate of indulging his sexual passions, has becomes AIDS-infected through Chet. As his fear and anger mounts, he abandons the shallow Chet and returns to Saul who has never stopped caring for his ex-lover. As the disease manifests itself, Rich passes through the various stages of denial, anger and acceptance. Meanwhile, those about him—including his unaccepting brother (Allan Scarfe), his sister-in-law (Julie Ganton) and, of course, Saul—cope or not cope with the pending tragedy. As the end draws painfully near for Rich, Saul is willing to buy pills on the black market so his friend can commit suicide, planning to join his friend in death. Instead, the two draw the curtains around Rich's hospital bed, so they can renew their ties by making love in private. Saul willingly risks his safety so they can affirm their regained love.

Variety reported, "Using the contemporary catastrophic disease to illustrate the meaning of love, *As Is*, is a stinging event . . . [William S.] Hoffman, who wrote his story with unrelenting power and with frankness about the gay scene—and with language so strong it smarts—has developed a rhythm that draws the viewer in with a forcefulness missing from telefilms about sickness. . . . Despite the brutal language and the candid studies of gay life, *As Is*, is beautifully suited to the intimacy of tv, where it is kept within its own boundaries." While Walter Kendrick (*Village Voice*) acknowledged "This portrayal of gay life is franker and less abashed than anything ever shown on cable, not to mention network, television," he found that the "stagy stylization" of Hoffman's writing "doesn't quite work on the tube; it clashes with the blatant naturalism of videotape and comes out looking affected." According to Kendrick, "despite Robert Carradine's impassioned performance, it's difficult to see Rich as anything more engaging than an overaged brat in the throes of terminal self-indulgence." Miles Beller (*Hollywood Reporter*) weighed, "dramatist Hoffman does infuse this work with liberal doses of comedy . . . such an approach gives added significance to it. . . . As a salient story, *As Is* is something too seldom seen on television."

As Is suffers from over-theatricality. The dialogue, betraying its stage origins, is self-consciously arty (i.e., when Rich mourns the loss of the wild old days of gay life: "I love sleaze . . . the whiny self pity of a rainy Monday night in a leather bar.") Nevertheless, *As Is* makes an impact because of its impassioned presentation, avoiding the gloss that marred another mainstream study of AIDS, *An Early Frost* (1985), q.v. Certainly, dramas about the gay lifestyle had come a great distance since *The Boys in the Band* (1970), q.v., and *As Is* would be a major stepping stone

to the later, slicker, *Longtime Companion* (1990), q.v.

11. Avenging Angel (New World Pictures, 1985), color, 93 min. R-rated.

Producers, Sandy Howard, Keith Rubenstein; director, Robert Vincent O'Neil; screenplay, O'Neil, Joseph Michael Cala; art director, Stephen Marsh; set decorator, Patti Hall; music, Chris Young; stunt coordinator, Vincent Deadrick Jr.; special effects, Greg Landerer, Gary Bentley; cameras, Peter Lyons Collister, Bryan England; editor, John Bowey.

Cast: Betsy Russell (Angel [Molly Stewart]); Rory Calhoun (Kit Carson); Robert F. Lyons (Detective Andrews); Susan Tyrrell (Solly Mosler); Ossie Davis (Captain Moradian); Barry Pearl (Johnny Glitter); Ross Hagen (Ray Mitchell); Tim Rossovich (Teddy Butts); Estee Chandler (Cindy); Steven M. Porter (Yo-Yo Charlie); Paul Lambert (Arthur Gerrard); Frank Doubleday (Miles Gerrard); Richard DeHaven (Terry); Tracy Robert Austin (Pat); Michael A. Andrews (Mike); Karin Mani (Janie Soon Lee); Carl Bressler (Professor Garfield); Leroy Daniels (Bootblack); Bill Cakmis (Security Guard); Joseph Michael Cala (Sanitarium Guard); Billy Beck (Tall Man); Liz Sheridan (Nurse); Tony Lorea (Man in Bowler); Laura Burkett (Blonde Hooker); Robert Tessier (Tattoo Artist); Jan Peters (Businessman); Hoke Howell (Seven Fingers Sid); Edward Blackoff (Studs); Dick Valentine (Cop); Paul Mousie Garner (Joe Borenstein); Jeanne Lucas (Shopping Cart Sally); Charlene Jones (Hooker); Claudia Templeton (Claudia); Howard Honig (Baylor); Debi Sue Voorhees (Roxie); Charles Shires, Richard Acunto (Spectators); Jessica O'Neil (Little Buck).

One year following the box-office hit *Angel* (1984), q.v., that film's director/ scripter (Robert Vincent O'Neil) created this sequel.

Four years have elapsed since the story-line end of *Angel*. Molly Stewart (Betsy Russell) is about to graduate from law school. Her career transformation and education has been financed by L.A. police detective Andrews (Robert F. Lyons). When he and Janie Soon Lee (Karin Mani), an undercover police person posing as a hooker, are killed by hoodlums, Molly returns to Hollywood, bent on avenging their deaths. She learns from her former landlady, the crotchety lesbian Solly Mosler (Susan Tyrrell) that their pal Kit Carson (Rory Calhoun), a former Western movie stuntman, has grown old and addled, and is stuck in a mental institution. Angel breaks into the asylum and releases her friend.

Disguised as a street hooker, Angel, along with Solly, Kit and street magician Yo-Yo Charlie (Steven M. Porter), track the murderers. The clues leads to underworld figure Arthur Gerrard (Paul Lambert) who is plotting to control all Hollywood Boulevard businesses so he can operate his vice rings more easily. The vigilante crew capture Gerrard's son, Miles (Frank Doubleday). When Miles tries to escape, he dies in a shootout with Kit. In the showdown, Gerrard is finished off by the gun-toting Solly.

Variety printed, "The pic largely duplicates the *Angel* formula. Softcore sleaze, taut thighs, car chases and beau-coup gunplay are accompanied by a raft of 'colorful' street characters who make unwanted claims on the audience's attention." Michael Wilmington (*Los Angeles Times*) agreed that the new Molly was "more opulent" but that "once again, it's her ragtag street associates who provide most of the movie's fun, especially Susan Tyrrell as an engagingly foul-mouthed lesbian landlady."

With its lack of zest, *Avenging Angel* was not as popular as the original feature, even with Susan Tyrrell and Rory Calhoun repeating their oversized characterizations. Despite its shortcomings and because of the reputation of *Angel*, the new picture was profitable enough to inspire *Angel III: The Final Chapter* (1988), q.v.

12. The Balcony (Continental Distributing, 1963), 84 min. Not rated.

Producers, Ben Maddow, Joseph Strick; assistant producer, Rosemary Kaye; director, Strick; based on the play *Le balcon* by Jean Genet and the English adaptation by Bernard Frechtman; screenplay, Maddow; art directors, John Nicholson, Jean Owens, Gabriel Scog-

namillo; music conductor, Robert Craft; assistant director, Helen Levitt; sound editors, Verna Fields, Jeanne Turner; camera, George Fosley; editor, Chester W. Schaeffer.

Cast: Shelley Winters (Madame Irma); Peter Falk (Police Chief); Lee Grant (Carmen); Ruby Dee (Thief); Peter Brocco (Judge); Kent Smith (General); Jeff Corey (Bishop); Joyce Jameson (Penitent); Arnette Jens (Horse); Leonard Nimoy (Roger, the Rebel Leader).

French playwright Jean Genet's allegorical play *Le balcon* (1956) had been translated into English by Bernard Frechtman in 1957. Because of its impressive origin and its stage success, this dark fantasy could be produced as a low-budget, independent film in the "new" Hollywood. It broke new ground in sexual permissiveness on screen, but it confused too many critics and moviegoers to be a box-office success.

A revolution has broken out in the streets of an unnamed city. However, inside Madame Irma's (Shelley Winters) whorehouse, known as "The Balcony" and located on a movie soundstage, Irma's gals earn hefty fees for making their customers' bizarre fantasies come true. One of the clients thinks of himself as the Bishop (Jeff Corey), and he earnestly listens to the confessions of a penitent (Joyce Jameson). The arrogant General (Kent Smith) is contemptuous of his faithful horse (Arnette Jens). A third customer, the Judge (Peter Brocco), finds pleasure in licking the shoes of a timorous thief (Ruby Dee).

Meanwhile, Irma's lover, the Chief of Police (Peter Falk), appears, alerting her that the Queen and several other state officials are either dead or now in hiding. The Police Chief suggests that Irma could stymy the revolutionaries—headed by the idealistic Roger (Leonard Nimoy)—if she pretends to be the Queen. Although she refuses, her condescending clientele (the Bishop, the General, the Judge) agree to perform their charades in public. Their bizarre parading through the city contributes to the downfall of the revolution.

The three pompous figureheads return to the Balcony, determined to retain their new-found power. They fight with one another, while the love-starved Police Chief breaks into Irma's room, halting her liaison with Carmen (Lee Grant), Irma's bookkeeper and lover. When Roger appears demanding to be the new Chief of Police, he—now attired in the police chief's uniform—and Carmen play out Roger's fantasy. Later, Roger and the Police Chief argue. Irma orders her girls to strip the two men. The latter, draped only in towels, are sent out into the street.

Variety, which agreed that this was "one of the most original and 'adult' American films in years," acknowledged, "This is never an easy film to watch, but also it is never boring or pretentious, and often it is acidly funny." The trade paper endorsed, "Presiding over the macabre revels is Shelley Winters, the madam who designs the illusions and is all the more ominous for her complete, almost tender detachment." On the other hand, the British *Monthly Film Bulletin* concluded, "The most disappointing thing about this film . . . is that it should be so pedestrian in its approach to the subject. Genet's brothel is a concept rather than a place, and Joseph Strick threw away his trump card by setting the scene on what is so obviously the sound stage of a film studio. Although the sham sets are superficially effective enough, one feels that inspiration has given way to economy. . . . And a general staginess of presentation applies. . . ."

A mini-trend in the Hollywood of the early 1960s was to present bordello madams as lesbians. In *Walk on the Wild Side* (1962), q.v., it had been tough-as-nails Barbara Stanwyck lusting for her worker Capucine. In *The Balcony*, it was shrill Shelley Winters hankering for sedate Lee Grant, whom she promotes from man-pleaser to accounts-keeper. In their roles, Winters and Grant share a kiss, leading *Variety* to report of the "comparativley gentle moment when the madame restrains her young office assistant, Lee Grant (for whom she has a lesbian lech), from returing to her original job with the rest of the girls."

13. Basic Instinct (Tri-Star, 1992), color, 127 min. R-rated.

Executive producer, Mario Kassar; producer, Alan Marshall; associate producers, William S. Beasley, Louis D'Esposito; director, Paul Verhoeven; screenplay, Joe Eszterhas; production designer, Terence Marsh; art director, Mark Billerman; set designers, Steve Berger, Barbara Mesney; set decorator, Anne Kuljian; costumes, Ellen Mirojnick; special makeup effects, Rob Bottin; makeup, David Craig Forrest; music, Jerry Goldsmith; assistant director, D'Esposito; second unit director, M. James Arnett; stunt coordinators, Arnett, Charles Picerni; sound, Fred Runner; camera, Jan De Bont; editor, Frank J. Urioste.

Cast: Michael Douglas (Detective Nick Curran); Sharon Stone (Catherine Tramell); George Dzundza (Gus); Jeanne Tripplehorn (Dr. Beth Gardner); Denis Arndt (Lieutenant Walker); Leilani Sarelle (Roxy); Bruce A. Young (Andrews); Chelcie Ross (Captain Talcott); Dorothy Malone (Hazel Dobkins); Wayne Knight (John Correli); Daniel Von Bargen (Lieutenant Nilsen); Stephen Tobolwosky (Dr. Lamott); Benjamin Mouton (Harrigan); Jack McGee (Sheriff); Bill Cable (Johnny Boz); Stephen Rowe, Mitch Pileggi (Internal Affairs Investigators); Mary Pat Gleason (Juvenile Officer); Freda Foh Shen (Berkeley Registrar); William Duff-Griffin (Dr. Myron); David Wells (Polygraph Examinier); Bradford Englis (Campus Policeman); Mary Ann Rodgers, Adilah Barnes (Nurses); Irene Olga Lopez (Maid); Juanita Jennings (Receptionist); Craig C. Lewis (Bartender at Police Bar); Michael David Lally, Peter Appel (Detectives); Michael Halton (Bartender at Country Western Bar); Keith A. McDaniel (Featured Dancer); Eric Poppick (Coroner's Guy); Ron Cacas (Policeman); Elsie Sniffen (Roxy's Friend); Ken Liebenson, Lindy Rasmusson, Byron Berline, Eddie Dunbar, Tod McKibbin (Doo Wah Riders Band Members); Julie Bond (Hand Puppet Model).

"If you think you're fucked up and you go see this movie and you're not sexually aroused by it—you're probably not as fucked up as you think you are. . . . This is supposed to be a sexy crime film, but no

Sharon Stone and Michael Douglas in *Basic Instinct* (1992).

cop acts like a cop and no situation conveys a motive." (Michael Ventura, *LA Weekly*)

Ever since Joe Eszterhas, who had written *Jagged Edge* (1985), was paid a reported $3 million to script *Basic Instinct*, this film became a high profile Hollywood production. When Michael Douglas was signed for mega-millions to star in this cop crime thriller of obsessive love, the movie became associated immediately with Douglas's earlier hit, *Fatal Attraction* (1987). When Dutch-born director Paul Verhoeven was attached to the San Francisco-set movie, it was insured that *Basic Instinct* would overflow with visual violence on the order of the filmmaker's slam-bang *RoboCop* (1987) and *Total Recall* (1990). As soon as word leaked that this exotic tingler revolved around a bisexual ice pick murderess, gay and lesbian groups began protesting loudly, a campaign which accelerated up to and through the film's much-anticipated opening (ironically providing the movie with just the ticket-selling publicity the gay rights activists were hoping to counter). At the last minute, Verhoeven made editing cuts in the movie (removing moments of gore and explicit sex) so the picture would receive an R-rating rather than a commercially debilitating NC-17 one.

However, when *Basic Instinct* was released, most viewers seemed to agree with Owen Gleiberman (*Entertainment Weekly*) who gave the picture a C+, reasoning, "Beneath its heavy-breathing fripperies . . . the movie is mechanical and routine, a muddle of Hitchcockian red herrings and standard cop-thriller ballistics. . . . There are four unusually lengthy and explicit sex scenes, but these centerpiece couplings depend on the sort of officially 'hot' devices . . . that are no longer shocking, or even very titillating. Most of the scenes make such a big point of being daring . . . that they're less erotic than showy. At one point the characters go to an ambisexual dance club and the leering 'decadence' is shoved in our faces. You half expect the

place to be called Dante's Inferno." For the author, seldom has a contemporary mainstream American movie boasted so many sick, mind-game playing characters or a director who thrived so enthusiastically on manipulating his audience into so many blind alleys.

At his San Francisco mansion, ex-rock star Johnny Boz (Bill Cable) is found murdered, his bloody corpse tied to the bedposts and his body punctured with multiple ice pick jabs. Detective Nick Curran (Michael Douglas) is assigned to the highly publicized case. An immediate suspect is Boz's sleek, rich, brainy girlfriend, Catherine Tramell (Sharon Stone), the last person to be seen with the victim. She arouses the police's suspicion on another level. She had written a recent novel (*Love Hurts*) detailing a very similar murder of a rock star. The law officers at her questioning insist, "Ah ha!" to which she replies "No way!", claiming she would not be that stupid to commit a crime she had already detailed so publicly in her book.

As the tale proceeds, Curran and Tramell have an eerie immediate attraction for one another. Unexplainably, he has a sixth sense about her abnormal psychological profile. On her part, she knows *everything* about him: from the suicide of his wife, to his bouts with booze, drugs and being trigger-happy. In short order, Nick learns that Catherine is an icy cool seductress who thrives on sexual encounters, including those with her tough girl-friend, Roxy (Leilani Sarelle). After Roxy attempts to run Curran down and is herself killed, it is learned that Roxy and another woman—a platonic older friend (Dorothy Malone) of Catherine's—share a disturbing similarity: each, at one time, have burst into unexplainable rage, and committed multiple murders.

Curran's cop pal and best friend, Gus (George Dzundza), warns Nick to stay away from beautiful, crazy, dangerous Catherine—that she is stalking him. However, the cat-and-mouse game thrills Curran, especially whenever Tramell whines

"Everybody that I am close to dies!" As the twisted Nick and Catherine proceed to bed down, Curran's sometime girlfriend, police psychologist Dr. Beth Gardner (Jeanne Tripplehorn), becomes intrigued clinically while subjectively jealous. Later, it is revealed that Beth, whose doctor husband died six years ago mysteriously, was Catherine's college classmate and that they had slept together at least once. Each woman now maintains that the other became obsessively possessive of the other. Not until Gus's gory death and Beth's death is the murderer's identity revealed. At the denouement, Nick and Catherine retire to the bedroom for therapeutic sex, with an eerie scene of deja vu referring to the opening murder scene.

Kenneth Turan (*Los Angeles Times*) concluded: "*Basic Instinct* is a reminder of the difference between exhilaration and exhaustion, between tension and hysteria, between eroticism and exhibitionism. The line may be fine, but it is real enough to separate the great thrillers from the also-rans. And *Basic Instinct* is not a great thriller. . . . [Even] though bisexual and lesbian characters do appear only in non-role model roles, *Basic Instinct* feels more contemptuous of women in general than specifically anti-gay. And despite liberal amounts of both male and female nudity, the celebrated sex scenes have all the feeling and finesse of aggressive board checking in the Stanley Cup finals. . . . If *Basic Instinct*'s characters go in too few directions, its plot goes in too many. . . ." Mark Goodman (*People*) complained, "Verhoeven has such fun conjuring up old film noir tricks (dirty secrets, false endings) that he has no time left to attend to plot. . . ."

In contrast, Todd McCarthy (*Daily Variety*) felt that, "*Basic Instinct* is Grade A, high-gloss, ultra classy pulp fiction . . . [Picture] is not anti-gay, and anyone who has seen all of Paul Verhoeven's previous work would know that he has shown more interest in and sympathy for his characters' distinctive and varied sexualities than

99% of all other directors. . . . At the same time, film is very arguably misogynistic, but no more so than a thousand other films. . . . After a decade marking time mostly in schlockers, Stone has a career-making role here. . . .Frank, provocative, daring and dangerous, she embodies what men both crave and fear, and she exists only in fiction. But Stone brings her vividly to life for a couple of hours." For Duane Bryge (*Hollywood Reporter*), "Eszterhas' screenplay is riveting: abrupt plot turns spring naturally from the lead character's pathologies. Even character inconsistencies and plot lapse are brushed over by Paul Verhoeven's full-throttle direction. . . . However, the whole escape often careens into overkill. Jerry Goldsmith's appropriately tempestuous score . . . is employed by Verhoeven to oversaturation level." Michael Ventura (*LA Weekly*), argued that "To be insulted by such tripe is to take it too seriously," and admitted that the film had "one brief saving grace: a marvelous cameo by Dorothy Malone, who at age 67, and in less than 60 seconds of camera time, gives a master lesson in how a screen actor portrays sexuality, complexity and intrigue."

In its first fourteen weeks of domestic distribution, *Basic Instinct* grossed $108,648,808 at the box-office, proving that hype of any sort is an aphrodisiac. By the time *Basic Instinct* was released, other movies had jumped onto the bandwagon of featuring a bisexual murderess. For example, the CBS-TV movie *In the Eyes of a Stranger* (1992), featured a maverick cop (Richard Dean Anderson) protecting a murder witness (Justine Bateman) who not only has a criminal lust for money, but admits that her girlfriend (Cynthia Dale) was once her pimp and her lover. And so the cycle continues.

14. Becket (Paramount, 1964), color, 148 min. Not rated.

Producer, Hal Wallis; director, Peter Glenville; based on the play *Becket ou l'honneur de Dieu* by Jean Anouilh as translated by Lucienne Hill; screenplay, Edward Anhalt; production designer, John Bryan; art director, Maurice Carter; set decorator, Robert Cartwright; costumes, Phyllis Dalton; makeup, Charles Parker; music, Laurence Rosenthal; assistant director, Colin Brewer; sound, Buster Ambler; camera, Geoffrey Unsworth; editor, Anne V. Coates.

Cast: Richard Burton (Thomas Becket); Peter O'Toole (King Henry II); John Gielgud (King Louis VII of France); Donald Wolfit (Gilbert Folliot, Bishop of London); Martita Hunt (Queen Matilda); Pamela Brown (Queen Eleanor); Paolo Stoppa (Pope Alexander III); Gino Cervi (Cardinal Zambelli); David Weston (Brother John); Felix Aylmer (Archbishop of Canterbury); Percy Herbert, Niall MacGinnis, Christopher Rhodes, Peter Jeffrey, Michael Miller, Peter Prowse (Henry II's Barons); Inigo Jackson (Robert de Beaumont, Duke of Leicester); Sian Phillips (Gwendolen); Veronique Vendell (French Girl); Gerald Lawson (Old Peasant); Jennifer Hilary (Peasant's Daughter); John Phillips (Bishop of Winchester); Frank Pettingell (Bishop of York); Hamilton Dyce (Bishop of Chichester); Paul Farrell (Farmer); Rose Howlett (Farmer's Wife); Linda Marlowe (Farmer's Daughter); Patrick Newell (William of Corbeil); Riggs O'Hara (Prince Henry); Geoffrey Bayldon (Brother Philip); Graham Stark (Pope's Secretary); Victor Spinetti (French Tailor); Magda Knopke (Girl on Balcony); Wilfrid Lawson (Old Soldier); Edward Woodward (Clement); Tutte Lemkow, Michael Anthony (Courtiers).

Becket was based on Jean Anouilh's French play (1959) which later (1960), in an English-language translation by Lucienne Hill, opened on Broadway starring Laurence Olivier (Thomas Becket) and Anthony Quinn (Henry II). As adapted to the screen, this U.S.-British co-production was a lusty spectacle in which gorgeous cinematography and splendid locales aided the lengthy narrative drama of the turbulent love/hate relationship between Henry II (1133–1189), the great grandson of William the Conqueror, and Thomas Becket (1118–1170). On screen, director Peter Glenville (who had supervised the Broadway stage version) opened up the drama to take advantage of on-location filming in England.

What remained unchanged in *Becket* was the complex bond between the two lead characters, a subtext of which (far more emphatic in the film than on the Broadway stage) was King Henry II's strong yearning for Thomas Becket. This element did not go unnoticed by the critics. *Newsweek* magazine commented that playwright Anouilh, "by descending to the realm of the psychiatric and implying a sexual attraction between the two, muddies the issues." Andrew Sarris (*Village Voice*) observed that of the main players, "O'Toole plays the King as a lovesick Queen." This was another illustration of Hollywood stretching itself to a new realism in the more permissive 1960s, even if it hid behind the cloak of historical fact. This period drama gave new meaning to the buddy film genre.

Opening in 1170, with King Henry II (Peter O'Toole) of England at the coffin of the murdered Thomas Becket (Richard Burton), Archbishop of Canterbury, Henry recalls the time years ago when the two were best friends. Back then, the excitable and impulsive Henry relied heavily on the friendship and counsel of the witty Becket, the London-born son of Saxon parents. With any excuse, Henry is pleased to be away from the staid Queen Eleanor (Pamela Brown) and the disdainful Matilda (Martita Hunt), the Queen Mother. Henry and Becket spend their time womanizing, drinking and hunting, always in each other's company. (At one point the haughty Queen mother complains of Henry's "unnatural" fixation on Becket.) In a moment of good will, the capricious Henry appoints Becket to the Chancellorship of England, much to the horror of his high-ranking advisors, including the Archbishop of Canterbury (Felix Aylmer) and Bishop Folliot (Donald Wolfit) of London. To everyone's amazement, including Becket's, the royal appointment sobers his nature, leading to conflicts with the fun-loving King.

The gap between the two men is widened after the possessive Henry insists on having Becket's mistress, Gwendolen (Sian Phillips) for himself. In her grief, Gwendolen kills herself, widening the gap between the two former friends. Later, a recalcitrant Henry appoints Thomas as Archbishop of Canterbury, which convinces Becket to insist that the will of God must now come before king. The two men collide continually, causing Thomas to resign from office and flee to France. (At one point, a court observer notes that Henry reacts to Thomas's rejection of their friendship "as if Becket were a woman.")

In France, King Louis VII (John Gielgud) offers Becket asylum. Eventually, duty-bound Thomas returns to England where he is greeted triumphantly by the Saxon population. This display of support leads the petulant Henry to wish aloud that he could be rid of Becket. Several of his barons take the thought as a command and murder Becket at the altar at Canterbury. Grieved by Thomas's death and knowing that it is political, the King allows himself to be publicly chastised by having Saxon monks flog him. Thereafter, he proclaims the martyrdom of Becket who is to be honored as a saint.

Bosley Crowther (*New York Times*), while agreeing that *Becket* has the look of "stately substance and historical authenticity," was more concerned about the movie's focus on Henry's "shattering realization that his love [for Becket] has been spurned." For the disturbed Crowther, "This rather intimate insight into the nature of the clash exposes to us a Henry who is not in the history book. This is a flabby, ranting monarch who is played by Peter O'Toole with a vast range of wild and frightened feelings chasing across his face and through his eyes." In contrast, Crowther was more comfortable with Burton's characterization, "There is little give in Mr. Burton's performance, little spirituality, little warmth. He is probably very close to the Becket of history."

Variety granted that *Becket* was "Richly mounted, vividly realized costumed drama with exceptional dialog. An exciting film. . . ." It too speculated on the multilayered relationship between the two historical characters. "The latency of homosexuality in the relationship is more than hinted." The British *Monthly Film Bulletin* chose not to deal with the film's sexual innuendos, instead noting that director Peter Glenville's "half-hearted attempts to open out the play seem clumsy or irrelevant. . . . O'Toole is effective, if mannered, and delivers the coarser of Anouilh's tirades with due relish; but Burton, though adequate in the early scenes is detached, even distant, and hardly suggests Becket's spiritual development."

Shot in 35mm and blown up to 70mm for road show engagements, *Becket* grossed $5 million in distributors' domestic film rentals. The picture received an Academy Award for Best Screenplay—Based on Material from Another Medium. It also received ten (!) other Oscar nominations: Best Picture (*My Fair Lady* won); Best Actor (Richard Burton and Peter O'Toole; Rex Harrison of *My Fair Lady* won); Best Supporting Actor (John Gielgud; Peter Ustinov of *Topkapi* won); Best Director (George Cukor of *My Fair Lady* won); Best Cinematography—Color (*My Fair Lady* won); Best Art Direction—Set Decoration—Color (*My Fair Lady* won); Best Sound (*My Fair Lady* won); Best Music Score (*Mary Poppins* won); Best Editing (*Mary Poppins* won); Best Costume Design—Color (*My Fair Lady* won). Peter O'Toole would play King Henry II again on camera in the British-made *The Lion in Winter* (1968), a historical drama which featured the homosexual relationship between the King's son (Anthony Hopkins)—the later Richard the Lion-Hearted and king of England—and the King of France (Timothy Dalton). Actress Sian Phillips, who played Gwendolen in *Becket* was then married to Peter O'Toole. Earlier, in 1962, Peter O'Toole, who had a penchant for playing tortured, sensitive characters, starred in the British-made *Lawrence of Arabia*.

15. Ben-Hur (Metro-Goldwyn-Mayer, 1959), color, 1959. 212 min. Not rated.

Producer, Sam Zimbalist; director, William Wyler; based on the novel *Ben-Hur: A Tale of the Christ* by General Lew Wallace; screenplay, Karl Tunberg, (uncredited): Maxwell Anderson, S. N. Behrman, Christopher Fry, Gore Vidal; art directors, William Horning, Edward Carfagno; set decorator, Hugh Hunt; costumes, Elizabeth Haffenden; makeup, Charles Parker; music, Miklos Rozsa; associate directors, Andrew Marton, Yakima Canutt, Mario Soldati; third unit director, Richard Thorpe; assistant directors, Gus Agosti, Alberto Cardone; sound supervisor, Franklin Milton; sound, Sash Fisher, William Steinkamp; special camera effects, Arnold Gillespie, Robert MacDonald; camera, Robert L. Surtees; second unit camera, Pietro Portalupi; editors, Ralph E. Winters, John Dunnings.

Cast: Charlton Heston (Judah Ben-Hur); Jack Hawkins (Quintus Arrius); Stephen Boyd (Messala); Haya Harareet (Esther); Hugh Griffith (Sheik Iderim); Martha Scott (Miriam); Sam Jaffe (Simonides); Cathy O'Donnell (Tirzah); Finlay Currie (Balthasar); Frank Thring (Pontius Pilate); Terence Longden (Drusus); Andre Morell (Sextus); Marina Berti (Flavia); George Relph (Tiberius); Adi Berber (Malluch); Stella Vitelleschi (Amrah); Jose Greci (Mary); Laurence Payne (Joseph); John Horsley (Spintho); Richard Coleman (Metellus); Duncan Lamont (Marius); Ralph Truman (Aide to Tiberius); Richard Hale (Gaspar); Reginald Lal Singh (Melchoir); David Davies (Quaestar); Dervis Ward (Jailer); Claude Heater (The Christ); Mino Doro (Gratus); Robert Brown (Chief of Rowers); John Glenn (Rower #42); Maxwell Shaw (Rower #43); Emile Carrer (Rower #28); Tutte Lemkow (Leper); Howard Lang (Hortator); Ferdy Mayne (Captain of Rescue Ship); John Le Mesurier (Doctor); Stevenson Lang (Blind Man); Aldo Mozele (Barca); Thomas O'Leary (Starter at Race); Noel Sheldon (Centurion); Hector Ross (Officer); Bill Kuehl (Soldier); Aldo Silvani (Manin Nazareth); Diego Pozzetto (Villager); Dino Fazio (Marcello); Michael Cosmo (Raimondo); Aldo Pial (Calvary Officer); Remington Olmstead (Decurian); Victor De La Fosse (Galley Officer); Enzo Fiemonte (Galley Officer); Hugh Billingsley (Mario) Tiberio Mitri (Roman at Bath); Pietro Tordi (Pilate's Servant); Jerry Brown (The Corinthian); Otello Capanna (The Byzantine); Luigi Marra (Syrian); Cliff Lyons (Lubian); Edward J. Auregul (Athenian); Joe Yrigoyan (Egyptian); Alfredo Danesi (Armenian); Raimondo Van Riel (Old Man); Mike Dugan (Seaman); Joe Canutt (Sportsman).

"Ben-Hur is the ultimate Technicolor meditation on homoerotic, S&M and master/slave relationships, as Judah Ben-Hur, Charlton Heston endures enough whipping, degradation, forced bondage and beatings to make even the most jaded masochist wince. . . . Looking at it now [1990], Ben-Hur's homoerotic subtext is the film's most obvious draw." (Dave Gardetta, *LA Weekly*)

General Lew Wallace's enormously popular novel, *Ben-Hur, A Tale of the Christ* (1880), led to a successful American stage version in 1899 and to several screen adaptations. The first was a one-reel silent version in 1907 by the Kalem Film Company. Almost two decades later, Metro-Goldwyn-Mayer Pictures produced a then staggeringly expensive ($4 million) silent remake of the religious spectacular starring Ramon Novarro (Ben-Hur) and Francis X. Bushman (Messala), with direction by Fred Niblo. One of the several unit directors for the famous Roman circus maximus chariot scene was William Wyler. In 1959, Wyler was hired to direct MGM's lavish ($15 million), sprawling sound remake of this religious melodrama. He admitted later that what attracted him to the epic story was the Jews' fight for their freedom. Nevertheless, Wyler always insisted that *Ben-Hur* "was never intended to be anything more or less than an adventure story with no artistic pretentiousness at all . . ." He accomplished that and far more.

During the reign of the Roman Empire's Augustus Caesar, Judah Ben-Hur (Charlton Heston) is born into a wealthy Jewish family. At about the same time, Jesus Christ is born.

Several years later, Messala (Stephen Boyd), a boyhood friend of Judah Ben-Hur returns to Jerusalem after years in Rome. He is now a centurion in the Roman army and rising star in the imperial

Stephen Boyd and Charlton Heston in *Ben-Hur* (1959).

service. He and Ben-Hur, a wealthy prince of Judea, share a reunion at the Roman garrison which Messala now commands. Messala is also welcomed by Judah's mother, Miriam (Martha Scott) and by Judah's sister, Tirzah (Cathy O'Donnell). When Messala pressures Ben-Hur to reveal the names of Jewish patriots who oppose Roman rule, Judah's refusal to cooperate earns him Messala's enmity. During a parade welcoming the arrival of the new Roman governor, Judah and his family watch from their palace roof. A tile accidentally breaks off and falls, striking the governor's head. Immediately, Messala and his soldiers arrest the innocent family. Judah is sentenced to the Roman galleys for life; Miriam and Tirzah remain imprisoned.

Three years pass. In the ship galleys, Ben-Hur is chained to the oar of a Roman flagship, ruled by a new commander, Quintus Arrius (Jack Hawkins). The sadistic Arrius takes a liking to the defiant, muscular Ben-Hur; he is even amused by the slave's belief that his God will help him survive the ordeal to gain revenge on his enemy, Messala. During the preparations for a coming battle, Arrius orders that Ben-Hur's leg be unshackled. After the vessel is rammed, the brawny Judah is able to break free. He releases the other galley prisoners and rushes on deck to find the ship being boarded by pirates. When Arrius falls overboard, Judah jumps in to save the Roman consul. They are rescued by another Roman ship and learn that the imperial forces have won the naval engagement. The grateful Arrius adopts Judah, bringing him to Rome as his son.

Ben-Hur is taught the methods of Roman warfare. However, despite the advantages he leaves behind, he returns to Judea to search for his mother and sister. Finding his faithful steward, Simonides (Sam Jaffee), he learns that the man has saved and even increased the family's wealth. Meanwhile, Judah becomes fascinated with Simonides's daughter, Esther (Haya Harareet).

Searching for his relatives, Judah encounters Sheik Ilderim (Hugh Griffith), a wealthy Arab who owns four splendid white horses. The eccentric Ilderim persuades Ben-Hur to compete against Messala, a powerful force in Jerusalem, in an upcoming chariot race. By now, Messala has discovered that Miriam and Tirzah contracted leprosy during their years in prison. He sends them to the Valley of Lepers, but allows Judah to think they are dead. The wrathful Ben-Hur wins the thundering race, while Messala is fatally injured. Before he dies, Messala goadingly tells Judah of his relatives' fate. (By this time, Esther has found Miriam and Tirzah and has been bringing them food. At their request, she has not told Ben-Hur of their fate.)

As Judah continues to look for his loved ones, he encounters a man preaching to a large crowd, the same carpenter who once gave him water at Nazareth when Ben-Hur was being marched off as a galley slave. Later, Judah finds himself engulfed by the mob who is following the preacher to his crucifixion by the Romans. After Christ's death on the cross, there is a period of stormy darkness, followed by a lighting storm. Miriam and Tirzah seek refuge in a cave. In the midst of the tempest, they discover that they have been cured miraculously. In the springtime rain that follows, Ben-Hur is reunited with his mother, sister and the loving Esther.

In judging the colossal *Ben-Hur*, an enthusiastic Bosley Crowther (*New York Times*) stated that the filmmakers "have managed to engineer a remarkably intelligent and engrossing human drama" and approved of Wyler et al for stressing "the powerful and meaningful personal conflicts that are strong in this old heroic tale. . . . . Charlton Heston is excellent as Ben-Hur—strong, aggressive, proud and warm—and Stephen Boyd plays his nemesis, Messala, with those same qualities, inverted ideologically." *Variety* rated the movie a "Blockbuster to top all previous blockbusters," adding, "The big difference between *Ben-Hur* and other spectacles, biblical or otherwise, is its sincere concern for human beings. . . . they arouse genuine emotional feeling in the audience." One mainstream critic unmoved by this lavish production was Dwight MacDonald (*Esquire* magazine) who insisted, "watching Ben-Hur was like waiting at a railroad crossing while an interminable freight train lumbers past, often stopping completely for a while."

At the time of production, MGM made much of the extravagant nature of *Ben-Hur* which utilized at the Cinecitta Studios in Rome 300 sets, 100,000 costumes, 1,500,000 props, 10,000 extra and 78 Yugoslavian horses trained for the critical circus chariot race. No publicity, at the time, was given to the fact that one of the uncredited script collaborators, Gore Vidal, had introduced a sub-theme of Messala and Judah Ben-Hur having been lovers years before, a relationship which Messala hopes to rekindle when they reunite in Jerusalem as adults. According to Vidal, this subtext was engineered with the approval of William Wyler, the endorsement of Stephen Boyd, but without the direct knowledge of the conservative Charlton Heston. If this script angle is true, a new dimension is present in the reunion scenes between Ben-Hur and Messala, who once saved Judah's life ("The best thing I ever did," the Roman insists).

Their love-hate relationship laces through the remainder of the film, leading Messala to observe cynically at one point "Is there anything so sad as unrequited love?" After the chariot race, as Messala lies dying, he insists "there is enough of a man still left there for you to hate." He dies saying, "It goes on Judah . . . the race is not over." Like a jealous lover, he knows that even death cannot separate his linkage to Ben-Hur, for the latter has yet to find his mother and sister and cannot forget that it was Messala who punished and divided the family.

The British *Monthly Film Bulletin* noted: "Freudians may find little difficulty in categorizing the relationship of Ben-Hur and Messala, as it burgeons from slow, strong handshakes to whip-slashings and a blood-drenched death scene. But in fact the whole thick and tear-bedaubed conception is a Victorian one, embracing as it does Frank Thring's portrayal of Pontius Pilate as an exquisite, Oscar Wildean quean, Haya Harareet's dewy-eyed slave girl, a wilting orgy reminiscent of *Intolerance*, and the sudden switch in Jack Hawkins' Quintus Arrius from a sort of nineteenth-century flogging headmaster to a Dickensian uncle figure."

Bowing as a road show attraction, *Ben-Hur* would gross $36,550,000 in distributors' domestic film rentals over the years (which included several theatrical reissues). The picture won a record number of Academy Awards—eleven Oscars: Best Picture, Best Actor (Charlton Heston), Best Supporting Actor (Hugh Griffith); Best Director; Cinematography —Color; Art—Set Direction—Color; Sound, Editing, Music Scoring, Special Effects, Costumes—Color. The only category *Ben-Hur* lost was Best Screenplay—Based on Material from Another Medium (*Room at the Top* won), probably because of the arbitration dispute as to whom should received screenplay credit.

The first choice to play Ben-Hur was Rock Hudson; when his studio (Universal) refused to loan him out, Marlon Brando and Burt Lancaster were considered, before Charlton Heston was hired for the role. Contenders for the role of Messala included Victor Mature and Steve Cochran, before Irish actor Stephen Boyd became the studio's choice. Cathy O'Donnell who played Tirzah was William Wyler's sister-in-law. It was Wyler's decision to hire American actors to play the Jewish roles; with British performers for the Romans in order to heighten the differences on camera between the two struggling forces.

16. Best Friends (Crown International, 1975), color, 83 min. Not rated.

Producer, Noel Nosseck; associate producer, Paul D. Corvan; director, Nosseck; screenplay, Arnold Somkin; art director, Jodie Tillen; makeup, Peter Deval; music, Rick Cunha; sound, Jeff Wexler; camera, Stephen M. Katz; editor Robert Gordon.

Cast: Richard Hatch (Jesse); Suzanne Benton (Kathy); Doug Chapin (Pat); Ann Noland (Jo Ella); Renee Paul (Dancer); Ralph Montgomery (Bar Boss); Roger Bear (Kola); John McKee (Recreational Vehicle Salesman); Bonnie Erkel (Doreen); Julie Clinch (Brenda); Michael Gordon (Truck Driver); Ray Willinski, Richard Tress, Wade Wilson (Band).

Shot on location in Arizona, this low-budget entry—an artless mix of the buddy film and road picture genres—focused heavily on repressed homosexuality. Most of the production values are crudely handled and the acting is often amateurish. However, given the time period of its production *Best Friends* is an amazingly strong study of (semi)-closeted gays. More blatant in its intentions that most mainstream pictures of its vintage, it is still couched in sufficiently veiled terms that its theme might slip pass any undiscerning viewer but yet be understood by the cognoscenti.

Jesse (Richard Hatch) and Pat (Doug Chapin), childhood friends, have been recently discharged from the Army, having served in Vietnam. As a lark before settling down to civilian blue collar life, they agree to drive a recreational vehicle cross country to Stockton, California, so they can have an almost free vacation. Joining them are Kathy (Suzanne Benton), whom Jesse plans to marry, and Jo Ella (Ann Noland) who is paired off with Pat. At first, Pat's restlessness (he even buys a motorcycle to have freedom on the road while the others ride in the confining RV), seems a result of his injury gained in the service. However, before long, he is pressuring his more conventional pal to break free—of women and responsibilities—and join him on the open road. ("Just you and me, pick up and go," he urges.) When Jesse counters that he cannot desert Kathy, the frustrated Pat reasons, "There are going to be so many other girls. The one you got is not that special!"

The more naive Jesse is puzzled by his friend's behavior. When he tells Pat "I can't go with you," the other is deeply-upset. Before long, Pat tells Jo Ella that he cannot marry her, as she expects, ambiguously explaining, "I'm doing you a favor." Desperate to separate Jesse and Kathy, Pat convinces Jo Ella that Jesse really likes her. Pat arranges for the two of them to be alone so, expectedly, they will make love. Pat, who has told Kathy all along that Jesse cannot be loyal to any one woman, makes sure Kathy learns of the betrayal. Nevertheless, she soon forgives Jesse.

As the quartet make their uneasy way westward, Pat is frantic to keep Jesse away from Kathy. At one point, he lures Kathy onto a pathway where he knows there is a rattlesnake. That fails to remove his competition. Stymied, he makes a senseless pass for Kathy, leading to another confrontation between the two friends:

Still not realizing/accepting the forces that keep drawing him back to the troubled Pat, Jesse wavers in his allegiance to Kathy. Then Pat asks the ultimate of his pal; to give up Kathy so he can have her. Jesse is shocked by this demand. Later, in a scuffle with the increasingly jealous and distraught Pat, Kathy is shot by Pat. In the confusion that follows, Pat harps back to the old days, when everything was so much simpler and happier—when he and Jesse were always together.

Variety reported, "The repressed homosexuality of the contemporary buddy-buddy films is made almost overt in *Best Friends*, a badly-done . . . release. . . . Everything is pitched on the stupidest, most primitive emotional level. . . . It's all childishly salacious, unbelievable, and lacking in a coherent point of view."

Eleven years later, Hollywood would re-examine a possible homosexual underlying theme of buddy films in *The Boys Next Door* (1986), q.v.

17. The Best Man (United Artists, 1964), 102 min. Not rated.

Producers, Stuart Millar, Lawrence Turman; director, Franklin Schaffner; based on the play by Gore Vidal; screenplay, Vidal; costume supervisor, Dorothy Jeakins; art director, Lyle Wheeler; set decorator, Richard Mansfield; makeup, Ben Lane; music, Mort Lindsey; assistant director, Dick Moder; sound, Jack Solomon; camera, Haskell Wexler; editor, Robert Swink.

Cast: Henry Fonda (William Russell); Cliff Robertson (Joe Cantwell); Edie Adams (Mabel Cantwell); Margaret Leighton (Alice Russell); Shelley Berman (Sheldon Bascomb); Lee Tracy (Art Hockstader); Ann Sothern (Mrs. Sue Ellen Gamadge); Gene Raymond (Dan Cantwell); Kevin McCarthy (Dick Jensen); Mahalia Jackson (Herself); Howard K. Smith (Himself); John Henry Faulk (T. T. Claypoole); Richard Arlen (Oscar Anderson); Penny Singleton (Mrs. Claypoole); George Kirgo (Speechwriter); George Furth (Tom); Anne Newman (Janet); Mary Lawrence (Mrs. Merwin); H. E. West (Senator Lazarus); Michael MacDonald (Zealot); William R. Eberson (Governor Merwin); Natalie Masters (Mrs. Anderson); Blossom Rock (Cleaning Woman); Bill Stout (Himself); Tyler McVey (Chairman); Sherwood Keith (Doctor).

The Best Man (1960), Gore Vidal's witty comedy-drama about the behind-the-scenes intrigue involved in the battle within a political party for the U.S. presidential nomination, ran for 520 performances on Broadway. One of Vidal's plot points in both the play and the film was to have one of the contenders be accused of homosexual activity in his past. As in the stage original, the movie adaptation emphasized the irony that, frequently in politics, the best man does *not* win.

In Los Angeles at the Ambassador Hotel, liberal former Secretary of State William Russell (Henry Fonda) and ultra conservative Senator Joe Cantwell (Cliff Robertson) are the chief combatants in the race to gain their party's Presidential nomination at the national convention in California. Each hopes to win the useful endorsement of the dying ex-President, Art Hochstader (Lee Tracy), a devious cracker

Advertisement for *The Best Man* (1964).

barrel politician. Hochstader refuses to support Russell because he is too intellectual and not decisive enough; he turns against ruthless Cantwell because the latter, not realizing Hochstader was leaning in his direction—he foolishly antagonized the former Chief executive.

Determined to still win the nomination, the unscrupulous Cantwell plans to release information that Russell once had a nervous breakdown (it was brought about by overwork.) Meanwhile, Dick Jensen (Kevin McCarthy), Russell's campaign manager, sets up a meeting between Russell and Sheldon Bascomb (Shelley Berman). The latter claims to have evidence that during World War II military duty in the Aleutians, Cantwell was guilty of practicing homosexual acts. Despite the urging of his associates that he resort to Cantwell-like smear tactics, Russell is unwilling to do so. Cantwell, however, has no such scruples and releases the information on Russell's medical history. Surprising everyone, Russell steps down from the campaign, turning over his support to a dark-horse rival, Governor Merwin (William R. Eberson). The latter wins his party's endorsement. The matter settled, Russell and his wife (Margaret Leighton), who had temporarily reconciled during the convention, agree to give their marriage a fresh start.

Bosley Crowther (*New York Times*) applauded "the head-on clash of two threatening character assassins that was made so engrossing on the stage is even more vivid, energetic and lacerating on the screen. . . . Franklin Schaffner has shrewdly directed the film to emphasize the rasp of a convention as well as of individuals." While crediting Henry Fonda, Cliff Robertson and Lee Tracy (of the Broadway cast) with sterling performances, Crowther complained "The drama goes almost out the window in the crucial confrontation scene" between Cantwell and Bascomb. In the first place, the details of the charge are much too involved and confused, and, in the second place, the role

. . . is atrociously played. Shelley Berman, a stand-up comedian, plays it as though he's struggling for laughs." *Variety* decided that "Although not an especially fresh or profound piece of work, it is certainly a worthwhile, lucid and engaging dramatization. . . . Sly references and character similarities to certain controversial politicians will help, too."

Just as the earlier *Advise and Consent* (1962), q.v.—which also co-starred Henry Fonda—had used homosexuality as a controversial pivotal point to gain audience interest, so did *The Best Man*. Although the question of Cantwell's sexual habits during his wartime tour of duty in the Quartermasters Corp is a central issue in *The Best Man*, the subject matter is handled discreetly in the film. When questioning the sniveling Bascomb about his accusation against Cantwell, the word homosexuality is never employed. Hochstader asks the nervous informant, "Do I understand by the way you are slowly beating around the bush that Joe Cantwell is what we used to call, when I was a boy, a degenerate?" In the screen version, Russell refuses to accept Bascomb's testimony as valid: "I don't believe it. No man with that awful wife or those ugly children could be anything but normal." (The implication is that had Cantwell actually been "proven"—let alone been—gay, then Russell might have gone along with the smear tactics to rid himself of his opponent.)

The Best Man was released in a presidential election year, just as the Broadway version had debuted in an earlier campaign time. However, it was not a major box-office hit. *Variety* predicted one of the reasons for its lack of great general appeal, "there will be those who will be offended by some of its points-of-view." Another factor was that feature films dealing cynically with politics, such as *The Best Man* and the earlier *Advise and Consent*, generally fail to attract the mass market of filmgoers, who want more traditional screen fare. *The Best Man* received one Oscar nomination: Best Supporting Actor (Lee Tracy). However, Peter Ustinov (*Topkapi*) won.

18. The Betsy (Allied Artists, 1978), color, 120 min. R-rated.

Presenter, Emanuel L. Wolf; producers, Harold Robbins, Robert Weston; associate producer, Jack Grossberg; director, Daniel Petrie; based on the novel by Robbins; screenplay, Walter Bernstein, William Bast; production designer, Herman A. Blumenthal; set decorators, James Payne, Sal Blydenburgh; costumes, Dorothy Jeakins; makeup, Del Armstrong; music, John Barry; assistant directors, Wolfgang Glattes, Jack Sanders; stunt coordinator, William Couch; sound, Lee Alexander Rimas Tumasonis; special effects, Greg Auer; camera, Mario Tosi; editor, Rita Roland.

Cast: Laurence Olivier (Loren Hardeman Sr.); Robert Duvall (Loren Hardeman III); Katherine Ross (Sally Hardeman); Tommy Lee Jones (Angelo Perino); Jane Alexander (Alicia Hardeman); Lesley-Anne Down (Lady Bobby Ayres); Joseph Wiseman (Jake Weinstein); Kathleen Beller (Betsy Hardeman); Edward Herrmann (Dan Weyman); Paul Rudd (Loren Hardeman Jr.); Roy Poole (Duncan); Richard Venture (Mark Sampson); Titos Vandis (Angelo Luigi Perino); Clifford David (Joe Warren); Inga Swenson (Mrs. Craddock); Whitney Blake (Elizabeth Hardeman); Carol Williard (Roxanne); Read Morgan (Donald); Charlie Fields (Loren III, as a Boy); Robert Phalen (Man); Nick Czmyr (Bellhop); Norman Palmer, Fred Carney, Maury Cooper, Russell Porter (Board Members); Teri Ralston (Hotel Clerk); Warney H. Ruhl (Security Guard); Patrick J. Monks (Helicopter Pilot); William Roerick (Secretary of Commerce); William B. Cain (Butler); Mary Petrie (Nurse); H. August Kuehl (Guest); Robert Hawkins (Retired Man); Sadie Hawkins (Retired Lady); Anthony Steere (Car Driver).

"God bless Laurence Olivier. And God only knows what the incomparable actor of the Western world is doing in a piece of hilarious idiocy like *The Betsy*. Taking away a zillion dollars, one hopes." (Jack Kroll, *Newsweek* magazine)

In mid-1970s Detroit, Loren Hardeman III (Robert Duvall) heads a huge car manufacturing corporation founded by his grandfather, Loren Hardeman Sr. (Laurence Olivier). Loren III is intent on diversifying the firm and opposes the 86-year-old patriarch's insistence on building a compact car to revive the automobile segment of the conglomerate. Meanwhile, Angelo Perino (Tommy Lee Jones), a talented young car designer and expert auto racer, is brought in by Loren Sr. to construct a new vehicle, the Betsy, named for Loren III's daughter (Kathleen Beller). Before long, both Betsy and Lady Roberta Ayres (Lesley-Anne Down)—Loren III's British mistress—are rivals for Angelo's affections. Later, Perino is dismissed by Loren III, but his decision is vetoed by the combined voting strength of his estranged wife Alicia (Jane Alexander) and his grandfather.

Flashbacks reveal that in 1936, Loren Jr. (Paul Rudd), a homosexual, had been removed from his corporate position for mishandling a labor union dispute. Later, when Loren Jr. discovers his wife (Katharine Ross) in bed with his father, he shoots himself, a suicide witnessed by his boy, Loren III (Charlie Fields). When Loren Jr.'s lover, Joe Warren (Clifford David), attempts to blackmail the dead man's father, Loren Sr. has him killed by Angelo Luigi Perino (Titos Vandis). When the latter is deported to Italy, Loren Sr. agrees to look after young Angelo.

Back in the present, Angelo gains control of the Bethlehem corporation. He keeps Loren III in charge and retains the support of Loren Sr. against hoodlum financier Jake Weinstein (Joseph Wiseman), the man who financed his campaign to get in charge of the corporation.

Janet Maslin (*New York Times*) concluded, "For the most part, the director, Daniel Petrie, has a classier cast than he knows what to do with. . . . Without much of a plot, *The Betsy* often sags, and a movie this frivolous has no business being dull." Kevin Thomas (*Los Angeles Times*) agreed and added, "Alas, heavy-breathing intrigues of sex and power prove more tedious than steady. . . . Olivier's patriarch is the only, truly fully dimensioned role created by Robbins' adapters." *Newsweek*'s Jack Kroll chided, "See Oliver chew out his homosexual son. Watch him try, at the age of 86, to put the make on a juicy broad. . . . Watch him show the suffering cast . . . how to kid a ridiculous script without losing your integrity."

Nevertheless, *The Betsy* managed to gross $7,850,000 in distributors' domestic film rentals, largely based on the appeal of Olivier's campy performance and the lure of a trashy Harold Robbins-based screenplay which covered the gamut of sleaze: incest, homosexuality, adultery and corporate backstabbing.

19. Beyond the Valley of the Dolls (Twentieth Century-Fox, 1970), color, 109 min. X-rated.

Producer, Russ Meyer; associate producers, Red Hershon, Eve Meyer; director, Russ Meyer; story, Roger Ebert, Russ Meyer; screenplay, Ebert; art directors, Jack Martin Smith, Arthur Lonergan; set decorators, Walter M. Scott, Stuart A. Reiss; makeup, Dan Striepeke; music, Stu Phillips; additional music, William Loose; songs: Phillips and Bob Stone; Phillips and Carey; Paul Marshall; assistant directors, David Hall, C. E. Dismukes; sound, Richard Overton, Don Minkler; special camera effects, Jack Harmon; camera, Fred Koenekamp; editors, Dann Cahn, Dick Wormel.

Cast: Dolly Read (Kelly MacNamara); Cynthia Myers (Casey Anderson); Marcia McBroom (Petronella "Pet" Danforth); John LaZar (Ronnie "Z-Man" Barzell); Michael Blodgett (Lance Rocke); David Gurian (Harris Allsworth); Edy Williams (Ashley St. Ives); Erica Gavin (Roxanne); Phyllis Davis (Susan Lake); Harrison Page (Emerson Thorne); Duncan McLeod (Porter Hall); James Iglehart (Randy Black); Charles Napier (Baxter Wolfe); Henry Rowland (Otto); Princess Livingston (Matron); Stan Ross (Disciple); Lavelle Roby (Vanessa); Angel Ray (Girl-in-Tub); Veronica Erickson (Blonde Date); Haji (Cat Woman); Karen Smith (Redhead); Sebastian Brook (Art Director); Bruce V. McBroom (Photographer); Ian Sander (Boy-in-Tub); Koko Tani (Assistant); Samantha Scott (Cynthia); Tea Crawford (Kathy Page); Health Jobes (Makeup Man); John Logan (Escort); Susan Reed (Fashion Model); Robin Bach, Christopher Riordan (Gay Boys); Ceil Cabot (Mother); Mary Carroll (Middle-Age Woman); Joseph Cellini (Man in Flowered Pants); Jackie Cole, Cissy Colpitts (Women); Frank Corsentino (Hippie Boy); Mibb Curry (White-Haired Gentleman); Coleman Francis (Rotund Drunk); Charles Fox (Earnest Man); Pamela [Pam] Grier (4th Woman); T. J. Halligan (Science Teacher); Rick Holmes (Man with Glasses); Marshall Kent (Dr. Downs); Michael Kriss (Young Actor); Tim Laurie, George Strattan (Gay Men); Bebe Louie (Hippie Girl); Lillian Martin (Nurse); Ashley Phillips (Fashion Model); Garth Pillsbury (Man with Newspaper); Big Jack Provan (Father); Joyce Ree (Marion Harrisburg); Bert Santos (Taxi Driver); The Strawberry Alarm Clock, The Sandpipers (Themselves).

In retrospect, more amazing than the fact that a major studio in 1970 Hollywood was willing to release this X-rated softcore porno junk, was the fact that the movie's screenplay was by future film critic Roger Ebert. The opening credit card on the movie attests this picture is *not* a sequel to the studio's earlier and equally vulgar (in a different way) *Valley of the Dolls* (1967), q.v. However, it "like *Valley of the Dolls* deals with the oft-times nightmare world of show business, but in a different time and context." Nevertheless, Jacqueline Susann, the author of *Valley of the Dolls*, attempted unsuccessfully to halt the release of this film claiming that the movie by its title association would damage her reputation as a writer. She later sued the studio for utilizing her book's title in naming the new movie. (She won a settlement posthumously.)

Three girls—Kelly MacNamara (Dolly Read), Casey Anderson (Cynthia Myers) and Petronella "Pet" Danford (Marcia McBroom)—who belong to a pop singing group arrive in Los Angeles, hopeful of persuading Kelly's wealthy aunt, Susan Lake (Phyllis Davis), to finance their careers in the music industry. Before long, the trio is managed by Ronnie "Z-Man" Barzell (John LaZar), a hip hermaphrodite, who guides them to fame. Romantically, Pet bounces from law student

David Gurian and Edy Williams in *Beyond the Valley of the Dolls* **(1970).**

Emerson Thorne (Harrison Page) to boxer Randy Black (James Iglehart), Kelly abandons the group's earlier manager, Harris Allsworth (David Gurian), for a slick gigolo, Lance Rocke (Michael Blodgett), and Casey teams with Roxanne (Erica Gavin), a lesbian designer. Meanwhile, Kelly pursues dishonest attorney Porter Hall (Duncan McLeod), intent on forcing him to get for the girls, a fair share of Susan's wealth.

While the singing trio are performing on a TV show, Harris, who has been hiding in the rafters of the stage set, attempts suicide. His fall leaves him wheelchair-bound. Later, Barzell, under the influence of peyote, goes crazy and launches into mass homicide, including the beheading of Lance. The killings shock Kelly into taking a new perspective of life, while the trauma of events relieves Harris of his paralysis.

Variety was unimpressed with the finished product: "Film is a heavy-handed put-on (many will consider themselves put-upon) with sex and violence, starring a group of relative newcomers whose abilities remain unknown. . . ." Mike Wallington (British *Monthly Film Bulletin*) noted, "if one can resist walking out, the last half hour is quite manic, culminating in the most ludicrously outrageous climax for some time. . . ."

Because of or in spite of its frequently crude and stupid excesses, this X-rated parody, made at a cost of $1.5 million, grossed a strong $7 million in distributors' domestic film rentals. Many found an unpleasant parallel between the movie's gory finale and the real-life Sharon Tate massacre committed by Charles Manson's followers in 1969. In 1979, Russ Meyer produced/directed *Beneath the Valley of the Ultra Vixens*. Its script was co-authored by R. Hyde, a pseudonym for Roger Ebert.

20. Beyond Therapy (New World Pictures, 1987), color, 93 min. R-rated.

Executive producer, Roger Berlind; producer, Steven M. Haft; associate producer, Scott Bushnell; director, Robert Altman; based on the play by Christopher Durang; screenplay, Durang, Robert Altman; production designer, Steve Dunn; art directors, Annie Senechal, Arnaud De Moleron; costumes, Claudia Perino; makeup, Roland Rebeiro De Abreu, Dominique De Vorges; music, Stephen Altman, Gabriel Yared; assistant directors, Yann Gilbert, Patrick Cartoux; sound, Philippe Lioret, Daniel Belanger, Bruno Lambert; camera, Pierre Mignot; supervising editor, Mignot; editor, Jennifer Auge.

Cast: Julie Hagerty (Prudence); Jeff Goldblum (Bruce); Glenda Jackson (Charlotte); Tom Conti (Stuart); Christopher Guest (Bob); Genevieve Page (Zizi); Chris Campion (Andrew); Sandrine Dumas (Cindy); Bertrand Bonvoisin (Le Gerant); Nicole Evans (Cashier); Louis-Marie Taillefer (Le Chef); Matthew Lesniak (Mr. Bean); Laure Killing (Charlie); Gilbert Blin, Vincent Longuemare (Waiters); Francoise Armel, Sylvie Lenoir, Annie Monnier, Jeanne Cellard, Helen Constantine, Yvette Prayer, Joan Tyrrell (Zizi's Friends).

First presented off-Broadway briefly in early 1981, Christopher Durang's comedy, *Beyond Therapy*, was re-mounted for Broadway the next year. The new production, starring John Lithgow, Dianne Wiest, Peter Michael Goetz, Kate McGregor-Stewart, Jack Gilpin and David Pierce lasted for twenty-one performances. Six years later, Robert Altman co-scripted and directed this frantic comedy, a French-style farce. Like Martin Scorsese's *After Hours* (1985), q.v., also set in New York City, this picture throws together assorted exaggerated urban types, who seem eccentrically diverting, but who, on closer examination, are essentially cardboard figures. By the 1980s, it was expected that any such broad-range study of metropolitan lifestyle, would contain at least one homosexual and/or bisexual character.

Anxious to reach out in new romantic directions, Bruce (Jeff Goldblum) arranges to meet Prudence (Julie Hagerty), a young woman who answered his personal ad, at "Les Bouchons," one of Manhattan's many French bistros. The encounter is a fiasco. The lunch hour is over and the kitchen is closed; Prudence, who is more edgy than Bruce, is dismayed to learn that her date is a bisexual who is living with his lover, Bob (Christopher Guest). (Bruce: "I swing both ways. Do you?. . . . Have I upset you?" Prudence: "No, it's just that I hate gay people.") The neurotic Bruce and Prudence retreat to their respective therapists—he to Charlotte (Glenda Jackson), who handles her patients like erring children and she to Stuart (Tom Conti), who has a passion for sleeping with his women patients. (Charlotte and Stuart have adjacent offices and frequently engage in therapeutic sex.) Another guest that afternoon at "Les Bouchons" was Zizi (Genevieve Page), Bob's possessive mother, who quickly tells her wispy son that he is about to be betrayed.

Later, Prudence answers another personal ad using a pseudonym and is amazed to discover, upon reaching "Les Bouchons," that her date is once again Bruce, who had resorted to a different name for himself. This time the couple enjoy each other's company, and Bruce invites her to his place for dinner. Bob, an anxious witness to the budding romance at his apartment, is non-plussed. (Bob to Prudence: "I don't think bi-sexuality exists, do you? I think everyone is basically gay, don't you?") Later, Bruce convinces the disgruntled Bob to confer with Charlotte. Meanwhile, Prudence, still fighting off Stuart's advances, meets again with Bruce at "Les Bouchons." By now, the glib Charlotte has dragged the sulky Bob to the restaurant. She wants him to meet her gay son Andrew (Chris Campion), a waiter there, who is looking for a new roommate. Others convening at the eatery are the melodramatic Zizi, grieving for her son's broken romance, and Stuart, disguised as a waiter and hoping to score with Prudence.

Urged by Charlotte to express his feelings, Bob fires a pistol at Bruce and Prudence. Pandemonium erupts until it is discovered that he was shooting blanks. Bruce and Prudence agree to fly to Paris to honeymoon, Bob and Andrew are mutually attracted to each other, and Bob and Zizi reconcile. As for the libidinous Charlotte and Stuart—they react in typical form by rushing off to the checkroom for a recuperative sexual fling.

Despite the talented cast, *Beyond Therapy* irritated many media reviewers. Mike McGrady (*Newsday*), "the performances are not at issue here. Coherence is. Meaning is. The film doesn't hang together, add up, or make sense." David Edelstein (*Village Voice*) decided, "Unfortunately, Robert Altman . . . has no handle on the material. Altman's forte is loopy, off-speed naturalism, not loony tunes, and he nestles Durang's characters—who have a pop-out clarity—in one of his trademark nattering menageries."

In 1990, Robert Altman would admit of this fiasco, "I wanted to make a pure, unabashed romantic comedy—about bisexuality. Unfortunately, we had terrible synchronicity. It came out right when the AIDS issue hit the public, and the critics just went ape." Although set in New York City, *Beyond Therapy* was filmed in Paris.

21. The Big Combo (Allied Artists, 1955), 89 min. Not rated.

Producer, Sidney Harmon; director, Joseph Lewis; screenplay, Philip Yordan; production designer, Rudi Feld; set decorator, Jack McConaghy; Miss Wallace's wardrobe; Don Loper; makeup, Larry Butterworth; music, David Raksin; assistant directors, Mack Wright, Robert Justman; special camera effects, Jack Rabin, Louis DeWitt; camera, John Alton; editor, Robert Eisen.

Cast: Cornel Wilde (Lieutenant Leonard Diamond); Richard Conte (Mr. Brown); Brian Donlevy (Joe McClure); Jean Wallace (Susan Lowell); Robert Middleton (Captain Peterson); Lee Van Cleef (Fante); Earl Holliman (Mingo); Helen Walker (Alicia Brown); Jay Adler (Sam Hill); John Hoyt (Nils Dreyer); Ted Corsia (Bettini); Helen Stanton (Rita); Roy Gordon (Audubon); Whit Bissell (Doctor); Philip Van Zandt (Mr. Jones); Steve Mitchell (Bennie Smith) Brian O'Hara (Malloy); Rita Gould (Nurse); Michael Mark (Hotel Clerk); Donna Drew (Miss Hartleby); Baynes Barron (Young Detective).

The Big Combo was one of several features made together by the husband-and-wife team of Cornel Wilde and Jean Wallace. Since its unheralded release, *The Big Combo* has gained a reputation as an incisive study of the corruption that power exerts on *both* sides of the law. One of the intriguing, understated aspects of this expose of mobsters, molls and crusading law enforcers, was the homosexual relationship of two thugs (Lee Van Cleef, Earl Holliman) who share not only workday camaraderie but an after hours apartment.

Experienced police detective Leonard Diamond (Cornel Wilde) is fixated on exposing local urban crime baron Mr. Brown (Richard Conte) and winning away his seductive mistress, Susan Lowell (Jean Wallace). When not pursuing the jaded blonde socialite, Diamond is at loggerheads with Captain Peterson (Robert Middleton). Diamond willingly bends the law to achieve his goal: he stages false arrests, etc. to harass Brown and his gangland confederates. In return, the equally egotistical Brown assigns hit men/lovers Fante (Lee Van Cleef) and Mingo (Earl Holliman) to eradicate this troublesome policeman. The killers, under the direction of underworld lieutenant Joe McClure (Brian Donlevy), torture Diamond—amplifying sounds on a radio beyond the victim's tolerance. Despite everything, Diamond survives and gathers evidence from Brown's execution of McClure and his team of underlings. Assisted by Brown's alcoholic ex-wife (Helen Walker), the lawman pursues his prey. The climatic showdown takes place at a desert airplane hangar where Diamond guns down the aggressive

Cornel Wilde and Jean Wallace in *The Big Combo* (1955).

Brown. With the case resolved, Diamond and Susan go off together.

Howard H. Thompson (*New York Times*) rated this picture "shrill, clumsy and rather old-fashioned." *Variety* judged: "Grim meller of honest cop versus syndicate for the action trade. . . . While approving that "Performances are in keeping with the bare-knuckle direction by Joseph Lewis," the trade paper emphasized, "Since Philip Yordan's original screenplay doesn't follow a credible line, there's not much sense . . . used to plot the course of this shocker."

Years later, in 1980, Tom Milne (British *Monthly Film Bulletin*) would reevaluate, "Rarely since the Expressionist Twenties in Germany, in fact, has torment so invaded the screen, with virtually every character either in mortal terror . . . or nursing an aspiration to love, however, tainted, that is crushed beneath the burden of corruption. . . ." Carl Maceck (*Film Noir: An Encyclopedic Reference to the American Style*, 1988) observed: "*The Big Combo* is filled with violence of a brutal and erotic nature. The homosexuality of Mingo and Fante is smothered in an atmosphere of murder and sadistic torture, as they refine the conventions of violence into a sexual ritual. Joseph H. Lewis's direction strongly points to a crude sexual bias throughout the film."

Among the more resourceful performances in *The Big Combo* are those of Brian Donlevy and Helen Walker. Not to be overlooked is the touching, shaded characterization provided by Earl Holliman. In every way, his Mingo is the student to Fante's (Lee Van Cleef) teacher. It is Holliman's character who suggests that perhaps someday the duo should retire from their dangerous careers and live peacefully. When Fante is killed, Holliman's Mingo reveals his soft inner shell, sobbing for his fallen comrade/lover. Like so many Hollywood films of this period that relied on suggestion to imply daring situations and relationships, there is a telling scene in *The Big Combo*. The setting is late at night in Mingo and Fante's bedroom, where each is asleep in his twin bed (just like parallel heterosexual couples of this period). The phone rings—it is a new assignment—and the bare-chested Fante, the masculine aggressor of the duo, answers the phone to take instructions. Like the good "wife," Mingo waits patiently by to learn what is to happen next.

22. The Big Doll House (New World Pictures, 1971), color, 93 min. R-rated.

Executive producers, Eddie Romero, John Ashley; producer, Jane Schaffer; director, Jack Hill; screenplay, Don Spencer; production designer, Ben Otico; set decorator, Bobby Bautista; makeup, Antonio Artiesda; wardrobe, Felisa Salcedo; music, Hall Daniels; assistant director, Maria S. Abelardo; special effects, Teofilo C. Hilario; camera, Freddie Conde; supervising editor, Millic Paul; editor, Cliff Fenneman.

Cast: Judy Brown (Collier); Roberta Collins (Alcott); Pam Grier (Grear); Brooke Mills (Harrad); Pat Woodell (Bodine); Sid Haig (Harry); Christiane Schmidtmer (Miss Dietrich); Kathryn Loder (Lucian); Jerry Franks (Fred); Jack Davis (Dr. Phillips); Gina Stuart (Ferina); Letty Mirasol (Leyte); Shirley De Las Alas (Guard); and: Siony Cordona, Myrna De Vera, Kathy McDaniels.

"The *Big Doll House* (1971) is set 'somewhere in a banana republic' (and you can bet your life the innuendo is intentional). . . . Lesbianism is rife and while there are no sexually explicit acts (these are not, of course, hardcore films and, indeed, these days barely rate as softcore) there is none of the pussyfooting around the subject that was imposed upon earlier moviemakers. All the stereotypes are here. . . ." (Bruce Crowther, *Captured on Film*, 1989)

Hollywood had come a great distance from such genre studies as *Caged* (1950) and *Women's Prison* (1955), qq.v., which hinted at but never explicitly stated the sexual activity that went on behind bars. In his essay, "Women in Prison Films," Jim Morton wrote for *Re/Search: Incredibly Strange Films* (1986):

"By the end of the sixties the archetypal roles of the WIP [women in prison] films had been established, i.e.: The Queen Bee: dominant female prisoner who lords it over the others. The New Fish: usually the lead actress, in jail for the first time. The Sadistic Warden: more often than not the one who proves to be the root of all evil and unrest in the prison. The Hooker with the Heart of Gold: a street-smart dame who knows the ropes and befriends the New Fish, for better or worse. The Dyke Guard: sometimes named 'Ruby'; no WIP film would be complete without one."

Director Jack Hill made several derivative features for Roger Corman's New World Pictures, all filmed inexpensively in the Philippines. Often featuring Pam Grier, they were crudely constructed affairs, but had a vitality and spontaneity that helped offset their shortcomings. Produced for a minimal $125,000, the R-rated *The Big Doll House* earned a whopping $5 million in distributors' domestic film rentals.

Cultivated Miss Dietrich (Christiane Schmidtmer) is the warden of a run-down prison in a tropical country. Her chief underling is the sadistic Colonel Mendoza of the secret police. Another staff member is the newly-arrived Dr. Phillips (Jack Davis) who crusades to improve prison conditions. The inmates include Bodine (Pat Woodell), a political prisoner, Harrad (Brooke Mills), a junkie who killed her baby and Grear (Pam Grier), a hooker who, while with a trick, overheard political information she should not have—and received a 30-year jail sentence.

In this hell, self-contained Grear displays a fondness for redheaded-convict Collier (Judy Brown). A staunch individualist, Grear makes no bones about her bad feelings about the opposite sex. As she philosophizes: "All men are filthy! All they ever want to do is to get at you. . . . I'm not goin' to let a man's filthy hands touch me again!" The only individual who awes tough-as-nails Grear is Lucian (Kathryn Loder), the brutal, sadistic prison guard. Always playing both sides against the middle, Grear is a stool pigeon for the warden, but is not above rifling through Dietrich's office for useful information.

Later, during a prison break, several inmates escape. In the process, Harrad kills the double-crossing Grear and, in turn, is shot down by the guards.

With its various heterosexual and homosexual episodes, *The Big Doll House* was an exercise in titillation. Much of the movie's success should be credited to 5' 8" Pam Grier who displayed a strong screen presence. She would appear in other such excursions, such as *The Big Bird Cage* (1972) and *Women in Chain* (1972).

23. Billy Budd (Allied Artists, 1962), 123 min. Not rated.

Executive producer, A. Ronald Lubin; producer/director, Peter Ustinov; based on the novelette *Billy Budd, Foretopman* by Herman Melville and the play by Louis O. Coxe, Robert H. Chapman; screenplay, Ustinov, DeWitt Bodeen, (uncredited) Robert Rossen; production designer, Don Ashton; costumes, Anthony Mendleson; makeup, Bob Lawrence, music/ music conductor, Anthony Hopkins; assistant director, Michael Birkett; special effects, George Blackwell; sound, Charles Crafford, Charles Poulton, Len Shilton; camera, Robert Krasker; editor, Jack Harris.

Cast: Terence Stamp (Billy Budd); Peter Ustinov (Captain Edward Fairfax Vere); Robert Ryan (Master-at-Arms John Claggart); Melvyn Douglas (The Dansker); Ronald Lewis (Jenkins); David McCallum (Lieutenant Wyatt); John Neville (Lieutenant John Ratcliffe); Paul Rogers (Lieutenant Philip Seymour); Lee Montague (Squeak); Thomas Heathcote (Payne); Ray McAnally (O'Daniel); Robert Brown (Talbot); John Meillon (Kincaid); Cyril Luckham (Alfred Hallam); Niall MacGinnis (Captain Neil Graveling); and: Victor Brooks, Barry Keegan.

Based on a novelette by Herman Melville (1819–1891) written over the five year period before the author's death, *Billy Budd* was first published in 1924. It was dramatized by Louis O. Coxe and Robert H. Chapman as *Uniform of Flesh* (1949) and revised as *Billy Budd* (1951). Like Melville's classic novel, *Moby Dick* (1851), *Billy Budd* is an allegorical study of good and evil clashing on the high seas, with both factions destroying one another. An underlying theme in *Billy Budd* is the unstated magnetic attraction the innocent, (i.e. virginal) young Billy holds for the sinister Claggart. By casting extremely handsome Terence Stamp in the film's title role, this movie adaptation became a more overt study of homosexual frustration leading a man—here the villain—to his doom and, in the process, destroying the naive hero—here oblivious to his physical mystique.

In August 1797, during England's war with France, merchant seaman Billy Budd (Terence Stamp) is impressed into service in the British Navy aboard the H.M.S. *Avenger*. The cheerful young sailor is so intrinsically good that he cannot see the bad in others. Thanks to his nautical skills, his pleasing nature and charm, he soon wins the friendship of everyone aboard. The one exception is the vicious and despised master of arms, John Claggart

Terence Stamp in *Billy Budd* (1962).

(Robert Ryan), who is amazed by the new-comer's honest soul ("I sometimes think you hate yourself," Billy says to the master-at-arms). Unable to make Billy fearful of him and bow to his control, the frustrated Claggart hopes to ruin Budd by trumping up a charge that he is inciting a mutiny.

The ship's captain, Edward Fairfax Vere (Peter Ustinov), is aware that Claggart is lying. He asks Billy to counter the accusation. However, the young man is so overwhelmed by Claggart's unfounded charge that he becomes speechless (a frequent impediment of his in moments of crisis). Unable to talk, he strikes out at his accuser. The latter falls, hits his head and dies. At the court-martial aboard ship, the others officers concur that the mishap was an accident. However, Vere is honor-bound to insist that naval jurisprudence, not everyday justice, must prevail, especially at a time when the British Navy is experiencing a rash of mutinies. As such, Budd must be punished for murdering a

superior officer. The board reluctantly decrees that Billy be hanged. At the public hanging on the ship, Billy stuns the mutinous crew into submission by shouting out "God bless Captain Vere!" as he is about to die. Greatly touched by Budd's action, Vere considers removing himself from command. However, a French warship appears and, in the skirmish, Vere dies.

The British *Monthly Film Bulletin* judged, "Although the film was made on board ship for the sake of authenticity, Ustinov concentrates his camera so much and so closely on his actors that it might well have been shot in a studio tank for all the feeling it gives of a group of men caught up in the mysterious, purifying power of the sea. . . . . Ustinov's prosaic direction relies heavily on his actors, and within the limits demanded they serve him well." For *Variety*, "Where Ustinov has slipped is in the development and delineation of the character he himself plays—the overly conscientious Captain Vere. . . . As executed in histrionic-directorial overlap by Ustinov, the character is not as sharply defined as it must be. Audience compassion is never properly aroused." In retrospect, Vito Russell noted in *The Celluloid Closet*, (1987), "Although, under the new [Motion Picture Association of America] Code, villainous homosexuals sometimes wanted the hero sexually, their homosexuality served as an illustration of their pathology and thus illuminated their villainy. . . . Innocent and irresistible is how Melville created *Billy Budd*, and Ustinov [in *Billy Budd*] left it that way. But the homoeroticism in the film comes as much from Stamp's angelic embodiment of Melville's Billy as it does from the lechings of the fascinated Claggart."

With location scenes shot in Spain, *Billy Budd*, was released originally in a 123-minute version, but was later trimmed to 112 minutes. Despite its sterling cast, this feature was considered too arty and too unlavish in its stagey black-and-white settings to be a commercial success.

24. Biloxi Blues (Universal, 1988), color, 106 min. PG-13-rated.

Executive producers, Joseph M. Caracciolo, Marykay Powell; producer, Ray Stark; director, Mike Nichols; based on the play by Neil Simon; screenplay, Simon; production designer, Paul Sylbert; set decorator, John Alan Hicks; costumes, Ann Roth; makeup designs, Kevin R. Trahan; music, Georges Delerue; assistant directors, Michael Haley, James Skotchdopole, Carla Corwin, Glen Trotiner; stunt coordinators, Whitey Hughes, Rick LeFevour; sound, Allan Byer, Roy B. Yokelson; special effects, Daniel Ottesen, Kevin Brink, John Ottesen; camera, Bill Butler; editor, Sam O'Steen.

Cast: Matthew Broderick (Eugene Morris Jerome); Christopher Walken (Sergeant Merwin J. Toomey); Matt Mulhern (Joseph T. Wykowski); Corey Parker (Arnold B. Epstein); Markus Flanagan (Roy W. Selridge); Casey Siemaszko (Donald J. Carney); Michael Dolan (James J. Hennessy); Penelope Ann Miller (Daisy Hannigan); Park Overall (Rowena); Alan Pottinger (David P. Peek); Mark Evan Jacobs (Pinelli); Dave Kienzle (Corporal); Matthew Kimbrough (Spitting Cook); Kirby Mitch-ell, Allen Turner, Tom Kagy (Diggers); Jeff Bailey (Mess Hall Corporal); Bill Russell (Rifle Instructor); Natalie Canerday (Girl at Dance); A. Collin Roddey (Private Roddey); Christopher Ginnaven (Corporal Ginnaven); Morris Mead (Corporal Mead); David Whitman (Tower Officer); Norman Rose (Newsreel Announcer); Michael Haley (Corporal Haley); Ben Hynum (Private Lindstrom); Andy Wigington (Corporal Wigington); Christopher Phelps (Private Phelps); Scott Sudbury (Private Sudbury); Katherine Barry, Ed Bradley, Charles Dietz, John Fedinatz, Lee R. Jones, Shirley Jordan, Tina E. Kalimos, John Anthony Lack, Conan McCarty, Albert Owens, Virginia Sandifur, Craig Sechler, Jeffrey Shafer, David James Sharp (Additional Voices).

Comedy writer maven Neil Simon wrote three autobiographical plays (*Brighton Beach Memoirs*, 1984, *Biloxi Blues*, 1985, and *Broadway Bound*, 1986) about his endearing alter ego Eugene Morris Jerome. The second in the popular trilogy, which ran for 524 performances on Broadway, won a 1985 Tony Award as Best Play. For the screen version of *Biloxi Blues*, Matthew Broderick, Penelope Ann Miller, Park Overall and Matt Mulhern recreated their stage roles. Set during World War II, the comedy/drama focuses on the Brooklyn-born hero during his hectic weeks of basic training in boot camp in Biloxi, Mississippi and how the experience pushes him into manhood. For many viewers, a highlight of Eugene's rite of passage is his visit to a local prostitute (Park Overall) where he loses his virginity. An almost throwaway segment of the boot camp story is the discovery that one of Eugene's barracks mates is homosexual.

At the Biloxi, Mississippi boot camp, Eugene's fellow raw recruits include braggart Roy Selridge (Markus Flanagan), intellectual but exasperating New York Jew Arnold Epstein (Corey Parker), brawny Joseph Wykowski (Matt Mulhern) as well as the less obtrusive Donald Carney (Casey Siemaszko) and farmboy James Hennessy (Michael Dolan). Assessing his peers, flippant Eugene, who hopes to become a writer and thus keeps a daily journal, insists, "It was hard to believe these guys had mothers and fathers who were worried about them." The bewildered newcomers are placed under the control of martinet drill Sergeant Merwin J. Toomey (Christopher Walken). When not coping with the sadistic, unpredictable Toomey or outmaneuvering one another in the daily tedium, the young men develop a camaraderie of sorts.

One weekend, while on a pass, the young men visit the local prostitute in town and there do manly things. That accomplished, Eugene, in particular, now considers himself a man, better able to cope with Sergeant Toomey and the confining life on base. He also meets a convent-school girl (Penelope Ann Miller) with whom he falls in love, but he knows that this infatuation cannot last.

Because they are both New Yorkers, Eugene feels a kinship for the stand-offish Epstein and writes in his diary: "But often I hold back showing my love and affection because I think he might misinterpret it. I have the instinctive feeling that Arnold is . . . homosexual and that bothers me." When these private observations are made public—ironically when Arnold grabs the diary and reads aloud from it—the now-stigmatized Epstein says rhetorically to the gaping onlookers, "Do you see why I find life so interesting, because here is a man who in three weeks has come to the brilliant conclusion that . . . his most esteemed and dearest friend is a fairy." Not sure how to take the situation, the recruits react by rote and immediately steer clear of Epstein, who as it turns out, is not gay.

Some time later, Private Lindstrom (Ben Hynum) is caught in the barracks' bathroom having sex with another soldier. The latter flees out an open window, but Lindstrom is caught, leading Toomey to bark: "Damm it Lindstrom! Why didn't you tell the Army what you were and save them the trouble of a court-martial?" Later, to pressure the troops into forcing the guilty one into confessing, all base privileges and passes are cancelled. Arnold, who seems the obvious "culprit" to the others, remains non-plussed. A few days later, the sweating soldiers are surprised when a jeep full of MPs pulls up and arrests Hennessy as the homosexual who had been involved with Lindstrom in the bathroom.

Out of this sobering episode, Eugene learns two lessons. His having idly accused Arnold in his diary of being gay was sufficient to make him one in the eyes of the others. Jerome realizes now that people usually believe what is written. He now tells himself, "Responsibility was my new watch word." As for Hennessy, Jerome recalls he was the only one who defended ethnic and racial minorities in the barracks against the bigotry of many of the redneck recruits. Jerome reflects, "Hennessy was the only guy in the platoon who stood up for both Epstein and me. That fact didn't even occur to me until I saw him being driven off to prison." Eugene has learned that homosexuals, caught in a repressive straight world, have extra empathy for other minorities who are also outcasts of the norm. As such, Jerome has begun to think of people as individuals not as stereotypes.

As the film concludes, the war ends before the boys can be shipped overseas. The untested recruits head home on the troop train. In a voice-over, Eugene relates that later he became a writer and that one of the plays he writes is *Biloxi Blues*.

Michael Wilmingham (*Los Angeles Times*) wrote, "The movies made from Neil Simon's plays often tend to be bright and superficial, buzzing with wisecracks like some comedy display window. But *Biloxi Blues* is an exception; it has some marvelous moments." Richard Schickel (*Time* magazine) agreed, "it is the tone of the picture that makes it so beguiling. . . . *Biloxi Blues* is truly pensive. It is a memory not yet embalmed in wistfulness, a blend of harsh reality and blurring fantasy." In contrast, Roger Ebert (*New York Post*) felt that "*Biloxi Blues* may indeed be based on memories from Neil Simon's experiences . . . but it seems equally based on every movie ever made about basic training, and it suffers by comparison with most of them . . . and tells us less about the characters than we already know. It is also curiously depressing; it evokes nostalgia without creating it." Katherine Dieckmann (*Village Voice*) concurred: "This is the most nicey-nice coming-of-age movie dealing with boot camp, sexual identity, and borderline psychosis one could imagine. . . ."

Made at an estimated negative cost of $19,000,000, *Biloxi Blues* earned $19,466,043 in distributors' domestic film rentals.

25. Black Eye (Warner Bros., 1974), color, 98 min. PG-rated.

Executive producer, Jack Reeves; producer, Pat Rooney; associate producer, Larry Noble; director, Jack Arnold; based on the novel *Murder on the Wild Side* by Jeff Jacks; screenplay, Mark Haggard, Jim Martin; art directors, Charles Pierce, John Rozman; music, Mort Garson; assistant directors, Clark Paylow, David Hamburger; sound, Bud Alper, Gene Ashbrook, Andrew Gilmore; camera, Ralph Woolsey; editor, Gene Ruggiero.

Cast: Fred Williamson (Shep Stone); Rosemary Forsyth (Miss Francis); Teresa Graves (Cynthia); Floy Dean (Diane Davis); Richard Anderson (Raymond Dole); Cyril Delevanti (Talbot); Richard X. Slattery (Bill Bowen); Larry Mann (Reverend Avery); Bret Morrison (Max Majors); Susan Arnold (Amy Dole); Frank Stell (Chess); Nancy Fisher (Vera Brownmiller); Teddy Wilson (Lindy); Gene Elman (Lou Siegal); Wayne Sutherland (Worm); Jim Malinda (Pusher); Joanne Bruno (Moms); Belinda Balaski (Mary); Edmund Penny (Marcus Rollo); and: Marie Cheatham, Bob Minor, John Moskoff, Nick Ramus, Clyde Ventura.

One of the delights of the rash of black action feature films of the early 1970s was the species' guiding principle of "anything goes!" If mainstream Hollywood had been decorous about any aspect of steamy street life, black exploitation movies broke through those barriers. The results might be crude, overstated and highly calculated, but there was no denying the energy and blatancy of these pieces, all filled with an array of hoodlums, drug dealers, prostitutes, pimps and the inevitable good guys. Any or all of these types would often display voracious sexual appetites, which, depending on the occasion, could be heterosexual or homosexual.

When black police lieutenant Shep Stone (Fred Williamson) murders a drug dealer who was responsible for his sister's death, he is suspended from the force. He becomes a private eye, based at a California beach town. His girlfriend is black Cynthia (Teresa Graves), a bisexual who is having a relationship with a white fashion designer, Miss Francis (Rosemary Forsyth). Not long after finding the body of a prostitute (Nancy Fisher) in his apartment building, Stone is pummeled by the killer, Chess (Frank Stell), who uses a cane as his weapon.

Later, Shep is given an undercover assignment on the case by Lieutenant Bill Bowen (Richard X. Slattery). The trail leads Stone to porno filmmaker Max Majors (Bret Morrison), which proves to be a dead end temporarily. Meanwhile, Raymond Dole (Richard Anderson) hires Stone to locate his missing daughter, Amy (Susan Arnold). Shep tracks her to a dissident born-again organization headed by the crooked Reverend Avery (Larry Mann). Before long, the clues draw Stone to Chess and to his fancy cane which once contained drugs. Soon, two thugs relieve Stone of the cane. Max Major and his underlings think Shep is lying about not having the drug cache. The scene shifts to an ocean-side service of Avery's followers, where Dole fires at Avery and almost kills Amy before Stone interrupts him. It turns out that Amy is not Dole's daughter, but rather a pusher who removed the drugs from the cane to assist Avery's cause.

Variety weighed, "Fast black private-eyer with plenty of values for action trade. . . .That it rates okay . . . is due particularly to efforts of Fred Williamson

Fred Williamson, Floy Dean, Brett Morrison and Rosemary Forsyth in *Black Eye* **(1974).**

. . . and rugged direction by Jack Arnold, who knows how best to take advantage of such elements as bruising fights, exciting auto chases and other facets of the genre." Lawrence Van Gilder (*New York Times*) was more critical of this self-mocking thriller: "What could have been an almost savage commentary, juxtaposing the traditional private eye to a modern California background of Jesus freaks, pornographic film makers, the narcotics trade and transitional sexual styles, stutters over the script and its performances."

26. Black Widow (Twentieth Century-Fox, 1987), color, 102 min. R-rated.

Executive producer, Laurence Mark; producer, Harold Schneider; director, Bob Rafelson; screenplay, Ronald Bass; production designer, Gene Callahan; set decorators, Jim Duffy, Buck Henshaw, Rick Simpson; costumes, Patricia Norris; makeup, Dorothy Pearl; music, Michael Small; additional music/songs, Peter Rafelson; assistant directors, Tommy Thompson, Nilo Otero, Liz Ryan; sound,

David MacMillan; special effects, Allen Hall, Jerry Williams; camera, Conrad L. Hall; underwater camera, Al Giddings; editor, John Bloom.

Cast: Debra Winger (Alexandra Barnes); Theresa Russell (Catharine); Sami Frey (Paul Nuytten); Dennis Hopper (Ben Dumers); Nicol Williamson (William Macauley); Terry O'Quinn (Bruce); Lois Smith (Sara); D. W. Moffett (Michael); Leo Rossi (Shelley); Mary Woronov (Shelley); Rutanya Alda (Irene); James Hong (Shin); Diane Ladd (Etta); Wayne Heffley (Etta's Husband); Raleigh Bond (Martin, the Houston Attorney); Donegan Smith (Reporter); Danny Kamekona (Detective); Christian Clemenson (Artie); Arsenio "Sonny" Trinidad (Tran); Thomas Hill (Attorney); Darrah Meeley (Dawn); Johnny "Sugarbear" Willis (James); Kathleen Hall (Young Girl); George Ricord (Italian Man); Richard E. Arnold (Doctor); Bea Kiyohara, Allen Nause (Clerks); Chris S. Ducey (Poker Player); Tee Dennard (Sid); David Mamet (Herb); Gene Callahan (Mr. Foster); John L. Sostrich (Priest); Juleen Murray (Attendant); Denise Dennison (Stewardess); Robert J. Peters (Steward); Rick Shuster, Al

Cerullo (Helicopter Pilots); David Kasparian (Limo Driver); Mick Muldoon (Doorman); Marcia Holley, Julie Robinson (Underwater Diving Doubles).

"*Black Widow*, with its good, flashy star-performances by Debra Winger and Theresa Russell, comes on with the seductiveness of an expensive perfume that inevitably evaporates before the night is over." (Vincent Canby, *New York Times*)

Drab, dedicated statistician Alex Barnes (Debra Winger), a member of the U.S. Department of Justice's Special Investigative Unit, becomes suspicious when a computer search alerts her that two men (a publisher and a Mafia figure), married recently to younger women, both died in their sleep from a rare syndrome known as Ondine's Curse. The evidence indicates that, in both cases, the young brides were the same person. Meanwhile, the strikingly attractive Catharine (Theresa Russell), who has again changed her appearance, has married Dallas, Texas manufacturer Ben Dumers (Dennis Hopper). She laces his bourbon with a slow-acting poison that will kill him while she is conveniently elsewhere. Thereafter, Catharine picks her next victim—wealthy William Macauley (Nicol Williamson), a Seattle museum curator and anthropologist.

Against the Department's better judgment, workaholic, frumpy Alex is permitted to go to Seattle to pursue her hunch about the murders. By now, Catharine has wed Macauley. Pretending to be a journalist, Alex interviews Macauley, unsure whether to tell him of her misgivings. Before long, he too is dead. Obsessed by the case and the murderess, Alex pursues Catharine to Hawaii. There she engages a seedy detective, Mr. Shin (James Hong), to track down Catharine, but she finds her quarry herself. Getting to know the uninhibited Catharine, Alex is impressed by her attitudes regarding sex, wealth and the fact that she insists she loved her various husbands.

Presently, Catharine has targeted international financier, Paul Nuytten (Sami Frey), as her next victim, despite the fact that he will not commit to her. Meanwhile, Catharine encourages Alex to spruce herself up and to pursue Nuytten herself. Although intrigued by Catharine, Alex soon suspects (especially after a narrow escape while they are scuba diving) that Catharine knows why Alex instigated their friendship. Belatedly, Alex realizes that Catharine has manipulated her pursuit of Paul, as a means of pushing him into marrying Catharine. After Catharine and Paul wed, the bride, who had earlier hired Shin to take photos of Alex and Nuytten together, kills the private detective, leaving the pictures near the corpse.

After Catharine leaves on a sudden trip, the distraught Alex is convinced that Nuytten will be poisoned. She warns him, but he rejects her notion, claiming that both he and Catharine have made new wills, leaving all their money to charity. (As it turns out, the wills have clauses allowing the surviving spouse to veto the charity bequest.) When Catharine returns from her trip, she is told that her husband is dead, that Shin's body has been found and that Alex is linked to both homicides. Catharine visits Alex in jail, confessing that she had incriminated her, but insisting that she will always remember their friendship. Suddenly, Paul and a telltale witness from the past, Sara (Lois Smith), appear. It has all been a set-up to trap Catharine into confessing. With the case over, the now liberated Alex leaves Hawaii.

Charles Sawyer (*Films in Review* magazine) praised the R-rated *Black Widow*, judging this stylish *film noir* an "original" in which "Everything works beautifully here; stunning performances by two very talented actresses . . . lovely scoring . . . and a witty and unpredictable script. . . ." On the other hand, most other critics had reservations. David Denby (*New York* magazine) recorded that "*Black Widow* is an elegant-looking movie, a thriller without conventional scare tactics. . . .

Theresa Russell and Debra Winger in a publicity pose for *Black Widow* (1987).

Most of the movie . . . is sunlit and gleaming. The plot is meant to flow out of the characters—and specifically out of women's needs, women's drives. All of this amounts to a fresh, nonexploitative approach to suspense. I wish to God it had worked. . . ."

For Mike McGrady (*Newsday*), "For half this movie, as the husbands are being killed and the puzzle pieces are being assembled, *Black Widow* is terrific—gripping and entertaining. It starts to stall,

however, as the hunt ends and the relationships begin. . . . Nothing damages a thriller more than gaps in basic logic."

What gained *Black Widow* so much attention, beyond its two stars and the return of director Bob Rafelson to filmmaking, was the multi-layered, (deliberately?) ambiguous relationship of its two leading female characters. There was a lot of printed debate about whether the two characters are or are not supposed to be (quasi-) gay in the story. David Edlestein (*Village

Voice) pointed out, "*Black Widow* has an irresistible notion: that Alex, who has too much integrity to settle for any man but her absent prince, becomes fatally attracted to Catharine." For Judith Williamson (*New Statesman*), when Alex and Catharine meet "the social dimension gives way to the psychosexual. Rafelson claims that 'Catharine brings out Alex's femininity, teaches her more about the feminine qualities in herself'; and the supposedly natural nature of these qualities is suggested by the backdrops of jungle and erupting volcano against which both women play out their affairs with the same man. . . . And the hint of sexual attraction between the women is just left in void." For David Denby of *New York* magazine, "the moods grow heavy with insinuation, including the suggestion (undeveloped) of a lesbian attraction between the two, but the explosion of temperament we have been waiting for never happens."

For whatever reasons which led the makers of *Black Widow* to hold back (if indeed they ever intended to go further), it remained for such features as *Lianna* (1983), *Desert Hearts* (1985) and *Henry and June* (1990), qq.v., to more fully explore the on-screen potentials of women in love.

Black Widow grossed $11,500,000 in distributors' domestic film rentals.

27. **Blood and Concrete** (I.R.S. Media, 1991), color, 97 min. R-rated.

Executive producers, Miles A. Copeland III, Paul Colichman, Harold Welb; producer, Richard LaBrie; director, Jeffrey Reiner; screenplay, LaBrie, Reiner; production designer, Pamela Woodbridge; art director, Wendy Guidery; set decorator, Robert Stover; costumes, Jan Rowton; makeup, Susan Reiner; music, Vinny Golia; assistant directors, Gregory Everage, David Cass; stunt coordinator, Tim Trella; sound, Giovanni Di Simone; special effects coordinator, Kevin McCarthy; camera, Declan Quinn; editors, LaBrie, Reiner.

Cast: Billy Zane (Joey Turks); Jennifer Beals (Mona); James LeGros (Lance); Darren McGavin (Hank Dick); Nicholas Worth (Spuntz); Mark Pellegrino (Bart); Harry Shearer (Sammy Rhodes); William Bastiani (Mort); Pat Cupo (Stone); Pat O'Bryan (Barton); Tracey Coley (Ack); Ellen Albertini Dow (Old Lady); Lyvingston Homes (Thelma); Andy Prieboy, Steven Brenner, Dorian MacDougall (Mona's Band Members); Eric Helms, Lantz Krantz, Robert Lundstrom (Lance's Band Members)..

This is another excursion onto the seamy streets of Hollywood, where life is cheap and the people cheaper.

Not-so-smart car thief Joey Turks (Billy Zane) gets into a scrape with drug dealer Mort (William Bastiani) when he tries to steal his TV. Bleeding from a knife wound earned in the skirmish, he hides out at a cemetery where he stumbles across drugged-out singer Mona (Jennifer Beals) who is about to slit her wrists. The two burned-out souls make passionate love back at her pad. When Mort is found dead, Turks is the chief suspect hunted by the police—gun-punchy Hank Dick (Darren McGavin)—and by underworld figures— including hefty homosexual hoodlum Spuntz (Nicholas Worth)—who want the drugs stash missing from Mort's possession. While Joey and Mona elude their pursuers so they can scrape together the cash to leave town, Lance (James Le Gros), her underground rock singer ex-lover, reappears on the scene. Eventually, escaping Hank Dick as well as fat, decadent Spuntz and his muscle-bound henchman (Mark Pellegrino), the couple leave L.A., bound for Las Vegas ("a quiet restful town").

Eric Mankin (*LA Reader*) observed, "The film consists of about five scenes (mostly involving the Pellegrino or McGavin character threatening the Zane character) each played two or three times almost without variation. Given that the number of locations is also sharply limited, after a couple of [plot] laps, the audience starts feeling trapped in some kind of feature-length looping session." Less offended with this scummy New Age *film noir* was Duayne Byrge (*Hollywood Reporter*): "While most of this sludge is about as creative as a parking ramp, there are lumps of bright lunacy, both in the script and in Jeff Reiner's frantic direction. *Daily Variety* judged it a "hip, funny whodunit . . . a stylish, well-paced romp that scores high in entertainment value. . . . [Picture] captures the drug-heightened atmosphere of this seedy, comic nightworld in a way that recalls, on a more modest scale, Martin Scorsese's *After Hours* [1985, q.v.]."

28. Born Innocent (NBC-TV, September 10, 1974), color, 100 min. Not rated.

Executive producers, Robert W. Christiansen, Rick Rosenberg; producer, Bruce Cohn Curtis; director, Donald Wrye; teleplay, Gerald DiPego; set decorator, Philip Abramson; costumes, Bruce Walkup; makeup, Bruce Hutchinson; music, Fred Karlin; assistant director, Ken Swor; sound, David Ronne; camera, David M. Walsh; editor, Maury Winetrobe.

Cast: Linda Blair (Chris Parker); Joanna Miles (Barbara Clark); Kim Hunter (Mrs. Parker); Richard Jaeckel (Mr. Parker); Allyn Ann McLerie (Emma Lasko); Mary Murphy (Miss Murphy); Janit Baldwin (Denny); Nora Heflin (Moco); Tina Andrews (Josie); Mitch Vogel (Tom Parker); Sandra Ego (Janet).

U.S. network television usually trailed a few years behind Hollywood's filmmakers in reaching new levels of permissiveness while exploring "mature" subjects. The TV movie, *The Glass House* (1972), q.v., had dealt somewhat with the viciousness of life behind bars in a men's prison, including inmates being forced into homosexual acts. However, that aspect was presented through dialogues. Two years later, *Born Innocent*, changed all that with its depiction of the grim fate that awaited new charges in a juvenile detention home. One of this TV movie's most exploited (and best remembered) aspects was the realistic sequence in which the heroine (Linda Blair) is raped by her peers in the dormitory showers.

In an unnamed western city, fourteen-year-old Chris Parker (Linda Blair) is jailed merely for being a runaway, a "crime" she has committed several times during the past two years. Made a court ward, she is sent to a juvenile detention home. Although a sympathetic superintendent, Barbara Clark (Joanna Miles), is in charge, it is the staff's tough Emma Lasko (Allyn Ann McLerie) who has direct supervision of Chris and the others. Chris's roommate is suicidal Janet (Sandra Ego), a pregnant young Indian girl, and soon, Chris's best friend is Josie (Tina Andrews), a black inmate who has been a prostitute since the age of ten. Before long, Chris becomes the target of teenage lesbian Moco (Nora Heflin), who resents the newcomer for being too independent and for resisting her advances. One evening, Moco and her followers attack Chris in the showers and rape her.

Overwhelmed by her oppressive surroundings, the bewildered Chris attempts to escape, but is caught. Later, she wins enough good conduct points to be given a four-day pass to visit her blue collar parents (Richard Jaeckel, Kim Hunter) who naively think that the detention center is the best remedy for their rebellious daughter. The desperate Chris takes a bus to Tucson to see her older brother (Mitch Vogel), hoping he will help her. However, he is overwhelmed by his own problems and rebuffs her. As a result, she is dispatched back to the dreaded, sterile detention center, where she becomes another of the hardened inmates. Her dire fate is now sealed!

Sue Cameron (*Hollywood Reporter*) described this telling telefeature as a "massive, brutal, indictment of the juvenile justice system in the United States and also a statement against uncaring parents." Cameron judged that it was "at times too sensationalistic, but basically a sensitive and successful attempt."

Several months after *Born Innocent*, CBS-TV, would present its own "mature" version of the hell that awaited young incarcerated women. In subsequent years—more so in theatrical features than on TV—women-behind-bars movies would continue to explore homosexuality, usually as an excuse to include highly exploit able interludes, generally filled with one-dimensional representations of lesbians. Linda Blair, who had risen to fame in *The Exorcist* (1973), would appear in other prison genre pieces, such as *Chained Heat* (1982) and *Red Heat* (1985).

In later TV showings of *Born Innocent*, the controversial shower scene was often trimmed or deleted.

29. The Boston Strangler (Twentieth Century-Fox, 1968), color, 116 min. Not rated.

Producer, Robert Fryer; associate producer, James Cresson; director, Richard Fleischer; based on the book by Gerold Frank; screenplay, Edward Anhalt; art directors, Jack Martin Smith, Richard Day; set decorator, Walter M. Scott, Stuart A. Reiss, Raphael Bretton; costumes, Travilla; makeup, Dan Striepeke; music, Lionel Newman; assistant director, David Hall; sound, Don Bassman, David Dockendorf; split screen image, Fred Harpman; special effects, L. B. Abbott, Art Cruickshank, John C. Caldwell; camera, Richard H. Kline; editor, Marion Rothman.

Cast: Tony Curtis (Albert DeSalvo); Henry Fonda (John S. Bottomly); George Kennedy (Detective Phil DiNatale); Mike Kellin (Julian Soshnick); Hurd Hatfield (Terence Huntley); Murray Hamilton (Sergeant Frank McAfee): Jeff Corey (John Asgeirsson); Sally Kellerman (Dianne Cluny); William Marshall (Attorney General Edward W. Brooke); George Voskovec (Peter Hurkos); Leora Dana (Mary Bottomly); Carolyn Conwell (Irmgard DeSalvo); Jeanne Cooper (Cloe); Austin Willis (Dr. Nagy); Lara Lindsay (Bobbie Eden); George Furth (Lyonel Brumley); Richard X. Slattery (Ed Willis); William Hickey (Eugene T. Rourke); Eve Collyer (Ellne Ridgeway); Gwyda Donhowe (Alice Oakville); Alex Dreier (News Commentator); John Cameron Swayze (TV Commentator); Shelley Burton (David Parker); Elizabeth Baur (Harriet Fordin); Dana Elcar (Louis Schubert, Esq.); James Brolin (Sergeant Phil Lisi); George Tyne (Dr. Kramer); William Traylor (Arnie Carr); Carole Shelley (Dana Banks); Karen Huston (Pat Bruner); Enid Markey (Edna); Dorothy Blackburn (Minnie); Almira Sessions (Emma Hodak); Isabella Hoops (Bertha Blum); Richard Krisher (Tom); Arthur Hanson (Commmissoner); Walter Klavun

(Chief of Police); Tim Herbert (Cedric); Matt Bennett (Harold); Penny Williams (Mae); Janis Young (Louise Parker); George Fisher (Mr. Taylor); David Lewis (Judge Schroeder); Pam McMyler (Grace); Greg Benedict (Dick Matheson); Tom Aldredge (Harold Lacey); Marie Thomas (Gloria); Gina Harding (Audri); Nancie Phillips (Barbara Wise); and: Tommy Flanders.

Between 1962 and 1964, a real-life serial killer known as "The Boston Strangler" murdered and raped thirteen women in the Massachusetts capitol. As demonstrated within this superior manhunt study, it was standard procedure in such police investigations to focus part of the investigation on known "deviates," a wide-reaching group which included, at the time, homosexuals, The latter fell within the "deviate" definition because the law and medical science, as did much of the general public, considered gay people to be mentally sick individuals capable of any sort of errant behavior/crime.

The Boston police are baffled when several elderly women are strangled in the Boston area, apparently the work of a single killer. When the homicidal maniac turns his murderous attention to younger victims, Attorney General Edward A. Brooke (William Marshall) orders his assistant, John Bottomly (Henry Fonda), to take charge of the "Strangler Bureau" to coordinate information on the serial killer. The law brings in a wide variety of suspects for questioning, but to no avail.

One victim, Dianne Cluny (Sally Kellerman), survives the killer's assault, but she cannot remember the attacker's face. However, she does recall that she bit the man's hand. Later, Albert DeSalvo (Tony Curtis), a maintenance man with a wife (Carolyn Conwell) and two young children, is arrested for breaking into an apartment. His persistent refusal to admit his guilt in this matter, despite the concrete evidence, leads to his incarceration at Boston City Hospital. There, while being tested for mental competency, small teeth marks are noted on his hand. Bottomly

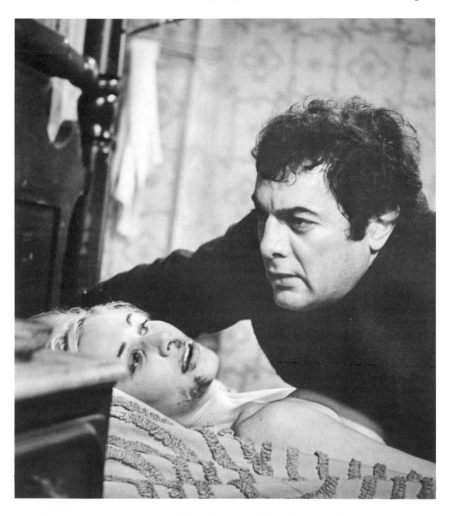

Sally Kellerman and Tony Curtis in *The Boston Strangler* (1968).

knows all too well that DaSalvo's shaky mental state plus the quesitonable legality surrounding the man's interrogation will prevent a successful prosecution. Nevertheless, he continues to question the schizophrenic man. Finally, DeSalvo politely admits that he is the Strangler. While this confession is considered legally irrelevant, DeSalvo is given a life sentence for robbing and assaulting four women—who survived to testify in court against him.

Renata Adler (*New York Times*) was no fan of this slickly executed drama: "*The Boston Strangler* represents an incredible collapse of taste, judgment, decency, prose, insight, journalism and movie technique and yet—through certain prurient options that it does not take—it is not quite the popular exploitation film that one might think." Jan Dawson (British *Monthly Film Bulletin*) noted, "whereas the most distressing thing to emerge from [Gerald] Frank's study was that, of the scores of suspects questioned, DeSalvo was clearly the most likable (one is tempted to say normal) . . . the picture that Fleischer paints is more reassuring to civic pride. . . . Inevitably then, the film never captures the real nightmare of a maniac killer let loose in a maniac world, and Fleischer further simplifies the moral complexity of the situation by turning De-Salvo into an old-fashioned Jekyll and Hyde schizophrenic." In contrast, *Variety* applauded the feature for its "telling, low-key, semi-documentary style" and for being "a triumph of taste and restraint."

In the course of the investigation within *The Boston Strangler*, the top police administrators order their subordinates to conduct a dragnet: "Now each of you is getting a list of known sex offenders. Bring in the people you usually ignore, peepers, men's room queens, exhibitionists, subway jostlers, dirty word offenders." One of the men caught in this round-up is Terence Huntley (Hurd Hatfield), a middle-aged, polished antique dealer who happens to be a homosexual. Searching his apartment, the police find he has a set of the collected works of the Marquis de Sade, suggesting to the lawmen that this suspect may be attuned to violent acts. Bottomly stalks his prey to a sedate gay bar, where he questions him for not responding to phone messages left with his landlady:

Huntley: I never answer calls unless I know who they are.

Bottomly: Why not?

Huntley: Because I'm too vulnerable. . . .[the type] people continually harass and blackmail.

Bottomly: Have you any idea why I want to talk to you?

Huntley: Well, whenever there are unsolved sex crimes, the police crack down on us. I think it is ridiculous.

Absorbing this reflection, Bottomly questions Huntley about his lesbian landlady (Eve Collyer), then decides this avenue of investigation is also worthless. The conversation ends with:

Huntley: [Was it that] you're curious about us?

Bottomly: Let's say I'm slumming. I was rude. I'm sorry.

Although the sequence is short, it is telling and very well-handled by Hurd Hatfield, best known for playing the title role in *The Picture of Dorian Gray* (1945).

Using Gerold Frank's best-selling book (1966) as a basis, *The Boston Strangler* earned $8 million in distributors' domestic film rentals. When the movie was later shown on Boston TV a few years after its theatrical release, a postscript voice-over was spliced in, stating that DeSalvo was found stabbed to death in his Walpole, Massachusetts prison cell on November 26, 1973.

The Boston Strangler appeared in the same year as *The Detective* and *No Way to Treat a Lady*, qq.v., two other Hollywood murder mysteries which wove homosexual suspects into their plots.

30. The Bostonians (Almi, 1984), color, 120 min. Not rated.

Executive producers, Michael Landes, Albert Schwartz; producer, Ismail Merchant; associate producers, Connie Kaiserman, Paul Bradley; director, James Ivory; based on the novel by Henry James; screenplay, Ruth Prawer Jhabvala; production designer, Leo Austin; art directors, Tom Walden, Don Carpentier; set decorator, Richard Elton; costumes, Jenny Beavan, John Bright; makeup, Jeanne Richmond; music, Richard Robbins; assistant directors, David Appleton, Ron Peck; sound, Ray Beckett, Alan Snelling, Scott Kent; camera, Walter Lassally; editors, Katherine Wenning, Mark Potter.

Cast: Christopher Reeve (Basil Ransom); Vanessa Redgrave (Olive Chancellor); Madeleine Potter (Verena Tarrant); Jessica Tandy (Miss Birdseye); Nancy Marchand (Mrs. Burrage); Wesley Addy (Dr. Tarrant); Barbara Bryce (Mrs. Tarrant); Linda Hunt (Dr. Prance); Nancy New (Mrs. Luna); John Van Ness Philip

(Henry Burrage); Wallace Shawn (Mr. Pardon); Maura Moynihan (Henrietta Stackpole); Martha Farrar (Mrs. Farrinder); Peter Bogyo (Mr. Gracie); Dusty Maxwell (Newton); Charles McCaughan (Music Hall Policeman); J. Lee Morgan (Music Hall Official); Lee Doyle (Mr. Filer); De French (Patient); Jane Manners (Maid); Janet Cicchese (Irish Washerwoman); Scott Kradolfer (Tough Boy); June Mitchell (Party Guest); Richard Robbins (Man Turning Music).

In their several joint movies to date, producer Ismail Merchant, director James Ivory and scriptwriter Ruth Prawer Jhabvala have turned frequently to the works of Henry James (*The Europeans*, 1979) and E. M. Forster (*A Room with a View*, 1986; *Maurice*, 1987) for their source material, turning out meticulous productions of arthouse variety. In *The Bostonians*, based on James's anti-feminist novel (1886) about Boston Brahmins, the moviemakers decorously deal with an underlying theme of homosexuality (here lesbianism), a subject they would treat more explicitly in the British-produced *Maurice*. What makes *The Bostonians'* subtext so unexploitive is the subtlety of presentation (even though it is much clearer than the ambiguity of the book original) and the fact that this feature is such a class production based on a literary classic.

In 1876 Boston, neurotic Olive Chancellor (Vanessa Redgrave), involved in the evolving women's movement, attends a meeting held by Miss Birdseye (Jessica Tandy), a veteran social reformer. There, Verena Tarrant (Madeleine Potter), whose father (Wesley Addy) is a faith healer/ spiritualist, makes an impassioned speech on women's rights. Olive is so moved by Verena's eloquence that she invites the attractive young woman to stay at her house (for a fee paid by the Tarrants) to learn more about the suffragette movement. Meanwhile, Olive's lawyer cousin, the impoverished Southerner, Basil Ransome (Christopher Reeve), is equally drawn to Verena. To be near Verena, the opportunistic Basil tolerates the advances of Olive's flirtatious sister, Mrs. Luna (Nancy New). Basil pursues Verena when she visits New York, but he lets slip his very chauvinistic point of view as well as his growing affection for her.

The shocked Verena is easily persuaded by the comforting Olive to depart for Cape Cod so they can prepare for a major lecture meeting to be held at the Boston Music Hall. Undaunted, Basil follows the women to Cape Cod and quickly forces the idealistic Verena into a dilemma: should she pursue her activist's role which includes a closer relationship with the possessive Olive, or should she abandons her fervent political beliefs to be with the attractive Basil. At the Music Hall conclave, Ransome's presence in the audience upsets Verena so much that she cannot give her keynote speech. Olive staunchly takes her place, while Verena rushes off to marry Basil in New York.

David Sterritt (*Christian Science Monitor*) championed the movie: "the story doesn't exactly gallop along—this is Henry James, after all—but it canters with an easy, flowing grace. Add a long list of vivid characters, and a mood as rich and proud as old Boston itself, and you have a hearty entertainment that's as thoughtful and engaging (if not so deep or imposing) as its source."

As to the gay sub-theme, Sheila Benson (*Los Angeles Times*) found, "the film makers must, necessarily, make the novel's pulsating undertone explicit. . . . Things are put a good deal more strongly in the film, although they have not vulgarized but only underscored James' subtext."

David Edelstein (*Village Voice*) concluded, "Some forbidden longings are more tedious than we ever dreamed— even the longings of the repressed, 19th century lesbian Olive Chancellor. . . ." In contrast, Jerry Parker (*Newsday*) found "what makes the film unique is the way it ascribes to the suffragettes an amorous dimension of their own . . . which divests Olive's love for Verena of any 'taint' of lesbianism in the narrow sense. Its most graceful, affecting, most sheerly enviable scenes are of this tender, flirtatious phalanstery of women, reading the classics of feminisms over each other's shoulders or strolling arm in arms along the beach. . . . or squealing with delight at a fireworks display."

31. The Boys in the Band (National General Pictures, 1970), color, 117 min. R-rated.

Executive producers, Dominick Dunne, Robert Jiras; producer, Mart Crowley; associate producer, Ken Utt; director, William Friedkin; based on the play by Crowley; screenplay, Crowley, production designer, John Robert Lloyd; assistant art director, Robert Wrightman; set decorator, William C. Gerrity; costumes, W. Robert La Vine; wardrobe supervisor, Joseph W. Dehn; makeup, John Jiras; assistant directors, Gerrity, Fred Gallo; sound, Jack C. Jacobsen; camera, Arthur J. Ornitz; editor, Jerry Greenberg.

Cast: Frederick Combs (Donald); Leonard Frey (Harold); Cliff Gorman (Emory); Reuben Greene (Bernard); Robert La Tourneaux (Cowboy); Laurence Luckinbill (Hank); Kenneth Nelson (Michael); Keith Prentice (Larry); Peter White (Alan).

Depending on one's own sexual lifestyle and/or empathies, *The Boys in the Band*, was or was not cathartic and/or revelatory. The hit off-Broadway play (1968) and the two-year later movie version, which used the same cast, became beacons of hope and illumination for gays at a time when most of them were still severely discriminated against in all walks of life. For many gays, the trend-setting drama provided them with the courage to come out of the closet and go public with their sexual orientation. In contrast, for more cosmopolitan gays, *The Boys in the Band* was already light years behind the changing community scene and was regarded as simplistic pop psychology about the angst ("You show me a happy homosexual and I'll show you a gay corpse") of stereotypical characters in the lavender world. On the other hand, for anyone homophobic, *The Boys in the Band* was like a red flag being waved furiously in front of a nervous bull. In the midst of all the controversy engendered by the play/movie, there existed a segment of critics and viewers who actually took the work at face value, judging it on whatever degrees of creativity and entertainment values it possessed.

In the decades that followed *The Boys in the Band*, two social changes had occurred: *One*—a far greater number of gays and lesbians had made their alternative lifestyle known and this, in turn, had made the general public much more aware of the homosexual culture; *Two*—the disastrous effects of AIDS in the 1980s and thereafter has not only drastically changed the sexual and romantic habits of both gays and straights, but it has tremendously changed how everyone views and deal with the gay world. Thus, while the movie of *The Boys in the Band* remains relevant to the history of the gay culture, it now seems more to be a dated museum piece.

In his Manhattan apartment, Michael (Kenneth Nelson), a guilt-ridden Catholic, and his quasi-lover Donald (Frederick Combs) are making last-minute preparations for their friend Harold's (Leonard Frey) thirty-second birthday party. Michael receives an anxious phone call from his old Georgetown University classmate, Alan (Peter White), who begs to come by and talk. The glib Michael, who has not yet admitted his homosexuality to his former roommate, is worried what the conservative Alan, now married and a Washington, D.C. attorney, will think of Michael's gay guests.

Before long, the partygoers arrive. There is swishy Emory (Cliff Gorman), an excessively effeminate interior decorator, Bernard (Reuben Greene), a considerate black young man employed at a Doubleday Book Shop, ex-married teacher Hank (Laurence Luckinbill) and Larry (Keith Prentice). The latter is Hank's artist lover, who has a strong libido and promptly begins flirting with Donald. Also arriving on the scene is the muscular, but empty-headed, blond stud Cowboy (Robert La

Laurence Luckinbill, Keith Prentice, Kenneth Nelson, Cliff Gorman and Frederick Combs in *The Boys in the Band* (1970).

Tourneaux), who reveals he is Emory's birthday gift for Harold. Later, a very distraught Alan appears. Very quickly, he gets into a scuffle with the obviously gay Emory. Finally, the guest of honor appears. Cynical and venomous Harold targets the foibles and emotional vulnerabilities of the guests. Michael, the most insecure of the group, goes on the offensive to hide his fears. He insists that everyone play a truth game, in which each player must call the one individual he loves most. Michael demands that the equivocating Alan join in the game. Pushed into action, Alan reluctantly declares his love over the phone. Michael thinks the call was directed to an old classmate of theirs. However, it turns out to have been to Alan's wife, whom he was on the verge of divorcing.

The party finally disbands. Before Harold departs with his hustler gift in tow, he finishes his devastating dissection of the brittle Michael, pointing out that with his unresolved guilts, Michael is a misfit in both the gay and straight world.

Vincent Canby (*New York Times*), believing that Mart Crowley's approach to his production's once taboo subject matter may be out of date, admitted, " My reservations . . . all have to do with the source material which sounds too often as if it had been written by someone at the party. . . . If I heard him correctly. . . . He's saying something to the effect that life can't be one, long, continuous matinee. It's cheap sentiment, borrowed, I suspect, from the Late Late Show." On the other hand, Canby reported, "Except for an inevitable monotony that comes from the use of so many close-ups in a confined space, [William] Friedkin's direction is clean and direct, and under the circumstances, effective. All of the performances are good. . . ."

Variety concluded, "It's a tight little band of queen stereotypes, no more or less realistic for their lavender world than the typical American outfit in those World War II battle programmers." The trade paper acknowledged, "despite its often tedious postulations . . . and the stagey posturing of the actor, the too literately faithful adaptation . . . has enough bitchy, back-biting humor, fascinating character studies, melodrama and, most of all, perverse interest to draw and hold substantial audiences." To Pauline Kael (*The New Yorker*), who preferred the stage version of the drama, "the actors [in the screen adaptation] are no longer fresh in their roles, and Friedkin, by limiting the number of actors in the frame to those directly involved in the dialogue and by the insistence of his closeups, forces our attention to the pity-of-it-all." The *Catholic Film Newsletter* chose to interpret the movie as commenting "with wit and passion on the desolation and waste which chill this way of life . . . with all its anxiety, bitterness, depression and solitude."

The Boys in the Band was Mart Crowley's first play. (He was, at one time, the private secretary of Robert Wagner and Natalie Wood.) The play was written in a five-week period and reputedly earned the playwright more than $1 million. The film adaptation which Crowley produced and wrote, was shot economically with New York City location work to open up the drama.

Because of its specialized material, BOYS IN THE BAND (promoted with the catch line "It's not a musical" hoping to give unsuspecting filmgoers a clue/ warning about this R-rated picture) was not a mainstream release and thus did not become a box-office hit. In retrospect, Vito Russell in *The Celluloid Closet* (1987) noted:

"It was a gay movie for gay people, and it immediately became both a period piece and a reconfirmation of the stereotypes. . . . The film industry showed no sign of seeing *The Boys in the Band* as anything but a diversion in a business that was always on the lookout for a novel angle. During the Seventies Hollywood did not relinquish the stereotypes of the Crowley play but moved steadily toward solidifying them."

32. The Boys Next Door (New World Pictures, 1985), color, 88 min. R-rated.

Executive producers, Mel Pearl, Don Levin; producers, Keith Rubinstein, Sandy Howard; associate producers, Michael S. Murphy, Joel Soisson; director, Penelope Spheeris; screenplay, Glen Morgan, James Wong; production designer/art director, Jo-Ann Chorney; set decorator, Barry Franenberg; costumes, Gail Viola; special makeup effects, Mark Shostrom; music, George S. Clinton; assistant directors, Eric Jewett, Warren Lewis, Scott White, Michael A. Masciarelli, Steven Pomeroy; stunt coordinator, Dan Bradley; sound, Craig Felburg; special effects, Joe Quinlivan; camera, Arthur Albert; editor, Andy Horvitch.

Cast: Maxwell Caulfield (Roy Alston); Charlie Sheen (Bo Richards); Christopher McDonald (Detective Woods); Hank Garrett (Detective Hanley); Patti D'Arbanville (Angie); Paul C. Dancer (Chris); Richard Pachorek (Boyfriend); Lesa Lee (Girlfriend); Kenneth Cortland (Dwayne); Moon Zappa (Nancy); Dawn Schneider (Bonnie); Kurt Christian (Shakir); Do Draper (Mr. Heaton); Blackie Dammett (Bartender); Phil Rubinstein (Gutfield); James Carrington (Ross); Grant Heslov (Joe Gonzales); Michael Lewis (Kanter); Leonard O. Turner (Sergeant); Vance Colvig (Old Man); Jeff Prettyman (Al); Claudia Templeton (Girl at Beach); Ron Ross (Drunk); Carlos Guitarlos (Patient); Helen Brown (Old Woman at Beach); Hettie Lynne Hurtes (Anchorwoman); Sarah Lily (Female Officer); Jimmy Ford (Bob, the Jock); James Bershad (Student); Joseph Michael Cala (Gas Station Owner); Mary Tiffany, Marilou Conway (Women); Mark Stanton, Kevin Kendall (Students); Kenneth Gilan Sr. (Older Guard); Carmen Filpi (Bum); Christina Beck (Punk Girl); John Davey (Watkins); Geof Brewer, Jadie David (Security Guards); Toby Iland (Tom);

Richard Halpern (Boy); John Escobar, Ray Lykins (Policemen); Texacala Jones, Pinkie Tessa, Terquila Mockinbird, Maggie Ehrig, Ted Quinn (Street Band).

"Certainly, one feels by the end that if the boys had decided to go to bed rather than to Los Angeles . . . then all this might never have happened. What is peculiar, however, is the extent to which this aspect recurs . . . without ever achieving any real resonance. Visually, it surfaces most self-consciously during an interlude when the youths are watching TV in their hotel room and an overhead shot of Maxwell Caulfield on the bed functions exactly as a beefcake pin-up. But the image remains a symptom of a love . . . which the film refuses to articulate." (Steve Jenkins, British *Monthly Film Bulletin*)

If the ineffective *Best Friends* (1975), q.v., crudely depicted some of the frustrations caused by repressed homosexual love between buddies, the frequently mesmerizing *The Boys Next Door* took the thesis several giant steps forward as this "road picture" chronicles the murderous spree of two teenagers. A good deal of the new picture's success was due to actors Maxwell Caulfield and Kenneth Cortland in particular and, especially, to the resourceful direction of Penelope Spheeris, who would later make the blockbuster, *Wayne's World* (1992).

Having graduated from high school in a small southwestern town, Roy Alston (Maxwell Caulfield) and Bo Richards (Charlie Sheen), extremely close pals, are not looking forward to their bleak, blue color future working at the local factory. In a restless mood, the two moody troublemakers gatecrash a graduation party. Next, anxious for something different, they head to Los Angeles for a last big weekend, deciding to be "totally prehistoric." Once there, Roy attempts to con a gas station owner (Joseph Michael Cala) out of a few dollars. When the man is not fooled, Roy viciously beats him up. Gravitating to the beach, the boys pick on an old lady (Helen Brown). When a group of girls come to the woman's rescue and taunt Roy and Bo as being "queer," Roy attempts to run down one of them with his car.

After driving and drinking along Hollywood Boulevard and the Sunset Strip, the agitated duo find themselves in West Hollywood's gay district. Roy and Bo meet Chris (Paul C. Dancer) who takes them to a local bar and then asks them back to his apartment. It is Roy, intrigued/repelled by Chris's come-on (which Roy engineered), who nonchalantly shoots the man with a gun he finds in the apartment. Los Angeles police detectives Mark Woods (Christopher McDonald) and Ed Hanley (Hank Garrett) tie together the gas station beating with the homicide, after questioning Chris's frantic young lover (Kenneth Cortland). Next, the fugitives track a young couple (Richard Pachorek, Lesa Lee) whom Roy kills out of jealousy for their normalcy.

By now, Bo is angry with his friend's escalating random acts of violence. To pacify him, Roy insists that he has calmed down, having rid himself of the "bad stuff" tearing at him inside. The troublemakers meet lonely Angie (Patti D'Arbanville) at a late night bar and she take them to her apartment. When Bo and Angie make love, a jealously enraged Roy kills her. Meanwhile, the police have tracked the suspects and follow them to a shopping mall, where the teenage perpetrators are surrounded. A panicked Roy demands that Bo hand over his gun. Bo refuses, then shoots his friend. When asked why he did it, Bo responds, "I had to."

Vincent Canby (*New York Times*) concluded, "the film . . . is as chilly as Terence Malick's *Badlands* [1973], if not as poetic. It's lean and unsentimental. . . . It's also exceptionally well acted. . . .*The Boys Next Door* is much more than just another teen-agers-go-wrong movie." Patrick Goldstein (*Los Angeles Times*) rated it "a provocative new film" and complimented director Spheeris for "etching a grim, unsettling portrait of two teen-agers tormented by frustration and despair. . . . [I]ts lack of sentimentality gives it a rugged moral force—-it doesn't soften the twisted fury that sends these kids careening into a crazed death trip."

On the other hand, Rex Reed (*New York Post*) judged the entry "a sick, violent study . . . that is as dull as it is pointless. . . . by failing to explore where their troubles began, the lurid story of her [Spheeris's] 'boys next door' turns from an exploration movie to a cheap, trash exploitation movie." *Variety* decided, "the film itself doesn't live up to the expectations. Even if intentions are worthy, it emerges glib and uninvolving. . . . One of the problems . . . is the casting. With conventional clean-cut good looks, Caulfield and Sheen clearly resemble the title, but they fail to adequately project the 'angry stuff' within. The result is one-dimensional characters. . . ."

One of the most affecting aspects of this film is Kenneth Cortland's performance as the young lover of the gay murder victim, who grows increasingly distraught as the (not-too-sympathetic) police interrogate him about his friend's murder. In his screen time, Cortland creates a fully-realized portrait, a rarity allowed in the genre, even in the mid-1980s.

33. The Broadway Melody (Metro-Goldwyn-Mayer, 1929), color sequences, 104 min. (Also silent version.) Not rated.

Producer, Harry Rapf; director, Harry Beaumont; ensemble numbers staged by George Cunningham; story, Edmund Goulding; screenplay, Sarah Y. Mason; dialogue, Norman Houston, James Gleason; titles, Earl Baldwin; art director, Cedric Gibbons; costumes, David Cox; music director, Nacio Herb Brown; songs: Brown and Arthur Freed; George M. Cohan; Willard Robison; camera, John Arnold; sound, Douglas Shearer, Wesley Miller, Louis Kolk, O. O. Ceccarini, G. A. Burns; editors: (sound version) Sam S. Zimbalist, (silent version) William Le Vanway.

Cast: Anita Page (Queenie Mahoney); Bessie Love (Hank Mahoney); Charles King (Eddie Kearns); Jed Prouty (Uncle Jed); Kenneth Thomson (Jock Warriner); Edward Dillon (Dillon, the Stage Manager); Mary Doran (Flo, the Blonde); Eddie Kane (Francis Zanfield); J. Emmett Beck (Babe Hatrick); Marshall Ruth (Stew); Drew Demarest (Turpe); James Burrows (Singer); James Gleason (Jimmy Gleason, the Music Publisher); Ray Cooke (Bellhop); Nacio Herb Brown (Pianist at Gleason's).

In Hollywood's transition from silents to talkies in the late 1920s, it was rightly assumed that moviegoers would be enthralled by the novelty of movie musicals where, at last, they would be able to hear singing and dancing on the silver screen. As the first such effort from a major studio, *The Broadway Melody* was considered innovative and exciting in its day. Moviegoers flocked to theatres showing it and the movie won an Academy Award as Best Picture of 1928–1929. In its bid to establish the all-talking, all-singing, all-dancing screen genre, *The Broadway Melody* sought to be racy and "authentic" in creating its backstage theatre story of romance and ambition. One of the cliches it perpetuated was that costume designers were frequently gay men with a strong love of working with women's clothing, a model already depicted in the silent *Irene* (1926), q.v.

Vaudeville dancer Eddie Kearns (Charles King) writes "Broadway Melody," a song which proves to be a hit. He is hired by Zanfield (Eddie Kane), a Broadway producer, to perform the number in an upcoming revue. Seeing this as an opportunity to be reunited with "Hank" Mahoney (Bessie Love) the older sister member of a vaudeville act, Eddie convinces she and her sister, Queenie (Anita Page), to leave their small-town circuit and come to New York. Once there, both sisters are hired by Zanfield (who thinks Queenie has talent, but must take Hank as part of the package). Before long, Eddie is more interested romantically in Queenie, but, loyal to her sister, Queenie becomes a mistress to a wealthy show backer (Kenneth Thompson) hoping to have money to keep Eddie and Hank together. Later,

Hank realizes that Eddie and Queenie love one another and convinces Eddie to win Queenie away from her keeper. As a result, Eddie and Queenie are reunited, while Hank finds a new partner for her small town vaudeville act.

Mordaunt Hall (*New York Times*) reported that *The Broadway Melody* was "teeming with the vernacular of the bright lights and back-stage argot" and that "although the audible device worked exceedingly well in most instances, it is questionable whether it would not have been wiser to leave some of the voices to the imagination, or, at least to have refrained from having a pretty girl volleying slang at her colleagues." According to Hall, "So far as its entertainment value is concerned, it is a matter whether one likes to see and hear so much of the upsets of chorus girls and their ilk." *Variety* printed, "It's the first flash New York has had as to how the studios are going after musical comedy numbers and there's no question of the potent threat to the stage producers. . . . . Paradoxically enough, *Broadway Melody* . . . is basically going to draw on its story, the performances of its two lead girls and simply the novelty rather than the quality of the interpolated numbers."

Unreported in the rash of reviews praising and/or dissecting *The Broadway Melody*, was any mention of the three scenes featuring a very angular performer as the fluttery, Broadway costume designer, all a-twitter as opening night approaches. On one occasion, he rushes on stage during a rehearsal carrying a white ermine coat. Very excited, he interrupts Zanfield, who is discussing the show with several tuxedo-clad associates/flunkies. Zanfield is not impressed by the garment:

Zanfield: What? Two grand for a coat worn less than three minutes? I won't pay it!

Designer: But you said ermine! It's a gorgeous garment, isn't it?

At this juncture, one of the underlings grabs the wrap from the costumer, slaps it over his shoulders and mocks:

"Oh! Isn't it gorgeous. In fact, it's the gorgeousest thing I've ever saw, you sweet little cutie."

The interlude ends with the designer storming off in a huff, with one of the inebriated onlookers following after the artist. One of his friends stops him from pursuing the simmering costumer, yelling "Come back here, unconscious!"

Later, on opening night, the chorus girls are having problems with the designer's oversized hats, too large for them to get out of the dressing room door comfortably.

Designer: Girls! Girls! My hats. Be careful of my hats! I won't allow you to ruin them!

Wardrobe Mistress: Say listen. I told you they were too high and too wide.

Designer: Well, big woman. I designed the costumes for the show, not the doors for the theatre.

Wardrobe Mistress: I know that. If you had, they'd have been in lavender.

Since "lavender" was considered synonymous by the smart set with effeminate men who were "that way," knowing viewers had no doubts as to the sexual persuasion of the costume designer. However, gays were not the only minority to be poked fun at in *The Broadway Melody*. One of the characters with a far larger role was the agent Uncle Jed (Jed Prouty) who has a speech impediment which causes him to stutter.

Besides inspiring the flood of imitative screen musicals that followed, *The Broadway Melody* led to several studios sequels: *The Broadway Melody of 1936* (1935), *The Broadway Melody of 1938* (1937) and *The Broadway Melody of 1940* (1940). Finally, it was remade as the budget picture, *Two Girls on Broadway* (1940), starring Lana Turner, Joan Blondell and George Murphy.

34. Buddies (New Line Cinema, 1985), color, 81 min. Not rated.

Producer, Arthur J. Bressan Jr.; associate producer, John Hartis; director/screenplay,

Bressan; makeup, Nina Port; music, Jeffery Olmstead; sound, Steve Hirsch; camera, Carl Tettelbaum; editor, Bressan.

Cast: Geoff Edholm (Robert Willow); David Schachter (David Bennett); Billy Lux (Edward); David Rose (Steve); Libby Saines (Mrs. Bennett); Damon Hairston (Gym Instructor); Tracy Vivat (Nurse); Susan Schneider (Sylvia Doulgas); Joyce Korn (Lynn).

"The picture . . . is unerring in its presentation of gay sensibilities and the variety of responses to them. Nothing is glossed over, and the touching aspects of both the [AIDS] disease and personal commitments are presented truthfully." (Archer Winsten, *New York Post*)

Although there had already been several plays dealing with AIDS, *Buddies* was billed as the first "dramatic movie" about the repercussions of the epidemic-proportion disease. Written in five days by porno filmmaker Arthur J. Bressan Jr. and shot in 16mm over a nine-day period, the movie led Richard Goldstein (*Village Voice*) to report, "*Buddies* rushes in where no other dramatic work about AIDS has dared to tread. It shows us sex; not the memory of sex or its disparagement, not the platonic embrace that will have to suffice for homosexual passion on prime time. . . . I can't remember a more riveting moment in any film than the image in *Buddies* of a dying man masturbating while being held by his friend."

David Bennett (David Schachter), a typesetter, is working on a book dealing with AIDS. Although he is still in the closet about his gay lifestyle, the book persuades him to volunteer to work with AIDS patients. He is assigned to Robert Willow (Geoff Edholm), a seasoned political activist, who has been hospitalized after suffering two attacks of pneumonia. Unsure of what to expect, the cautious David is surprised by Robert's candidness about his lifestyle and his belief in gay pride/political advocacy. Before long, David brings several of the patient's possession from his home to the hospital. Together they watch home

movies of Robert and his ex-lover Edward (Billy Lux).

During one of their dialogues, Robert admits that if he had one full day of feeling good again, he would spend it making love with Edward and then flying to Washington to picket the White House on behalf of AIDS research funds. On another occasion, the two new friends screen old porno movies, and David holds Robert while the later masturbates. By now, both David's mother (Libby Saines) and his lover (David Rose) wonder at the growing relationship between David and Robert. Later, it is Robert who convinces David to come out publicly by assisting a reporter with an AIDS article. When the interview is printed, David rushes to the hospital to show Robert the piece. However, his friend has died. David flies to Washington where he takes his stand in front of the White House, holding his "fight AIDS" placard.

Vincent Canby (*New York Times*) observed, "The characters say exactly what might be expected, and say it more often than would be necessary to get the point across; the performances are unrelievedly sincere. Still, if *Buddies* . . . is on the blunt side, at least it tells its story as plainly as possible." Mark Finch (British *Monthly Film Bulletin*) wrote, "*Buddies* turns its limited budget to advantage. Bressan uses two first-time performers and only three locations to suggest the isolation felt by people with AIDS; other voices are heard off-screen, but we never see where they come from. . . . . *Buddies* is, of course, instructive (it was made to raise money for AIDS organisations), but it welds this impulse with a pleasure and commitment to gay politics that seems almost exclusively addressed to politically defined audiences. . . ."

35. A Bump in the Night (CBS-TV, January 6, 1991), color, 100 min. Not rated.

Executive producer, Robert Halmi; co-executive producers, JoBeth Williams, Barry

Krost; supervising producer, Carl Clifford; producer, Craig Anderson; director, Karen Arthur; based on the novel by Isabelle Holland; teleplay, Christopher Lofton; production designer, Tom Wells; makeup, Suzanne Willet; music, Gary William Friedman; sound, Felipe Borrero; special effects, Matt Vogel; camera, Tom Neuwirth; editor, Geoffrey Rowland.

Cast: Meredith Baxter-Birney (Martha "Red" Tierney); Christopher Reeve (Lawrence Muller); Wings Hauser (Patrick Tierney); Corey Carrier (Jonathan Tieney); Richard Bradford (Sergeant Peter Mooney); Geraldine Fitzgerald (Mrs. Beauchamps); Shirley Knight (Katie Leonard); Terrence Mann (Ben Nicolaides); Richard Joseph Paul (Jeff Donner); Anne Twomey (Sarah Jenny); Leslie Gail (Cheryl Mason); Travis Swords (Barry Weller); Audra Blaser (Marguerite); Ella L. Cox (Julia); William Cameron (Roger Freemantle); Leonara Nemetz (Francine); David Early (Salesman); Anne Kittridge (Waitress); Zachary Mott (Sal).

A Bump in the Night was advertised with the teaser: "Tonight, a sinister stranger, an unspeakable crime, a courageous mother. . . . A film every parent must see!" The made-for-television movie had several highly exploitable items, all geared to grab viewership for this thriller: (1) Meredith Baxter-Birney known for her wholesome mother's role on the TV sitcom "Family Ties" (1982—1989) playing an alcoholic; (2) Christopher "Superman" Reeve as a gay pedophile and (3) child pornography. But as Rick Sherwood (*Hollywood Reporter*) cautioned, "*A Bump in the Night* is about an hour-and-a-half too long and pretty much a waste of time. The telefilm tries to be about so many things that it winds up as nothing at all. . . ."

In Brooklyn Heights, Martha "Red" Tierney (Meredith Baxter-Birney), once an award-winning investigative journalist for the *New York Times*, has allowed her career to get sidetracked. She has turned to alcohol, hoping it will restore her optimism and fortitude, but it has not. As a result, her novelist husband, Patrick (Wings Hauser), has divorced her, and their eight-year old son, Jonathan (Corey Carrier), is too frequently left to his own

devices both before and after his private school day. Meanwhile, pedophile Lawrence Muller (Christopher Reeve), a former college professor of Literature, learns about Jonathan through a contact, Cheryl Mason (Leslie Gail), who provides candidates for child pornography kingpin Ben Nicolaides (Terrence Mann). Receiving the boy's picture (sold to Cheryl by a photographer friend of Patrick), Muller salivates, "He's perfect. He's absolutely lovely!"

Before long, Muller has tricked Jonathan into playing hookey from school and spending the day with him, which is to climax in a sexual foray. Belatedly, Red wakes from her drunken fog and learns from the school that her son is missing. Teaming with her ex-husband, as well as Sergeant Peter Mooney (Richard Bradford) she uses her detecting skills to track her son to an abandoned apartment where Muller has stashed him. Thanks to Jonathan's ability to play hide-and-seek and thus keep himself from Muller's clutches, the boy remains unharmed. When the police close in, the pursued Muller falls to his death. With their child now safe, Red and Patrick decide to reconcile.

Ray Loynd (*Los Angeles Times*) reported generously, "If all this sounds lurid, a first-rate cast, Christopher Lofton's taut teleplay . . . and director Karen Arthur's crisp pace creates a crackling movie. . . . This is certainly Reeve's most challenging role to date, and his character's gracious demeanor, intense surface and sick obsession are totally convincing. . . . Meredith Baxter-Birney delivers a portrait of alcohol burnout that, if not original, is a distinguished and modulated performance." *TV Guide* kindly rated the "disturbing well-acted psychological drama and crime story" three stars.

Wasted in this scatter-shot production, filmed in Pittsburgh, were Geraldine Fitzgerald as an eccentric old neighborhood woman who loves cats and Shirley Knight as Baxter-Birney's drink-happy neighbor.

36. Bus Riley's Back in Town

(Universal, 1965), color, 93 min. Not rated.

Producer, Elliott Kastner; director, Harvey Hart; screenplay, Walter Gage [William Inge]); art directors, Alexander Golitzen, Frank Arrigo; set decorators, John McCarthy, Oliver Emert; costumes, Jean Louis, Rosemary Odell; makeup, Bud Westmore, Frank McCoy, Dick Cobos, Dorothy Parkinson; music, Richard Markowitz; songs, Markowitz and Jacques Wilson; choreographer, David Winters; assistant directors, Terence Nelson, Bill Gilmore; sound, Waldon O. Watson, Lyle Cain, Corson Jowett; camera, Russell Metty; editor, Folmar Blangsted.

Cast: Ann-Margret (Laurel); Michael Parks (Bus Riley); Janet Margolin (Judy Nichols); Brad Dexter (Slocum); Crahan Denton (Spencer, the Undertaker); Jocelyn Brando (Mrs. Riley); Kim Darby (Gussie Riley); Larry Storch (Howie); Mimsy Farmer (Paula); Brett Somers (Carlotta); Nan Martin (Mrs. Nichols); Lisabeth Hush (Joy); Ethel Griffies (Mrs. Spencer); Alice Pearce (Housewife); Chet Stratton (Benji); David Carradine (Stretch); Marc Cavel (Egg Foo); Parley Baer (Mr. Griswald).

Distinguished American playwright/novelist William Inge (1913–1971) was hired by Universal Pictures to write an atmospheric screen original, *Bus Riley's Back in Town*, hoping it might turn out to be another major hit like the author's *Picnic* (1955). Instead, the trouble-plagued production turned out to be a nightmare as Inge's drama of small-town life went through myriad plot changes to accommodate studio demands that Ann-Margret (then in her shrill would-be-siren period) be made the movie's focal point instead of newcomer Michael Parks. As a result, much of the picture was rewritten and reshot. Inge was so disgusted with the end results, that, when the picture was released, he demanded his name be removed from the credits (hence the use of the pseudonym, Walter Gage, for the movie's screenwriter).

Ex-Naval serviceman Bus Riley (Michael Parks) returns to his midwestern hometown after three years and is greeted by his mother (Jocelyn Brando) and his tomboyish sister, Gussie (Kim Darby).

Deciding not to fall back into old patterns, he considers the possibility of going to work for his bachelor mortician friend, Spencer (Crahan Denton). However, when the older man suggests that Bus come to "live" with him, he panics and leaves and returns home to live. Despite promptings, Bus refuses to return to being a garage mechanic; instead he becomes an "atomic" vacuum cleaner seller, working in the sales territory supervised by Slocum (Brad Dexter). Meanwhile, Bus's one-time-fiancee, Laurel (Ann-Margret), who jilted him to marry an older, wealthy man, learns Riley is home again. When her husband goes away on business, Laurel convinces Bus to renew their romance.

Judy (Janet Margolin), a friend of Gussie, whose mother (Nan Martin) dies in a fire, comes to live with the Rileys. Mrs. Riley tries to foster a romance between Bus and Judy. When Judy later leaves town to be with her father, Bus is surprised that he misses her. By now, Bus realizes the meaninglessness of both his sales position and his affair with Laurel. As such, he quits his job with Slocum, ends his situation with Laurel, and returns to working at the garage, hoping to woo back Judy.

Many critics responded favorably to the movie in parts, if not to Ann-Margret in particular. According to the British *Monthly Film Bulletin*, "One's main regrets about this charming little film are that the super-glossy Universal production values don't give the mood a chance, and that Ann-Margret as a predatory bitch is about as provocative as a kitten pretending to be a sexy lioness." Howard Thompson (*New York Times*) applauded "this low-keyed drama of a young Navy veteran's search for self-fulfillment" for being "so honest, sensitive and thoughtful on several levels." However, *Variety* analyzed that the movie has "a slickness and surface polish that makes a most attractive package but boxoffice endurance must rest with the film's dramatic impact and that is where the trouble lies." In assessing the supporting cast, the trade paper added, "Crahan Denton, as a latently homosexual undertaker, does demonstrate, in three knee-pats and a single line, how to quickly establish a morally-sick type, but other roles are routinely written and played, several almost caricatures of early Inge types."

Bus Riley's Back in Town was a box-office flop.

37. Busting (United Artists, 1974), color, 92 min. R-rated.

Executive producer, Hal Polaire; producers, Irwin Winkler, Robert Chartoff; associate producer, Henry Gellis; director/screenplay, Peter Hyams; set decorator, Ray Molyneaux; music, Billy Goldenberg; assistant director, Fred R. Simpson; stunt coordinator, Hal Needham; sound, Andrew Gilmore; special effects, Richard Albain; camera, Earl Rath; editor, James Mitchell.

Cast: Elliott Gould (Michael Keneely); Robert Blake (Patrick Farrel); Allen Garfield (Carl Rizzo); Antonio Fargas (Stephen); Michael Lerner (Marvin); Sid Haig (Rizzo's Bouncer); Ivor Francis (Judge Simpson); William Sylvester (Mr. Weldman); Logan Ramsey (Dr. Berman); Richard X. Slattery (Desk Sergeant); Margo Winkler (Mrs. Rizzo); John Lawrence (Sergeant Kenfick); Cornelia Sharp (Jackie); Erin O'Reilly (Doris); Danny Goldman (Mr Crosby); Nick St. Nicholas (Magenta [Harold Connors]); Ibycus (Phillip Lampson); Howard Platt (Carletti); Jack Knight (Hyatt); Mimi Doyle (Mrs. Rosen); Jessica Rains (Receptionist); Carl Eller (Huge Black Man); John Furlong (Policeman); Kai Hernandez (Hooker); Napoleon Whiting (Rizzo's Butler); Andy Stone (Rizzo's Son); Dominique Pinassi (Rizzo's Daughter); Ron Cummins (Keneely's New Partner); Elaine Partnow (Duty Nurse); Karen Anders, Dee Carroll (Nurses).

In the wake of the highly-successful *Dirty Harry* (1971) and *Serpico* (1973), Hollywood increased its production of police action pictures. Many of them, like *The New Centurions* (1972) depicted all too accurately police homophobia; others like *The Laughing Policeman* (1973) and *Freebie and the Bean* (1974), qq.v,—as had the earlier *The Detective* (1968), q.v.—utilized a gay villain. In *Busting*, gays are not only the victims of vice squad harassment, but they are repeatedly the butt of snide treatment by the judicial system.

Opposed by their corrupt superiors and by wary colleagues, unorthodox L.A. vice squad officers Michael Keneely (Elliott Gould) and Patrick Farrel (Robert Blake) persist in going after vice lord, Carl Rizzo (Allen Garfield). When they arrest Jackie (Cornelia Sharp), part of Rizzo's prostitution ring, the two honest cops are disgusted to learn that pivotal evidence in the arrest mysteriously disappears. As a result, the case is tossed out of court. Undaunted by their inability to get a search warrant, Michael and Patrick break into an apartment utilized by Rizzo's drug pushing underlings. They chase the fleeing punks through a crowded supermarket and kill two of Rizzo's stooges. As a result of their overzealous, reckless activity, Keneely and Farrel are demoted to humiliating "toilet duty" (i.e., staking out a public park bathroom where gays cruise).

Later, the two cops are beaten up badly and are assigned new partners. Nevertheless, they pursue Rizzo in their off-duty hours, hounding the gangster by following him everywhere, even to breaking into a birthday celebration he is having. Later, when they are told that Rizzo has been hospitalized with a supposed heart attack (allegedly caused by their harassment), the lawmen have a hunch that he will use his hospital room as a half-way point in his drug dealings. Their guess proves true and leads to a frantic car chase. When cornered finally, Rizzo has the last laugh. He informs his disgruntled pursuers that he is confident he will beat the rap and receive only a minor sentence. Knowing this to be true, Keneely is completely disillusioned.

Judith Crist (*New York* magazine) suggested, "if you don't take it seriously it's a wild and incredible caper . . . keep your mind a blank and your morality in abeyance and you'll be entertained." On the other hand, Vincent Canby (*New York Times*) felt, "It's not great but it's a cool,

Robert Blake and Elliott Gould in *Busting* (1974).

intelligent variation on a kind of movie that by this time can be most easily identified by the license numbers on the cars in its chase sequence. . . . . Mr. Hyams . . . brings off something of a feat by making a contemporary cop film that is tough without exploiting the sort of right-wing cynicism that tells us all to go out and buy our own guns. . . .*Busting* hardly overturns any film traditions, but it gives a little life to an exhausted genre." Opposing this view was John Raisbeck (British *Monthly Film Bulletin*): "too often the film settles for the easy laugh . . . which precludes any deeper statement; while the final scene . . . given the lack of any previous urgency in Elliott Gould's monotonously weary performances—[is] robbed of its intended weight."

Within *Busting*'s episodic framework, there are several scenes devoted to exploiting (for cheap laughs and titillation value) gay locales and/or stereotypes—depicted in overstated terms from a homophobic point of view. At one point, Keneely and Farrel are ordered by their sergeant (Richard X. Slattery) to follow up a complaint about the after-hours live shows being given at the Cavern, "a fruit bar" in the seamier part of town. The undercover officers are ordered to infiltrate the place and lead the way for a police bust.

Within the bar, the swishy Stephen (Antonio Fargas), who is pointedly sucking on a soda bottle, takes a lustful interest in the plain-clothes Keneely, the latter smart-mouths: "Him [i.e. Farrel] and me are very tight. We're going to pick out drapes next week." Before long, the police, who have been waiting in hiding outside the establishment, break up the gathering. In the ensuing free-for-all, the two vice officers emerge from the round-up bruised, but nonchalantly cocky about doing their job. (None of the law enforcers are concerned about the violated constitutional rights of these minority targets, people considered oddities, not human beings.)

Keneely: That creep [one of the drag queens] took a hunk out of my leg!

Cop: Boy, fruits are something!

Later, at the courthouse hearing, several of the Cavern's arrested patrons are ushered before Judge Simpson (Ivor Francis). Among them is Harold Connors (Nick St. Nicholas), a drag queen better known as Magenta. The latter complains that he was placed in a holding cell with a "whole bunch of animals." This causes the unsympathetic court officials to chortle. Later, after Harold is released on $250 bail, the intolerant judge admonishes the defendants' lawyer (Danny Goldman), "Tell your clients not to break their high heels on the way out." This prompts a big laugh from the onlookers.

Such exaggerated sequences as the above, in which a few types of gay persons and activities were depicted as the norm, led to a great deal of protest. Homosexual civil rights groups objected to the abuse taken in the picture by gays who were being depicted as highly effeminate freaks. Filmmaker Peter Hyams responded to the gay rights furor with:

"If I were homosexual and saw what goes on in *Busting*, I'd be mad not at the movie but at the society it reflects accurately. If I didn't show how mercilessly homosexuals are treated by the police, I'd be lying. I expected to be applauded for daring to show what really happens to homosexuals in courtrooms, not attacked for exploiting them."

In the midst of so many police thriller movies, *Busting* was not a large moneymaker. Originally, Elliott Gould's role in the film was to have been played by Ron Leibman who left the project over "artistic differences."

38. By Design (Atlantic, 1982), color, 93 min. Not rated.

Executive producers, Louis M. Silverstein, Douglas Leiterman; producers, Beryl Fox, Werner Aellen; associate producers, James R. Westwell, Harold J. Savage, Michael Zolf; director, Claude Jutra; screenplay, Joe Weisenfeld, Jutra, David Earnes; production designer, Reuben Freed; set decorators, Kimberley Richardson, Sandy Arthur, Ann Marie Corbett, Sea Kirby; costumes, Winston; makeup, Phyllis Newman; music/music arranger, Chico Hamilton; assistant directors, Don Granbery, Derek Gardner, Scott Mathers; sound, Larry Sutton; camera, Jean Boffety; second unit camera, John Searle; editor, Tony Trow.

Cast: Patty Duke Astin (Helen Hunter); Sara Botsford (Angie Olaffsen); Saul Rubinek (Terry); Mina Mina (R. B. Corcoron); Alan Duruissean (Sven); Clare Coulter (Ms. Hirshorn); Jeannie Elias (Cowgirl); Anya Best (Pineapple); Patricia Best (Her Mother); Jan Filips (Paul); Robert Benson (Henri); Joseph Flaherty (Veteran Father); William Samples (Inseminator); Jim Hibbard (Carl); Ralph Benmurgie, Steve Witkin (Window Dressers); Gabe Cohen (Family Man); Robin McCullough (Cafeteria Waiter); Bill Reiter (Construction Worker); Nabuko Hardychuk (Mo); Andre Olch (Angie's Baby); Scott Swanson (Mr. Potter); Enid Rose, June Round, Maggie Robertson, Connie Barnes, Xana Dwornyk (By Design Models); Maria West (Secretary); Shirley Barclay, Linda Hendersen (Hospital Nurses); Jenny Bernice, Debby Douglas, Rod Lew, Wendy Foster, Tish Monaghan, Jean Murphy, Mildred Perera (Sewers and Cutters); Don Granbery (Maitre d'); Eliza Wu (Cashier).

"By setting its story in the fashion business . . . where gayness is stereotypically more common than in more prosaic professions—*By Design* marks itself as a slightly soapy romantic comedy, as opposed to a Serious Treatment of an Important Issue. However, as such, it's an advance over the Stanley Kramer school of bringing controversial subjects into entertainment movies, and then pompously stirring up a spurious 'balanced argument,' before plumping, with mock courage, for the impeccably liberal attitude." (Kim Newman, British *Monthly Film Bulletin*)

Contented lesbian couple Helen Hunter (Patty Duke Astin) and Angie Olaffsen (Sara Botsford) own By Design, a small, struggling fashion firm in Vancouver,

British Columbia. Determined to do everything their own way, they resist a tempting offer by entrepreneur R. B. Corcoran (Mina Mina) to buy their company. Meanwhile, Helen, the older of the two, develops a strong maternalistic urge and convinces Angie that they should have a child. Because they are gay, their application is rejected by an adoption agency; they rule out artificial insemination. As an alternative, they agree to have Terry (Saul Rubinek), their randy, fashion photographer friend, who has always been drawn to Helen, become her male lover—briefly. On the night chosen for the coupling, Helen, Angie and Terry get inebriated. After leaving Helen and Terry to their lovemaking, Angie is in an obvious vulnerable state. She allows Sven (Alan Duruissean) to pick her up and seduce her.

Before long both Helen and Angie find themselves pregnant. Terry becomes their California sales manager and, soon By Design becomes a successful venture. Terry returns in time for Helen's delivery, but her baby boy is stillborn. On the other hand, Angie gives birth to a healthy baby girl. As for Terry, he learns that his Los Angeles model girlfriend, Suzie (Sonia Zimmer), is pregnant with their child.

By Design, with its shaky pacing, poor production values and inept acting (even from Academy Award winner Patty Duke Astin) received mixed reviews. *Variety* cited the "awkwardness of Jutra's direction," the film's "unnecessary claustrophobic feel" and "The misfired attempt at injecting humor into a basically serious area." As for the movie's star, Patty Duke Astin, *Variety* found it "irritating to watch as tears well up in her eyes every time a young child enters the frame. She appears totally uncomfortable in her lesbian role. . . . [O]nly Rubinek as the libidinous photographer overcomes script and direction." On the other hand, Pauline Kael (*The New Yorker*) judged it a "buoyant, quirky sex comedy" and observed that "What holds the movie together is the bond between the two women, who

couldn't be more unlike [i.e. tall, airy Angie; short, serious Helen]." Kim Newman (British *Monthly Film Bulletin*) was partial to the overall results: "the script, by three men, isn't without its contrivances . . . and banalities. . . .but it does have it share of witty lines. . . ."

The best aspect of this lightweight vehicle is the casualness with which it explores its lesbian theme, especially in contrast to the strident *Walk on the Wild Side* (1962), q.v., the high caricature of *The Killing of Sister George* (1968), q.v. and the heavily symbolic *The Fox* (1968), q.v. One wishes the screenplay had provided more comic observations on the run-of-events; as it stands, there are a few mini-gems—Angie saying to Helen: "There are many things we can share, but making babies isn't one of them." Then too, insufficient advantage is taken of the movie's unique story twists.

By Design was filmed in Vancouver, British Columbia. The movie's score is by jazz musician Chico Hamilton.

39. Cabaret (Allied Artists, 1972), color, 124 min. PG-rated.

Producer, Cy Feuer; associate producer, Harold Nebenzal; director, Bob Fosse; based on the play *Cabaret* by Joe Masteroff, John Kander and Fred Ebb, the play *I Am a Camera* by John Van Druten and the writings of Christopher Isherwood; screenplay, Jay Presson Allen; production designer, Rolf Zehetbauer; art director, Jurgen Kiebach; set decorator, Herbert Strabel; costumes, Charlotte Flemming; choreographer, Fosse; songs, Kander and Ebb; music director, Ralph Burns; assistant directors, Douglas Green, Wolfgang Glattes; camera, Geoffrey Unsworth; editor, David Bretherton.

Cast: Liza Minnelli (Sally Bowles); Michael York (Brian Roberts); Helmut Griem (Maxiilian van Heune); Joel Grey (Master of Ceremonies); Fritz Wepper (Fritz Wendel); Marisa Berenson (Natalia Landauer); Elisabeth Neumann-Viertel (Fraulein Schneider); Sigrid Von Richthofen (Fraulein Maur); Helen Vita (Fraulein Kost); Gerd Vespermann (Bobby); Ralf Wolter (Herr Ludwig); Georg Hartmann (Willi); Ricky Renee (Elke); Estrongo Nachama (Cantor); Kathryn Doby, Inge Jaeger, Angelika Koch, Helen Velkovorska, Gitta Schmidt, Louise Quick (Kit-Kat Dancers); Greta Keller (Voice on

Helmut Griem and Michael York in *Cabaret* (1972).

Phonograph); Oliver Collignon (Young Nazi); Mark Lambert (Singing Voice of the Young Nazi).

Over the years, a great deal of entertainment mileage has been squeezed from Christopher Isherwood's story of life among the decadent society set of 1930s Germany. *Cabaret* began in 1939 as a short story, "Goodbye to Berlin," and appeared later in Isherwood's compilation, *Berlin Stories* (1954). Meanwhile, the short narrative provided the basis for John Van Druten's Broadway play, *I Am a Camera* (1951). Julie Harris, who starred in the stage adaptation, also played the lead in the 1955 British movie version. Eleven year later, in 1966, Joe Masteroff adapted Van Druten's work into a Broadway musical, *Cabaret*. With music and lyrics by John Kander and Fred Ebb, and starring Joel Grey, Jill Haworth and Bert Convy,

the show became a mega hit. Six years later, Bob Fosse directed the movie version of *Cabaret*, shot on location in West Germany.

In 1931 Berlin, young American Sally Bowles (Liza Minnelli), a confused romantic with an uninhibited libido, is an entertainer at the sleazy Kit Kat Klub. There the sinister Master of Ceremonies (Joel Grey), grins wickedly as he tells one and all that outside in the streets life is bleak (the Depression, the political turmoil from the rising Nazi Party), while inside "life is beautiful." Before long, giddy Sally meets an aimless Britisher, Brian Roberts (Michael York), who also has a room at her boarding house. He is a recent University graduate, come to Berlin to sharpen his German. To earn money, Brian gives English lessons. Among his pupils are the wealthy Jewess, Natalia Landauer (Marisa Berenson), and the adventurer Fritz Wendel (Fritz Wepper), one of Sally's many friends. Before long, Fritz falls in love with Natalia, but she refuses to marry him, fearful that he will suffer the problems befalling Jews at the hands of the increasingly powerful Nazis. Eventually, Fritz admits he is Jewish and he and Natalia marry.

Meanwhile, bubbly Sally is attracted to the charming, rich Baron Maximilian von Heune (Helmut Griem), who bestows lavish gifts and good times on her and Brian. When Sally admits she has slept with von Heune, Roberts confesses he has too. Later, after Max leaves Berlin, Sally informs Roberts that she is pregnant, but unsure whom the father is. He offers to marry her, but she declines, instead secretly having an abortion. At this point, Brian bids farewell to Berlin and Sally. She remains at the Kit Kat Klub, convinced her big show business break will come any day.

For Roger Greenspun (*New York Times*), "*Cabaret* is one of those immensely gratifying imperfect works in which from beginning to end you can literally feel a movie coming to life . . . The film gains a good deal from its willingness to isolate its musical stage. . . .so that every time we return to the girls and their leering master . . . we return, as it were, to a sense of theater. . . . Everybody in *Cabaret* is very fine, and meticulously chosen for type, down to the last weary transvestite. . . . ." Pauline Kael (*The New Yorker*) was even more enthralled: "*Cabaret* is a great movie musical, made, miraculously, without compromises. . . . We see the decadence [of Berlin] as garish and sleazy, and yet we see the animal energy in it, and the people driven to endure. . . . No one has ever made a musical that looked better than this one. . . ."

John Russell Taylor (British *Monthly Film Bulletin*) rated *Cabaret* "a stylish, sophisticated entertainment for grown-up people." He pointed out, "the main drama, the developing triangle of Brian, Sally and Max, is very well handled, particularly in the nicely ambiguous sequence of the country weekend. . . . Michael York contributes another of his studies of the puppy-like schoolboyish young English gentleman who is such a puzzlement to foreigners, and is considerably more likely as an Isherwood self-portrait than was Laurence Harvey in *I Am a Camera*. . . ."

With its atmospheric mixture of musical diversion, depravity, cruelty, self-indulgence, etc., the bisexuality of Michael York's Brian Roberts was a subtheme blown out of proportion because of its controversial nature, especially in 1972. In *Something for Everyone* (1970), q.v., York had played a menacing user who plies his charm with both sexes. In *Cabaret* he is the quasi-hero, a confused young man generally repressing his true sexual feelings except for a slip-up when he sleeps with the Baron. While most of *Cabaret*'s other main characters— especially the Master of Ceremonies and Sally—are direct about their feelings, Brian remains an enigma whom the heroine decides cannot be counted on to provide her with a "normal" family life. Author Christopher Isherwood, on whom Brian Roberts's character was drawn, once said of the movie Cabaret, "I felt as though his homosexual side was used as a kink in the film—like bed wetting—and that he was really supposed to be basically heterosexual."

Cabaret grossed $20,250,000 in distributors' domestic film rentals. Its soundtrack album—featuring such songs as "Maybe This Time" and the title tune— remained on *Billboard* magazine's best-selling album chart for over a year. *Cabaret* won eight Academy Awards: Best Actress (Liza Minnelli); Best Supporting Actor (Joel Grey); Best Director; Cinematography; Art Direction—Set Direction; Sound; Scoring; Editing. It was nominated for two additional Oscars: Best Picture (*The Godfather* won); Best Screenplay—Based on Material from Another Medium (*The Godfather* won).

Originally, Gene Kelly was to have directed *Cabaret*, but backed out when his wife became seriously ill; Barbra Streisand had been the first choice to play Sally Bowles but refused the offer before she knew that Bob Fosse would direct the movie.

40. Cage Without a Key (CBS-TV, March 14, 1975), color, 100 min. Not rated.

Executive producer, Douglas S. Cramer; producer, Buzz Kulik; associate producer, Robert Mintz; director, Kulik; teleplay, Joanna Lee; art director, Ross Bellah; set decorator, Audrey Blasdel-Goddard; makeup, Ben Lane, Carl Silvers; music, Michel Legrand; assistant director, Thomas McCrory; camera, Charles F. Wheeler; editor, Roland Gross.

Cast: Susan Dey (Valerie Smith); Jonelle Allen (Tommy Washington); Sam Bottoms (Buddy Goleta); Michael Brandon (Ben Holian); Anne Bloom (Joleen); Karen Carlson (Betty Holian); Edith Diaz (Angel Perez); Susie Elene (Suzy Kurosawa); Dawn Frame (Sarah); Katherine Helmond (Mrs. R. C. Little); Vicky Huxtable (Jamie); Karen Morrow (Mrs. Turner); Lani O'Grady (Noreen); Margaret Willock (Wanda Polsky); Marc Alaimo (Workman); Lewis Charles (Liquor Customer); Jerry Crews (Supervisor); Edward Cross (Social Worker); Ann D'Andrea (Mrs. Smith); Joella Deffenbaugh (Girl in Corridor); Al Dunlap (Liquor Counterman); Annette Ensley (Rosie); Carol Carrington (Juvenile Hall Matron); Dan Evanilla (Coach); Harvey J. Goldenberg (Mr. Feiner); Basil Hoffman (Judge); Elizabeth Lane (Miss McGinnes); Carmen Martinez (Miss Marquez); Miko Mayama (Mrs. Little's Secretary); Allan Miller (Phil Kenneally); Tom Newman (Mr. Watkins); Gary Pagett (Station Duty Officer); Andrew Rubin (Russo); R. B. Sorko-Ram (Auto Club Driver); Richard Williams (Booking Officer).

In the wake of NBC-TV's high-rating *Born Innocent* (1974), CBS-TV concocted its own variation of the young woman trapped behind bars. In this bleak, derivative study, Susan Dey—best known as a co-star of the sitcom "The Partridge Family" (1970–74)—took over the chores that Linda Blair had handled in *Born Innocent*.

In flashback, the narrative relates the background of seventeen-year-old Valerie Smith (Susan Dey) who has been sentenced to the San Marcos School for Girls. A recent high school graduate, she had the misfortune of accepting a ride from an acquaintance, Buddy Goleta (Sam Bottoms). When she reject his sexual advances, he forces her to "participate" in a liquor store robbery. In the process, a victim dies and both Valerie and Buddy are arrested. To get even with Valerie for having rebuffed him, Buddy, who makes a deal with the authorities, claims that she was an active partner in the holdup. Valerie, who has a record (for having been caught smoking pot) is sentenced to the San Marcos reformatory.

The once gentle Valerie is bewildered by her nasty surroundings and finds it hard to relate to the other inmates. Among the ring leaders at San Marcos are a black girl, Tommy Washington (Jonelle Allen) and an Oriental girl, Suzy Kurosawa (Susie Elene). Each attempts to draw Valerie into their crowd. The crafty Suzy takes a dislike to Valerie and does her best to get the latter in trouble with officials. Later, the tough Noreen (Lani O'Grady) attempts to sexually molest Valerie, but Tommy comes to her rescue.

Before Valerie's hellish sojourn ends, another inmate, angry with her outspokeness, aims a pot of boiling fat at her while they are on kitchen duty. Valerie escapes injury, but fourteen-year-old Sarah (Dawn Frame) is badly scalded. Another day, while on the volleyball court, the vicious Suzy aims a ball directly at Wanda (Margaret Willock) who later dies. Bludgeoned by so much violence about her, Valerie becomes emotionally hardened as time passes. Eventually, thanks to her former attorney (Michael Brandon) and his wife (Karen Carlson), Buddy is trapped into admitting Valerie's innocence in the holdup. However, just before she is to be released, Suzy stabs Tommy who dies in Valerie's arms.

TV Guide magazine politely called *Cage Without a Key* "overdrawn." *Daily*

Variety was more critical: "the unbelievable circumstances of the narrative, the overburden of standard primetime brutality—murder by gunshot, by knifing and by scalding—and over-ripe thesping by all hands would have made it laughable if it hadn't been boring to tears." In contrast, Sue Cameron (*Hollywood Reporter*) wrote approvingly that *Cage Without a Key* was "a fabulous movie about how terrible the juvenile justice system is, as well as the appalling conditions in young women's prison."

Thanks to the casting of Susan Dey in the pivotal lead role, *Cage Without a Key* won a strong viewership.

41. Caged (Warner Bros., 1950), 96 min. No rating.

Producer, Jerry Wald; director, John Cromwell; screenplay, Virginia Kellogg, Bernard C. Schoenfeld; art director, Charles H. Clarke; set decorator, G. W. Bernsten; costumes, Leah Rhodes; makeup, Perc Westmore, Ed Voight; music, Max Steiner; assistant director, Frank Mattison; sound, Stanley Jones; camera, Carl Guthrie; editor, Owen Marks.

Cast: Eleanor Parker (Marie Allen); Agnes Moorehead (Ruth Benton); Ellen Corby (Emma Varges); Hope Emerson (Evelyn Harper); Betty Garde (Kitty Stark); Jan Sterling (Smoochie [Gita Krosky]); Lee Patrick (Elvira Powell); Olive Deering (June Roberts); Jane Darwell (Isolation Matron); Gertrude Michael (Georgia Harrison); Sheila Stevens (Helen); Joan Miller (Claire Devlon); Marjorie Crossland (Cassie Jenkins); Gertrude Hoffman (Millie); Lynn Sherman (Ann); Queenie Smith (Mrs. Warren); Naomi Robison (Hattie Cassidy); Esther Howard (Grace); Marlo Dwyer (Julie Klein); Wanda Tynan (Meta Minnelli); Peggy Wynne (Lottie Brannigan); Frances Morris (Mrs. Foley); Edith Evanson (Miss Barker); Yvonne Rob (Elaine Mullen); Ann Tyrell (Edna); Eileen Stevens (Infirmary Nurse); June Whipple (Ada); Sandra Gould (Skip); Grace Hayes (Mugging Matron); Taylor Holmes (Senator Donnolly); Don Beddoe (Commissioner Walker); Charles Meredith (Chairman); George Baxter (Jeffries); Guy Beach (Mr. Cooper); Harlan Warde (Dr. Ashton); Bill Hunter (Guard); Barbara Esback, Marjorie Wood, Evelyn Dockson, Hazel Keener, Jane Crowley (Matrons); Gail Bonney, Doris Kemper (Lovyss Bradley); Ezelle Poule, Margaret Lambert, Eva Nelson, Rosemary O'Neil, Jean Calhoun, Nita Talbot, Marie Melish, Pauline Creasman, Joyce Newhard, Helen Eby-Rock, Sheila Stuart, Claudia Cauldwell, Tina Menard, Carole Shanon, Glayds Roach, Virginia Engels (Inmates); Bill Haade (Laundryman); Ruth Warren (Miss Lyons); Davison Clark (Doctor); Pauline Drake (Doctor's Wife); Gracille LaVinder (Visiting Room Matron); Bill Wayne (Ada's Father); Doris Whitney (Woman Visitor); Grace Hampton, Helen Mowery, Helen Spring, Frances Henderson (Women).

If James Cagney's kinetic *White Heat* (1949) rejuvenated Hollywood's prison picture genre, *Caged*, also released by Warner Bros., was a landmark in women-behind-bar movies. Viewers were properly shocked by its graphic account of a guileless young woman (Eleanor Parker) landing in prison where, instead of being reformed, she is transformed into an hardened convict. Not that seasoned moviegoers had not seen the subject many times before on the screen. However, seldom had a motion picture handled the subject so expertly and so uncompromisingly. Among the many vivid types paraded forth in *Caged*, two have special relevance to this book—sadistic prison matron Evelyn Harper (Hope Emerson) and vice queen, Elvira Powell (Lee Patrick), a temporary prisoner.

Nineteen-year-old, pregnant widow Marie Allen (Eleanor Parker) is shipped to prison for participating in a gas station holdup with her late husband. Sympathetic superintendent Ruth Benton (Agnes Moorehead) assigns the bewildered Marie to relatively light work in the prison laundry. Meanwhile, in the overcrowded jail dormitory, Marie is placed under the jurisdiction of matron Evelyn Harper (Hope Emerson). The latter is a towering, big-boned sadist, who augments her salary by extorting bribes from her charges who want special favors. When Harper learns that the cowered Marie has no one on the outside to give her money to pay-off Evelyn, she vents her anger on the new-

Ellen Corby (left), Jan Sterling (center) and Eleanor Parker (with kitten) in *Caged*
(1950).

comer. Later, long-time convict Kitty Stark (Betty Garde), who is paid to find new talent for a shoplifting ring in the civilian world, tries to recruit Marie. However, the young woman refuses the offer. She believes idealistically that she will be able to lead a lawful existence when once released.

As a result of Evelyn's harassments, Marie gives premature birth to her baby, which she is forced to give up for adoption. At her first parole hearing, Marie is hopeful of gaining the board's sympathy, but they reject her cause because, if released, she has no potential job or home. Overwhelmed by the thought of six additional months in this hell hole, Marie fights back against Harper's abuses, which leads to a small riot by the convicts. Marie is placed in solitary and Harper, unknown to Superintendent Benton, gleefully clips

the young woman's hair as a final humiliation. When Benton does learn of this action, she demands Evelyn's resignaton. However, the latter uses her connections to retain her job.

Meanwhile, the sophisticated Elvira Powell (Lee Patrick) returns to prison as an inmate. She is a high-level worker in the shoplifting/vice ring and now, briefly on the inside, takes over from Kitty the task of recruiting apprentices. Harper uses Elvira's power play to get even with the uncontrollable Kitty. Unable to tolerate the matron's escalating taunts any further, Kitty explodes and kills Harper by stabbing her in the neck with a fork.

The now cynical, toughened Marie turns to Elvira to engineer a phony job for her on the outside. Finally paroled, Marie leaves confinement, reconciled to starting her criminal career on the outside.

In retrospect, it is startling how many critics in 1950 refused to accept the grimness depicted in *Caged* as an accurate reflection of reality. *Harrison's Reports*, while acknowledging that *Caged* was a "fine production," editorialized, "it is hardly believable that the brutality and inhumanness depicted in this picture could possibly exist in any prison in these days." Thomas M. Pryor (*New York Times*) insisted "*Caged* is a cliche-ridden account of institutional brutality and depravity" and "it does not necessarily follow, as the picture insists, that prisons breed hardened criminals."

Ironically, the reviewers were proven wrong, for the public responded to the well-crafted *Caged*. The movie went on to win three Academy Award nominations: Best Actress (Eleanor Parker; Judy Holliday won for *Born Yesterday*); Best Supporting Actress (Hope Emerson; Josephine Hull won for *Harvey*); Best Original Story (*Sunset Boulevard* won). Discussing the growing reputation of *Caged* over the years from revivals, TV showings, etc., Doug McClelland weighed in *Eleanor Parker; Woman of a Thousand Faces* (1989), "*Caged* does indeed remain the definitive dramatic portrait of women behind bars and was directly responsible for the installation of reform programs at many women's penal institutions." But the surest sign of how trend-setting *Caged* was, would be the rash of imitations that followed, including *Women's Prison* (1955), q.v., *Girls in Prison* (1956), q.v., and the very pallid *House of Women* (1962), the diluted remake of *Caged*.

Although the motion picture production code in 1950 condoned tacitly assorted acts of viciousness and homicide on camera, Hollywood moviemakers were restrained from being explicit about mainstream permissive love, let alone from dealing directly with alternate lifestyles such as homosexuality. Thus, scenarists Virginia Kellogg (who had authored the screen story for *White Heat* and who spent two months researching *Caged* in four different women's prisons) and Bernard C. Schoenfeld had to play scripting games. They hinted at the lesbian situations behind bars with various plotline suggestions, character development, and even giving the audience signals by the way certain characters dressed. Occasionally, the characters voiced a few toss-away hints, such as Kitty's remark, "If you stay in here too long you don't think of guys at all. You get out of the habit."

In the film, mannish Evelyn Harper remains a multi-dimensional monster, a savage bully in this ghetto of society's rejects. One prisoner says of the vicious jailer, "Don't kid me. Harper's first name is filth." This oversized tyrant, who claims to have men friends on the outside, is much more comfortable lording it over her women charges, especially singling out the "fresh meat" (the new inmates) for her scrutiny. She thrives on receiving little presents from "my gals" and in exchange for such gifts, provides drugs, communication to the outside, and easy prison work assignments. What makes the frightening, corrupt Evelyn Harper so complex is her "feminine side." This facet of her personality leads this butch tyrant to gobbling caramels, reading romance novels, having a decorous nip of liquor now and again (from the bottle stashed under her mattress), and, as if to substantiate that she is a desirable (!) woman, dressing up in her garish outfits for her days-off visits to her boyfriends outside the walls. Clearly, Evelyn Harper thrives on S & M (sadomasochistic) games and if, in *Caged*, she does not wear leather and use a whip on her charges, her personality is depicted as a tough master who thrives on her contorl of her covey of female slaves in the "bull pen."

In contrast to Evelyn Harper, there is Elvira Powell, who demonstrates that not all lesbians are as basic and crude as Harper. With her close-cropped hair-do, the mature, well-dressed Elvira makes a vivid impression midst the drab and often disheveled women prisoners. Setting up camp in prison, the experienced Elvira knows the score and with a quick glance around the population, picks out a likely possibility. Turning to the young, attractive Marie, and flashing her a very friendly smile, she asks an onlooker, "Who's the cute new trick?" Elvira's look alone is worth a thousand words.

Vito Russo points out in *The Celluloid Closet* (1987):

"In the prison of *Caged*, where the pretenses of polite society are ripped away, there is an astonishing amount of lesbianism. The world of *Caged* is a total underworld, corrupting and brilliantly drawn. Like the reflections of homosexuality in the *cinema noir* of the Forties, lesbianism appears here as a product of an outlaw social structure—it comes with the territory."

42. **Caged Heat** (New World, 1974), color, 83 min. R-rated. (a.k.a.: *Renegade Girls*)

Executive producer, Samuel Gelfman; producer, Evelyn Purcell; director/screenplay, Jonathan Demme; art director, Eric Thiermann; music, John Cale; assitant director, David Osterhout; sound, Alex Vanderkar; special effects, Charlie Spurgeon; camera, Tak Fujimoto; editors, Johnna Demetrakis, Carolyn Hicks, Michael Goldman.

Cast: Juanita Brown (Maggie Cromwell); Roberta Collins (Belle Tyson); Erica Gavin (Jacqueline Wilson); Ella Reid (Pandora Williams); Lynda Gold (Crazy Annie); Warren Miller (Dr. Randolph); Barbara Steele (McQueen); Toby Carr Rafelson (Pinter); and: John Aprea, Carmen Argenziano, George Armitage, Cindy Cale, Mickey Fox, Layla Gallaway, Essie Hayes, Valley Hoffman, Keisha, Gary Littlejohn, Dorothy Love, Hal Marshall, Carol Miller, Leslie Otis, Amy Randall, Bob Reese, Mike Shack, Rainbeaux Smith, Cynthia Songey, Ann Stockdale, Irene Stokes, Joe Viola, Patrick Wright.

Jonathan Demme, who later directed such well-regarded entries as *Something Wild* (1987) and *The Silence of the Lambs* (1991), made his directorial debut with *Caged Heat*. It was a low-budget trash outing that mixed women-behind bars and women's gang motifs. Besides the cult fa-

vorite Barbara Steele, the cast of *Caged Heat* included softcore pornography actress Erica Gavin and equally attractive Roberta Collins. The latter had already starred in such genre pieces as *The Big Doll House* (1971), q.v. and *Women in Cages* (1972). As was expected in such exploitation exercises, perversions ran rampant behind bars and the R-rated picture did it best to present the full gamut— as much as the production code and the running time would permit. As a result, much of the lesbian aspect was merely suggested, such as some of the prisoners holding hands and looking longingly at one another.

In California, sentenced on a robbery charge, Jacqueline White (Erica Gavin) begins her stay at the Connorville Women's Prison, a tough institution controlled by the harsh staff, including the sadistic, crippled Warden McQueen (Barbara Steele) —who releases her repressions through wild sexual fantasies—and her accommodating assistant, Pinter (Toby Carr Rafelson). When a prisoner, Pandora Williams (Ella Reid), is placed in solitary confinement on a trumped-up charge, her friend, Belle Tyson (Roberta Collins), steals food for her deprived pal. Belle is caught, but, later, she kills the informant. As punishment, Belle is selected to be a guinea pig for lobotomy surgery by the unprincipled Dr. Randolph (Warren Miller). Meanwhile, the now rebellious Jacqueline, joined by the resourceful Maggie Cromwell (Juanita Brown), escapes. They return eventually to Connorville just in time to save Belle. In the process, McQueen and Randolph are taken hostage and, as the convicts escape once again, they die in the shootout.

In *The Illustrated Guide to Film Directors* (1983), David Quinlan approved of *Caged Heat* for having "a style which transcended its origins. . . . Demme made the most of the personalities of the actresses involved. . . ." Tony Rayns (British *Monthly Film Bulletin*) rated the budget feature "an indefatigable melodrama in which the variously corrupt, sick and frustrated figures of authority happen to wind up dead, while the rough-talkin', hard-actin' renegade women themselves get their way." Rayns also noted, "its arguably the first film of its kind since [Roger Corman's] *Bloody Mama* [1970] that manages to indulge all the statutory exploitation scenes (from shower scenes to depraved medical malpractice) without ever becoming either gratuitous or condescending."

Chained Heat was filmed at Los Angeles' Lincoln Heights jail.

43. California Suite (Columbia, 1978), color, 103 min. PG-rated.

Producer, Ray Stark; associate producer, Ronald L. Schwarzy; director, Herbert Ross; based on the play by Neil Simon; screenplay, Simon; production designer, Albert Brenner; costumes, Ann Roth, Patricia Norris; makeup, Charles Schram; music, Claude Bolling; assistant directors, Jack Roe, Carla Reinke; sound, Al Overton Jr.; sound effects, Sam Shaw; camera, David M. Walsh; supervising editor, Margaret Booth; editor, Michael A. Stevenson.

Cast: Alan Alda (Bill Warren); Michael Caine (Sidney Cochran); Bill Cosby (Dr. Willis Panama); Jane Fonda (Hannah Warren); Walter Matthau (Marvin Michaels); Elaine May (Millie Michaels); Richard Pryor (Dr. Chauncy Gump); Maggie Smith (Diana Barrie); Gloria Gifford (Lola Gump); Sheila Frazier (Bettina Panama); Herbert Edelman (Harry Michaels); *At the Hotel*: Denise Galik (Bunny); David Sheehan (Himself); Michael Boyle (Desk Clerk); Len Lawson (Frank); Gino Ardito (Plumber); Jerry Ziman (Man on Phone); Clint Young (Doorman); David Matthau (Bellboy); James Espinoza (Busboy); Buddy Douglas (Page); Armand Cerami (Charley); Joseph Morena (Herb); Brian Cummings, William Kux, Zora Margolis (Autograph Seekers); Rita Gomez, Tina Menard (Maids); Lupe Ontiveros, Bert May, Eddie Villery (Waiters); *At the Academy Awards*: Army Archerd (Himself); Judith Hannah Brown (Oscar Winner); Gary Hendrix (Her Date); Jack Scanlan, Bill Steinmetz (Public Relations Men); Paolo Fredianai (Young Man); *At the Airport*: Dana Plato (Jenny Warren); Nora Boland (Passenger); David Rini (Airline Representative); John Hawker (Sky Cab); Frank Conn (Bobby): Colleen Drape, Kelly Harmon, Tawyn Moyer, Leslie Pagett, Vicki Stephens, Nan Wylder, Linda Ewen (Stewardesses); *In Beverly Hills*: David Sato (Salesman); Christopher Pennock (Cop).

Master funnyman Neil Simon wrote *California Suite* (1976) as a counterpoint to his earlier stage hit, *Plaza Suite* (1968). When adapting *California Suite* to the screen, besides opening up the action beyond the Beverly Hills Hotel, he also utilized different sets of lead actors as stars for each segment, unlike the play, which relied on two teams of key performers for the entire show. Thus, the movie intercut between the contrasting four stories, rather than unfolding the four playlets as separate entities.

Assorted guests check into Los Angeles' swank Beverly Hills Hotel. They include prim Hannah Warren (Jane Fonda), who has flown in from New York because Jenny (Dana Plato), her teenage daughter, has flown off to be with Hannah's exspouse Bill (Alan Alda), a screenwriter. British stage actress Diana Barrie (Maggie Smith) has been Oscar-nominated and is on hand for the Academy Award ceremonies, joined by her antique dealer husband, Sidney Cochran (Michael Caine). Chicago physicians, Dr. Willis Panama (Bill Cosby) and Dr. Chauncey Gump (Richard Pryor), and their wives (Sheilah Frazier, Gloria Gifford) are on the last lap of their problem-plagued vacation. Marvin Michael (Walter Matthau) is in Los Angeles for his nephew's Bar Mitzvah, having arrived in town before his wife, Millie (Elaine May).

In due time, demanding, career-driven Hannah comes to realize that Bill, who has undergone many changes since becoming a film industry success, is better equipped to cope with their daughter. As for Diana, she loses her Oscar bid, and is even further tested when confronted by new evidence of Sidney's homosexual liaisons. However, remembering that they still rely on one another greatly, they reconcile. Meanwhile, as a gift for Oscar, his brother (Herbert Edelman) hires a hooker, Bunny (De-

Maggie Smith and Michael Caine in *California Suite* **(1978).**

nisc Galik), but the lark turns into a disaster when Millie arrives and discovers the sleeping prostitute in their bedroom suite. Millie's price for forgiveness is a massive shopping binge in Beverly Hills. When Chauncey's hotel reservations are fouled up, he and his wife are forced to bunk in cramped quarters with Willis and Bettina. The close quarters leads to quarrels, and the couple's feuding is carried over to the tennis courts the next morning. Their highly competitive match ends with the quartet flying home in bandages.

Vincent Canby (*New York Times*) judged *California Suite* "the most agreeably realized Simon film in years. It all works . . . not only because the material is superior Simon, but also because the writer and director have assembled a dream cast." For Canby, the chief joys among the performers were Maggie Smith "who has her best screen role since *The Prime of Miss Jean Brodie* [1969]" and Michael Caine "who is seldom acknowledged as the fine

actor he is." *Variety* agreed that the "Simon 'touch' is present everywhere" but that here Simon "displays his serious bent for the first time to film audiences."

However, Michael Sragow (*Los Angeles Herald-Examiner*) was put off by this latest Neil Simon venture, feeling it was filled with "a kind of discount classicism. . . . Movie audiences may be wising up to Simon's shallowness—and this misanthropy which makes every character a butt. . . . Simon has been hailed for tackling 'serious' emotional conflicts [in the Fonda-Alda and Smith-Caine segments]. . . .But the only way Simon can deal with these subjects is to reduce the people to tackling dummies." Gene Siskel (*Chicago Tribune*) rated the movie 2½ stars, judging that the picture "is a mess of contrary emotions that don't work well together." As to the Smith-Caine episode, he found it the "best" and a "delightful put down of the whole Oscar business." However, he pointed out, the vignette concludes with a serious discussion that "comes out of nowhere but nevertheless is played with some sensitivity."

While the serious overtones of the Fonda-Alda segment seemed forced, the Smith-Caine episode runs as smoothly as a Noel Coward playlet. Unlike the other vignettes which are a New Yorker's jibes at the eccentricities of California lifestyle, the Smith-Caine portion is a telling satire of the Oscar race hoopla. It also has the added dimension of a sexually mismatched couple reaching a compromise to satisfy their mutual emotional needs.

Middle-aged Diana is very realistic about her see-sawing acting career. She finds humor in finally earning Oscar nomination recognition "for a nauseating little comedy" and knows in her heart-of-hearts that she cannot win.

Edgy about the Award show and nervous about the state of her twelve-year-old marriage, Diane would love to find fault with her heavy-drinking husband, but he remains level-headed in the face of her mounting hysteria. When he selects the proper outfit for her to wear to the Awards, she snaps: "Damn it! I wish you didn't have such good taste!" Another of Sidney's good qualities is that as an ex-actor he understands the professional tensions, she is suffering. He assures her that he does not mind living in her shadows ("I'm never bored with your life") and that, in fact, being wed to a public figure is good for his antique business ("I am a minor celebrity once removed").

After Diane loses the Award, the couple attend the after-show banquet, where Sidney spends a curiously long time conversing with a handsome young actor. Back in their hotel suite, the frustrated Diane questions her spouse:

Sidney: He was at our table. We shared a butter plate.

Diane: How incredibly spreadable.

The confrontation becomes more direct, as Diane jabs jealousy at her bisexual husband for his homosexual affairs ("There was a time when I thought you'd give *it* all

up for me") and for his sometimes wanting a man ("Now is not a good time to discuss biological discrepancies."). He successfully attempts to soothe her.

Reconciled anew to their future togethe in England—which will be more of the same—they caress. In a touching fade-out, she asks that he keeps his eyes open as they make love.

To Neil Simon's credit, and especially to his co-stars, this portion of *California Suite* is a well-realized blend of comedy and drama. It speaks volumes about the anxieties of a union in which one party not only cheats, but with a member of the same sex, making it impossible for the other spouse to compete with a rival.

Promoted as "The best two-hour vacation in town!" the combination of Neil Simon and a star-studded cast insured *California Suite* of hit status, in spite of mediocre reviews. It grossed $28,386,000 in distributors' domestic film rentals. *California Suite* won one Academy Award: Best Supporting Actress (Maggie Smith). It was nominated for two other Oscars: Best Screenplay—Based on Material from Another Source (*Midnight Express* won); and Best Art Direction (*Heaven Can Wait* won). Michael Caine would again play a bisexual character in *Deathtrap* (1982), q.v.

44. Camille (Metro-Goldwyn-Mayer, 1936), 108 min. Not rated.

Producers, Irving Thalberg, Bernard Hyman; associate producer, David Lewis; director, George Cukor; based on the novel and play *La Dame aux Camelias* by Alexandre Dumas, fils; screenplay, Zoe Akins, Frances Marion, James Hilton; art directors, Cedric Gibbons, Frederic Hope; set decorator, Edwin B. Willis; costumes, Adrian; music, Herbert Stothart; choreographer, Val Raset; sound, Douglas Shearer; camera, William Daniels, Karl Freund; editor, Margaret Booth.

Cast: Greta Garbo (Marguerite Gautier [Camille]); Robert Taylor (Armand Duval); Elizabeth Allen (Nichette); Jessie Ralph (Nanine); Henry Daniell (Baron de Varville); Lenore Ulric (Olympe); Laura Hope Crews (Prudence); Rex O'Malley (Gaston); Russell

Hardie (Gustave); E. E. Clive (Saint Gaudens); Douglas Walton (Henri); Marion Ballou (Corinne); Joan Brodel [Joan Leslie] (Marie Jeanette); June Wilkins (Louise); Fritz Leiber Jr. (Valentin); Elsie Esmonds (Mme. Duval); Edwin Maxwell (Doctor); Eily Malyon (Therese); Mariska Aldrich (Friend of Camille); John Bryan (DeMusset); Rex Evans (Companion); Eugene King (Gypsy Leader); Adrienne Matzenauer (Singer); Georgia Caine (Streetwalker); Mabel Colcord (Madame Barjon); Chappel Dossett (Priest); Elspeth Dudgeon (Attendant); Effie Ellsler (Grandma Duval); Sibyl Harris (Georges Sand); Maude Hume (Aunt Henriette); Olaf Hytten (Croupier); Gwendolyn Logan (Governess); Ferdinand Munier (Priest); Barry Norton (Emile); John Picorri (Orchestra Leader); Guy Bates Post (Auctioneer); Zeffie Tilbury (Old Duchess).

Four years after Alexandre Dumas, fils's novel, *La Dame aux Camelias*, was published in 1848, the author adapted his romantic story for the French stage. The famous story dealt with the Parisian needle worker, Marguerite Gautier, who abandons poverty to become a celebrated courtesan in nineteenth century France. She gains her nickname—"the lady of the camelias" through her love of that exquisite flower. Because she leads such a risque life outside the bounds of good taste, her friends include several uninhibited companions, including the very dandified, effeminate, Gaston.

Over the years, there had been many screen adaptations of *Camille*, providing a showcase vehicle for such stars as Sarah Bernhardt (1912), Clara Kimball Young (1915), Theda Bara (1917), Alla Nazimova (1921) and Norma Talmadge (1927). When Greta Garbo's *Anna Karenina* (1935) succeeded so admirably, MGM top executive Irving Thalberg looked for an appropriate follow-up screen vehicle. He and director George Cukor finally chose *Camille*. In re-adapting the classic love story to the screen, every effort was made to make the move contemporary, without sacrificing the mood. To accede to 1930s mores, the plot was altered from the hero agonizing over the heroine's sordid past to his jealous reaction to her ties to the demanding Baron de Varville.

In 1847 Paris, courtesan Marguerite Gautier (Greta Garbo), a one-time shopgirl, is presently being financed by her latest keeper, the disdainful Baron de Varville (Henry Daniell). Although no longer young and having seen too much of the world, Marguerite refuses to become hard and cynical. She remains generous and thoughtful to her friends, including Nichette (Elizabeth Allan)—whose wedding she finances—and an assortment of bohemian types: the lewd Prudence (Laura Hope Crews), the hussy Olympe (Lenore Ulric) and the epicene Gaston (Rex O'Malley). At the theatre, Marguerite encounters Armand Duval (Robert Taylor), a handsome but naive young bachelor. When the couple fall in love, the demanding Baron scolds her for succumbing to Duval. Next, Armand's father, the elderly General Duval (Lionel Barrymore), warns Marguerite that, if she persists in marrying his son, her reputation will sully both his career and life.

Realizing the truth of the General's words, she breaks with Armand. Misfortune strikes again when she contracts tuberculosis. She is forced to sell her possessions to cope with pressing bills. Before long, she is abandoned by most of her selfish, one-time associates; her loyal maid Nanine (Jessie Ralph) and Gaston are among the few who remains faithful. When Armand learns of Marguerite's plight, he rushes to her bedside, proclaiming his eternal love. She dies cradled in his arms, content in the knowledge that Armand loves her truly.

The prestige period production was warmly received by the critics. Frank S. Nugent (*New York Times*) affirmed, "Greta Garbo's performance is in the finest tradition: eloquent, tragic, yet restrained. . . . Through the perfect artistry of her portrayal, a hackneyed theme is made new again, poignantly sad, hauntingly lovely." Howard Barnes (*New York*

Herald-Tribune) enthused, "It is likely that Miss Garbo still has her greatest role to play, but she has made the Lady of the Camellias, for this reviewer, hers for all time."

At the time of release, everyone seemed so preoccupied with Garbo's pivotal performance and the sumptuous production values, that little attention was given to the minor hangers-on in Marguerite's circle. (Nugent of the *New York Times* did compliment the "good, sound, supporting performances.") In the mid-1930s, few movie watchers gave much specific thought to Gaston, the bachelor, a sissified member of Marguerite's bohemian entourage who frequently carries a fluffy poodle in his arms. However, in retrospect, especially given director George Cukor's homosexual lifestyle, one can appreciate the little touches and indications provided in Rex O'Malley's characterization.

Made at a $1,500,000 production cost, *Camille* was a tremendous commercial success. Garbo won her third Best Actress Oscar nomination for the movie, but lost the Academy Award to Luise Rainer (*The Good Earth*). Over the years, there would be several other screen and TV adaptations of *Camille*, but the Garbo version (now computer colorized) remains the definitive edition.

45. Caprice (Twentieth Century-Fox, 1967), color, 98 min. Not rated.

Producers, Aaron Rosenberg, Martin Melcher; associate producer, Barney Rosenzweig; director, Frank Tashlin; story, Martin Hale, Jay Jayson; screenplay, Jayson, Tashlin; art directors, Jack Martin Smith, William Creber; set decorators, Walter M. Scott, Jerry Wunderlich; costumes, Ray Aghayan; makeup, Ben Nye, Harry Maret; music, Frank DeVol; song, Larry Marks; assistant director, David Silver; sound, Harry M. Lindgren, David Dockendorf; special camera effects, L. B. Abbott, Emil Kosa Jr.; camera, Leon Shamroy; aerial camera, Nelson Tyler; editor, Robert Simpson.

Cast: Doris Day (Patricia Fowler); Richard Harris (Christopher White); Ray Walston (Stuart Clancy); Jack Kruschen (Mathew Cutter); Edward Mulhare (Sir Jason Fox); Lilia Skala (Mme. Piasco); Irene Tsu (Su Ling); Larry D. Mann (Inspector Kapinsky); Maurice Marsac (Auber); Michael Romanoff (Butler); Lisa Seagram (Mandy); Michael J. Pollard (Barney); Fritz Feld (Swiss Innkeeper); and: Leon Shamroy.

After her early screen musicals, Doris Day reached a new peak of success by co-starring with Rock Hudson in the saucy *Pillow Talk* (1959), leading to several other sex comedies in the 1960s. However, by the time of the awkward *Caprice*, Day's movie career was fast winding down. This inept spoof of James Bond-type espionage intrigue proved to be bottom-of-the-barrel.

Patricia Fowler (Doris Day) works for Femina Cosmetics owned by Sir Jason Fox (Edward Mulhare). She is arrested in Paris for trying to sell a radical new deodorant formula to Fox's rival, Matthew Cutter (Jack Kruschen). It develops that Fox concocted the scheme to get Pat hired by Cutter. Her task is now to acquire Cutter's revolutionary new hair spray which stays dry—no matter what. The process is being developed by Cutter's chief cosmetician, the very eccentric Dr. Stuart Clancy. Meanwhile, Pat comes into contact with the campy Christopher White (Richard Harris), a double agent, who pries from her that her father, an Interpol agent, was killed on the Swiss ski slopes while on the trail of a drug ring.

When Pat learns that Clancy's invention is the work of his Swiss-based mother-in-law, Madame Piasco (Lilia Skala), she heads there. Later, White saves Pat from being killed on the ski slopes and reveals that he is the Interpol agent assigned to replace her late father. By now, Pat and Christopher are convinced that Clancy murdered her dad. What they do not realize is that Fox and Clancy are partners in dope trafficking. After Clancy dies trying to murder Pat, she is abducted by Sir Jason in his helicopter. White shoots the culprit, leaving the bewildered Pat to fly the craft to Paris where she lands on the Eiffel Tower. White is on hand to greet her.

Doris Day in *Caprice* (1967).

The critics were very unhappy with this mishmash. Bosley Crowther (*New York Times*) blamed director/co-scripter Frank Tashlin for creating a "jumble of wacky and feeble comedy" filled with "cluttered chichi and comedy claptrap." As for the star, Crowther complained, "she appears to have reached that stage where massive wigs and nutty clothes and acrobatics cannot conceal the fact that she is no longer a boy." British *Monthly Film Bulletin* found the plot "incoherent and indeed barely comprehensible" and said of the cast, "Richard Harris understandably seems ill-at-ease throughout and Doris Day undetermined in what key to perform, but Ray Walston as a tricksy chemist with transvestite ambitions hovers exactly on the knife-edge between *Psycho* and *Charley's Aunt.*"

Indeed, in this sloppy comedy caper, there are many baffling aspects, not the least of which is the confounding villain, Dr. Stuart Clancy. The film presents him as a bizarre cosmetologist with a penchant for dressing in women's clothes and who loves working with women. (Since so little in *Caprice* makes sense, the illogic of Clancy's offbeat character is not unexpected.)

As Clancy is revealed to be so "abnormal" in his sexual orientation, it is no surprise to find that he is the plot's dastardly, vicious killer, a man who falls to his death after a final tussle with the heroine. Interestingly, Crowther (*New York Times*) was less concerned with this facet than wondering why the script called for Day to be "so brittle and tough and Mr. Harris should be so swively." Crowther concluded that filmmaker Tashin had in mind a role reversal for the two leading players. By extension, this, perhaps, explains why Ray Walston's Clancy is neither straight, nor gay in any coherent sense.

Location scenes for *Caprice* were accomplished in Switzerland, Paris and Los Angeles.

46. Car Wash (Universal, 1976), color, 97 min. PG-rated.

Producers, Art Linson, Gary Stromberg; associate producer, Don Phillips; director, Michael Schultz; screenplay, Joel Schumacher; art director, Robert Clatworthy; set decorator, A. C. Montenaro; costumes, Daniel Paredes; makeup, Chuck Crafts; music, Norman Whitfield; songs: Whitfield, Whitfield and Rose Royce; Lequeint "Duke" Jobe and Henry Garner; assistant directors, Phil Bowles, Richard Hashimoto, Dan Franklin; sound, Willie D. Burton, Robert L. Hoyt; camera, Frank Stanley; editor, Christopher Holmes.

Cast: Franklyn Ajaye (T. C.); Sully Boyar (Mr. B.); Richard Brestoff (Irwin); George Carlin (Taxi Driver); Professor Irwin Corey (Mad Bomber); Ivan Dixon (Lonnie); Bill Duke (Duane); Antonio Fargas (Lindy); Michael Fennell (Calvin); Arthur French (Charlie); Lorraine Gary (Hysterical Lady); Darrow Igus (Floyd); Leonard Jackson (Earl); DeWayne Jessie (Lloyd); Lauren Jones (Hooker); Jack Kehoe (Scruggs); Henry Kingi (Goody); Melanie Mayron (Marsha): Garrett Morris (Slide); Clarence Muse (Snapper); Leon Pinkney (Justin); The Pointer Sisters (The Wilson Sisters); Richard Pryor (Daddy Rich); Tracy Reed (Mona); Pepe Serna (Chuco); James Spinks (Hippo); Ray Vitte (Geronimo); Ren Woods (Loretta); Carmine Caridi (Foolish Father); Antonie Becker (Charlene); Erin Blunt (Lonnie's Son); Reginald Farmer (Daddy Rich's Chauffeur) Ricky Fellen (Hysterical Lady's Son); Ben Fromer (Man Behind); Cynthia Hamwy (Bandaged Man's Wife); Ed Metzger (Arresting Cop); Antar Mubarak (Sonny Fredericks); John Linson, Derek Schultz (Foolish Father's Sons); Mike Slaney (Bandaged Man); Al Stellone (Oldsmobile Owner); Jackie Toles (Calvin's Mother); Janine Williams (Lonnie's Daughter); Otis Sistrunk (Otis); Timothy Thomerson (Ken); Jason Bernard (Parole Officer); Jay Butler (AM Disc Jockey); Rod McGrew, J. J. Jackson (PM Disc Jockeys); Sarina Grant, Billy Bass (Newscasters).

"The movie's put together with a manic energy, we never even quite get introduced to half the people in the cast, but by the movie's end we know them, and what they're up to, and we like them. . . . All of this is held together by the music, which is nearly wall-to-wall, and by the picture tremendous sense of life. . . . [The] screenplay and the direction juggle the characters so adroitly, this is almost a wash-and wax M*A*S*H [1970]". (Roger Ebert, *Movie Home Companion*, 1991)

On a typical day at the Dee-Luxe Car Wash in Los Angeles. Lonnie (Ivan Dixon) arrives to open the Wash. Other employees appear, including: T. C. (Franklyn Ajaye), who has a yen for Mona (Tracy Reed), a waitress at the restaurant across the street; Lindy (Antonio Fargas), a flashy homosexual; the guilt-ridden Scruggs (Jack Kehoe), who has just cheated on his wife Charlene (Antonie Becker) and is afraid to tell her. Others (almost all black) employed at the De-Luxe, owned by Mr. B. (Sully Boyer), include Chuco (Pepe Serna), Goody (Henry Kingi), Hippo (James Spinks),

Justin (Leon Pinkney), the militant Duane (Bill Duke) and gum-chewing, chunky cashier, Marsha (Melanie Mayron).

During the day, a hooker (Lauren Jones) bolts from a taxi and, pursued by the cabbie (George Carlin) for not having paid her fare, hides in the ladies' room. Irwin (Richard Brestoff), Mr. B's pretentious hippie son who is a Maoist, insists on working on the assembly line at the Wash and is made fun of by the others. Daddy Rich (Richard Pryor), the flamboyant evangelist and his helpers (the Pointer Sisters) pull up in a fancy limousine (whose license plate spells "TITHE"), only to have Duane call him a capitalistic pimp. Justin's girlfriend, Loretta (Ren Woods), shows up, argues with him over his refusal to return to college, and breaks off their relationship. Hippo gives the hooker, with her several personality-altering wigs, his transistor radio in exchange for a quick go-round at sex. Chuco tries to frighten Marsha, while Mr. B flirts with her. (On her part, she prefers polishing her finger nails than keeping the Wash's books. During the day, she loses a contact lens in a cold cream jar.) Lonnie's parole officer (Jason Bernard) visits the Wash as do his children (Erin Blunt, Janine Williams). T. C. wins a radio contest and, buoyed by his success, maneuvers Mona to date him. Meanwhile, a suspected mad bomber (Professor Irwin Corey) makes a brief appearance. An apologetic Loretta reconciles with Justin, while the still-angry Charlene drive up to the establishment in a truck and tosses out Scruggs's suitcase. As the work day ends, Lonnie closes the shop. When Duane attempts to rob the Wash, Lonnie convinces him to hand over the gun and then comforts his distraught friend. The day is over.

Vincent Canby (*New York Times*) rated *Car Wash* "a cheerful, somewhat vulgar, very cleverly executed comedy. . . . *Car Wash* has the rhythm, beat and drive of the rock songs that are playing throughout the film . . . all reflecting a certain mindless contemporary mood without saying any-thing whatsoever about it." *Variety* reported that *Car Wash* "takes an audience on a whirlwind spin through the nuttiest autolaundromat ever seen on the screen. An enormous, and enormously talented, cast is put through its paces masterfully by director Michael ·Schultz. . . ."

If Richard Pryor was the best known cast members to 1970s audiences, veteran black actor Clarence Muse (as Snapper) was a familiar face to older filmgoers. By this juncture, the black action movies were a drug on the marketplace. Antonio Fargas, a frequent player in the black exploitation genre, had previous played a wide-eyed, effeminate homosexual in *Busting* (1974) and *Next Stop, Greenwich Village* (1976), qq.v. In *Car Wash*, he is the swivel-hipped, queen-ish Lindy whose workday uniform is accented with a long scarf, gold jewelry and a careful check of his makeup. He is the one who insists he is "more man than you'll ever be, and more woman than you'll ever get." (This moxie led Canby of the *New York Times* to describe his character as "the homosexual whose wrist is limp and whose mouth is loud.") With his vocal personality, Lindy might be a stereotype. However, he was anything but the meek, closeted gay so often pictured by Hollywood. This character makes no bones about what he is, and blasts the black militant Duane, who insists that Lindy's de-masculinization is another example of white society castrating black manhood.

The carefully-budgeted *Car Wash* grossed a large $8,534,564 in distributors' domestic film rentals and with its free-wheeling spirit and form, continues to be a popular revival item on TV, cable and video cassette.

47. Cat on a Hot Tin Roof (Metro-Goldwyn-Mayer, 1958), color, 108 min. Not rated.

Producer, Lawrence Weingarten; director, Richard Brooks; based on the play by Tennessee Williams; screenplay, Brooks, James Poe; art directors, William A. Horning, Urie McCleary; set decorators, Henry Grace, Robert

Priestley; costumes, Helen Rose; makeup, William Tuttle; assistant director, William Shanks; sound, Dr. Wesley I. Miller; special effects, Lee LeBlanc; camera, William Daniels; editor, Ferris Webster.

Cast: Elizabeth Taylor (Maggie Pollitt); Paul Newman (Brick Pollitt); Burl Ives (Big Daddy Pollitt); Jack Carson (Gooper Pollitt); Judith Anderson (Big Mama Pollitt): Madeleine Sherwood (Mae Pollitt); Larry Gates (Dr. Baugh); Vaughn Taylor (Deacon Davis); Patty Ann Gerrity (Dixie Pollitt); Rusty Stevens (Sonny Pollitt); Hugh Corcoran (Buster Pollitt); Deborah Miller (Trixie Pollitt); Brian Corcoran (Boy Pollitt); Vincent Townsend Jr. (Lacey); Zelda Cleaver (Sookey); Tony Merrill, Jeanne Wood (Party Guests); Bobby Johnson (Groom).

"Homosexuality has generally been regarded as a distaseful subject for the motion picture screen, and all reference to it has therefore been eliminated from MGM's adaptation of *Cat on a Hot Tin Roof*. . . . [Thus] much of the time [the film] seems directionless, like a hurricane without an eye. Mr. Williams, our best contemporary playwright, deserves better than this." (Hollis Alpert, *Saturday Review*)

Tennessee Williams's controversial and steamy drama, *Cat on a Hot Tin Roof* debuted on Broadway on March 24, 1955. It was an immediate hit. Brooks Atkinson (*New York Times*) raved that it was "Mr. Williams's finest drama. It faces and speaks the truth." Starring Barbara Bel Geddes, Ben Gazzara, Burl Ives, Mildred Dunnock, Pat Hingle and Madeleine Sherwood, it won both the Pulitzer Prize and the Drama Critics Awards as the Best Play of the 1954–55 season. MGM acquired the screen rights as a vehicle for Grace Kelly. However, by the time the studio had adjusted the storyline to meet Production Code approval, Kelly had married Prince Rainier of Monaco and retired. Elizabeth Taylor was substituted in the title part. Richard Brooks, who had directed the studio's *Tea and Sympathy* (1956), q.v., another stage-to-screen story dealing with homosexuality, was placed in charge of molding *Cat on a Hot Tin Roof* into a via-

ble item. What emerged was structurally perplexing; perhaps Hollywood's most bizarre revamping of a mature stage subject since Lillian Hellman's *The Children's Hour*, dealing with lesbianism, was twisted into a heterosexual romantic tale, *These Three* (1936), q.v.

In the present-day deep South, Big Daddy Pollitt (Burl Ives) returns to his plantation from an Eastern medical clinic. He believes he is in good health. However, his family and friends, on hand to celebrate Big Daddy's birthday, learn that he has terminal cancer. They attempt to keep the news from him and his wife, Big Mama (Judith Anderson). Meanwhile, Brick (Paul Newman) and his randy, attractive wife, Maggie (Elizabeth Taylor), have severe domestic problems. His drinking has escalated and he insists that she had an affair with his best friend, Skipper, who has since committed suicide. While they feud, Big Daddy's other son, Gooper (Jack Carson), has his own agenda. He and his equally grasping wife, Mae (Madeleine Sherwood)—who have five "no neck" bratty children—use Brick's alcoholism and Maggie's childlessness to woo Big Daddy's into their camp.

Despite his faults, Brick remains Big Daddy's favorite son and the dying man admits a partiality for the comely Maggie. Hoping to force Brick into accepting adult responsibilities, Big Daddy pushes his offspring into facing up to himself. In the confrontation, Maggie proves she was never unfaithful to Brick and that, actually, he was the one who led (by having feet of clay) the idolizing Skipper into killing himself. In the heated argument, Brick lets slip that Big Daddy is dying. At first shaken by the news, Big Daddy quickly recovers his courage. He taunts Brick that if he has the courage to face death, Brick should have the strength to face life. Gaining new perspectives, Brick and Maggie renew their love, much to the chagrin of Gooper and Mae.

Bosley Crowther (*New York Times*)

announced, "An all-fired lot of high-powered acting is done in *Cat on a Hot Tin Roof*. . . . And what a pack of trashy people these accomplished actors perform!" As to the storyline alteration (i.e. ignoring the play's intimation of a homosexual attraction between Brick and Skipper), Crowther reported, "the ways in which these [scripting] problems are solved do not represent supreme achievements of ingenuity or logic in dramatic art. . . . No wonder, the baffled father, in trying to find out what gives, roars with indignation: 'Something's missing here!'" The British *Monthly Film Bulletin* agreed with Crowther: "Censorship difficulties admittedly make it impossible to show homosexuality as the root of Brick's problem, but Brooks does not appear to have the skill to make convincing the motives he has substituted. Most of Williams' exhilarating dialogue has been left out or emasculated. . . . Brooks' handling, at its best detached, at its worst chaotically melodramatic, seldom excited and completely lacks attack."

With all the pre-production hoopla about bringing the controversial *Cat on a Hot Tin Roof* to the screen, the production was almost bound to be a success. It received an unexpected boost of attention when, during production, Elizabeth Taylor's husband (producer Mike Todd) died in a plane crash in New Mexico on March 22, 1959. After three weeks of mourning, a thinner and weaker Taylor resumed filming on the movie. *Cat on a Hot Tin Roof* grossed a large $8,785,162 in distributors' domestic film rentals. The movie was nominated for six Oscars: Best Picture (*Gigi* won); Best Actor (Paul Newman; David Niven won for *Separate Tables*); Best Actress (Elizabeth Taylor; Susan Hayward won for *I Want to Live!*); Best Director (Vincente Minnelli won for *Gigi*); Best Screenplay—Based on Material from Another Medium (*Gigi* won); Best Cinematography—Color (*Gigi* won). Ironically, Burl Ives who did a superior job of recreating his stage role as Big Daddy was not

even nominated for *Cat on a Hot Tin Roof*, but won the Best Supporting Actor Oscar that year for *The Big Country*.

For the 1974 Broadway revival of *Cat on a Hot Tin Roof*, Tennessee William rewrote the third act and made other revisions. To date, the play has been twice adapted for American TV as drama specials. The 1976 version starred Natalie Wood, Robert Wagner and Laurence Olivier. The 1986 edition cast Jessica Lange, Tommy Lee Jones and Rip Torn in the key roles.

48. Chastity (American International, 1969), color, 85 min. R-rated.

Producer, Sonny Bono; director, Alessio De Paolo; screenplay, Bono; costumes, Sadie Hayes; makeup, Stanley Campbell; music, Bono; music arranger/conductor, Don Peake; assistant director, William Lukather; sound, Gilbert D. Marchant, Duane Hensel; camera, Ben Coleman; editor, Hugo Grimaldi.

Cast: Cher (Chastity); Barbara London (Diana Midnight); Stephen Whittaker (Eddie); Tom Nolan (Tommy); Danny Zapien (Cab Driver); Elmer Valentine (1st Truckdriver); Burke Rhind (Salesman); Richard Armstrong (Husband); Joe Light (Master of Ceremonies); Dolly Hunt (Church Lady); Jason Clarke (2nd Truckdriver); and: Autumn.

Long before the endearingly unique Cher played a lesbian in *Silkwood* (1983), q.v., or won an Academy Award for *Moonstruck* (1987), her then husband, Sonny Bono, starred her in a vanity production, *Chastity*. Bono believed so much in the project that he mortgaged the couple's Beverly Hills mansion to raise the needed $300,000 to finance the project. It was a costly whimsy, for this disjointed, pretentious R-rated feature was a commercial dud.

Searching for meaning to life outside establishment society, a dissatisfied teenager who has renamed herself Chastity (Cher) embarks on a tour of the American southwest. She aims to stretch her realities, without sacrificing her virtue. On the road she hitches a ride from a burly truck driver (Elmer Valentine), but rejects his

Cher in *Chastity* (1969).

sexual advances when they share a motel room. In Tucson, she meets Eddie (Stephen Whittaker), a law student who gives her a place to sleep. The following morning she leaves, frustrated by her new attempts to fit in with society. Next, she hitchhikes to Mexico. There she talks with a drug-pushing street vendor (Danny Zapien), who is also a procurer for Diana Midnight's (Barbara London) whorehouse. When Chastity admits a desire to be a hooker, he directs her to Diana's bordello, where she becomes an employee of sorts. However, after conning a customer out of money, Chastity again renounces reality for spoiling her fantasy world. Meanwhile, Diana, who reminds Chastity of her mother, seduces the confused young woman. Then, rejecting the lesbian, Chastity returns to Arizona to see Eddie, who wants to marry her. However, frightened by commitment, she leaves again.

Babbling about her traumatic childhood—she was molested by her father—Chastity rushes onto the highway, still the frightened, dissatisfied loner.

Vincent Canby (*New York Times*) panned, "There may . . . be a movie out there, but it escapes Sonny, Cher and [director] Alessio de Paola. . . . The film does have a couple of moments of genuine humor." The *Hollywood Reporter* argued, "What this movie lacks is conviction, coherence, or the slightest capacity to compel sympathy for Chastity. . . . Peroxide blonde madam Diana Midnight proves that you don't have to look to another picture to find a more inept performer than our leering leading lady."

The print ads for this fiasco teased, "Meet Chastity . . . she picked another name for herself, but not for any reason you'd think. She's a bummer, a loser, using men like a drunk uses drink. Pick her up if you want, but be warned. She's not just a girl, she's an experience." By the time this inept movie was released, Sonny's and Cher's child, Chastity, was born on March 4, 1969.

49. The Chelsea Girls (Film-Makers' Distribution Center, 1966), color sequences, 210 min. Not rated.

Producer/director, Andy Warhol; screenplay, Warhol, Ronald Tavel; music, The Velvet Underground; camera, Warhol.

Cast: *Reel 1:* Nico, Eric Emerson, Ari; *The Pope Ondine Story:* Ondine (Pope); and: Angelina "Pepper" Davis, Ingrid Superstar, Albert Rene Ricard, Mary Might, International Velvet, Ronna; *The Duchess:* Brigid Polk; *The John:* Ed Hood (Ed); Patrick Flemming (Patrick); Mario Montez (Transvestite); and: Angelina "Pepper" Davis, International Velvet, Mary Might, Gerard Malanga, Albert Rene Ricard, Ingrid Superstar; *Hanoi Hanna (Queen of China):* Mary Might (Hanoi Hanna); and: International Velvet, Ingrid Superstar, Angelina "Pepper" Davis: *The Gerard Malanga Story:* Marie Menken (Mother); Gerard Malanga (Son); Mary Might (Girl Friend); *The Trip and Their Town (Toby Short):* Eric Emerson; *Afternoon:* Edie Sedgwick (Edie); and: Ondine, Arthur Loeb, Donald Lyons, Dorothy Dean; *The Closet:* Nico, Randy Borschedit.

"As the first Factory film to pressure its way up from 'underground' screenings to Broadway, *Chelsea Girls* effectively marked the turning-point in [Andy] Warhol's switch from 'aesthetic' experimentation to commercial movie-making. It has, however, everything in common with the early 'primitive' phase of Factory film-making. . . ." (Tony Rayns, British *Monthly Film Bulletin*)

Set in various rooms at New York City's (in)famous Chelsea Hotel, *The Chelsea Girls* presents several cinema verite episodes—shown simultaneously by using a split screen effect—of the building's bizarre tenants. At any given time, there is sound on only one of the two reels being shown; four of the reels are in color. The action ranges from the simplistic (Nico cutting her hair while playing with her

baby in the kitchen), to fantasy ("Pope" Ondine hearing the sex life confessions of Ingrid Superstar), to bizarre sexual hallucinating (sadistic Mary Might verbally and physically abusing several "girls"), to the mundane (Ed Hood fighting and then making love to a young man [Patrick Flemming] he has brought back to his room).

For Dan Sullivan (*New York Times*), "At its best, *The Chelsea Girls* is a travelogue of hell—a grotesque menagerie of lost souls. . . . At its worst it is a bunch of home movies in which Mr. Warhol's friends, asked to do something for the camera, can think of nothing much to do. . . . Mr. Warhol lets us spy on several sets of characters at once: Lesbians, homosexuals, drug addicts and other denizens of the Lower Depths, 1966." Sullivan's two chief complaints about this underground marathon were: (1) "Mr. Warhol's infantile way with his camera and sound equipment" and (2) "the utter banality of so much that goes on." *Variety* summed up: "No form, no substance, lots of deviation, limited but special audience. . . ."

Tony Rayns (British *Monthly Film Bulletin*) was more engrossed by the avante garde movie: "The cast of *Chelsea Girls* . . . are in many cases spectacularly interesting people; and even those who are not take on an interest because of the manner in which they are presented. . . ."

The Chelsea Girls was shot at Manhattan's Chelsea Hotel, as well as at city locales and in Cambridge, Massachusetts. Several of the cast—Ingrid Superstar (Ingrid Von Scheven), International Velvet (Susan Bottomly), Ondine (Bob Olivio), Mary Might (Mary Woronov)—were frequent players in Warhol's underground film projects and had gained a certain celebrity status for being so unabashedly outre about their different sexual lifestyles. Production assistant Paul Morrissey would later direct several features himself, including: *Trash* (1970), *Heat* (1972), *Forty Deuce* (1982), qq.v.

50. The Children's Hour (United
Artists, 1961), 107 min. Not rated. (British release title: *The Loudest Whisper*)

Producer, William Wyler; associate pro-
ducer, Robert Wyler; director, William Wyler;
based on the play by Lillian Hellman; adaptor,
Hellman; screenplay, John Michael Hayes; art
director, Fernando Carrere; set decorator, Edward
G. Boyle; costumes, Dorothy Jeakins; makeup,
Emile La Vigne, Frank McCoy; music, Alex
North; assistant directors, Robert E. Relyea,
Jerome M. Siegel; sound, Fred Lau, Don Hall Jr.;
camera, Franz F. Planer; editor, Robert Swink.

Cast: Audrey Hepburn (Karen Wright); Shir-
ley MacLaine (Martha Dobie); James Garner
(Dr. Joe Cardin); Miriam Hopkins (Mrs. Lily
Mortar); Fay Bainter (Mrs. Amelia Tilford);
Karen Balkin (Mary Tilford); Veronica Cart-
wright (Rosalie); Jered Barclay (Grocery Boy)
and: Mimi Gibson, Debbie Moldow, Diane
Mountford, William Mims, Florence Mac-
Michael, Sallie Brophy, Hope Summers.

With its sensational pedigree, the film
version of *The Children's Hour* should
have been far better. As Bosley Crowther
(*New York Times*) gaped, "It is hard to
believe that Lillian Hellman's famous
stage play, *The Children's Hour*, could
have aged into such a cultural antique in
the course of three decades. . . ."

Lillian Hellman's strong psychological
drama, *The Children's Hour*, debuted on
Broadway in 1934 and ran for 691 performances. It dealt with the disastrous effects
that rumors (of lesbianism) can have on
individuals, especially to one who has not
come to terms with her sexuality. Movie
producer Samuel Goldwyn brought the
stage hit to the screen in 1936, but was
forced by industry censorship to not only
change its title (to *These Three*, q.v.) but
to restructure the pivotal character assassination to that of adultery. William Wyler, who directed the unsatisfying *These
Three*, always wanted to present the drama
on screen in its intended form. Finally, in
1962, with the change in the film industry
code censorship, he directed the remake
which had a working title of *Infamous*. It
proved to have been definitely not worth
the wait.

Decorous Karen Wright (Audrey Hepburn) and restrained Martha Dobie (Shirley MacLaine) operate a small private
academy for girls. Buoyed by their successful partnership, they are unmindful
of having to cope with an ongoing disci-
plinary problem—spoiled brat Mary Tilford (Karen Balkin), the twelve-year-old
granddaughter of elderly Mrs. Amelia
Tilford (Fay Bainter), the town's most significant citizen. When the teachers punish
Mary for lying, she reacts by telling her
doting grandmother a much bigger lie, one
that leads Mrs. Tilford to conclude that
Karen and Martha are sharing a sinful relationship. The shocked Mrs. Tilford with-
draws Mary from the school and urges
other parents to do the same. Bewildered,
then angered by the accusation, Karen and
Martha sue Mrs. Tilford for slander. Their
case is lost when Lily Mortar (Miriam
Hopkins), Martha's thoughtless aunt, sur-
renders to local pressure and fails to testify
in their behalf.

With their school's reputation destroyed,
Karen must face another reality. She realizes that Mary's deceit has created grave
doubts in the mind of her fiance, Dr. Joe
Cardin (James Garner). She breaks off
their engagement. Later, a numbed Karen
suggests to Martha that they begin life
anew elsewhere—where no one knows of
their past. However, the shock of the scandal has made Martha appreciate that, all
along, she has been suppressing her love
for Karen. ("I've ruined your life, and I've
ruined my own. I feel so damn sick and
dirty I just can't stand it anymore.")
Shamed by her realization, she hangs
herself. Thereafter, Mary's lie is exposed,
but it is too late, even for Karen. After
Martha's funeral, she leaves town, rigidly
walking past Joe, Mrs. Tilford and the
other contrite townfolk.

Crowther of the *New York Times* analyzed the "several glaring holes in the
fabric of the plot" in which "the hint [of
lesbianism] is intruded with such astonish-
ment and it is made to seem such a shattering thing (even without evidence to

Audrey Hepburn and Shirley MacLaine in *The Children's Hour* (1961).

support it) that it becomes socially absurd. . . . More incredible is . . . [the film's] assumption of human credulity." Additionally, the disenchanted Crowther observed, "it is not too well acted, except by Audrey Hepburn . . . [who] gives the impression of being sensitive and pure. . . . Shirley MacLaine . . . inclines to be too kittenish in some scenes and does too much vocal handwringing toward the end." *Variety*, in an over generous mood, rated the movie "Somewhat dated, but bold, brisk and faith remake. . . . Wyler's direction is arresting, penetrating and sensitive."

Several creative problems drag down *The Children's Hour*. It starts with an overly solemn, even lugubrious tone, which badly diminishes the impact of the later tragedy. (Shooting the movie as an arty, low-keyed black-and-white production did not help matters.) If Audrey Hep-

burn was out of place as the head mistress of a small town American girls' school, irrepressible Shirley MacLaine—everyone's favorite on-camera hooker—was a far greater casting stretch. (Some said that Hepburn and MacLaine should have switched roles.) With her constant fidgeting hands and twitching mouth, it is hard to focus on MacLaine's characterization. She is especially lost in Martha's pivotal confession scene in which she informs Karen, "I remember the first time I saw you running across the quadrangle [at college]. I remember thinking what a pretty girl. . . ." and then admitting (with embarrassing hysterics), "I have loved you the way they said as long as I can remember." The less said about James Garner's non-performance the better; he wanders through the plodding movie looking embarrassed beyond belief. Miriam Hopkins, who had played Karen in *These*

Three, may be flibberty-gibbet as the selfish aunt, but, at least, she displays energy. Comparisons are always odious, but Karen Balkin as the malicious fabricator in no way matchs the memorably vicious young Bonita Granville of *These Three*.

What made *The Children's Hour* so old-fashioned and artificial in 1962 was that it promised so much and delivered so little in its discussions of "this *thing*" which everyone discusses as so dirty. For example, relevant scenes from Hellman's play in which Martha's love for Karen blossoms and leads to her jealousy of Karen's boyfriend were not included in the film adaptation. A filmed courthouse scene in which the judge brands Karen and Martha for having had "sinful sexual knowledge" of another was deleted on reconsideration by the filmmakers. Whereas in the stage version, Martha hangs herself for understanding her lesbian nature, in the movie it is the impact of the lie rather than her now uncloseted lifestyle which apparently causes her to kill herself. In fact, at one point in the pre-release of *The Children's Hour*, director Wyler seriously considered changing the movie's finale to allow Karen to leave the cemetery service with her ex-boyfriend.

The Children's Hour was promoted with an ad campaign which boasted "The landmark drama that shattered a screen taboo!" It carried a "not recommended for children" qualifier, although it did receive the movie industry's code of approval. Rushed into special limited release at the end of 1961 to qualify for Oscar consideration, the movie received five Academy Award nominations: Best Supporting Actress (Fay Bainter; Rita Moreno won for *West Side Story*); Cinematography: Black-and-White (*The Hustler* won); Art Direction—Set Direction: Black-and-White (*The Hustler* won); Sound (*West Side Story* won); Costume Design: Black-and-White (*La Dolce Vita* won).

While *The Children's Hour* was neither artistically nor commercially successful, it did pave the way for Hollywood's new "maturity," but one where—for years to come—homosexuals would be depicted as outcasts who either kill themselves or others.

51. The Choirboys (Universal, 1977), color, 119 min. R-rated.

Executive producers, Pietro Bregni, Mario Bregni, Mark Damon; producers, Merv Adelson, Lee Rich; associate producer, William Aldrich; director, Robert Aldrich; based on the novel by Joseph Wambaugh; screenplay, Christopher Knopf; art director, Bill Kenney; set decorator, Raphael Bretton; costumes, Tom Dawson, Yvonne Kubis; makeup, Tom Ellingwood; music/songs, Frank DeVol; assistant directors, Malcolm Harding, Cheryl Downey; sound, James Contreras; special effects, Henry Millar; camera, Joseph Biroc; editors, Maury Winetrobe, William Martin, Irving Rosenblum.

Cast: Charles Durning ("Spermwhale" Whalen); Louis Gossett Jr. (Calvin Motts); Perry King (Baxter Slate); Clyde Kusatu (Francis Tanaguchi); Stephen Macht (Spencer Van Moot); Tim McIntyre (Roscoe Rules); Randy Quaid (Dean Proust); Chuck Sacci (Cheech Sartino); Don Stroud (Sam Lyles); James Woods (Harold Bloomguard); Burt Young (Sergeant Dominic Scuzzi); Robert Webber (Deputy Chief Riggs); Jeanie Bell (Fanny Forbes); Blair Brown (Kimberly Lyles); Michele Carey (Ora Lee Tingle); Charles Haid (Sergeant Nick Yanov); Joe Kapp (Hod Carrier); Barbara Rhodes ("No Handle" Hadley); Jim Davis (Captain Drobeck); Phyllis Davis (Foxy/Gina); Jack DeLeon (Luther Quigley); George DiCenzo (Lieutenant Frank "Hardass" Grimsley); David Spielberg (Lieutenant Finque); Vic Tayback (Pete Zoony); Michael Wills (Alexander Blaney); Susan Batson (Sabrina); Claire Brennon (Carolina Moon); Gene Chronopoulos, Dimitri Logothetis (Card Players); Dianne L. Dixon, Maria O'Brien (Hod Carriers' Wives); Lani Kaye Harkless (Police Secretary); Louise Lorimer (Operator Fox); John Steadman (Odello); Cheryl Smith (Tammy); Maile Souza (Sheila Franklin); Lomax Study (Businessman); Ta-Tanisha (Melissa); Hatsuo Uda (North Vietnam Soldier); Bill Walker (Tilden); Ben Young (Vice Officer); Suzanne Zenor (Blonde at Party); Alex Brown, Howard Curtis, Gary Davis, Jon K. Greene, James Halty, Jim Kingsley, John R. McKee, Jim Winburn, Dick Ziker (Policemen).

Drawing on his years as a member of the Los Angeles Police Department, Joseph Wambaugh wrote *The Choirboys* (1975), one of his several books dealing with the enormous pressures and responsibilities of being a law enforcer. Sadly, Wambaugh's well-regarded novel was trashed in this episodic, farcical screen adaptation. What emerged on screen was a mindless, dehumanizing exercise, devoid of compassion for life's victims on either side of the law. *The Choirboys* was made in heavy-handed fashion by Robert Aldrich, whose directorial skills had been more appropriate to directing another type of servicemen—World War II soldiers—in his hit movie, *The Dirty Dozen* (1968).

Ten Los Angeles cops assigned to night watch duty are known as "The Choirboys" because of their custom of meeting in MacArthur Park after/during their mind-numbing shift to indulge in drugs, drink and women. Back at the precinct, Lieutenant Frank "Hardass" Grimsley (George DiCenzo) holds tight reins on his unorthodox crew; especially "Spermwhale" Whalen (Charles Durning) who is nearing retirement. Rebellious Whalen evens the score by entrapping Grimsley at a motel with a hired prostitute. Ironically, racist Roscoe Rules (Tim McIntire) is named Officer of the Month, although he is an insensitive policeman, baiting, for example, a would-be jumper into committing suicide. Francis Tanaguchi (Clyde Kusatu) thrives on dressing like Dracula and playing pranks on Rules and Lieutenant Finque (David Spielberg). Three of the unit—meek Harold Bloomguard (James Woods), bully Sam Lyles (Don Stroud) and clean-cut Baxter Slate (Perry King)— are reassigned to the vice squad. Bloomguard is made a fool of by street hookers, while Slate is discovered to be a slave client of a prostitute (Phyllis Davis) who specializes in sadism. When Lyles fails to show any compassion for Slate's sexual obsession, the latter commits suicide.

Upset by Slate's death, Lyles gets roaring drunk at the next choirboy "practice" and is stashed in a police van to quiet him. However, Lyles, as a result of harsh Vietnam War experiences, suffers from extreme claustrophobia and goes berserk. Escaping the truck, he runs amuck, fatally shooting a young homosexual (Michael Wills) cruising the park. When the squad attempts a cover-up, Deputy Chief Riggs (Robert Webber) forces the truth from Whalen. Thereafter, Spermwhale retires and buys a fishing boat. Later, he is told by a former duty buddy, Calvin Potts (Louis Gossett Jr.), that Riggs has punished the men for their part in the park murder. However, Potts insists, none of Los Angeles' "finest" hold it against Whalen for caving into pressure—each of them would have done the same thing. Conscience-stricken Spermwhale confront Riggs and, by outbluffing his former superior, gets his friends reinstated. Spermwhale is the squad's new hero.

Vincent Canby (*New York Times*) decided, "Though it's the kind of film that's designed for people who don't read much, it can be followed only by someone who has some familiarity with the book. However, anyone who liked the book will probably be appalled by the movie." For Canby, *The Choirboys* was "cheap and nasty without having any redeeming vulgarity and absolutely no conviction of truth." Richard Shickel (*Time*) argued that Robert Aldrich has "directed without nuance, jerking the movie to fitful life with occasional shocks—a beating here, a murder there, over in the corner some sick sad sex. . . . It amounts to a lot of stupid dirty jokes. . . ."

The crude, rude *The Choirboys* takes puerile delight in debasing all sorts of minorities who are outside the "norm": ethnics, would-be suicides, prostitutes, homosexuals, etc. One of the few characters in the "comedy" with any sense of decency is Sergeant Dominic Scuzzi (Burt Young), the precinct cop who is continually mistaken for the building janitor. When a young man, Alexander Blaney (Michael Wills) is entrapped and arrested

Charles Durning and Louis Gossett Jr. in *The Choirboys* (1977).

for cruising MacArthur Park, he is bought before Scuzzi:

Scuzzi: Kid, how long have you had this problem?

Blaney: [Terrified and crying] I've known three years that I'm this way. My mother and father can't understand that. . . . To be arrested. I've never been. . . .

Scuzzi: Kid, if I let you go. Do you promise never to go back.

The much-relieved Blaney leaves the precinct. But in an ironic twist, he returns to his old haunts, looking for quick sex pick-ups in the park, and it is he who is shot dead by the rampaging Rules. Like the suicide death of Baxter Slate, Blaney's fate not only provides a plot surprise, but also it is geared to comfort middle-of-the-road viewers that anyone deviating sexually from the norm, must pay a deadly price.

Produced at a cost of $6,000,000, *The Choirboys* earned $6,849,542 in distributors' domestic film rentals. The U.S. Catholic Conference condemned the picture for its depiction of aberrational sexual habits. Joseph Wambaugh would sue Universal Pictures et al in 1977 for "crudely" altering his work; the $1 million suit was settled out of court.

52. A Chorus Line (Columbia, 1985), color, 113 min. PG-13-rated.

Producers, Cy Feuer, Ernest H. Martin; director, Richard Attenborough; based on the stage play by James Kirkwood, Nicholas Dante Marvin Limsich, Edward Kliban, from a concept by Michael Bennett; screenplay, Arnold Schulman; production designer, Patrizia Von Brandenstein; art director, John Dapper; set decorator, George DeTitta; costumes, Faye Poliakin; makeup, Allen Weisinger; music, Hamlisch; songs, Hamlisch and Edward Kliban; music/music director, Ralph Burns; choreographer, Jeffrey Honraday; assistant directors, Robert Girolami, Louis D'Esposito; sound, Chris Newman, Arthur Bloom, Michael Farrow; camera, Ronnie Taylor; additional camera, Richard Kratina, Peter Norman; aerial camera, Do Sweeney; editor, John Bloom.

Cast: Michael Blevins (Mark Tabori); Yamil Borges (Diana Morales); Sharon Brown (Kim); Gregg Burge (Richie Walters); Michael Douglas (Zach); Cameron English (Paul San Marco); Tony Fields (Al DeLuca); Nicole Fosse (Kristine Erlick); Vicki Frederick (Sheila Bryant); Jan Gan Boyd (Connie Wong); Michelle Johnston (Bebe Benson); Janet Jones (Judy Monroe); Pam Klinger (Maggie Winslow); Audrey Landers (Val Clark); Terrence Mann (Larry); Charles McGowan (Mike Cass); Alyson Reed (Cassie); Justin Ross (Greg Gardner); Blane Savage (Don Kerr); Matt West (Bobby Mills); Pat McNamara (Robbie); Sammy Smith (Doorman); Timothy Scott (Boy with Headband); Bambi Jordan (Girl in Yellow Trunks); Mansoor Najee-Ullah (Cab Driver); Peter Fitzgerald (Dancer with Gum); John Hammil (Advertising Executive); Jack Lehnert (Poster Man); Gloria Lynch (Taxi Passenger); Gregg Huffman (Misfit Boy Dancer); Richard DeFabees, Melissa Randel, Jeffrey Cornell, Karen Prunczik, Jennifer Kent (Reject Dancers); Eric Aaron, Khandi Alexander, Annemaire, David Askler, Michele Assaf, Bryant Baldwin, Buddy Balou, Carol Baxter, Tina Bellis, Robin Brown, Ida Broughton, Anna Bruno, Brian Bullard, Cheryl Burr, Bill Bushnell, Roxan Cabalero, Sergio Cal, Joe Anthony Cavise, Linda Cholodenko, Cheryl Clark, Christine Colby, Alexander Cole, Anne Connors, Leslie Cook, Alice Cox, Frank Cruz, Amy Danis, Kim Darwin, Gary-Michael Davies, John DeLuca, Anita Ehlrer, Rickee Farrell, Denise Faye, Penny Fekany, Felix, Angel Ferreira, Scott Fless, Ed Forsyth, William Gabriner, David Gibson, Sandra Gray, Darrell Greene, Michael Scott Gregory, Tonda Hannum, Niki Harris, Laura Hartman, D. Michael Heath, Sonya Hensley, Dawn Herbert, Linda Hess, Regina Hood, Craig Innes, Cindy Lauren Jackson, Reed Jones, Bob Kellet, Barbara Kovac, Stanley Kramer, Andrew Kraus, Wayde Laboissoniere, Michael Lafferty, Brett Larson, Barbara LaVorato, Rodney Alan McGuire, Mia Malm, Monique Mannen, Celia Marta, Frank Mastrocola, Liz McLellan, Nancy Melius, Gwendolyn Miller, Brad Miskell, Gregory Mitchell, Debi A. Monahan, Edd Morgan, Bob Morrisy, Charles Murray, Ron Navarre, Arleen Ng, Reggie O'Gwyn, Alan Onickel, Lorena Palacios, Peggy Parten, Keri Lee Pearsall, Helene Phillips, Vick Regan, Daryl Richardson, Tia Riebling, Michael Rivera, Debbie Roche, Leora Ron, Adrian Rosario, Elissa Rosati, Patricia Ruck, Michelle Rudy, Mark Ruhala, George Russell, Lynne Savage, Anna Louise Schaut, Jeanna Schweppe, Kimry Smith, Jody Speruto, Ty Stephens, Leslie Stevens, Mary Ellen Stuart, William Sutton, Scott Taylor, Kirby Tepper, Christopher Todd, Evelyn Tosi, David Vernon, Linda Von Germer, Bobby Walker, James Walski, Robert Warners, Marsha Watkins, Faruma Williams, Melanie Winter, Scott Wise, Lily Lee Wong, Leslie Woodies, Barbara Yeager (Dancers).

The eventual hit musical, *A Chorus Line*, began off-Broadway in 1975 and moved that year onto Broadway where it won nine Tonys and a Pulitzer Prize. During its phenomenally long run, *A Chorus Line* became an industry unto itself, spawning road companies in the U.S. and abroad. When the screen version was released in 1985, it was anti-climactic, unable and unwilling to live up to a decade's worth of expectations. Gone on screen was much of the energy and excitement that had characterized the stage original. Gone was much of the exposition of two of its gay characters—Greg and Paul. Britisher Richard Attenborough, a strange choice for the directing assignment, claims that he diminished the Greg character and made the Paul role more manly because, "when it was first presented to audiences on the stage it was shocking. But in 1985 to be shocking you would have to deal with AIDS." Obviously, Sir Richard missed the point (as he did with so much else in transferring the landmark musical to the screen). In the play original, the authors included the gay characters' monologues as representing just another of the many chorus-line types of the Broadway theatre scene. Their reflections were not meant to be shocking, just to add to the atmosphere of reality, in this case, about two performers who happen to be gay.

Blane Savage, Jan Gan Boyd, Gregg Burge, Michelle Johnston, Audrey Landers, Vicki Frederick, Matt West, Yamie Borges, Pat McNamara, Nicole Fosse and Charles McGowan in *A Chorus Line* **(1985).**

Established Broadway director/choreographer Zach (Michael Douglas) is casting a new musical. From the many dancers who audition, he and his assistant, Larry (Terrence Mann), narrow the choices to sixteen. Zach informs the semi-finalists that the next cut will reduce the chorus group to four men and four women; each of whom must BE their parts. As such, he must know more about each of them to make his selection properly. Reluctantly or openly, as the case may be, the candidates reveal their stories.

Bobby Mills (Matt West), a mess at sports, never lived up to the expectations of his athletic father; Mike, who sings "I Can Do That," insists he began dancing only because his sister was taking lessons; In "At the Ballet" thirtyish Sheila Bryant (Vicki Frederick) tells of her snobbish dad who claims to have married beneath him, while Bebe Benson (Michelle Johnston) and Maggie Winslow (Pam Klinger) dis-

cuss their parents and the dance world; street-smart Al DeLuca (Tony Fields) does his best to bolster the impression made by his shy wife, Kristine (Nicole Fosse); in "Surprise," black Richie Walters (Gregg Burge) shines as a dancer; the Oriental Connie Wong (Jan Gan Boyd) would love to have a part that allows her to act; self-deprecating Greg Gardner (Justin Ross) jokes about being a double-minority— Jewish and gay; in "Dance Ten, Looks Three" Val Clark (Audrey Landers) explains how plastic surgery improved her career chances; Puerto Rican Diana Morales (Yamil Borges) recalls in "Nothing" her fears of revealing herself in a Method acting class; Don Kerr (Blane Savage), who has a family to support, is anxious not to lose his waiter's job because of the audition; tall Texan Judy Monroe (Janet Jones) wisecracks; in "Hello Twelve" seventeen-year-old Mark Tabori (Michael Blevins) expresses his nervousness at this, his first dance audition; and Puerto Rican Paul San Marco (Cameron English), who altered his last name to seem Italian, remembers how his parents' reacted to learning he was gay.

By now, Cassie (Alyson Reed), Zach's one-time girlfriend who left him to try her luck in Hollywood, has shown up at the theatre. Having failed in the movies, she badly needs a job—even in the chorus line and reflects on her fateful choices in "What I Did for Love." During the run-through of a number, Paul injures his knee and is taken to the hospital. After practicing the routine "One," Zach dismisses Al, Connie, Don, Greg, Judy, Kristine, Maggie and Sheila. The remaining eight have a new Broadway show in which to appear.

David Sterritt (*Christian Science Monitor*) pinpointed several of the movie's flaws, including the use of Richard Attenborough whose "movies tend to look like the logistical exercise they are, full of ideas and cinematic but oddly cold at their core." For Sterritt, "the show's format proves too slippery for the director to manage properly. . . . [The] sex-related material, which may have seemed daring when the play was new, will grate on the sensibilities of some viewers even when it's now downright trite or vulgar." Sheila Benson (*Los Angeles Times*) noted the film "travels in fits and starts. [Michael] Bennett's choreography has been all but erased. . . . Every chance we have at momentum or empathy is sabotaged by casting, by cutting away (even whacking off the dancers' feet). . . ." Rex Reed (*New York Post*) reasoned, "Instead of enhancing a great work of art, the movie version only ends up truncating it. . . . The obnoxious 'opening up' process . . . robs the chorus line of necessary dramatic presence by taking the audience on an unnecessary tour of the back-stage dressing rooms and even the street outside the theater."

Filmed largely at Broadway's venerable Mark Hellinger Theatre, *A Chorus Line* grossed a relatively modest $9,828,487 in distributors' domestic film rentals. It received two Oscar nominations: Best Sound (*Out of Africa* won); Best Editing (*Witness* won). Of the movie's cast, Vicki Frederick, Pam Klinger, Alyson Reed, Justin Ross and Matt West had appeared in one or another stage company of the landmark musical.

53. Cleopatra Jones (Warner Bros., 1973), color, 89 min. PG-rated.

Producer, William Tennant; co-producer, Max Julien; director, Jack Starrett; story, Julien; screenplay, Julien, Sheldon Keller; art director, Peter Wooley; set decorator, Cheryal Kearney; music/music director, J. J. Johnson; additional music, Carl Brandt, Brad Shapiro, Joe Simon; title theme, Simon; assistant director, Julien; stunt coordinator, Ernest Robinson; hapkido karate master, Bong Soo Han; sound, Bud Alper; camera, David Walsh; editor, Allan Jacobs.

Cast: Tamara Dobson (Cleopatra Jones); Bernie Casey (Reuben Masters); Shelley Winters (Mommy); Brenda Sykes (Tiffany); Antonio Fargas (Doodlebug); Bill McKinney (Officer Purdy); Dan Frazer (Detective Lou Crawford); Stafford Morgan (Sergeant Kert); Mike Warren (Andy); Albert Popwell (Matthew Johnson); Caro Kenyatta (Melvin Johnson); Esther Rolle (Mrs. Johnson); Paul Koslo; Joseph A. Tornatore (Mommy's Hoods); Hedley Mattingly (Chauffeur); George Reynolds, Theodore Wilson (Doodlebug's Hoods); Christopher Joy (Snake); Keith Hamilton (Maxwell Woodman); Angela Gibbs (Annie); John Garwood (Lieutenant Thompkins); John Alderman (Mommy's Assistant).

Cleopatra Jones was one of the more delightfully raunchy black action pictures. Not since *King Kong* Vs. *Godzilla* (1963) had the cinema depicted two such oversized rivals as sleek, 6' 2" black former model Tamara Dobson and bulky one-time Academy Award winner Shelley Winters. The chief villain of this piece was not one of fast-talking, fast-living black street characters who peppered the plotline, but a big, bad white mama who happens to be lesbian.

C.I.A. agent Cleopatra Jones (Tamara Dobson) supervises the laying waste of an

Tamara Dobson and Shelley Winters in *Cleopatra Jones* **(1973).**

enormous field of opium poppies in Turkey. This $30 million loss reverberates back to Los Angeles, where underworld gang leader and drug trafficker, Mommy (Shelley Winters), demands revenge for this "atrocity." She shrieks to her quaking henchmen about Cleopatra: "I want her black ass back heeerre!!" To trap the ace super agent into coming to California, Mommy order crooked cop Purdy (Bill McKinney) to raid a halfway house run by Cleopatra's boyfriend, Reuben Masters (Bernie Casey). The trick works and Jones returns to Los Angeles, where she agrees to help police Detective Lou Crawford (Dan Frazer) smoke out the corrupt lawmen and to wipe out the crooks bribing them. Cleopatra turns to her contact, Tiffany (Brenda Sykes), who is the girlfriend of dope pusher, Doodlebug (Antonio Fargas); he, in turn, works for Mommy. When Mommy captures Tiffany,

resourceful Cleopatra comes to her speedy rescue. The showdown occurs in an auto junkyard, where the hulking criminal intends to crush Cleopatra and Tiffany in a car-compressing machine. Instead, it is Mommy who dies, while her underlings are rounded up by Cleopatra and her karata-knowledgeable pals.

Variety enthused that *Cleopatra Jones* "is a good programmer" and that "Instead of the formula uptight, hip-flip-clip dialog, a more extensive use of casual black colloquialisms lends more depth to the milieu, making the characters more real though no less intense at the right moments." Janette C. Tolbert (*Encore* magazine) guaranteed, "This thrilling and sometimes funny movie will have you on the edge of your seat, jabbing your neighbor in the ribs, and yelling 'Right on, Cleo! Do it, mama! *Cleopatra Jones* is definitely not to be missed."

Within *Cleopatra Jones*, Shelley Winters's Mommy was the screen's butchest, most sadistic (stereotypical) creation since Mercedes McCambridge stalked through *Johnny Guitar* (1954) and *Touch of Evil* (1958). (Shelley Winters had played a lesbian in *The Balcony*, 1962, q.v., and played a variation of one in *S.O.B.*, 1981). Mommy, who clomps and screams through the film in her favorite leather coat and assortment of wigs, definitely has an eye for the girls, especially her revolving-door array of female helpers who assuage her frustrations when things go wrong. *Variety* reacted strongly to her over-the-top, grotesque performance, which it found "an embarrassingly vulgar characterization as a lesbian-type gangleader" The trade paper explained: "Winters for years, has popped up in flamboyant cameo roles, but never so strident, never so shrill, and never so pitiable for the gauche effort, as she appears here."

Cleopatra Jones grossed $3,250,000 in distributors' domestic film rentals and its soundtrack album by J. J. Johnson sold well over 500,000 copies. Ernest Robinson and the Black Stuntmen's Association fleshed out the movie's action sequences. With its box-office success, there was little doubt that a follow-up vehicle was in the wings. *Cleopatra Jones and the Casino of Gold*, q.v., emerged two years later.

54. Cleopatra Jones and the Casino of Gold (Warner Bros., 1975), color, 94 min. R-rated.

Producer, William Tennant; director, Chuck Bail; based on characters created by Max Julien; screenplay, Tennant; art director, Johnson Tasao; music, Dominic Frontierre; assistant directors, Bobby Canavarro, William Chaung Kin; stunt coordinator, Eddy Donno; Chinese fighting instructors, Tang Chia, Yuen Shian Yan; sound, Cyril Swern; special effects, Nobby Clark, Milt Rice; camera, Alan Hume; editor, Willy Kemplen.

Cast: Tamara Dobson (Cleopatra Jones); Stella Stevens (Bianca Jovan [The Dragon Lady]); Tanny (Mi Ling); Norman Fell (Stanley Nagel); Albert Popwell (Matthew Johnson); Caro Kenyatta (Melvin Johnson); Chan Sen (Soo); Christopher Hunt (Mendez); Lin Chen Chi (Madalyna); Liu Loke Hua (Tony); Eddy Donno (Morgan); Bobby Canavarro (Lin Ma Chen); Mui Kwok Sing (Benny); John Cheng (David); Tony Lee (Lao Di); Rich King (Mr. Han); Gigo Tevzadze (Chew Lun); Lok Sing (Mike); Paul Chen (Man in Walled City); Victor Kahn (Man in Hallway).

The fat lady (Shelley Winters) may have sung her final song at the end of *Cleopatra Jones* (1973), q.v., but it was not over for super-tall, super-cool, super agent, Cleopatra Jones (Tamara Dobson). Warner Bros. dispatched her on another screen assignment in this follow-up to the earlier hit. By now, the black exploitation film cycle was fast winding down, having done itself in with too many imitative entries. What had seemed fresh in *Cleopatra Jones* now seemed tired in this poorly assembled action entry, which erred in taking its heroine out of her own milieu (the streets of Los Angeles) and making her a dependent stranger in a foreign land. Like the far superior predecessor, the new adventure featured a white lesbian villainess, this time enacted by Stella Stevens.

When Bianca Jovan, a.k.a. the wicked Dragon Lady (Stella Stevens), captures two U.S. government agents—Matthew Johnson (Albert Popwell) and his brother Melvin (Caro Kenyatta)—their fellow operative, Cleopatra Jones (Tamara Dobson) arrives in Hong Kong to rescue them from the clutches of the drug cartel. Needing local help, Cleopatra teams with perky private investigator Mi Ling (Tanny), the latter buoyed by several tough motorcyclists. (Only later does Jones discover that Mi Ling and her helpers are actually Hong Kong undercover cops.) While Cleopatra and Mi Ling search for the Johnson boys, the sinister Dragon Lady is attempting to corrupt the duo into joining forces with her. Cleopatra and Mi Ling come to the Dragon Lady's casino in Macao where they lead a raid on the arch criminal's headquarters. In the fight to the finish,

Cleopatra subdues her wily opponent. With the drug trafficking under control for the time being, Cleopatra leaves Hong Kong.

Vincent Canby (*New York Times*) was disappointed by the sequel's poor showcasing of the lead actress: "Miss Dobson is a large, beautiful overwhelming presence whose real sexuality is denied by her movie role and by costumes that seem to have been designed for a female impersonator. With little to do but pose in bizarre outfits in between shoot-outs and bouts of martial arts action, the title character is effectively reduced to a joke." *Variety* dismissed this installment for "Running the gamut of cliches in both chopsocky and blaxploitation genre."

Because *Cleopatra Jones and the Casino of Gold* was an American-Hong Kong co-production made in conjunction with producer Run Run Shaw, a great deal of screen time was devoted to the martial art skills of Tanny and the other Orientals in the cast. The underrated Stella Stevens had little to do in her brief screen time, beyond looking sleek in exotic outfits and hinting at her preference for female companionship. *Variety* noted, "she occasionally has enjoyable moments of nefariousness, recalling roles once played by Gale Sondergaard [*The Letter*, 1940], or by Ona Munson in Josef von Sternberg's *Shanghai Gesture* [1941]." Vincent Canby (*New York Times*) who judged this picture "trashy" and "expansionist nonsense," noted that in handling her lesbian role "the irrepressible Stella Stevens plays [it] for something more than the little it's worth."

55. Compulsion (Twentieth Century-Fox, 1959), 103 min. Not rated.

Producer, Richard D. Zanuck; director, Richard Fleischer; based on the novel by Meyer Levin; screenplay, Richard Murphy; art directors, Lyle R. Wheeler, Mark-Lee Kirk; set decorators, Walter M. Scott, Eli Benneche; costumes, Charles Le Maire, Adele Palmer; makeup, Ben Nye; music, Lionel Newman; assistant director, Ben Kadish; sound, Eugene Grossman, Harry M. Leonard; camera, William C. Mellor; editor, William Reynolds.

Cast: Orson Welles (Jonathan Wilk); Diane Varsi (Ruth Evans); Dean Stockwell (Judd Steiner); Bradford Dillman (Artie Straus); E. G. Marshall (Horn); Martin Milner (Sid); Richard Anderson (Max Steiner); Robert Simon (Lieutenant Johnson); Edward Binns (Tom Daly); Robert Burton (Mr. Straus); Louise Lorimer (Mrs. Straus); Wilton Graff (Mr. Steiner); Gavin MacLeod (Padua); Terry Becker (Benson); Russ Bender (Edgar Llewellyn); Gerry Lock (Emma); Harry Carter, Simon Scott (Detectives); Voltaire Perkins (Judge).

When fourteen-year-old Robert Franks was murdered on May 21, 1924 by two law students (nineteen-year-old Nathan Leopold and eighteen-year-old Richard Loeb) at the University of Chicago, the killers had no other motive than their desire to commit the "perfect" crime. At their highly-publicized trial that fall, the affluent defendants had high-profile Clarance Darrow as their able attorney. As a result, instead of receiving the death sentence, they were sentenced to 99 years plus life. Meyer Levin, who had been a campus mate of the two killers in the 1920s, wrote a best selling novel (1956) on the notorious crime which was turned into a popular Broadway play (1957).

In 1924, young and well-to-do Judd Steiner (Dean Stockwell) and Artie Straus (Bradford Dillman) are superior law students at the University of Chicago. In their extremely close relationship, it is the callous Artie who controls the sensitive, dependent Judd. Neither accepting nor relying on anyone else but each other, they contemptuously consider themselves above society's rules. One day, they kidnap and murder the young Kessler boy, merely for the pleasure of outwitting the authorities. However, complications arise when Judd's eyeglasses are found near the scene of the crime and are traced to him. Although the duo have constructed solid alibis, they are undone by the casual remark of the Steiner's chauffeur (Terry Becker). Their aghast parents hire a bril-

Bradford Dillman and Dean Stockwell in *Compulsion* **(1959).**

liant criminal attorney, Jonathan Wilk (Orson Welles), to handle the case. Quickly understanding that his clients are guilty, Wilk, nevertheless, mounts a strong defense (i.e. admitting his clients guilt—which rules out a jury trial—but insisting that the young men are mentally sick, if not legally insane). Wilk delivers an emotional plea to the judge (Voltaire Perkins) against capital punishment. As a result, the culprits are sentenced to life imprisonment. Neither Judd nor Artie are remorseful, rather both leave the courtroom bitter toward Wilk for not attempting an acquittal strategy.

In his very favorable review, A. H. Weiler (*New York Times*) reported that first-time producer Richard D. Zanuck and director Richard Fleischer had "fashioned a documentary-like fiction that moves as briskly as exciting melodrama while it dramatically probes the characters of its principals. . . . Orson Welles contributes a comparatively short but the fin-

est portrayal to this searching drama. . . . Bradford Dillman emerges as an actor of imposing stature as the bossy, over-ebullient and immature mama's boy. Dean Stockwell's delineation of the quiet, sensitive Judd is equally effective. . . ." *Variety* credited the movie with bringing "the two brilliant young deviates to life with searching clarity, a superb sense of dramatic pacing and a certain bold honesty. . . ."

Variety noted, "That the boys have a homosexual relationship is quite clear, though the subject is not overstressed." Weiler of the *New York Times*, in describing the two lead characters, noted the screenplay's "showy inference of homosexuality." Because Hollywood was a few years away—*The Children's Hour* (1961) and *Advise and Consent* (1962), qq.v.—from delving into the subject of homosexuality in a more open manner, script writer Richard Murphy had to couch the sexual orientation of Judd and Artie in subtle terms.

In retrospect, Nick Roddick (*Magill's American Film Guide*, 1983), points out: "One way in which the film has not aged well, however, is in its cautious treatment of the homosexuality of its two central protagonists. Hailed as courageous at the time, the film in fact portrays Judd's and Artie's homosexuality as very little more than an adjunct to their psychopathic behavior, ever bit as sinister and even, perhaps, as dangerous."

The Leopold-Loeb case had already inspired a prior movie, Alfred Hitchcock's *Rope* (1948), q.v., and would be the subject of *Swoon* (1992), q.v. Despite the studio's claim that *Compulsion* was not a recitation of the Leopold-Loeb case, Nathan Leopold sued the filmmakers for $1,500,000 in October 1959. (Interestingly, this was just about the amount the movie grossed in domestic distribution.)

56. Consenting Adult (ABC-TV, February 4, 1985), color, 100 min. Not rated.

Executive producer, Martin Starger; supervising producer, Dennis E. Doty; producers, Ray Aghayan, David Lawrence; associate producer, Edward D. Markley; director, Gilbert Cates; based on the novel by Laura Z. Hobson; teleplay, John McGreevey; art director, Grame Murray; set decorator, Rondi Johnson; costumes, Toni A. Spadafora; makeup, Tom Case, Jo-Ann Wabisca; music, Laurence Rosenthal; camera, Frank Stanley; editor, Melvin Shapiro.

Cast: Marlo Thomas (Tess Lynd); Martin Sheen (Ken Lynd); Barry Tubb (Jeff Lynd); Talia Balsam (Margie); Ben Piazza (Dr. Mark Waldo); John Terlesky (Pete Roberts); Corinne Michaels (Claire Wister); Matthew Laurance (Nate); Joseph Adams (Stuart); Richard Sargent (Pat Malone); Thomas Peacocke (Dr. Daniels); Moira Walley (Sue Wister); Jeff Irvine (Hank); Dave Sayer (Counterman); Rebecca Staples (Maribel); Kim Kondrashoff (Dev); Roman Podhora (Ray); Peter Glashi (Mark); John Ormerod (Kerry).

"They were the perfect family. Happy. Loving. Together. . . . But sometimes the truth can tear a family apart. For the Lynds, it began when their only son told them, 'I am homosexual.'" (Advertisement for *Consenting Adult*)

Veteran fiction writer Laura Z. Hobson had shocked an earlier generation with her book, *Gentleman's Agreement* (1947) dealing with anti-Semitism. *Consenting Adult* (1975) focused on a young man admitting to his family that he is gay. Once again, Hobson had written a slick book geared to gain readership through its sensational topic rather than from superior prose or deft characterization. It took ten years for this novel to be adapted into a made-for-television movie, a nervous Hollywood having earlier decided against making it into a theatrical feature. By then (1985), the AIDS epidemic had erupted and drastically changed the gay lifestyle so cautiously depicted in Hobson's outside-looking-in novel. However, the TV adaptors of *Consenting Adult* were content to retain a pre-AIDS milieu in exploring the dimensions of an alternate lifestyle in which each and every point-of-view is examined (laboriously). As presented on screen, the story is NOT so much about the son's dealing with his homosexuality, as it is with his manipulative mother (star Marlo Thomas in a very harsh performance) who must cope with her child's "sickness."

Over-achieving college sophomore Jeff Lynd (Barry Tubb), has spent most of his years trying to please his demanding father, Ken (Martin Sheen), who owns a local car dealership. One day, Jeff makes a private confession to his mother, Tess (Marlo Thomas)—that he is homosexual. ("I know you don't want to believe it. I don't want to believe it either," he explains. "I've been fighting against it for years. But it's true and it just gets truer.") The flabbergasted woman, guilt-ridden that it may be her fault he is different, refuses to accept the news. She grabs at straws to avoid the truth (i.e. that the uptight son has yet to have any sexual experiences, let alone a homosexual one). In unenlightened fashion, this very manipulating woman ponders why such a thing is happening to her. Reluctantly, she tell Ken, who is recuperating from a stroke,

Barry Tubb and Marlo Thomas in *Consenting Adult* (1985).

partially brought on by the pressures of their faltering marriage.

Ken proves to be more intractable than Tess, especially after Jeff stops treatments with Dr. Daniels (Thomas Peacocke), a psychiatrist who claims to have good results in "curing" this type of "sickness." Insisting he is not diseased, an angry Jeff admits that recently he has been with a man and that now he is sure he is gay. This revelation makes Tess even more unyielding. Reacting to his parents' homophobia, Jeff cuts his ties with them. He lives for a time with his understanding sister (Talia Balsam) and brother-in-law (Matthew Laurance).

Finally, brooding Ken reaches the point of wanting to reestablish communication with his son. He writes him a letter saying "I'm not ready to embrace the whole homosexual world, but I will not give up my son." However, he dies before he can mail it. After the funeral, Tess gives the note to Jeff. As he leaves to return to college, the unforgiving Tess announces coldly, "It's your life, Jeffie. You have to live it your way." She would rather be alone than abandon her inflexibile viewpoint. However, after months of reflection, she calls him at Christmas and invites he and his lover (Joseph Adams) to spend the holidays with her.

Daily Variety observed that "John McGrevey's often compelling teleplay plays to the bleachers in attempt to cover all bases" while acknowledging that it is "meticulously crafted as far as producing and acting. . . .. Marlo Thomas as Tess does a remarkable job of showing a woman's gradations from prevailing materialism to vulnerability; the telefilm's focus most certainly is on her. . . . Barry Tubb's Jeff is solid. . . ." *TV Guide* magazine rated this high-profile TV movie three stars. *Daily Variety* assessed, "Thought-provoking, often cheerless, *Consenting Adult* explores myths, shadows and suspicions as they pertain to the mother in the case. . . .. Marlo Thomas as Tess does a remarkable job of showing a woman's gra-

Barry White in *Coonskin* (1975).

dations from prevailing maternalism to vulnerability. She makes her the genuinely hurt character in the telefilm . . . Barry Tubb as Jeff is solid."

Presented very much in the fashion of a disease-of-the-week TV movie, *Consenting Adult*, wanting to appeal to a larger audience, devoted very little screen time to the son's homosexual lifestyle, beyond showing a few brief scenes of his response to being picked-up by a young man (Jeff Irvine) in a coffee shop and his resultant panic. Typical of the film's attitude was the interchange between Jeff and his jock college roommate (John Terlesky). When the latter learns the embarrassing truth about the person who *was* his good friend and who *had* shared the same room, he screams "How can this be happening to me!" The movie, thus, is not about the "different" son, but about *everyone* else— the heterosexual people—with whom, so

went the network's philosophy, the bulk of the viewership would empathize.

This same inverted philosophy would govern another trend-setting TV movie, *An Early Frost* (1985), q.v., which, nevertheless, was a better presentation of the subject matter on all scores. *Consenting Adult* was filmed in Vancouver, British Columbia. In *That Certain Summer* (1972), q.v., Martin Sheen had been cast as a gay man having a relationship with Hal Holbrook's character.

57. Coonskin (Bryanston, 1975), color, 82 min. R-rated. (a.k.a.: *Streetfight*)

Producer, Albert S. Ruddy; director/ screenplay, Ralph Bakshi; music, Chico Hamilton; assistant director, Johnnie Vita; still photographers, Bakshi, Vita; camera, William A. Fraker; animation camera, Ted C. Bemiller; editor, Donald W. Ernst.

Cast: Barry White (Samson/Brother Bear); Charles Grodone (Preacher/Brother Fox); Scatman Crothers (Pappy/Old Man Bone); Philip [Michael] Thomas (Randy/Brother Rabbit).

Ralph Bakshi had a reputation for creating raucous, raunchy R-rated feature-length cartoons such as *Fritz the Cat* (1971), *Heavy Traffic* (1973) and *The Nine Lives of Fritz the Cat* (1974). For *Coonskin*, he updated Uncle Remus tales to an odyssey of several animal cartoon figures who leave the South to explore life on the hep streets of Harlem. Among the characters encountered are Snowflake, a smart-mouthed black transvestite. Richard Eder (*New York Times*) approved of filmmaker Bakshi for "making a most serious and difficult kind of artistic commitment in trying to capture black Harlem's human condition by heightening rather than softening its miseries."

Coonskin is framed by the live-action story of two black convicts somewhere in the South waiting in the prison exercise yard through the night for their escape car to finally appear. To fill in the time, Pappy (Scatman Crothers) tells the restless Randy (Philip [Michael] Thomas) a fable.

Facile Brother Rabbit (the voice of Philip [Michael] Thomas), an undisciplined Fox (the voice of Charles Grodone) and a confused bear (the voice of Barry White) set out for the north. Their road trek ends in Harlem. En route, they deal with a wide assortment of types, ranging from the Mafia to the police. During their colorful adventure, they encounter stereotypes of both races (as well as a smooth-talking Puerto Rican), including a redneck Southern sheriff, a black garbage picker, a shapely blue-eyed, blonde femme fatale named Miss America (who lures several blacks to their death), and a street-smart black stripper. Then, there is Snowflake, the jive-talking drag queen son of the New York Godfather. This "lousy, no-good queer" has a penchant for furtive sex in the back of trucks down by the docks and relishes being pummeled by macho men.

As this inventive parable ends on an upbeat note—the trio are victorious over their enemies—the movie returns to live action. It is now daybreak. The convicts make their fumbling prison break and drive off to freedom.

Variety concluded, "*Coonskin* is by no means avant garde; the story of young men who start essentially the same but turn out differently is as old as mankind; and the contemporary urban plot turns are drawn from the treasury of modern pulp dramaturgy. . . . *Coonskin* seems to be telling it 'the way it was'. . . ." Frank Rich (*New York Post*) decided, "The most likely candidates to be offended by *Coonskin* are actually white women and gays. These characters, more than the film's blacks, seem to take us to the bottom of Bakshi's personal obsessions."

Originally, in 1974, Paramount Pictures was to have released *Coonskin*. However, C.O.R.E. (Congress of Racial Equality) blasted the animated feature for being racist ("It depicts blacks as slaves, hustlers, and whores") and Paramount dropped its distribution plans. When the movie was released by independent Bryanston Pictures in 1975, there were picket lines and a lot of media hype about this controversial animated study of ghetto life. However, the movie received few theatrical bookings. When it was later offered on videocassette, the movie was heavily re-edited, retitled (*Streetfight*) and boasted a different musical score.

58. Cover Me Babe (Twentieth Century-Fox, 1970), color, 89 min. R-rated.

Producer, Lester Linsk; director, Noel Black; screenplay, George Wells; art directors, Jack Martin Smith, Dale Hennesy; set decorators, Walter M. Scott, Robert De Vestel; wardrobe, Jerry Kobald, Bruce Walkup; music, Fred Karlin; assistant director, Richard Glassman; sound, Richard Overton, David Dockendorf; special camera effects, Art Cruickshank; camera, Michel Hugo; editor, Harry Gerstad.

Cast: Robert Forster (Tony); Sondra Locke (Melisse); Susanne Benton (Sybil); Robert Fields (Will); Ken Kercheval (Jerry); Sam Waterston (Cameraman); Michael Margotta

(Steve); Mike Kellin (Derelict); Floyd Mutrux (Ronnie); Maggie Thrett (Prostitute); Jeff Corey (Paul); Regis Toomey (Michael); Mitzi Hoag (Mother); Franklin Townsend (Transvestite); Mello Alexandria (Male Puppet); Linda Howe (Female Puppet); Michael Payne, Carmen Argenziano (Students).

"*Cover Me Babe* . . . is the sort of movie that needs the words of a critic less than it requires the services of an analyst, displaying, as it does, a compulsive need to ridicule itself, to deny its basic intelligence and to fail." (Vincent Canby, *New York Times*)

Tony Hall (Robert Forster) is a prize-winning film major at a Los Angeles college. Melisse (Sondra Locke), the star of his acclaimed short movie, breaks off with film instructor Will Ames (Robert S. Fields) to move into Tony's apartment. To get even, the jealous Will refuses Tony's application for a grant for his next cinema project. While searching for funding, the driven filmmaker shoots his new documentary (a study of human depravity). To gain cinema verite footage, he thinks nothing of setting Melisse against another student actor, Jerry (Ken Kercheval), a situation which backfires when Jerry nearly rapes Melisse. Further into the project, the amoral Tony convinces his ex-girlfriend, Sybil (Susanne Benton), to seduce Ronnie Shields (Floyd Mutrux), a gay acquaintance, whom Hall has mocked. This latest on-camera experiment fails when Will breaks up the filming. By now, Melisse is so disillusioned with the obsessed Tony that she leaves him. The intrepid moviemaker is unbothered by losing Melisse, or by news that the film studio he hoped would finance the movie has backed out of the deal.

Variety judged this little-seen effort as "Tasteless, ludicrous and artistically offensive," and insisted that director Noel Black directed the misfire in "fumbling 1968 avant garde fashion." To be noted in this celluloid mess are fine character performances by Mike Kellin (as a bum) and by Regis Toomey (as an old-time movie director).

59. Cruising (United Artists, 1980), color, 106 min. R-rated.

Producer, Jerry Weintraub; associate producer, Burtt Harris; director, William Friedkin; based on the novel by Gerald Walker; screenplay, Friedkin; production designer, Bruce Weintraub; art director, Edward Pisoni; set decorator, Robert Drumheller; costumes, Robert de Mora; makeup, Allan Weisinger; special makeup effects, Robert Norin; music, Jack Nitzche; assistant director, Alan Hopkins; sound, Kim Ornitz; camera, James Contner; editor, Bud Smith.

Cast: Al Pacino (Steve Burns); Paul Sorvino (Captain Edelson); Karen Allen (Nancy); Richard Cox (Stuart Richards); Don Scardino (Ted Bailey); Joe Spinell (Patrolman DiSimone); Jay Acovone (Skip Lee); Randy Jurgensen (Detective Lefransky); Barton Heyman (Dr. Rifkin); Gene Davis (Da Vinci); Sonny Grosso (Detective Blasio); Larry Atlas (Eric Rossman); Allan Miller (Chief of Detectives); Edward O'Neil (Detective Schreiber); Michael Aronin (Detective Davis); James Remar (Gregory); William Russ (Paul Gaines); Mike Starr (Patrolman Desher); Steve Inwood (Martino); Keith Prentice (Joey); Leland Starnes (Jack Richards); Robert Pope (DaVinci's Friend); Leo Burmester (Water Sport); Bruce Levine (Dancer); Charles Dunlap (Three Card Monte); Powers Boothe (Hankie Salesman); James Sutorious (Voice of Jack); Richard Jamieson (Spotter); James Ray Weeks (Seller); David Winnie Hayes (Bouncer); Carmine Stipo (Bartender); James Hayden (Cockpit Coke Man); Todd Winters (Tugboat Mate); and: Robert Carnegie, Dennis Shea, Larry Silvestri, Lawrence Lott, Penny Gumeny, Ray Vitte, Joseph Catucci, Dan Sturkie, Sylvia Gassell, Henry Judd Baker, Kevin Johnson, Louie Grenier, Burr DeBenning, Mike Barbera, Robert Duggan, Linda Gary.

"You don't have to be homosexual to dislike *Cruising*, but the gay community is not wrong to worry that William Friedkin's movie plays like a recruiting poster for an Anita Bryant parade. It is like taking a Hamburg brothel as the site for an examination of heterosexuality. You don't quite get the full picture of the subject." (Charles Champlin, *Los Angeles Times*)

More than occasionally, 1960s and 1970s American movies (e.g.: *The Detec-*

tive, 1968, *Freebie and the Bean*, 1974, *The Eiger Sanction*, 1975, qq.v.) revealed the crass murderer to be gay. This calculated trend was pushed to a new extreme in *Cruising*, based on Gerald Walker's novel (1971). Here, the serial killer not only is homosexual but he targets gays as his victims. Because of *Cruising*'s nasty plotline and its mean-spirited depiction of a narrow segment of the homosexual scene as the whole lifestyle, gay rights activists strongly protested the movie. Not until *Basic Instinct* (1992), q.v., would the gay community again react so strongly against the overt bias of an American-made film.

A rash of brutal stabbing murders occurs in New York City, and the victims are all gay. Police Captain Edelson (Paul Sorvino) asks Steve Burns (Al Pacino), a young heterosexual patrolman, to go undercover to solve the homicides, promising to promote him to detective if he succeeds. Steve's girlfriend, Nancy (Karen Allen), has doubts about Burns accepting such a dangerous task. However, he takes the assignment and moves to Greenwich Village to be closer to the gay scene. There he meets his neighbor, Ted Bailey (Don Scardino), a would-be playwright who supports his dancer lover, Gregory (James Remar). In the following days, Burns studies the gay scene, especially the sado-masochistic subculture. As he hangs out at the bars and cruising areas, he focuses on Skip Lee (Jay Acovone) as a possibile suspect. With the help of backup lawmen, he entraps the man at a hotel one night. Although Skip has a knife in his possession (similar to the one used in the killings), he proves to be innocent.

By now, Burns's personality is becoming attracted to the gay scene and he is becoming absorbed in his new lifestyle. Because of his obsession with the case and his confusion over his new feelings, he is worried about losing Nancy and is almost ready to quit the project. However, additional clues lead him to Stuart Richards (Richard Cox), a man with a severe father complex. He stakes out the man's apart-

ment and puts pressure on the suspect, hoping he will crack. Meanwhile, Steve and Gregory have a violent quarrel. Later, luring Stuart to the park, Burns and Richards scuffle. After capturing the suspect, Richards is booked on suspicion of committing the murders. Having achieved his goals, Burns is promoted to police detective. A short time later, Ted is found dead in his apartment, apparently killed in a lover's argument.

David Denby (*New York* magazine) reported, "*Cruising* is a truly sordid experience, and not because it's about the heavy-leather gay-bar scene and a killer who preys on homosexuals. The movie is sordid and depressing because it's been made without insight or love and from the depths of a soul about the size of a thumbtack. . . .. Here is a movie about sex and the violence that sometime grows out of sex, and the movie has less eroticism than *Star Wars*." To the disgruntled Joseph Gelmis (*Newsday*), "The voyeuristic style of *Cruising* alternates between hitting the audience over the head and between the eyes. . . . The movie insinuates obliquely that the undercover cop realizes he's a latent homosexual when he poses as one. The movie can even be interpreted as implying that the shock of recognition may have transformed the cop into the same kind of killer as the one he was hunting. . . . Why bother to wallow in the perverse stuff and then keep us in the dark about the true character of the one person in the movie we're supposed to care about?"

David Ansen (*Newsweek*) concluded, "No wonder *Cruising* is murky. [Director William] Friedkin shows no sign of having digested or thought through his material." Vincent Canby (*New York Times*), no champion admitted that "The performances are not bad, but they aren't great either. Mr. Pacino, I suspect, knows what his character is up to even when Mr. Friedkin won't acknowledge it."

A great many were surprised when *Cruising* was given an R-rating rather than an expected X. This action led *Variety* to editorialize: "If this is an R, then the only X left is actual hardcore." Heeding the protests generated by the picture in advance of its actual release, United Artists re-edited *Cruising*, removing a portion of the plot's controversial sadism and gore, making the remaining storyline even more ambiguous and confusing.

All the hoopla surrounding *Cruising* helped it gross $6,788,141 in distributors' domestic film rentals. Al Pacino, who had played a cop in the earlier and far superior *Serpico* (1973), would play a New York police detective again in the thriller, *Sea of Love* (1989). William Friedkin had earlier directed *The Boys in the Band* (1970), q.v.

60. Dawn: Portrait of a Teenage Runaway (NBC-TV, September 27, 1976), color, 102 min. Not rated.

Producer, Douglas S. Cramer; associate producer, Wilford Lloyd Baumes; director, Randal Kleiser; teleplay, Dalene Young; art director, James G. Hulsey; set decorator, Rick Simpson; costumes, Tom Welsh, Jo Ann Eaas; makeup, Karl Silvera; music, Fred Karlin; songs: Fred Karlin and Meg Karlin; Joan Jett and Kim Fowley; assistant director, Mitchell Gamson; sound, Bud Alper; special effects, Marlowe Newkirk; camera, Jacques R. Marquette; editor, Carroll Sax.

Cast: Eve Plumb (Dawn Wetherby); Leigh McCloskey (Alexander "Alex" Duncan); Lynn Carlin (Dawn's Mother); William Schallert (Harry); Anne Seymour (Counterwoman); Joan Prather (Susie); Marguerite DeLain (Frankie Lee); Bo Hopkins (Swan); Georg Stanford Brown (Donald Umber); David Knapp (Dr. Roberts); Stephanie Burchfield (Randy); Diane Sommerfield (Joanne); Kaaren Ragland (Melba); Anne Ramsey (Librarian); Paul Bryar (Counterman); Queenie Smith (Old Woman); Paul Sorensen (Police Sergeant); David Terhune (Tom); Brad Trumbull (Man); John Rose (Salesman); Romo Vincent (Fat Man); Sylvia Anderson (Sumi).

American network television in the mid-1970s, hunting for daring topics to dangle in front of viewers, turned to the exploitation of teenagers—especially young women—locked up in reformatories (*Born Innocent*, 1974, *Cage without a Key*, 1975, qq.v.). When that subject lost its novelty, media decision-makers turned to adolescent prostitution for exploitation. *Dawn: Portrait of a Teenage Runaway* was one of the first examples to appear on national American television. Typically, it promised more than it delivered due to the constraints of network censorship. Nevertheless, this made-for-TV movie was pathbreaking. Not only did it offer Eve Plumb (one of TV's "The Brady Bunch") as a street hooker, but it gave her a storyline boyfriend, a bisexual hustler.

In Tucson, Arizona, Dawn Wetherby (Eve Plumb), the fifteen-year old child of an alcoholic single mother (Lynn Carlin) is neglected at home (which includes a younger brother) and alienated at school. To assert herself, she runs off to Hollywood, California. Once there, her adolescent dreams of making a fresh start are soon shattered. She cannot find honest work, because she is underage and lacks needed work papers. Life on the scuzzy streets proves scary and depressing. Eventually, she turns to the "easy" life on the Sunset Strip; she becomes a streetwalker. Later, advised by another prostitute (Marguerite DeLain) that she needs a protector, she goes to work for a pimp, Swan (Bo Hopkins). True to type, he is a baffling mixture of sweetness and viciousness.

Dawn's life continues downhill. The only cheerful thing that happens is meeting Alexander "Alex" Duncan (Leigh McCloskey). He is also a teenage runaway (from Oklahoma), one who has drifted into gay/straight hustling to survive. Almost immediately, Dawn and Alex are drawn to one another. However, the tension of coping with their lurid lifestyles takes it toll, despite the helpful efforts of social worker Donald Umber (Georg Stanford Brown). Eventually, Alex confronts the sinister Swan over Dawn's future. The encounter nearly costs the young man his life.

Kay Gardella (*New York Daily News*) rated the film: "In all its seedy reality . . .

[the telefilm] reflects what these young runaways go through." Gardella noted, " . . . [The] film . . . will carry the usual advisory saying it's intended for 'mature audiences.' Unfortunately, the only people that stand to benefit by it are gullible teenagers." Morna Murphy (*Hollywood Reporter*) found faults, noting that the "Sentimentalization of the story makes it basically unconvincing. . . . Randal Kleiser allows his actors to spill out their emotions even when their motivations are patently false."

Despite critics' mixed reactions, the TV movie gained high ratings and producer Douglas S. Cramer put a sequel into production almost immediately. NBC-TV's *Alexander: The Other Side of Dawn* (May 16, 1977), q.v., would focus primarily on young adult Alex (Leigh McCloskey) as he deals with life in the seamy part of Hollywood. Eve Plumb, in an almost supporting part, would repeat her characterization of Dawn Wetherby in the sequel.

61. Deathtrap (Warner Bros., 1982), color, 116 min. PG-rated.

Executive producer, Jay Presson Allen; producer, Burtt Harris; associate producer, Alfred de Liagre Jr.; director, Sidney Lumet; based on the play by Ira Levin; screenplay, Allen; production designer, Tony Walton; art director, Edward Pisoni; set decorator, George DeTitta Sr.; costumes, Walton; makeup, Joe Cranzano, Tony Lloyd; music, Johnny Mandel; assistant directors, Harris, Mark McGann; sound, James Sabat; special visual effects, Bran Ferren; camera, Andrzej Bartkowiak; editor, John J. Fitzstephens.

Cast: Michael Caine (Sidney Bruhl); Christopher Reeve (Clifford Anderson); Dyan Cannon (Myra Bruhl); Irene Worth (Helga Ten Dorp); Henry Jones (Porter Milgrim); Joe Silver (Seymour Starger); Tony DiBenedetto (Burt, the Bartender); Al LeBreton (Handsome Actor); Reverend Francis B. Creamer Jr. (Minister); Stewart Klein, Jeffrey Lyons, Joel Siegel (Themselves); Jenny Lumet (Stage Newsboy); Jayne Heller (Stage Actress); George Peck, Perry Rosen (Stage Actors).

The chief gimmick of *Deathtrap*, based on Ira Levin's hit Broadway production

(1978), is that it is a play within a play within a play. The danger of such a contrivance is that, in retrospect, some viewers will react adversely to having been manipulated and duped by the experience. On the other hand, the virtue of such a gimmick is its potential prompting of more curious individuals to rescreen the film to understand how the filmmakers built the diverting layers of illusions. A secondary surprise of *Deathtrap* is the storyline revelation that the two quite masculine lead characters—one of whom is married—are gay lovers. Had this premise dealing with homosexuality been used a decade earlier in a mainstream Hollywood film, it would have caused a far greater stir, or not been able to be filmed at all.

Glib Sidney Bruhl (Michael Caine) is acclaimed as America's foremost whodunit playwright; he wrote *The Murder Game*, the longest running thriller in Broadway's history. However, now he is convinced he is washed up, having suffered his fourth consecutive Broadway flop. On the other hand, his supportive, well-to-do-wife, Myra (Dyan Cannon) refuses to take his creative dry streak seriously. Meanwhile, Sidney invites one of his former students, Clifford Anderson (Christopher Reeve), to their East Hampton, Long Island house. Bruhl halfseriously admits that his plan is to steal Anderson's just-finished mystery play, and to present it to producers as his own. Clifford arrives and Sidney kills him, burying the corpse in the garden. Later that night, a blood-soaked Anderson reappears, scuffling with Sidney and frightening Myra—who has a bad heart—to death. Then, it unfolds that the two men are actually lovers and that they have plotted together to kill Bruhl's spouse.

Clifford moves into the house, ostensibly as Sidney's secretary. Before long, Bruhl discovers that the opportunistic Anderson (who has a prison record from youthful follies) is writing a new play, *Deathtrap*, a barely disguised version of

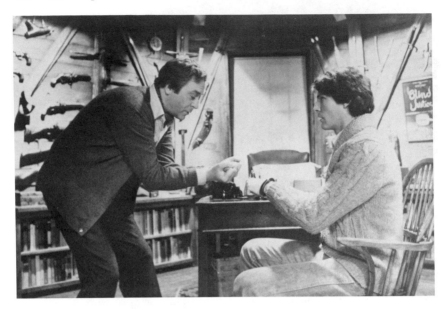

Michael Caine and Christopher Reeve in *Deathtrap* (1982).

how Myra really died. Initially angered, Sidney eventually agrees to collaborate with Clifford on completing the drama. However, in actuality he is plotting to kill Clifford as they write the second act. Not to be outdone, the wily Anderson gains the upper hand. Then, having absorbed all the tricks of Bruhl's writing craft, he smugly prepares to leave. Meanwhile, Sidney, who had been handcuffed with props/decorations in the house, gets free and wounds Anderson with a nearby crossbow. At this juncture, psychic Helga Ten Dorp (Irene Worth), a neighbor, returns to the house, having a premonition of brewing trouble. The frustrated Bruhl is just about to kill her when Anderson grabs his leg. The scene shifts to a stage, as two performers struggle to the death. After a curtain call, Helga Ten Dorp, the author of *Deathtrap*, revels in having a Broadway hit show.

Janet Maslin (*New York Times*) affirmed that "the cast of *Deathtrap* meets the demands of the material with delightful en-

thusiasm and ease. . . ." David Ansen (*Newsweek*) complimented, *"Deathtrap* still contains its fair share of claptrap, but it's become a dandy little movie, faithful to Levin's flamboyant theatricality yet artfully transcribed by a cinematic style that gives the illusion of reality." Judith Crist (*Saturday Review*) observed, "Beyond the plot, the major satisfaction is in seeing [Christopher] Reeve leave Clark Kent and Superman far behind and give us a multi-faceted and freshly fascinating character. He, Caine, and Lumet keep our eyes on the action and make it easy to avoid the plot holes." Andrew Sarris (*Village Voice*) was less charmed, "Lumet neither ruins *Deathtrap*, nor transcends it. He just lets it sit there amid his very meagre and earthbound mise-en-scene. . . ." John Pym (British *Monthly Film Bulletin*) granted the professionalism of the piece, but emphasized, "And yet, and yet. . . .*Death-trap* is a shameless concoction. . . . ."

Because *Deathtrap* is geared as a theatrical puzzle, the focus is on a succession of bon mots with the polished cast smoothly delivering glib remarks. As such, depth of characterization is not possible, which means that the romantic relationship between Sidney and Clifford never gets beyond an artificial level (even when they briefly embrace). Unsurprisingly, Michael Caine gives a marvelously facile performance. While Christopher Reeve is stiffly competent as the sociopath, it is Dyan Cannon who provides a welcome light note as the excitable, shrill victim. The one sour note of the casting is the hammy interpretation of the heavily-accented Scandinavian psychic by veteran actress Irene Worth. Michael Caine had previously played a bisexual in *California Suite* (1978), q.v., while Christopher Reeve would play a homosexual pedophile in *A Bump in the Night* (1991), q.v. Ira Levin had earlier authored the book and play which provided the basis for *Compulsion* (1959), q.v.

The artful *Deathtrap* grossed $9 million in distributors' domestic film rentals.

62. **Deathwatch** (Beverly Pictures, 1966), 88 min. Not rated.

Producers, Leonard Nimoy, Vic Morrow; director, Morrow; based on the play *Haute Surveillance* by Jean Genet; screenplay, Barbara Turner, Morrow; art director, James G. Frieburger; music, Gerald Fried; camera, Vilis Lapenieks; supervising editor, Irving Lerner; editor, Verna Fields.

Cast: Leonard Nimoy (Jules LaFranc); Michael Forest (Greeneyes); Paul Mazursky (Maurice); Gavin MacLeod (Emil); Robert Ellenstein (Guard).

Actor Vic Morrow and his wife, Barbara Turner adapted this wordy, confining drama, which Morrow directed. It was produced by Morrow and co-star Leonard Nimoy, the latter having gained great fame that year as Mr. Spock on TV's "Star Trek." As a movie, *Deathwatch* was an arty, black-and-white feature which had only limited theatrical release. It was based on the 1949 play by French writer Jean Genet, a drama which was presented on Broadway in 1958 in a translated version. The picture was produced on a tight budget ($120,000), with the majority of the scenes set in a solitary jail cell. It was one of (if not) the first non-pornographic American features to gear its promotional campaign to a gay audience.

Petty thief Jules LeFranc (Leonard Nimoy) finds himself sharing a cell in a French prison with Greeneyes (Michael Forest). The latter is an infamous killer soon to die on the guillotine. LeFranc, who has always regarded himself as an inferior outsider, takes pleasure in sharing space with such a notorious figure. The situation changes when Maurice (Paul Mazursky), a homosexual prisoner, is reassigned to the cell. Very soon he stirs up LeFranc's envy by catering in every possible way to the illiterate Greeneyes. Before long, Jules and Maurice are sharp competitors, fighting for Greeneyes's approval. Finally, to win his idol's favor, LeFranc chokes Maurice to death. However, this fails to gain Greeneyes's admiration because the strangulation was a calculated willful act rather than one of spontaneous passion. The scorned LeFranc is once more an outsider.

Howard Thompson (*New York Times*) decided that "this prison drama . . . is not so hot, not even with some ripe four-letter words. . . . This is a slow, static, talky picture. . . . Only in the climatic murder does *Deathwatch* become simple, moving and real. Shorn of homosexual coils, it means absolutely nothing." Admitting the limitations of this specialized movie, especially because "There is little action," the trade paper praised the performers, judging Nimoy "excellent as the 'outsider' not quite accepted by prison society, even though he has withstood extreme tortures in solitary confinement. Forest and Mazursky both give fine performances in respective parts as the king of the prison inmates and a weak homosexual."

63. **Desert Hearts** (Samuel Goldwyn Co., 1985), color, 96 min. R-rated.

Producer, Donna Deitch; co-producer, Cami Taylor; associate producer, Carol Jefferies; di-

63. Desert Hearts [110]

rector, Deitch; based on the novel *Desert of the Heart* by Jane Rule; screenplay, Natalie Cooper; production designer, Jeannine Oppewall; art director, David Brisbin; set decorator, Rosemary Brandenburg; costumes, Linda Bass; makeup, Richard Arrington; music supervisors, Terri Fricon, Gay Jones; assistant directors, George Perkins, Whitney Hunter; sound, Austin Kinney; camera, Robert Elswitt; editor, Robert Estrin.

Cast: Helen Shaver (Vivian Bell); Patricia Charbonneau (Cay Rivvers); Audra Lindley (Frances Parker); Andra Akers (Silver [Sylvia]); Gwen Welles (Gwen); Dean Butler (Darell); James Staley (Art Warner); Katie La Bourdette (Lucille; Alex McArthur (Walter Parker); Tyler Tyhurst (Buck Ucker); Denise Crosby (Pat); Antony Ponzini (Joe Lorenzo); Brenda Beck (Joyce); Sam Minsky (Best Man); Patricia Frazier (Change Girl); Sheila Balter (Raodside Waitress); Tom Martin (Red Cap); Joan Mankin (Casino Waitress); Frank Murtha (Minister); Dave Roberts (Lon); Bob Blankman (Croupier); Ron Fisher (Drunk Gambler); Gene Skaug (Announcer); Donna Deitch (Hungarian Gambler).

"It's probably obligatory to say that *Desert Hearts* isn't just a lesbian heartthrob movie, but a truly universal film of yearning and romance and the wish to belong. Sure, all true, but no big deal. What's really amazing is that it is a lesbian heart-throb movie." (Ruby Rich, *Village Voice*)

If the intimate, independently-filmed *Lianna* (1983), q.v., directed by a male (John Sayles) caused a mild sensation for its explicit view of the lesbian lifestyle, then the female-directed, R-rated *Desert Hearts* created more controversy, with its uncompromisingly frank lovemaking scene between the two lead actresses.

In 1959, 35-year-old Vivian Bell (Helen Shaver), an English literature professor at Columbia University, comes to Reno, Nevada to process her divorce. The haughty, inhibited woman stays at the dude/divorce ranch operated by Frances Parker (Audra Lindley). There she is introduced to Frances's son, Walter (Alex McArthur), and Frances's stepdaughter, the unpretentious, buoyant Cay Rivvers (Patricia Charbon-

neau). The latter is a sculptress who lives in a guest cottage on the spread and works at a casino in town with her pal, Silver Dale (Andra Akers), a one-time singer now a blackjack dealer. At the casino, Cay rebuffs the sexual advances of her boss, Darrell (Dean Butler), while pursuing a relationship with a co-worker, Gwen (Gwen Welles).

While the insecure Vivian becomes friends with Cay and Gwen and shares pleasantries with the lonely Walter, the very direct Frances grows increasingly concerned that her family is splitting apart. After an engagement party for Silver and her boyfriend (Antony Ponzini), Cay drives Vivian to a secluded, nearby lake. There she kisses her new friend, but the latter rebuffs her advances. Because of the gossip generated by Cay and Vivian leaving the party together, Frances demands that Vivian leave the ranch. Bothered by her stepmother's actions, Cay follows Vivian to the motel where she has moved. There the two women make love, argue and reconcile. Afterwards, Cay and Frances try to breach their barriers, with Cay explaining the relevance of her connection with Vivian. With her divorce finalized, Vivian leaves for New York. She convinces Cay to join her aboard the train, hoping that before they reach the next station, she can convince the younger woman to remain with her.

Rex Reed (*New York Post*) reported that *Desert Hearts* "looks at lesbians in Reno with clear, focused, unsentimental eyes. . . . [It's] a far cry from the anguished, suicidal case studies of lesbians the screen has offered in the past. It's interesting, offbeat, made with great sincerity, and refreshingly honest. . . ." Michael Musto (*Saturday Review*) congratulated the movie because it "confronts its lesbian theme like few films before it, with unflinching integrity, not dark lighting and fadeouts." However, Musto noted, the feature "doesn't always make its integrity translate into gripping drama." Ruby Rich (*Village Voice*) reported, "Deitch has transformed the original prose into a visually impressive movie, one that shifts smoothly between dreamy western landscapes and understated period settings. . . . *Desert Hearts* isn't perfect. Where the script stays from one-liners, it frequently falters. . . . But the film is immensely aided by some terrific performances in the supporting roles.

Adam Mars-Jones (*New Statesman*) found a structural flaw in *Desert Hearts*: "There are liable to be at least four areas of painful change for a woman who in maturity ceases to define herself as heterosexual—all of them judiciously dramatised in John Sayles's admirable film *Lianna* (1983) [q.v.]. Her financial standing may suffer if she has been dependent on a man; her social links with assumed friends will be tested; if she has children, her access to them may be restricted; and her expectations of what a sexual relationship can give her are likely to need recasting. . . . None of these conflicts affect Vivian in *Desert Hearts*. . . . [Her] transition has been smoothed for her." David Denby (*New York*) noted that "the sex, when it finally arrives, has some real heat. . . . The only other good thing in the movie is the performance of veteran Audra Lindley. . . . *Desert Hearts* is one of the new independent films that's not about much of anything *but* homosexuality. . . ." On the other hand, Sheila Benson (*Los Angeles Times*) found the movie's frank lovemaking scene "forced" and judged the picture to be "a taut, fatally careful movie with no looseness—and no abandon—to it and no feeling for detail that would let these characters really live."

Based on Jane Rule's 1964 novel, it was a conscious decision to retain *Desert Hearts*' period setting of 1959, because, according to filmmaker Donna Deitch, "no one goes to Reno to get a divorce anymore. More importantly, it would have been futile with this book; the story takes place in a particular time and a particular place." It took Deitch over two years to raise the needed $850,000 to produce this project, which proved to be a mild moneymaker.

64. The Detective (Twentieth Century-Fox, 1968), color, 114 min. Not rated.

Producer, Aaron Rosenberg; director, Gordon Douglas; based on the novel by Roderick Thorp; screenplay, Abby Mann; art directors, Jack Martin Smith, William Creber; set decorators, Walter M. Scott, Jerry Wunderlich; costume designer, Moss Mabry; makeup, Dan Striepeke; Mr. Sinatra's makeup, Layne Britton; music, Jerry Goldsmith; assistant director, Richard Lang; sound, Harry M. Lindgren, David Dockendorf; special camera effects, L. B. Abbott, Art Cruickshank; camera, Joseph Biroc; editor, Robert Simpson.

Cast: Frank Sinatra (Detective Joe Leland); Lee Remick (Karen Leland); Jacqueline Bisset (Norma MacIver); Ralph Meeker (Lieutenant Curran); Jack Klugman (Dave Schoenstein); Horace McMahon (Farrell); Lloyd Bochner (Dr. Wendell Roberts); William Windom (Colin MacIver); Tony Musante (Felix Tesla); Al Freeman Jr. (Robbie Loughren); Robert Duvall (Nestor); Pat Henry (Mercidis); Patrick McVey (Tanner); Dixie Marquis (Carol Linjack); Sugar Ray Robinson (Kelly); Renee Taylor (Rachel Schoenstein); James Inman (Teddy Leikman); Tom Atkins (Harmon); James Dukas (Medical Examiner); Sharon Henesy (Sharon); Jan Farrand (Karen's Friend at the Theatre); Marion Brash (Prostitute); Earl Montgomery (Desk Clerk); Peg Murray (Girl at Party); Frank Reiter (Tough Homosexual); Peter York (Decent Boy); Mark Dawson (Desk Sergeant); Jose Rodriguez (Boy in Police Station); Tom Gorman (Prison Priest); Lou Nelson (Procurer); Richard Krisher (Matt Henderson); Jilly Rizzo (Bartender); Arnold Soboloff, George Plimpton, Phil Sterling, Don Fellows, Paul Larson, Ted Beniades (Reporters).

"Perhaps the nicest thing that can be said about *The Detective* is that it is a film of transition. It deals with subject matter available to the new Hollywood in a style that reflects the old." (Vincent Canby, *New York Times*)

In the late 1960s, hot-tempered, opinionated Frank Sinatra, who happened to be a decent actor and an extraordinary singer, made a trio of (police) detective pictures. All three were directed by Gor-

64. The Detective

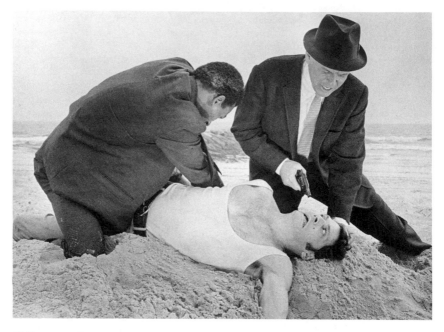

Al Freeman Jr., Tony Musante and Frank Sinatra in *The Detective* (1968).

don Douglas for Twentieth Century-Fox release: *Tony Rome* (1967), q.v., *Lady in Cement* (1968) and *The Detective*. These action entries were pseudo-tough, quasi-topical, and filled, expectedly, with macho wisecracks, shapely actresses, off-screen pals of the swinging star, and a blatant undercurrent of homophobia. In *The Detective*, based on Roderick Thorp's novel (1966) which had a midwestern setting, Sinatra had two highly exploitable topics to guarantee the picture's success: police corruption and homosexuality.

The naked body of homosexual Teddy Leikman (James Inman), the scion of a department store magnate, is found in his Manhattan apartment. Cynical New York police detective Joe Leland (Frank Sinatra) is assigned the case. More than one of Joe's superiors suggests that a hasty wrap-up of the high-profile case will hasten Leland's department promotion. The trail leads the tough law enforcer to Leik-

man's mentally unstable ex-roommate, Felix Tesla (Tony Musante). With the right prompting and pressure, the paranoid beach bum admits hysterically to having committed the crime. As a result, Tesla is sentenced to die in the electric chair. Leland is among those who attend the execution, and the harrowing experience bothers the veteran cop. Away from work, Leland is unable to repair his marriage with his libidinous wife Karen (Lee Remick).

At a later occasion, wealthy widow Norma MacIver (Jacqueline Bisset) insists to Joe that her husband, Colin (William Windom), did not accidentally fall from the roof of a racetrack grandstand. Workaholic Leland reopens the case and discovers a department conspiracy to hush up the evidence, especially by Lieutenant Curran (Ralph Meeker). When Joe questions his co-workers too deeply on the subject, he is almost murdered. Delving further, he uncovers that a crooked land development group called "Rainbow" includes many prominent city officials on the Borough Planning Commission. While investigating records at the office of MacIver's psychiatrist/friend, Dr. Wendell Roberts (Lloyd Bochner), Joe finds a tape which discloses the details of Rainbow. It also establishes that MacIver, a closeted gay, had killed Leikman and then destroyed himself. Fully realizing the repercussions ahead, Joe determines to expose the municipal corruption. He resigns from the New York police department, admitting, "I spent twenty years of my life living for the department. Now I'm going to start living for myself. It's not too easy to rub out all those years in your life."

Vincent Canby (*New York Times*) heavily criticized the feature which "haphazardly, even arrogantly, mixes the real and the fake. Although it makes some valid comments about contemporary society, it exploits its lurid subject matter in a showoffy, heavy-handed way designed as much to tease as to teach compassion. . . . Mr. Sinatra . . . has the waxy, blank look of a movie star as he moves through grimly authentic big city settings. The young muscle man [Tony Musante] from whom Mr. Sinatra wheedles the murder confession is appropriately savage and simpering. Then he opens his mouth in a cry of anguish and we see, in a close-up, all the dental work the actor had done so as to be presentable in pictures." Jan Dawson (British *Monthly Film Bulletin*) had mixed feelings about this thriller: "though the dialogue takes advantage of Hollywood's liberalised censorship code (the detective can comment on semen stains on the sheets and refuse to 'lick ass'), the possible realism is further vitiated by the physical appearance of the numerous homosexuals, who all look as if they had strayed on to the set from the chorus of *West Side Story*."

Within *The Detective*, veteran detective Joe Leland is shown to be a liberal with surface sympathy for the lower classes, and even for the hookers who make a public nuisance of themselves on the streets ("They've got to make a living too," he cracks.) In comparison to his bigoted confreres, especially policeman Nestor (Robert Duvall) who enjoys bashing "queers," Joe is "tolerant" of alternative lifestyles. However, in actuality, he goes along with demeaning, illegal police sweeps of gay haunts (bars, back alleys, etc.) in which homosexuals are randomly rounded up (constitutional civil rights to one side) in the search for the killer. When browbeating the unhinged "fruit" Tesla into confessing, the actually narrow-minded Leland looks like he has just smelled manure, disdaining to associate, even on a professional level, with such garbage. By Leland's standards, the suspect is trash, not just because he may have committed the killing, but because he is a faggot. This philosophy is substantiated later in the script of *The Detective* when MacIver's confesses to the murder Tesla died for, stating "I felt more guilty about being a homosexual than a murderer. . . ."

The Detective was shot partially on location around the boroughs of New York City and grossed $6.5 million in distributors' domestic film rentals. It received a publicity boost when Sinatra's then-wife, Mia Farrow, dropped out of the cast and was replaced by Jacqueline Bisset. Moreover, the movie was scorned by gay rights groups protesting the exploitive depiction of the picture's homosexual characters. *The Detective* was among the first of Hollywood's feature films to show heterosexual filmgoers where gays supposedly spent their time (i.e., bars, back alleys, etc.), a negative representation that was far-fetched and stereotypical.

65. A Different Story (Avco Embassy, 1978), color, 106 min. R-rated.

Executive producer, Michael F. Leone; producer, Alan Belkin; associate producers, James Freiburger, Joy Sheldon Davis; director, Paul Aaron; screenplay, Henry Olek; set decorator, Lee Poll; costumes, Robert Demora, Agnes Lyon; makeup, Ron Walters; music, David

Frank; song, Bob Wahler; assistant directors, Erwin Stoff, Donald Gold; sound, William Teague, Thomas Dodington; camera, Philip Lathrop; second unit camera, Michael Werk; editor, Lynn McCallon.

Cast: Perry King (Albert); Meg Foster (Stella); Valerie Curtin (Phyllis); Peter Donat (Sills); Richard Bull (Mr. Cooke); Barbara Collentine (Mrs. Cooke); Guerin Barry (Ned); Doug Higgins (Roger); Lisa James (Chris); Eugene Butler (Sam); Linda Carpenter (Chastity); Allan Hunt (Richard I); Burke Byrnes (Richard II); Eddie C. Dyer (Bernie); Richard Altman (Phyllis's Neighbor); Richard Seff (Justice of the Peace); George Skaff (Mr. Hashmoni); Sid Conrad (Salesman); Trent Dolan, Dan Mahar (Deputies); Ted Richards III (Justin); Clarke Gordon (Taylor); Gypsi DeYoung (Mrs. Taylor); Marion Perkins (Receptionist); Florence Di Re (Fitter); Gay Kleimenhapen (Patternmaker); Marie Denn (Coordinator); Kathryn Jackson (Nurse): Hatsuo Uda, Peter Furuta (Businessmen); Jennifer Dumas (Model); Eric Helland (Doorman); Philip Levien (Chicken Man); Stephen Nichols (Man at Bath); Derek Flint (Little Albert #1); Joshua Hansen (Little Albert #2).

For its time, this was an extremely daring movie for Hollywood to produce, even when mid-stream, the movie caves in to anti-gay bias. It bold subject matter, even badly handled, led *After Dark* magazine to overstate, "A breakthrough movie in every sense."

In Los Angeles, Albert (Perry King), a handsome young Belgian, is the lover and chauffeur of middle-aged Sills (Peter Donat), a famous orchestral conductor. When Sills tires of Albert and finds a new, younger boyfriend, the adrift Albert moves into an empty house, where he is discovered one day by real estate agent, Stella (Meg Foster). Learning of his plight (his broken relationship, his lack of work papers), she invites him to stay the night at her place. Albert is surprised to find out later that she is also gay and that she too is dealing with an ex-romance, the neurotic Phyllis (Valerie Curtin). (It is also established that each of them has sampled heterosexual sex and found it wanting.) It is decided that Albert can remain at

Stella's, the agreement being he will do the household chores while she continues to be the aggressive business person.

Time passes. When immigration authorities track down Albert for not having a proper passport, Stella marries him so he can remain in the country. Their platonic relationship continues happily until one night, while celebrating his birthday, they get drunk and make love. They realize they have fallen in love romantically, and together they cope with Stella's break from the suicidal Phyllis. When Stella becomes pregnant, Albert finds a responsible job in a clothing design firm. Stella gives birth to a baby boy and quits her firm to care for their child. Meanwhile, Albert's career escalates, but simultaneously. because he has become a workaholic. their relationship weakens. One night, Stella drops by Albert's office and discovers him making love to a female model. This shock causes her to leave him. Later, the apologetic Albert woos her back.

Janet Maslin (*New York Times*) wrote of this PG-rated entry: "The movie's use of their homosexuality is indeed exploitative, insensitive, and offensive in a variety of ways. Even worse, it is unconvincing. . . . Mr. King is much worse than the movie, which is no mean accomplishment. Miss Foster is much better, with an aggressive vitality that lets her upstage Mr. King at every turn. . . . the film's notion of reversing sex roles is not without comic potential [See *Turnabout*, 1940]. But there's something quite ugly about its manner of accepting sexual stereotypes in the first place, just for the sake of shuffling them around." For *Variety*, "*A Different Story* certainly is. . . . a first-class production whose only—but serious—flaw is a Henry Olek script that begins with brilliant cleverness but dissolves by fade-out into formula banality. . . . The abrupt plot change [midway]—which abandons everything that has come earlier, except for Curtin's freak-out stereotype of the neurotic and suicidal homosexual ex-lover—dissipates most of the earlier appeal of the story. One would think that both Foster and King are 'cured' or 'born again.' "

With its "novel twist being homosexuality" (*TV Guide*) it was a foregone conclusion in 1978 that such a theatrical feature would have limited audience appeal, despite its titillation value. One of its more reprehensible moments occurs when Stella catches Albert with someone in his executive office shower. As she opens the shower door, both Stella and the viewer are teased into believing from the glimpses of bare buttocks in the steamy water that the other party is a man— Albert has "slipped"! Another cheap shot in *A Different Story* occurs in the opening scenes where Albert has assumed the homemaker's duties. A door-to-door salesman stops Stella as she leaves the house for the office. The fuller brush seller inquires, "Are you the lady of the house?" An amused Stella refers him to a nonplussed Albert.

66. Distortions (Cori Films, 1987), color, 96 min. PG-rated.

Executive producer, Marie Hoy; coproducer, Daniel Kuhn; associate producer, Richard Bennett Warsk; director, Armand Mastroianna; screenplay, John Goff; technical supervisor, Gary Graver; camera, John Dirlam; editor, Jack Turner.

Cast: Olivia Hussey (Amy); Piper Laurie (Aunt Margot); Steve Railsback (Scott); Rita Gam (Mildred); June Chadwick (Kelly); with: Terence Knox, Edward Albert, Tom J. Castronova, Leon Smith.

This *Gaslight*-style ripoff is one of those minor thrillers that went directly to home video release, buoyed solely by an intriguing cast, including the always fascinating Piper Laurie. To spice the movie's ambiance, several of the characters display lesbian leanings. The opening sequence reveals a young man being murdered—seemingly in an argument with his gay lover—and his car then being pushed over a cliff.

After the death of her husband (Edward Albert), distraught Amy (Olivia Hussey) is invited by her Aunt Margot (Piper Laurie), who has more than a casual interest in her sexually, to stay at her house. Thanks to the scheming Margot who dopes her charge with drugs and contrives a variety of spectre-like visions, Amy is nearly driven mad. She is convinced that her husband is not dead, but that he has come back to haunt her. As she fights to retain her sanity, she relies increasingly on Scott (Steve Railsback), a sympathetic law man.

Variety panned: "About every threadbare and overworn cliche in the suspense genre has been written into this supremely predictable and humdrum drama. . . ." *The Phantom's Ultimate Video Guide* (1989) labeled it "competent but unexciting."

67. Doctors' Wives (Columbia, 1971), color, 102 min. R-rated.

Producer, M. J. Frankovich; director, George Schaefer; based on the novel by Frank G. Slaughter; screenplay, Daniel Taradash; production designer, Lyle R. Wheeler; set decorator, Marvin March; costumes, Moss Mabry; makeup, Frank Prehoda; music, Elmer Bernstein; song, Bernstein, Alan and Marilyn Bergman; assistant director, Philip L. Parslow; sound, Les Fresholtz, Arthur Piantadosi; camera, Charles B. Lang; editor, Carl Kress.

Cast: Dyan Cannon (Lorrie Dellman); Richard Crenna (Dr. Pete Brennan); Gene Hackman (Dr. Dave Randolph); Carroll O'Connor (Dr. Joe Gray); Rachel Roberts (Della Randolph); Janice Rule (Amy Brennan); Diana Sands (Helen Straughn); Cara Williams (Maggie Gray); Richard Anderson (District Attorney Douglas); Ralph Bellamy (Jake Porter); John Colicos (Dr. Mort Dellman); George Gaynes (Paul McGill); Marian McCargo (Elaine McGill); Scott Brady (Sergeant Malloy); Anthony Costello (Mike Traynor); Kristina Holland (Sybil Carter); Mark Jenkins (Lew Saunders); Vincent Van Lynn (Barney Harris); Ernie Barnes (Dr. Penfield); Paul Marin (Dr. Deemster); William Bramley (Dr. Hagstrom); John Loremer (Elderly Doctor).

With such an engaging cast, it is a pity that this sleazy vehicle, based on a trashy

Frank Slaughter novel was so dull. Dyan Cannon, at her box-office peak, was the nominal star of this claptrap. However, her flashy role as a sex-hungry bitch lasted for a brief reel and then poof, like the rest of the film, she evaporated. As an added attraction for voyeuristic filmgoers, *Doctors' Wives* boasted a character with a lesbian past.

At the card table at a private party, five doctors debate the finances of their private Western Clinic. Meanwhile, their wives avidly discuss life and sex. Lorrie Dellman (Dyan Cannon), scoffs at her friends' naivete, insisting that she has or will sleep with each of their spouses as part of her personal survey on lovemaking techniques. Soon thereafter, randy Lorrie is murdered by her jealous brain surgeon husband, Mort (John Colicos), who catches her having sex with her boyfriend-of-the moment. The other wives rush to the local hospital, desperate to know which one of their husbands was shot. It proves to be Paul McGill (George Gaynes), which his wife Elaine (Marian McCargo) finds ironic as she has begun a relationship with Mike Traynor (Anthony Costello), a hard-edged young intern.

Shocked by the scandal, the other couples (re)examine their domestic relationships. Dave Randolph (Gene Hackman) is told by his wife Della (Rachel Roberts) that she had a gay experience in her past; he forgives her. Urologist Joe Gray (Carroll O'Connor) worried about his ex-wife's serious drinking habit, pays a timely visit to her and saves her from drowning herself; they reconcile. Amy Brennan (Janice Rule), knowing of Pete Brennan's (Richard Crenna) illicit romance with black nurse Helen Straughn (Diana Sands), turns to drugs, hoping it will make her uninhibited enough to please him in bed. Meanwhile, Helen's young son is discovered to have an unusual brain disorder. Pete convinces the district attorney (Richard Anderson) to release Mort long enough to operate. Before he will perform the surgery, Mort de-

mands money from the others and assistance in escaping. Brennan accedes for the child's sake, and Mort saves the youngster. However, he is stopped from making a get-away by Jake Porter (Ralph Bellamy), Lorrie's revenge-seeking father, who shoots him dead. Now Pete must decide whether to remain with Amy or leave with Helen.

Roger Greenspun (*New York Times*), admitting the schlock nature of *Doctors' Wives*, decided: "[director George Schaefer] shepherds his cast through what can only have been for them sustained embarrassment and manages almost too successfully to minimize the nonsense in a cinema the first principle of which is the shock cut between operating room and bedroom." *Variety* agreed that the lackluster film had "some technically excellent suburban nouveau riche physical value appropriate to the plot" but that "Daniel Taradash's script is choppy, diffused and laugh-provoking at the wrong places, while George Schaefer's direction is lethargic. . . ." Tom Milne (British *Monthly Film Bulletin*) dismissed the offering: "Despite earnest stabs at *art nouveau* in the dialogue ('An orgasm a day keeps the doctor away') and the hospital scenes (real life operations sparing no grisly detail), this is traditional Hollywood at its worst."

For all its faults, one of the movie's sturdier moments, despite its voyeuristic intent, occurs when Della confesses her indiscretion three years ago. According to Della, it occured one night while Dave was out of town, when Lorrie removed a cinder from Della's eye:

"She said 'Go to the bedroom and lie down and I'll get it out.' . . . The way she touched me. It was a hot night. I wore a filmy blouse and no bra. . . . I remember she said, 'Some people are stage struck, some are clothes struck. I'm sex struck. . . .' Lying there in the bed I told her to stop. She said I was chicken. She kept stroking my face. It seemed so natural, not at all ugly. That crazy little half-slip she had on. It had cherubs on it. . . . I wanted her to touch me, just then . . . never after, even though she tried. Just once, once only. That night. . . . I hated her. Hated her every moment since. She touched my shoulder with her tongue. . . . She touched me so gently along my leg. Kissed me. It was wonderful to be . . . to be. . . ."

At that juncture, Dave, hurt and angry, slaps her hard. Then, shocked by the strong admission/reaction, they hug and reconcile. End of scene. Thanks to the restraint of Rachel Roberts and Gene Hackman, the sequence transcends its lewd purpose.

68. Dog Day Afternoon (Warner Bros., 1975), color, 130 min. R-rated.

Producers, Martin Bregman, Martin Elfand; associate producer, Robert Greenhut; director, Sidney Lumet; based on the magazine article by P. F. Kluge, Thomas Moore; screenplay, Frank Pierson; production designer, Charles Bailey; art director, Doug Higgins; set decorator, Robert Drumheller; costumes, Anna Hill Johnstone; assistant directors, Burtt Harris, Alan Hopkins; sound, James Sabata; camera, Victor J. Kemper; editor, Dede Allen.

Cast: Al Pacino (Sonny Wortzik); John Cazale (Sal); Charles Durning (Detective Sergeant Moretti) Chris Sarandon (Leon); Sully Boyar (Mulvaney); Penny Allen (Sylvia); James Broderick (Sheldon); Carol Kane (Jenny); Beulah Garrick (Margaret); Sandra Kazan (Deborah); Marcia Jean Kurtz (Miriam); Amy Levitt (Maria); John Marriott (Howard); Estelle Omens (Edna); Gary Springer (Stevie); Lance Henriksen (Murphy); Judith Malina (Vi); Dominic Chianese (Vi's Husband); Marcia Haufrecht (Vi's Friend); Susan Peretz (Angie Wortzik); Floyd Levine (Phone Cop); Carmine Foresta (Carmine); Thomas Murphy (Policeman with Angie); William Bogert (TV Studio Anchorman); Ron Cummins (TV Reporter); Jay Gerber (Sam); Philip Charles Mackenzie (Doctor); Chu Chu Malave (Maria's Boy Friend); Lionel Pina (Pizza Boy); Dick Williams (Limo Driver).

Were it not based on a real-life case, this bizarre study of a foiled robbery would be hard to believe. However, it is so resourcefully directed by Sidney Lumet and buoyed by its cast—especially Al Pacino and the actors playing the celebrity-status-seeking bank workers—that the lengthy movie is a great treat.

On August 22, 1972, a very hot day, a trio of men step into a branch of the First Brooklyn Savings Bank, waving firearms at manager Mullvaney (Sully Boyar) and his hysterical staff. The youngest of the robbers, Stevie (Gary Springer), runs off in a panic, leaving perplexed Sonny Wortzik (Al Pacino) and sad-sack Sal (John Cazale) to complete the heist. As the distracted leader, Sonny is knowledgeable about bank procedures, but is frustrated to discover that the bulk of the bank's inventory for the day has been already removed to the central warehouse vault. When he sets fire to the records of on-hand cash, the smoke pouring through the building's ventilator system alerts the police. Soon thereafter, Sonny receives a call at the bank from New York detective Sergeant Eugene Moretti (Charles Durning), who announces that the bank is surrounded by armed cops. Adding to Sonny's mounting concerns is glum Sal, itchy to shoot the hostages and insistent he would rather die than be sent to jail. Matters are complicated by the hostages, some of whom refuse to take the situation seriously. Next, Sonny deals with Moretti, offering the lives of his hostages in trade for a plane to take he and Sal out of the country.

By now, an amused crowd has gathered to enjoy this stand-off between two robbers and the police, while solemn FBI agent Sheldon (James Broderick) watches the situation accelerate. Anxious to save lives, Moretti complies with Sonny's wild plan, with a prisoner being released at each stage of the game. As evening approaches, a nervous Sonny insists on seeing his wife. It turns out that it is not Angie (Susan Peretz), his real wife, that he wants to see, but his new spouse, transvestite Leon Sherman (Chris Sarandon). The latter, having been hospitalized for attempted suicide, arrives via police escort. Wearing pajamas and a bathrobe, Leon calls Sonny from a shop across the street, with the police listening to the conversation, begging him to surrender. The emotionally shaky Leon complains, "I didn't ask ya to go and rob a bank." He is not grateful for Sonny's gesture: i.e. knocking over the bank to finance a sex-change operation for his lover. As their conversation ends, Leon says to his hen-pecked mate, "Thanks a lot and bon voyage. Yeah, I'll see you in my dreams. Well, goodbye, huh."

As evening approaches and the police delay in meeting Sonny's demands, he fears the worst. He dictates his last wishes: as an ex-G.I., he wants a military funeral. He adds a postscript to his will, "To my darling wife, Leon, who I love more than any man has loved another man for eternity." Eventually, the two robbers and the remaining hostages are driven with police escort to Kennedy Airport. Once on the airstrip, the FBI shoot Sal dead. Sonny is captured, while the relieved hostages are freed. A postscript states that Sonny is serving twenty years in federal prison; that his wife Angie lives with her children on welfare; and that Leon is now "a woman and living in New York City."

Vincent Canby (*New York Times*) rated this as one of "[director] Sidney Lumet's most accurate, most flamboyant New York movies. . . .. [It is] beautifully acted by performers who appear to have grown up on the city's sidewalks in the heat and hopelessness of an endless midsummer. . . . Most of the time the film stays contained within the bank. This concentration in space and time is responsible for much of the film's dramatic intensity." Canby applauded Al Pacino's stellar performance and that of Chris Sarandon, the latter "played with just the right mixture of fear, dignity and silliness. . . . Of particular interest is Susan Peretz as Mr. Pacino's wife, in whom one sees the tangle of city distress, anger, sweetness and violence, which is one of the main things that *Dog Day Afternoon* is all about."

Richard Combs (British *Monthly Film Bulletin*) found virtues in the movie's method of character delineation "without each being a scene, a crisis or a monologue to establish the fact." On the other hand, Combs balanced, "the humour all too quickly and cosily encloses bandits and victims in a mutually fraught situation . . . and Lumet and [scriptwriter Frank] Pierson seem to have been at a loss to find a place, and a style, for the two FBI men who hover, impassively Dick Tracy-like, in the wings." When shown on television, *TV Guide* rated this expert comedy drama, its highest accolade: four stars.

The acclaimed *Dog Day Afternoon*, shot in New York, grossed a huge $22,500,000 in distributors' domestic film rentals. It received an Academy Award for Best Original Screenplay. It earned five additional Oscar nominations: Best Picture (*One Flew over the Cuckoo's Nest* won); Best Actor (Al Pacino; Jack Nicholson won for *One Flew over the Cuckoo's Nest*); Best Supporting Actor (Chris Sarandon; George Burns won for *The Sunshine Boys*); Best Director (Milos Forman won for *One Flew over the Cuckoo's Nest*); Best Editing (*Jaws* won).

Ironically, the real-life "Littlejohn" Wojtowicz gained little from his ill-fated robbery. On the other hand, the actual transvestite in the case sued Warner Bros. for $1 million and settled out of court; he later sued Patrick Mann (who novelized the story based on a 1972 *Life* magazine article and the screenplay) for $2 million.

In retrospect, Pauline Kael (*5001 Nights at the Movies*, 1991) assessed *Dog Day Afternoon* as "One of the best 'New York' movies ever made. . . . Lumet keeps so much low comedy and crazy melodrama going on in the bank, on the street, among the police, that he can risk the long, quiet scenes that draw us in. . . . Sarandon gives one of the finest homosexual performances ever seen in a movie; he's true to Leon's anguish in a remarkably pure way—he makes no appeal for sympathy."

Al Pacino in *Dog Day Afternoon* (1975).

69. Doing Time on Maple Drive

(Fox-TV, March 16, 1992), color, 100 min. Not rated.

Supervising producer, Gina Scheerer; producer, Paul Lussier; director, Ken Olin; teleplay, James Duff; production designers, Philip Vasels, Diane Hughes; set decorator, Lauren Gabor; makeup, Belinda Bryant; music, Laura Karpman; assistant directors, Jack Philbrick, Gere LaDue; stunt coordinator, Gary Jensen; sound, Bob Anderson; camera, Bing Sokolsky; editor, Elba Sanchez-Short.

Cast: James B. Sikking (Phil Carter); Bibi Besch (Lisa Carter); William McNamara (Matt Carter); Lori Loughlin (Alicen Hall); James Carrey (Tim Carter); Jayne Brook (Karen); David Bryon (Tom); Philip Lenton (Andy Paulson); Bennett Cale (Kyle Trainor); Mark Chael (Student Actor) Janice Lynde (Judy); George Roth (Dr. Norman); Parker Whitman (Gene); Danielle Michonne (Cindy); Toni Sawyer (Millie); Bodhi Elfman (Joe); Mike Marikian (Kevin); Courtney McWhinney (Clara).

Not since *Consenting Adult* (1985) and *An Early Frost* (1985), qq.v., has U.S. network TV focused so maturely on the subject of homosexuality and how a son's revelation of his gayness affects each member of a family about to fall apart. Despite the dramatic rough spots and plot lapses, *Doing Time on Maple Drive* is a powerful movie, efficiently directed by Ken Olin (best known as one of the stars of TV's "Thirtysomething"). Not only does this movie take into account the dangerous ramifications of coming out of the closet in the AIDS era, but it maturely reflects on gayness as a *lifestyle choice* not an admission of mental aberration. It also shows that, despite a growing awareness that homosexuals are people and not freaks, but because of the homophobia resurrected by the AIDS crisis, coming out in the 1990s is just as hard for a young adult as it was in the far more repressive past.

On the surface, Phil (James B. Sikking) and Lisa Carter (Bibi Besch) have a successful life. They own a thriving, upscale restaurant, have a well-appointed house (where an American flag is flown daily) in a nice neighborhood, and three attractive, grown-up children: Tim (James Carrey), Matt (William McNamara) and Karen (Jayne Brook). However, the reality is far different, as becomes obvious when the family gathers for Matt's pending marriage to the aristocratic Alicen Hall (Lori Loughlin). Phil, who once had been a Captain in the military service, treats his household like an erring Army squad who require constant browbeating and lecturing. A perfectionist who stalks through each day in an orderly fashion, he expects better than the best from each of his offspring.

As events shortly show, the family has fractured into self-contained units, each person hiding his/her real feelings from Phil the martinet. Tim, who flunked out of college and works at the family's business, is fed up with being treated as a failure by his dad and always compared to the high-achieving Matt; he has turned to alcohol. Karen, who had wanted to be a writer but who gave up this ambition when she married the financially struggling Tom, is so fearful of displeasing Dad that she would rather have a secret abortion (unbeknownst to her photographer husband) than bring a child into the world before her father thinks she is ready for one. As for handsome Matt, the gem of his parents' eyes, he is a high scorer academically and in sports; he is everything—so Phil insists—that Tim never was or never could be.

Alison finds a note written by Kyle Trainor (Bennett Cale), one of Matt's school friends, to her fiance, in which he reveals that Kyle and Matt had been lovers. A numbed Alison—who had subconsciously known the truth all along but loved Matt too much to admit it—breaks their engagement. Matt pleads with her not to let anyone know the real reason for their split. She agrees and leaves the Carter household. Deathly afraid of confessing the truth to his family, Matt becomes

increasingly frantic. Finally, in a moment of panic he drives off, eventually deliberately crashing his car into a tree. (As he later tells his super-controlled mother, "It's better to be dead than to tell you I'm gay.") He is badly bruised but not critically injured. During his brief recuperation, he tries reaching out to his family, wondering how to handle the shattering truth. Finally, pushed by his mother's refusal to deal with facts she has known for years—she once caught Matt and Tim together—he verbalizes what she has not accepted, that her son is gay. The intractable Lisa remains unsympathetic, but authoritarian Phil Carter makes an earnest effort to come to terms with the situation. He may not understand or like his son's lifestyle choice, but he loves the boy too much to shun him. ("You're my son, " he tells Matt. "That's all.") Meanwhile, Matt reaches out to repair his relationship with Kyle.

Richard Huff (*Variety*) alloted the telefeature "high marks for this sensitive, powerful drama about a dysfunctional family." He admitted that "For the first 40 minutes, it's hard to tell in what direction this telefilm is going" but that "James Duff's writing drives home the message without oversimplifying the situation. . . . As Matt, McNamara brings deep emotion and sympathy to the role. . . ." Laurence Vittes (*Hollywood Reporter*) rated it "a beautifully made melodrama" and pointed out, "What distinguishes *Doing Time on Maple Drive* from similar soapers is the patience with which the characters are first introduced and then dissected within the framework of their upper-middle-class white lifestyle. . . . As the center of the growing emotional storm, McNamara uses his Ricky Nelson looks and vulnerability to effectively mirror his and the others' torments."

Less won over by the production was Jeff Jarvis (*TV Guide*), who rated the telefilm a five on a scale of ten, reasoning, "The first big television movie about AIDS, *An Early Frost*, drew these emotions well. *Doing Time* sometimes draws them in Crayola." Lynne Heffley (*Los Angeles Times*) complained that this "broadly drawn soaper. . . .washes out along the way. . . . There are a few strong performances to lull viewers along. . . . James B. Sikking . . . scores high marks as the odious father but, like the rest of the cast, ultimately is defeated by the connect-the-dots wrap-up."

While the film's long-expected confrontation scene is contrived, it contains moments of dramatic resonance:

Phil: Did you really think we'd rather have you dead?

Matt: It's hard to know.

Then there is Matt's unleashing of years of pent-up feeling to his mother:

"I didn't choose this, I am this. . . . Mom, I didn't choose to be gay. Do you think I'd chose to be this different than everyone else? . . . That I'd choose to make you and dad this upset? . . . That I'd choose to lose someone as beautiful and wonderful as Alison? And what about AIDS? I mean, if someone wanted to be gay, would they want to be gay now?"

The movie's most telling interchange occurs between the parents, whom have proven to be the emotional reverse of what they seemed initially (mother is the sneering tyrant; dad is the repressed liberal):

Lisa: You're going to let him get away with it? . . . Embarrassing us.

Phil: Maybe it's not about us. Maybe it's about him.

Doing Time on Maple Drive was shot on location in Arcadia, California. Its title refers to a statement made by the teleplay's alcoholic son that he has already served his hard time in life, growing up in the stern household on Maple Drive. The movie is dedicated to cast member Philip Lenton, the 29-year-old actor, who died in early 1992.

70. Dracula's Daughter (Universal, 1936), 69 min. Not rated.

Associate producer, E. M. Asher; director, Lambert Hillyer; suggested by the story *Drac-*

ula's Guest by Bram Stoker; screen story, John Balderston, Oliver Jeffries; screenplay, Garrett Fort; art director, Albert D'Agostino; music, Heinz Roehmheld; sound supervisor, Gilbert Kurlan; special effects, John P. Fulton; camera, George Robinson; editor, Milton Carruth.

Cast: Otto Kruger (Dr. Jeffrey Garth); Gloria Holden (Countess Marya Zaleska); Marguerite Churchill (Janet Blake); Irving Pichel (Sandor); Edward Van Sloan (Dr. Von Helsing); Nan Gray (Lili); Hedda Hopper (Lady Esme Hammond); Gilbert Emery (Sir Basil Humphrey); Claude Allister (Sir Aubrey Vail); E. E. Clive (Sergeant Wilkes); Halliwell Hobbes (Constable Hawkins); Billy Bevan (Albert); Gordon Hart (Host); Douglas Wood (Dr. Townsend); Joseph E. Tozer (Dr. Graham); Eily Malyon (Miss Peabody); Fred Walton (Dr. Bemish); Christian Rub (Coachman); William von Brincken (Policeman); Edgar Norton (Hobbs); Guy Kingsford (Radio Announcer); David Dunbar (Motor Bobby); Paul Weigel (The Innkeeper); George Sorel (Police Officer); Douglas Gordon (Attendant); Eric Wilton (Butler); Agnes Anderson (Bride); William Schramm (Groom); Owen Gorin (Friend); Elsa Janssen, Bert Sprotte (Guests); John Blood (Bobby); Clive Morgan (Desk Sergeant); Hedwig Reicher (Wife); John Power (Police Official).

After the enormous success of its *Dracula* (1931), which starred Bela Lugosi, Universal produced this well-executed follow-up. It is an extremely atmospheric thriller, benefitting greatly from the lead performance of Gloria Holden as the exotic vampire. Here is a creature whose passion for fresh blood is especially focused on nubile young women. (At one point an unsuspecting young female says to Holden, "Why are you looking at me that way. Won't I do?" Holden, appraising her comely prey replies approvingly, "Yes. You will do very well, indeed.") The hinted-at lesbian theme in *Dracula's Daughter* would be explored far more explicitly in *The Hunger* (1983), q.v.

In London, following his killing of the vampire, Count Dracula, Dr. Von Helsing (Edward Van Sloan) vainly tries to convince the authorities—in particular Scotland Yard Inspector, Sir Basil Humphrey (Gilbert Emery)—that he has rid the world of a major menace. Refusing to believe in the possibilities of vampires, Humphrey keeps Von Helsing in custody. Psychiatrist Dr. Jeffrey Garth (Otto Kruger), a friend of the accused killer, offers his help in the case. Meanwhile, Jeffrey is introduced to Countess Marya Zaleska (Gloria Holden), a mysterious figure, who begs him for his help in ridding herself of an unstated obsession.

Later, Garth investigates the ravings of a dying girl at the hospital. Her description of events tie her attacker to Marya, and the pieces fall into place for Jeffrey. Later, the desperate Countess, who now craves Garth's eternal companionship, kidnaps the doctor's secretary/sweetheart, Janet Blake (Marguerite Churchill). She uses Janet as a bait to trap Jeffrey into being with her, intending to transform him into one of the undead, so he can share her life as a vampire. However, Sandor (Irving Pichel), Marya's prissy and jealous servant, wants his mistress to remain loyal to him alone. In a spiteful rage, Sandor drives a wooden stake through her heart. With Marya dead, Jeffrey and Janet plan to marry. As for Von Helsing, Sir Basil is now convinced of the reality of vampires and releases the defendant from his custody.

In a tongue-in-cheek manner, Frank S. Nugent (*New York Times*) wrote approvingly of *Dracula's Daughter*: "A chip off the old block, Miss Dracula manages to be lovely and deadly at the same time. She has not inherited the pointed canines of the late Count, but she wears a black cloak with equal effectiveness, and she always manages to leave her bloodless victims with those two telltale marks on the throat, just over the jugular vein." *Variety* reported, "For a change, this is a picture that is quite entertaining along with its shocks. . . ." *Harrison's Reports* approved of the slick horror venture, "It is eerie and at times horrifying. . . . Miss Holden does not resort to weird make-up. Nevertheless, she is sinister in appearance and manner, and at times terrifies the spectator by her action."

One of the joys of the polished *Dracula's Daughter* is its sense of humor, as when the vampire is offered a drink and she says pointedly, "Thank you. I never drink. . . .wine."

71. Drum (United Artists, 1976), color, 102 min. R-rated.

Producer, Ralph Serpe; director, Steve Carver; based on the novel by Kyle Onstott; screenplay, Norman Wexler; production designer, Stan Jolley; art director, Bill Kenney; set decorator, John McCarthy; costumes, Ann Roth; music director, Charlie Smalls; assistant directors, Peter Bogart, Al Shephard; stunt coordinator, Eddie Smith; sound, Robert Gravenor; camera, Lucien Ballard; editor, Carl Kress.

Cast: Warren Oates (Hammond Maxwell); Isela Vega (Marianna); Ken Norton (Drum); Pamela [Pam] Grier (Regine); Yaphet Kotto (Blaise); John Colicos (DeMarigny); Fiona Lewis (Augusta Chauvet); Paula Kelly (Rachel); Royal Dano (Zeke Montgomery); Lillian Hayman (Lucretia Borgia); Rainbeaux Smith (Sophie Maxwell); Alain Patrick (Lazare); Brenda Sykes (Calinda); Clay Tanner (Mr. Holcomb); Lila Finn (Mrs. Holcomb); Henry Wills (Mr. Gassaway); Donna Garrett (Mrs. Gassaway); Harvey Parry (Dr. Redfield); May R. Boss (Mrs. Redfield); Ilona Wilson (Elly Bee Rowe); Monique Madnes (May Ruth Rowe); Eddie Smith (Bruno); S. A. Lewis (Babouin); Harold Jones (1st Slave); Maurice Emanuel (2nd Slave); Larry Williams (3rd Slave); Julie Ann Johnston (1st Woman Guest); Jean Epper (2nd Woman Guest); Bob Minor (Cuban Slave).

Andy Warhol voted *Mandingo* (1975), a vulgar depiction of life on an 1840s Louisiana plantation, as his favorite bad picture of the year. Nevertheless, that tawdry study of depraved life among white masters and black slaves, grossed $8.6 million in distributors' domestic film rentals. Its success prompted producer Dino De Laurentiis to make this sequel, full of gaudy sado-masochistic situations, steamy passion and illogical plotting. More blatantly than its predecessor, the trashy *Drum* exploited homosexuality as a personality trait of some of its more depraved characters.

In 1860 New Orleans, Drum (Ken Norton) is a house slave at a fancy whorehouse. He does not know that its madam, Marianne (Isela Vega), is actually his mother rather than the one he assumes is his parent, her lesbian lover/maid, Rachel (Paula Kelly). After the muscular Drum rejects the sexual advances of Bernard D'Marigny (John Colicos), who has a lover (Alain Patrick), the white man spitefully forces Marianne to have Drum compete in a prize fight with the burly Blaise (Yaphet Kotto). Drum wins the contest and is rewarded with the slave woman Calinda (Brenda Sykes). As the couple start to make love, the lusting D'Marigny breaks into their tryst, wanting Drum for himself. When he fails, he traps Drum into a battle with Babouin (S. A. Lewis). During their skirmish, Rachel dies in an attempt to save Drum from harm.

Next, in order to save her boy from D'Marigny's further plots, Marianne sells Drum and Blaise to slave dealer Hammond Maxwell (Warren Oates). He brings them and slave girl Regine (Pamela Grier) to his plantation, Falconhurst. Once there, Sophie (Rainbeaux Smith), Maxwell's fiery daughter, sexually pursues both Drum and Blaise, leading to Blaise being chained, beaten and nearly castrated. Later, Augusta Chauvet (Fiona Lewis), a well-bred woman reduced to working as a chaperone for Sophie, arranges a dinner party at Falconhurst. D'Marigny and Marianne are among the invited guests. That evening, slave dealer Zeke Montgomery (Royal Dano) passes by the plantation with a group of chained blacks. He asks for shelter that night. Before dawn, Drum releases Blaise from his binds, who, in turn, instigates a slave revolt. In the ensuing fight, the plantation is set ablaze and Marianne dies. Hammond allows Drum to flee.

Vincent Canby (*New York Times*) warned of this potboiler: "There's more hot air than steam in the overwrought melodrama of *Drum*. . . . Not since Mandingo have I seen a film so concerned with such methods of humiliation as beating, shooting and castration. . . . Among the people in the film who don't look totally ridiculous are Mr. Oates, Fiona Lewis. . . . and Pam Grier. . . ." *Variety* revealed that *Drum* was a "grubby followup . . . which invites its own derisive audience laughter. . . . Ham acting like you wouldn't believe, coupled with nondirection. . . . The worst characterization in the film is that of John Colicos as a New Orleans dandy; got up like a drag act version of Bela Lugosi, and sporting an accent not heard outside of Pepe Le Pew cartoons. Alain Patrick plays his passive lover."

During the filming of *Drum*, Steve Carver replaced director Burt Kennedy. Paramount dropped out of its distribution deal for *Drum* because of the X-rating the movie received initially. By the time United Artists agreed to release the picture, the production had been chopped down for its R-rating. This stinker died from bad word-of-mouth. Norman Wexler wrote the screenplay for both *Mandingo* and *Drum*; boxer Ken Norton and actress Brenda Sykes appeared in both features, but had different character parts in each.

Among the many who responded unfavorably to *Drum* were those viewers who regarded the homosexual (would-be-seduction) scenes as another attempt by white Hollywood to put down the black race.

72. An Early Frost (NBC-TV, November 11, 1985), color, 104 min. Not rated.

Producer, Perry Lafferty; co-producer, Art Seidel; associate producers, Daniel Lipman, Ron Cowen; director, John Erman; story, Sherman Yellen; teleplay, Cowen, Lipman; art director, James G. Hulsey; set decorator, Phil Causman; costumes, Richard Bruno; music, John Kander; assistant directors, Stephen M. McEveety, Michael J. Schilz; sound, Keith Wester; camera, Woody Omens; editor, Jerrold L. Ludwig.

Cast: Gena Rowlands (Katherine Pierson); Ben Gazzara (Nick Pierson); Sylvia Sidney (Beatrice McKenna); Aidan Quinn (Michael Pierson); D. W. Moffett (Peter Hilton); John

Ben Gazzara and Aidan Quinn in *An Early Frost* **(1985).**

Glover (Victor DiMato); Sydney Walsh (Susan Maracek); Terry O'Quinn (Dr. Redding); Bill Paxton (Bob Maracek); Cheryl Anderson (Christine); Christopher Bradley (Todd); Sue Ann Gilfillan (Nurse Lincoln); Don Hood (Dr. Gilbert); Barbara Iley (Meredith); Scott Jacek (Phil); John Lafayette (Paramedic); Michael Prince (Norman Wesker, Esq.); Essex Smith (James); Lee Wilkof (Dr. Reisberg).

"In *An Early Frost* we see how AIDS affects a young man's mother, father, sister, brother-in-law and grandmother. There is no consideration given to the fact that this is happening to him—not them. . . . Such films are about the real people in our society, the straight people. Gays are the problem they have." (Vito Russell, *The Celluloid Closet*, 1987)

With the escalating AIDS epidemic making a global impact, U.S. network TV found valid reasons (including the potential of high prime time ratings) for dealing with the subject of homosexuality. ABC-TV's *Consenting Adult* (February 4, 1985), q.v., had focused on a family coping with their son being gay. *An Early Frost* went a step further; not only must the relatives deal with their high-achieving attorney son being homosexual, but also with the fact that he is dying of AIDS. This searing drama made a tremendous impact on a generally tunnel-vision public, not only as an educational experience, but also as superlative drama. *An Early Frost* won an Emmy for Outstanding Writing in a Miniseries or a Special and received thirteen other Emmy nominations. The TV movie's director, John Erdman, won the Directors Guild Award.

Upwardly mobile, young Chicago attorney Michael Pierson (Aidan Quinn) returns home to rural Pennsylvania for the thirtieth wedding anniversary celebration of his parents, Nick (Ben Gazzara), who operates a lumberyard, and Katherine (Gena Rowlands), a housewife and piano teacher. Michael is burdened by having recently learned that he has the AIDS virus and that his live-in lover, Peter Hilton (D. W. Moffett), may have been responsible for infecting him (having been unfaithful to workaholic Michael on several occasions). Angry with Peter's betrayal, Michael has broken off their relationship.

Michael feels a pressing need finally to tell his parents about his lifestyle. When the Piersons are confronted with the truth, Katherine is surprised but more concerned with her son's deteriorating health. ("This is still your home. We're still your parents," she insists.) On the other hand, macho Nick is repulsed by the overwhelming news. Hurt by his father's (ex-pected) response, Michael retorts, "I'm not going to apologize for what I am, because it has taken me too long to accept it." Later, the confused father acknowledges, "I never thought the day would come when you'd stand in front of me and I wouldn't know who you are."

Each member of the Pierson clan has a different response. Katherine's outspoken mother, Beatrice (Sylvia Sidney), is accepting of Michael's revelation, only concerned with his health crisis. Michael's sister, Susan (Sydney Walsh), despite her husband's (Bill Paxton) objection, is frantic about the potential of Michael infecting her children by his mere presence.

As Michael's health deteriorates further and he moves back and forth to the hospital for treatment, his parents quickly become AIDS-educated. Meanwhile, the physically worn-out Michael learns about facing up to his fatal disease from AIDS support groups and from talking with AIDS-dying patient, Victor DiMato (John Glover), whose own family rejected him because of his unpopular disease. The guilt-ridden Peter visit Michael, hoping to repair their relationship. When Michael later attempts suicide, Nick finally realizes that his love of his son is far more crucial than any other personal feelings. Before Michael returns to Chicago and to Peter, he and the other members of his family reconcile.

Gail Williams (*Hollywood Reporter*) praised this entry as "another pioneering NBC social issue drama. . . . *An Early Frost* is first and foremost a quality drama about the side of love that doesn't always come naturally, i.e., accepting loved ones for what they are. . . . [Aidan] Quinn delivers a haunting performance here that's restrained and deeply creative. His relationship with his lover, played by D. W. Moffett, is treated with an intriguing candor that accommodates both intimacy of commitment and realistic conflict."

TV Guide magazine gave this "affecting story" its highest rating—four stars. Steven H. Scheuer (*Movies on TV and*

Videocasette, 1991) endorsed, "Powerful, sensitively acted, and doubly effective for eschewing preachiness and remaining retrained in its portrayal of the plague of the 1980s." *Daily Variety* had mixed feelings, rating the production "a curious mixture of well-played scenes and dollops of bromides about homosexuality. . . . Stereotypes abound, but writers . . . have managed to create several telling segments. . . . A strong emotional telefeature, *An Early Frost* boasts superb acting, a sure purpose and polished production values. . . ."

Beyond its "upbeat" ending, there is a structural fault in *An Early Frost* in that it conforms too much to a requisite format of disease-of-the-week television. As such, the teleplay clumsily works in statistical and other vital information on the focal ailment, thus, at times, causing the characters to talk in textbook recitation fashion. Comparing the parallel roles of Marlo Thomas and Martin Sheen in *Consenting Adult* to those of Gena Rowlands and Ben Gazzara in *An Early Frost*, the latter actors give far more shaded, mature performances.

Seven years later, in *Doing Time on Maple Drive*, q.v., network TV would again return to the same subject matter, a son's coming out to his parents about his sexual lifestyle. By then, viewers were more aware of the gay lifestyle in general, and the drama could focus instead on individuals caught in conflict, not on representational points-of-view.

73. **The Eiger Sanction** (Universal, 1975), color, 128 min. R-rated.

Presenter, Jennings Lang; executive producers, Richard D. Zanuck, David Brown; producer, Robert Daley; director, Clint Eastwood; based on the novel by Trevanian; screenplay, Hal Dresner, Warren B. Murphy, Ron Whitaker; art directors, George Webb, Aurelio Curgnola; set decorator, John Dwyer; costumes, Charles Waldo; makeup, Joe McKinney; music, John Williams; assistant directors, Jim Fargo, Craig Huston, Victor Tourjansky; sound, James R. Alexander; special effects, Ben McMahan; camera, Frank Stanley; editor, Ferris Webster.

Cast: Clint Eastwood (Jonathan Hemlock); George Kennedy (Ben Bowman); Vonetta McGee (Jemima Brown); Jack Cassidy (Miles Mellough); Heidi Bruhl (Mrs. Montaigne); Thayer David (Dragon); Reiner Schoene (Freytag); Jean-Pierre Bernard (Montaigne); Brenda Venus (George); Gregory Walcott (Pope); Candice Rialson (Art Student); Elaine Shore (Miss Cerberus); Dan Howard (Dewayne); Jack Kosslyn (Reporter); Walter Kraus (Kruger); Frank Redmond (Wormwood [Andre Bach]); Siegfried Wallach (Hotel Manager); Susan Morgan (Buns); Jack Frey (Cab Driver).

For his fourth screen directorial assignment, Clint Eastwood chose this James Bond-like adventure. Despite its chilling mountain climbing sequences, the movie spy caper was bland and derivative; it sorely needed Sean Connery as its star. On the other hand, the disappointing film offered an unusual plot gimmick (for the time) of an interracial romance (Eastwood and black co-star Vonetta McGee). It also boasted the not-so-novel gambit of having one of its nasty villains be an epicene gay man—complete with pinky ring, natty clothing, a muscular henchman companion, and a fluffy poodle named Faggot. (This is the same movie that named its black femme fatale Jamima!)

Before he retired from spying, art professor Jonathan Hemlock (Clint Eastwood) used to be a U.S. government agent for the C2 intelligence division. Now, C2's director, Dragon (Thayer David), blackmails Jonathan into accepting an assignment to sanction (i.e. kill) two targets who have just murdered an operative in Switzerland. If Hemlock refuses the job, Dragon threatens to tell the Internal Revenue Service about Jonathan's undeclared art collection. Hemlock carries out the first sanction. En route home, he seduces a stewardess, Jemima Brown (Vonetta McGee), who later proves to be a C2 person. She steals the reward (cash and the letter-of-explanation to the I.R.S.) he received from Dragon. Now he must carry out the second assassination. To further stimulate Jonathan's interest, Dragon tells him that the dead operative was Hemlock's colleague/friend and that he was betrayed by Miles Mellough (Jack Cassidy), another department member.

Knowing that the second kill is to be a member of a mountaineer team climbing the dangerous north face of the Eiger peak in Switzerland, Jonathan trains at the Arizona headquarters of his old pal Ben Bowman (George Kennedy), who is to be a groundsman for the upcoming climb. There, Hemlock encounters Mellough and his muscle-bound bodyguard Dewayne (Dan Howard). He kills them when they try to eliminate him.

In Switzerland, Hemlock joins the climbers: Freytag (Reiner Schoene), Meyer (Michael Grimm) and Montaigne (Jean-Pierre Bernard). Montaigne dies in a sudden frost, and when they begin the descent, both Freytag and Meyer fall to their deaths. Ben saves Hemlock and the latter discovers that Ben is his prey (having been forced into his deceit by his daughter's drug addiction). Since three of the climbers have died, Dragon is content that Hemlock has carried out his final sanction. Jonathan lets Ben escape.

Kevin Thomas (*Los Angeles Times*) charitably decided, "*The Eiger Sanction* . . . is a splendid high adventure. . . . sleekly contemporary. . . . Jack Cassidy is quite uninhibited as an obnoxious effete spy. . . ." Vincent Canby (*New York Times*) judged, "*The Eiger Sanction* is a long, foolish but never boring suspense melodrama. . . . [Besides the mountain climbing sequences] The rest of the movie is the kind of tongue-in-cheek nonsense that Mr. Eastwood . . . laboriously intended." *New York* magazine rated this effort "stilted, self-conscious, belabored and boring." The publication chided Jack Cassidy's performance as "insulting to homosexuals." Richard Combs (British *Monthly Film Bulletin*) concluded, "all the villains have been constructed from prefabricated Bond models . . . [including] the mincingly, queer ex-colleague now turned traitor whom the

hero disposes of with relish about halfway through."

The Eiger Sanction grossed a modest $6,736,532 in distributors' domestic film rentals. Location work was accomplished at Totem Pole in Monument Valley, Arizona and in the Bernese Oberland of Switzerland.

74. Everything You Always Wanted to Know About Sex, But Were Afraid to Ask (United Artists, 1972), color, 87 min. R-rated.

Executive producer, Jack Brodsky; producer, Charles H. Joffe; associate producer, Jack Grossberg; director, Woody Allen; based on the book by Dr. David Reuben; screenplay, Allen; production designer, Dale Hennesy; set decorator, Marvin March; makeup, Paul Stanhope Jr.; music/music director, Mundell Lowe; assistant directors, Fred T. Gallo, Terry M. Carr; sound, Jack Solomon; camera, David M. Walsh; supervising editor, James T. Heckert; editor, Eric Albertson.

Cast: Woody Allen (Victor/Fabrizio/Fool/Sperm); John Carradine (Dr. Bernardo) Lou Jacobi (Sam Waterman); Louise Lasser (Gina); Anthony Quayle (The King); Tony Randall (Operator); Lynn Redgrave (The Queen); Burt Reynolds (Switchboard); Gene Wilder (Dr. Ross); Jack Barry (Himself); Erin Fleming (The Girl); Elaine Giftos (Mrs. Ross); Toni Holt (Herself); Robert Q. Lewis (Himself); Heather MacRae (Helen); Sidney Miller (George); Pamela Mason (Herself); Regis Philbin (Himself); Titos Vandis (Milos); Stanley Adams (Stomach Operator); Oscar Beregi (Brain Control); Alan Caillou (Fool's Father); Dort Clark (Sheriff); Geoffrey Holder (Sorcerer); Jay Robinson (Priest); Ref Sanchez (Igor); Baruch Lumet (Rabbi Baumel); Robert Walden (Sperm); H. E. West (Bernard Jaffe); Don Chuy, Tom Mack (Football Players); Inga Neilson (Royal Executioner).

According to Woody Allen, "This picture contains every funny idea I've ever had about sex, including several that led to my own divorce." In its wildly antic way, this seven-episode R-rated comedy sharply satirizes typical obsessions, misconceptions and fantasies that the average person "enjoys" on a wide spectrum of sexual topics. Allen was inspired by Dr. David Reuben's essentially inane questions-and-answers book to make this, his third feature. Any movie that can weave such diverse personalities as Gene Wilder, Burt Reynolds, Lynn Redgrave, Tony Randall and Regis Philbin into 87-minutes of shenanigans deserves a special award.

The segment titles almost speak for themselves: "Do Aphrodisiacs Work?" "What Is Sodomy?" "Why Do Some Women Have Trouble Reaching an Orgasm?" "Are Transvestites Homosexuals?" "What Are Sex Perverts?" "Are the Findings of Doctors and Clinics Who Do Sexual Research Accurate?" and "What Happens During Ejaculation?"

In the fourth episode, "Are Transvestites Homosexuals?" Sam Waterman (Lou Jacobi) and his wife, Tess, dine at the surburban home of their daughter's pretentious in-laws to be. During the meal, Sam excuses himself to go to the bathroom. Once upstairs, he investigates his hostess' closet, and soon indulges his passion for dressing in female attire and decks himself out in his hostess' red skirt, blouse, red hat, purse, and even her silk underwear. When the others come looking for Sam, he sneaks out of the house into the street. There a thief grabs his purse. When a policeman investigate the hullabaloo, everyone rushes out of the house to see what is happening. Holding a handkerchief to his nose (to hide his moustache), the agitated Sam is the "perfect" picture of a hysterical matron, insisting that he is Jasmine Glick, and that he is three months pregnant (to explain his pot belly). However, his wife soon makes a revelation: "My God! She's my husband!" This leads to an intriguing discussion, full of absurdist logic and satire.

The nonsensical skit certainly does not resolve its thematic question—the answer is actually "not that frequently"—but it is inspired lunacy. Vincent Canby (*New York Times*) reported on this anthology: "[The movie] is uneven, but if you're an Allen

freak, as I am, it doesn't make any difference." Canby added, "some of the sketches aren't absolutely great, but each has at least some great moments in it." As for the "Are Transvestites Homosexual?" episode, Canby complimented Lou Jacobi for his "beautifully played" skit characterization. Lee Beaupre (*Variety*) admitted, "The result is probably his weakest screen effort to date, but the titillating comic promise of having the zany lamebrain spoof current sexual mores should keep the boxoffice humming until word-of-mouth takes hold.": As to the Lou Jacobi sketch, Beaupre observed, "Female impersonation is always a surefire laugh-getter with less discriminating audiences, and Allen milks the yocks for what little they're worth."

Everything You've Always Wanted to Know About Sex may not have won any Academy Awards, but it grossed an impressive $8,827,924 in distributors' domestic film rentals.

75. Fame (Metro-Goldwyn-Mayer/United Artists, 1980), color, 134 min. PG-rated.

Producers, David de Silva, Alan Marshall; director, Alan Parker; screenplay, Christopher Gore; production designer, Geoffrey Kirkland; art director, Ed Wittstein; set decorator, George DeTitta; costumes, Krista Zea; makeup, Joseph Cuervo; music, Michael Gore; songs: Michael Gore and Dean Pitchford; Dominic Bugatti and Frank Musker; Michael Gore, Robert F. Colesberry and Lesley Gore; Michael Gore and Leslie Gore; Paul McCrane; Anthony Evans; choreographer, Louis Falco; assistant directors, Colesberry, Raymond L. Greenfield; sound, Chris Newman, Arthur Bloom, Chuck Irwin; camera, Michael Seresin; editor, Gerry Hambling; additional editor, Yoshio Kishi.

Cast: Eddie Barth (Angelo); Irene Cara (Coco Hernandez); Lee Curreri (Bruno Martelli); Laura Dean (Lisa Monroe); Antonia Franceshi (Hilary Van Doren); Boyd Gaines (Michael); Albert Hague (Professor Shorofsky); Tresa Hughes (Mrs. Finsecker); Steve Inwood (Francois Lafete); Paul McCrane (Montgomery MacNeil); Anne Meara (Mrs. Sherwood); Joanna Merlin (Miss Berg); Barry Miller (Ralph Garcy [Raul Garcia]); Jim

Moody (Farrell); Gene Anthony Ray (Leroy Johnson); Maureen Teefy (Doris Finsecker); Debbie Allen (Lydia); Richard Belzer (Richard, Master of Ceremonies at *Catch a Rising Star*); Frank Bongiorno (Truck Driver); Bill Britten (Mr. England); Eric Brockington (Plump Eric); Nicholas Bunin (Bunsky); Cindy Canuelas (Cindy); Nora Cotrone (Topless Student); Mbewe Escobar (Phenicia); Gennady Filimonov (Violinist); Victor Fischbarg (Harvey Finsecker); Penny Frank (Dance Teacher); Willie Henry Jr. (Bathroom Student); Steven Hollander, Ted Lambert, Loris Sallahian (Drama Students); Sang Kim (Oriental Violinist); Darrell Kirkman (Richard III); Judith L'Heureux (Nurse); Nancy Lee (Oriental Student); Sarah Malament (Dance Accompanist); James Manis (Bruno's Uncle); Carol Massenburg (Shirley—Leroy's Partner); Isaac Mizrahi (Touchstone); Raquel Mondin (Ralph's Sister); Alba Ooms (Ralph's Mother); Frank Oteri (Schlepstein); Traci Parnell (Hawaiian Dancer); Sal Piro (Master of Ceremonies at *Rocky Horror Picture Show* Screenng); Leslie Quickley (*Towering Inferno* Student); Ray Ramirez (Father Morales); Ilse Sass (Mrs. Tossoff); Dawn Steinberg (Monitor on Stairs); Jonathan Strasser (Orchestra Conductor); Yvette Torres (Ralph's Little Sister); Frank X. Vitolo (Frankie); Stefanie Zimmerman (Dance Teacher); Tracy Burnett, Greg De Jean, Laura Delano, Michael DeLorenzo, Aaron Dugger, Niesha Folkes, Karen Ford, Robin Gray, Hazel Green, Eva Grubler, Patrick King, Cynthia Lochard, Julian Montenaire, Holly Reeve, Kate Snyder, Meg Tilly, Louis Venosta, Philip Wright, Ranko Yokoyama (Principal Dancers).

"Our film, I hope, will be a microcosm of New York. It's the glamour of the Great White Way of Broadway and the squalor of 42nd Street . . . the fine line between a Julliard Scholarship and dancing topless at the Metropole. . . . A dozen races pitching in and having their own crack at the American Dream." (Alan Parker, the director of *Fame*)

What now seems a studied cliche—no more than an updating of the old Judy Garland-Mickey Rooney "let's put on a show!" theme—appeared to be remarkably fresh in 1980. (When released, some referred to *Fame* as the younger set's *A Chorus Line*, q.v.) *Fame*'s generated

$7,798,235 in distributors' domestic film rentals, won Oscars and spawned a long-running TV series adaptation (1982–87). One of the many types to be found in *Fame*'s cast of characters was a sensitive homosexual, who changes from being a closeted gay to being a self-reliant, if still self-effacing, outsider. By the end of the film he no longer needs his analyst to tell him that he is worthy of love even if his actress mother is always on the road working and his father had deserted the family. Like *Fame*'s other representational "kinds" (a chip-on-the-shoulder black, a mother-controlled Jewish girl, etc.), the movie broke no new ground in depicting these types. Rather, *Fame*'s virtue is its boundless energy and the marvelous music.

At Manhattan's High School for the Performing Arts, teenagers audition for admission in front of the selection committee of teachers: acting, Angelo (Eddie Barth), dance, Miss Berg (Joanna Merlin) and music, Professor Shorofsky (Albert Hague). Among those applicants who are accepted at the School are: Doris Finsecker (Maureen Teefy), a Jewish girl with an over-possessive mother (Tresa Hughes); Ralph Garcy (Barry Miller)—actually Raul Garcia—a Puerto Rican would-be stand-up comic; Coco Hernandez (Irene Cara), a highly ambitious songstress; Leroy Johnson (Gene Anthony Ray), a talented modern dancer from the black ghetto; well-to-do Lisa Monroe (Laura Dean) with mixed feelings about the world of ballet; Italian Bruno Martelli (Lee Curreri), fixated on becoming a fine electronic musician; and Montgomery MacNeil (Paul McShane), an overly-introverted homosexual.

During their four years at Performing Arts, each student comes to term with himself/herself. The Freddie Prinz-obsessed Ralph gains only temporary success at a comedy club; Coco learns a harsh lesson about life's users from a porno filmmaker (Steve Inwood); Leroy discovers from his teacher (Anne Meara) that other people have feelings and is later accepted by the Alvin Ailey Dance Company. As for Montgomery, thanks to the friendship of Doris, who breaks away from her mother's control, he admits to himself and others that he is gay, and that he is a person. At their graduation concert, the students perform a rousing "I Sing the Body Electric."

Charles Champlin (*Los Angeles Times*) championed *Fame*: "It is ablaze with energy and abloom with young and unfamiliar faces. . . . Paul McCrane is a sensitive young actor-singer who is discovering sadly that he is gay." More critical was David Denby (*New York*) who noted that the filmmakers "turn *Fame* into a near hysterical lament over the miseries of show business. By the end, these eight kids, who haven't even graduated from high school, are smiling through tears like a group of teen Pagliaccis. . . . After a while . . . we realize that every seemingly spontaneous and authentic moment has been tightly, even rigidly, planned to make a point."

Stephen Harvey (*Saturday Review*) emphasized, "Unfortunately [director Alan] Parker isn't content to let his tinsel fable alone—he wants to stun us with gritty pathology as well. . . . While telling his class that he is homosexual Montgomery unburdens himself of such howlers as 'gay used to be such a happy word.' . . . Throughout, Montgomery is the homosexual equivalent of the characters Sidney Poitier played in those queasily liberal movies on race 15 years ago—a sexless saint who just wants to be understood."

Fame won two Oscars: Best Song ("Fame") and Best Score. It received Oscar nominations for: Best Screenplay— Written Directly for the Screen (*Melvin and Howard* won); Best Editing (*Raging Bull* won). Paul McShane would play another sensitive, gay loner in *The Hotel New Hampsire* (1984), q.v.

76. The Fan (Paramount, 1981), color, 95 min. R-rated.

Executive producer, Kevin McCormick; producer, Robert Stigwood; associate producers, John Nicolella, Bill Oakes; director, Edward Bianchi; based on the novel by Bob Randall; screenplay, John Hartwell, Priscilla Chapman; production designer, Santo Loquasto; art director, Paul Eads; set decorator, Leslie Bloom; costumes, Jeffrey Kurland, Tom McKinley; makeup, Joseph Cuervo, Margaret Sunshine; music, Pino Donaglio; songs, Marvin Hamlisch and Tim Rice; choreographer, Arlene Phillips; assistant directors, Herb Gains, Bill Eustace; stunt coordinator, James Lovelett; sound, Arthur Bloom; camera, Dick Bush; editor, Alan Heim.

Cast: Lauren Bacall (Sally Ross); James Garner (Jake Berman); Maureen Stapleton (Belle Goldman); Hector Elizondo (Inspector Raphael Andrews); Michael Biehn (Douglas Breen); Anna Maria Horsford (Emily Stolz); Kurt Johnson (David Branum); Feiga Martinez (Elsa); Reed Jones (Choreographer); Kaiulani Lee (Miriam, Douglas's Sister); Charles Blackwell (John Vetta): Dwight Schultz (Director); Dana Delany (Saleswoman); Terence Marinan (Young Man in Bar); Lesley Rogers (Heidi); Parker McCormick (Hilda); Robert Weil (Pop); Ed Crowley (Caretaker); Gail Benedict (Assistant Choreographer); D. David Lewis (Pianist); Griffin Dunne (Production Assistant); Themi Sapountzakis (Markham); Jean DeBaer (Stage Manager); Liz Smith (Herself); Haru Aki, Rene Ceballos, Cliff DeRaita, Edyie Fleming, Linda Haberman, Sergio Lopez-Cal, Jamie Patterson, Justin Ross, Stephanie Williams, Jim Wolfe (Dancers); Thomas Saccio (Prop Man); Victoria Vanderkloot (Pen Thief); James Ogden (Drummer); Terri Duhaime (Nurse); Donna Mitchell (Hostess); Hector Osorio (Doughnut Vendor); Lionel Pina (Customer); Miriam Phillips (Woman on Steps); Jack R. Marks, George Peters (Doormen); Esther Benson, Eric Van Valkenburg, Ann Pearl Gary, Madeline Moroff, Leo Schaff (Fans); James Bryson, J. Nesbit Clark, Tim Elliott, Paul Hummel, Jacob Laufer (Stagehands).

The Fan has about as much relationship to how a Broadway musical is mounted, as the lumbering movie does to being a well-paced thriller. This dud is notable only for providing the mature Lauren Bacall with a major screen vehicle. Likewise, portraying the movie's slasher villain—a compulsive fan turned homicidal stalker—as a confused bisexual won the picture no fans

Michael Biehn in *The Fan* (1981).

among gay rights groups. This inept film died quickly at the box-office. It was based on a 1977 novel, which predated the rash of celebrity killings (i.e., John Lennon) and murder attempts (i.e., President Ronald Reagan), but strove to capitalize on the public's fascination with such homicidal behavior.

Veteran Broadway star Sally Ross (Lauren Bacall) finds that her life is frequently lonely. She is protected from everyday annoyances by her loyal personal secretary, Belle Goldman (Maureen Stapleton). One of Belle's chores is to answer Sally's fan mail. The psychotic Douglas Breen (Michael Biehn), who works at a local record shop, is one of the actress's many admirers. He pours out his feelings in letters to Sally ("I am your greatest fan. I want nothing from you, only your happiness. I adore you as no one has or ever will.") Breen gets furious at the stock responses he receives from Sally via Belle. Particularly angered by Belle's recent terse note, Breen attacks her on a sub-

way platform, razor-slashing her face. Later, Sally's leading man/boyfriend, David Branum (Kurt Johnson), is attacked in a swimming-pool by the razor-wielding Douglas. Meanwhile, police Inspector Raphael Andrews (Hector Elizondo) investigate the attempted killings. Several days later, Sally's apartment is broken into and ransacked by Douglas, who murders the maid (Feiga Martinez).

The terrorized Sally retreats to her East Hamptons beach house, while the musical (*Never Say Never*) she is preparing, embarks on out-of-town tryouts with her understudy. Sally's ex-husband, Jake Berman (James Garner), arrives in town from Los Angeles, admitting to her that he still loves her. When Breen's burned body is discovered—actually the charred corpse of a gay man (Terence Marinan) Douglas picked up in a bar—Sally decides it is safe to return to the city. Her show opens successfully, while Jake and she reconcile. However, left alone for a few minutes in the theatre, she is confronted by blade-wielding Breen. Fed up with being a victim, she turns aggressively angry. She berates Douglas, who cowers hysterically. She then grabs his razor and stabs him.

Vincent Canby (*New York Times*) perceived that *The Fan* "has several things going for it, and they're all named Lauren Bacall." Canby reported, "The movie's producers have been so piously disassociating *The Fan* from front-page events—those involving real-life homicidal fans of one stripe and another—that one can't help suspecting that they aren't quite as dismayed as they profess to be." An annoyed David Denby (*New York*) wrote, "You know who the killer is from the beginning, and you get sick of watching him stalk and then attack one person after another. . . . . the killer's mentality remains baffling (he appears to be homosexual, but his letters are full of heterosexual swagger." One of the movie's few endorsers was Richard Schickel (*Time*) who found that the expensively-mounted slasher movie "has an emptily sophisticated air that, strangely, works for it. . . . If the ending is a preachy letdown, what goes before it makes *The Fan* a surprisingly worthwhile exercise in suspense. . . ."

Made at a cost of $9 million and shot partially on location in New York, *The Fan* was promoted with the tag line, "This is the story of a great star and a fan who went too far." Only snatches of Marvin Hamlisch-Tim Rice's songs ("Hearts Not Diamonds," "A Remarkable Woman" are used in the film's rehearsal/show scenes.)

77. The Fiend Who Walked the West (Twentieth Century-Fox, 1958), 101 min. Not rated.

Producer, Herbert B. Swope Jr.; director, Gordon Douglas; suggested by the story by Eleazor Lipsky and the screenplay *Kiss of Death* by Ben Hecht, Charles Lederer; new screenplay, Harry Brown, Philip Yordan; art directors, Lyle R. Wheeler, Walter M. Simonds; set decorators, Walter M. Scott, Chester Bayhi; costumes, Adele Balkan; music supervisor, Leon Klatzkin; assistant director, David Silver; special camera effects, L. B. Abbott; camera, Joe MacDonald; editor, Hugh S. Fowler.

Cast: Hugh O'Brian (Daniel Slade Hardy); Robert Evans (Felix Griffin); Dolores Michaels (May Mathieson); Linda Cristal (Ellen Hardy); Stephen McNally (Sheriff Emmett); Edward Andrews (Judge Parker); Ron Ely (Jim Dyer); Ken Scott (Paul Finney); Emile Meyer (Ames); Gregory Morton (Attorney Gage); Shari Lee Bernath (Janie); Georgia Simmons (Mrs. Finney); David Leland (Prison Storekeeper); Al Wyann, Irving Steinberg (Convicts); Clegg Hoyt (Siddell); Ed Hinton (Guard); Billy McCoy (Deputy Sheriff); Terry Becker (Lew Lane); Frank Donahue (Sam, the Bank Guard); Gordon Wynn (Deputy); Frank Scannell, Bernard Nedell (Drunks); Ned Weaver (Coyne); Max Wagner (Court Clerk); Bob Adler (Jeffords); Stan Kamber (Prager); Harry Carter (Leacock); June Blair (The Girl).

In the late 1950s, the morality of Hollywood films was still relatively simple and pure. In this period, movie characters who diverted from the "norm" were *de rigeur* the villains of the piece, and if they had unique characteristics (i.e. divergent sexual orientations, psychotic fixations, etc.), these were generally only suggested by indirection. Similarly to the same year's *The Left-Handed Gun*, q.v., *The Fiend Who Walked the West* forced filmgoers to pay strict attention to catch the hints that its celluloid scoundrel's only interest in women was in intimidating or beating them up and that he was a closet homosexual. When released, reviewers missed these connotations, instead noting only the movie's excessive violence and that the film was a loose remake of *Kiss of Death* (1947), an urban thriller which had starred Richard Widmark (the evil one) and Victor Mature (the good guy).

Desperate for money to support his family on their tiny ranch, Daniel Hardy (Hugh O'Brian) joins in robbing a bank. He is caught, while the other three criminals escape. In jail at Fort Smith, he refuses to reveal his cohorts' identity, foolishly thinking they will share the bounty with his family. Dan's cellmate is Felix Griffin (Robert Evans), a handsome, sadistic loner serving a short sentence. (Griffin, who says of women: "Never one as good as men," recounts with crackling relish to his new pal of how several females in his life all met with disastrous fates.) One day, Hardy reveals to Griffin the name of a fellow robber. When Felix is released, he visits the man (Ken Scott), viciously killing both he and his crippled mother (Georgia Simmons). Griffin locates the hidden loot at their spread, and then burns down the ranch. Next, he calls on Hardy's pregnant wife, Ellen (Linda Cristal), and so terrorizes her that she suffers a miscarriage.

When Griffin moves into town with his new mistress, May Mathieson (Dolores Michaels), Sheriff Emmett (Stephen McNally) becomes suspicious, especially after his deputy, Jim Dyer (Ron Ely), is found murdered. Suspecting Griffin of the killings, Emmett arranges for Dan to escape from prison to entrap Griffin. The ploy works as Felix falls into the web. However, at Felix's trial, Griffin's tricky lawyer (Gregory Morton) gains his client's freedom. Dan knows that Felix will seek revenge one day soon. Meanwhile, May is found dead of a broken neck. The desperate Hardy forces a showdown with Felix at the local saloon and kills the latter in self-defense.

Variety decided "There isn't much rhyme or reason to the whole thing, though it does allow [actor Robert] Evans to emerge as one of the most vicious, cold-blooded killers to hit the screen for some time. He does a very creditable job within the confines of the script. . . ." The trade paper added, "there are moments when it appears that director Gordon Douglas is striving for tongue-in-cheek effects as the mad killer leers and sneers at his intended victims."

Shot in widescreen CinemaScope but economical black-and-white *The Fiend Who Walked the West* boasted two future screen/TV Tarzans in its cast: Ron Ely and Ken Scott.

78. Five Easy Pieces (Columbia, 1970), color, 96 min. R-rated.

Executive producer, Bert Schneider; producers, Bob Rafelson, Richard Wechsler; associate producer, Harold Schneider; director, Bob Rafelson; story, Adrien Joyce [Carol Eastman], Bob Rafelson; screenplay, Joyce; interior designer, Toby Rafelson; costumes, Bucky Rous; assistant director, Sheldon Schrager; sound, Charles Knight; camera, Laszlo Kovacs; editors, Gerald Shepard, Christopher Holmes.

Cast: Jack Nicholson (Robert Eroica Dupea); Karen Black (Rayette Dipesto); Billy "Green" Bush (Elton); Fannie Flagg (Stoney); Sally [Ann] Struthers (Betty); Marlena MacGuire (Twinky); Richard Stahl (Recording Engineer); Lois Smith (Partita Dupea); Helena Kallianiotes (Palm Apodaca); Toni Basi (Terry Grouse); Lorna Thayer (Waitress); Susan Anspach (Catherine Van Ost); Ralph Waite (Carl Fidelio Dupea); William Challee (Nicholas Dupea); John Ryan (Spiecer); Irene Dailey (Samia Glavia).

"*Five Easy Pieces* was more than just another counterculture movie pitting a misfit against the Establishment. It was a picture that tried to show man's eternal quest to find meaning in life by discovering his true self. . . . What sets *Five Easy Pieces* apart from other road films is that we come to know the hero's roots." (David Zinman, *50 Grand Movies of the 1960s & 1970s,* 1886)

Certainly the major highlight of *Five Easy Pieces* is the classic restaurant scene in which Jack Nicholson orders "a plain omelet, no potatoes, tomatoes instead, a cup of coffee and wheat toast" and then must deal with the feisty waitress (Lorna Thayer), who insists "No substitution!" This landmark scene, like the film itself, was a plea for individuality in a control-happy society. However, there are other gems within this road picture as this raging, non-conformist returns home to explore his roots. One of the daffiest encounters occurs when this anti-hero and his girlfriend give a lesbian couple a ride.

Although Robert Dupea (Jack Nicholson) was trained as a classical pianist, he prefers working in the California oil

Jack Nicholson in *Five Easy Pieces* **(1970).**

fields. After learning his waitress girlfriend, Rayette Dipesto (Karen Black), is pregnant, he heads to Los Angeles to visit his pianist sister, Partita (Lois Smith). She tells him that their father (William Challee) is critically ill. Reluctantly, Robert takes the sexy but witless Rayette with him on the trip home to Puget Sound. En route, they pick up two lesbians—Palm Apodaca (Helena Kallianiotes) and Terry Grouse (Toni Basil)—whose incessant chatter aggravate the hyper-tense Dupea. Embarrassed by Rayette's lack of class, he leaves her at a nearby motel while he visits his stroke-victim father. At the house, he is attracted to his brother's (Ralph Waite) girlfriend, Catherine Van Ost (Susan Anspach), a young pianist. They make love that night. The next day, the bored Rayette appears uninvited and Robert must defend her against the snobbery of his family's friends. Unable to communicate with his

dying father, Robert leaves with Rayette. Realizing he cannot fit into either world—the oil fields or his family's intellectual environment—the dysfunctional Robert abandons Rayette at a highway gas station. He then hitches a ride on a truck.

Roger Greenspun (*New York Times*) had mixed feelings about this feature which "on reflection seems both more carefully studied and more coldly casual than profoundly understood. . . . The acting is generally good, but except for Karen Black's pathetically appealing vulgarian, it lives in bits and pieces. . . ." A more responsive *Variety* rated this "an absorbing, if nerve-wracking, film that qualifies as one of the top-quality entries of the year. . . . [It is] significant that relaxed 'enjoyment' is possible only in those segment of the film which seem to be inserted as sops to the current marketplace; set pieces of varying lengths, involving a

Lesbian hitchhiker who's obsessed with cleanliness. . . . These are all well-directed bits, extraordinarily well-acted, but they violate [director Bob] Rafelson's overall approach. . . ."

Within *Five Easy Pieces*, the lesbian couple scene works at several levels: a real-life absurdity, comic relief (from a condescendingly straight point-of-view), and a comparison of different types of outsiders (Robert and the gay lovers). The contest of wills begins when Dupea stops to help two distressed travelers (Palm, Terry), whose car has broken down on the highway. The two women are heading to Alaska and they accept a ride from the bemused macho Robert and the confused Rayette. Dupea is immediately sorry he made the gesture as Palm rambles on endlessly about the destroyed environment and her reactions to it. The dim-witted, but womanly, Rayette cannot relate to the passengers, who are anything but subservient, feminine individuals.

Almost as quickly as the lesbian couple appear in the storyline, they disappear, having served their purposes in the picture.

Five Easy Pieces received four Academy Award nominations: Best Picture (*Patton* won); Best Actor (Jack Nicholson; George C. Scott won for *Patton*); Best Supporting Actress (Karen Black; Helen Hayes won for *Airport*); Best Screenplay (*Patton* won). The movie grossed $8.9 million in distributors' domestic film rentals.

79. Flesh (Sherpix, 1968). color, 105 min. Not rated.

Producer, Andy Warhol; director/screenplay/camera, Paul Morrissey.

Cast: Joe Dallesandro (Joe); Geraldine Smith (Gerry); John Christian (Young Man); Maurice Bardell (Artist); Barry Brown (Boy on Street); Candy Darling (Blonde on Sofa); Jackie Curtis (Redhead on Sofa); Geri Miller (Terry); Louis Waldon (David); Patti D'Arbanville (Gerry's Girl Friend).

Kitschy Andy Warhol (1929–1988) displayed his exuberant, creative talents in so many mediums, that some unkindly souls labeled him "the high priest of camp." Nevertheless, with his exalted status in the art community, all his projects took on a legitimacy, often beyond their worth. One of his contributions to the changing American cinema was his underground film Factory which released a large number of cinema verite exercises, frequently provocation mainly for their blatant titles and their inordinate length: e.g., *Blow Job* (1964), *My Hustler* (1965) and *The Chelsea Girls* (1966), q.v. These often crude, amateurish efforts were filled with daring —for the time—subject matter. As such, they proved important to a growing liberalization of the viewing public. Since the art establishment would review his screen work, the public would as a consequence, attend showings, thus viewing sexual lifestyles and acts that formerly had been exclusively the subject of "blue" films.

In 1968, Paul Morrissey, a protegee of Warhol's, took over directorial duties at the Factory. One of Morrissey's first ventures was *Flesh*. It starred Joe Dallesandro as an attractive, incoherent, street-tough hustler who sleeps with men and women— anyone, to survive financially and to stay amused.

Joe (Joe Dallesandro), a young Manhattan hustler, rents a rundown East Village apartment. His wife, Gerry (Geraldine Smith), prompts her lazy spouse to venture out and earn the $200 needed for her friend's (Patti D'Arbanville) abortion. Joe earns $20 by tricking with a male customer (John Christian) he picks up on the street. Matters improve when an aging British artist (Maurice Bradell) gives him $100 for posing for sketches. Again, on the street, Joe teaches a young hustler (Barry Brown) how to succeed in their business. Later, he encounters a pal (Louis Waldon) from a Village gym, whom he convinces to loan him money. Heading home, Joe visits with Terry (Geri Miller), a topless dancer, who is one of his former girlfriends. While she performs fellatio on him, two transvestites (Jackie Curtis,

Candy Darling) sit on the nearby sofa reading old movie magazines. Home again, Joe learns that his wife's friend, now there, does not need an abortion after all. The trio lie down on the bed. While Joe falls asleep, the two women amuse themselves together.

Flesh received more mainstream notice than had the Factory's *My Hustler* (1965), directed by Andy Warhol. While *Flesh* was notable for its sexual permissiveness, the critics were not enthusiastic. A.H. Weiler (*New York Times*) complained, "as produced in gaudy color, a haphazard sound track and slapdash editing, it becomes transparently clear that *Flesh* is simply what its title shouts. . . . Joe Dallesandro, as the bi-sexual hooker, who is sleeping when the film opens is, nevertheless, indefatigable." *Variety* rated the picture a "hapless erotica freakout." When distributed abroad in 1970 in an abbreviated 89-minute version, Claire Johnston (British *Monthly Film Bulletin*) praised the production because "the structure of the film is deliberate and even aesthetic, beginning and ending as it does with Joe Dallesandro asleep, suggesting the circularity of experience. . . ."

Several members of the cast went on to mainstream careers, including Joe Dallesandro, Patti D'Arbanville and Barry Brown. To be noted in the cast are transvestite performers Candy Darling and Jackie Curtis, fixtures of the Film Factory.

80. Flesh Gordon (Mammoth, 1973), color, 78 min. X-rated.

Producers, Howard Ziehm, William Osco; associate producer, Walter R. Cichy; directors, Michael Benveniste, Ziehm; screenplay, Benveniste; art director, Donald Harris; costumes, Ruth Glunt; makeup, Bjo Trimbo; music/music director, Ralph Ferraro; sound, John Brasher; special effects, Ziehm, Lynn Rogers, Cichy; visual effects, David Allen, Jim Danforth; camera, Ziehm; editor, Abbas Amin.

Cast: Jason Williams (Flesh Gordon); Suzanne Fields (Dale); Joseph Hudgins (Dr. Flexi Jerkoff); William Hunt (Emperor Wang); John Hoyt (Professor Gordon); and: Mycle Brandy, Nora Wieternik, Candy Samples, Steven Grummette, Lance Larsen, Judy Ziehm, Donald Harris, Linus Gator, Susan Moore, Mark Fore, Maria Aranoff, Rick Lutze, Sally Alt, Duane Paulsen, Leonard Goodman, Patricia Burns, Linda Shepard, Mary Gavin, Dee Dee Dailes.

This tacky softcore spoof of the hallowed Flash Gordon comic strips and movie serials (of the late 1930s), proved surprisingly popular at the box-office. With its crude jokes aimed at titillating both gay and straight audiences, it could have been offensive to all. Instead, it was a pleasant, slapdash outing that was so (deliberately?) bad, it was good fun. As the movie's foreword promises, these new adventures were made "with the spirit of the old but the outrageousness of the new."

With the world beset by a manic sex ray which prompts unbridled orgies, Flesh Gordon (Jason Williams), along with Dale Ardor (Suzanne Fields) and Dr. Flexi Jerkoff (Joseph Hudgins), set off in the latter's rocket ship to trace the source of the ray to the distant planet of Porno. Once there, they are attacked by assorted creatures and underlings of the Emperor Wang (William Hunt). A benevolent spirit, Amora, Queen of Magic, provides Flesh with a protective weapon against Wang's sex ray. Thereafter, the resourceful Gordon and Jerkoff prevent Wang from marrying the unwilling Dale. However, she later is dispatched by the vengeful Wang into the lesbian underworld. With the assistance of the gay Prince Precious, the rightful heir to Porno who has a strong yen for musuclar Flesh, the forces of good eventually destroy Wang and his sinister ray machinery. Returning to Earth, Flesh, Dale and Jerkoff are relieved to discover that normalcy reigns again.

According to Vincent Canby (*New York Times*), "What wit the film possesses has gone into the physical production in the re-creation of the kind of badly proportioned miniatures used in the original serial, and in the barren exterior locations." Geoff Brown (British *Monthly Film Bulletin*)

Steven Grummette in *Flesh Gordon* (1973).

was not amused, "Parodying something which is almost a parody in itself is a dangerous game to play, and the makers of *Flesh Gordon* play it badly. Their script remains on the same flat-footed level as the dialogue in the serials, and the single big joke (the transformation of every character and situation from the Flash Gordon mythology into porno terms) wears thin within ten minutes, though some of the conceits raise a laugh through their sheer idiocy. . . ."

Made over a two-year period on a $2 million budget, the independently-produced feature grossed $5.3 million in distributors' domestic film rentals. It was re-issued in 1975, re-edited to a R-rated version. Over the years, *Flesh Gordon*, with its standout monsters created by David Allen, has become a minor cult favorite.

In 1991, Howard Ziehm, who had directed *Flesh Gordon*, brought out *Flesh Gordon Meets the Cosmic Cheerleaders*, made for $3 million. In this heterosexual follow-up, the intrepid hero journeys through space to find the villains who are causing men on Earth to be impotent. Aboard for this pornographic odyssey are Flesh Gordon (Vince Murdocco), Dale Ardor (Robyn Kelly), Dr. Flexi Jerkoff (Tony Travis) and they battle such forces as the Evil Presence (Bill Hunt), Master Bator (Bruce Scott) and Robunda Hooters (Morgan Fox). Excessively crude, this abysmal sequel received some publicity when, because of its NC-17-rating, it temporarily was denied advertising space in several major newspapers. Kirk Honeycutt (*Hollywood Reporter*) rated it a "demented curio." Gregory Soloman (*LA Reader*) insisted, "it crosses the line from plain bad taste to distastefully ugly."

81. A   Florida   Enchantment

(General Film Co., 1914), 5 reels. Not rated.

Director, Sidney Drew; based on the novel by Archibald Clavering Gunter, Fergus Redmond; screenplay, Eugene Mullen and/or Maguerite Bertsch; camera, Robert A. Stuart.

Cast: Sidney Drew (Dr. Fred Cassadene); Edith Storey (Lillian Travers); Charles Kent (Major Horton); Jane Morrow (Bessie Horton); Ada Gifford (Mrs. Stella Lovejoy); Ethel Lloyd (Jane); Lillian Burns (Malvina); Grace Stevens (Miss Constancia Oglethorpe); Allan Campbell (Mr. Stockton Remington); Cortland Van Duesen (Charley Wilkes); Frank O'Neil (Gustavus Duncan).

A Florida Enchantment was based on the 1891 novel by Archibald Clavering Gutner and Fergus Redmond, which had been turned into a Broadway stage production in 1896. The silent picture was a unique forerunner of moviemakers' occasional penchant for stories dealing with sex-role changes (e.g.: *Turnabout*, 1940, *Goodbye, Charlie*, 1964, and *Switch*, 1991, q.v.). What made the storyline more unique/confusing was that after the main characters switch sexes, they do not change gender clothing, and their resultant pursuit of the same sex leads to all kinds of assumptions by onlookers. Unfortunately, the movie's ending is a cop-out preventing any real assessment of the movie's deeper implications.

While vacationing at a resort hotel in St. Augustine, Florida, a northerner, Lillian Travers (Edith Storey), is shocked to find her fiance, Dr. Fred Cassadene (Sidney Drew) romancing another woman. In a pique of jealous rage, she remembers having an antique box from Africa which contains a note detailing that the enclosed seeds were harvested from the Tree of Sexual Change. She impulsively swallows one of the pellets. It changes her into a man, complete with moustache, which she hastily shaves off. Still wearing female attire, she is persuaded by the drug to flirt with the women guests at the spa. The same thing occurs when she encourages Jane (Ethel Lloyd), her mulatto maid to take one too; the latter becomes a sex-hungry valet. Time passes and Lillian and Jane head off to New York City dressed as men. Meanwhile, Fred assumes that Lillian has been killed and that this newcomer is her murderer. To prove her story, Lillian has the suspicious doctor try the magical potent. He becomes a woman (still dressed as a man he pursues his male friends). Next, he borrows a dress, dives into the ocean and begins to drown. Suddenly, Lillian awakens to find that it has all been a bizarre dream.

The New York Dramatic Mirror noted that "while Edith Storey made quite an attractive man, Sidney Drew is far from a handsome woman." Sime Silverman (*Variety*) was put off by the movie's premise, insisting "The thing started off like a comic opera, but it lapsed into a weary, dreary, listless collection of foolish things." In contrast, *Motography* complimented the film's "large and competent cast."

A Florida Enchantment was filmed in St. Augustine and other Florida locales.

82. Fortune and Men's Eyes

(Metro-Goldwyn-Mayer, 1971), color, 102 min. R-rated.

Producers, Lester Persky, Lewis M. Allen; co-producer, Donald Ginsberg; director, Harvey Hart; based on the play by John Herbert; screenplay, Herbert; production designer, Earl G. Preston; costumes, Marcel Carpenter; music, Galt MacDermot; songs: Michael Greer; MacDermot, MacDermot and William Dumaresq; choreographer, Jill Courtney; assistant director, Arthur Voronka; sound, Joseph Champagne; camera, George Dufaux; editor, Douglas Robertson.

Cast: Wendell Burton (Smitty); Michael Greer (Queenie); Zooey Hall (Rocky); Danny Freedman (Mona); Larry Perkins (Screwdriver); James Barron (Holyface Peters); Lazaro Perez (Catso); Jon Granik (Sergeant Gritt); Tom Harvey (Warden Gasher); Hugh Webster (Rabbit); Kirk McColl (Guard Gasher); Vance Davis (Sailor); Robert Goodlier (Doctor); Cathy Wiele (Cathy); George Allard (Fiddler); Modesto (One-Eye); Michel Gilbert (Young Prisoner); Robert Saab (Drummer); A. Zeytounian (Pianist).

"The film has an unliberated, craven homosexual personality. I won't try to pin this mentality to its proper origins . . . but to its incapacity for sincerity, its subversiveness; to the fabulous, epic bitchiness of the institutionalized faggot. Gay and proud it is not. Elusive, self-destructive and cruel it is." (Richard McGuinness, *Village Voice*)

In February 1967, John Herbert's thoughtful drama of degrading life in a dormitory cell inside a Canadian penal reformatory was presented off Broadway. Once incarcerated in jail himself, Herbert conceived his play as a plea for prison reform. His aim was to change the situation where sexual hunger behind bars leads to role playing and ultimately becomes a power tool, which ends by debasing all concerned. The production ran for 383 performances. In October 1969, Sal Mineo directed a revamped version, also off-Broadway, which added, highly exploitable on-stage nudity and simulated sexual acts. The new production—which distorted Herbert's original intentions— ran for 231 performances and then toured the U.S.

Jules Schwerin, impressed by the 1967 play version, was hired to direct the MGM feature. However, after nine weeks of shooting at Quebec Prison, he was let go by the film's producers who wanted the movie to sensationalize homosexuality and nudity as box-office bait, as well as highlight the campy nature of its drag queen character, Queenie. Harvey Hart completed the movie, which was touted with the campaign slogan: "What goes on in jail is a crime!" *Fortune and Men's Eyes* was a far cry from the fictional prisons depicted in the James Cagney/Pat O'Brien/George Raft movies of the 1930s. Its real antecedents lay in the Jim Brown-Gene Hackman *Riot* (1969), q.v.

For possessing marijuana, nineteen-year-old college student Smitty (Wendell Burton) is sentenced to six months of detention at a Canadian jail for young men. Behind bars, he meets his cellmates: the

effeminate, baleful, Shakespeare-quoting Mona (Danny Freedman); the strong, silent Rocky (Zooey Hall); and Queenie (Michael Greer), a highly flamboyant gay man. When Queenie makes sexual overtures, the uptight Smitty rejects him, despite warnings from the cross-dresser that he would do better to pick Queenie over some of the others in the prison. Later, Smitty is nearly gang-raped by other convicts, but is rescued by Rocky. The naive newcomer is grateful until he realizes that he now owes Rocky, and that his "old man" has the right—according to prison tradition—to have him sexually anytime he wants. Giving in to the inevitable, Smitty becomes Rocky's boy. Later, after the jealous Queenie taunts him, Smitty fights Rocky and is the victor. He is now his own man. The humiliated Rocky, no longer cast in the male's role, commits suicide. Queenie, deeply upset by Rocky's death, causes a furor when he does a frantic bump-and-grind strip at a Christmas variety show attended by the warden and his wife.

Now the cock of the walk, Smitty demands that Mona become his boy. The latter refuses, explaining that to be humiliated by one he loves (i.e., Mona's feelings for Smitty) is too agonizing. The stunned Smitty suddenly realizes how, like Rocky before him, he has been dehumanized by prison life.

Paul D. Zinmann (*Newsweek*) was one of the few to find virtues in the screen adaptation: "for all its failings . . . [it] remains a powerful and often shocking film. Director Harvey Hart makes us feel that confinement itself is the more horrible of prison conditions." In contrast, A. H. Weiler (*New York Times*) felt the adaptation "shortchanged" moviegoers because it "vacillates between an explicit, largely homosexually slanted dramatization and an implied, surface indictment of callous penal practices that does little justice to either approach." For Weiler, "[The] acting honors go to Michael Greer as the uninhibited homosexual . . . who is often

Danny Freedman (center) and Michael Greer (right) in *Fortune and Men's Eyes* (1971).

fascinatingly funny and campy in a larger-than-life role."

Addison Verrill (*Variety*) rated the movie a "dud" explaining: "What emerges is ineptly filmed soap opera centering about the latest cinematic 'fate worse than death': homosexual rape. . . . Obviously, MGM did not want an X rating on the film, so *Fortune* is almost discreet in the male frontal nudity and sex act department. One brief genital flash and two 'demure' sodomy sequences are remarkably restrained, but the dialog makes up for those lapses." As to Michael Greer, who had performed in the 1969 stage revival drama and who had played a similar flaming queen in *The Gay Deceivers* (1969), q.v., Verrill decided, "When his material meshes with his delivery . . . he's great, but the grotesque campiness of it all works against establishing a sympathetic characterization. Still

his performance will give whatever legs it may have in urban keys.

Like the prior year's *The Boys in the Band*, q.v., *Fortune and Men's Eyes* was too specialized to make box-office headway among mainstream Americans, even if the compromised movie had been faithful to, or improved upon, its stage original.

83. Forty Deuce (Island Pictures, 1982). Color, 89 min. Not rated.

Producer, Jean Jacques Fourgeaud; director, Paul Morrissey; based on the play by Alan Browne; screenplay, Browne; music, Manu Dibango; sound, Larry Schaff; camera, Francois Reichenbach, Stefan Stapasik, Steven Fierberg; editor, Ken Aleuto.

Cast: Orson Bean (Mr. Roper); Kevin Bacon (Rickey); Mark Keyloun (Blow); Harris Laskaway (Augie); Tommy Citera (Crank); John Anthony (John Noonan); Carol Jean Lewis (Black Woman).

Based on Alan Browne's off-Broadway play (1981), which he adapted for the screen, this little-seen feature continued director Paul Morrissey's screen studies of male hustlers. Unlike his earlier *Flesh* (1968) and *Heat* (1972), qq.v., this movie had a great deal more structure because of its stage origins. The play cast repeated their assignments for the screen version, a movie whose plotline (i.e. a centerpiece corpse) reminded more than one viewer of Alfred Hitchcock's *Rope* (1948), q.v.

The opening half of the feature, played in comedic terms, is set on raunchy 42nd Street—hence the film's title—where teenage prostitute Rickey (Kevin Bacon) hopes to finance a drug deal by selling a runaway youth to a wealthy client, Mr. Roper (Orson Bean). However, the boy, who is staying at Rickey's apartment, is later found dead from a dope overdose. This does not stop the manipulative Rickey from wanting his finder's fee from the drugged-out Roper, who is led to believe that he killed the youth. The second half of the movie, utilizing a split-screen technique, is set in the claustrophobic apartment.

Frank Rich (*New York Times*) assessed, "Mr. Browne appears to have the real lowdown on his subject. As his variously pathetic boys discuss and practice the vicissitudes of their trade in a shabby hotel room, they speak in a colorful argot that is too baroque to be invented . . . Let social historians note that *Forty Deuce* may be the first play to simulate even an unintentional act of homosexual-sadomasochistic-pedophilic necropilia." Kevin Thomas (*Los Angeles Times*) advised, "Shot through with savage humor; this is definitely not for the squeamish." *Variety* noted, "Thanks to excellent location camerawork, the film captures the rawness of living in that environment." Reviewing the theatrically unreleased movie at the 1984 New York Gay Film Festival, the *Village Voice* observed, "The director's decision (based more, it would seem, on economics than aesthetics) to

film the last few reels in quickly shot split-screen scenes drains the drama and leaves the play a shambles . . . Most of *Forty Deuce's* first hour is still remarkable, with fine work from Kevin Bacon."

Kevin Bacon, who would rise to screen prominence with *Diner* (1982) and *Footloose* (1984), had won an Obie Award for appearing off-Broadway in the original cast of *Forty Deuce*.

84. The Fox (Warner Bros., 1968), color, 110 min.

Producer, Raymond Stross; associate producer, Howard Koch; director, Mark Rydell; based on the novella by D. H. Lawrence; screenplay, Lewis John Carlino, Koch; art director, Charles Bailey; makeup, Mel Brooke; music/music conductor, Lalo Schifrin; song, Oscar Brand; assistant director, Burtt Harris; sound, Des Dollery; camera, Bill Fraker; editor, Thomas Stanford.

Cast: Sandy Dennis (Jill Banford); Keir Dullea (Paul Grenfel); Anne Heywood (Ellen March); Glyn Morris (Realtor).

"Ten years ago, this motion picture could not possibly have been made. Even a year ago, *The Fox* could not have been made . . . not quite this way!" (Advertisement for *The Fox*)

D. H. Lawrence was best known for his erotic novel, *Lady Chatterly's Lover* (1928), but his novella *The Fox* (1922) proved to be a landmark of cinematic free expression. Filmed in Canada—mostly around Toronto—this feature took Lawrence's symbolic story (i.e. the masculine fox grabbing his prize, in this case, a woman) and converted it into a graphic depiction of lesbians in love. Like the same year's *The Killing of Sister George*, q.v., it was far more graphic than the merely hinted-at special relationships of certain women in prior movies. The film was made during a transitionary period in the 1960s, when the film industry's production code in the U.S. was breaking down and before the inauguration of the industry's classification rating system in the fall of 1968.

Far out in the country, during a cold,

bleak winter, the domesticated Jill Banford (Sandy Dennis) and the more mannish Ellen March (Anne Heywood) eke out a living on their chicken farm. Their success is hampered by a rapacious fox and by their refusal to be compulsive workers. Later, Ellen comes across the maurading fox but has a strange compunction not to shoot it.

Merchant seaman Paul Grenfel (Keir Dullea), the grandson of the farm's prior owner, appears one day and persuades the women to let him stay there during his shore leave. Before long, he has decided to marry Ellen. Ellen, who notes parallels between Paul and the fox, is drawn to the newcomer and they become lovers. Meanwhile, the very jealous Jill does her best to place Paul in a bad light with Ellen. When Grenfel leaves the farm briefly, Jill convinces Ellen to abandon her marriage plans; she writes him a letter breaking off their romance. Paul returns to the farm to find the women chopping down a tall tree. As he takes charge of the axe, he warns Jill to move from the tree's path. She refuses his suggestion and is killed by the falling trunk. Selling the farm, Ellen and Paul go off together.

The controversial *The Fox* received a full spectrum of responses from reviewers and audiences. Wanda Hale (*New York Daily News*) rated it with four stars, praising its "honesty', while Tony Mastroianni (*Cleveland Press*) ranked it as "a Great Big Yawn. . . . If a lesbian relationship was barely implied in Lawrence's story it is made explicit in the film. It is one of several tasteless scenes." Renata Adler (*New York Times*) decided, "The trouble with the movie is that Sandy Dennis's acting in the first half hour is terrible (later, the strain becomes an asset), that the autoerotic scenes are interminable, that the lovemaking is ambitious but ludicrously cross-cut with a chase through the snow. . . . What is good is the intelligence with which the ambiguities are kept . . . and a certain courage in following every exaggeration through." More than one re

viewer noted the changes made to the book original (i.e. far more explicit sex scenes, Jill's death being suicidal rather than Paul's murderous ploy, etc.). Several contemporary critics were baffled by the lesbians' role-playing. Pauline Kael (*The New Yorker*) wondered, "If Ellen isn't afraid of sex with men, what's she doing playing house in the woods with that frumpy Jill?"

While the makers of *The Fox* protested they were not being daring just for the sake of daring, Anne Heywood's much-discussed on-camera masturbation scene, as well as the women characters' lovemaking was sufficient to shock the public (mostly into seeing the film). Interestingly, in retrospect, it is Keir Dullea's performance as the determined, unambivalent male which holds up best.

The economically-made *The Fox* grossed $8.6 million in distributors' domestic film rentals. It was a profitable lesson not lost on Hollywood filmmakers.

85. **Frankie & Johnny** (Paramount, 1991), color, 118 min. R-rated.

Executive producers, Alexandra Rose, Charles Mulvehill; producer, Garry Marshall; co-producer, Nick Abdo; director, Marshall; based on the play by *Frankie and Johnny in the Clair de Lune* by Terrence McNally; screenplay, McNally; production designer, Albert Brenner; art director, Carol W. Wood; set designer, Harold L. Fuhrman; set decorators, Kathe Klopp, Kathleen Dolan; costumes, Rosanna Norton; makeup, Sheryl Berkoff, Naomi Beth Dunne; music, Marvin Hamlish; assistant directors, Ellen H. Schwartz, Bettiann Fishman, Nandi Bowe; second unit director, Abdo; sound, Keith A. Wester, Andrea Lakin, Samuel E. Kaufman; special effects supervisor, Thomas R. Ward; camera, Dante Spinotti; second unit camera, Steve Yaconelli; editors, Battie Davis, Jacqueline Cambas.

Cast: Al Pacino (Johnny); Michelle Pfeiffer (Frankie); Hector Elizondo (Nick); Kate Nelligan (Cora); Nathan Lane (Tim); Jane Morris (Nedda); Greg Lewis (Tino); Al Fann (Luther); Glenn Plummer (Peter); Sean O'Bryan (Bobby); Fernando Lopez (Jorge); Ele Keats (Artemis); Phil Leeds (Mr. DeLeon); K. Callan (Frankie's Mother); Shannon Wilcox (Chris

Sandy Dennis, Keir Dullea and Anne Heywood in *The Fox* **(1968).**

tine, the Hooker); Tim Hopper (Lester); Harvey Miller (Mr. Rosen); Goldie McLaughlin (Helen, the Waitress); Marvin Braverman (Officer Joe); Frank Campanella (Retired Customer); Julie Paris (Pregnant Customer); Allan Kent (Racetrack Customer); Bud Markowitz (Juggler Customer); Elizabeth Kerr (Senior Citizen Customer); Marty Nadler (Rude Customer); Jeff Michalski (Seizure Customer); Diane Frazen (Marge, the Whispering Customer); Hyman Fishman (Cora's Customer); Ronny Hallinn (Biker Customer); Harvey Keenan (Salesman Customer); Pricilla Phillips, Joy Rosenthal (Snooty Customers); Robert Brunner (Accident Driver); Mark Scarola (Garment Worker); Karin Calabro (Dental Technician); Flora Berniker (Flora): Steve Restivo (Night Cook); Nick Gambella (Night Busboy); Hope Alexander-Wills, Barbara Mealy, Barbara London (Night Waitresses); Al Sapienza (Peter's Roommate); Diane Kent (Nick's Wife); Tracy Reiner (Attorney at Party); Eugenie Bravos (Grandma); Gene Bravos, Shirley Kirks (Greek Dancers); Joli Lallo (Jorge's Girlfriend); Ira Glick (Mutzie Calish); Dey Young (Johnny's Ex-Wife); Paul Tinder (New Husband); Barbara Marshall (Helen's Nurse); Scott A. Marshall (Sidewalk Preacher); Laurie Quinn (Pretty Girl Bowler); Zachary Weintraub (Handsome Bowler); Lucinda Crosby (Abused Neighbor); Shane Ross, Richard Gillis (Sexy Neighbors); Robert Ball (Haircombing Neighbor); Frank Buxton (Minister); Dee Dee Pfeiffer (Frankie's Cousin); Betiann Fishman (Aunt Betty); Lori Marshall (Party Guest); Krista H. Davis, Kelly McCray, Blair Richwood (Bus Riders).

On the Broadway stage (1987), Terrence McNally's romantic comedy, starring Kathy Bates and F. Murray Abraham, was unaffecting, understated and unglamorous. As a major Hollywood film, it became an overblown star vehicle for Al Pacino and Michelle Pfeiffer, who had previously co-starred in *Scarface* (1983). *Entertainment Weekly* rated the romantic comedy a B+: "It's clear from the outset that *Frankie & Johnny* is going to fall squarely in the tradition of inspirational Hollywood romance. . . . *Frankie & Johnny* could have used more of an edge." The publication pointed out, "And Frankie has been given an affectionate, mildly bitchy gay neighbor (Nathan Lane)

Michelle Pfeiffer and Nathan Lane in *Frankie & Johnny* (1991).

who feels a little too much like a cozy stereotype from another era."

After eighteen months in jail on a fraud charge, wise-cracking Johnny (Al Pacino) comes to New York City where he finds work as a short order cook at the Apollo Cafe, an inexpensive downtown diner owned by Nick (Hector Elizondo). Before long, the sex-hungry Johnny is flirting with all the waitresses, but is especially drawn to cynical Frankie (Michelle Pfeiffer), a drab loner. Determined to date her, he pursues the distrusting Frankie, and finally—goaded by her gay neighbor Tim (Nathan Lane) not to be so reclusive—she goes out with him. After a passionate evening with Frankie, Johnny becomes more aggressive, while Frankie retreats from the relationship. Meanwhile, Johnny makes an abortive visit to see his ex-wife and children in the suburbs, but realizes he is no longer part of their lives. Eventually, the emotionally crippled Frankie and Johnny admit their love and need for each other.

Ella Taylor (*LA Weekly*) analyzed, "Like all Garry Marshall's work, whether in film or television, *Frankie & Johnny* is a sitcom peopled with types rather than characters." But, Taylor admitted "though the feelings are forever revved up to top register, and the comedy's as broad as you can find outside prime time—full of New York jokes, immigration jokes, gay-man jokes, single-woman jokes—there's wry good humor and directness to the movie." Lizzie Francke (British *Monthly Film Bulletin*) was unimpressed by the "bunch of freshly added support characters [who] reek of old stock" and chided the filmmakers for "not forgetting that a girl's best friend is her gay neighbour."

In a role that once would have been played by James Coco or, before gays were depicted on screen, by Eve Arden, Nathan Lane's Tim appeared as the sharp-tongued neighbor. He is the one who dispenses romantic advice to his neighbor, Frankie, while coping himself with a string of bad romances. He has wry per-

ception on life, and especially on his own
foibles. Not defensive about his own sexual orientation, he enjoys several witty in-
terchanges with Johnny:

Johnny: You know, I have a cousin
who's gay.

Tim: [Pleasantly] Most people do.

While the character of Tim was no more
or less sharply defined than the other ethnic, emotional and social class types of
this movie, the Gay and Lesbian Alliance
Against Defamation (GLAAD) was a tremendous booster of the picture, ignoring
the limited boundaries of Tim's persona.
"We're GLAD that . . . *Frankie & Johnny*
includes some of the most accurate and
positive portrayals of gay people we've
seen in some time. . . .[It][includes a gay
man and his lover as Pfeiffer's neighbors.
They have some of the best lines in the film
and at one point they are seen in bed with
their arms wrapped [around] each other."

Despite the extensive promotional campaign, filmgoers found the love story too
coyly artificial. *Frankie & Johnny* grossed
only $9.8 million in distributors' domestic
film rentals. George Carlin would play a
similar-type gabby gay New York City
neighbor to Nick Nolte in *The Prince of
Tides* (1991).

86. Freebie and the Bean (Warner Bros., 1974), color, 112 min. R-rated.

Executive producer, Floyd Mutrux; pro-
ducer, Richard Rush; associate producer, Tony
Ray; director, Rush; story, Mutrux; screenplay,
Robert Kaufman; art director, Hilyard Brown;
set decorator, Ruby Levitt; music, Dominic
Frontiere; assistant directors, Chris Seitz, Lorin
Salob; second unit director/stunt coordinator,
Chuck Bail; sound, Barry Thomas; special ef-
fects, Sass Bedig; camera, Lazlo Kovacs; edi-
tors, Frederic Steinkamp, Michael McLean.

Cast: Alan Arkin (Benito "Bean" Vasquez);
James Caan (Freebie Waters); Loretta Swit (Mil-
dred Meyers); Jack Kruschen (Albert "Red"
Meyers); Mike Kellin (Lieutenant Rosen);
Linda Marsh (Barbara); Paul Koslo (Whitey);
John Garwood (Meyers's Chauffeur); Alex
Rocco (District Attorney); Valerie Harper (Con-
suelo Vasquez); Christopher Morley (Gason);

Chuck Bail (Suspect); and: Monte Stickles,
Kathy Witt.

In the early 1970s, the onslaught of cop
buddy films and TV series so escalated
that *Freebie and the Bean*, made in 1973,
sat on the shelf for nearly a year before
it was unleashed. This banal exercise
boasted two major goals: (1) how infantile
can we make the destructive cop partners?
(2) can we beat the Hollywood record for
on-camera mayhem (i.e. body counts, de-
molished cars). Like the prior year's *The
Laughing Policeman*, q.v., also set in San
Francisco, the film's prime killer just happens to be gay, this time a transvestite.

WASP-ish Freebie Waters (James Caan)
and Mexican-American Benito "Bean"
Vasquez (Alan Arkin) are very casual San
Francisco plainclothes cops in search of a
big case to crack. One night, while sifting
for clues through the garbage of gangland figure Albert "Red" Meyers (Jack
Kruschen), the team uncovers evidence
which links the gangster to the local numbers racket. Inspired by the hope of a departmental promotion, they pursue additional leads. These clues, in turn, take
them to a man called Motley, who *might*
be the needed major witness in the case
against Meyers. One of the lawmen's informants tells them Motley is out of town,
and that Detroit mobsters have ordered a
contract for Meyers's death. Freebie and
the Bean arrest Meyers on a trumped-up
charge, believing jail is the safest haven
for him.

After Meyers's lawyer engineers his release, the cops shadow the suspect around
town, saving him from the active hit man.
Meanwhile, Freebie and the Bean interrogate Gason (Christopher Morley), Motley's lover, who insists his roommate has
not returned to the Bay City. Later, the
policemen watch Meyers driving off with
a striking woman in his Mercedes. Suspicious, they follow the car to the sports
stadium where the Super Bowl game is in
progress. When Bean pulls open the rear
door of Meyers's chauffeur-driven ve-

Alan Arkin and James Caan in *Freebie and the Bean* (1974).

hicle, he is shot twice by the woman, who is actually Gason in drag. Gason yanks Meyers into the stadium as a hostage, but the latter dies of a heart attack. Freebie chases the killer into the ladies room. There, in a violent shootout, Gason dies.

Belatedly, Freebie learns from Meyers's wife, Mildred (Loretta Swit), that she had planted the evidence in the garbage can, hoping it would lead to Meyers being sent to prison, so she could marry her boyfriend—Lieutenant Rosen (Mike Kellin), Freebie and the Bean's superior officer. The discouraged Freebie is also told that Motley was murdered as he arrived at the San Francisco airport, effectively ending the case he and Bean had been building for the past year. Disgusted by the turn-of-events, Freebie drags himself into the ambulance that is carting away Bean's body. Suddenly, Bean tosses off the blanket covering him, and announces he is fine. The two pals wrestle wildly, causing the ambulance to zoom out of control and crash into a pole. The cops are tossed out the back door into a row of garbage cans. They are back just where they began on the case.

A bored Vincent Canby (*New York Times*) reported, "this year's final cop comedy [the movie was released on December 25, 1974], seems the worst of the lot, probably because it has a cast of otherwise good actors doing bits of business . . . as if they thought they could upstage all of the movie's automobiles, which are seldom still. . . .. The best performance is that of Valerie Harper (television's Rhoda), who is seen briefly as Bean's wife. . . . The rest of the time the movie is serio-comic trash." *Variety* branded the entry as "Tasteless" and alerted: "The purported 'humor' between the two stars largely hinges on Caan's delivery of what are nothing more than repeated racist slurs on Arkin's character's Chicano ancestry." Clyde Jeavons (British *Monthly Film Bulletin*) critiqued, "A researcher of the future hunting for a single film which might summarise Hollywood's favourite thematic elements of the early Seventies would not have to look much further than this frenetic farce. Platonic male love affair, police corruption, comic violence, cynicism in high places, San Francisco, gay villains, the car chase—they are all here in spades (and yes, there is plenty of racial backbiting as well)."

87. **Fried Green Tomatoes** (Universal, 1991), color, 130 min. PG-13-rated.

Executive producers, Ane Marie Gillen, Tom Taylor, Norman Lear; producers, Jon

Avnet, Jordan Kerner; co-producers, Martin Huberty, Lisa Lindstrom, Ric Rondell; associate producers, Deborah Love, Barbara Ling; director, Avnet; based on the novel *Fried Green Tomatoes at the Whistle Stop Cafe* by Fannie Flagg; screenplay, Flagg, Avnet; production designer, Barbara Ling; art director, Larry Fulton; set decorator, Deborah Schutt; costumes, Elizabeth McBride; makeup, Fern Buchner; music, Thomas Newman; assistant directors, Love, Jeff Rafner; stunt coordinator, Kerrie Cullen; sound, Mary Ellis; camera, Geoffrey Simpson; editor, Debra Neil.

Cast: Kathy Bates (Evelyn Couch); Jessica Tandy (Ninny Threadgoode); Mary Stuart Masterson (Idgie Threadgoode); Mary Louise Parker (Ruth Jamison); Nick Searcy (Frank Bennett); Cicely Tyson (Sipsey); Chris O'Donnell (Buddy Threadgoode); Stan Shaw (Big George); Gailard Sartain (Ed Couch); Tim Scott (Smokey Lonesome); Gary Basarba (Grady Kilgore); Lois Smith (Mama Threadgoode); Jo Harvey Allen (Teacher with Mirror); Macon McCalman (Prosecutor); Richard Riehle (Reverend Scroggins); Ranor Scheine (Curtis Smoote); Grace Zabriskie (Eva Bates); Reid Binion (Young Julian); Afton Smith (Leona Threadgoode); Danny Nelson (Papa Threadgoode); Nancy Atchison (Little Idgie); Constance Shulman (Missy); Haynes Brooke (Older Julian); Ginny Parker (Ruth's Mother); Tres Holton (Boy at Supermarket); Ronald McCall (Ocie); Wallace Merck (KKK Man); David Dwyer (Hooded Man); Lashondra Phillips (Young Naughty Bird); Catherine Larson, Missy Wolff (Girls); Latanya Richardson (Janeen); Grayson Fricke (Buddy Jr.); Enjolik Oree (Older Naughty Bird); Genevieve Fisher (Peggy Hale); Tom Even (Judge); Bob Hannah (Defense Attorney); Ted Manson (Bailiff); Carole Leon-Mitchell (Sue Otis); Evan Lockwood (Tim); Suzi Bass (Nurse).

Fried Green Tomatoes, a star vehicle for Academy Award-winners Kathy Bates and Jessica Tandy, is many things to many people. It is a parallel (1920s–1930s and the 1980s) character study of two women in the American South establishing their independence; it is a Gothic murder mystery; it is a memory play of atmospheric southern life long gone. It is also a quietly stated study of (un)requited lesbian love, of two women sharing friendship, obstacles and joys as their reliance on one another deepens over the years. Within *Fried Green Tomatoes*, the affection between Idgie and Ruth may or may not have ever been physical, and it may or may not have been acknowledged or rejected by Ruth. As such, the lesbian subtext remains a deliberate undercurrent to the main thrust of this comedy drama.

In present-day Alabama, frumpy Evelyn Couch (Kathy Bates) accompanies her husband Ed (Gailard Sartain) on a visit to his aged mother at a nursing home. While he is occupied, menopausal Evelyn—full of low self-esteem and uncharted other miseries—chats with an elderly patient, Ninny Threadgoode (Jessica Tandy). During many conversations over the weeks, Ninny captivates Evelyn with anecdotal personal stories of southern life during the Depression era.

Tomboy Idgie Threadgoode (Mary Stuart Masterson) has always been a rebellious child. When her beloved brother, Buddy (Chris O'Donnell), dies accidentally on the railroad tracks, she runs away, preferring a vagrant's life in the nearby woods. Later, at the family's prompting, Ruth Jamison (Mary-Louise Parker), Buddy's grief-stricken fiancee tries winning Idgie's confidence, hoping to civilize this maverick. Soon Idgie and the well-bred Ruth, both so very different, become nurturing friends, sharing adventures and confidences. Idgie feels rejected when Ruth marries Frank Bennett (Nick Searcy) and moves to another county. When Idgie finally visits Ruth, she discovers that Frank is a sadistic bully who beats his wife, but that Ruth is too fearful of him to leave. Gutsy Idgie, aided by black Big George (Stan Shaw), "kidnaps" the pregnant Ruth. Back in Whistle Stop, the two women, helped by Sipsey (Cicely Tyson), open the Whistle Stop Cafe, which becomes famous for its barbecued meats, fried green tomatoes and its two inseperable owners who treat blacks with respect. Ruth gives birth to Buddy Jr. (Grayson Fricke), who, one day, will himself be injured on the railroad

Mary-Louise Parker and Mary Stuart Masterson in *Fried Green Tomatoes* (1991).

tracks (losing an arm in the accident). Meanwhile, the vengeful Frank shows up in town, threatening to even the score. That night he is murdered (by Sipsey), his body disposed of (in the barbecue roast), and the participants hope that he will be forgotten. However, a sheriff (Ranor Scheine) from Frank's county investigates, refusing to be stymied by Idgie's and Ruth's lack of cooperation. Eventually, Frank's car is dragged out of the river and Idgie, whom witnesses once heard threatening the deceased, is placed on trial. Thanks to the creative testimony of the local preacher (Richard Riehle), Idgie goes free. Thereafter, Idgie and Ruth live happily, watching Buddy Jr. grow up. Tragedy strikes when Ruth develops cancer and dies.

As a result of Ninny's inspiring stories of friendship, candy-chomping Evelyn re-examines her life. She diets, takes self-assertiveness classes, and gains self-respect as a successful door-to-door cosmetic salesperson. Although Ed is baffled by the boisterous, new Evelyn (who calls herself "Tawanda" in randy moments), Ninny encourages Evelyn's emotional growth at each step.

Wanting to repay Ninny for all that she has done, Evelyn insists that she come stay with she and Ed. En route to their new life, they visit the cemetery where Ruth is buried. Suddenly, Evelyn, looking at Miss Threadgoode, put together the missing pieces of the puzzle. She just may have the answer to the question of "What ever happened to Idgie?"

With two such stellar actresses, critics expected more of *Fried Green Tomatoes* than it offered. Henry Sheehan (*LA Weekly*) insisted that filmmaker Jon Avnet "simply doesn't have the vocabulary to suggest undercurrents of feeling, and as the film progresses, it sheds, rather than acquires, meanings." He observed that the "Idgie-Ruth friendship, which starts out with explicit hints of lesbianism, scurries for cover in a melodramatic tale of murder." Owen Glieberman (*Entertainment Weekly*) gave the film a B-, reasoning that "compared with the recent *Rambling Rose* (which it sometimes resembles), *Fried Green Tomatoes* is pushy, didactic, and not very well directed."

Fried Green Tomatoes was nominated for two Academy Awards: Best Supporting Actress (Jessica Tandy; Mercedes Ruehl won for *The Fisher King*) and Best Screenplay Based on Material from Another Medium (*The Silence of the Lambs* won). Despite reviewers' reservations, it proved to be immensely popular with filmgoers, grossing $75,696,907 at the box-office in its first 22 weeks of domestic distribution

Concerning the film's lesbian subtheme, director Jon Avnet was quoted as saying, "You can take it how you want to. I had no interest in going into the bedroom." Co-scripter Fannie Flagg (who wrote the original 1987 novel) insisted, "It's not a political film at all. It's about the possibilities of people being sweet and loving to each other." Nevertheless, the Gay and Lesbian Alliance Against Defamation (GLAAD) gave the movie a Media Award for its positive depiction of lesbians in a film.

88. **Funny Lady** (Columbia, 1975), color, 136 minutes.

Producer, Ray Stark; director, Herbert Ross; story, Arnold Schulman; screenplay, Schulman, Jay Presson Allen; production designer, George Jenkins; set decorator, Audrey Blasdel; costumes, Ray Aghayan, Bob Mackie, Shirley Strahm; makeup, Don Cash; music director, Peter Matz; choreographer, Betty Walberg; songs: John Kander and Fred Ebb; Vincent Youmans, Edward Eliscu and Billy Rose; Harold Arlen, E. Y. Harburg and Rose; Harry Warren, Mort Dixon and Rose; James V. Monaco, Fred Fisher and Rose; Oscar Levant, Dixon and Rose; Arthur Fields, Fred Hall and Rose; Harry Akst, Grant Clarke and Rose; Joseph Meyer, Ballard MacDonald and Rose; Al Jolson, Dave Dreyer and Rose; Jack Murray and Ben Oakland; assistant directors, Jack Roe, Stu Fleming, Dodie Fawley; sound, Jack Solomon; special camera effects, Albert Whitlock; camera, James Wong Howe; editor, Marion Rothman.

Cast: Barbra Streisand (Fanny Brice); James Caan (Billy Rose); Omar Sharif (Nick Arnstein); Roddy McDowall (Bobby Moore); Ben Vereen (Bert Robbins); Carole Wells (Norma Butler); Larry Gates (Bernard Baruch); Heidi O'Rourke (Eleanor Holm); Samantha Huffaker (Fran); Matt Emery (Buck Bolton); Joshua

Shelley (Painter); Corey Fischer (Conductor); Garrett Lewis (Production Singer); Don Torres (Man at Wedding); Raymond Guth (Buffalo Handler); Gene Troobnick (Ned); Royce Wallace (Adele); Byron Webster (*Crazy Quilt* Director); Lilyan Chauvin (Mademoiselle); Cliff Norton (Stage Manager); Ken Samson (Frederick Martin—Daddy); Colleen Camp (Billy's Girl); Alana Collins (Girl with Nick); Jackie Stoloff (Mrs. Arnstein); Bert May (Assistant Stage Manager); Ben Busch (Ned's Secretary); Maggie Malooly (Gossip Columnist); Jodean Russo (Woman at Wedding); Larry Arnold (Maitre D' in Billy's Club); Shirley Kirkes (Singer in Billy's Club); Jerry Trent, Toni Kaye and Gary Menteer (*Paper Moon* Tap Trio); Deborah Sherman (Billy's Secretary); Dick Winslow (Fritz), Dick De Benedictis (Rehearsal Pianist); Louis Da Pron (Choreographer); Hank Stohl (Radio Director); Diane Wyatt (Baruch's Secretary); Tom Northam (Magazine Executive); Tod Durwood (Photographer); Brett Hadley, Jack Frey, Jadeen Vaughn (Acquacade Assistants); Paul Bryar (Cleaning Man); Maralyn Thomas, Phil Gray (Radio Singers); Frank L. Pine (Pilot); Bill Baldwin (Radio Announcer).

Techniques may have changed drastically in the 46 years since *The Broadway Melody*, q.v., but the same backstage stereotypes were being trotted forth in new Hollywood musicals about life on the Great White Way. The representative types still included the gay chorus boy. In this follow-up to *Funny Girl* (1968), Barbra Streisand was again the bombastic star, Fanny Brice; this time her confidant was ever-amiable, ever-sympathetic, ever-obliging Bobby Moore (Roddy McDowall), who used to be a stage hoofer before becoming the theatre queen's lady-in-waiting. It was the same sort of role McDowall had played in *Inside Daisy Clover* (1965), q.v.

The sequel picks up where *Funny Girl* left off in tracing the career of the Broadway legend, Fanny Brice (Barbra Streisand). In 1930, she is headlining the latest edition of *The Ziegfeld Follies* and has a young daughter, Fran (Samantha Huffaker). Although she is divorced from smooth crook Nick Arnstein (Omar Sharif), she still adores the man. Meanwhile, Fanny meets brash, young songwriter-club owner Billy Rose (James Caan). Although they are opposites, the two are attracted to each other. The uncouth, ambitious Rose wants to star Fanny in spectacular stage shows. The two fall in love, but Nick re-enters the scene. For a time, Nick and Fanny renew their romance, yet Arnstein realizes he is wrong for Fanny. He leaves again. She returns to Billy Rose, who stars her in *Crazy Quilt*. Fanny marries Rose and, for a spell, they are content. However, on a surprise trip from Hollywood to Cleveland, she discovers Billy is having an affair with his aquacade swimming star, Eleanor Holm (Heidi O'Rourke). As a result, Fanny and Rose divorce. Years pass. Fanny encounters an older, wealthier Billy Rose who again hopes to star Fanny on Broadway. Although she declines the offer, there is a suggestion that she might change her mind.

Roddy McDowall's Bobby Moore does not have much footage in *Funny Lady*— does anyone in a Barbra Streisand vehicle? —but his presence is felt. Bobby, who thinks the ambitious Billy is not good enough for Fanny, is always anxious to prove the name-dropper is a phony:

Moore: Ruth Etting! My ass.

Rose: That's swell, dear. Anytime I want your ass, I'll know what to call it.

When *Funny Lady* premiered, Pauline Kael (*The New Yorker*) decided, "The moviemakers weren't just going to make a sequel to *Funny Girl*—they were going to kill us. . . . The picture is overproduced and badly edited, with a '40s-movie-heartbreak plot. A great deal of talent has been badly used." *Variety* acknowledged "However much of a letdown the plot becomes, there's no denying the superior integration of drama, comedy, show music and personal dramatic music en route. . . . The breath and depth of Streisand's screen abilities and assurance have reached total maturity. . . . Roddy McDowall has another one of those formula handholder-to-

the-leading-player 'go-for' parts he usually gets. . . ."

Funny Lady was not as successful as its predecessor. Made at a cost of $8.5 million, it grossed $19,313,000 in distributors' domestic film rentals. It received five Oscar nominations: Original Song, "How Lucky Can You Get," (*Nashville* won); Scoring (*Barry Lyndon* won); Cinematography (*Barry Lyndon* won); Costumes (*Barry Lyndon* won); and Sound (*Jaws* won).

89. Garbo Talks (Metro-Goldwyn-Mayer, 1984), color, 105 min. PG-13-rated.

Producers, Burtt Harris, Elliott Kastner; associate producer, Jennifer M. Ogden; director, Sidney Lumet; screenplay, Larry Grusin; production designer, Philip Rosenberg; costumes, Anna Hill Johnstone; set decorators, Philip Smith, James Godfrey; makeup, Joe Cranraro; music, Cy Coleman; assistant director, Alan Hopkins; sound, James Sabat; camera, Andrej Bartkowski; editor, Andrew Mondshein.

Cast: Anne Bancroft (Estelle Rolfe); Ron Silver (Gilbert Rolfe); Carrie Fisher (Lisa Rolfe); Catherine Hicks (Jane Mortimer); Steven Hill (Walter Rolfe); Howard Da Silva (Angelo Dokakis); Dorothy Loudon (Sony Apollinar); Harvey Fierstein (Bernie Whitlock); Hermione Gingold (Elizabeth Rennick); Richard B. Shull (Shepard Plotnick); Michael Lombard (Mr. Morganelli); Ed Crowley (Mr. Goldhammer); Nina Zoe, Betty Comden (Greta Garbo); Alice Spivak (Claire Rolfe); Maurice Sterman (Dr. Cohen); Antonia Rey (Puerto Rican Nurse); Court Miller (*Romeo and Juliet* Director); Denny Dillon (Elaine); Karen Shallo (Harriet); Maxwell Alexander (Roger Kellerman); Peter Gumeny (Arresting Officer); Stephen Burks (Black Officer); Tony DiBenedetto, Burtt Harris (Construction Workers); Mervyn Nelson (Movie Shop Owner); John Ring (Garbo's Doorman); Anne Gartlan (Garbo's Maid); Jose Santan (Sanchez/Orderly); Jennifer M. Ogden (Nurse); David Hammil (Ferry Conductor); Roderick Cook (Von Klammer); Mary McDonnell (Lady Capulet); Leila Danette (Augusta); Nadine Darling, Joan de Marrais (Flea Market Saleladies); Ethel Beatty (Lady in Jail); Adolph Green, Francesco Scarvullo, Arthur Schlesinger Jr., George Plimpton, Pat Kennedy Lawford (Themselves); Didi

Catherine Hicks and Ron Silver in *Garbo Talks* (1984).

D'Errico (Actors Equity Receptionist); Harry Madsen (Delivery Man).

What a wonderful conceit for a little movie!

All her life, eccentric New Yorker Estelle Rolfe (Anne Bancroft) has been an active champion of lost causes and is never shy about speaking her piece, even if it lands her in jail—which it frequently does. One of the eccentric woman's many obsessions is watching Greta Garbo movies on TV. Eventually, Estelle's successful husband, Walter (Steven Hill) can take no more, and the couple divorce (he eventually remarries). Meanwhile, their downtrodden accountant son, Gilbert (Ron Silver), is married to the ultimate American Jewish princess, Lisa (Carrie Fisher).

When Estelle learns that she is dying of cancer, she tells Gilbert that she has one wish before she dies—to meet the elusive Garbo in person. Agreeing to this "mission impossible," the loving Gilbert de-

votes himself to satisfying his mother's "simple" request. In the process, he antagonizes his overbearing office superior (Richard B. Shull), gets to know flighty, would-be-actress, Jane Mortimer (Catherine Hicks), discovers how oppressive his shallow wife is and finds that life has many positive options. Determined to fulfill his quest, the driven Gilbert begs elderly celebrity photographer Angelo Dokakis (Howard Da Silva) to help him stalk the reclusive Garbo. The trail leads them all over New York City. One of Gilbert's tips takes him to Fire Island, where the Swedish actress is known to vacation. He misses his prey, but shares conversation with well-meaning Bernie Whitlock (Harvey Fierstein).

Finally, Gilbert crosses paths with Garbo; blurts out his request, and is amazed when the celebrity comes with him to the hospital. Garbo spends an hour with the dying woman, which pleases Estelle tremendously. Soon thereafter, Mrs.

Rolfe passes away. Gilbert, the wimp-turned-man, is ready to start life anew, especially now that Lisa has gone out West and he is developing a real rapport with Jane.

Sheila Benson (*Los Angeles Times*) applauded, "A novella of a movie, it is smart, edged with particularly New York humor, and amazingly unsentimental with a subject that could have become a real tooth-rooter. . . . The tracking of Garbo involves four wonderful vignettes: [including] . . . Harvey Fierstein; a quiet sociable Fire Islander to whom Gilbert can finally talk. . . ." On the other hand, David Denby (*New York*) found "The movie is poorly directed, but there are two marvelous performances. As an ancient lady of the stage and screen, Hermione Gingold creates a wonderful portrait of theatrical vanity. . . . Bancroft is so forceful that she burst this stupid movie at its seams." For an unimpressed J. Hoberman (*Village Voice*): "[Carrie] Fisher, of all people, adds a welcome touch of vinegar as Silver's spaced-out, bitch wife. The rest of the cutie pies . . . [Bancroft et al] are strictly from the Cabbage Patch."

Gilbert's vignette with Bernie Whitlock, a veteran salesman at the Queen's Boulevard branch of Alexander's Department Store, occurs when they meet on the ferry boat to Fire Island, carrying its mostly gay clientele. Bernie, who admits, "The older I get, the less I care about sex," cannot figure out why straight-looking Rolfe is heading to Fire Island. When they reach their destination and Gilbert fails to track down Garbo, Bernie does his best to be hospitable. Even knowing that his new acquaintance is married, he remains the optimist. When they part, Bernie shouts to Rolfe to drop by the store sometime. The episode portrays another lonely New Yorker reaching out in contemporary society.

Harvey Fierstein and Anne Bancroft would re-team for the screen version of *Torch Song Trilogy* (1988), q.v.

90. The Gay Deceivers (Fanfare Films, 1969), color, 91 min. R-rated.

Producer, Joe Solomon; associate producer, Paul Rapp; director, Bruce Kessler; story, Abe Polsky, Gil Lasky; screenplay, Jerome Wish; art director, Archie Bacon; set decorator, Ray Boltz; costumes, Norman Saling; makeup, Brian Perrow; music/music conductor, Stu Phillips; assistant director, Christopher Morgan; sound, Phil Mitchell; camera, Richard C. Glouner; editors, Renn Reynolds, Reg Browne.

Cast: Kevin Coughlin (Danny Devlin); Lawrence Casey (Elliot Crane); Brooke Bundy (Karen); Jo Ann Harris (Leslie Devlin); Michael Greer (Malcolm de John); Sebastian Brook (Craig); Jack Starrett (Lieutenant Colonel George Dixon); Richard Webb (Mr. Devlin); Eloise Hardt (Mrs. Devlin); Jeanne Baird (Mrs. Conway); Marishka (Carolyn); Mike Kopscha (Psychiatrist); Joseph Tornatore (Sergeant Kravits); Robert Reese (Real Estate Agent); Christopher Riordan (Duane); Doug Hume (Corporal); David Osterhout (Stern); Marilyn Wirt (Sybil); Ron Gans (Freddie); Rachel Romen (Dorothy); Tom Grubbs (Paul); Louise Williams (Bunny); Randee Lynne (Sheryl); Meredith Williams (Phil); Harry Sodoni (Georgette); Lenore Stevens (Laverne); Trigg Kelly (Jackie); Tony Epper (Vince).

"A sick joke at the expense of homosexuals, whose presumed mannerism of speech and behaviour are grotesquely parodied to occasionally amusing but more often tasteless effect." (British *Monthly Film Bulletin*)

In Los Angeles, good friends Danny Devlin (Kevin Coughlin) and Elliot Crane (Larry Casey) scheme to avoid being drafted into the Army and being shipped to Vietnam. They pose as gays and, as a result, the draft board exempts them. However, suspicious board officer Dixon (Jack Starrett) places them under personal surveillance. To insure their draft status stays the same, the two men move into an apartment building known to be full of homosexuals. Their landlord, Malcolm de John (Michael Greer), and his live-in lover, Craig (Sebastian Brook), are delighted with the handsome new tenants.

Danny constantly reminds Elliot not to

give away their gambit by dating women. On the other hand, Devlin is engaged to Karen (Brooke Bundy) and she insists on seeing the new pad. When she does, she, like the Devlins (Richard Webb, Eloise Hardt) and his sister Leslie (Jo Ann Harris), become suspicious of the flamboyant interior decorations (inherited from a past tenant). By now, busybody Malcolm wonders at the procession of straights parading in and out of Danny and Elliot's apartment. The pressures of the masquerade leads to a night out on the town, where Elliot gets involved in a brawl in a gay bar, Karen—concerned about Danny's sexual leanings—breaks their engagement.

In despair, Danny admits the truth to the draft board. To his surprise he is rejected. As it happens, Dixon and his underlings are actually gays, and do NOT want straights in the Army.

Variety noted the missed opportunities in this R-rated misadventure: "As is, it is an uneven situation piece with a great plot and a serious of unfilled incidents ranging from screaming camp to tender romantics. . . . Uneven starts and stops in the momentum of the film weakens the twist ending . . . Film is too much the formula Hollywood comedy. . . .Greer's flaming faggot portrayal is brilliant for the stereotype swish. But it is his own finesse that makes the role the best of the film. His sense of timing and talent for extending the humor of a situation is marvelous."

The problem with *The Gay Deceivers* is that it wants to have it both ways. It hoped to titillate heterosexuals with its "eavesdropping" on the "humorous" gay lifestyle. On the other hand, it intended to win homosexuals over with its self-deprecating humor, the oversized performance of acerbic Michael Greer ("I may not know my flowers, but I know a bitch when I see one") and Lawrence Casey's flexing in his swimwear. At the same time, concerned that viewers might misinterpret the macho nature of both

leads, the picture grows timid and self-conscious. And it protests a great deal.

The same year as this low-budget film's release, Michael Greer was playing a very serious variation of the flamboyant queen in an off-Broadway revival of *Fortune and Men's Eyes*, a part he would repeat in the screen version (1971), q.v. Kevin Coughlan had played a gay character in *Wild in the Streets* (1968), q.v.

91. The Gay Divorcee (RKO, 1934), 107 min. Not rated.

Producer, Pandro S. Berman; director, Mark Sandrich; based on the musical play *The Gay Divorce* by Dwight Taylor and Cole Porter, and the novel *The Gay Divorce* by Taylor; screenplay, George Marion Jr., Dorothy Yost, Edward Kaufman; art directors, Van Nest Polglase, Carroll Clark; costumes, Walter Plunkett; songs: Con Conrad and Herb Magidson; Mack Gordon and Harry Revel; Porter; music director, Max Steiner; choreographers, Dave Gould, (uncredited) Fred Astaire, Hermes Pan; special effects, Vernon Walker; camera, David Abel; editor, William Hamilton.

Cast: Fred Astaire (Guy Holden); Ginger Rogers (Mimi Glossop); Alice Brady (Hortense Ditherwell); Edward Everett Horton (Egbert Fitzgerald); Erik Rhodes (Rodolfo Tonetti); Eric Blore (Waiter); Lillian Miles, Betty Grable (Hotel Guests); Charles Coleman (Valet); William Austin (Cyril Glossop); Paul Porcasi (Nightclub Proprietor); E. E. Clive (Customs Inspector); George Davis, Alphonse Martell (French Waiters); Charles Hall (Call Boy at Dock); and: Art Jarrett.

Not only was *The Gay Divorcee* the first starring feature for the new screen team of Fred Astaire and Ginger Rogers, but it showcased the type of sissy friend/servant/companion to the hero, so often found in 1930s American movies. Here, the type was performed to the hilt by Edward Everett Horton, but the assignment might easily have been handled by the cast's Eric Blore or Erik Rhodes (or by such other character actors as Franklin Pangborn or Grady Sutton). While the movie industry's production code could now dictate the surface features of such milquetoast characterizations, Horton, who knew of what he spoke, took the stock part to new levels in *The Gay Divorcee*. He is the hero's light-hearted pal, a man with a passion for toy dolls, who is known to his friends as Aunt Egbert and admits that his family once nicknamed him Pinky.

The underlying attitude of Egbert Fitzgerald, however, is just one of the many sophisticated ingredients in the top-flight *The Gay Divorcee*. With Astaire and Rogers dancing to "The Continental" and songs like "Night and Day," "Don't Let It Bother You" and "Let's K-nock K-nees" (performed by Betty Grable and Edward Everett Horton), *The Gay Divorcee* solidified the popularity of Astaire and Rogers.

Mimi Glossop (Ginger Rogers) wants a divorce and her Aunt Hortense (Alice Brady) and foggy attorney, Egbert Fitzgerald (Edward Everett Horton), ship her off to a British resort. There, a hired correspondent (Erik Rhodes) will provide the impression that they are lovers, giving Mimi a legal basis for her divorce. En route, Mimi meets American dancer Guy Holden (Fred Astaire). He pursues her to the Brighton resort hotel where she thinks he is the co-respondent, causing her to dislike him. On the other hand, when Rodolfo arrives, Guy believes he is Mimi's lover. Eventually, the confusions are sorted out, and Guy and Mimi begin their romance in earnest.

Andre Sennwald (*New York Times*) rated this RKO release "an entirely agreeably photoplay which sings, dances and quips with agility and skill." Of the stars, he noted: "Both as a romantic comedian and as a lyric dancer Mr. Astaire is an urbane delight, and Miss Rogers keeps pace with him even in his rhythmic flights over the furniture." As to the supporting cast: "For subsidiary humor there are Alice Brady as the talkative aunt; Edward Everett Horton as the confused lawyer with his first case. . . ." *Variety* agreed that "This musical has everything for audi-ence satisfaction. . . . Alice Brady and Edward Everett Horton, as the sub-team, are more than just good foils."

Based on the Broadway show, *The Gay Divorce* (1932), in which Astaire had starred with his sister, Adele, the film proved to be a box-office smash. The movie won an Academy Award for Best Song ("The Continental"). It received four additional Oscar nominations: Best Picture (*It Happened One Night* won); Best Score (*One Night of Love* won); Best Interior Decoration (*The Merry Widow* won); Best Sound (*One Night of Love* won).

92. Georgia, Georgia (Cinerama Releasing Corp., 1972), color, 91 min. R-rated.

Executive producer, Quentin Kelly; producer, Jack Jordan; director, Stig Bjorkman; screenplay, Maya Angelou; music, Sven Olaf Waldorf; song, Angelou; choreographer, Herman Howell; camera, Andreas Bellis; editor, Sten-Goran Camitz.

Cast: Diana Sands (Georgia Martin); Dirk Benedict (Michael Winters); Minnie Gentry (Albert Anderson); Roger Furman (Herbert Thompson); Terry Whitmore (Bobo); Diane Kjaer, Lars Eric Berenett, Stig Engstrom, Artie Sheppard, James Thomas Finlay Jr., Andrew Bates Jr., Randolph Henry, Tina Hedstrom, Beatrice Wendin.

A year before her untimely death from cancer, talented Diana Sands appeared in this low-key entry: an American production shot in Scandinavia by Swedish director Stig Bjorkman. The R-rated feature tried earnestly to reflect several points of views, especially black sensibilities, reducing it to a talky, unconvincing celluloid forum of ideas instead of drama.

Exhausted black American entertainer Georgia Martin (Diana Sands) arrives in Stockholm for a concert engagement, accompanied by her anti-white companion, Alberta Anderson (Minnie Gentry), and her gay road manager, Herbert Thompson (Roger Furman). Soon, Georgia meets Michael Winters (Dirk Benedict), a white American deserter (from the Vietnam War) who is employed as a photographer for a local magazine. While Georgia and Michael begin an intense romance, Bobo (Terry Whitmore), a black American deserter, hounds the songstress to become a spokesperson for their causes. When she refuses, Bobo stirs up the bigoted Alberta against the celebrity. The latter is already furious with Georgia for coupling with Winters—he is white and besides, Anderson is strongly attracted to the performer. The story ends with the disturbed Alberta killing Georgia.

Variety reported, "Maya Angelou has packed her first script with just about as many of the black-white cliches as it will stand, then the producers added a few of their own.. Occasionally . . . some good things happen but the overall impression is that of an amateurish, poorly-written, poorly-directed and mostly ineptly-played film." In retrospect, Donald Bogle (*Blacks in American Films and Television*, 1988) decided this was a "Startling but uneven and rather frustrating drama." As to the roles played by Sands, Gentry and Furman: "all three are fascinating objects (they're almost abstractions) but not a one is a wholly believable character, and the relationships among the three . . . are left foundering and underdeveloped."

93. Gilda (Columbia, 1946), 110 min. Not rated.

Producer, Virginia Van Upp; director, Charles Vidor; story, E. A. Ellington; adaptor, Jo Eisinger; screenplay, Marion Parsonnet; art directors, Stephen Goosson, Van Nest Polglase; set decorator, Robert Priestly; costumes, Jean Louis; music directors, Morris W. Stoloff, Marlin Skiles; songs, Allan Roberts and Doris Fisher; choreographer, Jack Cole; assistant director, Art Black; sound, Lambert Day; camera, Rudolph Mate; editor, Charles Nelson.

Cast: Rita Hayworth (Gilda); Glenn Ford (Johnny Farrell); George Macready (Ballin Mundson); Joseph Calleia (Obregon); Steven Geray (Uncle Pio); Joe Sawyer (Casey); Gerald Mohr (Captain Delgado); Robert Scott (Gabe Evans); Ludwig Donath, Lionel Royce (Germans); Don Douglas (Thomas Langford); Saul Z. Martel (Little Man); George J. Lewis (Huerta); Rosa Rey (Maria); Jerry De Castro (Doorman); Robert Kellard, Ernest Hilliard, Frank Leigh, Rodolfo Hoyos, Jean Del Val, Paul Regas, Phil Van Zandt (Men); Fernando Eliscu (Bendolin's Wife); Frank Leyva (Argentine); Forbes Murray, Sam Flint (Americans); Oscar Lorraine, Jean DeBriac (Frenchmen); Herbert Evans (Englishman); Eduardo Ciannelli (Bendolin); Robert Tafur (Clerk); Russ Vincent (Escort); Erno Verebes, Eugene Borden (Dealers); Alphonse Martell, Leon Lenoir (Croupiers); Soretta Raye (Harpy); J. W. Noon, Noble G. Evey (Bunco Dealers); George Sorel, Jack Chefe, Albert Pollet, Lou Palfy (Assistant Croupiers); Sam Appel (Black Jack Dealer); Jack Del Rio (Cashier); Juli Abadia (Newsman/Waiter); Cosmo Sardo, Paul Bradley, Nina Bara, Ruth Roman, John Tyrrell (Bits); Ted Hecht (Social Citizen); Leander DeCordova (Servant); Fred Godoy (Bartender); Lew Harvey, John Merton (Policemen); Herman Marks, Carli Elinor, Joseph Palma, Alfred Paix, Herman Marks, Ralph Navarro (Waiters); Ramon Munox (Judge); Argentina Brunetti (Woman); Sam Ash (Gambler).

For most of her fans, *Gilda* remains the high-water mark of beautiful Rita Hayworth's screen career. Embedded within this tale of a femme fatale and her lovers is the complex relationship between the two lead male characters—played by Glenn Ford and George Macready. While the script calls for each to be conventionally magnetized by the sultry leading lady, they are strongly bound to one another. Near the opening of *Gilda*, Macready, brandishing his phallic, knife-concealing cane, saves Ford from a trio of toughs who intend to roll him for his gambling winnings. Macready says (symbolically) to Ford about his trusty weapon: "It is silent when I wish it to be silent. It talks when I wish it to."

Ford: Is that your idea of a friend?
Macready: Yes.

Later, Macready makes a revealing statement to Ford on the evening Rita first appears at Macready's home: "You never thought I'd have a woman in the house."

Johnny Farrell (Glenn Ford), is a pugnacious, sarcastic young gambler. He becomes the confidential assistant to sinister Ballin Mundson (George Macready), the owner of a thriving Buenos Aires gambling casino. (It develops that Mundson is the secret head of an international combine dealing in tungsten, a cartel first sponsored by the Nazis.) Soon after Germany's World War II surrender, Ballin departs on a trip. He returns with a bride, Gilda (Rita Hayworth), not realizing that she and Johnny once had an affair. Mundson makes Farrell responsible for Gilda and Johnny endures her taunts and covers up her flirtations with other men. After killing a Nazi agent, Mundson flees the country. He fakes an ocean plane crash so everyone will believe he is dead. Farrell takes charge of the casino, marries the insolent Gilda and pays her back for the taunts he endured from her. Mundson makes a sudden return, insisting that Johnny and Gilda have betrayed him. He is stopped from shooting them by an employee (Steven Geray), who stabs Ballin. Secret police agent Obregon (Joseph Calleia), who has been tracking Mundson's activities for months, rules that the killing is self-defense. As for Johnny and Gilda, they forgive one another and leave Argentina to start life anew.

Harrison's Reports predicted, "This melodrama of love and hate . . . should go over well with adult audiences, in spite of the fact that the story is a vague and confusing one. . . ." Bosley Crowther (*New York Times*), no fan of the sensual picture nor Rita Hayworth, observed, "Glenn Ford . . . shows, at least, a certain stamina and poise in the role of the tough young gambler, but his is a thankless role. And George Macready is icy and unbending as the Germanic casino proprietor. . . ." *Variety* advised, "when things get trite and frequently far-fetched, somehow, at the drop of a shoulder strap, there is always Rita Hayworth to excite the filmgoer."

Despite the critics' frosty reaction to the movie, *Gilda* was a huge box-office success, grossing over $3 million. It led to several other Rita Hayworth-Glenn Ford screen teamings, including *An Affair in Trinidad* (1952). In later years, when questioned about the underlying sado-masochistic relationship between Johnny and Ballin, Glenn Ford admitted he always understood the subtext. In contrast, director King Vidor said that theory was nonsense. The viewer must decide for himself.

For the record, it was Anita Ellis who dubbed Rita's singing in *Gilda*, including the movie's erotic number, "Put the Blame on Mame, Boys."

94. Girlfriends (Warner Bros., 1978), color, 86 min. PG-rated.

Producer, Claudia Weill; co-producer, Jan Saunders; associate producers, Pat Churchill, Lilly Kilvert; director, Weill; story, Vicki Polon, Weill; screenplay, Polon; art director, Patrizia von Brandenstein; costumes, Bonnie Daziel, Jody Coy-Cooper, Susan Becker; music, Michael Small; songs, Tom Griffith; assistant director, David Streit; sound, Maryte Kavaliauskas; camera, Fred Murphy; editor, Suzanne Pettit.

Cast: Melanie Mayron (Susan Weinblatt); Anita Skinner (Anne Munroe); Eli Wallach (Rabbi Gold); Christopher Guest (Eric); Bob Balaban (Martin); Gina Rogak (Julie); Amy Wright (Ceil); Viveca Lindfors (Beatrice); Mike Kellin (Abe); Jean de Baer (Terry); Kenneth McMillan (Cabbie); Russell Horton (Photo Editor); Tania Berezin (Rabbi's Wife); Kathryn Walker (Carpel's Receptionist); Roderick Cook (Carpel); Kristoffer Tabori (Charlie); Stacey Lomoe-Smith (Rebecca); Norma Mayron (Mrs. Weinblatt); Regina David (Rabbi's Receptionist); Amy Wright (Ceil); Ted Lambert (Rabbi's Son); Tania Berezin (Rabbi's Wife); Kathryn Walker (Carpel's Receptionist).

Long before she gained prominence as a co-star of TV's "thirtysomething" (1987–91), Melanie Mayron, the self-absorbed cashier of *Car Wash* (1978), q.v., made an early career mark in this sensitive, feminist screen study. Like other movies of the period which offered a cross-section of Big Apple life, a gay figure was included in the storyline for several purposes: to make the urban mix realistic, to add mild titillation, and, more importantly, to clarify for viewers that the moody, soul-

Melanie Mayron and Amy Wright in *Girlfriends* **(1978).**

searching heroine who wants a career *and* love is quite heterosexual. (A similar situation exists in Elaine May's *Sheila Levine Is Dead and Living in New York*, 1975, q.v.)

Now a college graduate, chubby, Jewish New Yorker Susan Weinblatt (Melanie Mayron) supports herself photographing bar mitzvahs and weddings. She is sponsored by middle-aged, married Rabbi Gold (Eli Wallach), with whom she enters an increasingly personal relationship. When her roommate, Anne Munroe (Anita Skinner), marries the unconventional Martin (Bob Balaban), insecure Susan becomes concerned with her own single status. Meanwhile, her attraction to college teacher Eric (Christopher Guest) is short-lived. Inspired by ambitious photographer friend Julie (Gina Rogak), Susan attempts to become professionally more aggressive. She and Eric make another go at a relationship.

After an out-of-town visit to Anne and Martin, schleppy Susan gives hitchhiker Ceil (Amy Wright) a ride. Susan allows Ceil, a hopeful dancer, to temporarily share her apartment, knowing that she is lesbian. Later, agitated by her own problems, Susan asks the irresponsible Ceil to leave and Julie moves in. Still later, Susan begins a live-in relationship with Eric. On another visit to Anne, now pregnant, each woman admits their hidden thoughts of the other. Later, at an art gallery showing of her photo work, Susan and Eric renew their friendship. Thereafter, Susan reaffirms her friendship with Anne, who, in turn, is reunited with her spouse.

Harold C. Schonberg (*New York Times*) admitted, "It's all very sad and, at its core, rather sentimental. But Claudia Weill keeps the film from degenerating into pathos. . . . For the most part, however, this is a slice-of-life cinema, realistically acted and filmed, with a good deal of charm under the quiet desperation. . . . Most of the charm comes from Melanie Mayron as Susan." *Variety* enthused, "It's the work of a technically skilled and assured director. . . . Each performance is a little gem and so are the character developed. . . . They look and act like people, which is a relief."

Made on a $500,000 budget by former documentary filmmaker Claudia Weills, *Girlfriends* was a modest hit. It is frequently revived on television, where *TV Guide* rates the drama three stars for being "a sensitive study of a woman . . . adjusting to life alone."

95. Girls in Prison (American International, 1956, 86 min. Not rated.

Producer, Alex Gordon; director, Edward L. Cahn; screenplay, Lou Rusoff; art director, Don Ament; music/song, Ronald Stein; camera, Frederick E. West; editor, Ronald Sinclair.

Cast: Richard Denning (Reverend Fulton); Joan Taylor (Anne Carson); Adele Jergens (Jenny); Helen Gilbert (Melanee); Lance Fuller (Paul Anderson); Jane Darwell (Matron Jamieson); Raymond Hatton (Pop Carson); Phyllis Coates (Dorothy); Diana Darrin (Meg); Mae Marsh (Grandma); Laurie Mitchell (Phyllis); Diane Richards (Nightclub Singer); Luana Walters, Riza Royce (Female Guards).

Variety summarized: "*Girls in Prison* is as routine as its title, an overlength jail yarn with telegraphic situations which reduce movements to a walk." Ever since *Caged* (1950), q.v., revitalized the women-behind-bars genre, Hollywood filmmakers had been exploiting the box-office potentials of a jailhouse filled with love-starved women. American International Pictures, which catered to the youth set, took the cinema's new maturity (in depicting prison stories) one step further and produced a fantasy mix of bondage, cheesecake and tough action. The "unnatural" sexual attitudes of some of the prisoners were depicted by those characters acting particularly butch and "mannish."

Anne Carson (Joan Taylor) is stuck in prison for five years for having helped Paul Anderson (Lance Fuller) in a bank robbery. Before starting her hard time, she thought she could cope with the tough life, but she learns differently. Her jailmates include a forbidding lineup of rough sorts: the off-kilter Dorothy (Phyllis Coates), Jenny (Adele Jergens) and Melanee (Helen Gilbert). While the prison chaplain (Richard Denning) attempts to rehabilitate Anne, Jenny and Melanie pressure her into revealing where she hid the heist loot. During an earthquake, Jenny and Melanie force Anne to escape with them. Jenny dies in the process, while Melanie and Anne go to her father (Raymond Hatton) thinking he might know where the loot is. Paul shows up and in the scuffle Jenny dies, before Paul is overwhelmed by the law. Anne turns the ill-gotten money over to the law and returns to prison, hoping for a new future.

96. The Glass House (CBS-TV, February 4, 1972), color, 100 min. (a.k.a.: *Truman Capote's The Glass House*)

Executive producer, Roger Gimbel; producer, Robert W. Christiansen, Rich Rosenberg; director, Tom Gries; story, Truman Capote, Wyatt Cooper; teleplay, Tracy Keenan Wynn; wardrobe, Bruce Walkup; makeup, Robert Stein; music, Billy Goldenberg; assistant director, Mike R. Moder; sound, Herman Lewis; camera, Jules Brenner; editor, Gene Fowler Jr.

Cast: Vic Morrow (Hugo Slocum); Clu Gulager (Brian Courtland); Billy Dee Williams (Lennox Beach); Kristoffer Tabori (Allan Campbell); Dean Jagger (Warden Auerbach); Alan Alda (Jonathan Paige); Luke Askew (Bibleback); Scott Hylands (Ajax); Edward Bell (Sinclair); Tony Mancini (Steve Berino); G. Wood (Pagonis); Roy Jenson (Officer Brown); Alan Vint (Bree).

It used to be that a fate-worse-than-death was reserved for chaste female screen characters who would rather die than submit and/or survive rape at the hands of a man. In the early 1970s, as mores changed and industry codes eased up, Hollywood feature films (*Fortune and Men's Eyes*, 1971, q.v.) and even network TV began dealing with homosexuality behind bars. This watershed TV movie, with its story co-authored by Truman Capote, made gay rape one of the many prison horrors it examined. Sue Cameron (*Hollywood Reporter*) judged, "Without a doubt, this movie will have more effect in bringing about prison reform than any number of riots or demonstrations around the country."

Among the fresh arrivals at a Utah prison are liberal college professor Jonathan Paige (Alan Alda), serving a short term on a manslaughter charge. Another newcomer is guitar-playing seventeen-year-old Allan Campbell (Kristoffer Tabori), starting a five-year sentence for drug-selling. Once inside the gates, the new convicts discover that the institution is not run by the aged Warden Auerback (Dean Jagger), but by rough convict Hugo Slocum (Vic Morrow), who controls the prison population with his muscle-bound convicts/thugs.

The well-bred Jonathan advises street-smart Allan not to join Slocum's circle. However, the teenager begins doing errands for the gang leader, anxious to gain his favor. Belatedly, he understands the price to be paid for becoming Slocum's new "boy." When he rejects these sexual advances ("It's either me or everybody" says Slocum), the tough convict retaliates by having his henchmen gang rape Allan in the gym room. The distraught Campbell later jumps to his death from the third-floor cell tier. Angered by Allan's death, Paige gathers evidence against the cocaine-snorting Slocum and his crowd, eventually winning the support of the black faction, headed by Lennox (Billy Dee Williams). In the showdown, Paige shoots Slocum, but, in turn, is killed by a prison guard (Clu Gulager).

Daily Variety admitted, "Prison dramas do not offer much opportunity for variations on the basic facts of life about men in enforced confinement" but agreed that *The Glass House* "succeeded as engrossing tv fare by underplaying the violence and concentrating sensitively on the pressures and inadequacies of the penal system. . . .

The trade paper commended the "authentic sounding dialog," the effort to "mesh exploitable incidents realistically with its main storyline" the avoidance of "the temptation to be preachy" and the "Good acting." In contrast, Tom Milne (British *Monthly Film Bulletin*) decided, "the script is much too busy with melodrama to explore its themes. . . . Less outrageous than *Fortune and Men's Eyes*, it is even less convincing, and light years behind *Riot in Cell Block 11* [1954]."

Filmed at the Utah State Prison, the grim drama received an Emmy Award for Best Direction, and editor Gene Fowler Jr. received an Emmy nomination.

97. The Glitter Dome (Home Box Office-Cable, November 18, 1984), color, 95 min.

Executive producer, Frank Konigsberg; producers, Stuart Margolin, Justis Greene; associate producer, Barry Jossen; director, Margolin; based on the novel by Joseph Wambaugh; teleplay, Stanley Kallis; production designer, Douglas Higgins; art director, Michael Bolton; set decorator, Rose Marie McSherry; costumes, Csilla Marki; makeup, Sandy Cooper Smith; music, Margolin; second unit director, David H. Banks; assistant directors, Gordon Mark, Warren Carr, David Rose; stunt coordinator, V. John Wardlow; sound, Rob Young; special effects, George Ertschbamer; camera, Michael Watkins, Fred Murphy; editor, M. S. Martin.

Cast: James Garner (Al Mackey); Margot Kidder (Willlie); John Lithgow (Marty Welborn); John Marley (Captain Woofer); Stuart Margolin (Herman Sinclair); Paul Koslo (Griswold Veals [Mr. Wheels]); Colleen Dewhurst (Lorna Dilman); Alex Diakun (Weasel); Billy Kerr (Ferret); William Taylor (Officer Gibson Hand); Dusty Morean (Buckmore Phipps); Christianne Hirt (Peggy Farrel [Jill]); Tom McBeath (Flameout Farrell); Dixie Seatle (Amazing Grace); Dale Wilson (Lloyd/Bozeman); Julian Munoz (Elliot Ramos); Sal Lopez (Chuey Verdugo); Real Andrews (Maxine); Stephen Chang (Minh Nguyen); Dawn Luker (Gladys); Claudine Melgrave (Yacht Woman); Colin Skinner (Yacht Man); Harvey Miller (Harvey Himmelfarb); Enoid Saunders (Eleanor St. Denis); Alistair MacDuff (Malcolm Sinclair); Clara

Kamuude (Whore); William Nunn (Detective Simon); Preston Ford (Detective Schultz); Beau Kazar (Hockey Player); Christopher Martini (Danny); Michelle Martini (Karen); Max Martini (Steven); Benson Fong (Wing, the Bartender).

The Glitter Dome was based on Joseph Wambaugh's 1981 novel. Like so much of that author's work, *The Glitter Dome* delved into the psyches of police officers surviving the grinding pressures of often deadly and deadening careers. In the course of this telefilm, full of cynicism ("Halloween in Hollywood is redundant") and funny wisecracks (a hooker says to the impotent Mackey "It takes a stiff rod to catch a big fish"), the focal Los Angeles law enforcers lock horns with a wide array of Hollywood types. Not the least of these individuals is a young homicide victim's lesbian lover, a middle-aged film editor. As played by the resourceful Colleen Dewhurst, the cameo scene at her home is handled memorably, full of nuance and dimension. Because this feature was a made-for-cable venture, it could be more mature in its gritty presentation of life in the City of Angels.

Los Angeles police detective Al Mackey (James Garner) and Marty Welborn (John Lithgow) are not exceptionally bright, but the middle-aged lawmen have learned that if they ask sufficient questions and are patient, eventually they will usually get lucky on a case. They are assigned to investigate the murder of Malcolm Sinclair, head of American Studios. The twice-divorced Mackey and the currently-separated Welborn hunt for clues. Their search leads them from Herman Sinclair (Stuart Margolin), the unscrupulous nephew of the deceased, to unemployed cinematographer Griswold Veals (Paul Koslo), the latter known as the roller-skating "Mr. Wheels." Others implicated in the caper are Jill (Christianne Hirt), a teen-age hooker who is later found dead, and Lloyd (Dale Wilson), a porno moviemaker.

It develops that the slimy Lloyd was involved with Jill and the devious Veals in a child porno racket financed by the late movie mogul. Later, Lloyd is killed fleeing a police raid, while his cohort, Minh Nguyen (Stephen Chang), is severely wounded. Mackey improvises a dying declaration that he claims to have "obtained" from Nguyen and closes the file. Meanwhile, Welborn, stunned because one of his young informants (Julian Munoz) died due to his (Welborn) having carelessly revealed his source, commits suicide. Marty leaves Al a farewell note which causes the cop to realize that the movie mogul's actual killer was Jill's vengeful dad (Tom McBeath). Now satisfied that justice has been served, the casual, cynical Mackey returns to the Glitter Dome—a police bar hangout—where he reunite with Willie (Margot Kidder), a movie star he met during his investigation of this case.

Daily Variety judged, "*Glitter Dome* rolls around in a lot of dirt, but the story's good, the situations credible, the ending satisfactory. . . . Telefilm revels in unseemly action and characters, reflecting street stuff not always easy to assimilate. . . .. Garner extends his fine acting style, and Dewhurst emphatically steals her scenes with her presence." Gail Williams (*Hollywood Reporter*) conceded, "We've see it all before . . . [but] still, this is an absorbingly styled production. . . ."

One of the noteworthy aspects of Colleen Dewhurst's performance here is her forthrightness in playing her minority character. Her Lorna Dilman refuses to be cowed by the law, meeting the disconcerting stares of James Garner's cop head-on. She is unapologetic for having loved another woman (the young Jill), but realistic that the sizeable age difference doomed the relationship from the start.

Shot largely in Vancouver and Victoria, British Columbia, *The Glitter Dome* was directed by Stuart Margolin who co-starred with James Garner on his "The Rockford Files" series (1974–80).

Kim Stanley, Joyce Van Patten and Joan Linville in *The Goddess* (1958).

98. The Goddess (Columbia, 1958), 105 min. Not rated.

Producer, Milton Perlman; director, John Cromwell; screenplay, Paddy Chayevsky; art director, Edward Haworth; set decorators, Richard Meyerhoff, Tom Oliphant; costumes, Frank L. Thompson; makeup, Robert Jiras; music, Virgil Thompson; assistant director, Charles H. Maguire; camera, Arthur J. Ornitz; editor, Carl Lerner.

Cast: Kim Stanley (Rita Shawn [Emily Ann Faulkner]); Betty Lou Holland (Mother); Joan Copeland (Aunt); Gerald Hiken (Uncle); Burt Brinckerhoff (Boy); Steven Hill (John Tower); Gerald Petrarca (Minister); Linda Soma (Bridesmaid); Curt Conway (Writer); Joan Linville (Joanna); Joyce Van Patten (Hillary); Lloyd Bridges (Dutch Seymour); Bert Freed (Lester Brackman); Donald McKee (R. M. Lucas); Louise Beavers (Cook); Elizabeth Wilson (Secretary); Roy Shuman, John Lawrence (G.I.s); Chris Flanagan (Emily Ann, at Age 4); Patty Duke (Emily Ann, at Age 8); Mike O'Dowd, Sid Raymond (Men); Margaret Brayton (Mrs. Woolsy); Werner Klemperer (Mr. Woolsy);

Fred Herrick (The Elder); Gail Haworth (Emily's Daughter).

Long-thought to be a loosely-based retelling of the Marilyn Monroe saga, *The Goddess*'s director, John Cromwell, once suggested that the movie derived more from Ava Gardner's life story. Whatever the truth, *The Goddess*, for all its artiness, is a captivating, compassionate character study of a tortured movie celebrity. It starred famed stage actress Kim Stanley in her motion picture debut. The Paddy Chayefsky screenplay was Oscar-nominated, but lost to *The Defiant Ones*. During the plot, one of the many characters drawn to the movie star "heroine" is her competent, brusque secretary/companion (Elizabeth Wilson) who has a far-ranging interest in her employer. As she tells her employer's ex-husband "You take care of your little girl [his and the star's child] and I'll take care of mine. . . . I'll take good care of her. . . . I kind of love her."

The Goddess is divided into three sections. "Portrait of a Young Girl" tells of Emily Ann Faulkner (Chris Flanagan), a four-year-old illegitimate child, unwanted by her impoverished mother (Betty Lou Holland). As she grows into adulthood, Emily Ann (Kim Stanley) gains a reputation as a loose woman. Her one ambition is to become a movie star. Meanwhile, she weds a troubled soldier, John Tower (Steven Hill), intrigued that his dad was a Hollywood actor. After she gives birth to a baby, Tower abandons her. Emily Ann leaves the unwanted infant with her mother and heads for California and fame. In "Portrait of a Young Woman" Emily is now a Hollywood starlet, known as Rita Shawn. She uses sex to gain the attention of industry starmakers and her career rises. She marries ex-prizefighter, Dutch Seymour (Lloyd Bridges), but that mismatch ends when he discovers her being unfaithful. In "Portrait of a Goddess" six years have passed since her divorce from Dutch. By now, Rita is an established Hollywood name, but she is a lonely, alcoholic recluse. She brings her burned-out mother to California, but that reunion proves unfortunate and Rita is soon again on her own. When her parent dies, she attends the funeral. At the service, the drunken Rita encounters John Tower and their thirteen-year-old daughter (Gail Haworth). John is repulsed by the highly neurotic Rita. Finally, except for her protective paid nurse/secretary (Elizabeth Wilson), the movie goddess is alone.

Bosley Crowther (*New York Times*) reported, "Paddy Chayefsky's favorite subject, the abrasive force of loneliness . . . is scored for ironic tragedy in his first original screen drama. . . . It comes off a fine dramatic film. . . . Kim Stanley is brilliant. . . . Elizabeth Wilson is harsh as a nurse. . . ." *Harrison's Reports* noted, "Both in dialogue and depiction, no punches are pulled in the film's presentation of sex, and alcoholism." In reviewing this "Semi-poetic, semi-realistic melodrama, *Variety* rated it "an episodic and self-consciously artistic effort," The trade journal decided "There is too much that is cliche" and "There is also too much left unexplained and unpenetrated. . . . The basic weakness of Chayefsky's screenplay is that it is not truly a Hollywood story." *Variety* granted that Kim Stanley is "undeniably a movie personality in the fullest sense" and that "Elizabeth Wilson is a standout as the secretary and nurse to Miss Stanley in her final scenes."

An appreciative addition to the film was famed music critic/classical comper Virgil Thompson's fine score.

99. The Grasshopper (National General Pictures, 1970), color, 96 min. R-rated.

Producers, Jerry Belson, Garry Marshall; director, Jerry Paris; based on the novel *The Passing of Evil* by Mark McShane; screenplay, Belson, Marshall; art director, Tambi Larsen; set decorator, Donald J. Sullivan; costumes, Donfeld; makeup, Gustaf M. Norin; music, Billy Goldenberg; assistant directors, James Rosenberger, Joe Nayfack, Francis X. Shaw Jr.; sound, John Muchmore; special effects, Thol O. Simonson; camera, Sam Leavitt; editor, Aaron Stell.

Cast: Jacqueline Bisset (Christine); Jim Brown (Tommy Marcott); Joseph Cotten (Richard Morgan); Corbett Monica (Danny); Ramon Bieri (Rossevelt Dekker); Christopher Stone (Jay Rigney); Roger Garrett (Buck); Stanley Adams (Buddy Miller); Dick Richards (Lou Bellman); Tim O'Kelly (Eddie Molina); Stefanianna Christopherson (Libby); Ed Flanders (Jack Bishop); Wendy Farrington (Connie); Sandi Faviola (Kyo); Eris Sandy (Vicky); John David Wilder (Timmy); Jay Laskay (Manny); Jim Smith (Larry); Therese Baldwin (Gigi); Chris Wong (Billy); Kathalyn Turner (Ann Marie); William H. Bassett (Aaron); Marc Hannibal (Walters): David Duclon (Miller's Son); Jessica Myerson (Saleswoman).

In the process of breaking through old taboos, the New Hollywood made some dreadful films. On the other hand, sometimes the exploitation values of a feature were so overemphasized that the picture's

Jacqueline Bisset and Jim Brown in *The Grasshopper* **(1970).**

merits were lost in the shuffle. Such was the case with the comedy drama, *The Grasshopper*, starring radiant Jacqueline Bisset, and directed by ex-actor Jerry Paris.

Discouraged by her dull home town life, nineteen-year-old Christine Adams (Jacqueline Bisset) joyfully leaves British Columbia for Los Angeles. She plans to visit her former boyfriend, Eddie Bishop (Tim O'Kelly). However, in Utah, her car breaks down, and she is forced to hitchhike. Lounge comedian Danny Raymond (Corbett Monica) gives her a ride, and takes her to Las Vegas. She is intrigued by the glitz, but proceeds on to California. A short time later, the restless Christine returns to Las Vegas, finding work as a casino showgirl. Her new friends include: homosexual chorus boy Buck Brown (Roger Garrett), rock musician Jay Rigney (Christopher Stone) and black Tommy Marcott (Jim Brown), a former professional gridiron champ. Tommy is now a pub-

lic relations worker for the hotel. Rushing into a romance, Christine and Tommy marry and the couple soon relocate to Los Angeles. Again, she becomes fidgety. However, before she can leave Tommy, he is killed by associates of tycoon Rosie Dekker (Ramon Bieri), a crook she rejected in Las Vegas.

Returning once more to the gaming capital, she cannot find honest work because Dekker has blackballed her. Instead, she becomes a high-priced prostitute, which leads to her meeting urbane, wealthy Richard Morgan (Joseph Cotten). He suggests they marry, but not wanting such a commitment, she continues as a call girl, with Jay now her pimp. Later, he runs off with their bank account. Alone and drug-dependent, the rebellious Christine persuades a sky writer to spell out the word "fuck" in the air. Still later, she is booked on a morals charge by the police. In three short years, her life has dead-ended.

Roger Greenspun (*New York Times*) championed *The Grasshopper* as "a film of ordinary ambitions and of limited but sometimes stunning success. . . . [The] film repeatedly transcends its own vulgarity . . . and improves upon the conventions that keep it moving." *Variety* described the feature as "a very commercial package" that "keeps a convincing sense of reality, punctuated with bright flashes of humor that are no less real. . . . It is the dark side of the Hollywood story. . . ." Besides appreciating Bisset's "screen magnetism" and the "mystique of reality" about Brown's stiffly-played stud role, the trade paper recorded, "In its cinematic capturing of the grueling backstage marathon behind the sequins and boa feathers of Vegas, the camaraderie among 'the kids' in the chorus, and the sympathetic friendships between the gay chorus boys and the straight girls, and threadmill of backslapping, *The Grasshopper* achieves [a] realistic, dehoked picture of Vegas." Less impressed, Richard Combs (British *Monthly Film Bulletin*) described *The Grasshopper* as "A gaudy modern morality play" done in a "summary television sketch manner." The unconventional *The Grasshopper*, which did passable business at the box-office is definitely worth viewing.

100. The Group (United Artists, 1966), color, 150 min. Not rated.

Producer, Sidney Buchman; director, Sidney Lumet; based on the novel by Mary McCarthy; screenplay, Buchman; production designer, Gene Callahan; set decorator, Jack Wright Jr.; costumes, Anna Hill Johnstone; makeup, Irving Buchman; music supervisor, Charles Gross; music director, Robert De Cormier; assistant directors, Dan Eriksen, Tony Belletier; sound, Dennis Maitland; camera, Boris Kaufman; editor, Ralph Rosenbloom.

Cast: Candice Bergen (Elinor "Lakey" Eastlake); Joan Hackett (Dottie Renfrew); Elizabeth Hartman (Priss Hartshorn); Shirley Knight (Polly Andrews); Joanna Pettet (Kay Strong); Mary-Robin Redd (Pokey Prothero); Jessica Walter (Libby MacAusland); Kathleen Widdoes (Helena Davison); James Broderick (Dr.

Ridgeley); James Congdon (Sloan Crockett); Larry Hagman (Harold Peterson); Hal Holbrook (Gus Leroy); Richard Mulligan (Dick Brown); Robert Emhardt (Mr. Andrews); Carrie Nye (Norine); Philippa Bevans (Mrs. Hartshorn); Leta Bonynge (Mrs. Prothero); Marion Brash (Radio Man's Wife); Sarah Burton (Mrs. Davison); Flora Campbell (Mrs. MacAusland); Bruno di Cosmi (Nils); Leora Dana (Mrs. Renfrew); Bill Fletcher (Bill, the Actor); George Gaynes (Brook Latham); Martha Greenhouse (Mrs. Bergler); Russell Hardie (Mr. Davison); Vince Harding (Mr. Eastlake); Dorene Lang (Nurse Swenson); Chet London (Radio Man); Baruch Lumet (Mr. Schneider); John O'Leary (Putnam Blake); Hildy Parks (Nurse Catherine); Lidia Prochnicka (The Baroness); Polly Rowles (Mrs. Andrews); Douglas Rutherford (Mr. Prothero); Truman Smith (Mr. Bergler); Loretta White (Mrs. Eastlake); Ed Holmes (Mr. MacAusland); Richard Graham (Reverend Garland); Arthur Anderson (Pokey's Husband): Clay Johns (Phil).

With customary chutzpah, Hollywood tackled Mary McCarthy's best-selling history (1963) of the lives and loves of eight Vassar graduates of the Class of 1933 who "go forth to play a role in every sphere of the nation's life." In book form, *The Group* was a formless but still trenchant social history; on screen, it was high-gloss soap opera. The plot-heavy movie, which required a score card to keep pace with its anguished heroines, had two strong points: (1) the much-discussed chosen actresses for this high-profile production and, (2) the ultimate casting of screen newcomer Candice Bergen, daughter of beloved ventriloquist Edgar Bergen, in the daring role of Elinor "Lakey" Eastlake, the high-toned lesbian. On both counts, the movie proved anticlimactic to the publicity generated about it.

A fresh group of confident women graduate from Vassar's hallowed campus in the midst of the Depression. Coldly-efficient Elinor "Lakey" Eastlake (Candice Bergen), the group's chief and "law unto herself," embarks on a European sojourn. Boston Brahmin Dottie Renfrew (Joan Hackett) has a brief affair in Greenwich Village be-

Mary Robin Redd, Kathleen Widdoes, Joan Hackett, Elizabeth Hartman, Jessica Walter, Candice Bergen and Shirley Knight in *The Group* **(1966).**

fore turning to a proper marriage. The idealistic Priss Hartshorn (Elizabeth Hartman) abandons her dream of working for a New Deal poverty program in order to marry, suffering two miscarriages before giving birth to a baby boy. Practical Polly Andrews (Shirley Knight) has an abortive romance with an artist (Richard Mulligan), before meeting a reliable young doctor (James Broderick) at the hospital where she works. Insecure Kay Strong (Joanna Pettet) works at Macy's Department Store to support her would-be playwright husband, Harold Peterson (Larry Hagman), an alcoholic philanderer. Wealthy, bright Helena Davison (Kathleen Widdoes) is pushed by her domineering parents into abandoning her hope of becoming a teacher. Instead, she sublimates her frustrations with solitary travel. Ambitious Libby MacAusland (Jessica Walter) finds herself succeeding as a Manhattan literary agent, but failing in her personal relationships. As for uncomplicated Pokey Prothero (Mary-Robin Redd), she enthusiastically settles for marriage and gives birth to two sets of twins.

In 1939, the group reunite to greet Lakey upon her return from war-engulfed Europe. As soon as they spot the Baroness (Lidia Prochnicka), her wealthy mannish companion, it is clear why Lakey, the lesbian, has remained on the sophisticated Continent for so long. (Pokey observes of the Baroness, "That dame must tote a pair of brass knuckles!") The revelation about Lakey causes the group to recall their college dorm days when they thought nothing of parading around naked in front of one another. Later, at an engagement celebration for Polly's upcoming marriage, the women listens to war news on the radio. Polly, missing Kay who has been recuperating from a nervous breakdown brought on by her disastrous marriage, calls her. The distraught Kay, thinking that planes passing over her apartment building are invading German aircrafts, excitedly leans out the window, and falls to her death.

Under Lakey's guidance, her friends arrange the funeral. At the services, the always cool Lakey rebuffs the unwanted Harold Peterson, who has shown up at the cemetery.

Bosley Crowther (*New York Times*) chided, "Sidney Lumet must be kidding. His film . . . is such a feeble and foolish contemplation . . . that it must be a spoof of something. . . . If it is seriously intended—it is the worst misfire of a movie in many a year. . . . It is hard to believe that Mr. Lumet . . . could have let himself stage such grotesque pictures of New York office and apartment living as are in this film, or that he could have directed reasonably skillful actors to behave as fatuously as his people do here." The disgruntled Crowther added, "Candice Bergen is plausible as a Paris expatriate who comes back at the end of the picture in the company of a German countess with a (get this!) mannish look. (A quick hint of Lesbianism at the very end is the only naughty thing in the film.)"

Without noting that the filmmakers had downplayed her role in the screenplay and editing, *Variety* observed, "Biggest letdown, and doubly so because her few scenes are so effective and played so well, is the part played by Candice Bergen. . . . [Her] treatment in Buchman's script will puzzle the audience, as her few scenes at the beginning and at the end don't match with the billing and important promotion she receives." (*Variety* referred to her as "the ambisextrous leader of the Group.") Pauline Kael (*The New Yorker*) noted that *The Group* dealt with Lakey's lesbianism with so much "discretion that United Art-

ists publicity men threw out the ad campaign they'd prepared to exploit it."

At the cemetery finale to *The Group*, there is a symbolic shot of the severely-dressed Lakey in her smart red car, a marked contrast to the sedate other members of the group in their standard black limousines. As always, Lakey is an outsider.

The advertising for *The Group* touted, "This is The Group. . . . Lakey. . . . Mona Lisa of the smoking room for women only!" Regardless of the exploitive elements *The Group* was not a box-office hit.

101. Guess What We Learned in School Today? (Cannon Group, 1970), color, 96 min. R-rated.

Executive producers, Dennis Friedland, Christopher C. Dewey; producer, David Gil; associate producer, James V. Clarke; director, John G. Avildsen; story, Eugene Price; screenplay, Price, Avildsen; music, Harper MacKay, Joan Andre Gil; songs: Moose Charlap and Joan Andre Gil; MacKay; sound, Michael Scott Goldbaum; camera/editor, Avildsen.

Cast: Richard Carballo (Lieutenant Roger Manley); Devin Goldenberg (Robbie Battle); Zachary Haines (Lance Battle); Jane MacLeod (Rita Battle); Yvonne McCall (Dr. Lily Whitehorn); Rosella Olson (Eve Manley); Diane Moore (Lydia); Larry Evers (Al); Stanton Edgehill (Billie); Iris Brooks (Lulu); Jean David (Mrs. O'Reilly); Brett Morrison, Robert Emerick (Radio Voices); Daphne Gil (Dancing Girl); George Pollack (Waiter); Elizabeth Grusky (Elizabeth); Andrew Kay (Young Man in Pool); Natalie Rogers, Margaret Steele (Women in Pool); Tim Lewis (Mike Avalon); Bradley Price (Bradley); Gene Price (Marine Captain); Judy Price (Dance Teacher); Philip Price (Philip); Jan Saint (Mailman); Lou Stanishia (Karate Teacher); Ches Turner (Little Boy); Sandra Wolf (Betty); Catherine Avildsen (Opening Voice).

"With 'sex education' films having reached new heights of solemn didacticism and clinical detail, it's extremely refreshing to find the Institute for Interpersonal Relations (who sponsored John Avildsen's film) allowing its plea for greater tolerance to be made within the traditions of the low budget sex comedy." (David McGillivray, British *Monthly Film Bulletin*)

Vice Squad Lieutenant Roger Manley (Richard Carballo) is so determined to unearth corruption everywhere that he arrests innocent young women on false charges. While on duty, he submits to the advances of black prostitute Billie (Stanton Edgehill). Later, he discovers that his sex partner is actually a male transvestite. Nevertheless, he pursues the relationship. Meanwhile, several local families attend a lecture given by Dr. Lily Whitehorn (Yvonne McCall) of the nearby Institute for Interpersonal Relations. Lily hopes to introduce sex education into the local high school system, while Manley agitatedly insists this is merely another Communist plot to corrupt American youth.

As several individuals from the community study at the Institute, the ever-snooping Roger realizes that during the course of his many surveillances, he has become tremendously attracted to seventeen-year-old Robbie Battle (Devin Goldenburg). Shocked by his realization, he hangs himself. However, he is saved by Billie, who announces that he is an undercover detective. Thereafter, he arrests Manley for improper behavior while on duty and for making homosexual advances.

Variety rated this a "Fairly amusing takeoff on suburban sex hangups. . . . Too witty for sexploiter use, it is free in its nudity if subdued in erotics . . . It is a promising pic, brightly played. . . ." The release of *Guess What We Learned in School Today?* (and such similar movies as *Cry Uncle*, 1970) led Pauline Kael (*The New Yorker*) to editorialize: "though the absence of solemnity about sex in pornospoofs is a relief, and the sex jokes can have a fizzy, liberated humor . . . after a while it isn't enough that they're being done; you want them to be done with some comic polish and style."

In the same year that *Guess What We Learned in School Today?* was released, United Artists distributed the Carl Reiner-directed comedy, *Where's Poppa?*, q.v. The latter was an equally irreverent, but more professional, satire. It too had a male character who discovers that his sex partner is another male. He then shrugs his shoulders and decides to have more of the same. It was another step in Hollywood's transition towards a more honest dealing with a minority sexual lifestyle: what was today treated as a joke (so as not to offend the mainstream) could tomorrow be dealt with legitimately, or even better yet, as not worthy of special apologetic attention.

102. **The Handmaid's Tale** (Cinecom, 1990), color, 109 min. R-rated.

Executive producer, Wolfgang Glattes; producer, Daniel Wilson; associate producers, Gale Goldberg, Alex Gartner; director, Volker Schlondorff; based on the novel by Margaret Atwood; screenplay, Harold Pinter; production designer, Tom Walsh; costumes, Coleen Atwood; makeup, Jeff Goodwin; music, Ryuichi Sakamoto; assistant director, Anthony Gittelson; sound, Danny Michael; camera, Igor Luther; editor, David Ray.

Cast: Natasha Richardson (Kate); Faye Dunaway (Serena Joy); Aidan Quinn (Nick); Elizabeth McGovern (Moira); Victoria Tennant (Aunt Lydia); Robert Duvall (Commander); Blanche Baker (Ofglen); Traci Lind (Ofwarren/Janine); David Dukes (Doctor); Zoey Wilson (Aunt Helena); Kathryn Doby (Aunt Elizabeth); Reiner Schoene (Luke); Lucia Hartpeng (Cora); Karma Ibsen Riley (Aunt Sara); Lucile McIntyre (Rita); Gary Bullock (Officer on Bus); Allison Holmes (June); J. Michael Hunter (Preacher); Robert Raiford (Dick); Miriam Bohnet (Alma); Julian E. Bell (TV Announcer); David Barnes (Guard); James A. Carleo III (Angel at Desk); Jim Grimshaw (Eyein Van); Ivan Migel (Eye); Doris Boggs (Aunt); Annemarie Fenske (Aunt Christina); Linda Pierce (Another Wife); Nina Lynn Blanton (Third Wife); Rhesa Reagan Stone (Mrs. Warren); Sara Seidman (Handmaid); Muse Watson (Guardian); Janell McLeod (Martha): Elke Ritschel (Hostess); Jane Learned (Nun); Randall Haynes (Condemned Man); Rhonda Bond (Black Woman); Mil Nicholson (Wardress); Robert Penz, Tom McGovern (Guards); Danny Simpkins (Walter); James G. Martin Jr. (Steve);

Elizabeth McGovern in *The Handmaid's Tale* (1990).

Stefanie J. Chen (Ofglen #2); Ed L. Grady (Old Man); Molly Sandick (Baby); Blair Nicole Struble (Jill); Bill Owen (TV Announcer #2).

This elaborate women's rights parable is set in a bleak future where war is always raging somewhere. Because society has abused its choices, decisions are made for the survivors by the state. Wars, ecological disasters, etc. have sterilized most of the world, and the remaining fertile females must breed to restock society. As such, gender benders (i.e. lesbians) are a severe threat to the new order. These outsiders must be whipped (literally) into conformity. Based on Margaret Atwood's strongly feminist novel, this should have been a frightening, thought-provoking movie, but was not even buoyed by Faye Dunaway's over-the-top performance.

Sometime in the future, ultra-conservative, puritanical forces control the United States, now known as the Republic of Gilead. Because most women on Earth are sterile, the few remaining fertile ones are prize commodities, rounded up to be handmaids to breed children for the republic. When Kate (Natasha Richardson) attempts to escape from the U.S. to Canada, her husband (Reiner Schoene) is shot, her daughter Jill (Blair Nicole Struble) disappears and Kate is dispatched to the training camp. There, her teacher is the pious Aunt Lydia (Victoria Tennant). Kate makes friends with Moira (Elizabeth McGovern), a lesbian (whom she later helps to escape), and tries to soothe Janine (Traci Lind), who has lost her grip on reality.

Kate is assigned to the household of a top-ranking Commander (Robert Duvall) where, following the story of Rachel in the Book of Genesis, she is to lie between the officer and his wife, Serena Joy (Faye Dunaway), to conceive a child on their behalf. Time passes, but Kate fails to become pregnant, as the Commander proves to be sterile. Meanwhile, contrary to policy, the Commander becomes emotionally intrigued with Kate. The impatient Serena Joy secretly orders Kate to mate with the Commander's chauffeur, Nick (Aidan

Quinn). Kate and Nick soon fall in love and he promises to help her find her child, whom Serena Joy insists is safe. At an orgy at a state house of pleasure, Kate encounters Moira, whose escape failed. After being tortured, Moira was assigned to be a permanent "party" girl. Considering the option—being sent to the colonies plagued with toxic dumps—she has accepted her fate. "Free booze, free drugs. You only work nites. . . . Not bad, really."

Kate is recruited by her monitor, Ofglen (Blanche Baker), to join the underground resistance. After killing the Commander, Nick rescues her and takes her to a mountain hideaway. Now pregnant with Nick's child, Kate hopes someday to rejoin her daughter.

Ralph Novak (*People*) favored this "extraordinarily well-acted, cleanly presented film." Praising the cast, Novak cited, "Elizabeth McGovern nicely mixes defiance and playfulness as a lesbian rebel. . . ." In contrast, Roger Ebert (*Movie Home Companion*, 1991) in his two star review, reflected on the film's flaws: "For all its anger, *The Handmaid's Tale* is curiously muted. Natasha Richardson's passivity . . . is a distraction. . . . Duvall and Dunaway provide the best moments. . . . At the end of the movie we are conscious of large themes and deep thoughts, and of good intentions drifting out of focus."

In ten weeks of domestic distribution, *The Handmaid's Tale* grossed a disappointing $5,534,500 at the box-office.

103. Happy Birthday, Gemini

(United Artists, 1980), color, 107 min. R-rated.

Executive producer, Alan King; producer, Rupert Hitzig; co-producer, Bruce Calnan; director, Richard Benner; based on the play *Gemini* by Albert Innaurato; screenplay, Benner; production designer, Ted Watkins; costumes, D. Lynne MacKay; music, Rich Look, Cathy Chamberlain; assistant director, Rob Malenfant; camera, James B. Kelly; editor, Stephan Fanfara.

Cast: Madeline Kahn (Bunny Weinberger); Rita Moreno (Lucille Pompi); Robert Viharo (Nick Geminiani); Alan Rosenberg (Francis Geminiani); Sarah Holcomb (Judith Hastings): David Marshall Grant (Randy Hastings); Timothy Jenkins (Herschel Weinberger); David McIllwraith (Sam Weinberger); Maura Swanson (Mary O'Donnel); Richard Easley (Judge); John William Kennedy (O'Donnel); Michael Donaghue (Father McBride); Alberto de Rosa (Dominique); Michael Holton (Court Clerk); A. Frank Ruffo (Jerry); Dwayne McLean (Eddie); Jeff Wincott (Taxi Driver).

This flop was based on Albert Innaurato's Broadway comedy *Gemini* (1977), which was still running at the time this movie version was released. With a plotline full of exaggerated ethnic types, it was adapted and directed for the movies by Richard Benner, which led a displeased Kevin Thomas (*Los Angeles Times*) to note: "This is not the first time film maker Richard Benner's handling of gay themes has misfired. In his earlier but better *Outrageous* [1977, q.v.] he drew an unfortunate equation between a female impersonator . . . and a mentally unstable young woman." David Sterritt (*Christian Science Monitor*) chided, "Its very dubious plot is developed with an egregious lack of taste. The dialogue abounds with crass ethnic humor. The characters are uniformly and sometimes aggressively unattractive. Everyone shouts all the time."

WASPy, rich Randy Hastings (David Marshall Grant) and his equally pretentious sister, Judith (Sarah Holcomb) pay a surprise visit to their Harvard classmate, Francis Geminiani (Alan Rosenberg), at his working-class, South Philadelphia home. Judith thinks she loves the sensitive Francis, a scholarship student, but he—preparing to celebrate his twenty-first birthday—is convinced he wants her brother. Meanwhile, Francis's crude, loud-mouth father, Nick (Robert Viharo), a butcher whose wife deserted him years before, is having a relationship with his shop worker, Lucille Pompi (Rita Moreno). Next door, the promiscuous, vulgar

Bunny Weinberger (Madeline Kahn), a former stage performer, lives with her obnoxious, overweight son (Timothy Jenkins). Having declared his sexual preference, Francis's relatives, neighbors, friends, etc., rally to his support.

Variety explained why the Broadway success was a movie mess: "this one has a hard time translating its contrived situations and semi-absurdist caricatures . . . to the realism of film. And when it does eventually shift gears to reveal the 'humanity' underlying its otherwise gross or pathetic characters, no one will believe it for a minute."

In the effort to drag box-office appeal into the movie, comedienne Madeline Kahn's role as the off-kilter, harpy neighbor was enlarged into a super-caricature at the expense of the rest of the characters, including that of opera-loving, confused Francis Geminiani. To tidy up the film's storyline with a happier ending than the more ambiguous play provided, the movie has the robust butcher father accepting his son's lifestyle declaration, and the hero's ex-girlfriend becoming his good pal.

Happy Birthday, Gemini disappeared quickly from the box-office.

104. Haunted Summer (Cannon Group, 1988), color, 115 min. R-rated.

Executive producers, Menahem Golan, Yoram Globus; producer, Martin Poll; associate producers, John Thompson, Mario Cotone; director, Ivan Passer; based on the novel by Anne Edwards; screenplay, Lewis John Carlino; production designer, Stephen Grimes; art director, Francesco Chinaese; costumes, Gabriella Pescucci; effects makeup, Manlio Rocchetti; music, Christopher Young; assistant directors, Carlos Quintero, Mauro Sacripanti; stunts/fencing, Franco Fantasia; sound, Drew Kunin; special effects, Ditta Corridori, Gino De Rossi; camera, Guiseppe Rotunno; editor, Cesare D'Amico.

Cast: Eric Stoltz (Percy Shelley); Philip Anglim (Lord Byron); Alice Krige (Mary Godwin); Laura Dern (Claire Clairmont); Alex Winter (Dr. John Polidori); Giusto Lo Pipero (Berger); Don Hodson (Rushton); Terry Rich-

Madeline Kahn, Rita Moreno and Robert Viharo in *Happy Birthday, Gemini* **(1980).**

ards (Fletcher); Peter Berling (Maurice); Alise McLain (Elise).

"Ultimately, it's about the artist-as-rebel. But it's less psychological vivisection than elegant romance, a sweet-tempered comedy of manners and morals. The poets are not sacred beasts but holy fools." (Michael Wilmington, *Los Angeles Times*)

Elsa Lanchester had impersonated Mary Wollstonecraft Shelley (1795–1851)—who wrote *Frankenstein*—in the prologue to *The Bride of Frankenstein* (1935). In the mid-1980s, a trio of features dealt with the specter-laden summer in 1816 when Mary and the poet Percy Shelley, sojourned with the scandalous George Gordon, Lord Byron at a villa near the shores of Lake Geneva. The three movies were Ken Russell's British-made *Gothic* (1986), Gonzalo Suarez's Spanish-produced *Rowing with the Wind* (1988), and *Haunted*

Summer. The latter is an underrated, semi-precious gem, filled with exuberant if excessive performances. Drifting in the shadows of this romantic account of famous personalities is the would-be-writer, Dr. Polidori, who is sexually magnetized by the bisexual Byron.

In 1816, Percy Shelley (Eric Stoltz) and his mistress, Mary Godwin (Alice Krige), travel through Switzerland with her half-sister, Claire Clairmont (Laura Dern). Claire schemes to meet up with the indulgent Lord Byron (Philip Anglim), who deserted her after their brief London affair. While Mary is put off by the cynical Byron who does his best to rebuff Claire, Percy and Byron appreciate one another's creative accomplishments. To extend their time together, Percy, Mary and Claire accept Byron's offer to visit him at the Villa Diodata, nearby Lake Geneva. Joining the group is the brooding Dr. Polidori (Alexander Winter), who is drawn physically to the club-footed Byron and jealously regards the intruders with suspicion.

At the villa, Mary is agitated by Byron's cavalier attitude towards Polidori, his assessment of Shelley's too sweet nature and by his ridicule of her beliefs in women's rights. On his part, Byron is intrigued by Mary's rejection and continues to pursue her. Later, Byron convinces Shelley to experiment with opium, allegedly to expand his creative process. In truth, Byron hopes to use the power of suggestion during the test to cause a splinter between Percy and Mary. In actuality, the drug overwhelms the impressionable Shelley and he collapses. Mary dares the perpetrator to try the drug himself. Byron accepts the challenge, during which a monster appears and kisses him on the mouth. Later, Mary informs the shaken Lord Byron that the specter was actually Polidori (whom Byron had banished after he admitted a publisher had offered him a large bribe to expose his relationship with Byron). Byron admits that what frightened him most of all was gaining such a shocking insight into himself.

The next morning, Percy and Mary, along with Claire (pregnant with Byron's child), leave their host and travel on to Italy.

Variety reported, "What's fatally lacking here is any feeling of passion or eroticism, and that's crucial to this tale of scandalous relationships. . . . Yet given this combustible material, all [director Ivan] Passer can come up with are a couple of excessively long and conventionally filmed love scenes notable only for their lack of excitement." The trade paper complimented Alice Krige for her "delicate performance" but decided "standout in the acting stakes is Laura Dern, giving another beautiful performance. . . . Alex Winter has moments as Polidori, forever being humiliated by his lover Byron. . . ."

In comparing *Haunted Summer* to *Gothic*, Michael Wilmington (*Los Angeles Times*) judged, "The flamboyant Russell dragged the nightmares up and waved them

around. Passer keeps them buried, teasing them almost to the light. . . . *Haunted Summer* . . . is not a film for everyone. Some audiences, jazzed up to the point where they take no pleasure in poetic language and poetic scenery, may not enjoy it at all."

Originally, before his final illness sidetracked him, John Huston was to have directed *Haunted Summer*.

105. **The Haunting** (Metro-Goldwyn-Mayer, 1963), 112 min. Not rated.

Producer, Robert Wise; associate producer, Denis Johnson; director, Wise; based on the novel *The Haunting of Hill House* by Shirley Jackson; screenplay, Nelson Gidding; production designer, Elliot Scott; set decorator, John Jarvis; costume supervisor; Maude Churchill; Claire Bloom's clothes, Mary Quant; makeup, Tom Smith; music/music director, Humphrey Searle; assistant director, David Tomblin; sound supervisor, A. W. Watkins; sound, Gerry Turner; special effects, Tom Howard; camera, Davis Boulton; editor, Ernest Walter.

Cast: Julie Harris (Eleanor Vance); Claire Bloom (Theodora); Richard Johnson (Dr. John Markway); Russ Tamblyn (Luke Sanderson); Lois Maxwell (Grace Markway) Fay Compton (Mrs. Sanderson); Valentine Dyall (Mr. Dudley, the Caretaker); Rosalie Crutchley (Mrs. Dudley); Diane Clare (Carrie Fredericks); Ronald Adams (Eldridge Harper); Freda Knorr (2nd Mrs. Crain); Janet Mansell (Abigail Crain, at Age Six); Pamela Buckley (1st Mrs. Crain); Howard Lang (Hugh Crain); Mavis Villiers (Landlady); Verinia Greenlaw (Dora Fredericks); Paul Maxwell (Bud Fredericks); Claud Jones (Fat Man); Susan Richards (Nurse); Amy Dalby (Abigail Crain, at Age Eighty); Rosemary Dorken (Abigail's Companion).

At the time of initial release, *The Haunting*, shot in atmospheric and economical black-and-white, was considered "artful" (*Variety*) but not sufficiently commercial. Today, this complex film is accepted as a cult classic. In *5001 Nights at the Movies* (1991), Pauline Kael writes that *The Haunting* is "An elegantly sinister scare movie, literate and expensive (although basically a traditional ghost story) with those two fine actresses Claire Bloom

Claire Bloom and Julie Harris in *The Haunting* **(1963).**

and Julie Harris. . . . This 'old dark house' movie is set in a marvellous Victorian gothic pile in New England, and it's good fun." Based on Shirley Jackson's novel, *The Haunting of Hill House* (1959), *The Haunting* is noteworthy for its direct presentation of homosexuality, in this case personified by the Greenwich Village lesbian played by Claire Bloom. Above all, *The Haunting* is light years ahead of *The Children's Hour* (1961), q.v., in treating the subject of two women with "unnatural feelings."

In Massachusetts, Dr. John Markway

(Richard Johnson), an anthropologist, decides that Hill House, with its long history of death-cursed owners and occupants, would be an excellent backdrop for his psychic research. He rents the house from the elderly Mrs. Sannerson (Fay Compton) who announces she has willed Hill House to her irresponsible nephew, Luke Sannerson (Russ Tamblyn). When Markway explains why he wants Hill House and that he, a married man whose wife Grace (Lois Maxwell) scoffs at the supernatural, will be staying there alone with two female subjects, she suggests that Luke join the group as a chaperone. Markway's subjects are: Eleanor Vance (Julie Harris), a lonely spinster who once had a supernatural experience when she was ten and who has spent her life caring for her now-deceased, mother; and the New Yorker, Theodora (Claire Bloom), a nonconformist business person and lesbian from New York City, with sharp extrasensory perceptions.

Hardly have they settled in at Hill House, than they begin hearing threatening noises for which Markway has no ready explanation. Timid Eleanor is convinced the "haunted" house is beckoning to her and regards the building as a breathing object. Meanwhile, the self-sufficient Theodora is drawn to Eleanor, but the latter is attracted to handsome Dr. Markway. The strange, unexplainable sounds and trembling persist. At this point, Markway's demanding wife, Grace, appears on the scene, hoping to convince her husband to abandon his strange experiments. By now, Eleanor has lost grasp with reality. The others agree that she must leave Hill House.

As Eleanor drives away, a force pulls at the car's steering wheel. Unexpectedly, Grace, appears in the road. To avoid running her over, Eleanor swerves and crashes into a tree—the same one under which a previous owner's wife had died. Markway concludes that Hill House is haunted "It didn't want her to leave and her poor bedeviled mind wasn't strong enough to stop her. . . ." Self-contained Theodora has a different theory: "Maybe not poor Eleanor. It was what she wanted; to stay here. She had no place else to go. The house belongs to her now too. Maybe she is happier."

As the film ends, Eleanor's voice-over intones: "We who walk here, walk alone. . . ."

Bosley Crowther (*New York Times*) was unimpressed, "before this antique chiller drags to an ectoplasmic end, you'll agree that it does have just about everything in the old-fashioned blood-chilling line except a line of reasoning that makes a degree of sense. . . . [I]t looks as though this film simply makes more goose pimples than sense, which is rather surprising and disappointing for a picture with two such actresses, who are very good all the way through it, and produced and directed by the able Robert Wise." Crowther ridiculed the movie's logic, at the same time putting it down by ignoring the sexual makeup of Theodora: "Some clear intimations that Miss Harris is obsessed by the notion that she killed her mother might remotely explain why she has hallucinations, hears noises and all that sort of thing. But Miss Bloom also hears them, and she doesn't seem to be obsessed, except perhaps by a disposition to hug Miss Harris as often as she can."

Variety judged that "Audiences will respond to the film's intermittent terror passages, thanks to the skill of Wise, his cast and his crew, but are apt to find the whole unsatisfactory. . . . After elaborately setting the audience up in anticipation of drawing some scientific conclusions about the psychic phenomena field, the film completely dodges the issue in settling for a half-hearted melodramatic climax that is a distinct letdown." As to the performances, the trade paper viewed, "The acting is effective all around. Miss Harris delivers an expertly agitated portrayal. . . . The lovely Miss Bloom subtly conveys the unnatural forces at play within her character . . ."

Tom Milne (British *Monthly Film Bulletin*), who had mixed feelings about *The Haunting* ("Wise's camera is so determinedly zooming"), was underwhelmed by some of the casting: "Julie Harris, all fluttering eyelids and quivering sensibility . . . but Claire Bloom gives a sharply intelligent performance as the Lesbian Theo, who is doubly tormented as her special powers of perception enable her to read all the emotionally repressed Eleanor's feelings. Richard Johnson is adequate. . . ."

With her severe costuming and bits of business, it is established early on in *The Haunting* that Theodora is not heterosexual. Thus, the dialogue takes on double meanings as the two female characters combat the supernatural at Hill House and are forced to relate to one another:

Eleanor: What are you afraid of Theo?

Theodora: Of knowing what I really want. [Her knowing look is matched by a sharp visual response from Eleanor.]

Later, Markway, concerned about his subjects safety, suggests they share a room:

Eleanor: Oh, but that's my room. My very own room. . . .

Theodora: Don't get all hung up, Nell. We'll have fun. Like sisters.

Not yet willing to accept the indecorous truth, Eleanor, the repressed spinster, insists upon asking if Theodora has ever been married to a man. The other replies, "No" with such a knowing look that anybody would get the message.

Due as much to the morality of the 1960s as to consistency in the screen characters, Theodora and Eleanor never physically consummate their ambiguous relationship in *The Haunting* beyond clutching one another in moments of fear. Nevertheless, despite its hesitant nature, *The Haunting* provided a foreshadowing that lesbianism, Hollywood-style, was coming out of the closet.

106. Heat (Andy Warhol Release, 1972), color, 100 min. R-rated.

Producer, Andy Warhol; associate producer, Jed Johnson; director, Paul Morrissey; screen idea, John Hallowell; screenplay, Morrissey, Hallowell; music, John Cale; camera, Morrissey; editors, Lara Idel, Johnson.

Cast: Sylvia Miles (Sally Todd); Joe Dallesandro (Joey Davis); Andrea Feldman (Jessie); Pat Ast (Lydia, the Motel Manager); Harold Childe (Harold); Bonnie Walder (Bonnie); and: Ray Westal, P. J. Lester, Eric Emerson, John Hallowell, Gary Koznocha, Pat Parlemon.

Paul Morrissey, an Andy Warhol disciple, had already directed Joe Dallesandro in *Flesh* (1968) and *Trash* (1970), qq.v.. At the time, these raw offerings were regarded as very avant garde for their daring sexual naturalness. With his strong emphasis on presenting and depicting working-class types as his movies' focal characters, Morrissey went in a different direction from his mentor.

Ex-child star, Joey Davis (Joe Dallesandro), is now an unemployed adult, surviving in Los Angeles by hustling. He lives at a seedy motel run by blowsy Lydia (Pat Ast), and has sex with her in exchange for free rent. Anxious for any sort of acting work, he considers performing in a stage sex act with two brothers, also staying at the dumpy motel, or maybe—he fantasizes—pursuing a recording contract. Always wanting a fast dollar, the bored Joey becomes entangled with bisexual Jessie (Andrea Feldman). She is a former mental patient and ex-druggie, who cannot decide between Joey, her girlfriend (Bonnie Walder) or nothing.

Meanwhile, Jessie's rapacious mother, Sally Todd (Sylvia Miles), shows up on the scene. With moviemakers no longer anxious for her services, the middle-aged, ex-star is adrift. The much-married woman yanks Joey into her life, overwhelming him with her paranoia and sexual needs. To keep this stud, she promises him assorted rewards, including introducing him to industry power players. However, the very independent Joey leaves her. His later sexual adventures include an interlude with an older man, Harold (Harold Childe).

Vincent Canby (*New York Times*) found this sexually-permissive movie a refreshing lark. He described its lead performer, Dallesandro, with: "Joey wears his hair down to here and looks great and doesn't much care who does what to him as long as he doesn't have to do the work." Commenting on the film's deliberate parallels to *Sunset Boulevard* (1950), *Variety* saw, "Morrissey has given more fluidity than his other pix but relies mainly on actors in a series of well-meshed scenes as they play out the drama and comedy of a Hollywood that is sliding away. . . . Drugs are not a part of this scene. It is all ego, sex and the old film system." In retrospect, Pauline Kael (*5001 Nights at the Movies*, 1991) concluded, "A slack, depressive Paul Morrissey version of *Sunset Boulevard*, with Joe Dallesandro as a stud hustler. . . . It's meant to be a funny exploitation movie, but the comic moments are rare."

107. Henry & June (Universal, 1990), color, 136 min. NC-17-rated.

Producer; Peter Kaufman; associate producer, Yannoulla Wakefield; director, Kaufman; based on the book by Anais Nin; screenplay, Philip Kaufman, Rose Kaufman; production designer, Guy-Claude Francois; art director, Georges Glon; set decorators, Thierry Francois, Auguste Carriere; costumes, Yvonne Sassinot De Nesle; makeup, Didier Lavergne; music, Mark Adler; assistant directors, Eric Bartonio, Thierry Verrier; sound, Jean-Pierre Ruh; camera, Philippe Rousselot; editors, Vivien Hilgrove, William S. Scharf, Dede Allen.

Cast: Fred Ward (Henry Miller); Uma Thurman (June Miller); Maria De Medeiros (Anais Nin); Richard E. Grant (Hugo); Kevin Spacey (Osborn); Jean-Philippe Ecoffey (Eduardo Sanchez); Bruce Myers (Jack); Jean-Louis Bunuel (Publisher/Editor); Fedor Atkine (Spanish Dance Instructor); Sylvie Huguel (Emilia); Artus De Penguern (Brassai); Pierre Etaix (Henry's Friend #1); Pierre Edernac, Gaetan Bloom (Henry's Magician Friends); Alexandre De Gall (Henry's Clown Friend); Karine Couvelard (Osborn's Girlfriend); Louis Bessieres (Accordionist); Erika Maury-Lascoux, Claire Joubert (Contortionists); Brigitte Lahaie (Henry's Whore); Maite Maille (Frail Prostitute); Annie Fratellini (The Patronne); Frank Heiler (Steamship Agent); Stephanie Leboulanger (Prostitute Brushing Long Hair); Suzy Palatin (Bal Negre Performer); Samuel Ateba (Black Musician at Quat'z Arts Ball); Marc Maury (Man in Silent Film); Annie Vincent (Fat Prostitute); Maurice Escargot (Pop); Liz Hasse (Jean).

In 1990, the Classification and Rating Administration (CARA) of the Motion Picture Association of America (MPAA) and the National Association of Theatre Owners (NATO) revised its rating system, changing the X category to NC-17 (No Children Under 17 Admitted). Because of its explicit heterosexual and homosexual scenes, *Henry & June* both inspired and received the new NC-17 rating after appealing the X-rating given it. *Variety* determined, "*Henry and June* will be considered liberating by some and obscene by others. Its credentials as a serious, non-pornographic, treatment of the subject are unquestionable, but its length and subject matter may make it difficult commercially. . . ."

In 1931, Anais Nin (Maria De Medeiros) and her banker spouse, Hugo Guiler (Richard E. Grant), remain in Paris for the summer. While researching material on the literary career and value of D. H. Lawrence, the stifled Anais comes across a stack of erotic pictures in their flat and is surprised at how much they arouse her. Contrary to most of her husband's stuffy acquaintances, Anais is sparked by the unrestrained Henry Miller (Fred Ward), a struggling American writer. She meets his artistic acquaintances and learns of his captivating wife, June (Uma Thurman), whose past included having both a lesbian lover and a mysterious sponsor (Maurice Escargot). When Anais has an affair with Henry ("I want to know what you know. I want my life to match our life") it frees her sexual consciousness, improving her relationship with Hugo.

June returns to Paris to be with Henry again. Soon, June and Anais are drawn to

Maria De Medeiros, Fred Ward and Uma Thurman in *Henry & June* (1990).

one another emotionally and sexually, leading, at times, to a complex emotional/physical triangle. After June again leaves, both Henry and Anais start writing books on their experiences with June, each critical of the other's literary abilities. Henry completes his volume, *Tropic of Cancer*, and, as he is making a publication deal, June reappears. She is furious at having been exploited by Miller in his writings. Later, after she and Anais again go to bed, June senses that Anais and Henry have been lovers. As such, she condemns them both and vanishes. After her farewells to Henry, Anais—now fully liberated—leaves Paris with loyal Hugo.

Stephen Farber (*Movieline*) judged this film to be "An erotic masterpiece." *Variety* decided the "generally impressive" picture succeeds "In its depiction of Depression Paris and sexual candor" and that both Fred Ward and Maria De Medeiros give wonderfully perceptive performances. However, the trade paper judged, "Pic is less successful in gaining audience sym-

pathy for these hedonists," and that "the character of June . . . is ill-defined." Roger Ebert (*Movie Home Companion*, 1991) gave *Henry & June* three stars, but noted, "It's hard to find the purpose of the film, not always easy to care about the characters. . . ." Reflecting on the movie's NC-17 rating, Ebert wrote, "Americans seem more comfortable with sex when it's lurid and thrill-soaked. . . . when adults are seen freely and calmly making unorthodox sexual decision, we get all aflutter. . . . Censors by their nature are happier with sex when it is presented as sin." For Richard Combs (British *Monthly Film Bulletin*), "The major obstacles here . . . remain Henry Miller and Anais Nin, whose exploration of a new sensuality . . . is never divorced from stereotyped notions of writers writings. . . . The film might be construed as a kind of comedy about 'creativity,' but for all its scandalous sex scenes, it is too straitened by convention. . . ."

Henry & June grossed $4,981,328 in

Rutger Hauer and C. Thomas Howell in *The Hitcher* (1986).

distributors' domestic film rentals. It received one Oscar nomination: Cinematography, but lost to *Dances with Wolves*.

108. The Hitcher (Tri-Star, 1986), color, 97 min. R-rated.

Executive producers, Edward S. Feldman, Charles R. Meeker; producers, David Brombyk, Kip Ohman; co-producer, Paul Lewis; director, Robert Harmon; screenplay, Eric Red; production designer, Dennis Gassner; art director, Dins Danielson; set decorator, Lynda Burbank; music, Mark Isham; song, Mickey Jones; assistant directors, Craig Beaudine, Leigh Webb; sound, Art Names, Warren Hamilton Jr.; special effects, Art Brewer; camera, John Seale; second unit camera, Chuck Minsky; editor, Frank J. Urioste.

Cast: Rutger Hauer (John Ryder); C. Thomas Howell (Jim Halsey); Jennifer Jason Leigh (Nash); Jeffrey DeMunn (Captain Esteridge); John Hackson (Sergeant Starr); Billy "Green" Bush (Trooper Donner); Jack Thibeau (Trooper Prestone); Armin Shimerman (Interrogation Sergeant); Eugene Davis (Trooper Dodge); Jon Van Ness (Trooper Hapscomb); Henry Darrow (Trooper Hancock); Tony Epper (Trooper Con-

ners); Tom Spratley (Proprietor); Colin Campbell (Construction Man).

At one time or another, most drivers who have picked up a hitchhiker have experienced paranoia about these strangers (could he be a sociopath?). This theme was explored efficiently in Stephen Spielberg's *Duel* (1971) and *Road Games* (1981), with Stacy Keach and Jamie Lee Curtis. However, what gave *The Hitcher* a new texture was its more horrendous violence—generally suggested rather than visualized, Rutger Hauer's chilling performance, and its underlying theme of a homoerotic attraction between the stalking madman and his unwilling victim/executioner. *The Hitcher* forces the viewer to use his own imagination to fill in gaps created by the ambiguous storyline and symbolic characters ("You figure it out. . . .You figure it out" says the killer to the hero).

Young Jim Halsey (C. Thomas Howell), is earning free transportation by driving a car from Chicago to San Diego. He stops on a Texas highway to give a hitchhiker, John Ryder (Rutger Hauser), a lift. He wonders at his rash act, admitting "My mother told me never to do this." Before long, the sinister stranger, who carries a switchblade, admits that he has killed before and dares Halsey to prevent him from murdering again. The bewildered adolescent makes Ryder get out of the car. The man hitches another ride, this time with a family. Later, Jim finds the vehicle with everyone inside murdered and Ryder gone. When Ryder attempts to run Halsey down at a gas station, Jim's car is wrecked. Nash (Jennifer Jason Leigh), a waitress at a roadside diner, helps Halsey.

The teenager is later arrested for possessing Ryder's blood-caked knife. Falling asleep in his cell, he awakens to discover the law enforcers dead and the cell door open. Taking a gun, he escapes and commandeers a highway patrol car with its two troopers. Ryder drives alongside the police vehicle, shooting both troopers, and then zooms off. John later catches up with Jim, and together they flee the pursuing lawmen. Subsequently, Ryder kidnaps Nash and causes her gory death through dismemberment. He is later caught by the police, but, after killing his guards, flees. Finally, Jim runs the killer down, but, somehow, John gets up and Jim shoots him. There is an intimation now that Jim will embark on his own murderous spree along the highway.

Rex Reed (*New York Post*) approved of the film: "The marvelous thing that separates *The Hitcher* from ordinary slasher movies is the degree of artistry involved. . . ." Michael Wilmington (*Los Angeles Times*) thought, "Nothing **is** original, though the core of the movie seems to be a quasi-homosexual mentor-pupil assault. Ryder is as fixated on Halsey as Bruno on Guy in Hitchcock's *Strangers on a Train* [1951, q.v.] (whenever police or tolltakers are around, he goes coy: Grabbing Halsey's crotch, tenderly caressing his hand

or batting sullen blue come-hither eyes.)" Joseph Gelmis (*Newsday*) wrote, "As entertainment, it's a pointless obscenity. . . . But what makes *The Hitcher* even more appalling, as an enterprise, is that it is not the sleazy product of some schlock outfit." Janet Maslin (*New York Times*), no fan of this thriller, approved of Rutger Hauer's "certain evil panache" but admitted that C. Thomas Howell" remains a sincere young actor with no distinctive personality of his own."

109. The Hotel New Hampshire

(Orion, 1984), color, 110 min. R-rated.

Producer, Neil Hartley; director, Tony Richardson; co-producer, Jim Beach; associate producers, Bill Scott, Norman Twain; based on the novel by John Irving; screenplay, Richardson; production designer, Jocelyn Herbert; art director, John Meighen; costumes, Herbert; makeup, Diane Simard, Micheline Foisy; music director/arranger, Raymond Leppard; assistant directors, Bill Scott, Anne Murphy; stunt coordinator, Jerome Tiberghien; sound, Patrick Rousseau; special effects, Jacques Godbout, Louis Craig; camera, David Watkin; editor, Robert K. Lambert.

Cast: Rob Lowe (John Berry); Jodie Foster (Franny Berry); Paul McCrane (Frank Berry); Beau Bridges (Win Berry); Lisa Banes (Mary Berry); Jennie Dundas (Lilly Berry); Seth Green (Egg Berry); Nastassja Kinski (Susie, the Bear); Wallace Shawn (Sigmund Freud); Wilford Brimley ("Iowa Bob" Berry); Wally Aspell (Hotel Manager); Joelyn Richardson (Waitress); Jobst Oriwal (German); Linda Clark (German Woman); Nicholas Podbrey (Boy with Rifle); Morris Domingue (High School Band Conductor); Matthew Modine (Sterling "Chip" Dove/Ernst); Cali Timmins (Ernestine "Bitty" Tuck); Dorsey Wright (Junior Jones); Richard Jutras (Lenny Metz); Johnny O'Neil (Chester Pulaski); Colin Irving, Anthony Ulc, Nick Nardi (Chip Dove Gang Members); Charles Fournier (Howard Tuck); Anita Morris (Ronda Ray); Fred Doederlein (Finnish Doctor); Walter Massey (Texan); Young Sup Chung, Inhi Chung (Oriental Couple); Ada Fuoco (New Jersey Woman); Joan Heney (Connectcut Woman); Robert Thomas (Harold Swallow); Gayle Garfinkle (Doris Wales/Screaming Annie); Jonelle Allen (Sabrina Jones); Eli Oren (King of Mice); Roger Blay (Arbeiter); Timothy Webber (Schraubenschlussel): Janine Manatis (Schwanger); Jean-Louis Roux (Old Billig); Amanda Plummer (Fehlgeburt—"Miss Miscarriage"); Sharon Noble (Babette); Lorena Gale (Dark Inge); Jade D. Bari (Jolanta); Adrian Aron (American Woman); Arthur Grosser (American Man); Tara O'Donnell (American Daughter): Louis de Bianco (Bartender); Jyanna Honey (Bar Patron); Michele Scarabelli (Chip Dove's Girlfriend); Jeffrey Cohen (New York Journalist); Benoit Laberge (Bookstore Man); John Hutman, James V. Mathews (Reporters); Prudence Emery (Mean Reporter).

The screen version of *The Hotel New Hampshire*, like John Irving's earlier *The World According to Garp* (1982)—also directed by Tony Richardson—baffled many viewers who were unable to fathom its free-wheeling form, eccentric characters or satire. Within *The Hotel New Hampshire*, a large range of sexual expression is encompassed, including incest, rape, fetishism and homosexuality. In a cheap ploy, the filmmakers cast Paul McShane, who had played the gay student in *Fame* (1980), q.v., as Frank Berry, the sensitive outsider of *The Hotel New Hampshire*. They relied on his earlier characterization to flesh out his bare-bone role here: "I'm queer," he says. His sister replies "I know," and his brother consoles "It's ok." Outside of that brief interchange, the shadowy Frank operates in a near void, no friends, no lovers, no nothing.

In New England, school teacher Win Berry (Beau Bridges) has a large family: his wife Mary (Lisa Banes), homosexual oldest son Frank (Paul McCrane), dreamy John (Rob Lowe) and foul-mouthed Franny (Jodie Foster), and the youngest two children: Egg (Seth Green) and dwarfish Lilly (Jennie Dundas). There is also his father, football coach "Iowa Bob" (Wilford Brimley). Cherishing memories when he and Mary once worked at a resort hotel and even met vacationing Sigmund Freud (Wallace Shawn), Win turns a seminary into the Hotel New Hampshire. As the children grow up, Frank, a homosexual, is taunted at school by jock Chip Dove (Matthew Modine), while John and Franny thrive in each other's company. Chip and his pals rape Franny one Halloween night before she is rescued by John and Junior Jones (Colin Wright), a black athlete at the high school who adores Franny.

At the prompting of Freud, the Berry clan relocate to Vienna, but, upon reaching Europe, Mary and Egg die in a plane crash. At the Viennese hotel they are to run, they discover Freud's permanent guests include rabble-rousers, prostitutes, and the bisexual Susie (Nastassja Kinski), the latter coping with life through the protection of a bear suit. In an explosion set by radicals, Freud dies and Win is blinded. The Berrys return to the U.S. where Lilly writes a best-selling book (*Trying to Grow*) about her physical handicap (stunted growth). Using Lilly's royalties, they purchase the hotel where Win and Mary once worked, opening the third Hotel New Hampshire. To revenge her rape, Franny and John (who later make love together) concoct a plot in which Susie, the Bear symbolically rapes Chip. Subsequently, Lilly kills herself when her next book flops, Frank becomes a thriving literary agent, Franny and Junior Jones marry, while John hopes to give Susie enough confidence to abandon her bear skin protection. Meanwhile, all the dead figures return from the past: Mother, Lilly, Egg, Freud and his Bear, and Grandpa.

Vincent Canby (*New York Times*) reported, "The movie looks great, but Mr. Irving's modern fable . . . is less fabulous than flatulent. . . ." Sheila Benson (*Los Angeles Times*) explained, "Unlike *Garp*, these Irving characters have not made the leap from book to screen felicitously. There is no emotional umbrella here for the rain of disaster to come . . ." David Denby (*New York*) pointed out, "What happens to Franny—and to everyone else . . . is meant to shock us; what shocks us, however, is the way even the most extreme experiences can be made stupid, weightless, and empty of meaning." Rex Reed

---

Jodie Foster and Nastassja Kinski in *The Hotel New Hampshire* (1984).

(*New York Post*) observed, "Director Richardson heaps perverted people in our laps and expects us to think they're cute. He shows us the mad things they do, but he never analyzes their motivations for doing them."

The Hotel New Hampshire was a box-office failure. It was filmed on location in and around Montreal. Originally, Tony Richardson had planned to make two films from Irving's sprawling novel.

110. The House on 92nd Street

(Twentieth Century-Fox, 1945), 88 min. Not rated.

Producer, Louis de Rochemont; director, Henry Hathaway; story, Charles G. Booth; screenplay, Barre Lyndon, Booth, John Monks Jr.; art directors, Lyle Wheeler, Lewis Creber; set decorators, Thomas Little, William Sittel; costumes, Bonnie Cashin; makeup, Ben Nye; music, David Buttolph; assistant director, Melville Shyer; sound, W. D. Flick, Roger Heman; special camera effects, Fred Sersen; camera, Norbert Brodine; editor, Harmon Jones.

Cast: William Eythe (Bill Dietrich); Lloyd Nolan (Inspector George A. Briggs); Signe Hasso (Mr. Christopher [Elsa Gebhardt]); Gene Lockhart (Charles Ogden Roper); Leo G. Carroll (Colonel Hammersohn); Lydia St. Clair (Johanna Schmedt); William Post Jr. (Walker); Harry Bellaver (Max Coburg); Bruno Wick (Adolphe Lange); Harro Meller (Conrad Arnulf); Charles Wagenheim (Gus Huzmann); Alfred Linder (Adolph Klaen); Renee Carson (Luise Vadja); John McKee (Dr. Arthur C. Appleton); Edwin Jerome (Major General); Elisabeth Neumann (Freda Kassel); George Shelton (Jackson); Alfred Zeisler (Colonel Strassen); Reed Hadley (Narrator); Rusty Lane (Admiral); Salo Douday (Franz Von Wirt); Paul Ford (Sergeant); William Adams (Customs Officer); Lew Eckles, Fred Hillebrand (Policemen); Tom Brown (Intern); Bruce Fernald, Jay Wesley (FBI Agents); Benjamin Burroughs (Aide); Douglas Rutherford (Colonel); Frieda Altman, William Beach, Hamilton Benz, Henry Cordy, Mita Cordy, James J. Coyle, Hans Hansen, Kenneth Konopka, Scott Moore, Delmar Nuetzman, John Zak, Gertrude Wottitz, Bernard Lenrow (Saboteurs): George

Brandt (German Man); Yoshita Toagawa (Japanese Man); Sheila Bromley (Customer); Elmer Brown, Jack Cherry (Scientists); Victor Sutherland (Toll Guard); Stanley Tackney (Instructor); Robert Culler, Vincent Gardenia, Carl Benson, Frank Richards, Ellsworth Glath, Edward Michaels, Harrison Scott, Anna Marie Hortemann, Sara Strengell, Eugene Stuckmann, Marriott Wilson (Trainees); Frank Kreig (Travel Agent); Antonio J. Pires (Watchmaker); Danny Leone (Delivery Boy); Edward Marshall (Morgue Attendant); J. Edgar Hoover, Baron von Genin, Dr. Hans Thomson (Newsreel Footage); Edgar Deering (Cop).

"Very Good! It is a capably directed, well-acted, highly exciting spy melodrama. . . . The picture is . . . a glowing tribute to the FBI. . . ." (*Harrison's Reports*)

When *The House on 92nd Street* premiered, America was busy congratulating itself for winning World War II. Twentieth Century-Fox was in a self-congratulatory mood for having adopted the Italian neo-realism movement in this "just-the-facts-m'am" documentary-style drama, partially filmed *away* from California sound stages. At the time, little discussion focused on the peculiar chief villain of the piece, "Mr. Christopher," who happened to be a Nazi female operative in drag! Most viewers accepted this cross-dresser as a plotline convenience, an interesting diversion, but nothing much more. More sophisticated filmgoers, then and in later reappraisal, would make the connection between the dastardly Mr. Christopher—a "perverse" Nazi enemy agent—and such later butch blackguards as the lesbian Rosa Klebb (Lotte Lenya) of the British-made *From Russia with Love* (1964). It has frequently been part of the public's accepted conceit that depraved scoundrels were frequently sexual "deviants."

Suggested by a true-life case during World War II, the slickly- made *The House on 92nd Street* opens in 1939. It focuses on engineer Bill Dietrich (William Eythe), a young American of German descent, asked to do espionage work for Germany in the U.S. He agrees, but secretly tells FBI Inspector George A. Briggs (Lloyd Nolan), who counsels him on how he can help to trap these Axis agents. After extensive training in Germany, Dietrich returns to the U.S. to establish a hidden radio station to transmit information back to the fatherland. Dietrich works with the chief operatives at their New York City headquarters on 92nd Street, disguised as a dress shop/home supervised by Elsa Gebhardt (Signe Hasso). Through Dietrich's working with the spies, led by the mysterious Mr. Christopher, the FBI monitors the Germans' efforts to gather data on Process 97, the code name for part of the formula to the atom bomb. As the case builds, the Nazis discover Dietrich's true allegiance. However, the FBI rescue him and, in the process of rounding up the spy ring, Mr. Christopher is killed trying to escape. It is then learned that Christopher is actually Elsa Gebhardt.

Variety predicted (correctly): "This film will do biz because of its excellent exploitation possibilities. The FBI, in peace as in war, is still a pretty good boxoffice bet." Thomas M. Pryor (*New York Times*) noted that, "As the ring leader of the spies, Miss Hasso tends to be over-domineering at times. . . ." James Agee (*The Nation*) who ruled the film was "Unpersuasive" but "generally enjoyable," zeroed in on the "effective pseudo-naturalistic performances." He added that "none of whom, however, manage to suggest how spies, counterspies, and traitors who look and act like that are not identifiable to those interested at five hundred paces."

The House on 92nd Street won an Academy Award for Best Original Story.

111. The Hunger (Metro-Goldwyn-Mayer/United Artists, 1983), color, 98 min. R-rated.

Producer, Richard A. Shephard; director, Tony Scott; based on the novel by Whitley Strieber; screenplay, Ivan Davis, Michael Thomas; production designer, Brian Morris; art director, Clinton Cavers; set decorators, Ann Mollo, Janet Rosenbloom; costumes, Milena Canonero; makeup, Jane Royle; special makeup, Antony Clavet; music, Michel Rubini, Denny Jaeger; assistant directors, David Tringham, Michael Stevenson, Debbie Vertue; sound, Dan Neroda; camera, Stephen Goldblatt; additional camera, Hugh Johnson; editor, Pamela Power.

Cast: Catherine Deneuve (Miriam); David Bowie (John Blaylock); Susan Sarandon (Dr. Sarah Roberts); Cliff DeYoung (Tom Haver); Beth Ehlers (Alice Cavender); Dan Hedaya (Lieutenant Allegrezza); Rufus Collins (Charlie Humphries); Suzanne Bertish (Phyllis); James Aubrey (Ron); Ann Magnuson, John Stephen Hill (Disco Couple); Shane Rimmer (Jelinek); Bauhaus (Disco Group); Douglas Lambert (TV Host); Bessie Love (Lilybelle); John Pankow, Willem Dafoe (Phone Booth Youths); Sophie Ward, Philip Sayer (London House Couple); Lise Hilboldt (Waiting Room Nurse); Michael Howe, Edward Wiley (Interns); Richard Robles (Skater); George Camiller (Eumenes); Oke Wambu (Egyptian Slave).

It was not a novel moviemaking concept to exploit the (mis)adventures of lesbian vampires. Earlier there had been the European-made *Daughters of Darkness* (1971). In the English-language cinema, there had been, among others, the shaded performance of Gloria Holden in *Dracula's Daughter* (1936), q.v.. In the American-produced short subject, *Because the Dawn* (1988), a saxophone-playing vampiress seduces a woman sports photographer. The high-tech *The Hunger* updated that tradition, but won few plaudits in the process. David Ansen (*Newsweek*) labeled it "your basic decadent lesbian vampire movie. It's so chic, indeed, that the word 'vampire' is never uttered, although the slashed throats and gushing blood get the point across. This movie is a triumph of tony packaging."

In New York City, elegant Miriam (Catherine Deneuve), a beautiful, centuries-old vampire, and her lover, John Blaylock (David Bowie), whom she met in the 1700s, lure victims back to their Manhattan home, needing fresh blood to nourish their systems. Later, because of his badly-accelerating aging system, John rushes to the Park West Clinic, wanting advice from Dr. Sarah Roberts (Susan Sarandon), who is researching the longevity process. When she cannot see him, he leaves, having aged tremendously. After murdering another victim, the young Alice Cavender (Beth Ehlers), at Miriam's, he "dies." Miriam sets Blaylock's body in a coffin box in the attic, in the same room with other past lovers. Thereafter, New York Police Lieutenant Allegrezza (Dan Hedaya), tracks the vanished Alice to Miriam's. Later, Sarah arrives searching for John. She is informed by the icy Miriam that he has gone for treatment to Switzerland.

Drawn back to Miriam's by an indefinable force, Sarah and Miriam, make love and drink one another's blood. Meanwhile, Sarah's co-worker and lover, Tom Haver (Cliff De Young), is concerned about her peculiar behavior. A blood test reveals that Sarah's system contains a foreign element. Beginning to understand her own plight, Sarah confronts Miriam, only to learn that she now belongs to the vampire. (Miriam says, "After a while you will forget what you once were. You will begin to love me as I love you.") Hungering for blood, Sarah murders Tom when he follows her to Miriam's. Then, horrified by her misdeed, she kills herself. As Miriam brings Sarah's body to the attic room, she is attacked by her rotting past amours. In the process, she apparently falls to her death. Later, the house is sold. As for Miriam, she reenergizes elsewhere.

Rex Reed (*New York Post*) inquired, "Whatever happened to garlic, crucifixes and silver bullets? The decadent vampires in *The Hunger* are into Quaaludes, punk fashion, kinky sex and interior decorating. . . . For a vampire movie, it isn't remotely scary, and despite its nude lesbian makeout scenes . . . it's surprisingly unsexy, too." Sheila Benson (*Los Angeles Times*) summed up: "The film is absolutely beautiful, and dumb. It is also gruesomely unpleasant and very nearly unfathomable." Steve Jenkins (British *Monthly Film Bulletin*) disapproved: "This slick, vacuous surface might not have been disastrous were the accompanying narrative not so-hand-me-down and broken-backed. . . ."

Vincent Canby (*New York Times*) was more accepting: "What makes *The Hunger* so much fun is its knowing stylishness. . . ." But, Canby cautioned: "it is not, strictly speaking, a horror film. Rather, it is a film of visual sensation, not all of which are quite so explicit as the sight of Miss Deneuve making love to the innocent Miss Sarandon, while simultaneously giving her a blood transfusion. . . . Miss Sarandon puts her mark on the film with one of her now-obligatory nude scenes. . . ."

The Hunger, not a box-office success, was the first feature of Tony Scott, previously known for his TV commercials. He is the brother of Ridley Scott (director of *Alien*, 1979, *Bladerunner*, 1982 and *Thelma and Louise*, 1991).

112. I Escaped from Devil's Island (United Artists, 1973), color, 87 min. R-rated.

Producers, Roger Corman, Gene Corman; director, William Witney; screenplay, Richard L. Adams; art director, Robert Silva; set decorator, Jose Gonzalez; costumes, Jodie Tillen; makeup, Carmen Palomino; music, Les Baxter; assistant directors, Jaime Contreras, Cliff Bush; sound, Jose Carlos; special effects, Raoul Faromar; camera, Rosalio Solano; supervising editor, Alan Collins; editors, Tom Walls, Barbara Pokras.

Cast: Jim Brown (Le Bras); Christopher George (Davert); Rick Ely (Jo-Jo); James Luis (Dazzas); Paul Richards (Major Marteau); Richard Rust (Sergeant Zamoora); Roland "Bob" Harris (Barber); Jan Merlin (Roenquist); Eduardo Rosas Lopez (Sergeant Brescano); Jonathan Dodge (Lieutenant Duplis); Quintin Bulnes (Sergeant Grissoni); Gabriella Rios (Indian Girl); Ana de Sade (Bedalia); Max Kerlow (Pelliserre); Aubert Knight (The Dealer); Enrique Lucero (Esteban); Aurora Nunez (Whore); Gaston Melo (Police Captain); and: Peter Goldberg, Stephen Whittaker, Sergio Martinez.

Beating the far more expansive *Papillon*, q.v., to the box-office by several

months, *I Escaped from Devil's Island* shared many plot parallels with that feature, including the character of a homosexual prisoner.

In 1918, black prisoner Le Bras (Jim Brown) is sentenced to a life term at the notorious French penal colony on Devil's Island. Defiantly insisting he will escape, Le Bras joins with two other convicts, Dazzas (James Luisi) and the man's sometimes transvestite lover Jo-Jo (Rick Ely) in making a breakout. Using a raft made of animal skins, they are joined in their escape by a pacifist, Davert (Christopher George). As Major Matteau (Paul Richards) and his troops pursue the prison-breakers, the latter suffer attrition of their numbers. Dazzas is killed by a shark, and Jo-Jo is arrested for pickpocketing. Before the authorities can interrogate (and torture) him, he hangs himself. Later, the injured Le Bras stands off the advancing lawmen so that Davert can escape aboard a departing ship.

Made quickly to exploit the remaining box-office appeal of black action star Jim Brown, *Variety* rated this effort a "slovenly, gamy potboiler. . . . Plot makes no pretense to proper motivation. . . ." As to the haphazard depiction of the gay characters, the *Variety* reviewer described Rick Ely's role as "a semi-transvestite, or something like that. . . ." In dismissing this rip-off of *Papillon*, David McGillivray (British *Monthly Film Bulletin*) wrote, "the similarities between the two plots stretch beyond mere coincidence. Once again, the four escapees from the penal colony represent brawn, brains, homosexuality and expendability. . . ."

113. The Incident (Twentieth Century-Fox, 1967), 99 min. Not rated.

Producers, Monroe Sachson, Edward Meadow; director, Larry Peerce; based on the teleplay *Ride with Terror* by Nicholas Baehr; screenplay, Baehr; production designer, Manny Gerard; set decorator, Robert Drumheller; costumes, Muriel Gettinger; makeup, Herman Buchman; music/music conductor, Charles Fox; assistant directors, Steve Barnett, Alex

Hapasas; sound, Jack Jacobsen; camera, Gerald Hirschfeld; editor, Armond Lebowitz.

Cast: Tony Musante (Joe Ferrone); Martin Sheen (Artie Conners); Beau Bridges (Private First Class Felix Teflinger); Brock Peters (Arnold Robinson); Ruby Dee (Joan Robinson); Jack Gilford (Sam Beckerman); Thelma Ritter (Bertha Beckerman); Ed McMahon (Bill Wilks); Diana Van Der Vlis (Helen Wilks); Mike Kellin (Harry Purvis); Jan Sterling (Muriel Purvis); Gary Merrill (Douglas McCann); Robert Fields (Kenneth Otis); Robert Bannard (Private First Class Phillip Carmatti) Victor Arnold (Tony Goya); Donna Mills (Alice Keenan); Kathleen Smith (Wilks's Daughter); Henry Proach (Derelict); Neal Hynes (Toll Booth Attendant); Ben Levi (Man Who Is Mugged); Martin Meyers (Poolhall Owner); Don De Leo (Mr. Carmatti); Nina Hansen (Mrs. Carmatti); Ted Lowrie (Host); John Servetnik (Bartender); Ray Cole, Barry Del Rae (Young Men); Nico Hartos (Policeman); Maxine McCrey (Black Woman).

Set largely within the confines of a Manhattan-bound subway car, this intense drama focuses on the effects the terrorizing by two mindless punks of the passengers, the latter a wide assortment of New Yorkers, including a troubled homosexual.

After mugging an old man (Ben Levi), two drunk young ruffians, Joe Ferrone (Tony Musante) and Artie Connors (Martin Sheen), jump aboard a subway bound for Grand Central Station. In the course of the trip, they intimidate and brutalize the other passengers. The riders include high school teacher Bill Wilks (Ed McMahon), his wife (Diana Van Der Vlis) and their youngster (Kathleen Smith); horny Tony Goya (Victor Arnold) and his timid date, Alice Keenan (Donna Mills); an elderly Jewish couple, Sam (Jack Gilford) and Bertha Beckerman (Thelma Ritter); a black racist (Brock Peter) and his pacifist wife (Ruby Dee); a passed-out drunken bum (Henry Proach); a frustrated married couple, Harry (Mike Kellin) and Muriel Purvis (Jan Sterling); a recovering alcoholic, Douglas McCann (Gary Merrill); a timid homosexual, Kenneth Otis (Robert

Fields), who had tried to pick up McCann at a rundown bar; and two soldiers on leave, Felix Teflinger (Beau Bridges) and Philip Carmatti (Robert Bannard).

As the hellish ride continues, none of the passengers try to defend any of the others, as each, in turn, is humiliated and frightened. Finally, Teflinger, a Southerner visiting town, confronts the two bullies. He uses his broken arm, encased in a plaster cast, as a weapon to fight off the knife-wielding punks. Although he is stabbed by Ferrone in the stomach, he is able to beat his assailant senseless. When the subway train reaches Grand Central, cops come aboard and cart off the two thugs. Carmatti drags his buddy onto the station platform. Meanwhile, the other passengers, shamed into silence, carefully step over the drunk, who has slept through the entire ordeal.

Bosley Crowther (*New York Times*) felt the movie adaptation had "inflated to appalling proportions" the urban problem. Crowther disliked the overabundance of the "carefully assorted and conspicuously identifiable social and ethnic types." Per the *Times'* reviewer, "Too many times one is reminded by little cliches or big gaucheries that these are only actors. . . ." A more lenient *Variety* weighed this a "very fine episodic drama" although admitting, "some overexposition and relaxed editing flag the pace."

The Incident falls back onto ready-made stereotypes in order to portray its large main cast by short vignettes. One of the lengthier explanatory sequences concerns the homosexual character, Kenneth Otis. Prior to the main subway ride, he is shown entering a seedy bar, timorously trying to make contact with a man, but then nervously rushing to the bathroom to throw up. While he is recuperating there, a middle-aged on-the-mend alcoholic, Douglas McCann, comes into the washroom. The jittery Otis contemplates approaching McCann sexually, but then backs off, frightened at risking rejection or anything worse. As each man makes his separate way to the subway stop, McCann observes Otis following him and gives him a self-righteous scornful look. (Why the homophobic Douglas would think anyone would want to seduce him is a plotline puzzlement.)

In the subway car horror that follows, crafty Artie Connors sizes up defensive Kenneth as a gay man. He teases his frightened victim by pretending he will side with Otis against the belligerent Ferrone. ("Maybe when we get off, we could go some place. A movie . . . I just want to talk to you . . . Do you trust me?") Then turning vicious, he grabs Otis by his necktie and screams, "You rotten fag! You make me want to puke!" Kenneth is more upset at being unmasked and made so vulnerable in public than he is about being potentially mugged. The other passengers, including the minority types (the Jewish couple, the black couple, etc.) display no compassion for this now-persecuted outsider. Tony Goya says nonchalantly to his date, "Ah, it looks like they got a hold of a queer." To make the humiliation complete, Connors sets a handkerchief on the immobilized Otis's head and makes Kenneth dance with him. After embracing Otis, Artie tires of the game and pushes the stunned man away: "Come on princess. You've been a naughty girl. You've got to sit in the corner." His spirit completely beaten, the gay man retreats into himself. The message of this sequence went beyond ordinary realistic drama.

The Incident was based on a "DuPont Show of the Week" TV drama , "Ride to Terror" (December 1, 1963). Shot in economical black-and-white, the movie was filmed for less than $900,000.

114. Inmates: A Love Story

(ABC-TV, February 13, 1981), color, 100 min. Not rated.

Executive producer, James S. Henerson, James G. Hirsch; producer, Bill Finnegan; associate producer, E. Darrell Hallenbeck; director, Guy Green; story, Delia Jordan; teleplay, Hirsch, Jordan; art director, Joe Aubel; music, Dana Kaproff; assistant directors, Nick Marck, Michael Green, Mary Ellen Canniff; sound, Pat Mitchell; camera, Al Francis; editor, Paul LaMastra.

Cast: Kate Jackson (Jane Mount); Perry King (Roy Matson); Pamela Reed (Sunny); Paul Koslo (Harold Virgil); Fay Hauser (Grace); Penelope Allen (Gloria); Craig T. Nelson (Daniels); Tony King (Jon); Paul Lieber (Thomas P. Eliot); Judith Chapman (Leslie Matson); Shirley Jones (Superintendent E. F. Crown); Tony Curtis (Flanagan); Maxayn Lewis (Shawna); Virginia Capers (Agnes); Ted Noose (Lieutenant Hodges); Arva Holt (Marty); Norma Donaldson (Lila); Peggy Walton-Walker (Clair); Duke Stroud (Sheriff); Rita Taggart (Salt); Cynthia Avila (Pepper); Randal Johnson (Tony); Ron Spivey (Mac); Janet Lee Parker (Bennett); S. John Launer (Chairman).

The gimmick of this high concept made-for-television movie was to exploit the potentials of life and love in a co-ed correctional facility. Among the prisoners serving time there are two lesbians—with the cutsy names of Salt and Pepper—with their own agenda for the beleaguered hero (Perry King). Unfortunately, the promising premise went unrealized on screen. *Daily Variety* dismissed the project as "a rambling, trite collection of characters trying to be outrageous." *TV Guide* rated the picture with only two stars.

Upscale account executive Roy Matson (Perry King) allows himself to be charged with professional wrongdoing to protect the corporate hierarchy whose attorney (Craig T. Nelson) insists that his prison stay will be very brief. The elitist Roy is sent to Greenleaf State Co-Correctional Institution, which has an experimental co-ed program run by Superintendent E. F. Crown (Shirley Jones). Before he learns humility within the prison compound, Matson is pummeled in the shower by a tough thug (Tony King) and his underlings and earns the enmity of the sadistic Harold Virgil (Paul Koslo). The corrupt Crown wants Roy to doctor the prison books in order to hide her graft, but he refuses. Meanwhile, two lesbian prisoners, Salt (Rita Taggart) and Pepper (Cynthia Avila),

Advertisement for *Inmates: A Love Story* (1981).

decide that Roy, the handsome stud, is the perfect choice to inseminate one of them. He refuses the unorthodox offer, earning him the dislike of even more people behind bars. Before he is released, Roy, whose own marriage is failing, finds love with a repentant cat burglar (Kate Jackson).

One of the few convincing performances in this tripe was by Tony Curtis as an old-timer prisoner who befriends the hero. Location work for this telefeature was accomplished at an unused correctional facility in Lancaster, California and at Ft. MacArthur, California.

115. Inside Daisy Clover (Warner Bros., 1965), color, 128 min. Not rated.

Producer, Alan J. Pakula; director, Robert Mulligan; based on the novel by Gavin Lambert; screenplay, Lambert; production designer, Robert Clatworthy; art director, Dean Tavoularis; set decorator, George James Hopkins; costumes, Edith Head, Bill Thomas; makeup, Gordon Bau, Ed Butterworth, Al Greenway; music, Andre Previn; songs, Andre Previn and Dory Previn; choreographer, Herbert Ross; assistant directors, Joseph E. Kenny, Jack Cunningham; sound, Russell Ashley; montage, John Hoffman; camera, Charles Lang; editor, Aaron Stell.

Cast: Natalie Wood (Daisy Clover); Christopher Plummer (Raymond Swan); Robert Redford (Wade Lewis); Roddy McDowall (Baines); Ruth Gordon (The Dealer); Katharine Bard (Melora Swan); Peter Helm (Milton Hopwood); Betty Harford (Gloria Goslett); John Hale (Harry Goslett); Harold Gould (Cop); Ottola Nesmith (Old Lady in Hospital); Edna Holland (Cynara).

"It is not clear from viewing the film whether the treatment should be regarded as satire, fantasy, up-the-establishment, charcoal-gray humor, social comment, a gross melodrama of manipulation, or, perhaps a bit of each." (Rudy Belmer, Tony Thomas, *Hollywood's Hollywood*, 1975)

Inside Daisy Clover might have been a good film or even a fun film. However, what survived on screen after heavy editing is a jumbled plotline, undefined characters, and badly mixed moods. The cast-

ing of this expensively-mounted period piece reflects its greater artistic problems. Strident Natalie Wood plays a charismatic fifteen-year-old gamin (she was 27 at the time) with a great singing voice (her voice was dubbed by Jackie Ward.) As for Robert Redford's badly-defined role as the narcisstic movie idol, it was originally conceived as that of a homosexual, but ended in the release print as being a barely-recognizable passive bisexual. Neither studio nor star wanted to risk depicting the character as a blatant homosexual.

In 1936 California, rebellious young tomboy Daisy Clover (Natalie Wood) lives in a shack on Venice Beach with her mentally unstable mother (Ruth Gordon). The latter is known as The Dealer because of her penchant for playing solitaire. Daisy loves to sing and sends a recording to Raymond Swan (Christopher Plummer), head of a major Hollywood studio. He screen tests Daisy and signs her to a movie contract. Meanwhile, Daisy's older sister (Betty Harford) and brother-in-law (John Hale) work with Swan to get Daisy's embarrassing mother, The Dealer, out of the way, by having her institutionalized. At a meet-the-industry party, Daisy is introduced to handsome screen star Wade Lewis (Robert Redford), with whom she spends the night. They soon marry, but the next morning he vanishes from their Arizona motel room. Back in Hollywood, the badly-perplexed Daisy learns the truth about her errant spouse—-he has found a new playmate. (Daisy is told, "Your husband never could resist a charming boy.")

Distraught, Daisy brings her mother to live with her at the beachhouse. However, the Dealer soon dies. This event leads to Daisy's nervous breakdown and her failed suicide attempt (turning on the stove gas jet). As she walks out of the house and down the beach, the gas-filled building explodes. Amused by the twists of fate which have made "America's Little Valentine" a has-been at seventeen, she vows to survive regardless.

Howard Thompson (*New York Times*)

gave the majority view: "There have been better pictures about Hollywood, but few as triumphantly, all-around bad. . . ." As to the characters, Thompson viewed, "They're all neurotic, in fact, and the crowning touch is Miss Wood's unsuspecting marriage to the studio's top glamour boy, a homosexual, personably played by newcomer, Robert Redford." Pauline Kael (*The New Yorker*) judged the movie "all portent, no content." She found Natalie Wood "brassy and mechanical, with wind-up emotions." However, Kael found that Robert Redford "in one of the most cryptic roles ever written, gives the only fresh performance in *Inside Daisy Clover*."

Inside Daisy Clover received three Academy Award nominations: Best Supporting Actress (Ruth Gordon; Shelley Winters won for *A Patch of Blue*); Best Art Direction—Set Decoration: Color (*Doctor Zhivago* won); Best Costume Design: Color (*Doctor Zhivago* won). Of the three Dory and Andrew Previn song numbers, "You're Going to Hear From Me" gained modest popularity.

116. Internal Affairs (Paramount, 1990), color, 115 min. R-rated.

Executive producers, Pierre David, Rene Malo; co-executive producer, David Streit; producer, Frank Mancuso Jr.; associate producers, Mara Trafficante, Pam O'Har; director, Mike Figgis; screenplay, Henry Bean; production designer, Waldemar Kalinowski; art director, Nicholas T. Preovolos; set designer, Clare Scarpulla; set decorators, Florence Fellman; costumes, Rudy Dillon; makeup, Julie Purcell; music, Figgis, Anthony Marinelli, Brian Banks; assistant directors, J. Stephen Buck, Joseph Christian Auer Jr.; stunt coordinator, Gary Hymes; sound, David Brownslow, Mark Curray; special effects co-ordinator, Paul Staples; camera, John A. Alonzo; second unit camera, Michael Ferris; editor, Robert Estritt.

Cast: Richard Gere (Dennis Peck); Andy Garcia (Raymond Avilla); Nancy Travis (Kathleen Avilla); Laurie Metcalf (Amy Wallace); Richard Bradford (Grieb); William Baldwin (Van Stretch); Michael Beach (Dorian Fletcher); Katherine Borowitz (Tova Arrocas); Faye Grant (Penny); Xander Berkeley (Rudy Mohr); John Kapelos (Steven Arrocas); John Capodice (Chief Healy); Victoria Dillard (Kee); Pamella D'Pella (Cheryl); Susan Forristal (Lolly); Allan Havey (Judson); Lew Hopson (Buster); Tyde Kierney (Sergeant Trafficante); Dinah Lenney (Newscaster); Scott Lincoln (Freddy); Julio Oscar Mechoso (Cousin Gregory); Harry Murphy (Surgeon); Billie Neal (Dorian's Wife); Heather Lauren Olson (Megan); Marco Rodriguez (Demetrio); Annabella Sciorra (Heather Peck); Arlen Dean Snyder (Captain Riordan); Deryn Warren (TV Reporter); Valerie Wildman (May); Elijah Wood (Sean); Domingo Adkins (Party Guest); Hamlet Arman (Carlos); Camilla Bergstrom (Surfer Chick); Mitchell Claman (Kevin); Mark A. Cuttin (Honor Guard Sergeant); Justin DeRosa (Latino Driver); Mike Figgis (Hollander); Geoffrey Grider (Dinner Guest); Father Andrew Herman (Priest); Brian Johnson (Busboy); Waldemar Kalinowski (Surgeon #2); Helen Lin (Dina); Frank Mancuso Jr. (Radio Cop); Christopher Raymond Mullane (Guard); Hank McGill (Medic); Jimmy Ortega (Oscar); S. Grant Sawyer (Surfer Dude); Richard B. Whitaker (Marksman).

". . . where *Internal Affairs* really succeeds is in its cracking narrative drive, moody atmospherics, and excellent performances, even in the smallest roles." (Julian Petley, British *Monthly Film Bulletin*)

Film noir police thrillers have been a Hollywood staple for decades, many of them detailing the power struggles between watchdog and corrupt lawmen who share a the-end-justifies-the-means philosophy. However, the gritty, superior R-rated *Internal Affairs* boasted particularly energetic performances from Richard Gere and Andy Garcia. The film also provided an understated characterization of a lesbian police officer, performed in deliberately casual style by Laurie Metcalf (of TV "Roseanne" fame).

In Los Angeles, newly-trained Internal Affairs investigator Raymond Avilla (Andy Garcia) is teamed with experienced Amy Wallace (Laurie Metcalf) to follow up on Van Stretch (William Baldwin), a police officer accused of corruption. Before long, the partners unravel a hornet's

Laurie Metcalf, Andy Garcia and Marco Rodriquez in *Internal Affairs* (1990).

nest of police corruption, all tied to well-liked officer Dennis Peck (Richard Gere). Meanwhile, the devious Peck toys with driven Raymond, suggesting that Avilla's wife, Kathleen (Nancy Travis), could be guilty of infidelity. Later, the much-married Dennis, who is having an affair with Van Stretch's wife, Penny (Faye Grant), has Van Stretch killed, and then arranges for the murderers to be eliminated.

Workaholic Raymond, who has earlier beaten up Peck, now is convinced that Kathleen and he are having an affair. His fears deepen when Peck slugs him and tells him it is all true about he and Kathleen. As a result, the frustrated, once by-the-books Avilla fantasizes about shooting Peck. Subsequently, he and Amy learn from Dennis's wife (Annabella Sciorra) that he has been moonlighting as a hired killer. In tracking Peck to his latest hit job, Amy is badly wounded and the crooked officer escapes. At Avilla's house, Dennis terrorizes the innocent Kathleen. When Peck resists arrest, Avilla kills him.

Variety approved of *Internal Affairs* for being "Stylish and slick" and "tightly constructed. The trade journal complimented Richard Gere for his "constant sense of menace" and Andy Garcia whose "quiet seething brings needed complexity and depth to a thinly drawn character." Of Laurie Metcalf, *Variety* printed, she "turns in the film's most memorable supporting role, terrific as Garcia's tough femme partner." Pauline Kael (*The New Yorker*) felt that "This sophisticated variant of the L.A. cops-and-coke-and-art-world thrillers has a creepy, rhythmic quality that sucks you in and keeps you amused . . . The subtext is ingeniously nasty; it's a dirty, sexy twist on the Iago-Othello relationship. . . . As Garcia's partner, a lesbian who doesn't try to ingratiate herself with anybody, Metcalf gives a strong, contained performance."

As the high-achieving Internal Affairs officer, competing in a tight circle of macho "brothers," Laurie Metcalf's Amy Wallace is a tough enforcer of department standards. While her chauvinistic co-workers are shown frequently with their mates or assessing the merits of the opposite sex, Amy is the overly-devoted worker always grinding away at the job. If her brusque demeanor in a man's world does not "give away" her sexual orientation, there is a telling moment while she and Raymond relax in their police car munching a fast-food lunch. A statuesque woman passes by and Wallace nearly flips around in her seat to oggle the shapely sight. This revealing facet of Amy's personality is not lost on her new teammate, but neither verbally comments on it. It gives a new twist to a later sequence when Raymond's unsuspecting wife jealously inquires about what his female partner is like.

Internal Affairs grossed $11 million in distributors' domestic film rentals.

117. **Irene** (First National, 1926), color sequences, 83 min. Not rated.

Presenter, John McCormick; director, Alfred E. Green; based on the play by James Montgomery; continuity, June Mathis; screenplay, Rex Taylor; art director, John D. Schulze; music, Harry Tierney, Joseph McCarthy; comedy construction, Mervyn LeRoy; camera, T. D. McCord; lighting effects, Lawrence Kennedy; editor, Edwin Robbins.

Cast: Colleen Moore (Irene O'Dare); Lloyd Hughes (Donald Marshall); George K. Arthur (Madame Lucy); Charles Murray (Pa O'Dare); Kate Price (Ma O'Dare); Ida Darling (Mrs. Warren Marshall); Eva Novak (Eleanor Hadley); Edward Earle (Larry Hadley); Laurence Wheat (Bob Harrison); Maryon Aye (Helen Cheston); Bess Flowers (Jane Gilmour); Lydia Yeamans Titus (Mrs. Cheston); Cora Macey (Mrs. Gilmour).

A bizarre conceit of 1920s cinema was to convert a Broadway musical into a silent movie—obviously unable to take advantage of the show's well-known songs on screen. *Irene* derived from a 1919 stage hit and reached the movies as a joyful romantic comedy starring irrepressible Colleen Moore as a wistful Irish lass. A more unusual aspect of the production was comedian George K. Arthur's performance

as Madame Lucy (!) the proprietress, or rather, the effeminate proprietor of the dress-making establishment where the heroine works as a model.

Leaving her Philadelphia tenement home, likable but ungainly Irene O'Dare (Colleen Moore) comes to New York City to find work. She encounters wealthy Donald Marshall (Lloyd Hughes), who arranges for her to have a position at a new fashion shop run by Madame Lucy (George K. Arthur). Through perseverence and much luck, Irene succeeds as a model. However, Donald's snobbish mother (Ida Darling) investigates Irene's background to confirm her fears that the young woman is unworthy of Donald's noble love. Although depressed by Mrs. Marshall's cruel discrimination, Irene still adores Donald. He has sense enough to realize her worth and declares his undying affection for her.

Mordaunt Hall (*New York Times*) enthused that star Colleen Moore was "nimble and versatile" in this vehicle. Furthermore, he discreetly observed that "George K. Arthur . . . does reasonably well with the effeminate part and is mildy amusing when he endeavors to design a gown with Irene as his model." *Variety* cheered, "One more bullseye for Colleen Moore. . . ." The trade paper added, "there is the effeminate modiste characterization of George K. Arthur . . . a gem of its kind. Nothing fresh, vulgar or objectionable about the way Arthur plays it, just 'sissified' and funny, so even the average lay mind will absorb it as desired. . . . [There is] little doubt that Arthur runs only second to Miss Moore for personal honors."

As Madame Lucy, George K. Arthur's prissy character has a penchant for mincing gestures (including extravagant pop-eyed reactions), lace handkerchiefs, and a swishy walk. When he first sets sights on the hoydenish Irene, he gaps in (title card) amazement: "As I live and hemstitch. She's impossible! Even I cannot make a peach melba from a prune!" Later, the haughty Madame Lucy and the compliant Irene, each fed up with their teacher-student chores, snap at one another:

Madame Lucy: You're impossible! . . . You walk almost like a man!

Irene: So do you!

When the popular *Irene* was remade in 1940, starring Anna Neagle and Ray Milland, the Madame Lucy character was homogenized into the unobtrusive character, Mr. Smith (Roland Young).

118. Jacqueline Susann's Once Is Not Enough (Paramount, 1975), color, 122 min. R-rated.

Executive producer, Irving Mansfield; producer, Howard W. Koch; director, Guy Green; based on the novel by Jacqueline Susann; screenplay, Julius J. Epstein; production designer, John DeCuir; art director, David Marshall; set decorator, Ruby Levitt; music, Henry Mancini; songs, Mancini and Larry Kusik; assistant director, Howard W. Koch Jr.; sound, Larry Jost; camera, John A. Alonzo; editor, Rita Roland.

Cast: Kirk Douglas (Mike Wayne); Alexis Smith (Deidre Milford Granger); David Janssen (Tom Colt); George Hamilton (David Milford); Melina Mercouri (Karla); Gary Conway (Hugh Robertson); Brenda Vaccaro (Linda Riggs); Deborah Raffin (January Wayne); Lillian Randolph (Mabel); Mark Roberts (Rheingold); John Roper (Franco); Leonard Sachs (Dr. Peterson); Jim Boles (Scotty); Ann Marie Moelders (Girl at El Morocco); Trudi Marshall (Myrna); Eddie Garrett (Maitre D' at Polo Lounge); Sid Frohlich (Waiter); Kelly Lange (Weather Lady); Maureen McCluskey, Harley Farber, Michael Millius, Tony Ferrara (Beautiful People).

"Everything that can happen between a man and a woman—and a woman and a woman happens before your eyes." (Advertisement for *Jacqueline Susann's Once Is Not Enough*)

Fortunately, authoress Jacqueline Susann died before this R-rated soap opera disaster was unleashed on the public. With its "name" cast, the film version diluted Susann's tawdry best-seller. Within its voyeuristic peek into life among the seamy jet set rich, the most exploitable item in the story was the lesbian relationship between a screen goddess (supposed to suggest Greta Garbo) and a Park Avenue socialite. The movie ad campaign described these two characters in purple prose: Karla (Melina Mercouri) . . . "From peasant to screen goddess—her rumored love life was real." Deidra (Alexis Smith) . . . "Untold wealth, untold marriages—her real love was a woman." Actually, because the parts were played by two such professionals, their few scenes together—chopped down to appease the censors—were relatively tasteful and believable.

Recovering from a serious motorcycle accident, virginal January Wayne (Deborah Raffin) comes to New York from Switzerland to be with her movie producer father, Mike (Kirk Douglas), now down on his luck. Father-fixated January is dismayed to learn that her father has married demanding, mega-millionaire Deidre Milford Granger (Alexis Smith), in order to gain for January a cushy lifestyle. The very independent January goes to work for *Gloss* magazine, edited by former school pal Linda Riggs (Brenda Vaccaro). January has an affair with Deidre's playboy cousin, David Milford (George Hamilton), whom she finds shallow. He, meanwhile has a relationship with the movie star Karla (Melina Mercouri), who is Deidre's secret lover. Later, January falls in love with the much-older cynical novelist, Tom Colt (David Janssen), which upsets daughter-obsessed Mike. Still later, Mike and Deidre die in a plane crash, January's affair with the heavy-drinking Tom fades, and our heroine, no longer innocent, must deal with life on her own (but helped by a $3 million insurance policy dad left her).

Critics and moviegoers alike roasted this inept screen offering. Thom Smith (*Palm Beach Post*) insisted "Once Is Plenty for Latest Susann Star Story." He explained: "the movie jumps from scene to scene like a rabbit eluding a hunter." Smith did note kindly, "The film is not the vehicle for great performances," but ob-

Melina Mercouri and Alexis Smith in *Jacqueline Susann's Once Is Not Enough* (1974).

served that Alexis Smith "is disappointing" in her role and that Melina Mercouri "is interesting, but her part is comparatively minor." Eric Hertz (*Women's Wear Daily*) insisted the picture was "a soap opera that has lost all its suds. . . . The enervated cast stumbles around as if it has leg irons on while the film drags to its denouement. . . ." A more generous Kevin Thomas (*Los Angeles Times*) described the picture "as old-style Hollywood hokum" and that "Alexis Smith and Kirk Douglas look terrific and perform with much flair. Miss Mercouri is wisely mischievous in her brief appearance."

Unlike the enormously successful *Valley of the Dolls* (1967) q.v., and the less popular *The Love Machine* (1971)—also adapted from Jacqueline Susann bestsellers, bad word-of-mouth kept audiences away from *Once Is Not Enough*. The highly-touted "forbidden" love scenes

(cooing remarks here, a prim kiss there, Karla massaging Deidre's neck, Deidre in a bath towel in Karla's bedroom) were, when all was said and done, very chaste. From the vantage point of time, Vito Russo in *The Celluloid Closet* (1987) decided that this movie featured "one of the most positively approached lesbian love scenes ever, and theirs was certainly the healthiest relationship in the film."

119. James Dean (NBC-TV, February 19, 1976), color, 99 min. Not rated.

Executive producers, Gerald I. Isenberg, Gerald W. Abrams; producers, William Bast, John Forbes; director, Robert Butler; teleplay, Bast; art director, Perry Ferguson II; set decorator, Sam Jones; costumes, Jimmy George; makeup, Fred Phillips; music, Billy Goldenberg; sound, Glenn Mabson; camera, Frank Stanley; editor, John A. Martinelli.

Cast: Stephen McHattie (James Byron Dean); Michael Brandon (Bill Bast); Candy

Clark (Chris White); Meg Foster (Dizzy Sheridan); Jayne Meadows (Reva Randall); Dane Clark (James Whitmore); Katherine Helmond (Claire Folger); Heather Menzies (Jan); Leland Palmer (Jan); Amy Irving (Norma Jean Brokner); Robert Foxworth (Psychiatrist); Chris White (Secretary); Brooke Adams (Beverly); Julian Burton (Ray); Robert Kenton (Mechanic); Judge Murdock (Judge); James O'Connell (Mr. Robbins); and: Rita Taggart, Wes Parker.

James Dean died in a car crash on September 30, 1955 at age twenty-four, but his legend certainly lives on. Among the several documentaries and biography-dramas produced since his death, one of the most unique is this 1976 telefilm. While it falls victim to a "And then he starred in this picture" scenario, it is a revealing—for its time—"love" story between actor/writer William Bast and James Dean, the bisexual rebel with a cause. To avoid offending prim viewers, the icon's minority lifestyle is only ambiguously suggested, and most of the "unrequited" love affair is portrayed as being the "problem" of the narrator, William Bast, who wrote (!) the teleplay. Covering all bases, this movie carried a let's-have-it-both ways disclaimer: "What you are about to see is one man's recollection of the actor as seen through the eyes of a friend. Like all memories it is intensely personal, elusive and incomplete. Yet it refuses to die."

In the present day, writer Bill Bast (Michael Brandon) confers with his psychiatrist (Robert Foxworth), in the hopes of exorcising the nightmarish guilt he still experiences concerning his late friend James Dean. The scene jumps back to 1950 when Bast and James Dean (Stephen McHattie) first meet at college in Los Angeles. "He was the last guy in the world I would have picked for a friend," Bast recalls. Drawn to this charismatic loner, Bill and James become good friends, sharing their love of acting and each other's company. However, Bast, whom the teleplay notes has had heterosexual relationships in his past, becomes jealous when Dean makes film industry contacts and must "pay back" a casting favor to agent Claire Folger (Katherine Helmond). Later, Bast is upset when his pal goes off alone on weekend dates with various women. Back in the present, Bill ponders, "I don't know why I stuck around so long . . . [but] he was beginning to grow on me. He gave me the feeling he really needed you."

As Dean's star rises, he moves out of their shared apartment. However, not long after Jimmy relocates to New York to study acting, Bast, who has decided to be a writer instead, gravitates to the Big Apple too. Shy, insecure and awed, Bill moves into the periphery of Dean's circle of friends, again an outsider as Dean cavorts with kookie Dizzy Sheridan (Meg Foster) and, later, becomes involved with aspiring actress Chris White (Candy Clark).

Turning coy, the TV movie craftily hedges its bets during a revealing hotel room sequence in which the two friends lounge about in their underwear. Tantalizingly structured on many levels, the scene ends ambivalently, leading the more naive viewer to wonder what it meant by suggesting that it is okay for an ARTIST to try anything for the sake of his craft.

Dean: Did you ever make it with another guy?

Bast: Are you serious?

Dean: I've got to prepare a scene for class.. .. It's about this guy who had a thing once with his best friend. Ever since it has been tearing him apart.

Bast: [With a knowing look] That's a rough one.

Dean: I don't mean kid stuff. I mean really? Did ya?

Bast: [Freezing up] Did you?

Dean: [Nonchalantly] Why not.

Bast: [Amazed] Ha, ha. Man, I've known you for flattening guys for even joking about it.

Dean: We owe it to our craft to experience everything we can . . . . Life's too short. I want to do it all. You know what they say, 'Don't knock it till you try it.'

Bast: Are you kidding? I wouldn't even known how to go about it. I mean if and when I was ready to experiment.

This leads to Dean ordering the "naive" Bast to dress and rush over to the Astor Bar in midtown Manhattan to pick up a man. Following instructions, Bill meets a businessman, but panics and calls Jimmy:

Bast: Dean-er, I don't think I'm ready for this. What the hell am I doing here?

Dean: Yeah, I guess it ought to be somebody you tamed first. Come on home.

When the confused Bast returns to the hotel, Dean is gone. The scene shifts to Hollywood where Jimmy has become a movie star, while Bill is making slow inroads as a screen writer. One September day in 1955 Jimmy plans to attend a car race near Salinas, California. The busy Bast declines to join his pal and the rest is history. Back in the present, a crying Bast admits to the therapist, "I never let him know how much I loved him." As a final scene, Bast visits his friend's grave and leaves a book, *The Little Prince*, by the tombstone.

Moyna Murphy (*Hollywood Reporter*) decided, "This is a bold script with inferences of homosexuality that might shock and offend some viewers, but what sticks out almost palpably is that this is an honest script. . . . Brandon and McHattie dominate the story with performances rich with nuance and dramatic credibility." *Daily Variety* confirmed, "It works and it works startling well. . . . What seems to be surface views of Dean quickly become more solid, and strong performances by others in the cast lend even more credence to the difficult subject. . . . Director Robert Butler eschews sensationalism, but the frankness of the sexual orientation investigates another level of the Dean character.

Like the previous year's *Best Friends*, q.v., *James Dean* was a daring exercise, despite its relative tentativeness in depicting the world of homosexual love. For the record, the long-underrated Stephen McHattie gives an uncanny impersonation of Dean, although it is too bad that Martin Sheen—in his younger years quite a Dean look-a-like—never had the opportunity to play the legendary Jimmy on camera.

120. JFK (Warner Bros., 1991), color, 189 min. R-rated.

Executive producer, Arnon Milchan; producers, A. Kitman Ho, Oliver Stone; co-producer, Clayton Townsend; associate producer, Joseph Reidy; director, Stone; based on the book *On the Trail of the Assassins* by Jim Garrison and *Crossfire: The Plot that Killed Kennedy* by Jim Marrs; screenplay, Stone, Zachary Sklar; production designer, Victor Kempster; art director, Alan R. Tomkins; set decorator, Crispian Sallis; costumes, Marlene Stewart; makeup, Ron Berkeley; music, John Williams; assistant directors, Joseph Reidy, Joseph R. Burns, Deborah Lupard; stunt coordinator, Webster Whinery; sound, Tod A. Maitland; camera, Robert Richardson; editors, Joe Hutshing, Pietro Scalia.

Cast: Kevin Costner (Jim Garrison); Sissy Spacek (Liz Garrison); Joe Pesci (David Ferrie); Tommy Lee Jones (Clay Shaw); Gary Oldman (Lee Harvey Oswald); Jay O. Sanders (Lou Ivon); Michael Rooker (Bill Broussard); Laurie Metcalf (Susie Cox); Gary Grubbs (Al Oser); John Candy (Dean Andrews); Jack Lemmon (Jack Martin); Walter Matthau (Senator Russell Long); Edward Asner (Guy Bannister); Donald Sutherland (Colonel X); Kevin Bacon (Willie O'Keefe); Brian Doyle-Murray (Jack Ruby); Sally Kirkland (Rose Cheramie); Beata Pozniak (Marina Oswald); Vincent D'Onofrio (Bill Newman); Tony Plana (Carlos Bringuier); Tomas Milan (Leopoldo); Jim Garrison (Earl Warren); Anthony Ramirez (Epileptic); Ray LePere (Abraham Zapruder); E. J. Morris, Cheryl Penland, Jim Gough (Plaza Witnesses); Perry R. Russo (Angry Bar Patron); Mike Longman (1st Newman); Pat Perkins (Mattie); Wayne Knight (Numa Bertel); Tom Howard (Lydon B. Johnson); William John Galt (Voice of Lyndon B. Johnson); Ron Jackson (FBI Spokesman); Sean Stone (Jasper Garrison); Amy Long (Virginia Garrison); Scott Krueger (Snapper Garrison); Allison Pratt Davis (Elizabeth Garrison); Pruitt Taylor Vince (Lee Bowers): Red Mitchell (Sergeant Harkness); Ronald von Klaussen, John S. Davies, Michael Ozag (Hobos); J. J. Johnson (Mobster with Broussard); Linda Flores Wade (Syvia Odio); Dale Dye (General Y); Nathan Scott (John

Chancelor); Jorge Fernandez (Miguel Torres); John Finnegan (Judge Haggerty); Michael Skipper (James Teague); Chris Robinson (Dr. Humes); Merlyn Sexton (Admiral Kenney); Ted Pennebaker (Arnold Rowland); Kristina Hare (Reporter); Loys Bergeron (Jury Foreman); Martin Sheen (Offscreen Narrator of Documentary Sequence); Jodi Farber (Jackie Kennedy); Steve Reed (John F. Kennedy Double); Columbia Dubose (Nellie Connally Double); Randy Means (Governor Connally Double).

"Some of the characterizations of the New Orleans gay underworld of the early '60s might seem offensive today. But it is part of an accurate portrayal of characters essential to the development of the story. . . . I am sensitive to the problems of picturing sexual relations in a psychotic and do not think *JFK* a case of that, but one purely of politics and power." (Oliver Stone in a published statement about *JFK*)

Few modern films have proven as controversial as *JFK*. As Andy Klein (*Los Angeles Reader*) outlined: "With the possible exception of Spike Lee, Oliver Stone is Hollywood's most in-your-face film maker. He wants to coax us into his moral universe, but, if coaxing doesn't work, he is more than willing to knock us down and lecture us. You have to applaud him for taking on important subjects that no one else with clout wants to handle, and you have to applaud louder on the occasions when he does it well. . . . On the other hand, there is something scary about his messianic arrogance. . . . *JFK* is clearly intended to remind us . . . that our culture will be forever haunted if we give up the quest for the truth about the central trauma of the postwar era or worse yet, if we willingly greedily opt to delude ourselves by accepting the most implausible 'official scenario.'"

After the assassination of President John F. Kennedy on November 22, 1963, New Orleans District Attorney Jim Garrison (Kevin Costner) studies the TV news coverage, including the later arrest of Lee Harvey Oswald (Gary Oldman). Meanwhile, in a local bar, one-time FBI agent and now private detective Guy Banister (Edward Asner) tell Jack Martin (Jack Lemmon), a friend and informant, that Kennedy was asking for it. Later, Oswald, insisting that he has been framed, is shot while in police custody by club operator, Jack Ruby (Brian Doyle-Murray). Magnetized by the case, Garrison follows up a New Orleans lead, bringing in a local pilot, David Ferrie (Joe Pesci), for questioning. Ferrie's hyperactive behavior convinces Garrison that the suspect knows far more than he is telling, but he has insufficient evidence to detain him further.

Upon reading the Warren Commission Report three years later, Garrison is struck by its inconclusiveness, contradictions, and the fact that many leads were not followed up, including activity in a nearby train yard and close to where JFK's motorcade passed. Studying and restudying the 8mm home movie taken by Abraham Zapruder (Ray LePere), an on-site witness to the killing, Garrison feels sure the truth has yet to be discovered and told. He becomes obsessed with the case, at the expense of his other professional activities or his family time with his patient wife (Sissy Spacek) and their small children. With staff attorney Bill Broussard (Michael Rooker) and investigator Lou Ivon (Jay O. Sanders) heading his team, Garrison starts an intensive investigation. One of his first observations is the proximity in New Orleans of the building where Banister (now dead) maintained his office front for CIA activities and the facilities of the FBI, CIA and the Office of Naval Intelligence.

Through his search of the records and further information from Ferrie, the trail leads Garrison to local businessman, Clay Shaw (Tommy Lee Jones), who, like Ferrie and a now-imprisoned hustler, whom they both knew, Willie O'Keefe (Kevin Bacon), is a homosexual. Garrison and his team "uncover" that Shaw was involved with anti-Castro Cubans, whom the district attorney is convinced were tied to the CIA's anti-Communist efforts. As the "evidence" mounts, Garrison forms a con-

Kevin Costner, Kevin Bacon and Michael Rooker in *JFK* (1991).

spiracy theory. It is his unpopular contention that the President was assassinated by a combination of high-level military command officers who joined with large military contractors to have Kennedy killed and to put war-favoring Vice President Lyndon Johnson, who would more likely favor an escalation in the Vietnam conflict, into the White House. According to Garrison's "proof," Clay was a military intelligence liaison operator directed to dupe Oswald. Much of Garrison's "findings" are confirmed by a one-time Pentagon official, Colonel "X" (Donald Sutherland).

With his elaborately-researched case ready, Garrison brings Shaw to trial. While he doubts that he really can get the defendant convicted, he welcomes the chance to present his findings to the public.

Owen Gleiberman (*Entertainment Weekly*) felt that "Stone has framed *JFK* as a classic cover-up thriller, like *Z* (1969) or *All the President's Men* (1976). . . . The real Garrison was a cocky troublemaker who, many say, had a way of coming up with theories and bending the facts to fit them. Stone turns him into a white knight, with Costner doing a Southern-gentleman variation on Eliot Ness. . . . The plot doesn't really make sense; it's just a dramatic frame on which Stone can hang the various conspiracy theories. Yet when it comes to dramatizing those theories . . . his filmmaking is so supple and alive, his obsession with the visual aspect of history so electrifying, that *JFK* practically roots itself in our imagination." Todd McCarthy (*Daily Variety*) described JFK as "electric, muckraking filmmaking" and that Stone's "contentious" point of view "and agitated manner will stimulate an enormous amount of thought and fresh debate." McCarthy noted the director's use of "a complex, jumbled style that mixes widescreen, archival footage, TV clips, black-and-white, slow motion, documdrama recreations, time jumps, repeated actions from various viewpoints, still photos, the Zapruder film and any other technique at hand." For the trade paper, "Where Stone takes this beyond the documentary, however, is in the film's fabulously rich parade of personalities. With superior character actors and a handful of stars portraying key secondary figures, the picture becomes an amazing collection of diverse types. . . . Particularly noteworthy in the huge cast are Joe Pesci as the volatile Ferrie; Tommy Lee Jones as the superbly smooth Clay Shaw. . . .Kevin Bacon as a trick of Shaw's who squeals. . . ."

For Kenneth Turan (*Los Angeles Times*), *JFK* was "Disturbing, infuriating yet undeniably effective," but concluded, it "is probably the most exposition-heavy film ever made. Exhaustive and exhausting, it so batters and blitzes you with details, incidents and occurrences . . . that when one of Garrison's minions finally squeals, 'I'm lost, boss,' there is not a person in the audience who won't know exactly how he feels." For Henry Sheehan (British *Monthly Film Bulletin*) "Ultimatley, the film fails because it cannot supply a cohesive glue for such a desperate and long-lived conspiracy."

While David Ansen (*Newsweek*) insisted "the film itself shouldn't be charged with homophobia" because of its trio of conspirators who are gay, David Ehrenstein, film critic of the gay newspaper, *The Advocate*, contended "The great thing about right-wing homophobes is that they come at your head on, rather than stab you when your back is turned. . . .What's at stake here is not so much Kennedy's assassination, but Oliver Stone's character assassinations of a gay man who has been dead for many years and is unable to defend him." Richard Jennings, executive director GLAAD/Los Angeles, a gay activist organization observed in reference to meeting with Oliver Stone and producer A. Kitman Ho, "They took the position that these characters are historically accurate people who really lived, or as in Kevin Bacon's case, were a composite of several real people . . . Certainly it was their view that some of the gay characters were sympathetically portrayed. But after seeing the film, we disagree. We have Kevin Bacon, who is a hustler, fascist and racist, and you've got David Ferrie, who looked bizarre because of a disease that left him bald, but you never find that out. You never know why, even though you learn later that he is receiving cancer treatment."

Despite the on-going high-profile furor caused by *JFK*, its commercial success, surprisingly, was not particularly spectacular. In eighteen weeks of domestic release, it grossed $69,741,131 at the box-office. It received two Academy Awards: Best Cinematography and Best Editing. It was nominated for five additional Oscars: Best Picture (*The Silence of the Lambs* won); Best Supporting Actor (Tommy Lee Jones; Jack Palance won for *City Slickers*); Best Director (Jonathan Demme won for *The Silence of the Lambs*); Best Screenplay—Adapted from Another Medium (*The Silence of the Lambs* won); Best Sound (*Terminator 2: Judgment Day* won).

To be noted in the large cast of *JFK* is the real-life Jim Garrison playing, ironically, Earl Warren, the head of the commission investigating the assassination.

121. Judgment (HBO-Cable, October 13, 1990), color, 90 min. Not rated.

Executive producer, Steve Tisch; producers, Dan Wigutow, Roy Hershman; co-producer, Donald C. Klune; director/teleplay, Tom Topor; production designer, Rae Fox; art director, Cecilia Montiel; set decorator, Anthony Stull; costumes, Karen Patch; makeup, Sheryl Berkoff; music, Cliff Eidelman; assistant directors, David Womark, J. Alan Hopkins, Daniel M. Stillman; sound, Steve Aaron; camera, Elmer Ragalyi; editor, Cynthia Scheider.

Cast: Keith Carradine (Pierre Guitry); Blythe Danner (Emmeline Guitry); Jack Warden (Claude Fortier, Esq.); David Strathairn (Father Frank Aubert); Michael Faustino (Robbie Guitry); Bob Gunton (Monsignor Beauvais); Mitchell Ryan (Dave Jarvis, Esq.); Robert Joy (Mr. Hummel); Steve Hofvendahl (Daniel Boussard); Mary Joy (Madeleine Broussard); Brad Sullivan (Kenneth Loring); Dylan Baker (Father Delambre); Bob Barnes (Mr. Poujade); Deborah Barone (Lucille Ar-

Advertisement for *Judgment* (1990).

naud); Christopher Caige (Joseph Brussard); Ann Christiansen (Grace Basile); Daisy Eagan (Justine Guitry); Richard Eagan (Psychiatrist); Otto Felix (Dr. Morgan); Crystal McKellah (Sabine Guitry); Stacy I. Robison (Molly Landry); Jeff Weiss (Father Vinion); James Scott Hess, Nicholas Wood, Jesse Zeigler (Altar Boys). Kimberly Bronson (Miss Haver).

Judgment is based on a true account of an incident that occurred in Louisiana in the 1980s. This made-for-cable movie is extremely earnest and occasionally pedantic (in suggesting the problem detailed is widespread throughout America). However, the production never exploits its volatile subject matter: the sodomizing of young boys by a lustful parish priest who considers himself above any laws and insists that he loves these children far better than their parents.

In the Lafayette Diocese of Louisiana, devout Catholics Pierre (Keith Carradine) and Emmeline Guitry (Blythe Danner) are pleased when Father Frank Aubert (David Strathairn) selects their young son, Robbie (Michael Faustino) to be an altar boy at St. Simon's Church. However, they are concerned that he may have problems absorbing the required rituals because of a learning deficiency. Nevertheless, the boy is anxious to start his new tasks. "Will God love me more?" the innocent child asks. Before long, the priest is pursuing his old habits: on a weekend retreat, he takes photos of the naked altar boys in the shower, stays with Robbie overnight in his sleeping bag, and continues to play with and sodomize the boy on later occasions. The badly-confused Robbie, fearful of betraying his molester, lets slip the truth to his family. Pierre, a struggling contractor, at first is unwilling to believe the facts, afraid of losing a Diocese building job. Emmeline, while despising the idea of warring with the Church, cannot ignore the situation.

Going through proper channels, the Church initially rejects their accusations, pressuring the couple in every way possible not to pursue their case. Soon, the Guitrys are joined in their complaint by other parents whose young sons have been molested. (Church officials, who had records of Aubert's past misdeeds, eventually offer a settlement to pay for the youths' therapy, but still refuse to dismiss Aubert.) Because their first attorney (Mitchell Ryan) is so quickly cowed by the Church, the Guitrys turn to veteran lawyer Claude Fortier (Jack Warden) to prosecute their case. With patience, Fortier convinces the frightened Robbie to testify to the molestations in open court. As a result, Father-Aubert is sentenced to twenty years of hard labor with no possibility of parole and the Guitry family is awarded $1.25 million. A postscript advises "Because of this case and others like it, most insurance carriers will no longer insure the Roman Catholic Church of the U.S. against the molestation of children."

Miles Beller (*Hollywood Reporter*) judged the film: "In spite of the theatrics that sometimes intrude on *Judgment*'s scripted events . . . this TV movie is compelling television . . . The sense of believers shaken by the sins of a man of the cloth is intensely conveyed by Carradine and Danner. As the wronged child, Faustino sharply portrays innocence taken advantage of. . . ." In contrast, *Daily Variety* focused on the fact that the telefilm omits "what happens to the boy and to his parents—their status in the community, their family life and, of enormous interest, their faith. . . .. Dramatization of events of such major importance should be fully told, not hidden behind fictional events and characters."

Judgment was filmed in Lakeview, Florida. Its director/scripter, Tom Topor was the author of the play/movie *Nuts* (1987).

122. Justine (Twentieth Century-Fox, 1969), color, 116 min. R-rated.

Producer, Pandro S. Berman; associate producer, Kathryn Hereford; director, George Cukor; based on the novels *The Alexandria Quartet* by Lawrence Durrell; screenplay, Lawrence

Elaine Church, Dirk Bogarde, Anouk Aimee and Michael York in *Justine* (1969).

B. Marcus; art directors, Jack Martin Smith, William Creber; set decorators, Walter M. Scott, Raphael Bretton; costumes, Irene Sharaf; makeup, Dan Striepeke, Ed Butterworth; music, Jerry Goldsmith; choreographer, Gemze de Lappe; assistant directors, Maurice Vaccarino; sound, Bernard Freericks, David Dockendorf; special camera effects, L. B. Abbott, Art Cruickshank; camera, Leon Shamroy; editor, Rita Roland.

Cast: Anouk Aimee (Justine); Dirk Bogarde (Pursewarden); Robert Forster (Narouz); Anna Karina (Melissa); Philippe Noiret (Pombal); Micheal York (Darley); John Vernon (Nessim Hosnani); Jack Albertson (Cohen); Cliff Gorman (Toto); George Baker (Mountolive); Elaine Church (Liza); Michael Constantine (Memlik Pasha); Marcel Dalio (French Consul General); Michael Dunn (Mnemjiam); Barry Morse (Maskelyne); Severn Darden (Balthazar); Amapola Del Vando (Mrs. Serapamoun); Abraham Sofaer (Proprietor); Stanley Waxman (Serapamoun); DeAnn Mears (Lady at Ball); Tutte Lemkow (Prisoner).

Hollywood had long been intrigued by the potentials of filming Lawrence Durrell's complex, sexually explicit, very literate *The Alexandria Quartet*, published between 1957–60. In the newly-permissive 1960s, Twentieth Century-Fox tackled this tale of interlocking relationships in perverse Alexandria. It was a decision the company came to regret bitterly. The production became a cause celebre as director Joseph Strick, filming in Tunisia, was replaced by George Cukor, who finished the movie mostly in Hollywood. En route, the shooting schedule dragged, and the cost of filming this very compressed version of Durrell's atmospheric four-part story spiraled out of control. To play the effeminate, nastily bitchy homosexual, Toto, in *Justine*, the studio hired actor Cliff Gorman. (At one point in pre-production Dirk Borgarde intended to tackle that part.) He had gained acclaim off-Broadway (1968) playing the swishy Emory in *The Boys in the Band*, a part he would recreate on screen (1970), q.v. Gorman's part in *Justine* is peripheral to most of the action in the final screen version. During the course of the story, at a masked ball, he gropes a character (Robert Forster) who pushes him away, and the flamboyant Toto—no more than a house pet to manipulative Justine—falls on a hat pin and dies, virtually unmourned.

In 1938 Alexandria, Egypt, the Jewish Justine (Anouk Aimee), a prostitute, and her wealthy husband, Nessim Hosnanis (John Vernon), a Coptic Christian, work to smuggle arms to Palestine. The mysterious Justine has a circle of lovers and friends which soon include: aloof British official Pursewarden (Dirk Bogarde), who is fixated on his blind sister, Lisa (Elaine Church), who, in turn, is admired by Pursewarden's superior, Mountolive (George Baker); the Irishman Darley (Michael York), a young school teacher/writer; the homosexual Toto (Cliff Gorman); and Naroux (Robert Forster), Justine's activist brother-in-law who abhors her continual unfaithfulness to Nessim.

Melissa (Anna Karina), a tubercular Greek belly dancer, has a close relationship with elderly, dying Jewish furrier Cohen (Jack Albertson), the latter one of Justine's many acquaintances. When Darley becomes friendly with Melissa, Justine fears he will learn of the Hosnanis's illegal activities through her. Thus she takes Darley as a lover. Jealous of Darley's dalliance with Justine, Melissa turns to Pursewarden and tells him of the Hosnanis's gun smuggling scheme. The primly patriotic Pursewarden feels compelled to inform Mountolive of Justine's plans and the Hosnanis are placed under house arrest. Horrified at his own actions, Mountolive commits suicide. Subsequently, as Darley is about to return to England, he visits the Hosnanis and finds that Justine has already charmed her captors.

Vincent Canby (*New York Times*) warned matter-of-factly that *Justine* has "necessarily been simplified, straightened out" and that "It's a movie of sexual confusion (a woman might look like a transvestite, and vice versa) and dark humor." However, he decided it is "a movie of so much opulence that the eye and ear are constantly persuading the mind to take a rest." A more realistic *Variety* reported that screenwriter Lawrence B. Marcus did not have "marked" success in creating a "comprehensive and smoothly-flowing narrative," that French actress Anouk Aimee" frequently cannot be understood," but that Michael York, the narrator of the story "delivers a persuasive performance." David Wilson (British *Monthly Film Bulletin*) complained that, among other faults, that "of Alexandria itself, the only constant in the four books, there is not a trace, unless one counts a few clumsily inserted Tunisian location shots and some painted backdrops of Hitchcockian audacity against which the characters are occasionally and uncomfortably superimposed."

Justine—an arty, mishmash—failed badly at the box-office.

123. The Killing of Sister George

(Cinerama Releasing Corp., 1968), color, 138 min. X-rated.

Producer, Robert Aldrich; associate producer, Walter Blake; director, Aldrich; based on the play by Frank Marcus; screenplay, Lukas Heller; art director, William Glasgow; set decorator, John W. Brown; costumes, Renie; makeup, Bill Turner; music, Gerald Fried; assistant directors, Daisy Gerber, Dennis Robertson; sound, Dick Church, George Maly, Dean Hodges; camera, Joseph Biroc; second unit camera, Brian West; editor, Michael Luciano.

Cast: Beryl Reid (June Buckridge [Sister George]); Susannah York (Alice "Childie" McNaught); Coral Browne (Mercy Croft); Ronald Fraser (Leo Lockhart); Patricia Medina (Betty Thaxter); Hugh Paddick (Freddie); Cyril Delevanti (Ted Baker); Sivi Aberg (Diana); William Beckley (Floor Manager); Elaine Church (Marleen); Brendan Dillon (Bert Turner); Mike Freeman (Noel); Maggie Paige (Maid); Jack Raine (Deputy Commissioner); Dolly Taylor (Tea Lady); Meier Tzelniker (Mr.

Katz); Cicely Walper (Mrs. Coote); Byron Webster (Jack Adams); Rosalie Williams (Mildred); Sam Kydd (Taxi Driver).

"The most sociopathic, and hence most evil, moment in *The Killing of Sister George* is not the one in which one woman sucks the breast of another and the two then kiss lustfully, nor the one in which degenerate women dance together in a London 'club,' but the one in which the character called 'George' attempts to fondle sexually two novitiate nuns. The scene of a brazen, and drunken attempt to corrupt the young is played for comedy." (Flavia Wharton, *Films in Review*)

Sometimes in film, by using caricature, delicate personal matters (often censurable) can be referred to more overtly rather than by a more usual subtle and indirect approach. Thus, by viewers reacting with "Oh, these people and situations can't be real," the filmmaker can make it easier for the audience to deal with once, or still, taboo subjects. Such was the case with *The Killing of Sister George*, based on a 1965 British play. Not that Robert Aldrich, who always had an eye for controversial commercialism, could ever be considered subtle. After all, he was the auteur of *What Ever Happened to Baby Jane?* (1962) and *The Dirty Dozen* (1967). It is interesting to note that in 1968, the same year *The Fox*, q.v., had shown that audiences could "cope" with films dealing with woman-to-woman love, Aldrich directed two features dealing with lesbianism: the R-rated *The Legend of Lylah Clare*, q.v., and the far more blatant, graphic, X-rated *The Killing of Sister George*.

In London, June Buckridge (Beryl Reid), is a co-star of the BBC-TV soap opera, "Applehurst," in the role of the perpetually cheery nurse Sister George (which has led to her nickname, "George."). Currently, the aging "George," who has a drinking problem, is worried about being written out of the long-running show. Meanwhile, at home, the butch lesbian George, who smokes cigars and clumps around her house, has a troubled relationship with the younger, child-like (hence her nickname "Childie") Alice McNaught (Susannah York), often taking out her frustration on the frilly blonde. Becoming paranoid about losing her TV role, George absents herself frequently from rehearsals or arrives at the studio drunk. She gets into serious problems with the network, when, one day while inebriated, she causes a ruckus in a taxi cab—frightening two young nuns with her bawdy remarks. A new network executive, the devious Mrs. Mercy Croft (Coral Browne) warns George that any further such behavior could cost her the role on "Applehurst." Mercy suggests that while the network may be tolerant of alternative lifestyles, the public would not be so kind if the truth about George were known. Relieved to have a reprieve, George jokingly invites the well-bred Mercy to join she and Childie at a lesbian club for a drink. There, Mercy, who is obviously interested in Childie, confides to the young woman that George is to be written out of the show the following week—to be killed off in a highway accident while riding her trademark motor scooter. Mercy offers to be Childie's new benefactor.

Mercy's prediction comes true and George is no longer part of "Applehurst." The only new work she is offered is the voice of Clarabelle Cow on a children's TV program. Meanwhile, the cast members of "Applehurst" throw George a farewell party. Arriving home drunk, she finds Mercy and Childie in bed together. An argument ensues and Childie goes to live with Mercy. The distraught George returns later that night to the deserted studio. After wrecking havoc on the sets, the dejected woman sits alone, pathetically rehearsing her Clarabelle dialogue: "Moo. . . . Moo. . . . Moo."

Renata Adler (*New York Times*) reported, "Beryl Reid, as George, seems to have become, since the play, just a whinnying, hissing granny on a single unconvincing note. . . . Miss York, whenever her face is in view, looks embarrassed." Regarding the seduction sequence between Browne and York, Adler noted, "The scene goes on for ages. . . . It is the longest, most unerotic, cash-conscious scene between a person and a breast there has ever been on screen, and outside a surgeon's office." It was Adler's observation that: "The prolonged, simultaneously serious and mocking treatment of homosexuals, I suppose inevitably turns vicious and silly—as homosexuality itself, inevitably has a degree of parody in it."

Variety perceived, "What the story is meant to depict, and what happens in Aldrich's film are not always the same." As to the cast, the trade paper judged, Reid "carries it off superbly, from her pre-title nastiness to the pathetic freeze-frame-out. . . . Miss Browne, with a role pitched at constant level, is excellent, if a bit too stilted at times. . . . But., Miss York's performance, and the responsible direction, are quite fuzzy. . . . [She] looks too old . . . and acts in far too ambivalent a fashion. . . . As her deceptions pile up, the contrast is just not there." Regarding the highly-touted sex scene, *Variety* decided, it "takes precisely five minutes to run its tasteless course. It is unnecessary, gratuitous, offensive and crude."

In England, Tom Milne (British *Monthly Film Bulletin*) judged, "Since most of the dialogue between George and Childie is pitched on the edge of hysteria anyway, Aldrich's excitable, attacking style stands him in good stead, and the scenes between Beryl Reid and Susannah York have a genuinely lacerating quality. . . ."

That some viewers in 1968 accepted this movie's exaggerated study of lesbianism (the ultra butch George, the baby doll passive partner and the discreet, reptilian Mercy) as an accurate portrayal of the real thing, is suggested by Richard Schickel (*Life*), "*The Killing of Sister George* re-creates with considerable realism . . . an odd, but real, corner of existence. . . . There is nothing soft or graceful about it;

the emphasis is on people using each other, not loving each other." In some states, including Connecticut and Massachusetts, the "offensive" sex scene was cut by state censors, although the X rating remained in force, an indication that the movie's subject per se, not its explicit depiction of sexual interplay, was the cause of the categorizing. As a result of the stigma attached by the X-rating and the critical reaction in general, *The Killing of Sister George* did badly at the box-office. A year later, *Midnight Cowboy*, q.v., was the first X-rated feature to win an Oscar. In 1970, the moral climate had changed so much that *The Boys in the Band*, q.v., would be given a R rating.

Susannah York would be involved on screen in another lesbian relationship in the British-made *X, Y & Zee* (1972).

124. Kiss of the Spider Woman

(Island Alive, 1985), color, 119 min. R-rated.

Executive producer, Francisco Ramalho Jr.; producer, David Weisman; associate producers, Jane Holzer, Michael Maiello, Jayme Sverner, Gustavo Halbreich, Altamiro Boscoli, Paulo Francini; director, Hector Babenco; based on the novel by Manuel Puig; screenplay, Leonard Schrader; production designer, Felipe Crescenti; costumes, Patricio Bisso; music, John Neschling, Nando Carneiro, Wally Badarou; camera, Rodolfo Sanchez; second unit camera, Lucio Kodato; editor, Mauro Alice.

Cast: William Hurt (Luis Molina); Raul Julia (Valentin Arregui); Sonia Braga (Leni Lamison/Marta/Spider Woman); Jose Lewgoy (Warden); Milton Goncalves (Pedro); Miriam Pires (Mother); Nuno Leal Maia (Gabriel); Fernando Torres (Americo); Patricio Bisso (Greta); Herson Capri (Werner); Denise Dummont (Michele); Nildo Parente (Leader of Resistance); Antonio Petrin (Clubfoot); Wilson Grey (Flunky); Miguel Falabella (Lieutenant); Luis Serra (Prison Doctor); Ana Maria Braga (Lidia); Luis Gilherme, Walmir Barros (Agents); Benjamin Cattan, Oswaldo Barreto, Sergio Bright, Claudio Curi (Nurse); Pericles Campos, Edmilson Santos, Walter Vicca, Kenichi Kaneko (Prisons Guards); Georges Schlesinger, Carlos Fabriello, Frederico Botelho (Jewish Smugglers): Silvio Band, Paulo Ludmer (Rabbis); Elvira Bisso (Maid).

Raul Julia and William Hurt in *Kiss of the Spider Woman* (1985).

Manuel Puig's acclaimed novel (1978), which the Argentinian later turned into a play, provided the framework for this superior screen adaptation. In dealing with the B-movie fantasy world of the homosexual prisoner, Puig's *Kiss of the Spider Woman* was ideally suited to the cinema medium. The movie version could flesh out the reveries of beleaguered Luis Molina (William Hurt) in the novel. Luis is a man who avoids dealing with much of life's everyday horrors by retreating to his dream world, a foreign country, a place to which he seduces his straight cellmate, Valentin Arregui (Raul Julia), into visiting. (During the course of *Spider Woman*, Arregui admits that his revolutionist hopes are also a dream and, like Luis's movie world fabrications, a way of avoiding real life and personal relationships.)

For structural, copyright and other reasons, the movies (*The Cat People, The Enchanted Cottage, I Walked with a Zombie*) retold by the effeminate prisoner in Puig's book are telescoped within the film

into an elaborately recalled movie scenario, *Her Real Glory* (a variant of *Casablanca*). One of the conceits of *Kiss of the Spider Woman* is having Luis be such an ostentatious gay man that most viewers would hardly question his sexual persuasion (and, hence, have little fear that they could be like him). Instead, and more importantly, moviegoers could focus on Luis's unique method of dealing with life as seen in contrast, and parallel to, his macho idealist cellmate.

In an unnamed South American police state country, Luis Molina (William Hurt), a store window dresser, has been jailed for "corrupting the morals of a minor." His cellmate is Valentin Arregui (Raul Julia), a journalist apprehended for giving his passport to revolutionist, Dr. Americo (Fernando Torres). To make time pass in their squalid surroundings, the flamboyant Luis—with plucked eyebrows and usually wearing a towel turban and kimono—recounts in romantic detail the plot of a heavily-romantic Nazi wartime movie he adores, which features a seductive leading lady, Leni Lamison (Sonia Braga). Meanwhile, Luis and Valentin break down the many barriers (political, emotional, intellectual) between them, barriers that in the outside world would have made them totally incompatible. They discuss their personal lives: Molina's unrequited attraction to unobtainable Gabriel (Nuno Leal Maia), a very masculine waiter; Arregui's conflicting loyalties to co-revolutionist, Lidia (Ana Maria Braga) and to the unreachable, beautiful Marta (Sonia Braga). Because the prison authorities are trying to get rid of Valentin, their political prisoner, by slowly poisoning him, both men become ill from eating the tainted food. The warden (Jose Lewgoy) and an undercover policeman, Pedro (Milton Goncalves), think they have coerced the seemingly weak-willed Luis into helping them gain the names of Valentin's confederates. In actuality, Molina has tricked the authorities in order to obtain groceries for the ailing Arregui.

In a daring tactic, Luis convinces the warden to let him leave the prison, insisting this will convince Valentin to confide the names of his underground associates. On the night before his "release," Molina tells the failing Arregui a fanciful account of a Spider Woman (Sonia Braga) caught on a tropical isle. Molina also confesses to his friend, that he has fallen in love with him. Now feeling compassion for Luis—whom he once regarded with revulsion as a tragic joke of a man—Valentin makes love with his cellmate. Released from prison, Molina is followed by Pedro, who trails him to a meeting with Lidia and other revolutionists. As the police dragnet is sprung, Lidia shoots Molina. Pedro attempts to gain information from the dying ex-prisoner, but he refuses to say anything. Meanwhile, in the prison, the newly-tortured Valentin is given a pain-killing drug in the infirmary. In his reverie, Marta rescues him and together they go to the isle of the Spider Woman.

Rex Reed (*New York Post*) cautioned, "Don't be turned off by the title. . . . [The movie] is an exotic, sobering film about politics and sex. . . . It's strictly for grownups. . . . Everything about *Kiss of the Spider Woman* is original and powerful, but the one smashing effect of lasting impact that towers above everything else is William Hurt's magnificent, three-dimensional performance as the pathetic homosexual with the heart of a woman trapped in the body of a man." David Ansen (*Newsweek*) observed, "One's initial impression of *Spider Woman* are uneasy . . . But the . . . []filmmakers] are setting stereotypes the better to explore and explode them." Sheila Benson (*Los Angeles Times*) rated the movie a "profoundly moving adaptation" and that Hurt provided a "rapturous characterization . . . both generous and acute, with succeeding levels that reveals themselves as the story deepens." On the other hand, Benson had problems with Bragia "The heavy makeup does her a disservice; she looks drawn, she moves inelegantly and she's entirely the wrong type for the role."

A U.S.-Brazilian co-production, shot in English in the low-budget, *Kiss of the Spider Woman* grossed $6,376,000 in distributors' domestic film rentals. The movie won an Academy Awards for William Hurt as Best Actor. The picture was nominated for three additional Oscars: Best Picture (*Out of Africa* won), Best Director (Sydney Pollack won for *Out of Africa*), Best Screen Based on Material from Another Medium (*Out of Africa* won). Originally, Burt Lancaster was to have played the lead role in the movie, but a heart attack forced him out of the project.

In mid-1992, Chita Rivera (Spider Woman), Brent Carver (Molina) and Anthony Crivello (Valentin) starred in Toronto in a London-bound musical version of *Kiss of the Spider Woman*, with book by Terrence McNally, music by John Kander, lyrics by Fred Ebb and the production directed by Hal Prince.

125. Knightriders (United Film Distribution Co., 1981), color, 145 min. R-rated.

Executive producer, Salah M. Hassanein; producer, Richard P. Rubinstein; associate producer, David E. Vogel; director/screenplay, George A. Romero; production designer, Cletus Anderson; makeup, Jeannie Jeffries Brown; music, Donald Rubinstein; assistant directors, Pasquale Buba, Clayton Hill, John Roddick; stunt coordinator, Gary Davis; sound, Fred Christie; special effects, Larry Roberts; camera, Michael Gornick; editors, Romero, Buba.

Cast: Ed Harris (Billy Davis); Gary Lahti (Alan); Tom Savini (Morgan); Amy Ingersoll (Linet); Patricia Tallman (Julie); Christine Forrest (Angie); Warner Shook (Pippin); Brother Blue (Merlin); Cynthia Adler (Rocky); John Amplas (Whiteface); Don Berry (Bagman); Amanda Davies (Sheila); Martin Ferrero (Joe Bontempi); Ken Foree (Little John); Ken Hixon (Steve); John Hostetter (Tuck); Harold Wayne Jones (Bors); Randy Kovitz (Punch); Michael Moran (Cook); Scott Reiniger (Marhalt); Maureen Sadusk (Judy Rawls); Albert Amerson (Indian); Ronald Carrier (Hector); Tom Dilco (Corncook); David Early (Bleoboris); John Harrison (Pellinore); Robert Williams (Kay); Taso N. Stavrakis (Ewain); Judy Barrett, Ian Gallacher, Donald Rubinstein (Trio); Jim Braffico (Lester Dream); Iva Jean Saraceni (Helen Dream); Chris Jessell (Boy Billy); Bingo O'Malley (Sheriff Rilly); Nann Mogg (Mrs. Rilly); Hugh Rose (Jess); Victor Pappa (Photographer).

George Romero, the craftsman who created *The Night of the Living Dead* (1968), had an engaging concept in *Knightriders*. This offbeat feature dealt with present-day knights jousting on motorcycles and their personal relationships and problems were made to parallel aspects of Camelot and the Arthurian legends. Unfortunately, the movie's inordinate length, its stagnant plotline and the overhackneyed characterizations spoiled this handsomely photographed project. Within *Knightriders*, the cycle show has a multi-racial entourage, which includes all kinds of life's dropouts, including dwarfs and the tournament announcer (Warren Shook), a good-natured young man who is uncertain if he is gay.

In their traveling Middle Ages show, which features bike riders in armor in a tournament on motorcycles, Billy Davis (Ed Harris) is King Arthur and offstage is their leader. He and Morgan (Tom Savini), rivals on the jousting turf, compete after hours for the affections of Linet (Amy Ingersoll), the show's Queen Quinevere. Angie (Christine Forrest) is Morgan's patient woman, while the group's mechanic, Rocky (Cynthia Adler) is a tough-riding female knight. Finally, Alan (Gary Lahti) and Julie (Patricia Tallman), a young runaway, are the production's youthful lovers. Providing "magic" on and off stage is Merlin (Brother Blue), a one-time doctor. As for Pippin (Warner Shook), the tournament's loud-speaker voice, the other troupe members acknowledge/accept that he is gay, but he still is not sure. (Eventually he meets a lover and finds happiness). Meanwhile, the cycle show is constantly harassed by redneck police, media hounds and crass agents, The lure of making big dollars causes Morgan and some of the others to leave the tournament for a spell. The idealistic Billy insists that his followers remain loyal to their utopian dream of bringing joy and truth to the public. Fearing that he has been corrupted by the crass world, Billy, who has lost a tournament battle to Morgan, symbolically hands his prop sword over to a classroom schoolboy, mounts his motorcycle, and drive off down the highway where he collides fatally with a truck.

Kevin Thomas (*Los Angeles Times*) found this "one-of-a-kind film" appealing: "To be enjoyed and appreciated fully. . . . [It] probably must be seen as a primitive work of art in which everything is inherently bold and unshaded." Vincent Canby (*New York Times*) was entertained, but had reservations: "Just as there is no real villain in the movie, there is no real damage to the daredevil riders during public performances. . . ." In contrast, Robert Asahina (*New Leader*) assessed, "Unfortunately, this film fairy tale of purity versus evil is only cartoon-deep." A turned-off

David Denby (*New York*) concluded, "It's hard to figure out what Romero is trying to say. My only guess is that he's making an elaborate allegory of his relations to his own crew and to the cult that has grown around him during his career as a highly personal low-budget filmmaker."

Unfortunately, *Knightriders* was not helped at the box-office, as it was released at about the same time as John Boorman's elaborate *Excalibur*, that director's very personal, very dark interpretation of the Arthurian legends.

126. The Kremlin Letter (Twentieth Century-Fox, 1970), color, 116 min. GP-rated.

Producers, Carter De Haven III, Sam Wiesenthal; director, John Huston; based on the novel by Noel Behn; screenplay, Huston, Gladys Hill; production designer, Ted Haworth; art directors, Elven Webb, Boris Juraga; set decorator, Dario Simone; costumes, John Furness; makeup, George Frost, Amato Barbini; music/music director, Robert Drasnin; music/music conductor, Toshiro Mayuzumi; assistant directors, Gus Agosti, Carlo Cotti; sound, Basil Fenton-Smith, Renato Cadueri; special effects, Augie Lohman; camera, Ted Scaife; editor, Russell Lloyd.

Cast: Bibi Andersson (Erika Boeck); Richard Boone (Ward); Nigel Green (The Whore [Janis]); Dean Jagger (The Highwayman); Lila Kedrova (Sophie); Michael MacLiammoir (Sweet Alice); Patrick O'Neal (Lieutenant Commander Charles Rone); Barbara Parkins (B. A.); Ronald Radd (Potkin); George Sanders (The Warlock); Raf Vallone (The Puppet Maker); Max Von Sydow (Colonel Vladimir Kosnov); Orson Welles (Aleksei Bresnavitch); Sandor Eles (Grodin); Niall MacGinnis (Erector Set); Anthony Chinn (Kitai); Guy Deghy (Professor); John Huston (Admiral); Fulvia Ketoff (Sonia); Vonetta McGee (Black Woman); Marc Lawrence (Priest); Cyril Shaps (Police Doctor); Christopher Sandford (Rudolph); Hana-Maria Pravda (Mrs. Kazar); George Pravda (Kazar); Ludmilla Dudarova (Mrs. Potkin); Dimitri Tamarov (Ilya); Pehr-Olof Siren (Receptionist); Daniel Smid (Waiter); Victor Beaumont (Dentist); Stephen Zacahrias (Dittomachine); Laura Forin (Elena); Sara Rannin (Mikahil's Mother); Rune Sandlunds (Mikhail); Sacha Carafa (Mrs. Grodin).

By 1970, moviegoers had been inundated with espionage screen dramas. With the ultra popular James Bond movie series as a genre benchmark, the tedious *The Kremlin Letter* failed on many scores: dull hero (Patrick O'Neal), highly convoluted plot, lengthy running time, etc. Not even its international name cast could salvage this film at the box-office. For many viewers, the chief highlight of this John Huston production was still-debonair George Sanders cavorting through the gloomy proceedings as a very mature drag queen spy (decked out in a revealing black satin sheath dress, blonde wig and long feather boa) who must seduce a top Russian spy. In his self-mocking performance, Sanders was a hoot and generated the bulk of publicity for *The Kremlin Letter*.

At stake is an embarrassing letter by an American agent to U.S. officials suggesting they join Russia in eliminating China's nuclear weapons. Both America and Russia want to gain possession of the incriminating paper. Ward (Richard Boone) recruits Lieutenant Commander Charles Rone (Patrick O'Neal) from the Navy to head a team to retrieve this treaty letter. Rone's recruited team soon includes Janis (Nigel Green), The Warlock (George Sanders)—an aged San Francisco drag queen—and B.A. (Barbara Parkins). B.A., whose father was an expert safecracker, and Rone fall in love. Meanwhile, an upper echelon Soviet official, Aleksei Bresnovitch (Orson Welles), monitors the growing intrigue over the missing document. After several murders in Moscow and B.A. being taken prisoner, Rone and Ward leave Russia, believing the tell-tale Kremlin Letter to be in Peking. Only then does Ward reveal himself to be the long-thought-dead Sturdevant, now a double agent working for Aleksei. Ward casually announces that if Rone carries out certain assassinations in New York City— of a Russian agent's wife and daughter— B.A. will be released. As for the so-called Kremlin Letter it was all a device created

George Sanders in *The Kremlin Letter* (1970).

by Ward to carry out his revenge agenda on various operatives.

Vincent Canby (*New York Times*) lamented that *The Kremlin Letter* was "an extravagant, depressing movie that dimly recalls . . . early Huston classics. . . . [As] with so many recent Huston films, the scale of everything . . . has been enlarged as if to disguise what looks to be the director's awful boredom with movies. . . ." Pauline Kael (*The New Yorker*) scoffed, "The picture is visually undistinguished. . . . *The Kremlin Letter* has a trick, unresolved ending that is miscalculated, because we don't give a damn." Nigel Andrews (British *Monthly Film Bulletin*) noted, "The film seems undecided whether to carry its burlesque elements through to their limit, or to keep things strictly serious. For instance, George Sanders' few extravagant appear-

ances (first seen rouged, mascaraed and bewigged as a nightclub drag queen, and ever after inseparable from his knitting) jostle with equally bizarre but darker scenes like that in which the kidnapped Potkin is forced to watch his daughter being seduced by a lesbian."

When interviewed on the set of *The Kremlin Letter*, veteran actor Sanders—two years away from committing suicide—would waggishly say of his high profile role: "I feel rather silly but acting queer seems to be the trend these days, so why fight it? Besides I have remarkable legs and I want to show off." On a later occasion, he would admit, "I really don't understand the film. It's too modern for me. I just do what I'm told." As for director Huston, he thought Sanders "was exactly right in voice and gesture" for his part in the transvestite sequences.

127. The Last Married Couple in America (Universal, 1980), color, 103 min. R-rated.

Executive producers, Gilbert Cates, Joseph Cates; producers, Edward S. Feldman, John Herman Shaner; associate producer, Marian Segal; director, Gilbert Cates; screenplay, Shaner; production designer, Gene Callahan; art director, Peter Smith; set decorator, Lee Poll; costumes, Edith Head, Vicki Sanchez; makeup, Ron Snyder, Emile LaVigne, Ed Butterworth; music, Charles Fox; song, Norman Gimbel and Fox; choreographer, Scott Salmon; assistant directors, Thomas Lofaro, Steve Lofaro; sound, Don Sharples; camera, Ralph Woolsey; editor, Peter E. Berger.

Cast: George Segal (Jeff Thompson); Natalie Wood (Mari Thompson); Richard Benjamin (Marv Cooper); Arlene Golonka (Sally Cooper); Alan Arbus (Al Squib); Marilyn Sokol (Alice Squib); Oliver Clark (Max Dryden); Priscilla Barnes (Helena Dryden); Dom DeLuise (Walter Holmes); Valerie Harper (Barbara); Bob Dishy (Howard); Mark Lonow (Tom); Sondra Currie (Lainy); Robert Wahler (Rick); Catherine Hickland (Rebecca); Charlene Ryan (Oriana Holmes); Murphy Dunner (Dr. Schallert); David Rode (Andy Thompson); David Comfort (Dick Thompson); Ricky Segall (Charlie Thompson); Stewart Moss (Donald); Colby Chester (Reggie); Delia Salvi (Bel Air Woman); Bebe Drake-Hooks (Policewoman); Edgy Lee (Liu); Mieko Kobayashi (Carol); Yvonne Wilder (Margrette); Billy Holms (Dave); George Pentecost (Roy); David Bennett (Ralph); Shari Summers (Maggie); Jenny O'Hara, William Bogert (Dancing Couple at Party); Robert Perault, Brad Maule (Young Men at Restaurant); Jan Jorden, Vernon Weddle (People at Soccer Game); G. Lewis Cates (Boy at Refreshment Stand); Jenny Neumann (Nurse); Lynne Marie Stewart (Receptionist); Oz Tortora (Patron at Tommy's).

"The Last Married Couple in America . . . wants to be hip and funny about that endangered species, long-term matrimony, and about divorce and sex— marital, fooling-around, swinging, homosexual, etc."* (Alex Keneas, *Newsday*)

Nothing is more depressing than a satirical comedy that falls flat, and *The Last Married Couple in America* does just that. It was another one of Natalie Wood's box-office failures in her final years. Like her earlier—and far more successful—*Bob & Carol & Ted & Alice* (1969). this film was supposed to poke sharp fun at contemporary suburban middle-class values. As a parallel to the array of unhappy heterosexual couples, there is the newlywed gay couple (Stewart Moss, Colby Chester) down the street, whose relationship soon comes unhinged.

In Los Angeles, architect Jeff (George Segal) and sculptor Mari Thompson (Natalie Wood) seem moderately content with their lives and their three children (David Comfort, David Rode, Ricky Segall). However, they are alarmed that all their friends' marriages are breaking up including Max (Oliver Clark) and Helena Dryden (Priscilla Barnes) as well as Marv (Richard Benjamin) and Sally Cooper (Arlene Golonka). They grow paranoid (and tempted) by being surrounded by "FMs" (Formely Married) which also includes-divorced Barbara (Valerie Harper) and thrice-divorced plumber Walter Holmes (Dom DeLuise) whose new wife (Charlene Ryan)—for the moment—is a hooker. After Jeff is unfaithful with Barbara and contracts gonorrhea, Mari throws him out, and then has a romantic fling herself with a tennis player. However, after encountering several other lusting souls, Mari and Jeff (who has reacted to his situation by becoming impotent) reunite, realizing being together is better than the alternatives they have seen.

Alex Keneas (*Newsday*) found the movie "so bereft of wit that its adult 'frankness' is smarmy/pubescent." Ron Edelman (*Films In Review*) observed, "George Segal and Natalie Wood, *The Last Married Couple in America*, are revoltingly hip. They socialize with a token gay couple (a decade ago, the pair would be black). They speak in the lingo of the ghetto (a white lady of the suburbs talking about a 'terrific lookin' dude' is now quite stylish, thank you). They curse in public. And, of course, they jog. . . . [It] is a morality tale that reduces the state of mod-

George Segal and Natalie Wood in *The Last Married Couple in America* (1980).

ern matrimony to ridiculous generalizations. . . ."

On the brief plus side, Natalie Wood looked radiant in her Edith Head wardrobe.

128. The Last of Sheila (Warner Bros., 1973), color, 120 min. PG-rated.

Executive producer, Stanley O'Toole; producer/director, Herbert Ross; screenplay, Anthony Perkins, Stephen Sondheim; production designer, Ken Adams; art director, Tony Roman; set decorator, John Harvins; makeup, Harry Frampton, Peter Frampton; music, Billy Goldenberg; assistant directors, William C. Gerrity, Michael Cheyko; sound, Cyril Swern; camera, Gerry Turpin; editor, Edward Warschilka.

Cast: Richard Benjamin (Tom); Dyan Cannon (Christine); James Coburn (Clinton Greene); Joan Hackett (Lee); James Mason (Philip); Ian McShane (Anthony); Raquel Welch (Alice); Yvonne Romain (Sheila Greene); Pierre Romain (Vittorio); Serge Citon (Guido); Robert Rossi (Captian); Elaine Geisinger, Elliott Geisinger (American Couple); Jack Pugeat (Silver Salesman); Martial (Locksmith); Maurice Crosnier (Concierge).

The Last of Sheila is a strange offering. Filled with convoluted red herring clues, flashbacks and thinly-veiled character traits borrowed from various real-life Hollywood personalities, this puzzler film proved too rarified a whodunit for general consumption. *Variety* wondered at the legitimacy of its premise, based "on the assumption that these film industry friends would keep such banal secrets from one another. Alcoholism, homosexuality, kleptomania, even criminal records are the very stuff of conversation these days. . . ."

In the midst of a Los Angeles party hosted by film producer Clinton Greene (James Coburn), his wife Sheila (Yvonne Romain) stalks out and is run down by an unrevealed hit-and-run-driver. A year later, Greene invites six friends—who had been at that party—on a week's cruise in the Mediterranean aboard his yacht, the *Sheila*. The guests include talent agent/gossip columnist Christine (Dyan Can-

non); movie sexpot Alice (Raquel Welch) and her manager spouse Anthony (Ian McShane); out-of-work veteran movie director Philip (James Mason); and novice screenwriter Tom (Richard Benjamin) and his wealthy, neurotic wife Lee (Joan Hackett).

Once aboard, Clinton sadistically informs his nervous guests (prey) that they are to play a game—"The Last of Sheila" —in which each will be given a card with a secret listed on it. Next, they will be provided with clues to help tie each guilt to the right suspect among them. (Greene announces that this whodunit will be the basis of his next film project in which everyone of them will participate.) The first go-round is to decide who, among them, is the shoplifter. That resolved, Christine is nearly murdered. The next category is "homosexual," but before that stigma can be placed on any of the party, Clinton is found murdered in a deserted monastery ashore. The paranoid players rush to reveal their "sins," with Lee admitting she was the hit-and-run driver and that she had killed Clinton to protect the secret. Lee later commits suicide, but Philip is unconvinced. Re-examining the clues he deduces that Tom, knowing that his wife accidentally killed Sheila, maneuvered Clinton's game to his own advantage: i.e., getting rid of Clinton (with whom he once had a brief affair) and eliminating Lee (for her insurance money). As Tom is about to silence Philip, Christine reappears. Trapped in his own deceit, Tom is blackmailed into financing the upcoming movie which Philip will direct and Christine will cast.

Pauline Kael (*The New Yorker*) insisted, "This is a glittering film with a deliberately expressionless cast." Jeff Millar (*Houston Chronicle*) agreed, "The film is intensely, cleverly—and considering the incredible complexity of the script— courageously directed by Herbert Ross." Less bedazzled, Tony Rayns (British *Monthly Film Bulletin*) decided, "Boasting the year's most impeccably chic

Richard Benjamin and James Mason in *The Last of Sheila* **(1973).**

credits—from Tony Perkins [and Stephen Sondheim) script to Halston gowns—*The Last of Sheila* easily scores as Hollywood's most extravagantly camp melodrama since *Beyond the Valley of the Dolls* [1970, q.v.]. . . . It's ultimately the kind of film that must have been more amusing to plot and shoot than it is to watch. . . ."

In retrospect, Vito Russell (*The Celluloid Closet*, 1987) found this movie to be "another instance of Hollywood and Broadway dragging homosexuality back to the realm of the dirty secret. . . ." Regarding the handling of Tom's secret from his dim, dark past, Russell emphasized, "Nobody is ever really homosexual in Hollywood on Hollywood; it is always something that people 'tried once' when they were nobody. . . ."

129. The Laughing Policeman
(Twentieth Century-Fox, 1973), color, 111 min. PG-rated. (British release title: *An Investigation of Murder*)

Producer/director, Stuart Rosenberg; based on the novel *Den Skrattande Polisen* by Per Wahloo, Maj Sjowall; screenplay, Thomas Rickman; set decorator, Doug Von Koss; music, Charles Fox; assistant director, Mike Moder; sound, Theodore Soderberg, Jerry Jost; camera, David Walsh; editor, Robert Wyamm.

Cast: Walter Matthau (Jake Martin); Bruce Dern (Leo Larsen); Lou Gossett [Jr.] (Larrimore); Albert Paulsen (Camerero); Anthony Zerbe (Lieutenant Steiner); Val Avery (Pappas); Cathy Lee Crosby (Kay Butler); Mario Gallo (Bobby Mow); Joanna Cassidy (Monica); Shirley Ballard (Grace Martin); William Hansen (Schwermer); Jonas Wolfe (Collins); Paul Koslo (Haygood, the Dealer); Lou Guss (Gus Niles); Lee McCain (Prostitute); David Moody (Pimp); Ivan Bookman (Rodney); Cliff James (Maloney); Gregg Sierra (Vickers); Warren Finnerty (Ripple); Matt Clark (Coroner); Joe Bernard (Avakian's Brother); Melvina Smedley (Maydola); Leigh French (Porno Store Cashier); Jim Clawin (Fowler); Anthony Costello (Dave Evans); John Francis (Russo); John Vick (Terry); Wayne Grace (Brennan); Cheryl Christiansen (Nurse); Jimmy Christy (Avakian); Dave Belrose (Ralph Martin); Dawn Frame

(Debbie Martin); Ellen Nance, Lavelle Robey (Receptionists); Hobart Nelson (Jail Guard); Gus Brujeman (Squad Captain); The San Francisco Strutter (Themselves).

The Laughing Policeman proved to be yet another bigoted Hollywood cops-and-robbers exercise in which the mass murderer proved to be—surprise, surprise—a homosexual. This gory, violence-packed feature, shot largely on location in San Francisco, was based on one of several detective novels set in Stockholm by the husband-and-wife writing team of Maj Sjowall and Per Wahloo. In its condescending, tourist-view tracking through the underbelly of the Bay City—frequently in an unrealistically depicted gay ghetto—it reveals a strong underpinning of prejudice against such minority groups as blacks, Hells Angels bikers and gay. These views are supposedly balanced within the script by having Walter Matthau's policeman be "liberal" in his beliefs and views. (He is the up-to-date law enforcer who tell his anti-gay partner who wants to arrest a closeted suspect, "You miss the point. Things are different today. Homosexuals don't hide anymore. They demonstrate.")

When his partner, Dave Evans (Anthony Costello) is among several passengers machined-gunned on a San Francisco bus, Jake Martin (Walter Matthau) is determined to hunt down the killer. Along with his new partner, fiery, less observant and homophobic Leo Larsen (Bruce Dern), Jake sorts through the seemingly unrelated clues. The obsessed Martin discovers that Evans had been re-examining an unsolved homicide case from a few years prior. The suspect in that case had been the dead woman's boyfriend, Camerero (Albert Paulsen) a well-connected businessman who is secretly gay. The trail leads in several misdirections, including a lesbian nurse (Joanna Cassidy) and a suspicious black pimp (Ivan Bokman). Eventually, persistent Martin and tag-along Larsen tie Gus Niles (Lou Guss), one of the dead people on the bus, to Camerero,

his one-time Army pal. To wrap up the investigation, Martin lets Camerero be aware that he knows he committed the bus massacre to get rid of Evans, who was on his and Niles's trail. This action, obviously, leads to the showdown in which the pursued Camerero boards a bus and, just before he can shoot Jake, is killed by Larsen.

A.H. Weiler (*New York Times*) reported that *The Laughing Policeman* "stands a good deal taller than the norm because of the expert guidance of Stuart Rosenberg . . . He is effectively aided by a fine script and a cast as convincing as a live cop or a dead gunman." Gene Siskel (*Chicago Tribune*) lauded, "*The Laughing Policeman* has more than its share of slam-bang slaughter, but it's real and distinguishing strength is an intelligent script that will have your mind working as much as those of the detectives on the case." In contrast, Caroline Lewis (British *Monthly Film Bulletin*) reacted unfavorably: in having as its investigator such an over-dedicated—and finally, robot-like and unmotivated—police officer, the film simply provides a gratuitous, tic-ridden portrait of both the crime and the detective. . . . Matthau, out of a desire perhaps to escape the humour which comes to him so naturally, overplays his grunts and monosyllables."

Unlike such predecessors as *Dirty Harry* (1971), *The Laughing Policeman* was not a box-office hit. Originally, John Cassavetes was to have played the Walter Matthau role as was Allen Garfield the Lieutenant Steiner part taken by Anthony Zerbe.

130. The Left-Handed Gun

(Warner Bros., 1958), color, 102 min. Not rated.

Producer, Fred Coe; director, Arthur Penn; based on the teleplay "The Death of Billy the Kid" by Gore Vidal; screenplay, Leslie Stevens; art director, Art Loel; set decorator, William Kuehl; costumes, Marjorie Best; music, Alexander Courage; song, William Goyen and Courage; assistant director, Russ

Saunders; camera, J. Peverell Marley; editor, Folmar Blangsted.

Cast: Paul Newman (Billy Bonney); Lita Milan (Celsa); John Dehner (Pat Garrett); Hurd Hatfield (Moultrie); James Congdon (Charles Boudre); James Best (Tom Folliard); Colin Keith-Johnston (Turnstall); John Dierkes (McSween); Bob Anderson (Hill); Wally Brown (Moon); Ainslie Pryor (Joe Grant); Martin Garralga (Saval); Denver Pyle (Ollinger); Paul Smith (Bell); Nestor Paiva (Maxwell); Jo Summers (Mrs. Garrett); Robert Foulk (Brady); Anne Barton (Mrs. Hill).

Many actors (from Roy Rogers to Audie Murphy to Emilio Estevez) have played the legendary Billy the Kid on screen, but not even in sex-obsessed Howard Hughes's *The Outlaw* (1943) had the young killer been suggested as a repressed homosexual. But then again, this arty, sparse film was based on a teleplay by iconoclastic Gore Vidal and directed by Arthur Penn (who also directed the movie version). Handsome Paul Newman, who had created the role on TV's "Philco Television Playhouse" (July 24, 1955), recreated his characterization in this black-and-white feature. Hurd Hatfield, most closely associated with the title assignment in *The Picture of Dorian Gray* (1945), was cast as a one-man Greek chorus, an epicene figure who favors holding a handkerchief to his nose, and who has a decided eye for the good-looking Billy. To "balance" the screenplay for 1950s audience, the outlaw, who prefers being with his male pals, dallies briefly with Celsa (Lita Milan), the wife of a good-natured locksmith (Martin Garralga).

In the 1880s, illiterate Billy Bonney (Paul Newman) seeks revenge for the murder of his beloved cattleman boss/mentor, Turnstall (Colin Keith-Johnston). Joined by boisterous pals Charles Boudre (James Congdon) and Tom Folliard (James Best) they pursue the killers: a sheriff (Robert Foulk) and a trio of rival cattlemen (Robert Anderson, Wally Brown, Robert E. Griffin). Fast-shooting Pat Garrett (John Dehner), who becomes involved in the

struggle between the hunters and the hunters, loses patience with Billy when Bonney disturbs Garrett's wedding by gunning down the last target at the ceremony. The angry Garrett is sworn in as sheriff, guns down Boudre and Folliard and captures Billy. The latter escapes, but in the final showdown is outdrawn by father-figure, Pat Garrett.

Harrison's Reports pointed out, "This time the glamour has been stripped from the characterization, and he [Billy the Kid] is presented as one who is a confused, irrational and at times unbalanced user of a gun. Paul Newman plays the part of the outlaw well. . . ." *Variety* reported, "The best parts of the film are the moments of hysterical excitement as the three young desperadoes rough-house with each other . . . and in the next instant turn to deadly killing without flicking a curly eyelash. . . . Newman dominates the picture but there are excellent performances from others including . . . Hurd Hatfield, a mysterious commentator on events." An annoyed Howard Thompson (*New York Times*) concluded, "The picture moves self-consciously, at a snail's pace . . . Poor Mr. Newman seems to be auditioning alternately for the Moscow Art Players and the Grand Ole Opry, as he ambles about, brooding, grinning or mumbling endlessly."

In the same year, Hollywood produced *The Fiend Who Walked the West*, q.v., another Western in which a similarly good-looking young killer (Robert Evans) has an unconventional sexual orientation.

131. The Legend of Lylah Clare

(Metro-Goldwyn-Mayer, 1968), color, 127 min. R-rated.

Producer, Robert Aldrich; associate producer, Walter Blake; director, Aldrich; based on the teleplay by Robert Thom, Edward DeBlasio; screenplay, Hugo Butler; art directors, George W. Davis, William Glasgow; set decorators, Henry Grace, Keogh Gleason; costumes, Renie; makeup, William Tuttle, Robert Schiffer; music, Frank De Vol; song, De Vol and Sibylle Siegfried; assistant directors, Cliff

Coleman, Dennis Donnelly, Daisy Gerber; stunt coordinator, John Indrisano; sound, Franklin Milton; special effects, Al Burke; camera, Joseph Biroc; editor, Michael Luciano.

Cast: Kim Novak (Lylah Clare/Elsa Brinkmann); Peter Finch (Lewis Zarkan); Ernest Borgnine (Barney Sheean); Milton Selzer (Bart Langner); Rossella Falk (Rossella); Gabriele Tinti (Paolo); Valentina Cortese (Countess Bozo Bedoni); Jean Carroll (Becky Langner); Michael Murphy (Mark Peter Sheean); Lee Meriwether (Young Girl); James Lanphier (1st Legman); Robert Ellenstein (Mike); Nick Dennis (Nick); Dave Willock (Cameraman); Coral Browne (Molly Luther); Peter Bravos (Butler); Ellen Corby (Script Girl); Michael Fox (Announcer); Hal Maguire (2nd Legman); Tom Patty (Bedoni's Escort); Vernon Scott (Himself); Queenie Smith (Hairdresser); Sidney Skolsky (Himself); Barbara Ann Warkmeister, Mel Warkmeister (Aerialists); George Kennedy (Matt Burke in *Anna Christie* sequence).

Even considering that such equally awful films as *Valley of the Dolls* (1967), q.v., and *The Oscar* (1967) beat it to the punch, *The Legend of Lylah Clare* ranks high on the list of ludicrous movies by and about Hollywood. (Then, too, rarely has Kim Novak been worse on camera.) In this grotesque excursion behind the kleig lights, a drug-crazed butch lesbian proves to be the crux of everyone's problems. That is saying something in this extravagantly eccentric movie, which reveals tinseltown to be full of wild nasties and unappetizing kooks.

Tormented Hollywood director Lewis Zarkan (Peter Finch) has been unable to work since the bizarre death of movie star Lylah Clare (Kim Novak) on their wedding night, two decades earlier. Then one day, Chicago actress Elsa Brinkmann (Kim Novak), a Lylah look-a-like, is brought to Zarkan's attention. He perversely agrees to film the long-discussed screen biography of Lylah's life. Things take a sick turn, when Elsa—exhausted by the coaching of the tyrannical Zarkan— finds herself "possessed" by the German-accented Lylah. In this posture, she reveals events that only the real, late star could have known. Now, having survived through the trouble-plagued production, Zarkin and Elsa, who are battling lovers, are having tremendous problems shooting the climactic scene in which Lylah dies. Lewis believes the stalemate is due to the possessed Elsa knowing how the movie legend really died. (Zarkan had discovered Lylah having an affair with dope-addicted Rossella (Rossella Falk], her "dialogue coach," and knowing that Lylah feared heights, had staged a fight with her at the top of a huge flight of steps. She had fallen to her death.) Now furious with Elsa for having an affair with their gardener (Gabriele Tinti), Zarkan restructures the final scene of their movie. He has Elsa/Lylah mount a sound stage trapeze. Ordered to look down, she falls (again) to her death. Later, after the patched-together movie is premiered, Lewis returns home where the vengeful Rossella, Zarkan's housekeeper, waits to shoot him.

Renata Adler (*New York Times*) chided, "*Lylah Clare* is not funny exactly . . . but it is kind of fun to watch. And the emotional-fossil put-on is done with sufficient care. . . ." Adler noted of the excessive plotline, "All the dyed, Eastern European lesbians on the set fall in love with her [Elsa Brinkmann] as they did with Miss Clare. So do the gardener, the public and Mr. Finch. It has to end badly. The laws of the legend factory leave no room for affairs of the heart." A polite *Variety* acknowledged, "A past master at creating mellerish hokum, Aldrich here once again builds his tensions. . . . Perhaps in trying overly to balance the mysterious ingredients with the barb-tossing expose of Hollywood manners and mores, pic tends to drag in spots. . . ."

The Legend of Lylah Clare had originated on TV as a "DuPont Show of the Week" (May 19, 1963) starring Tuesday Weld. Kim Novak had previously played dual roles in Alfred Hitchcock's *Vertigo* (1958), in which both her characters also died in falls. Robert Aldrich had dealt with the Hollywood milieu in *The Big Knife*

Peter Finch and Kim Novak in *The Legend of Lylah Clare* (1968).

(1955) and *What Ever Happened to Baby Jane?* (1962). The best few moments in *Lylah Clare* are provided by Coral Browne as the sharp-tongued, one-legged, bitchy gossip columnist. Later in 1968, Robert Aldrich, the director of the R-rated *Lylah Clare*, turned out the X-rated *The Killing of Sister George*, q.v., a far more direct, if broad study of lesbianism. Coral Browne would have a very pivotal role in that controversial picture.

132. Lenny (United Artists, 1974), 112 min. R-rated.

Executive producer David V. Picker; producer, Marvin Worth; director, Bob Fosse; based on the play by Julian Barry; screenplay, Barry; production designer, Joel Schiller; set decorator, Nicholas Romanac; costumes, Albert Wolsky; makeup, Bob Laden, Romaine Greene, Bill Farley; music supervisor, Ralph Burns; assistant directors, Ted Zachary, Douglas Green, Tommy Lofaro; sound, Dennis Mait-

land; camera, Bruce Surtees; editor, Alan Heim.

Cast: Dustin Hoffman (Lenny Bruce); Valerie Perine (Honey Bruce); Jan Miner (Sally Marr); Stanley Beck (Artie Silver); Gary Morton (Sherman Hart); Rashel Novikoff (Aunt Memma); Guy Rennie (Jack Goldstein); Frankie Mann (Master of Ceremonies at Baltimroe Strip Club); Mark Harris (San Francisco Defense Attorney); Lee Sandman (San Francisco Judge); Susan Malnick (Kitty Bruce, at Age Eleven); Martin Begley (New York Cop) Ted Sorrell, Clarence Thomas (New York Attorneys); Mike Murphy (New York District Attorney); Buddy Boylan (San Francisco Cop); George DeWitt (Comic); Judy LaScala (Chorus Girl); Glen Wilder, Frank Orsati (Hunters); Michelle Young (Nurse's Aide); Alison Goldstein (Kitty Bruce, at Age One); Belle Flower (Babysitter); Winston Lee (Chinese Waiter); Cindy Ember (Opening Stripper); Onyx, Rita Darlene Turner (Strippers); Monroe Myers (Hawaiian Judge); Lynette Bernay, Kim St. Leon, Sherry Greene (Dressing Room Girls); Jack Nagle

(Reverend Mooney); Eugene Monahan (Los Angeles Plainclothesman); Robert Parsons, Cecil Seay (Chicago Plainclothesman); Bud Atchison (New York Plainclothesman); Bruce McLaughlin (New York Judge).

Born Leonard Alfred Schneider in 1927, he became notorious as Lenny Bruce, the controversial club comedian who was frequently arrested in the U.S. for verbal "obscenity" on stage. A counterculture hero of the mid-1960s, he died in 1966 of an accidental drug overdose in Hollywood. *Lenny*, based on a 1971 Broadway play, stars Dustin Hoffman in a tour-de-force performance. Valerie Perrine appears as Bruce's wife, Honey, a stripper with lesbian tendencies, who claims "You do things on dope that normally wouldn't come into your mind to do." For her sympathetic performance, Perrine was Oscar-nominated and won the Best Actress Award at the Cannes Film Festival.

After his death, three of the people who knew Lenny Bruce (Dustin Hoffman) best, are interviewed about this controversial comedian: his mother Sally Marr (Jan Miner), his wife Honey (Valerie Perrine) and his agent Artie Silver (Stanley Beck). The oral history movie traces Lenny's life starting when he worked in a Baltimore club as a stand-up comic and met vulnerable Honey, a stripper. Despite the objections of his mother and agent, he marries Honey. Soon he is basing his club act on his own experiences, shocking his audiences. Because of his raw language, he is fired from an engagement in the Catskills by star comedian Sherman Hart (Gary Morton). Leaving the resort, Lenny and Honey are involved in a car accident. While Honey is hospitalized, he has an affair with a nurse's aide (Michelle Young), a situation Honey discovers. All these human situations become grist for Bruce's club act.

The couple move to California. By now a heavy drug user, the increasingly mercurial Lenny sets up Honey for a lesbian liaison while he looks on. He cruelly exploits the situation in his act. ("You notice comics will do endless fag jokes, but never dyke jokes. . . . You know why? Because dykes will push the shit out of you. . . . It's really hard to spook dykes, you know why? Because sometimes we're married to them.") Humiliated by his sadistic public exposure, Honey asks him why he never tells her to stop these gay scenes. He retorts with a mind-game distortion, "Why? You obviously dig that. That's cool." The emotionally stripped Honey is non-plussed.

In 1955, they have a daughter Kitty, but finally divorce two years later. Time passes and Lenny gains a reputation as a biting satirist performing in fashionable nightclubs. However, his use "of "obscene" material get him into hot legal water and starts his period of being in and out of court and jail. He becomes so preoccupied with the constitutional issues of freedom of speech involved in his cases that his stage act suffers. Honey, who had gone to jail on a drug charge, reappears, now wanting support money. Broke due to his ongoing legal fees, Lenny becomes increasingly drug-dependent. In 1966, he dies from substance abuse.

Vincent Canby (*New York Times*) disliked the gimmick of the staged on-camera interviews which "you never for a moment believe in" but he thought the truncated club act sequences were "brilliant." Reacting to the movie's claim of presenting "the real Lenny Bruce," Joel Siegel (*Washington Post*) labeled the movie a homage-driven distortion, labeling it "a simpering, simplistic white-wash in which the comedian literally dies for our sins."

Caroline Lewis (British *Monthly Film Bulletin*) found *Lenny* was "singularly unsuccessful at suggesting the complexity beneath the masks of this dangerous and tragic performer." While the *Hollywood Reporter* called the movie "a real downer" in which Bob Fosse's direction was "sullen," *Variety* summarized: "Hoffman's work is at or near his best, having gotten inside the Bruce character. Perrine's achievement lingers long after the film ends."

Made at a cost of $2.5 million, *Lenny* grossed $11,622,371 in distributors' domestic film rentals. It received six Academy Award nominations: Best Picture (*The Godfather Part II* won); Best Actor (Dustin Hoffman; Art Carney won for *Harry and Tonto*); Best Actress (Valerie Perrine; Ellen Burstyn won for *Alice Doesn't Live Here Anymore*); Best Director (Francis Ford Coppola won for *The Godfather Part II*); Best Screenplay Adapted from Other Material (*The Godfather Part II* won); Cinematography (*The Towering Inferno* won).

133. Lianna (United Artists Classics, 1983), color, 115 min. R-rated.

Producers, Jeffrey Nelson, Maggie Renzi; associate producers, Lauren Wingate, Douglas McKenna; director/screenplay, John Sayles; art director, Jeanne McDonnell; set decorator, Dena Roth; wardrobe, Louise Martinez; makeup, James Sarzotti; music, Mason Daring; choreographer, Marta Renzi; assistant directors, Carol Dysinger, Carolyn Brooks; sound, Wayne Wadhams, Aaron Nathanson; camera, Austin de Besche; editor, Sayles.

Cast: Linda Griffiths (Lianna); Jane Hallaren (Ruth); Jon DeVries (Didck); Jo Henderson (Sandy); Jessica Wight MacDonald (Theda); Jesse Solomon (Spencer); John Sayles (Jerry); Stephen Mendillo (Bob); Betsy Julia Robinson (Cindy); Nancy Mette (Kim); Maggie Renzi (Sheila); Madelyn Coleman (Mrs. Hennessy); Robyn Reeves (Job Applicant); Christopher Elliott (Lighting Assistant); Marta Renzi, D. David Porter (Dancers); Rochelle Oliver (Betty); Nancy-Elizabeth Kammer (Liz); Jean Passanante (Rose); Maggie Task (Evelyn); Marisa Smith, Amanda Carlin (Dick's Students); Madeline Lee (Supermarket Customer); Deborah Taylor (Receptionist).

'So, my old lady's a dyke. Big deal.' (Spoken by the young son in *Lianna*)

Affecting and sincere, *Lianna* is a far stronger exploration of lesbian love than the exploitive *Personal Best* (1982), q.v., or the more commercial *Desert Hearts* (1985), q.v., the latter directed by a woman

(as was Juliet Bashore's quasi *cinema verite* study, *Kamikaze Hearts*, 1986). For *Lianna*, Sayles—who created *The Brother from Another Planet* (1984), *Eight Men Out* (1988) and *The City of Hope* (1991)—served many functions as director, scenarist, editor and actor.

Lianna (Linda Griffiths), who quit college to marry, has two children: Spencer (Jesse Solomon) and Theda (Jessica Wight MacDonald). Now thirty-three, she wonders at the sacrifices made for her self-absorbed husband, Dick (Jon DeVries) who teaches literature and film at a small East coast university. Awakening to her needs, Lianna enrolls in night classes in child psychology and develops a crush on her teacher, Ruth (Jane Hallaren). One evening while Dick, who has had numerous affairs, is away, Lianna and the older Ruth dine together and then make love. Upon her confession of this affair to Dick, he uses the situation to bring about their divorce and to demand custody of the children. Unsure of how to become self-sufficient, Lianna turns to Ruth, who admits she cannot commit to a relationship which could adversely affect her career. Besides, she adds, she has a long-term lover back home. Now alone, the confused Lianna copes with propositions from her husband's womanizing associates (John Sayles) and deals with the rejection of her best friend, Sandy (Jo Henderson), who is baffled by Lianna's lifestyle admission. As for her children, little Theda feels betrayed while thirteen-year-old Spencer is more accepting. Gaining self-confidence, Lianna picks up Cindy (Betsy Julia Robinson) at a lesbian club, leading to a sexual episode. It confirms for the inexperienced Lianna that she is gay. With Ruth finally out of her life, and having patched up her friendship with Sandy, Lianna faces her future with surety.

Kevin Thomas (*Los Angeles Times*) found *Lianna* "tender, kindly and often funny," that "it glows with a bemused, humane sensibility," but "runs on too long." Regarding Canadian actress Linda

Griffiths, Thomas decided that her "Lianna is most appealing as a woman trying to build a new life for herself with dignity and good humor. Sayles invites us to laugh with—never at—Lianna as she tries to cope with life's absurdities." David Denby (*New York*) observed, "Sayles underdramatizes his material, but his untextured style may work for a lot of people; it may allow parts of the audience to concentrate more fully on the relationships." David Ansen (*Newsweek*) highlighted, "Sayles isn't half as dexterous with his camera as he is with his dialogue. But eventually the characters simply win you over. . . ." Richard Corliss (*Time*) approved that "By the end it has turned a 'problem drama' into a social comedy, full of cagey behavioral surprises and a lovely performance by Griffiths."

Based on a screenplay he wrote in 1978, Sayles shot *Lianna* in Hoboken, New Jersey for $300,000 in 16mm (later blown up to 35mm). Despite such later features as *Kamkikaza Hearts* (1986)—a docudrama of two porno actresses in love—*Lianna* remains the definite U.S. feature of lesbian love.

134. **Liberace** (ABC-TV, October 2, 1988), color, 100 min. Not rated.

Executive producers, Dick Clark, Joel R. Strote; producer, Preston Fischer; supervising producer, Arnold Shapiro; associate producer, John A. Martinelli; director, Billy Hale; teleplay, Anthony Lawerence, Nancy Lawrence; production designer, K. C. Fox; set decorator, Greg Grande; costumes, Dorothy Amos, Michael Travis; makeup, Dee Mansano; music, Gary William Friedman; choreographer, Stanley Holden; assistant director, Tom Snyder; consultants, Terry Clarkson, Jamie James; sound, Peter Bentley; camera, Thomas Burstyn; editor, Martinelli.

Cast: Andrew Robinson (Liberace); Rue McClanahan (Frances Liberace); John Rubinstein (Jamie James); Maris Valainis (Scott Thorson); Deborah Goodrich (Joanne Rio); Carmen Argenziano (Sam Liberace); Louis Giambalvo (Eddie Rio); Kario Salem (George Liberace); Robert Petkoff (Young Liberace); Debi A. Monahan (Bea Haven); Leslie Bevis

(Maxine Lewis); Romy Windsor (Jane); Gerald Hiken (John); Benjamin Cleaveland (Young George); Alba Francesca (Courtney); Thom Adcox (Darin); Tracy Shaffer (Lydia).

See Summary under **Liberace: Behind the Music**.

135. **Liberace: Behind the Music**

(October 9, 1988), color, 100 min. Not rated.

Executive producers, Peter Locke, Donald Kushner, Linda Yellin, Nancy Bein; producers, Murray Shostak, Bob Baylis; director, David Green; teleplay, Gavin Lambert; production designer, Ben Edwards; art director, Michael Joy; set decorator, Andre Chamberland; costumes, Jane Greenwood; makeup, Ann Brodie; music, Hagood Hardy; music director, Richard Gresko; assistant directors, Pedro Gandol; sound, Michael Charron; camera, Rene Verzier; editor, Yves Langlois.

Cast: Victor Garber (Liberace); Maureen Stapleton (Frances Liberace); Michael Wikes (George Liberace); Saul Rubinek (Seymour Heller); Frances Hyland (Florence); George Touliatis (Salvatore Liberace); Macha Grenon (Joanne Rio); Michael Dolan (Scott Thorson); Shawn Levy (Glenn Rivers); Paul Hipp (Elvis Presley); Kenneth Welsh (John Jacobs); Dianne Heatherington (Tessie); Stephen Watts (Jimmy); Rochelle Bruneau (George's Girl); Joan Heney (Serious Lady); Andrew Nicholls (Teenager); Shirley Merovitz (Lola); Gayle Garfinkle (1st Woman); Richard Zeman (Lola's Cop); Philip Pretten (TV Director); Amanda Straw (Gladys); Linda Smith (Jane); Victoria Kogan (Shirley); Sam Gesser (Bob); Bryan Elliot (New Chauffeur); Arthur Holden (TV Reporter); Mark Brennan (Blonde Player); James Rae (Photographer); Philip Spensley (Dr. Taylor); Barbara Jones, Susan Almgren (Nursing Sisters); Michaelle Sweeney (Nurse); Jose Miguel (Luis); and: Linda Dwyern, Karina Huber, Martine Aubin.

"Liberace's life was one of colossal denial, not only of his sexuality but of his prodigious and underappreciated musicianship. It would have made a fascinating movie, but instead, posthumously, the denial continues." (David Kipen, *Hollywood Reporter*)

Twenty months after Liberace's death (February 4, 1987) two rival U.S. networks aired competing TV-movies dealing

Jane Hallaren and Linda Griffiths in *Lianna* (1983).

with the famed pianist known for his kitchy song renditions. The biopics had lots of intriguing material with which to work in capturing the essence of this highly-successful performer. In his special way, "Mr. Showman" was a distinctive entertainer. For one thing, with his broad smile, wavy hair, nasal twang and theatrical gestures, Liberace had a uniquely recognizable presence. For another, he was renown for his glitsy stage wardrobe (ermine capes, flashy jewelry), his piano-top candelabra, and the gimmickry of his act (flying up into the stage rafters on guide wires, etc.). Then there was his ostentatious lifestyle (assorted homes, expensive cars, etc.) Added into the mix was his sexual orientation. Even in the more naive 1940s-1950s, some of the public thought this flamboyant, mother-devoted man, could not be heterosexual, no matter what he protested or did (i.e. his abortive engagement to a woman). In actuality, of course, he was not, but spent most of his

years repressing his homosexuality or, fearing professional repercussions, conducting a very private life—until events drew him out of the closet. With so much grist to draw upon, no wonder two networks rushed to film the life and loves of Liberace.

Both TV movies deal, to one degree or another, with the chronological events in the life of Wladziu Valentino Liberace. He was born in Wisconsin in 1919 to immigrant parents (his father, Salvatore, was Italian and his mother, Frances, was Polish). After his parents divorced, Liberace helped to support the household (which included his violin playing brother George) with his piano-playing. His piano work led to his show business career as a club entertaine, and he made his mark in early 1950s TV series. Later, his popularity waned in some mediums, but he remained a big draw in Las Vegas. His long-rumored homosexuality came to the fore when a past lover sued him for palimony

Rue McClanahan and Andrew Robinson in *Liberace* (1988).

and the usually reticent Liberace fought back in court. By the mid-1980s, he had contracted AIDS, a prognosis he refused to acknowledge publicly right up unto his death.

The first of the two movies, ABC-TV's *Liberace*, was sanctioned by the subject's estate and based "on his personal recollections', immediate indicators that the production would be a homage. Opening with the entertainer's Radio City Music Hall stand in 1986 New York, it flashes back to

1934 and moves forward. The strongest asset of this telefeature is Andrew Robinson's uncanny impersonation of Liberace, capturing not only the subject's vocal inflections and gestures, but the very look of the master showman. (Mike Garson provided the Liberace music styling.) In lesser roles, John Rubinstein is quietly effective as the star's long-time friend/publicist (their relationship is left discreetly ambiguous, especially since the real Jamie James was a project consultant). On the other hand, Rue McClanahan is embarrassingly bad as his Polish-accented mother, weakening this drama in which Frances is supposed to be a focal point. Equally nondescript are Deborah Goodrich as Joanne Rio, the Los Angeles girl Liberace almost marries—till, according to this account, her father (Louis Giambalvo) vetoes the union—and Maris Valainis as Scott Thorson, Liberace's assistant who brings his ex-lover's lifestyle out into the open with his legal suit.

This final action leads the film to the high-profile palimony suit where a female journalist asks the legend the question most of America would have liked to: "Do you still claim you're not a homosexual?" to which Mr. Showman responds "I'm not claiming anything. I just don't happen to believe that entertainers should publicly air their sexual or political tastes. . . . I've always admitted that my act borders on drag but I'm not a female impersonator. I have a general family audience appeal and I don't want to develop a gay following." Later, he tells the media, "But with a name like Liberace . . . I'm for anything that has L-I-B in it, and that includes gay lib."

Howard Rosenberg (*Los Angeles Times*) rated this first Liberace film "a flat-note, awesomely absurd story. . . . [It] offers no insights into the character of this outrageous performer. . . . Even worse it conceals and muffles it subject behind a veil of ambiguity, depicting him as a sort of asexual, hopelessly naive clod. . . . [Andrew] Robinson has the voice and

walk down, but . . . [has a] vacant expression revealing his own bafflement over the character he's playing. . . ." *Daily Variety* noted, "the vidbio . . . skips the tough years, showing his rise to fame as a surprisingly pleasant climb. . . . His personal life is touchier . . . The women with whom he has contact are malleable if not forward, while the young men are portrayed as shy intruders. . . . Robinson does a fine job of interpreting the complex Liberace despite the jetspeed approach of the telefilm."

A week later, CBS-TV promoted its telecast with: "The flamboyant legend of the master showman. What kind of life did he really live behind the glamor and the fame. The man revealed. *Liberace: Behind the Music.*" This presentation (dubbing in Liberace recordings for the piano playing sequences) relied heavily on the advice of the showman's long-time personal manager, Seymour Heller (not depicted in the earlier film). It omitted Liberace's loyal publicist, Jamie James (depicted in the earlier film). It too opens at Radio City Music Hall in the mid-1980s with the veteran entertainer flying on stage and joking, "Mary Martin. Eat your heart out." In comparison to Andrew Robinson's Liberace, Victor Garber is a dud. On the other hand, Maureen Stapleton excels as the mother who exerts such a strong influence on her son after the father deserted the family. She is on hand when, after the *Confidential* magazine scandal in the 1950s, her son insists to her, "I am not a homosexual." Expectedly, the telefilm makes a great deal of how Seymour Heller (played by Saul Rubinek) effectively managed the pianist's career over the years. A highlight of this presentation is the subject's early seduction by a chanteuse (Dianne Heatherington), and the teleplay suggests that the later breakup with his girl friend (Macha Grenon) turned the pianist gay. Much more is made of Liberace's seduction by/of Scott Thorson (Michael Dolan), portrayed as a rough street kid. This version takes Liberace to his last

Victor Garber in *Liberace: Behind the Music* (1988).

days, when he is dying of AIDS and ponders, "Now I could go public. Maybe get a message of sympathy from the press like Rock [Hudson] did, but I don't want to check out like that." The finale fades from the dying Liberace to the showman singing his trademark song, "I'll Be Seeing You."

Daily Variety reported that this second Liberace movie "crashes to earth all too soon . . . The 'unauthorized' version pounds home the idea that Liberace lived for image and self-indulgence; try making a hero out of that! . . . Victor Garber not even faintly resembling Liberace, goes all out with the vocal mannerism—most of the time. But there's never any doubt Garber's playing a role. . . .The *Hollywood Reporter* decided "*Behind the Music* is the stronger film dealing at great length with Liberace's years as a classical prodigy and his troubled relationship with his father. . . . Not saddled with Andrew Robinson's eerie resemblance to the late showman, Garber quietly harmonizes a series of grace notes into a fully nuanced performance." Howard Rosenberg (*Los Angeles Times*) found, "Victor Garber plays the lead . . . with sureness and nuanced credibility, effectively separating character from caricature . . . This Liberace seeks companionship in his own face, spending nearly as much time speaking to himself in mirrors . . . as communicating on stage. . . ." In comparing the two TV movie versions, Rosenberg noted, "Sexually ambivalent Liberace One eyed Scott [Thorson] as if he were a eunuch. Gay Liberace Two ogles Scott as if he were a chocolate eclair."

When all was said and done, the *Hollywood Reporter* observed, "It's a little dispiriting to think that two TV movies, separately developed and presumably antagonistic, should come out so interchangeable. . . . [It is] an indication of how slavishly they both conform to the rules of televised biography."

136. Lilith (Columbia, 1964), 114 min. Not rated.

Producer/director, Robert Rossen; based on the novel by J. R. Salamanca; screenplay, Rossen; production designer, Richard Sylbert; set decorator, Gene Callahan; costumes, Ruth Morley; makeup, Irving Buchman, Bill Herman, Robert Jiras; puppets, The Zoo, Gene Carlough; music/music director, Kenyon Hopkins; assistant directors, Larry Sturhahn, Bob Vietro, Allan Dennis; sound, Jim Shields, Richard Vorisek; camera, Eugene Shuftan, Tibor Sands; editor, Aram Avakian.

Cast: Warren Beatty (Vincent Bruce); Jean Seberg (Lilith Arthur); Peter Fonda (Stephen Evshevsky); Kim Hunter (Bea Brice); Anne Meacham (Mrs. Yvonne Meaghan); James Patterson (Dr. Lavrier); Jessica Walter (Laura); Gene Hackman (Norman); Robert Reilly (Bob Clayfield); Rene Auberjonois (Howie); Lucy Smith (Vincent's Grandmother); Maurice Brenner (Mr. Gordon); Jeanne Barr (Miss Glassman); Richard Higgs (Mr. Palakis); Elizabeth Bader (Girl at Bar); Alice Spivak (Lonely Girl); Walter Arnold (Lonely Girl's Father); Kathleen Phelan (Lonely Girl's Mother); Cecilia Ray (Lilith's Mother in Dream); Gunnar Peters (Her Chauffeur in Dream); L. Jerome Offutt (Tournament Judge); W. Jerome Offutt (Tournament Announcer); Robert Jolivette (Older Watermelon Boy); Jason Jolivette (Younger Watermelon Boy); Jeno Mate (Assistant to Dr. Lavrier); Ben Carruthers (Benito); Dina Paisner (Psychodrama Moderator); Pawnee Sills (Receptionist); Luther Foulk, Kenneth Fuchs, Steve Dawson, Michael Paras (Doctors); Morton Taylor (Ambulance Doctor); Joavan Curran, Rick Branda, Wade Taylor, Tony Lombard, David Barry, Frank Nonoia (Ambulance Attendants); Joanne Bayes, Barbara Lowe, Patsy Klein, Gwen Van Dam, Eadie Renaud (Nurses); Katherine Gregg, Edith Fellows, Page Jones, Olympia Dukakis, Mildred Smith, Cynthia McAdams, Wendell Phillips Jr., David Craig (Patients).

There are many parallels between societies and social groups, and that includes the contrasting worlds of the sane and insane. In *Lilith*, based on J. R. Salamanca's novel (1961), the title figure is beautifully angelic on the outside and devilishly corrupt on the inside. Following the tradition of medieval demonology, she is portrayed as the evil spirit luring people to their destruction. In this pretentiously arty cinema exercise, one of *Lilith*'s victims is a fellow female patient who is magnetized by this indiscriminate nymphomaniac.

Following the Korean War, distraught serviceman Vincent Bruce (Warren Beatty) returns to his Maryland hometown. Wanting to help humanity, he accepts a position at a nearby private mental institution as a trainee occupational therapist, working under the supervision of Bea Brice (Kim Hunter). Among the affluent patients there, he meets and falls in love with attractive Lilith Arthur (Jean Seberg), who lives in her own fanciful world. In the midst of their relationship, he finds that she is having an affair with another patient, Mrs. Meaghan (Anne Meacham). Reproaching Lilith for this, she tells Vincent: "I show my love for all of you, and you despise me!" Yet another inmate drawn to Lilith is Stephen Evshevsky (Peter Fonda), who commits suicide when she rebuffs him. Following Stephen's death, Lilith loses complete touch with reality, retreating into total madness. The shattered Vincent abandons his job, but asks a doctor (James Patterson) at the hospital there to help him survive.

Bosley Crowther (*New York Times*) found the affectations of *Lilith* repugnant, thus labeling the film "a gauzy, opaque work full of clever camera trickery . . . and loaded with symbolistic details that festival people usually love." A traditionalist, Crowther archly referred to the movie containing "some dark suggestions of a homosexual attachment between the heroine and an older patient, which agitates a flare of masculine jealousy." As to the acting, Crowther approved of Seberg, thought Beatty's interpretation was "muddy" and that "Anne Meacham is icy and mephitic as the older woman who lures [sic] the girl. . . ." *Variety* pinpointed the movie's problems: "Its subject of seduction in an insane asylum is neither pleasant nor conducive to mass entertainment. . . . Audience is left in as much of a daze as the hero is throughout most of the film." As to the performances, the trade paper objected to Beatty's "hesitation jarring to the watcher," but found "Miss Seberg is properly vague but is lovely in her role" and that "Good support is offered by [among others] Anne Meacham. . . .."

Lilith, which failed at the box-office, was originally to have been the official U.S. entry at the Venice Film Festival but was withdrawn after unfavorable earlier screenings. Location work for *Lilith* was accomplished in Barnesville, Great Falls and Rockville, Maryland. To be noted briefly in the cast as a patient is future Oscar winner Olympia Dukakis.

137. Little Big Man (National General Pictures, 1970), color, 147 min. GP-rated.

Producer, Stuart Millar; associate producer, Gene Lasko; director, Arthur Penn; based on the book by Thomas Berger; screenplay, Calder Willingham; production designer, Dean Tavoularis; art director, Angelo Graham; set decorator, George R. Nelson; costumes, Dorothy Jeakins; makeup, Dick Smith, Terry Miles; music, John Hammond; assistant directors, Mike Moder, Mack Harding; stunt coordinator, Hal Needham; special effects, Logan Frazee; camera, Harry Stradling Jr.; editor, Dede Allen.

Cast: Dustin Hoffman (Jack Crabb); Faye Dunaway (Mrs. Pendrake); Martin Balsam (Allardyce T. Merriweather); Richard Mulligan (General George A. Custer); Chief Dan George (Old Lodge Skins); Jeff Corey (Wild Bill Hickok); Amy Eccles (Sunshine); Kelly Jean Peters (Olga); Carol Androsky (Caorine); Robert Little Star (Little Horse); Cal Bellini (Younger Bear); Ruben Moreno (Shadow That Comes in Sight); Steve Shemayne (Burns Red in the Sky); William Hickey (Historian); James Anderson (Sergeant); Jesse Vint (Lieutenant); Alan Oppenheimer (Major); Thayer David (Reverend Silas Pendrake); Philip Kenneally (Mr. Kane); Jack Bannon (Captain); Ray Dimas (Young Jack Crabb); Alan Howard (Adolescent Jack Crabb); Jack Mullaney (Card Player); Steve Miranda (Younger Bear, as a Youth); Lou Cutell (Deacon); M. Emmett Walsh (Shotgun Guard); Emily Cho (Digging Bear); Cecelia Kootenay (Little Elk); Linda Dyer (Corn Woman); Dessie Bad Bear (Buffalo Wallow); Len George (Crow Scout); Norman Nathan (Pawnee); Helen Verbit (Madame); Bert Conway (Bartender); Earl Rosell (Giant Trooper); Ken Mayer (Sergeant) Bud Cokes (Man at Bar); Rory O'Brien (Assassin); Tracy Hotchner (Flirtatious Girl).

Long before the ultra liberal *Dances with Wolves* (1990) refocused attention on native Americans, *Little Big Man* dealt richly with nineteenth century American Indians, in what Richard Combs (British *Monthly Film Bulletin*) termed "a beautiful and complex satire on the divergence of fact and legend in the Old West." Among the several Cheyenne Indians whom the white man narrator (Dustin Hoffman) encounters over his long life is Little Horse (Robin Little Star), a blatant homosexual, who is not shunned by his society but venerated. As James J. Desmarais analyzes in *Magill's American Film Guide* (1983), "The film is ultimately pro-Indian. Indians are presented as possessing many desirable qualities unknown to most white men; they are more tolerant and understanding (as seen in their acceptance of a homosexual member of the tribe), and less jealous. . . . At the beginning of the film they are naive, fighting soldiers' guns with sticks. However, by the end of the film, they have learned to protect themselves."

A historian (William Hickey) chronicles the reminiscences of irritable 121-year-old Jack Crabb (Dustin Hoffman) from the time when, as a boy, he is captured and adopted by the "human beings" (what the Cheyenne Indian tribal members calls themselves). Later recaptured by the U.S. Army, Jack has the first of several encounters with the legendary Wild Bill Hickok (Jeff Corey) and, thereafter, with megalomaniacal General George Armstrong Custer (Richard Mulligan). Initially married to a white woman (Kelly Jean Peters), Jack's second mate is Sunshine (Amy Eccles), who dies, along with her child, in a camp raid by Custer and his troops. This shock leads to Crabb becoming a drunken hermit. Subsequently, he is accidentally drawn into the massacre at Little Big Horn, where his one-time tribal rival, Younger Bear (Cal Bellini), saves him. It is Jack who goes with the venerable Chief Old Lodge Skins (Chief Dan George) to the hills, where the latter waits to die at the family resting ground, but decides his time has not come. Jack and he return to the village and the jumps back to the present.

Variety described the proceedings as "a sort of vaudeville show, framed in fictional biography, loaded with sketches of varying degrees of serious and burlesque humor, and climaxed by the Indian victory over General George A. Custer. . . ." In describing the array of characters that Jack, the spectator, encounters—from the randy Mrs. Pendrake (Faye Dunaway) to an outrageous con artist (Martin Balsam) —*Variety* noted the presence of "Robert Little Star, the effeminate Indian thrown in for no-one-knows-what valid story purpose. . . ."

Little Big Man grossed $15 million in distributors' domestic film rentals. It received one Academy Award nomination: Best Supporting Actor (Chief Dan George; John Mills won for *Ryan's Daughter*).

138. The Living End (Strand Releasing, 1992), color, 92 min. R-rated.

Executive producers, Evelyn Hu, Jon Jost, Henry Rosenthal, Mike Thomas; producer, Marcus Hu, Jon Gerrans; co-producer, Jim Stark; associate producer, Andrea Sperling; director/screenplay, Gregg Araki; music, Cole Coonce; sound, George Lockwood; camera/editor, Araki.

Cast: Mike Dytri (Luke); Craig Gilmore (Jon); Mark Finch (Doctor); Mary Woronov (Daisy); Johnna Went (Fern); Darcy Marta (Darcy); Scott Goetz (Peter); Bretton Vail (Ken); Nichole Dillenberg (Barbie); Paul Bartel (Twister Master); Stephen Holman, Maggie Song (7-Eleven Couple).

Yet a new variation of the Road/Buddy picture, this film revolved around two gay men. *The Living End* finds Jon (Craig Gilmore), a writer, learning he is HIV+ and soon thereafter meeting a drifter, Luke (Mike Dytri), who is also HIV +. Jon is sensitive and calm; Luke is the opposite. When hot-tempered Luke kills a cop in a moment of anger, and then robs a bank, the two lovers find themselves on the run. The bewildered John meekly follows the mercurial Luke, the latter insisting, "We're totally free! We have nothing to lose." As they start their odyssey, they declare themselves, prophetically "Till death do us part!"

Made on a $20,000 budget by Los

Angeles underground filmmaker Gregg Araki, Amy Dawes (*Daily Variety*) approved of the concept, but was disappointed because "[the picture] doesn't take them anywhere but down in an edgy, irreverent but ultimately dead-end journey." Dawes observed that "Araki's dialogue can be wickedly clever" and "pic is occasionally fueled by a gleeful sick humor." Janet Maslin (*New York Times*) approved of the film for its "power of honesty and originality, as well as the weight of legitimate frustration. Miraculously, it also has a buoyant, mischievous spirit that transcends any hint of gloom. . . . Like *Thelma and Louise*, which it resembles on a more modest and desperate scale, *The Living End* uses crime as a way of extricating its characters from everyday society, and not as an occasion for passing moral judgment on their behavior. Getting out is what matters, not getting even." According to Jeff Menell (*Hollywood Reporter*), "Despite the approachable humor, the graphic gay sex will turn off most of the heterosexual audience. . . . Menell also noted, "this road flick loses its direction along the way, and ultimately winds up in a rambling, somewhat unsatisfying fashion. . . ."

139. Logan's Run (Metro-Goldwyn-Mayer/United Artists, 1976), color, 118 min. PG-rated.

Producer, Saul David; associate producer, Hugh Benson; director, Michael Anderson; based on the novel by David; screenplay, David Zelag Godman; production designer, Dale Hennesy; set decorator, Robert De Vestel; costumes, Bill Thomas; makeup, William Tuttle; music, Jerry Goldsmith; assistant director, David Silver; stunt coordinators, Glen Wilder, Bill Couch; sound, Jerry Jost, Harry W. Tetrick, William McCaughey, Aaron Rochin; camera, Ernest Laszlo; editor, Bob Wyman.

Cast: Michael York (Logan); Jenny Agutter (Jessica); Richard Jordan (Francis); Roscoe Lee Browne (Box); Farrah Fawcett-Majors (Holly); Peter Ustinov (Old Man); Michael Anderson Jr. (Doc); Gary Morgan (Billy); Denny Arnold (Runner #1); Glen Wilder (Runner

#2); Lara Lindsay (Woman Runner); Bob Neil (2st Sanctuary Man); Randolph Roberts (2nd Sanctuary Man); Carnilla Carr (Sanctuary Woman); Greg Michaels (Ambush Man); Roger Borden (Daniel); Michelle Stacy (Mary Two); Ann Ford (Woman on Lastday); Laura Hippe (New You Shop Customer).

In this PG-rated science fiction projection into the year 2274, the world has been ravaged by war, pollution and overpopulation. What remains is a new society, living in a vast geodome. Life is fun and carefree; discrimation against minorities (including homosexuals) no longer exists. However, there is a governmental rule that, at age thirty, all inhabitants must experience a mystical ceremony in which they are terminated and supposedly renewed. One of society's sandmen (security guards) is Logan (Michael York), who is shocked to learn that there is NO renewal. First as a bogus "runner" and then as a real rebel, he escapes from the dome with Jessica (Jenny Agutter), pursued by sandman/friend Francis (Richard Jordan), who is later killed. Outside the dome, they encounter an old man (Peter Ustinov) existing happily in the ruins of Washington, D.C. After causing the geodome city to self-destruct, many of the young people escape and are led by Logan and Jessica to the old man, proving that life after thirty can and does exist.

Vincent Canby (*New York Times*) noted, "*Logan's Run* is less interested in logic than in gadgets and spectacle, but these are sometimes jazzily effective and even poetic. Had more attention been paid to the screenplay, the movie might have been a stunner." *Variety* rated the production a "spectacular-looking escapist adventure as well as intelligent drama." Richard Combs (British *Monthly Film Bulletin*) described *Logan's Run* as "A cautionary tale for the Pepsi generation," questioning "why anyone would want to recreate Disneyland in the aftermath of world-wide destruction" and deciding "[Director] Michael Anderson handles his toy-town concept with a kind of squint-eyed concentra-

Peter Ustinov, Michael York and Jenny Agutter in *Logan's Run* (1976).

tion on getting his wafer-thin characters from A to B. . . ."

Logan's Run grossed $9,425,994 in distributors' domestic film rentals. It received two Academy Award nominations: Best Cinematography (*Bound for Glory* won); and Best Art Direction—Set Decoration (*All the President's Men* won). Nevertheless, this hit movie spawned a TV series, "Logan's Run" (1977–78) starring Gregory Harrison and Heather Menzies.

140. Lonesome Cowboys (Factory Films, 1968), color, 110 min. X-rated.

Executive producer, Paul Morrissey; producer/director/screenplay, Andy Warhol; camera/editor, Morrissey.

Cast: Viva (Ramona Alvarez); Tom Hompertz (The Drifter); Louis Waldon (Mickey, the Eldest Brother); Eric Emerson (Eric); Taylor Mead (The Nurse); Joe Dallesandro (Little Joe); Francis Francine (The Sheriff); Julian Burroughs (Julian, the Brother); Alan Midgette (Brother).

Shot in 16mm in Tucson, Arizona, this crude, extemporized exercise featured such regulars of Andy Warhol's film Factory as the androgynous Viva, stud Joe Dallesandro and the inestimable Taylor Mead. With the cast improvising much of the dialogue, the film's structure was obviously loose, the production values skimpy and the total effect produced more bewilderment than enjoyment, in a way similar to Paul Bartel's campy *Lust in the Dust* (1985). However, *Lonesome Cowboys*' exaggerated depiction of flighty, gay caballeros—while far from the norm of the gay community—was a distinct counterbalance to 1960s Hollywood movies which presented homosexuals as repressed and suicidal individuals or sociopathic killers.

In an Arizona ghost town, few civilians remain. There is the transvestite sheriff (Francis Francine), an exotic rancher, Ramona Alvarez (Viva), along with her ninny nurse (Taylor Mead), and the few remaining cowboys (Julian Burroughs, Alan Midgette, Eric Emerson, Louis Waldon). These men spend their time dancing a ballet, redoing their hairstyles and pondering their fate. They are also distracted by Little Joe (Joe Dallesandro), the blond who has drifted recently into their group. Later, the cowboys rape Ramona who, in turn, demands the sheriff take action. He is too preoccupied with his drag outfit to fulfill her request. Turning aggressive, Ramona seduces Little Joe and then decides they should die together since they reached such joyous perfection through lovemaking. He declines, instead riding off with one of the cowboys, heading for the wilds of California.

According to *Variety*, *Lonesome Cowboys*, "is simply an unedited but in-focus home movie for homosexuals and a 'drag' in every play on the word." When released in England in 1970, the (British *Monthly Film Bulletin*) judged that "Occasionally the variations are—in their tasteless way —very funny. . . ." In analyzing the film's flaws, the *Bulletin* concluded, "Part of the problem is that Warhol's cowboys, unzipping their flies with the same reflex alacrity that their conservative prototypes display in reaching for the holster, became at least as predictable as any old B-feature heroes; another part . . . is that the improvised satire is more than blunted by the self-admiring, stoned haziness of the non-performances."

141. **Longtime Companion** (Samuel Goldwyn Co., 1990), color, 100 min. R-rated.

Executive producer, Lindsay Law; producer, Stan Wlodkowski; co-producer, Lydia Dean Pilcher; director, Norman Rene; screenplay, Craig Lucas; production designer, Andrew Jackness; art director, Ruth Ammon; set decorator, Kate Conklin; costumes, Walker Hicklin; makeup, Nina Port; music, Greg DeBelles; song, Zane Campbell; assistant directors, Howard McMaster, Noga Isackson, Dolly Hall; sound, Paul Cote, Harold Rebhun; camera, Tony Jannelli; editor, Katherine Wenning.

Cast: Stephen Caffrey (Fuzzy [Alan]); Patrick Cassidy (Howard Palin); Brian Cousins (Bob); Bruce Davison (David Elders); John Dossett (Paul); Mark Lamos (Sean); Dermot Mulroney (John Deacon); Mary-Louise Parker (Lisa); Michael Schoeffling (Michael); Campbell Scott (Willy Wolf); Tanya Berezin (Office Manager); Welker White (Rochelle); Michael Pointek, Joyce Reehling (Office Workers); Marceline Hugot (Soap Opera Reader); Margo Skinner (Casting Director); Eric Gutierrez (Disco Bartender); Dan Brad O'Hare (Waiter); Philip Moon (Restaurant Bartender); Hazel J. Medina Neil (Triage Nurse); Annie Golden (Heroin Addict); Pi Douglass (Henry); Dan Butler (Walter); Alexandra Neil (Soap Actress); Brent Barrett (Soap Actor); Kelly Connell (Man with Soap Script); Bajika Puri (Dr. Seth); Freda Foh Shen (Nurse with Addict); Robi Martin (Transvestite); Robert Joy (Ron); Tony Shalhoub (Paul's Doctor); Sam Silver (Gym Instructor); David Drake (GMHC Volunteer); Michael Carmine (Alberto); Melora Creager, Jesse Hultberg, Lee Kimble (Finger Lakes Trio).

"It is a reflection on history, rather than on the film itself, that *Longtime Companion* is a simple film. The plot consists of nothing more than excerpts of the daily lives of a group of gay men between 1981 and 1989. By the film's end, however, daily life includes an omnipresent death threat in the form of the AIDS epidemic. Everyday life, and, horrifyingly, everyday death." (Gabrielle J. Forman, *Magill's Cinema Annual*, 1991)

This emotional narrative of interweaving lives opens in December 3, 1981, with a *New York Times* report about a new "gay" cancer proving deadly to homosexual men. The account is noted by several New Yorkers: Fuzzy (Stephen Caffrey), an attorney; his sister Lisa (Mary-Louise Parker); and her next-door neighbors, Paul (John Dossett) and Howard (Patrick Cassidy). On Fire Island, the article is read by well-to-do David Elders (Bruce Davison), his lover, Sean (Mark Lamos), as well as by his friends Willy Wolf (Campbell Scott), an actor and part-time gym instructor, and John Deacon (Dermot Mulroney). By mid-1982, John is dying of AIDS, while Willy has a role on a national TV soap opera as "Central Falls'" first gay character. In 1983 Sean, a scriptwriter for "Central Falls," has suspicious AIDS-like symptoms; David tells him not to worry.

Bruce Davison and Campbell Scott in *Longtime Companion* (1990).

The next year, Paul is hospitalized with an AIDS-induced brain lesion, while Sean's health is deteriorating. In the spring of 1985, Sean's condition has so declined, that David is writing his scripts, while Howard is fired from the TV program because it is rumored he has AIDS. Meanwhile, Paul's condition is terminal. Sean dies in January 1986 and, for his obituary in the *New York Times*, the group list David as Sean's "longtime companion." May 1987 finds the survivors gathered for David's memorial service and tribute. By the fall of 1988, both Willy and Fuzzy are involved actively with AIDS support groups, while Howard, HIV+, works for an AIDS benefit concert. In the summer of 1989, Fuzzy, Lisa and Willy are on Fire Island planning a pro-AIDS-support sit-in at a local health department office. Thinking back on the traumatic decade, they fantasize about seeing all their dead friends.

Dissenters of *Longtime Companion* protested that its story is (1) too pro-white, urban upper class, (2) fails to encom-pass lesbian participants in AIDS care/protests, (3) too passive in its presentation of the politics involving the AIDS epidemic, (4) manipulatively structured as a melodrama in the style of *La Ronde*. As Jim Farber (*Entertainment Weekly*) concluded, "Too bad the moviemakers were so intent on delivering their information-heavy message to a straight audience that they erased nearly every quirk and blemish of humanity that would make us care about the people affected. The characters here give off the same constipated, mannequin-like vibe we're accustomed to enduring from TV-movie portrayals of gay men." Comparing this movie to *As Is* (1986), q.v., Farber decided "Unlike the public-service-announcement approach of *Longtime Companion*, *As Is* is art. *Longtime Companion* **C-**, *As Is*: **A**."

On the other hand, Neal Gabler (*Video Review*) enthused, "*Longtime Companion* packs few surprises, which is obviously part of its effect . . . It is a grave, earnest, intimate movie . . . that makes its impact in small gestures rather than in loud, hyperdramatized ones. . . . *Longtime Companion* doesn't extrapolate from AIDS any more than most movies about the Holocaust extrapolate from it. . . . It seems designed instead to bear witness to a terrible time and a terrible pain. If it doesn't do more under the circumstances bearing witness seems sufficient, and *Longtime Companion* does it simply and movingly."

Farrah Anwar (British *Monthly Film Bulletin*) pointed out that, "The episodic story-telling . . . does not hamper the film's continuity. . . . Sentimentality is reined in by preventing performer and . . . soundtrack alike from manipulating emotions too gratuitously. . . . Even the film's more obvious moves to educate its audience about AIDS, both in terms of pathology (each of the victims is afflicted by a different spectrum of the 'syndrome'. . .) and sociology (the increased political activism of the survivors) are unobtrusively incorporated. Any narrative shortcoming that *Companion* may have . . . are negated by a clutch of excellent performances, with Bruce Davison superb as the mother hen of this unhappy brood."

In a movie filled with so much tragedy and death suffered by its characters, the impact could eventually blunt the viewer's emotions. However, two keys scenes recharge the audience's empathy. The most powerful is the tender moment when David, having nursed his lover through the long ordeal, tells his dying friend, Sean: "It's okay. You can go. Let go my baby. It's all right. Don't be afraid. I'm here. You let go of everything and don't hold on. . . . Don't worry. . . . Let go. No pain. . . . There you go." It is beautifully handled by Bruce Davison. The other occurs at the finale as a trio of survivors chat about the past and the future, and in a wish-fulfillment sequence envision a reunion with all their many departed friends. This roll-call of the dead tugs mightily at the heart strings.

Longtime Companion grossed $2,200,000 in distributors' domestic film rentals, its mainstream potential increased by its low-key approach and by the realization that its subject matter, AIDS, was no longer to be considered just a gay disease. Bruce Davison, who won a Golden Globe for his performance was Oscar-nominated as Best Supporting Actor, but lost to Joe Pesci (*GoodFellas*).

142. **Looking for Mr. Goodbar**

(Paramount, 1977), color, 135 min. R-rated.

Producer, Freddie Field; director, Richard Brooks; based on the novel by Judith Rossner; screenplay, Brooks; art director, Edward Carfagno; set decorator Ruby Levitt; costumes, Jodie Lynn Tillen; makeup, Charles Schram; music, Artie Kane; assistant directors, David Silver, Alan Brimfield; sound, Al Overton; camera, William A. Fraker; editor, George Grenville.

Diane Keaton (Theresa Dunn); Tuesday Weld (Katherine Dunn); William Atherton (James Morrissey); Richard Kiley (Mr. Dunn); Richard Gere (Tony Lopanto); Alan Feinstein (Professor Martin Engle); Tom Berenger (Gary Cooper White); Priscilla Pointer (Mrs. Dunn); Laurie Prange (Brigid Dunn); Joel Fabiani (Barney); Julius Harris (Black Cat); Richard Bright (George); LeVar Burton (Captain Jackson); Marilyn Coleman (Mrs. Jackson); Carole Malory (Marvella); Mary Ann Mallis (Principal); Jolene Dellenbach, Louie Fant (Teachers); Eddie Garrett (Bartender); Alexander Courtney (Arthur); Brian Dennehy (Surgeon); Richard Venture (Doctor); Robert Burke (Patrick); Robert Fields (Rafe); Richard O'Brien (Father Timothy); Tony Hawkins (Chuck); Caren Kaye (Rhoda); Richard Spangler (TV Announcer); Elizabeth Cheshire (Theresa, as a Child); Marilyn Roberts (Woman in Bar).

"There's one crucial thing that *Looking for Mr. Goodbar* doesn't make clear: Just because you find Mr. Goodbar doesn't necessarily mean you were looking for him. The heroine of Judith Rossner's bestseller *was* looking. Theresa was turned on to a particular flavor of self-destructive sexual experience. . . . What we might have gotten [but did not] is a movie about a character obsessed, and fascinated, by what the end might be. Even a movie about how she got to be that way." (Roger Ebert, *Home Movie Companion*, 1991)

Judith Rossner based her hit novel (1975) on a well-publicized 1972 New York City homicide case which fascinated case investigators because of the marked discrepancies between the lonely victim's daytime activities (teaching the handicapped) and her nighttime amusement (prowling the city's disco bars for quick sexual pickups). In *Looking for Mr. Goodbar*, director Richard Brooks's depiction of Manhattan hot spots was more Hollywood hallucination than Big Apple reality. But then, there were a lot of distortions in this screen adaptation, not the least of which were its annoying fantasy sequences about the victim's living/dead father. The reality, as depicted in the novel and underemphasized in the screen version was that (sub)consciously the self-destructive teacher was drawn irresitably to the hot-tempered man, a bisexual, who ends her life.

In the 1970s, independent Theresa Dunn (Diane Keaton), from a strict Roman Catholic family, completes college and bucks her stern father (Richard Kiley) by moving to Manhattan in an apartment beneath that of her airline steward sister, Katherine (Tuesday Weld). By day, Theresa teaches deaf children; at night she hangs out at singles' bars. To give herself energy for her split life, she turns to cocaine. Having had a bad relationship with her married college teacher (Alan Feinstein), she now becomes involved with solicitous social worker James (William Atherton). While she toys with the traditional James, she is far more excited about an uneducated hustling barfly, Tony Lapato (Richard Gere). However, she eventually tires of the sexy, restless Tony and, later, humiliates James when he attempts finally to make love to her. Subsequently, Tony, who has been living off another woman who has now thrown him out, returns, but she refuses to renew the relationship, calling the police when he becomes violent. On New Year's Eve, the restless Theresa returns to her favorite bar to escape the love-sick James. She tells the

bartender that she has resolved to quit the bar scene—tomorrow. Nevertheless, soon she is attracted to Gary (Tom Berenger), who has just had a fight with his lover (Richard Bright). "Why did you pick me?" he asks. "I don't know. You seem friendly. A nice smile." She takes him home, but while in bed she berates his masculinity, and in a frenzy (heightened by amyl nitrate) he rapes her and then stabs her to death.

A peculiar break in the movie's logic occurs during the exploitive developmental sequences prior to the meeting of Gary and Theresa. Unlike the rest of this picture, these fragments are not told from Terersa's point-of-view *and* they are played in a highly melodramatics manner. They begin with Gary storming out of a Village bar in drag, shouting "Look at us, we're a couple of freaks!", and followed by his meek, older lover, George (Richard Bright). Gary changes to jeans and a shirt, insisting to his whining keeper, "I've had it with you. . . . I'm cutting out of this." As Gary runs off down the street, his dependent friend calls out "Will you be back? . . . I'll wait for you at the apartment. Do you need some money?" To which Gary responds, "Shove it!" insisting "I'm a pitcher. Not a catcher." Much is made by director Brooks of volatile Gary's entrance into the disco where Theresa is surveying the scene. Just before they encounter, a man cruises the muscular Gary, leading the latter to snarl: "You think I'm queer, don't you? . . . You thought it! . . . Freak!" Thus, these scenes cinematically disjointed from the atmosphere of the rest of the movie, jarringly establishes the personality of Theresa's killer. As John Pym (British *Monthly Film Bulletin*) concluded, "That Theresa's death is engineered with heady, melodramatic artifice does not altogether detract from its irony, nor does it entirely prevent us from caring about the film's shadowy heroine."

Vincent Canby (*New York Times*) was displeased at how filmmaker Brooks turned converted Rossner's fine novel into "something glossy" full of material that "is artificial without in any way qualifying as a miracle fabric." Pauline Kael (*The New Yorker*) argued that Brooks has "lost the erotic, pulpy morbidity that made the novel a compulsive read; the film is splintered, moralistic, tedious." A more compliant *Variety* decided the filmmaker "again manifests his ability to catch accurately both the tone and subtlety of characters in the most repellant environments . . . [the] production is a major achievement for all concerned."

Looking for Mr. Goodbar grossed a huge $16.9 million in distributors' domestic film rentals. It received one Academy Award nomination; Best Cinematography (*Close Encounters of the Third Kind* won). Ironically, Diane Keaton, not nominated for *Mr. Goodbar*, won an Oscar that year as Best Actress for the comedy, *Annie Hall*. The *Goodbar* saga would be re-explored in the TV movie, *Trackdown, Finding the Goodbar Killer* (1983), q.v.

143. Love Child (Warner Bros., 1982), color, 97 min. R-rated.

Producer, Paul Maslansky; director, Larry Peerce; story, Anne Gerard; screenplay, Gerard, Katherine Specktor; art director, Don Ivey; set decorator, Richard A. Helfritz; makeup, Marie Del Russo; music, Charles Fox; song, Fox and Carly Simon; assistant directors, David Whorf, Paul Rose; sound, Howard Warren; special effects, J. B. Jones; camera, James Pergola; editor, Bob Wyman.

Cast: Amy Madigan (Terry Jean Moore); Beau Bridges (Jack Hansen); Mackenzie Phillips (J. J.); Albert Salmi (Captain Mark Ellis); Joanna Merline (Superintendent Helen Sturgis); Margaret Whitton (Jacki Steinberg); Lewis Smith (Jesse Chaney); Dennis Lipscomb (Arthur Brady); Anna Maria Horsford (Mara); Michael Shane (Judge Hare); Randy Dreyfuss (Jeff Striker); Rhea Pearlman (June Burns); Juanita Mahone (Cecily); Raymond Peters, Al Kiggins (Correctional Officers); Annette Fosaner (Woman in Yard); Norma Davids (Bonnie); Ronnie Mickey (Faith); Tame Connelly (Norma); Liba Carole May (Vicki); Lynn Lathan (Claudia); Sterling Swanson (Officer); Thomas Monshan (Broward Correctional Insti-

tution Officer); Alan Minor (County Jail Guard); Terry Jean Moore (Inmate).

In a rehash of the women-behind-bars type of film, this low-budget feature was based on an actual case in Florida where a nineteen-year-old prisoner gave birth to a baby whose father was a prison guard. Among the stereotypical characters in the plotline was a lesbian inmate who is infatuated with the heroine. As to the movie's effectiveness, Rex Reed (*New York Post*) weighed, "With its miraculously happy, upbeat ending, its condescending moral tone, and its swarm of prison-movie cliches, *Love Child* is strictly formula TV Movie of the Week fodder. . . ."

In 1977, young Terry Jean Moore (Amy Madigan) gets into trouble while hitchhiking in Florida with her cousin, Jesse Chaney (Lewis Smith). He holds up the driver who had given them a ride. When they are caught, he turns state's evidence and it is Terry who is sent to the Broward Correctional Institution on a fifteen-year sentence. In this prison without barbed wires or armed guards, she becomes the target of butch J. J. (Mackenzie Phillips), who wants a sexual relationship. When Terry says no, they become friends instead. Meanwhile, the new prisoner is befriended by sympathetic Jack Hansen (Beau Bridges), a veteran guard there. As their love relationship blossoms, she eventually becomes pregnant and confronts him with her condition. He admits he is married, and later resigns his post from the facility. Terry gives birth to her baby in the prison hospital and, finding a loophole in the state's statues, she gets to keep her baby at the facility. After 741 days in prison, Terry and her baby are paroled.

Janet Maslin (*New York Times*) concluded, "the truth must almost certainly have been stranger than the determinedly simple movie it has engendered. . . . [Director Larry Peerce's] portrait of Terry is so mild that the film's harsher touches seem gratuitous. . . . Even Mackenzie

Phillips, who swaggers along in a ducktail haircut and describes herself as 'a married man,' becomes positively humdrum before the film ends." Somewhat more enthusiastically, *Variety* rated the low-keyed picture "tasteful and sincere," applauding Amy Madigan for her "strong screen debut." Nevertheless, the trade paper noted that, "Sporting a short, greased-back hairdo, Phillips is striking in support, but both her and Bridges's roles remain functional. Phillips starts off as an aggressive rival to Bridges for Madigan's romantic affections, but the script abruptly turns her into just a nice-guy sounding-bound. More bite . . . would have helped the film."

144. The Loved One (Metro-Goldwyn-Mayer, 1965), 116 min. Not rated.

Executive producer, Martin Ransohoff; producers, John Calley, Haskell Wexler; associate producer, Neil Hartley; director, Tony Richardson; based on the novel by Evelyn Waugh; screenplay, Terry Southern, Christopher Isherwood; production designer, Rouben Ter-Arutunian; art director, Sydney Z. Litwack; set decorator, James Payne; costumes, Ter-Arutunian; makeup, Fmile LaVigne, Bunny Armstrong; music/music conductor, John Addison; assistant directors, Kurt Neumann, Les Gorall; sound, Robert Post; special effects, Geza Gaspar; camera, Wexler; supervising editor, Anthony Gibbs; editors, Brian Smedley-Aston, Hal Ashly.

Cast: Robert Morse (Dennis Barlow); Jonathan Winters (Wilbur Glenworthy/Harry Glenworthy); Anjanette Comer (Aimee Thanatogenos); Rod Steiger (Mr. Joyboy); Dana Andrews (General Brinkman); Milton Berle (Mr. Kenton); James Coburn (Immigration Officer); John Gielgud (Sir Francis Hinsley); Tab Hunter (Guide); Margaret Leighton (Mrs. Kenton); Liberace (Mr. Starker); Roddy McDowall (D. J. Jr.); Robert Morley (Sir Ambrose Abercrombie); Lionel Stander (Guru Brahmin); Ayllene Gibbons (Joyboy's Mother); Bernie Kopell (Assistant to Guru Brahmin); Asa Maynor (Secretary to D. J. Jr.); Alan Napier (English Club Official); Martin Ransohoff (Lorenzo Medici); Roxanne Arlen, Pamela Curran, Claire Kelly (Whispering Glades Hostesses); John Bleifer (Mr. Bogaloff); Bella

Bruck (Mrs. Bogaloff); Ed Reimers (Whispering Glades Minister); Paul H. Williams (Gunther Fry); "Miss Beverly Hills" (Orgy Dancer) Chick Hearn ("Resurrection Now" TV Announcer); and: Brad Moore, Dort Clark, Robert Easton, Don Haggerty, Warren Kemmerling, Reta Shaw, Barik Trone.

"What's funny about *The Loved One* (and although it's a bad movie, it is funny) is that just about everybody in it seems to be playing satyrs or sissies or faggots." (Pauline Kael, *The New Yorker*)

Ater a 1947 visit to Hollywood, English novelist Evelyn Waugh wrote *The Loved One* (1948), a biting short satire of tinseltown, its British film colony and the excessiveness of its local cemetery (Forest Lawn Memorial Parks). It took many years before Hollywood made a movie of this dubious subject matter. The results were flat and flabby, primarily because of the lifestyle that Waugh had caricatured had long vanished. In a cast that ranged (!) from John Gielgud to Tab Hunter, two stock comedy performances stood out: Liberace as a flamboyant gay casket salesman and Rod Steiger as the overly-fastidious Mr. Joyboy, obsessed with his gluttonous, gargantuan mother (Ayllene Gibbons).

Shortly after untalented British poet Dennis Barlow (Robert Morse) comes to Hollywood to stay with his uncle (John Gielgud), the latter, a studio art director, commits suicide when he is fired from the Megalopolitan film studios. Pompous Sir Ambrose Abercrombie (Robert Morley) requests young Barlow to coordinate the funeral service at Whispering Glades Memorial Park, Hollywood's most exclusive burial faciity. Before long, Dennis is employed by the Park at the sister cemetery for pets and falls in love with Park cosmetologist, Aimee Thanatogenos (Anjanette Comer). Aimee is also pursued by Mr. Joyboy (Rod Steiger), the head embalmer. She rejects both men and kills herself when the Reverend Glenworthy (Jonathan Winters) makes lewd advances to her. Her body is launched into the "celestial seren-

John Gielgud and Robert Morse in *The Loved One* (1965).

ity" of outer space as part of Glenworthy's complex scheme to eliminate the cemetery's buried caskets and convert the Park's expensive real estate into a senior citizen complex. A disillusioned Dennis returns to England.

Bosley Crowther (*New York Times*) reacted very negatively to this irreverent comedy: "What is offensive about it— what is hideous and gross—is the violent, undisciplined excessiveness of its morbid ribaldry. . . . Further intelligence is offended when the initial joke wears thin. . . ." *Variety* admitted, "Most of the subtlety of Waugh's approach is lost in an episodic screenplay . . . given often to sight gags." The trade paper reported of the cast: "Rod Steiger clothes his mortican part with oddball chracteristics: when he thinks femme [Anjanette Comer] loves him, he prepares bodies—

Loved Ones—with a smile on their face for her to make up; when her affections wane, their countenances are fierce. . . . A slick bit of casting has Liberace deserting his smile and sequined tails for the somber role of casket salesman, which he fulfills with a flair." A disenchanted Pauline Kael (*The New Yorker*) added, "There is something else offensive: the complacent assumption that things badly done are brilliant just because they may give offense. They give offense because they're badly done."

Touted as the motion picture with "something to offend everyone," *The Loved One*, shot in black-and-white, was a box-office dud. Among the many scripters who worked on this project at one time or another were Elaine May and Luis Bunuel. Location scenes were shot at Los Angeles' Greystone Mansion.

145. **Lust for Freedom** (Troma, Inc, 1988), color, 91 min. R-rated.

Executive producers, Lloyd Kaufman Jr., Michael Herz; producer, Eric Louzil; co-producer, Laurel A. Koernig; associate producers, William J. Kulzer, Riley Carsey; director, Louzil; screenplay, Craig Kusaba, Duke Howard, Louzil; art director, Riley Carsey; makeup, Wendi Tolkin; music, John Massari; assistant director, Rob Rosen; stunt coordinator, Kulzer; sound, Ann Krupa; camera, Ron Chapman; second unit camera, John Sprung; editor, Jay Kessel.

Cast: Melanie Coll (Gillian Cates); William J. Kulzer (Sheriff Coale); Judi Trevor (Ms. Pusker); Howard Knight (Warden Maxwell); Elizabeth Carlisle (Vicky); Deana Booher (Big Eddie); John Tallman (Jud); Rob Rosen (Peter Andrews); Shea Porter (Scruggs); Donna Lederer (Donna); Rick Crew (J.T.); Elizabeth Carroll (Sharon Clarke); Lon Stickel (Warren Clarke); Joan Tinei (Evelyn Clarke); Raymond Oceans (Petey); Dana Palmer (Susan Williams); Richard Vega (Bill Collins); Amy Lyndon (Mary Robinson); Lisa Stagno (Lynn); Michelle Bauer (Jackie); Denise Webb (Sally Hill); Adrian Scott (Karen); George J. Engelson (Doc Bass); Karl Anthony Smith (Cody Joe Dobson); Jan Washburn, Marc Christopher (Undercover Detectives); Terri Beck (Holly); Sam Crespi (Sam Potter); John Martin (Ron Peterson); Nick Kranovich (Cemetery Caretaker); Nealie Gerard (Waitress); Martha Garcia, Beverly Urman, Precious (Female Guards); Brian Scavo, Riley Carsey, Jim Cooper, Chuck Koernig (Male Guards).

The R-rated *Lust for Freedom* proved that filmmakers had learned little from *Caged* (1950), *Women's Prison* (1955), qq.v., or the myriad of subsequent imitations. This claptrap, part of a recurring trend of direct-to-video filmmaking, was re-edited with tongue-in-cheek from an abortive straightforward narrative (*Georgia County Lock-Up*). Despite its crude satirical thrusts and its exploitive chauvinistic cheesecake and hetero/homosexual behind-bars scenes, the movie is a dull clinker. Michael Wilmington (*Los Angeles Times*) quipped, it "gives us plenty of lust and little freedom . . . It looks as though it cost almost nothing to make. That's a relief."

The film opens with a preachy, self-mocking, narration by Gillian Gates (Melanie Coll), a burned-out ex-policewoman: "this is the story of the terror and torture I and others endured . . . until we finally gained our lust for freedom." Somewhere in Georgia County, California (near the Mexican border), Gillian is picked up by corrupt police working for Sheriff Coale (William J. Kulzer). She is accused of a crime (drug smuggling) she did not commit and sentenced to time behind bars. At the facility, she deals with sleazy Warden Knight (Howard Knight), who sits in his office in his underwear salivating over the shapely women prisoners and then sells their services to a lecherous old doctor (George J. Engelson) who makes porno movies. There is also the butch head matron, Ms. Pusker (Judi Trevor), who advise: "You're mine while you're in here. Do I make myself perfectly clear! All mine!" Several rapes, beatings, misjustices later—from a variety of villains (including heavy-footed female guards)— Gillian and others incite a riot and break out of the compound. Gillian has learned "there are times when we must all fight for what is ours. No one would ever have to suffer again if I could help it."

V. A. Musetto (*New York Post*) despised *Lust for Freedom* for being "badly dubbed, badly written and badly filmed" and for being "sexist, mean spirited and degrading to women." *Variety*, dismissed this "sexploitation mishmash" in which "Premise is simply an excuse for softcore sex scenes, ranging from 1960s soft porn-style whipping scenes and rape to a sensual lesbo coupling featuring familiar sex stars Crystal Breeze and Michelle Bauer."

146. **Mahogany** (Paramount, 1975), color, 109 min. PG-rated.

Producers, Rob Cohen, Jack Ballard; associate producer, Neil Hartley; director, Berry Gordy; story, Toni Amber; screenplay, John Byrum; art directors, Leon Erickson, Aurelio Crugnola; set decorators, James Ryan, Franco Fumagalli; costumes, Diana Ross; makeup, Wally Schwartz, Franco Corridon; music, Michael Masser; additional music, Gil Askey; song, Masser and Gerry Goffin; choreographer, Jho Jhenkins; assistant directors, Andrew Grieve, Robert Dahlin, Piero Amati; sound, Don Matthews; montage, Jack Cole; camera, David Watkin; editor, Peter Zinner.

Cast: Diana Ross (Mahogany [Tracy Chambers]); Billy Dee Williams (Brian Walker); Anthony Perkins (Sean McAvoy); Jean-Pierre Aumont (Cristiano Rosetti); Beah Richards (Florence); Nina Foch (Miss Evans); Marisa Mell (Carlotta Gavin); Lenard Norris (Wil); Ira Rogers (Stalker); Kristine Cameron (Instructress); Ted Liss (Sweatshop Foreman); Marvin Corman (Cab Driver); E. Rodney Jones (Radio Announcer); Daniel Daniele (Guiseppe); Princess Galitzine (Herself); Jacques Stany (Auctioneer) Bruce Vilanch, Don Howard, Albert Rosenberg (Designers); Roger Bill Brown, Michael Colton, C. Mitchell (Ad Agency Executives).

Three years after her stunning performance in *Lady Sings the Blues,* Diana Ross returned to the screen in *Mahogany*, a vanity production directed by her Motown Records mentor, Berry Gordy (who replaced director Tony Richardson) from a script by John Byrum (after discarding the version by Broadway composer/lyricist, Bob Merrill). To play her three contrasting suitors in this sudsy drama, Ross used Billy Dee Williams (her *Lady Sings the Blues* co-star), continental Frenchman Jean-Pierre Aumont, and Tony Perkins. Since *Psycho* (1960), the latter specialized in playing lip-quivering neurotics and disturbed gays (e.g. *Play It as It Lays,* 1972, q.v.). Perkins's bizarre, androgynous character in *Mahogany* is the quirky man who insists, "I refuse to let a really good obsession slip through my fingers."

In Chicago, Tracy Chambers (Diana Ross), lives in the tenements and works as a department store secretary. Although she falls in love with Windy City politician Brian Walker (Billy Dee Williams), a dedicated liberal, she sacrifices their romance to pursue her modeling career with international fashion photographer Sean McAvoy (Tony Perkins) in Rome. Renamed Mahogany, she becomes an indus-

try hit in Europe, which upsets the manically possessive Sean. Meanwhile, Tracy finds compassion with well-to-do Cristiano Rosetti (Jean-Pierre Aumont) and is briefly reunited with Brian, who comes to Rome after losing his election bid. Triggered by Tracy's insistence on independence, Sean attempts to kill himself and Tracy in his sports car. He dies in the crash, while she is badly injured. While Tracy recuperates at Rosetti's villa outside of Rome, Cristiano organizes a fashion show to showcase her new designs. It is a huge success, but she chooses to return to Chicago and to the poor but honest Brian, now running for Congressman.

Vincent Canby (*New York Times*) scoffed, "*Mahogany* is silly fiction—it's ridiculous—but it's been directed with undeniable energy and canniness. . . ." Canby acknowledged Ross's pleasing display of "a furious gutsiness and a ribald humor," and the asset of Tony Perkins "as the more than slightly bent photographer, a role that begins as a cliche but becomes increasingly idiosyncratic before it winds up as a cliche again. Mr. Perkins's strength as an actor helps to give shape to Miss Ross's performance." *Variety* rated this "contrived personality vehicle" a "mediocrity" which is "often unintentionally funny." For Geoff Brown (British *Monthly Film Bulletin*), "the badness of *Mahogany* is overwhelming. . . . Once the action shifts to Rome, the level of silliness rises steadily, with Anthony Perkins' fashion photographer parading his madness with a great deal of twitching. . . ."

On the strength of Diana Ross's popularity, the expensively-mounted turkey grossed $6,917,776 in distributors' domestic film rentals. The film received an Oscar nomination for its hit theme song, "Do You Know Where You're Going To?" but "I'm Easy" from *Nashville* won.

In *Mahogany*, Hollywood once again glossed over another gay character, afraid and/or indifferent to dealing with the "type" in a forthright manner. The quirkiness of Tony Perkins's characterization

Diana Ross in *Mahogany* (1975).

was buried within the conceit that an important creative artist such as Sean the photographer could/would/should be bitchily temperamental, too "busy" for dalliances with women, favor effeminate companions such as Giuseppe (Daniel Daniele), and know more about how a woman should dress and act than any living female. How much more dimensional the Sean character would have been if the film had "dared" to be direct.

147. Making Love (Twentieth Century-Fox, 1982), color, 113 min. R-rated.

Producers, Allen Alder, Daniel Melnick; associate producers, Barry Sandler, Dorothy Wilde; director, Arthur Hiller; story, A. Scott Berg; screenplay, Sandler; production designer, James D. Vance; set decorator, Rick Simpson; costumes, Bruce Walkup, Betsy Cox; makeup, Del Armstrong, Fred Blau Jr.; music, Leonard Rosenman; assistant directors, Jack Roe, John Kretchmer; sound, Maury Harris; camera, David M. Walsh; editor, William H. Reynolds.

Cast: Michael Ontkean (Zack); Kate Jackson (Claire); Harry Hamlin (Bart McGuire); Wendy Hiller (Winnie Bates); Arthur Hill (Henry); Nancy Olson (Christine); John Dukakis (Tim); Terry Kiser (Harrington); Dennis Howard (Larry); Asher Brauner (Ted); John Calvin (David); Gwen Arner (Arlene); Gary Swanson (Ken); Ann Harvey (Lila); Stanley Kamel (Charlie); Chip Lucia (Chip); Doug Johnson (Doug); Ben Mittleman (Ben); Mickey Jones (Cowboy Musician); Joe Medalis (Announcer); Erica Hiller (Lucie); Michael Shannon (Marty); Arthur Taxier (Don); Phoebe Dorin (Jenny); Mark Schubb (Josh); Carol King (Pam); Camilla Carr (Susan); Lili Haydn (Little Sister); Paul Sanderson (Bill); David Knell (Michael); David Murphy, Michael Dudikoff, John Starr, Charles Zukow, Scott Ryder (Young Men in Bar); Joanne Hicks, Stacey Kuhne, Stephanie Segal, Kedren Jones (Wives); Alexander Lockwood (Minister); Andrew Harris (Rupert); Michael Harris, Robert Mikels, Jason Mikels (Twins).

"An honest film about homosexual love is long overdue, but this one has had its mouth scrubbed with soap (or soap opera). Its characters, interestingly and appealingly presented at the outset, ultimately

Michael Ontkean, Kate Jackson and Harry Hamlin in a publicity pose for *Making Love* (1982).

have nowhere to go." (Arthur Knight, *Hollywood Reporter*)

At the time of production, *Making Love* was heralded as THE major studio Hollywood feature that would legitimize homosexuality as proper subject matter for mainstream features. It would take up where the British-made *Sunday, Bloody Sunday* (1971) had left off. It would accomplish what *A Different Story* (1978), q.v., did not, namely, present gay love not for ridicule or exploitation but as an alternative life style involving real and believable people. Instead, *Making Love* was a dullish soap opera full of diluted heterosexual premises, prejudices and role models. Viewed today in the perspective of the intervening AIDS crisis, *Making Love* seems even more puerile, as well as tedious in its exposition of its plot.

In Los Angeles, successful Dr. Zack (Michael Ontkean) and his TV executive wife, Claire (Kate Jackson) seem to be a contented young married couple. Re-luctantly, they leave their rented house and their landlady/friend, Winnie Bates (Wendy Hiller), to buy their own place. When Zack becomes increasingly inattentive to her, Claire attributes his manner to professional pressures. Actually, his perplexity about his growing gay sexual drive is repeatedly drawing him to the gay ghetto of West Hollywood, although he is too timid to experiment. When Bart (Harry Hamlin), a self-acknowledged gay writer, comes to Zack as a patient, he is intrigued with the attractive physician and eventually maneuvers him into bed. Having now expressed his gay feelings and "come out," Zack wants immediate commitment from Bart, while the latter finds emotional safety in one-night stands. This conflict leads to their breaking off their budding relationship.

Meanwhile, Claire, baffled by her disintegrating marriage, accepts a promotion with the TV network and temporary assignment in New York City. When she returns, Zack tells her the truth. At first shocked ("What are you telling me? That our whole marriage has been a lie?"), then full of self-guilt, Claire hopes therapy can cure Zack. Finally, she accepts his sexual choice and lets him go. Some years later, Zack, living with a lover in New York City, returns to Los Angeles for Winnie's funeral. After the service, Zack visits briefly with Claire and meets her husband (Dennis Howard) and their child (Andrew Harris).

Sheila Benson (*Los Angeles Times*) asked, "How could *Making Love* offend anyone? It is at such a distance from real life, real people. . . . It seems to have slid off the pages of the women's magazines. . . . How could an entire film built around the subject of homosexuality have not a trace of wit?" Robert Asahina (*New Leader*) criticized, "Gay liberation has turned into gay romanticization. . . . Evidently the film industry now feels free to have homosexuals in love as foolish as their heterosexual counterparts. . . ." Alex Keneas (*Newsday*) noted of this "extremely cautious" film, "Fox reportedly chose [Arthur] Hiller, the director of *Love Story* [1970], because it felt that he would deliver without generating controversy." Andrew Sarris (*Village Voice*) found the movie had "the look of a Los Angeles sitcom" and that "the Ontkean character has been rendered with such deadly solemnity that he makes both heterosexual and homosexual relationships seem singularly joyless."

As expected, *Making Love* was lurid in depicting transitory gay sex (quick pickups in back alleys, etc.), self-conscious in scenes of West Hollywood gay bars, and chaste in the scenes dealing with Zack and Bart's love-making (hugging, a few brief kisses, waking up in bed together). *Making Love*'s Zack emerges as an unfocused person (is he a confused heterosexual, an inexperienced bisexual or a naive homosexual or none of the above?). The depiction of Bart's character is done in pure stereotypical fashion: he is presented as a

pouty creative soul who loves old movies, is narcissistic, bodybuilds endlessly and is incapable of enduring relationships. Oh yes, he is super handsome. If anything conveys the underlying majority-view message of *Making Love*, it is the film's closing shot revealing heterosexual Claire and her family returning to the safety of their comfortable, "normal" upper middle class home, while Zack, the homosexual loner/outsider, drives off ALONE down the road. So much for the movie's objective point of view.

Worried how moviegoers would react to its "daring" subject matter, the movie was promoted with a let-me-have-cake-and-eat-it philosophy: "*Making Love* . . . is a love story that deals sensitively and candidly with a timely issue that audiences will want to discuss. . . . *Making Love* is bold but gentle. We are proud of its honesty." Before word of mouth—for being dull and a cheat—killed the box-office take, *Making Love* grossed $6,100,000 in distributors' domestic film rentals. Originally, Tom Berenger was to have played the Michael Ontkean role.

148. The Maltese Falcon (Warner Bros., 1941), 100 min. Not rated.

Producers, Hal B. Wallis, Henry Blanke; director, John Huston, based on the novel by Dashiell Hammett; screenplay, Huston; art director, Robert Haas; costumes, Orry-Kelly; makeup, Perc Westmore; music, Adolph Deutsch; assistant director, Claude Archer; sound, Oliver S. Garretson; camera, Arthur Edeson; editor, Thomas Richards.

Cast: Humphrey Bogart (Sam Spade); Mary Astor (Brigid O'Shaughnessy); Gladys George (Iva Archer); Peter Lorre (Joel Cairo); Barton MacLane (Detective Lieutenant Dundy); Lee Patrick (Effie Perine); Sydney Greenstreet (Kasper Gutman); Ward Bond (Detective Tom Polhaus); Jerome Cowan (Miles Archer); Elisha Cook Jr. (Wilmer Cook); James Burke (Luke); Murray Alper (Frank Richman); John Hamilton (Distirct Attorney Bryan); Walter Huston (Captain Jacobi, the Ship's Officer); Emory Parnell (Mate of the La Paloma); Robert Homas (Policeman); Creighton Hale (Stenographer); Charles Drake, William Hopper, Hank Mann (Reporters); Jack Mower (Announcer).

"The Maltese Falcon is a landmark film not only because it set the style and tone for the hardboiled detective genre but also because it established screen personas for most of its players. . . . The incomparable Peter Lorre is magnificent as the neurotic, fussy . . . effeminate, emotional Joel Cairo." (Danny Peary, *Cult Movies*, 1981)

In Dashiell Hammett's novel, *The Maltese Falcon* (1930), before secretary Effie Perine admits Joel Cairo into the inner sanctum of her boss, Sam Spade, she says, "This guy is queer." In Warner Bros.'s first screen version of Hammett's detective classic, *The Maltese Falcon* (1931), Joel Cairo, as played by Otto Matieson, is coyly introduced to private eye Spade (Ricardo Cortez) as if he is a precious woman, then the notion is dropped. In the 1936 diluted screen revamping, *Satan Met a Lady*, Arthur Treacher played a silly Britisher, Anthony Travers, the plotline equivalent to the Cairo character. However, nothing was made of his sexual orientation.

By 1941, when John Huston directed the third and best screen version of *The Maltese Falcon*, Huston wanted to be more authentic with the Joel Cairo character. There was no problem with depicting in broad strokes the sadistically vicious nature of Cairo, as detailed in Hammett's work. However, to circumvent the industry's production code which forbade portraying overt homosexual characters explicitly on screen, Peter Lorre's Cairo was made into a very fussy creature. He is always worried about getting his clothes mussed or soiled, and his frilly handkerchiefs and personal names cards are heavily scented with gardenias. To insure that the point got across, during the course of this celluloid caper, at one point Lorre's Cairo taunts Mary Astor's manipulative Brigid O'Shaughnessy that her feminine charms will not work on him, and she

kicks back in frustration. She also makes veiled references to a past episode involving Cairo and "that young boy in Istanbul." Astute moviegoers understood the subtext fully.

Soon after San Francisco detective Sam Spade (Humphrey Bogart) and Miles Archer (Jerome Cowan) are hired by the mysterious Brigid O'Shaughnessy (Mary Astor) to locate her vanished younger sister, Archer is killed. Before long, Spade is competing with a ruthless trio—Kasper Gutman (Sydney Greenstreet), Joel Cairo (Peter Lorre) and Wilmer Cook (Elisha Cook Jr.)—for a valuable black bird statue supposed to contain a fortune in gems. After jockeying back and forth for control of the elusive black falcon, it is discovered that the bird in hand is a fake, and that the real one is still in the hands of a Russian general. By now, the seductive Brigid has admitted that she killed Miles, and honor-bound Sam, who is greatly attracted to this deadly woman, turns her over to the police.

Bosley Crowther (*New York Times*) approved of the new version for being "brisk and supremely hard boiled" and noted: "Much of the quality of the picture lies in its excellent revelation of character." The *New York Herald-Tribune* complemented, "The film moves through its various sequences with an electric tension. . . . Peter Lorre is fine as the effeminate scoundrel who follows the 'fat man' around like a dog."

In fleshing out the homosexual villains of Hammett's original, there is also Elisha Cook Jr.'s Wilmer. He is the subservient henchman of the murderous trio, referred to as a gunsel, a slang word which originally meant a passive homosexual partner—a kept boy. The oversized Gutman—marvelously played by Sydney Greenstreet in his movie debut—continually expresses a strong "fondness" for Wilmer whom he regards "like a son." Then too, in his first scenes with Sam Spade, bulbous Kasper cannot keep his hands off the detective's knee.

Humphrey Bogart, Peter Lorre, Mary Astor and Sydney Greenstreet in *The Maltese Falcon* **(1941).**

The classic *The Maltese Falcon* received two Academy Award nominations: Best Picture (*How Green Was My Valley* won); Best Screenplay (*Here Comes Mr. Jordan* won). *The Maltese Falcon* was the movie which launched Humphrey Bogart's screen stardom; it also was the first of several film teamings by Peter Lorre and Sydney Greenstreet.

149. Manhattan (United Artists, 1979), 96 min. R-rated.

Executive producer, Robert Greenhut; producer, Charles H. Joffe; director, Woody Allen; screenplay, Allen, Marshall Brickman; production designer, Mel Bourne; set decorator, Robert Drumheller; costumes, Albert Wolsky, Ralph Lauren; makeup, Fern Buchner; music adaptor/arranger, Tom Pierson; assistant directors, Frederic B. Blankfein, Joan Spiegel Feinstein; sound, James Sabat; camera, Gordon Willis; editor, Susan E. Morse.

Cast: Woody Allen (Isaac Davis); Diane Keaton (Mary Wilke); Michael Murphy (Yale); Mariel Hemingway (Tracy); Meryl Streep (Jill); Anne Byrne (Emily); Karen Ludwig (Connie); Michael O'Donoghue (Dennis); Victor Truro, Tisa Farrow, Helen Hanft (Party Guests); Bella Abzug (Guest of Honor); Gary Weiss (TV Director); Kenny Vance (TV Producer); Charles Levin, Karen Allen, David Rasche (TV Actors); Damion Sheller (Isaac's Son, Willie); Wallace Shawn (Jeremiah); Mark-Linn Baker, Frances Conroy (Shakespearean Actors); Bill Anthony (Porche Owner #1); John Doumanian (Porsche Owner #2); Ray Serra (Pizzeria Waiter).

Seldom has Woody Allen used his neurotic schlemiel persona to better advantage than in his hugely popular *Manhattan*, an optimistic love song to the Big Apple employing George Gershwin's music for its soundtrack. As the archetypal, middle-aged Jewish intellectual, Allen's Isaac Davis is not only self-deprecating about his professional abilities as a TV comedy writer, but he is constantly worried about being bested by anyone and everyone, no matter what the arena: the work place, the cocktail party, the bedroom. Nowhere does his relationship paranoia zoom higher or his male ego crash lower than in dealing with his ex-wife, Jill (Meryl Streep), who prefers a lesbian relationship to living with erratic chauvinist Isaac. "Think of me as a detour on the highway of life," Jill blithely suggests to the uncomprehending man.

Although loving New York life, 42-year-old Isaac Davis (Woody Allen) is full of insecurities, resulting in frequent visits to his various therapists. He feels demeaned by writing TV comedy which he has abandoned to write a novel and he ponders the future with his current girlfriend, seventeen-year old drama student Tracy (Mariel Hemingway). Adding to his woes, Isaac has a unsteady truce with his ex-wife, Jill (Meryl Streep), who is raising their son, Willie (Damion Sheller), while living with another woman, Connie (Karen Ludwig). Davis is furious that Jill is writing a book (*Marriage, Divorce and Selfhood*) about their failed marriage, exposing his foibles to the world. Isaac's best friend is Yale (Michael Murphy), who is being unfaithful to his wife (Anne Byrne) with a divorcee, Mary Wilke (Diane Keaton). At first, Davis is put off by Mary's intellectual posturing, but his attraction to the quirky journalist soon turns compulsive. When Yale and Mary part company, Isaac is there to fill her emotional void, unmindful of the hurt he is causing the adolescent Tracy. Later, Mary realizes she prefers Yale and returns to him. Rejected yet again, Isaac retaliates by badgering Yale over his irresponsible behavior. Then, in a moment of self-discovery, Davis rushes to precocious Tracy, pleading with her to drop plans to study drama in London. However, she has determined that she needs her own emo-

tional space, but asks him asks to wait for her return.

Vincent Canby (*New York Times*) described *Manhattan* as "extraordinarily fine and funny" and the Allen's "most moving and expansive work to date." Canby reported, "The on-screen characters are beautifully played by, among others, Mr. Murphy and Miss Streep." Richard Combs (British *Monthly Film Bulletin*), approving of this comedy satirizing intellectual poseurs, pointed out, "Again Allen proves that he is the closest thing to an American [Ingmar] Bergman by providing splendid opportunities for the actresses who play the three women in Isaac's life: frustratingly brief in the case of Meryl Streep. . . . suffering most from *deja vu* in the case of Diane Keaton . . . and delightfully fresh in the case of Mariel Hemingway. . . ."

Within *Manhattan*, homophobia is merely another wrinkle in the character of the angst-ridden chauvinist, Isaac. It also provides opportunities for "humorous" potshots by Woody Allen at the frailty of a man losing his woman to another woman:

Isaac: I can't understand how you prefer her to me.

Jill: You can't understand? Well you knew my history when you married me.

Isaac: I know. My analyst warned me. But you were so beautiful that I got another analyst.

In his inability to let go, the obsessive Isaac—who in a fit of anger once tried to run Jill down in his car—taunts Jill's patient lover, Connie on every occasion. When his son displays drawing talents and Jill enthuses with motherly pride, Isaac snidely chides Connie, his "male" replacement, with: "But there's no way you could be the actual father." At *Manhattan*'s finale, Jill has the last laugh, for not only is her book showing signs of being a best-seller, but there is talk of turning it into a movie. While Karen Ludwig's cameo as Connie has almost no dialogue, Meryl Streep, then fast-rising to stardom, gives a casual, full-bodied presence to Jill, making her anything but a lesbian caricature.

Manhattan grossed a very sizeable $17,582,659 in distributors' domestic film rentals. The film received two Academy Award nominations: Best Supporting Actress (Mariel Hemingway; Meryl Streep won for *Kramer Vs. Kramer*); Best Screenplay Written Directly for the Screen (*Breaking Away* won).

150. Mannequin (Twentieth Century-Fox, 1987), color, 90 min. PG-rated.

Executive producers, Edward Rugoff, Joseph Farrell; producer, Art Levinson; associate producer, Catherine Paura; director, Michael Gottlieb; screenplay, Rugoff, Gottlieb; production designer, Josan Russo; art director, Richard Amend; set decorator, Elise "Cricket" Rowland; costumes, Lisa Jensen; music, Sylvester LeVay; choreographer, Vincent Paterson; assistant directors, Michael Haley, James Skotchdopole, Carla Corwin; sound, Jan Brodin; special effects, Phil Cory, Hans Metz, Ray Svedin; animation sequence, Sally Cruikshank; camera, Tim Suhrstedt; editor, Richard Lasey; additional editor, Frank Jiminez.

Cast: Andrew McCarthy (Jonathan Switcher); Kim Cattrall (Emmy); Estelle Getty (Claire Timkin); James Spader (Richards); G. W. Bailey (Felix); Carole Davis (Roxie); Stephen Vinovich (B. J. West); Christopher Maher (Armand); Meshach Taylor (Hollywood Montrose); Phyllis Newman (Emmy's Mother); Phil Rubenstein (Mannequin Factory Boss); Jeffery Lampert (Factory Worker); Kenneth Lloyd (Superdad); Jake Jundeff (Superkid); Harvey Levine (Balloon Boss); Thomas J. McCarthy (Head Gardener); R. L. Ryan (Pizzeria Manager); Glen Davish (Effete Executive); Steve Lippe (Male Sales Clerk); Lee Golden (Wino); Vernon R. DeVinney (Older Man in Boardroom); Olivia Frances Williams (Woman in Boardroom); Charles N. Lord (Man in Boardroom); Ben Hammer (Hans, Maitre d'); Jane Moore (Tina); Jane Carol Simms (Lupe); Judi Goldhand (Mrs Thomas); Lara Harris (Mannequin in Photo Window); Dan Lounsberry, Kitty Minehart (Senior Citizens); Katherine Conklin (West's Secretary); Andrew Hill Newman (Compactor Room Janitor); Bill Greene (Police Officer).

See summary under **Mannequin Two: On the Move.**

151. Mannequin Two: On the Move (Twentieth Century-Fox, 1991), color, 95 min. PG-rated.

Executive producer, John Foreman; producer, Edward Rugoff; co-producer, Malcolm R. Harding; associate producer, Kate Bales; director, Stewart Raffill; based on characters created by Rugoff, Michael Gottlieb; screenplay, Rugoff, David Isaacs, Ken Levine, Betty Israel; art director, Norman B. Dodge Jr.; set decorator, Scott Jacobson; costumes, Ernest Misko; makeup, David Craig Forrest; music, David McHugh; assistant directors, Roger La Page, Bruce Greenfield, Betsy Schrott, Steven Kossover; stunt co-ordinator, Gary Jensen; sound, Glenn Berkovitz, Morteza Rezvani, Thomas Brandau, Lawrence Hoff; special visual effects, Max W. Anderson; camera, Larry Pizer; editor, Joan Chapman.

Cast: Kristy Swanson (Jessie); William Ragsdale (Jason Wiliamson/Prince William); Meshach Taylor (Hollywood Montrose/Doorman); Terry Kiser (Count Spretzie/Sorcerer); Stuart Pankin (Mr. James); Cynthia Harris (Mom/Queen); Andrew Hill Newman (Andy Ackerman); Julie Foreman (Gail); John Edmondson (Rolf/Soldier); Phil Latella (Egon/Soldier); Mark Gray (Arnold/Soldier); Eric Weiss, Jackye Roberts (Mr. James's Assistants); John Casino (Horned Soldier); Laurie Wing (Old Queen); Julie Warder (Beauty Technician); G. James Reed (Furniture Salesman); Joanne Bradley, Christine Baur (Garbage Women); Alleton Ruggiero (Employee); Heather Henderson (Lipstick Girl); Sherry Wallen (Dress Saleswoman); Thom Christopher Warren (Albert); Wendy Worthington (Tour Guide); Jim Mital (Grip); Daphne Lynn Stacey (Cafe Waitress); Eva Andell (Jessie's Sister); Dana Dewes, Celeste Russi (Southside Girls); Chris Giannin (Cool Guy); Coco (Lead Dancer); Michael Stermel, Jerry Lyden, John Richman, Rocky Cathcart (Cops); Matt Meyers (Officer Al); Cliff McMullen (Mannequin Cop).

There was nothing fresh about the labored comic premise of *Mannequin* in which an inanimate store display figure comes beautifully to life. It had been used to far better effect in such films as *One Touch of Venus* (1948). What was ironic about *Mannequin* was that it pushed actor Meshach Taylor into the caricature role of a super-stereotypical swishy window

Advertisement for *Mannequin* (1987).

dresser. It was just the kind of flamboyance so carefully avoided in his masculine role as partner/confidant to several female interior decorators in the hit TV sitcom "Designing Women" (1986–93).

In 25 B.C. Egypt, Emmy (Kim Cattrall) refuses to marry a lowly camel manure dealer. Praying for divine help, she makes a quantum leap to present-day Philadelphia where her spirit inhabits a newly-assembled mannequin. The display form is delivered to Prince & Co. Department Store, where would-be sculptor Jonathan

Switcher (Andrew McCarthy) has just been given a job for saving the life of its owner, Claire Timkin (Estelle Getty). Once there, Jonathan becomes pals with window dresser Hollywood Montrose (Meshach Taylor), a flaming queen and finds himself in competition with smarmy store executive Richards (James Spader), who, in turn, is in cahoots with rival store owner B. J. Wert (Stephen Vinovich). Jonathan also runs afoul of blundering night watchman Felix (G. W. Bailey), and, most interesting of all for him, he discovers that, in the privacy of the store after closing time, one of the female mannequins comes charmingly to life as Emmy. By the finale, Prince & Co. has been saved from corporate take-over, the villains have been ousted, and, best of all, Emmy remains humanly alive. She and Jonathan marry in the department store window.

Roger Ebert (*New York Post*) assessed the film: "It's dead. I don't mean it's bad. A lot of bad movies are fairly throbbing with life. *Mannequin* is dead. . . . The supporting characters have been recycled out of failed sitcoms." For Mike McGrady (*Newsday*), *Mannequin* is pure drivel, but at least it's drivel that keeps kids off the streets." Janet Maslin (*New York Times*) rated the comedy "a state-of-the art showcase of perfunctory technique. . . . Several of those stock characters play upon racial and sexual stereotypes, and a few are drawn along obnoxiously homophobic lines . . . The Cadillac-driving figure is at least played with some energy by . . . Meshach Taylor. . . ."

The makers of *Mannequin* left *no* cliche unturned in devising Meshach Taylor's role, which comes across like a hyper frenetic Arsenio Hall in drag. Hollywood Montrose drives a pink Cadillac whose license plate reads "BAD GIRL." Dressed garishly in lavender, heavy jewelry, lots of makeup and sporting outre sunglasses, he gestures excessively, prances around, laughs wildly and talks in nonstop, self-mocking foolishness: "Albert left me. He said my thighs are too fat. Albert calls me cellulite city. It's those jelly donuts—they call me in the middle of the night."

To everyone's amazement, *Mannequin* grossed a whopping $18 million in distributors' domestic film rentals, proving a favorite among the teen set. It led inevitably to *Mannequin Two: On the Move*. Of the original cast, only scene-stealing Meshach Taylor returned. Better he should have stood at home. In the follow-up (not really a sequel), Jason Williamson (William Ragsdale) works at Philadelphia's Prince & Co. where Hollywood Montrose

(Meshach Taylor) is head of the window display department. When the store houses an exhibition of the riches of the medieval Bavarian kingdom of Hauptmann-Koenig, one of the stone statues comes to life as peasant girl Jessie (Kristy Swanson). Before long, Jason and his friends combat the grasping Count Spretzle (Terry Kiser), a descendant of the sorcerer who placed a curse on Jessie to prevent her from marrying another man. After many misadventures, including rescuing the abducted Jessie from a hot air balloon, Jason and his enchanted dream girl are reunited.

A turned-off Arion Berger (*LA Weekly*) complained of *Mannequin Two*: "It's one thing to introduce an evil count so ugly people gag when they look at him; it's entirely another to have Meshach Taylor as a mincing, simpering, outrageously dressed black gay choreographer . . ." Kevin Thomas (*Los Angeles Times*) concluded, "From start to finish *Mannequin Two: On the Move* (rated PG for some mild sexual innuendo) is insipid in the extreme." Henry Sheehan (*Hollywood Reporter*) branded this a "Tinny comedy pounded flat" and noted that, "Taylor gives forth with every gay designer cliche ever imagined, clearly trading on Middle America's stereotypes, but on the other hand, his character is also courageous and ingenious at key moments."

The abysmal *Mannequin Two* grossed only $1,850,000 in distributors' domestic film rentals, proving that some people have taste some of the time.

152. Marilyn: The Untold Story

(ABC-TV, September 28, 1980), color, 150 min. Not rated.

Producer, Lawrence Schiller; directors, John Flynn, Jack Arnold, Schiller; based on the book *Marilyn* by Norman Mailer and other sources; teleplay, Dalene Young; art directors, Jan Scott, Sidney Z. Litwack; set decorator, William Harp; makeup, Allen Snyder; music, William Goldstein; choreographer, Alex Romero; assistant directors, Gary M. La Poten, Debra Michaelson; sound, Don E. Parker; camera, Terry

K. Meade, Sol Negrin, Jim Phalen; editors, Jack Gleason, Patrick T. Roark.

Cast: Catherine Hicks (Marilyn Monroe); Richard Basehart (Johnny Hyde); Frank Converse (Joe DiMaggio); John Ireland (John Huston); Viveca Lindfors (Natasha Lytess); Jason Miller (Arthur Miller); Sheree North (Gladys Baker); Kevin Geer (Jim Dougherty); Tracey Gold (Young Norma Jean); Priscilla Morrill (Louella Parsons); John Christy Ewing (Lawyer); Bill Vint (Montgomery Clift); Larry Pennell (Clark Gable); Heath Jobes (Tom Ewell); Howard Caine (Billy Wilder); Brad Blaisdell (Jack Lemmon); Anthony Gordon (Laurence Olivier); Bruce Neckels (Tony Curtis); Anne Ramsey (Maid); and: Michael Fairman, J. P. Bumstead, Carole Tru Foster, Paul Larson, John Steadman, Janus Blythe, Sima Conrad, E. Brian Dean, Jim Greenleaf, James Hayden, Mae Marmy, Jessamine Milner, John Moskoff, Frank Pesce, Alex Romero, Lance Rosen, George Skaff, Cicely Wolper.

Of the several actresses who have played Marilyn Monroe (1926–1962) on screen, Catherine Hicks offered one of the most finely etched characterizations of the legendary sex symbol in *Marilyn: The Untold Story*. Hicks makes her role rise above a mere cardboard impersonation. In this lengthy, selective TV movie chronicle, one of the many people to have helped the icon on her path to stardom is drama coach Natasha Lytess, who, in real life, died two years after Marilyn. In the overall scope of this screen narrative, Natasha is seen only peripherally, with not much time or consideration given to her fleeting appearances. However, wanting to suggest the stronger-than-teacher relationship between the two women, the filmmakers cast Viveca Lindfors as the drama coach. Already, Lindfors had played lesbians in a succession of movies: *No Exit* (1962), *Sylvia* (1965), *Puzzle of a Downfall Child* (1970), qq.v., etc. Her mere presence in *Marilyn: The Untold Story* provided an easy, intended inference, even for those viewers who had little or no background information on Monroe's actual off-camera life.

In June 1962, screen star Marilyn Monroe (Catherine Hicks) has been fired from her latest movie, *Something's Gotta Give*. Alone in her house, except for her housekeeper (Anne Ramsey), and high on a mixture of champagne and pills, she thinks back on her troubled life. As a child in Los Angeles, when her mother (Sheree North) is committed to a mental asylum, she is raised in an orphanage and, later, various foster homes. Her teen-age marriage to Jim Dougherty (Kevin Geer) during World War II fails. Later, she is spotted by a photographer and begins modeling, including her infamous nude calendar posing. This work leads to tiny parts in movies, and Norma Jean—now Marilyn Monroe—takes acting lessons from the intense, possessive Natasha Lytess (Viveca Lindfors). Through the much older Johnny Hyde (Richard Basehart), a Hollywood talent agency executive, Marilyn wins a studio contract at Twentieth Century-Fox. After Hyde's death, she marries baseball star Joe DiMaggio (Frank Converse), a union doomed by their conflicting careers.

Wanting to become more than a sex symbol, Marilyn the star rebelliously leaves Hollywood to study acting at the Actors' Studio in Manhattan. There she meets famed playwright Arthur Miller (Jason Miller), who becomes her mentor and husband. Meanwhile, Natasha tries to reactivate her hold over Monroe, but the latter rejects her. After the failed movie *The Misfits* (1961), Marilyn and Miller end their relationship. Monroe has a nervous breakdown and, upon recovering, starts her new picture. Fired from the production for her tardiness, etc., she dies from an overdose of sleeping pills.

Steve Jenkins (British *Monthly Film Bulletin*) pointed out, "Its title notwithstanding, this . . . is very much Marilyn the oft-told story, a succession of familiar biographical incidents and events plus a dash of one-dimensional psychologizing. . . . While certain sections of Marilyn's life are conjured then dismissed . . . those granted more screen time hardly gain in resonance. In particular, the relationships with Natasha Lytess and Arthur Miller . . . remain unanalyzed and hopelessly cliched."

Marilyn: The Untold Story, which boasts three credited directors received Emmy nominations for Outstanding Actress (Catherine Hicks); Cinematography, Art Direction and Makeup. Just as new evidence continues to crop up about the tortured life and mystery-shrouded death of Marilyn, so there is a steady stream of (auto)biographies about those who knew or claimed to have known the "real" Monroe. One of the more interesting documents to surface in recent years were notes taken from an interview with Natasha Lytess in 1963 in which she claimed Monroe was *"mio amore*—my love." In retrospect, this reference gives added credibility to the quick brush stroke performance of Viveca Lindfors in *Marilyn: The Untold Story*.

153. Mass Appeal (Universal, 1984), color, 100 min. PG-rated.

Executive producer, Joan B. Kroc; producers, Lawrence Turman, David Foster; director, Glenn Jordan; based on the play by Bill C. Davis; screenplay, Davis; production designer, Philip Jefferies; set designer, Don Woodruff; set decorator, Robert Checchi; costumes, Shari Feldman, Bruce Walkup; makeup, Richard Blair; music, Bill Conti; assistant directors, James S. Simons, Debra Michaelson, Paul Rose, Paul Magwood; sound, Barry Thomas; Steve Maslow; camera, Don Peterman; editor, John Wright.

Cast: Jack Lemmon (Father Farley); Zeljko Ivanek (Mark Dolson); Charles Durning (Monsignor Burke); Louise Latham (Margaret); Alice Hirson (Mrs. Hart); Helene Heigh (Mrs. Hart's Mother); Sharee Gregory (Marion Hart); James Ray (Father De Nicola); Lois De Banzie (Mrs. Dolson); Talia Balsam (Liz Dolson); Jerry Hardin (Mr. Dolson); R. J. Williams (Boy); Noni White (Mother); Gloria Stuart (Mrs. Curry); Maggie Gwinn (Mrs. Quinn); F. William Parker (Mr. Hartigan); John Vargas (Scott Alvarez); Frank Robinson (Robin); Richard Doyle (Faculty Member); Terry Wills (Bill Kelly); Suzanne Kent (Mickey Kelly); Christopher Carroll (Salvatore Fitzgerald); John Devlin (Choir Leader); Ann Nelson (Miss Barber); John C. Becher (Mr. Jennings).

On the New York stage in 1980, *Mass Appeal* had been a two-character, two-act drama. For its screen version, the action was opened up, but, at heart, it remained a sometimes witty, if too contrived, study of a glib Catholic priest coming to terms with his smug religious beliefs when challenged by an idealistic, young seminarian. The latter, much to the dismay of several forces in the diocese, admits to having had an unorthodox background, including having experimented with both heterosexual and homosexual lovemaking.

Dedicated Catholic theology student Mark Dolson (Zeljko Ivanek) has unconventional views on his Church (i.e. women priest, etc.), which are at odds with those of pompous Monsignor Burke (Charles Durning), who heads the seminary. Meanwhile, Mark challenges Father Farley (Jack Lemmon), a well-liked but very casual, materialistic priest, during one of his "safe" joke-session sermons to his complacent parishioners. Later, when Mark protests Burke's ruling that two students are to be expelled for having expressed their "unnatural" love for each other, Farley comes to his rescue with hard-headed Burke. As such, Burke finds poetic justice in allowing Dolson a reprieve, by turning this troublemaker over to the liberal Farley to make him toe the mark.

During his first sermon at Farley's church, the brash Mark offends the upper middle class congregation with his tirade against the hypocritical rich. Monitoring the repercussions, Burke compiles evidence about Mark's suspect pre-seminary wild lifestyle when he was traveling abroad. Now convinced more than ever that Mark would make a good priest, Farley fights to prevent Dolson's expulsion from the Church. However, part of him fears bringing about his own downfall and his appeal is perfunctory. As the badly-disappointed Dolson prepares to leave the Church, he and Farley have an intense

Jack Lemmon and Zeljko Ivanek in *Mass Appeal* (1984).

confrontation. During their talk, Mark insists he cannot lie and sacrifice his principals. Sparked by the truths of Mark's arguments, the heavy-drinking priest embarks on a last-minute battle to help Dolson.

Michael Buckley (*Films in Review*) was in the minority when he rated *Mass Appeal* "One of the year's best pictures." In contrast, Michael Wilmington (*Los Angeles Times*) voted thumbs down on this movie adaptation: "As a saga of the struggle between spiritual idealism and the old theological soft-shoe, its heart is set too firmly on religious razzmatazz, the socko curtain line, on knocking 'em dead in the back pews." As to the cast, Wilmington decided: "These actors obviously relish the bite and sass of Davis' lines. . . ." Leo Seligsohn (*Newsday*) thought Jack Lemmon "lacks the range and resonance to make him believable . . ." Jack Kroll (*Newsweek*) also weighed that Lemmon was wrong for the role and that "even more strangely, that splendid young actor Zeljko Ivanek . . . fails to make young Mark Dolson an attractive embodiment of

impractical but indispensable idealism. Some of the fault lies with director Glenn Jordan, who makes *Mass Appeal* seem like a pilot for an unlikely TV series, 'Farley's Angels.'"

During the course of their verbal sparring throughout *Mass Appeal* there is the inevitable moment when Farley must learn the truth of the charges that Mark once had gay sexual experiences. While the interrogation is serious, the dialogue overly cute. The embarrassed Farley and the usually straight-forward Dolson talk in euphemistic terms about "staying down on the farm" (being sexual "normal" or even chaste) and "not seeing Paree" (experimenting in wild sex). Farley asks Mark "Have you ever seen Paree? And if you have seen Paree, were they Parisian-etes or Parisians?" Having come this far, the movie cheats by stepping back from the brink, with Dolson admitting that having once tried physical love of both sorts, he has abandoned that in favor of devoting himself to helping others. This scene led Vito Russo (*The Celluloid Closet*, 1987) to insist, "Fradulent claptrap posing as strong stuff about young priest admitting homosexual affair."

Despite Jack Lemmon's box-office appeal and snappy delivery ("It's your responsibility as a priest to raise common grief to the level of the inconsolable by saying something inane" or "It is no accident that the collection comes after the sermon, it's like a Nielsen rating"), *Mass Appeal* failed to get any favorite rating and did poorly at the box-office.

In the TV movie, *Our Sons* (1991), q.v., Zeljko Ivanek would play Ann-Margret's son, dying of AIDS.

154. Mean Dog Blues (American International, 1978), color, 108 min. R-rated.

Producers, Charles A. Pratt, George Lefferts; director, Mel Stuart; screenplay, Lefferts; art director, J. S. Poplin; set decorator, Don Sullivan; costumes, Bill Milton, Chris Zamiara; makeup, Michael Moschella; music, Fred Karlin; assistant directors, Kenneth Swor, Richard Luke Rothschild; stunt coordinator, Bill Couch; sound, Dwight Mobley; camera, Robert B. Hauser; editor, Housely Stevenson.

Cast: Gregg Henry (Paul Ramsey); Kay Lenz (Linda Ramsey); George Kennedy (Captain Omar Kinsman); Scatman Crothers (Mudcat); Tina Louise (Donna Lacey); Felton Perry (Jake Turner); Gregory Sierra (Jesus Gonzales); James Wainwright (Sergeant Hubbell Wacker); William Windom (Victor Lacey); John Daniels (Yakima Jones); Marc Alaimo (Guard); Edith Atwater (Linda's Mother); James Boyd (Sonny); Edward Call (Road Gang Guard); Christina Hart (Gloria Kinsman); Chris Hubbell (Elroy Smith); Stephen Johnson ("Mary" Emerson); Logan Ramsey (Edmund Oberlin); Gene Silva (Tonto); Lee Weaver (Cheatem); Ian Wolfe (Judge); David Lewis (Dr. Caleb Odum); Billy Beck (Deadman); Herb Armstrong (Bailiff); James Bacon (Court Clerk); Hunter van Leet (Guard at Conjugal Barracks); Kimberly Allan (Max); Andy Albin (Truck Driver); Georgie Paul (Masseuse); John Dennis (Deputy Sheriff); Bill Catching (Mr. Vogel).

"Only the open acceptance of prison homosexuality . . . distinguishes *Mean Dog Blues* from a bunch of similarly-themed pix, and provides the plot angle that leads to [star Gregg] Henry's inevitable escape attempt." (*Variety*)

When his car breaks down, county and western performer Paul Ramsey (Gregg Henry) hitchhikes to Nashville. Dishonest politician Victor Lacey (William Windom) and his wife Donna (Tina Louise) give him a lift. Later, the drunk Victor runs down a youngster and claims that Ramsey was at the wheel at the time. Paul is sent to a prison farm supervised by vicious Captain Omar Kinsman (George Kennedy) and his chief stooge, the sadistic Sergeant Hubbell Wacker (James Wainright). While Ramsey's pregnant wife, Linda (Kay Lenz), pressures the Laceys to come forward with the truth, Paul must deal with life in confinement. When not overworked or terrorized by his keepers, he is pursued sexually by guards and fellow inmates (one of the prisoners suggests, "It helps to be a little queer"), and by Kinsman's promiscuous sixteen-year-old daughter (Christina Hart). The latter leads Ramsey into a compromising situation which triggers Kinsman to order the prisoner into a deadly race with a killer Doberman. Ramsey wins the contest and the sympathetic prisoners riot to prevent the enraged camp Captain from killing him. Finally, Paul is released, and he and Linda reunite.

Variety admitted the exploitation picture had "fashioned the stock elements of the plot into an involving, and sometimes amusing story that has few surprises. . . . Thrown in the pot are the usual BCP [Bing Crosby Productions] ingredients of violence, sadism, sexual innuendo and final revenge, . . ." On the other hand, Paul Taylor (British *Monthly Film Bulletin*) sighed, "This warmed-over stew of every prison-farm picture from *I Am a Fugitive from a Chain Gang* to *Cool Hand Luke*, crudely packaged yet played with inapposite conviction by its leads, makes for rudimentary, tediously predictable melodrama."

155. Meatballs: Part II (Tri-Star, 1984), color, 97 min. PG-rated.

Executive producer, Lisa Barsamian; producers, Stephen Poe, Tony Bishop; director, Ken Wiederhorn; story, Martin Kitrosser, Carol Watson; screenplay, Bruce Singer; production designer, James William Newport; costumes, Sandi Love; makeup, Cheri Minns; music, Ken Harrison; assistant director, Robert P. Cohen; stunt coordinator, John Sherrod; sound, Bill Nelson; specical effects coordinator, Martin Becker; camera, Donald M. Morgan; editor, George Berndt.

Cast: Archie Hahn (Jamie/Meathead's Voice); John Mengatti (Flash, the Bash); Tammy Taylor (Nancy); Kim Richards (Cheryl); Ralph Seymour (Eddie); Richard Mulligan (Giddy); Hamilton Camp (Colonel Batjack Hershey); John Larroquette (Foxglove); Paul Reubens (Albert); Nick Ryan (Cop); David Hollander (Tommy McFee); Misty Rowe (Fanny); Viv Lorre (Tula); Joanne Giudici (Sally); Elayne Boosler (Mother); Nancy Glass (Daughter); Patti Kirkpatrick (Dibble Mother); Paul Stout (Larry); Scott Stout (Barry); Jonna King (Susie); Tim Bartell (Damien); Chad Sheets (Ted); Scott Nemes (Butterball); Jason Hervey (Steve); Felix Silla (Meathead); Vic Martinez (Indian Chief); Blackie Dammett (Palladin); Christian Brackett (Wild Eyes); Donald Gibb (Mad Dog); Vic Dunlop (Rene); Joe Nipote (Boomer).

With *Meatballs*'s (1979) huge $21.2 million in distributors' domestic film rentals, *Meatballs II* was a sure bet. But gone from this follow-up was director Ivan Reitman, star Bill Murray, and most of the crude but zany fun of the original. Linda Gross (*Los Angeles Times*) summarized, "As a second helping, *Meatballs Part II* is short on flavor. . . . What . . . [the filmmakers] have dished up is pretty pallid. . . ."

As part of their probation from jail, troublemaker Flash (John Mengatti) and his pal Eddie (Ralph Seymour) are sent to Camp Sasquatch as counselors in training under resort supervisor Giddy (Richard Mulligan). Among the radical campers— a full racial/ethnic mix—the most unique newcomer is an E.T.-like visitor from outer space. On the other side of the lake is Camp Patton, run by tyrannical, pint-size Colonel Batjack Hershey (Hamilton Camp) and his effete, mincing helper, Foxglove (John Larroquette). Their ambition is to gain control of Sasquatch. Before the asinine finale, the regenerated Flash, a boxing tyro, saves the day by winning the big match for Sasquatch against Camp Patton's Mad Dog (Donald Gibb). As for the extraterrestial—the best actor in this mess—he and his family re-orbit into outer space.

Variety panned this "Tame sequel" which haphazardly threw together such ingredients as "military bullies victimizing the good guys, girls looking for their first peek at male anatomy, gay jokes, and a bargain basement *E.T.* . . . Essential element missing here . . . is sympathetic characters. Hamilton Camp . . . is a cardboard fascist. Equally predictable is John Larroquette as his closet gay assistant."

While Pee Wee Herman (Paul Reubens) has a brief *Meatballs II* role, John Larroquette (of TV's "Night Court" fame) is on camera far longer, and looks rightfully ill-at-ease as the stock pansy buffoon played for cheap humor.

Meatball II earned under $4 million in distributors' domestic film rentals, but that did not prevent the arrival of the R-rated *Meatballs III* (1987), nor the production of *Meatballs IV* (1992) with Corey Haim and Jack Nance.

156. Midnight Cowboy (United Artists, 1969), color, 113 min. X-rated.

Producer, Jerome Hellman; associate producer, Kenneth Utt; director, John Schlesinger; based on the novel by James Leo Herlihy; screenplay, Waldo Salt; production designer, John Robert Lloyd; set decorator, Philip Smith; costumes, Ann Roth; makeup, Dick Smith, Irving Buchman; music supervisor, John Barry; song, Fred Neil; music arranger/conductor, George Tipton; sound, Abe Seidman; camera, Adam Holender; editor, Hugh A. Robertson.

Cast: Dustin Hoffman (Enrico "Ratso" Rizzo); Jon Voight (Joe Buck); Sylvia Miles (Cass); John McGiver (Mr. O'Daniel); Brenda Vaccaro (Shirley); Barnard Hughes (Towny

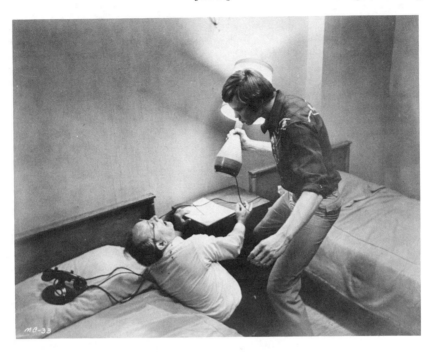

Barnard Hughes and Jon Voight in *Midnight Cowboy* **(1969).**

[Townsend]); Ruth White (Sally Buck); Jennifer Salt (Crazy Annie); Gil Rankin (Woodsy Niles); Gary Owen, T. Tom Marlow (Little Joe); George Eppersen (Ralph); Al Scott (Cafeteria Manager); Linda Davis (Mother on Bus); J. T. Masters (Old Cowhand); Arlene Reeder (Old Lady); Georgann Johnson (Rich Lady); Jonathan Kramer (Jackie); Bob Balaban (Young Student); Anthony Holland (TV Bishop); Jan Tice (Freaked-Out Lady); Paul Benjamin (Bartender); Peter Scalia, Vito Siracusa (Vegetable Grocers); Peter Zamaglias (Hat Shop Owner); Arthur Anderson (Hotel Clerk); Tina Scala, Alma Felix (Laundromat Ladies); Richard Clarke (Escort Service Man); Ann Thomas (Frantic Lady); Viva (Gretel McAlbertson); Gastone Rossilli (Hansel McAlbertson); Joan Murphy (Waitress); Al Stetson (Bus Driver); Ultra Violet, Paul Jabara, International Velvet, William Door, Cecelia Lipson, Taylor Mead, Paul Morrissey, Paul Jasmin (Party Guests).

". . . in this film the scenery is lovely and only the human race is vile." (*Variety*)

The X-rated *Midnight Cowboy* was a very strong film to be produced by Hollywood in the late 1960s. On one level it was a grim account of a baby-faced young man full of innocent dreams coping with grim reality in a grotesque city full of users. On another plane, it is a buddy movie about two lonely losers gaining strength from their mutual friendship. Coursing through this drama are assorted homosexuals, all of whom suffer from a far-ranging mix of repression, guilt and depression.

Unhappy with his dull life as a dishwasher in a small Texas town, Joe Buck (Jon Voight) boards a bus for New York City. Outfitted in a flashy cowboy outfit, naive Joe is convinced he can make his fortune in Manhattan as a professional stud. On the way he remembers random childhood events, including a gang rape of both Joe and his girlfriend Annie (Jennifer Salt). In the Big Apple, the gawky newcomer is promptly outwitted by a middle-aged hooker (Sylvia Miles). At a run-down bar, Joe meets Ratso Rizzo (Dustin Hoffman), a crippled minor thief who suggests he will be Buck's pimp. Later, when one of Ratso's contacts, the religious fanatic Mr. O'Daniel (John McGiver), propositions Joe, the terrified Buck flees the sordid hotel room. Angry at this deception, Joe and the tubercular Ratso fall out, but later patch up their differences.

Joe has little success in hustling clients of either sex for any money (the boy he encounters in the balcony of a 42nd Street movie theatre) or little money (the restless Shirley [Brenda Vaccaro]). By now, it is winter and Rizzo is very ill. Joe decides he will make his friend's lifelong dream of reaching Miami Beach come true. Needing bus fare for them, Joe goes to the hotel room of an aging homosexual (Barnard Hughes). Once there, he panics, severely beats the older man, and steals his cash. Aboard the bus, Rizzo dies just as they reach Miami. Joe puts his arm around the dead body of his one and only friend.

Vincent Canby (*New York Times*) judged, "It is tough and good in important ways, although its style is oddly romantic. . . . *Midnight Cowboy* often seems to be exploiting its material for sensational or comic effects, but it is ultimately a moving experience. . . ." Canby noted of the sterling cast that Voight was "equally fine as Joe Buck, a tall, handsome young man whose open face somehow manages to register the fuzziest of conflicting emotions within a very dim mind." Robert Landry (*Variety*) described *Midnight Cowboy* as a "Sassy, sexy, sordid saga." In contrast, Pauline Kael (*The New Yorker*) had reservations, "The director, John Schlesinger, uses fast cutting and tricky camerawork to provide a satirical background as enrichment of the story, but the satire is offensively inaccurate—it cheapens the story and gives it a veneer of almost hysterical cleverness." David Wilson (British *Monthly Film Bulletin*) found that the picture suffered from being "a little too neatly sewn up, certainly romanticised. . . ." Wilson added, "Voight convincingly suggests the essential vulnerability behind Joe's aggressively confident exterior, while Hoffman's Ratso . . . is a beautifully observed creation."

As an undercurrent in the film, there is the homosexuality or, at least, bisexuality, of its would-be gigolo. During the course of his New York misadventures, dense Joe, prodded by street-saavy Rizzo, realizes that his swaggering along the city streets draws more notice from males than females. However, being sexually closeted, Buck represses such notions. Nevertheless, he finds himself in three (failed) liaisons with gay men, the third ending in an outburst of brutality caused by his panic, frustration and confusion as to what he is supposed to feel as a hustler, or what he is coming to suspect about his own sexual orientation. Then there is the underlying texture of Ratso's multi-layered attraction to Joe, who is his complete physical opposite: healthy, handsome and not crippled. By interacting/living with Buck, Rizzo can sublimate into his friend's being; creating a situation full of homoeroticism, narcissism, etc.

The extremely daring *Midnight Cowboy*, made at a cost $3,200,000 earned a huge $20,499,282 in distributors' domestic film rentals. It won Academy Awards for Best Picture, Best Director and Best Screenplay: Based on Material from Another Medium It received Oscar nominations for Best Actor (Dustin Hoffman and Jon Voight; John Wayne won for *True Grit*), Best Supporting Actress (Sylvia Miles; Goldie Hawn won for *Cactus Flower*) and Best Film Editing (*Z* won). *Midnight Cowboy* was Hollywood's first X-rated motion picture to receive the Best Picture Academy Award. Two years later, the mainstream film was resubmitted to the Motion Picture Association of America where it was re-rated R, with NO cuts required. Its new R-rating demonstrated how mores had altered in only two years.

157. Midnight Express (Columbia, 1978), color, 120 min. R-rated.

Executive producer, Peter Guber; producers, Alan Marshall, David Puttnam; director, Alan Parker; based on the book by Billy Hayes with William Hoffer; screenplay, Oliver Stone; production designer, Geoffrey Kirkland; art director, Evan Hercules; costumes, Milena Canonero; makeup, Mary Hillman, Penny Steyne; music, Giorgo Moroder; song, David Castle; fight arranger, Roy Scammell; sound, Clive Winter; camera, Michael Seresin; editor, Gerry Hambling.

Cast: Brad Davis (Billy Hayes); Randy Quaid (Jimmy Booth); Bo Hopkins (Tex); John Hurt (Max): Paul Smith (Hamidou); Mike Kellin (Mr. Hayes); Norbert Weisser (Erich); Irene Miracle (Susan); Paolo Bonacelli (Rifki); Michael Ensign (Stanley Daniels); Franco Diogene (Yesil); Kevork Malikyan (Prosecutor); Gigi Ballista (Chief Justice); Mihalis Yannatos (Translator); Tony Boyd (Aslan); Peter Jeffrey (Ahmet); Ahmed El Shenawi (Negdir); Zanninos Zanninou (Turkish Detective); Dimos Starenios (Ticket Seller); and Yasfar Adem, Joe Zammit Cordina, Vic Tablkian, Raad Rawi.

"The film is like a porno fantasy about the sacrifice of a virgin. It rushes from torment to torment, treating Billy's ordeals hypnotically in soft colors—muted squalor— with a disco beat in the background. The prison itself is more like a brothel than a prison." (Pauline Kael, *5001 Nights at the Movies*, 1991)

Whatever the exact truths or fabrications of the tortuous odyssey portrayed, *Midnight Express* is compelling drama. It depicts graphically the hero's five years of brutal confinement in a Turkish prison, surviving his ordeal with the dream of one day, somehow escaping. During his horrendous detention, the protagonist intermingles with an assortment of bi- and/or homosexual captives and captors.

In 1970 Istanbul, American college student Billy Hayes (Brad Davis), returning to the U.S. with his girlfriend, Susan (Irene Miracle), is detained during a customs search. Because the officers find hashish concealed on his person, he is arrested. When he tries to escape confinement he is shipped to Sagamilcar, a rundown prison fortress, where he is sodomized by the chief guard, Hamidou (Paul Smith). The desperate Billy is sentenced to a term of four years and two months. He comes to know the corrupted British Max (John Hurt), already behind bars for seven years, and Erich (Norbert Weisser), the young Swede. The latter makes homosexual overtures to Billy which he rejects. Then there is another American, the off-kilter Jimmy Booth (Randy Quaid) who admits, "We're all crazy here." Jimmy tells Billy about the "Midnight Express" a prison term for escape. When Hayes's appeal is rejected and he is sentenced to thirty years in prison (as a lesson to foreigners), he joins with Jimmy and Max in an escape plan. Unfortunately, a fellow prisoner, Rifki (Paolo Bonacelli), informs on them. Jimmy is dragged away and, later, Rifki frames Max. As payback, the enraged Billy bites out the traitor's tongue. Still later, Susan visits the prison and sneaks Billy money which he uses to bribe the guards in his escape scheme. Once again he is caught and brought before Hamidou whom he accidentally kills in a scuffle. Dressed in the dead man's uniform, Hayes finally escapes. He crosses the border into Greece, arriving back in the U.S. three weeks later.

Christopher Lehmann-Haupt (*New York Times*) was angered by this adaptation of Billy Hayes's story to the screen: "I have no idea if the people who made the film, most of whom are English, have altered Billy Hayes's story out of simple stupidity or because of some unexplained grudge against the Turkish people." On the other hand, *Variety* appreciated that the "cast, direction and production are all very good" but noted, "[It is] difficult to sort out the proper empathies from the muddled and moralizing screenplay which, in true Anglo-American fashion, wrings hands over alien cultures as though our civilization is absolutely perfect." John Pym (British *Monthly Film Bulletin*) agreed with Pauline Kael and found that

Mike Kellin and Brad Davis in *Midnight Express* (1978).

director Alan Parker "has opted to play the whole story as a fairytale."

Midnight Express, shot on location in Malta, grossed $15,065,000 in distributors' domestic film rentals. It won two Academy Awards: Best Screenplay (Oliver Stone) and Best Original Score (Giorgio Moroder). It received four other Oscar nominations: Best Picture (*The Deer Hunter* won); Best Director (Michael Cimino won for *The Deer Hunter*), Best Supporting Actor (John Hurt; Christopher Walken won for *The Deer Hunter*); and Best Editing (*The Deer Hunter* won).

158. Mike's Murder (Warner Bros., 1984), 97 min. R-rated.

Producer, Kim Kurumada; associate producer, Jack Larson; director/screenplay, James Bridges; production designer, Peter Jamison; art director, Hub Braden; set decorator, R. Chris Westlund; costumes, April Ferry; makeup, Mark Reedall; music, John Barry; additional music, Joe Jackson; assistant directors, Albert Shapiro, Marty Ewing; sound, Michael Minkler, Richard Beggs; special effects, Bruce Mattox; camera, Reynaldo Villalobos; editor, Jeff Gouson, Dede Allen.

Cast: Debra Winger (Betty Parrish); Mark Keyloun (Mike); Paul Winfield (Phillip); Darrell Larson (Pete); Brooke Alderson (Patty) Robert Crosson (Sam Morris); Daniel Shor (Richard); William Ostrander (Randy); Gregory Hormel (Kid Drug Buyer); John Michael Stewart, Victor Perez (Tough Guys); Mark High (Ben); Ken Y. Namba (Sushi Chef); Ruth Winger (Betty's Mother); April Ferry (Boss Lady); Randy White (Boss Man); Robert Kincaid (Bodyguard); Kym Malin, Lori Butler, Dawn Abraham (Beautiful Girls); Freeman King, Alphonse Walter (Killers); James Carrington (Jim); Rebecca Marder, Bruce Marder (Cafe Workers); Sarah Zinsser (Girl in Video Tape); James Daley Ryan, Robert Johnstreet, Gordon Hoban (Police Technicians); Javier Jose Gonzales (Bus Stop Boarder); Cliff Jenkins (Bus Boarder); Aurelia Gallardo (Pancho's Waitress); Frank Cavestani (Charles); Spazz Attack (Himself); John B. Fran, MariSol Garcia (Blonde Punkers); Jennifer Dixon, Steve Solberg, Annie Johnes, Michael Uhlenkot (Party Goers).

James Bridges, who had directed Debra Winger in *Urban Cowboy* (1980), created this 1982 project as a showcase for the actress. Because of myriad production problems, the trouble-plagued film was long held up in release, then chopped from 109 to 97 minutes (to remove some violence) and with a revamped music score, tossed out into the marketplace by disenchanted studio executives. Rex Reed (*New York Post*) was quick to observe, 'The sleazy neon-lit atmosphere of Los Angeles after dark has served as a favorite setting for an endless stream of recent movies made by young directors. . . . None of them has the talent or perceptive eye of James Bridges. That's a chief reason why *Mike's Murder* is eerily, creepily, unnervingly effective."

Los Angeles bank teller Betty Parrish (Debra Winger) is flattered and intrigued when she meets and beds down with good-looking, scruffy Mike (Mark Keyloun). He temporarily disappears after their one-night stand, but over the next several months, they have several chance reunions, which renew her infatuation with this easy-living, mysterious character, whom she thinks earns his living teaching tennis. When she later learns that Mike has been murdered, she is driven to find out why. The obsession leads her to an assortment of people who "knew" the victim: a middle-aged photographer, Sam (Robert Crosson), and, then, Phillip (Paul Winfield). The latter, a thriving record producer, tells her that he first met Michael two years earlier on a cross-country drive during a stopover in Ohio and brought him to Los Angeles as his live-in companion. The self-contained Phillip, who has a new young boyfriend, admits that Mike "was always preparing faces for the faces he met." As it develops, the bisexual Mike and his pal, Pete (Darrell Larson), had stolen cocaine from a big-time dealer, who, thereafter, needed to teach both a lesson. (Pete is later gruesomely murdered while hiding out at Betty's house.) In the nightmarish unraveling of

the mystery, Betty sates her curiosity if not all of her fantasy about Mike.

Sheila Benson (*Los Angeles Times*) pointed out, "Writer-director James Bridges frames his chilling cautionary tale as a love story, although a story of powerful attraction might be closer to the truth . . . Where Bridges lets down is in giving Winger nothing to play, and in making Mike less than charismatic." Leo Seligsohn (*Newsday*) judged the movie a "slick, run-of-the-mill thriller" in which "the actors talk movie and act cinema, and if Winger seems almost real, it's merely a tribute to her style. . . ." Richard Corliss (*Time*) rejected the movie because: "Every cliche of existential anomie—the aimless driving, the heavy smoking, the elliptical dialogue, the motel-room angst—has been imported to the seedier suburbs of Los Angeles." In contrast, Pauline Kael (*The New Yorker*) thought that Bridges was being "original and daring"; she favored Winger's performance as "superb full-scale" and found that Winfield provides "a brief intense appearance . . . that's right up there with Winger's acting."

A box-office failure, *Mike's Murder* remains an atmospheric, if coy study of a charming punk/hustler whose luck runs out when he uses the wrong person at the wrong time.

159. Mountains of the Moon
(Tri-Star, 1990), color, 135 min. R-rated.

Executive producer, Mario Kassar, Andrew Vajna; producer, Daniel Melnick; associate producer, Chris Curling; director, Bob Rafelson; based on the novel *Burton and Speke* by William Harrison and original journals by Richard Burton and John Hanning Speke; screenplay, Rafelson, Harrison; production designer, Norman Reynolds; art directors, Maurice Fowler, Fred Hole; set decorator, Harry Cordwell; costumes, Jenny Beavan, John Bright; makeup, Christine Beveridge; music, Michael Small; choreographer, Eleanor Fazan; assistant director, Pat Clayton; sound, Simon Kaye; special effects, David Harris; camera, Roger Deakins; editor, Thom Noble.

Cast: Patrick Bergin (Captain Richard Francis Burton); Iain Glen (Lieutenant John Hanning Speke); Richard E. Grant (Laurence Oliphant); Fiona Shaw (Isabel Arundell Burton); John Savident (Lord Murchison); James Villiers (Lord Oliphant); Adrian Rawlins (Edward); Peter Vaughan (Lord Houngton); Delroy Lindo (Mabruki); Bernard Hill (Dr. David Livingstone); Matthew Marsh (William); Richard Caldicot (Lord Russell); Christopher Fulford (Herne); Garry Cooper (Stroyan); Roshan Seth (Ben Amir); Jimmy Gardner (Jarvis); Doreen Mantle (Mrs. Speke); Anna Massey (Mrs. Arundell); Peter Eyre (Norton Shaw); Leslie Phillips (Mr. Arundell); Frances Cuka (Lady Houghton); Roger Ashton-Griffiths (Lord Cowley); Craig Crosbie (Swinburne); Paul Onsongo (Sidi Bombay); Leonard Juma (Jemadar); Bheki Tonto Ngema (Ngola); Martin Okello (Veldu); Philip Voss (Colonel Rigby); Pip Torrens (Lieutenant Hesketh); Esther Njiru (Lema); Alison Limerick (Sorceress); Asiba Asiba (Nubian Servant); Ian Vincent (Lieutenant Allen); Ralph Nossek (Doctor); Stewart Harwood (Attendant); George Malpas (Lead Actor) Robert Whelan, Bill Croasdale, Renny Krupinski (Reporters); Rod Woodruff (Fencer); Fikile Mdeleni, Martin Ocham, Wilson Ng 'Ong' A, Rocks Nhlapo, Patrick Letladi, Konga Mbandu, Michael Otieno (Bearers) Fatima Said, Zam Zam Issa, Norta Muhammed, Pineniece Joshua (Somali Girls); Roger Rees (Edgar Papworth).

In some ways, *Mountains of the Moon* is a very modern film rendition of a certain type of movie—i.e., *Four Feathers* (1939) and *King Solomon's Mines* (1950)—that was made: full of obsessed Britishers exploring the depths of, and coping with, the natives of uncharted Africa. *Mountains of the Moon* focuses on two real-life, well-known nineteenth-century British explorers, Richard Burton and John Speke, trudging their way through East Africa in search of the elusive source of the Nile River. Unlike Hollywood movies of past generations, this one chose to touch upon the homoerotic relationship between the two highly competitive men. Moreover, it details the homosexual private life of Speke, in parallel to the overly heterosexual romantic life of Burton.

In the late 1850s, the Royal Geographical Society sponsors the return of two Brit-

ishers, Richard Burton (Patrick Bergin) and John Hanning Speke (Iain Glen) to East Africa in their quest to find the Nile's source. Both men have left behind romantic interests: Burton's impetuous, self-sufficient Isabel Arundell (Fiona Shaw) and Speke, his adoring publisher friend, Laurence Oliphant (Richard E. Grant), who has given his lover a publishing contract to write of the African scientific safari. During their trek, Burton is mauled by a lion—and soon must be carried by stretcher—while Speke suffers a gross infection due to a beetle invading his ear. Most of their native bearers and trackers defect as the group approach and make their way around Lake Tanganyika. Later, Ngola (Bheki Tonto Ngema) and his tribal followers capture the invading white men, leading to Speke's tending to Ngola's ailing sister. While the injured Burton remains behind at Ngola's village, the opportunistic Speke continues on, reaching Lake Victoria. Upon reuniting, Speke insists he has found the Nile's source, while Burton refuses to accept Speke's sketchy evidence that Lake Victoria is the searched-for source.

Speke returns to England before Burton and, through Oliphant's manipulations, is financed to a new much-heralded expedition to East Africa. Burton is hurt but not especially resentful of this turn-about situation. Meanwhile, Isabel diverts him by using her influence to gain him a consular post. Two years pass. Dr. David Livingstone (Bernard Hill) arranges that Burton and Speke (who has gained tremendous fame in the interval) debate their conflicting geographical theories. At this juncture, Speke becomes aware of Oliphant's past deceit in turning him against Burton. While home visiting his family, Speke dies (likely at his own hands) in a hunting accident. Thereafter, a mournful Burton is shown Speke's death mask by a sculptor (Roger Rees); he reshapes the feature to more closely resemble his late friend.

Variety noted of this well-mounted feature that it "never strays from its dramatic thrust to become merely picturesque." The trade journal rated it "an outstanding adventure film. . . . The male bonding theme of the two explorers is forcefully and tastefully told (with a key scene of intimacy as Speke cradles and kisses a feverish Burton midway through the pic.). . . ." John Pym (British *Monthly Film Bulletin*) determined, "There is something both playfully melodramatic and, at the same time, more than half serious about this handsomely shot historical epic. The playfulness extends, refreshingly, to Rafelson's reconstruction of high mid-Victorian life. . . . The seriousness . . . [of the two men's relationship] is altogether less confidently handled. Or rather its several strands are less fully developed. The heart of the story . . . [for the filmmakers] is the relationship between the two explorers, and particularly perhaps Speke's suppressed sexual longing for his more overtly manly comrade. But Africa . . . keeps getting in the way."

Ralph Novak (*People*) pondered, "why is *Mountains of the Moon* so coldly uninvolving? . . . For one thing, the richness of the explorers' lives make it difficult to cram them both into one movie. . . . Rafelson has failed to give the movie the historical perspective it demands. . . . [This] movie still basically focuses on how tough it was for two white men to trespass on a foreign continent. . . . [The] emotional and historical integrity of his story, not to mention fairness, were ill served by his limited perspective [in deemphasizing the black Africans in the storyline]."

Like similar past films of single-minded explorers (*Stanley and Livingstone*, 1939), *Mountains of the Moon*, despite the virtues of cast, characters and locales, was trapped by its inability to convey properly the obsessions driving these men through such perils. As such, the movie emerged irrelevant to most 1990s audiences. *Mountains of the Moon* earned a very unimpressive $1.5 million in distributors' domestic film rentals.

At one point in pre-production rock star David Bowie was considered for the role of Speke. Much of the history depicted in *Mountains of the Moon* had been traced in the 1972 six-hour TV docudrama, *The Search for the Nile*, featuring Kenneth Haigh and John Quentin. Director/co-scripter Bob Rafelson had dealt with lesbian relationships in *Five Easy Pieces* (1970) and *Black Widow* (1987), qq.v.

160. My Own Private Idaho

(New Line Cinema, 1991), color, 102 min. R-rated.

Executive producer, Gus Van Sant; co-executive producer, Allan Mindel; producer, Laurie Parker; director, Van Sant; based on a screen story by Van Sant and additional material suggested by the play *Henry IV* by William Shakespeare; screenplay, Van Sant; production designer, David Brisbin; art director, Ken Hardy; set decorator, Melissa Stewart; costumes, Beatrix Aruna Pasztor; makeup, Gina Monica; music, Bill Stafford; assistant directors, Kris Krengel, David Minkowski; sound, Reinhard Stergar, Robert Marts, Jan Cyr, Jon Huck; special effects, Tom Arndt; camera, Jon Campbell; editor, Curtiss Clayton.

Cast: River Phoenix (Mike Waters); Keanu Reeves (Scott Favor); James Russo (Richard Waters); William Richert (Bob Pigeon); Rodney Harvey (Gary); Chiara Caselli (Carmella); Michael Parker Digger); Jessica Thomas (Denise); Flea (Budd); Grace Zabriskie (Alena); Tom Troupe (Jack Favor); Udo Kier (Hans); Sally Curtice (Jane Lightwork); Robert Lee Pitchlynn (Walt); Mickey Cottrell (Daddy Carrol); Wade Evans (Wade); Matt Ebert, Scott Patrick Green, Tom Cramer (Coverboys); Vana O'Brien (Sharon Waters); Shaun Jordan, Shawn Jones (Cafe Kids); George Conner (Bad George); Oliver Kirk (Indian Cop); Stanley Hainesworth (Dirtman); Joshua Halladay (Baby Mike); Douglas Tollenen (Little Richard); Stephen Clark Pachosa (Hotel Manager); Lannie Swerdlow (Disco Manager); Wally Gaarsland, Byran Wilson, Mark Weaver, Conrad "Bud" Montgomery (Rock Promoters); Pat Patterson, Steve Vernelson, Mike Cascadden (Cop); Eric Hull (Mayor's Aide); James A. Arling (Minister); James Caviezel (Airline Clerk); Ana Cavinato (Stewardess); Melanie Mosely (Lounge Hostess); Greg Murphy (Carl); David Reppinhagen (Yuppie at Jake's); Tiger Warren

River Phoenix and Grace Zabriskie in *My Own Private Idaho* **(1991).**

(Himself); Massimo DeCataldo, Pao Pei Andreoli, Paolo Baiocco (Italian Street Boys); Mario Stracciarolo (Mike's Italian Client).

"You may not be sure exactly how you feel when *My Own Private Idaho* ends, but you'll sure as hell know you haven't seen another cookie-cutter movie . . . [His] third feature—the last in an informal trilogy of the streets that began with *Mala Noche* in 1986 [and includes *Drugstore Cowboy*, 1989]—leaves absolutely no doubt that Van Sant is the freshest new voice working in American movies." David Ansen (*Newsweek*)

For decades, Hollywood had been fighting against or striving to reach a point where it could present gay characters as dimensional human beings, not sociopathic villains, low comedy relief, or pitiable outcasts. Gus Van Sant's *My Own Private Idaho* reaches for that goal in a clever blend of sensitive forthrightness, commerciality (its two mainstream young stars), and with exaggerated symbolic lyricism (the weakest link in the offering).

Among young street hustlers in Port-land, Oregon, are Mike Waters (River Phoenix), a sweet but ratty young blond, who is obsessed about finding his long-vanished mother. He is a severe narcoleptic who, during stressful situations, collapses frequently into a catatonic heap. (This condition often leads to his being picked up by clients while unconscious and then awakening hours later in unfamiliar surroundings.) His best friend, and his opposite, is dark-haired Scott Favor (Keanu Reeves), the aristocratic son of Portland's mayor (Tom Troupe). Unlike the gay Mike, who has a deep crush on Scott, the latter is basically straight. He has sex with men only for money and to get back, so he claims, at his ultra conservative family. His "slumming" is part of his rebellion against his hypocritical, demanding father.

Determined to locate his mother, Mike convinces Scott to join him in an odyssey back to Idaho, and then, following up further clues provided by his alcoholic brother/father (James Russo), on to Rome, Italy. En route, they encounter a sleazy Continental salesman, Hans (Udo

Kier), who indulges in sex with both teenagers. In Italy, Scott, anxious to reaffirm
his sense of masculinity, becomes deeply
attracted to beautiful Carmella (Chiara
Caselli) and abandons his love-sick friend
for her. Back in the States, Scott, now
twenty-one, has come into a lucrative inheritance and rigidly abandons his former
friends. Meanwhile, much-older Bob Pigeon (William Richert), the leader of the
street urchins, who had befriended Scott
in his fledgling days, dies rejected by
Scott, paralleling the death of Scott's politician father. Pathetically lonely Mike is
left with his broken illusions.

Lawrence Fascella (*US*) reported,
"nothing could prepare you for this unapologetic, uncompromising piece of renegade cinema. . . . . *Idaho* is most effective at putting across a desperately
intimate sense of isolation." Van Sant's
most valuable models can be found in the
German films of the Seventies: the vision-
ary movies of Werner Herzog and the late,
great Rainer Werner Fassbinder (Van
Sant's nearest precursor as an openly gay
film director.) Abbie Bernstein (*Drama-
Logue*) complimented Van Sant: "The
tone of *My Own Private Idaho* doesn't so
much shift as expand, taking in everything
from beefcake magazine covers that come
to life and converse with each other, to
simple campfire confessions of love. He
gives Mike some endearingly odd dreams,
including one that contains an extremely
funny metaphor for orgasm, and keeps the
proceedings devoid of hysteria and finger-
pointing. . . . Van Sant prefers to illustrate the existence of modern-day American outlaws without commenting much on
what we're seeing. . . . There are no
killer pimps, no drug overdoses, not even
mention of AIDS; just a pervasive, melancholy rootlessness and the feeling that
anything might happen at any moment."

Henry Sheehan (*Hollywood Reporter*)
assessed, "the film's tonal richness, its
hipness and its plain humanity, as well as
the considerably canny casting of River
Phoenix and Keanu Reeves in lead roles,

mark this feature as one to watch. . . .
Van Sant emphasizes the vulnerable side
of Phoenix's persona, and not only does
the young actor deliver his best performance, he manages to limn a gay character who will probably have an enormous
appeal to young women."

Owen Gleiberman (*Entertainment
Weekly*), who rated the movie an A-,
pointed out, "Van Sant has his arty
side, and this time he's given it full reign.
One section is even lifted for Shakespeare's *Henry IV*, with a Falstaffian street
ringleader named Bob (played with strut-
ting, demonic gusto by the veteran director) lording it over his wolf pack of
boy runaways. Richert is a powerful presence, but the film—for nearly half
an hour—goes thud. The updated Eliz-
abethan dialogue is simply too much of a
conceptual stunt. . . . *My Own Private
Idaho* . . . often seems as rootless as poor
Mike. Yet the film has an authentic emotional lyricism."

Definitely not a mainstream film for
everyone's taste—despite the presence of
teen stars River Phoenix (who is superb)
and Keanu Reeves (who is adequate)—
My Own Private Idaho, nevertheless,
grossed $6,382,667 at the box-office in 23
weeks of domestic distribution. For his
work in *My Own Private Idaho*, Phoenix
was awarded the Best Actor at the 1991
Venice Film Festival and named Best Actor of 1991 by the National Society of Film
Critics.

161. My Two Loves (ABC-TV, April
7, 1986), color, 100 min. Not rated.

Executive producer, Alvin Cooperman; as-
sociate producers, Patty Newburger, Graham
Ford; director, Noel Black; teleplay, Reginald
Rose, Rita Mae Brown; art director, Christian
Kelly; set decorator, Fred Chalfy; costumes,
Deirdre Williams; makeup, Leslie Fuller; mu-
sic, Gary William Friedman; assistant direc-
tors, Mark McGann, Johnny Jensen; sound,
Danny Michael; camera, Arthur Albert; editor,
John A. Martinelli.

Cast: Mariette Hartley (Gail Springer);
Lynn Redgrave (Marjorie Lloyd); Barry New-

man (Ben Taylor); Sada Thompson (Dorothea); Sarah Inglis (Amy Springer); Robert L. Leonard (Larry Taylor); Eve Roberts (Dr. Patricia Hoffman); Arturo Tamaez (John); Thee Swan (Martha); Rachel Rey (Instructress); Ray Loberto (Melon Seller); Edwin Neal (Telephone Man); Diane Perella (Teacher); Lee Connally (Flower Vendor)

This made-for-TV movie, with strong feminist underpinnings, followed timidly and tritely in the path of such theatrical features as *Lianna* (1983) and *Desert Hearts* (1985), qq.v. Whereas the earlier telefeature, *A Question of Love* (1978), q.v., concentrated on the repercussions that a lesbian couple must endure from discrimination. *My Two Loves* had a different agenda. It wanted to explore and define the relationship between a confirmed lesbian and her new friend. The latter is a vulnerable widow uncertain whether her emotional/sexual responses to another female are based on desire or a reaction to loneliness. Unfortunately, *My Two Loves* was not a comfortable assignment for its very professional co-stars: Mariette Hartley seemed excessively uptight and Lynn Redgrave came across as bored with her assignment.

After the death of her physician husband, Gail Springer (Mariette Hartley) and her daughter, Amy (Sarah Inglis), sell their house and move into an apartment. Bewildered by the many new roles required of her as a single mother, Gail feels pressured when long-time friend, Ben Taylor (Barry Newman), now separated from his wife, dates her and quickly wants to get serious. Meanwhile, having rejoined the work force, Gail meets executive Marjorie Lloyd (Lynn Redgrave) on the job. The latter takes an immediate interest in the comely Gail, which the former initially misinterprets. Because Gail feels secure sharing girl talk, dinners, etc. with another woman, the friendship blossoms. Finally, one day the reality comes to a fore. Discovering that Marjorie is gay, perplexes Gail:

Gail: How could I have not known?

. . . You just don't look like what I'd expect a gay woman to look like. . . .

Marjorie: We don't all wear black leather and ride Harley Davidsons. I'm a relatively happy woman and I live as I please.

After absorbing the new situation, Gail insists: "I'm just an ordinary, garden variety heterosexual." However, patient Marjorie persists and soon the two women enter into a sexual/emotional affair. When Gail's mother, Dorothea (Sada Thompson) learns of the situation, she is not only disgusted and shamed, but worried about the effect it will have on teenaged Amy. (Eventually mother and daughter reconcile.) Being a honest soul, the liberated Gail—who is now seeing a therapist (Eve Roberts) to understand all the changes in her life—tells Ben the news. The personal relationships soon develop into a tug-of-war for Gail's affection between Marjorie and the chauvinistic, condescending Ben (he tells Marjorie "I'd be lying if I didn't say I was curious to meet you. You're very good looking. You don't look like one.").

Forced to make a choice between her two ardent suitors, Gail chooses neither, telling Marjorie "I'm ready to take, not to give. . . . You and I spent some of the tenderess moments of my life together. I just don't think we belong together, not right now anyway."

Variety was unimpressed with this unsubtle production filled with "silly melodramatic splurges," noting that it "insists on stock characters, coincidental entrances, convenient exits and trite dialog." The trade paper pointed out, "Telefilm has many important things to say . . . and fritters them away with high-strung confrontations and startlingly pedestrian dialog. . . ." *TV Guide* rated this production only two stars.

Since this was made for a TV audience, the movie was very discreet about its lovemaking scenes, ending sequences tactfully after the two female stars share a few kisses. With its pedantic discussion of the ramifications of being a lesbian in a still unaccepting society, *My Two Loves* shared many parallels with such features as *Consenting Adult* (1985) and *An Early Frost* (1985), qq.v., both dealing with man-to-man relationships. *My Two Loves* was shot on location in San Antonio, Texas.

162. Myra Breckinridge (Twentieth Century-Fox, 1970), color, 94 min. X-rated.

Producer, Robert Fryer; associate producer, James Cresson; director, Michael Sarne; based on the novel by Gore Vidal; screenplay, Sarne, David Giler, (uncredited) Vidal; special material, Mae West; art directors, Jack Martin Smith, Fred Harpman; set decorators, Walter M. Scott, Reg Allen, costumes, Theadora Van Runkle, Edith Head; makeup, Dan Striepeke; music supervisor/conductor, Lionel Newman; songs: John Phillips; Allen Jones, Alvertis Isbell, Otis Redding; choreographer, Ralph Beaumont; assistant director, Richard Glassman; sound, Don Bassman, David Dockendorf; special camera effects, L. B. Abbott, Art Cruickshank; camera, Richard Moore; editors, Danford B. Greene, Hugh K. Cummings.

Cast: Mae West (Leticia Van Allen); John Huston (Buck Loner); Raquel Welch (Myra Breckinridge); Rex Reed (Young Man [Myron Breckinridge]); Farrah Fawcett (Mary Ann); Roger C. Carmel (Dr. Montag); Roger Herren (Rusty); George Furth (Charlie Flager Jr.); Calvin Lockhart (Irving Amadeus); Jim Backus (Doctor); John Carradine (Surgeon); Andy Devine (Coyote Bill); Grady Sutton (Kid Barlow); Robert Lieb (Charlie Flager Sr.); Skip Ward (Chance); Kathleen Freeman (Bobby Dean Loner); B. S. Pully (Tex); Buck Kartalian (Jeff); Monty Landis (Vince); Tom Selleck (Stud); Peter Ireland (Student); Nelson Sardelli (Mario); William Hopper (Parole Officer); Genevieve Waite (Dentist's Patient); Charlene Jones (Masseuse).

More than two decades after it came and went, the hubbub over the X-rated *Myra Breckinridge* seems truly quaint. Based on Gore Vidal's then controversial novel (1968) about mixed sexuality and intellectualized nostalgia, the book was translated to the screen by novice British film director Michael Sarne. In the process, the filming developed into bizarre casting coups: the return of Mae West to mov-

iemaking after nearly thirty years, movie reviewer/interviewer Rex Reed given a chance at a lead screen part, etc. En route, it blew up into a three-ring circus when Mae West and more current sex bomb, Raquel Welch, battled over each other's screen billing, time, and wardrobe. Once completed, studio executives realized there was too little usable film footage and, in a panic, padded it with clips from a wild variety of 1930s and 1940s studio productions. Their action led to some actors and actresses (Loretta Young included) demanding that their "appearances" be excised from this tasteless mess.

After undergoing a sex-change operation, devoted film critic Myron Breckinridge (Rex Reed) is now Myra Breckinridge (Raquel Welch). All that remains of Myron is a hovering memory who watches over the proceedings. Stunningly attractive Myra, who claims no man will ever possess her, arrives at the Westwood, California screen acting school of Uncle Buck Loner (John Huston). She pretends to be Myron's widow, and demands her inheritance, including her rights to the land on which the acting academy is now situated. While working to crush Myra legally, the braying Buck offers her a staff job teaching position. Now entrenched in the academy, Myra unleashes her crusade to destroy American manhood. Her first target is to rape Rusty (Roger Herren), a handsome young stud student whom Myra insists is "the last stronghold of masculinity in this Disneyland of perversion." Once ravaged, he beats a hasty retreat to the beach home of Leticia Van Allen (Mae West), a veteran talent agent and songstress. Mary Ann (Farrah Fawcett), Rusty's perplexed girlfriend, asks Myra's help. Instead, she tries to seduce her, but neither party proves interested. By now, Buck's attorneys are convinced that Myron never died nor married. To prove she is really Myron, Myra raises her skirts and shows the assemblage her surgery scars. Rushing from the school, she is involved in a street accident, and, upon awakening

Rex Reed and Raquel Welch in *Myra Breckinridge* (1970).

in the hospital, she is once again Myron. Leaving the hospital, the resigned Myron soft-shoe dances down the street with his alter ego, Myra.

Vincent Canby (*New York Times*) thought once the rape scene is over, *Myra Breckinridge* "collapses like a tired, smirking elephant with no place to go . . . . The most intriguing thing about the picture is the continual rhythmical juxtaposition of fleeting clips from other movies that supply most of the filth and what little wit the movie has." In reviewing this X-rated feature—which debuted the same month as the studio's X-rated *Beyond the Valley of the Dolls*, q.v.—Variety noted, "The real offense is not in the visible, but in the strung-out crashing nature of the film's unfolding and resolution. . . . Film was an interesting try at a very elusive story."

As a curiosity piece, *Myra Breckinridge* garnered $4.3 million in distributors' do-

mestic film rentals. Years later, author Gore Vidal would have the final verdict: "*Myra Breckinridge* was not just a bad movie, it was an awful joke."

163. The Naked Cage (Cannon, 1985), color, 97 min. R-rated.

Executive producers, Menahem Golan, Yoram Globus; producer, Chris D. Nebe; director/screenplay, Paul Nicholas; art director, Alex Hajdu; set decorator, Marlene McCormick; wardrobe, Shelly Komarov; makeup, Lily Beyair; music, Christopher Stone; assistant director, Bradley Gross; stunt coordinator, Al Jones; sound, Morteza Rezvani; camera, Hal Trussell; editor, Warren Chadwick, Nino De-Marco.

Cast: Shari Shattuck (Michelle); Angel Tompkins (Warden Wallace); Lucinda Crosby (Rhonda); Christina Whitaker (Rita Morani); Faith Minton (Sheila); Stacey Shaffer (Amy); Nick Benedict (Smiley); Lisa London (Abbey); John Terlesky (Willy); Aude Charles (Brenda Williams); Angela Gibbs (Vonna); Leslie

Huntly (Peaches); Carole Ita White (Trouble); Seth Kaufman (Randy); Larry Gelman (Doc); Susie London (Martha); Valerie McIntosh (Ruby); Flo Gerrish (Mother); James Ingersoll (Father); William Bassett (Jordan); Nora Niesen (Bigfoot); Jennifer Anne Thomas (Mock); Chris Anders (Miller); Al Jones (Bartender); Sheila Stephenson (Bank Teller) Bob Saurman (Motorcycle Cop); Rick Avery (Security Officer); Christopher Doyle (Police Officer); Gretchen Davis, Beryl Jones, Michael Kerr (Prison Guards).

Smiley: I'm entitled to have a little fun on the job.
Warden: Keep your hands off the girls.
Smiley: What about you, Warden?

The above dialogue takes place at a woman's prison in *The Naked Cage*, and, once again, as had become *de rigueur* in women-behind-bars feature, the zoo keeper was a tough woman whose sexual preferences ran to the same sex. Paul Nicholas, who had directed the successful European-produced *Chained Heat* (1982), was on hand to explore/exploit the genre set pieces in this R-rated example of softcore pornography.

Attractive Michelle (Shari Shattuck), a bank teller, who lives on a ranch with her parents (James Ingersoll, Flo Gerrish), is involved innocently in a bank robbery when her rotten ex-husband (John Terlesky) decides he wants quick cash. No sooner has the bewildered Michelle arrived at the prison than a guard alerts the oh-so-innocent Michelle, "don't mess with the warden! Whatever she wants, give it to her." Before long, Michelle finds out that prisoners are not safe from *anyone* in this institution, which includes the sex-crazed guard Smiley (Nick Benedict), the butch bitch guard Martha (Susie London) and, of course, the infamous Warden Wallace (Angel Tompkins). The latter tells the dazed young woman, "As long as you stay loyal to me, I'll protect you and you'll have certain privileges." Michelle is amazed to learn that the Warden has a penchant for inviting the more appealing inmates to her suite for conversation, drinks

and whatever else the situation inspires. After enduring the hell behind bars for some time, the toughened Michelle is befriended during a riot by a friendly guard, Rhonda (Lucinda Crosby) who turns out to be an undercover law agent detailed to investigate prison corruption. After the prison riot ends, Warden Wallace is fired. Michelle is soon released and returns to her peaceful life on her parents' ranch.

Variety found difficulty treating the movie seriously: "Though they call it *The Naked Cage*, a woman's prison is actually kind of a nice place, with lots of showers and beds and they don't make the ladies wear brassieres or very long dresses or much of anything if they don't want to. If the menfolk don't believe they'll just have to go see for themselves." *The Phantom's Ultimate Video Guide* (1989) was more enthusiastic, acknowledging that director Nicholas "supplies vicious catfights aplenty, gratuitous nudity galore, and more seething inmate unrest than you could shake a nightstick at. Toss in racial hostilities, brutal prison power struggles, and a lively climactic riot."

164. Next Stop, Greenwich Village (Twentieth Century-Fox, 1976), color, 111 min. R-rated.

Producers, Paul Mazursky, Tony Ray; director/screenplay, Mazursky; production designer, Phil Rosenberg; set decorator, Ed Stewart; costumes, Albert Wolsky; makeup, Bob Jiras; music, Bill Conti; assistant directors, Terry Donnelly, Jonathan Sanger; sound, Dennis Maitland; camera, Arthur Ornitz; editor, Richard Halsey.

Cast: Lenny Baker (Larry Papinsky); Shelley Winters (Mrs. Lapinsky)); Ellen Greene (Sarah); Lois Smith (Anita); Christopher Walken (Robert); Dori Brenner (Connie); Antonio Fargas (Bernstein); Lou Jacobi (Herb); Mike Kellin (Mr. Lapinsky); Michael Egan (Herbert); Denise Galik (Ellen); John C. Becher (Sid Weinberg, the Producer); John Ford Noonan (Barney); Helen Hanft (Herb's Wife); Rashel Novikoff (Mrs. Tupperman, the Neighbor); Joe Madden (Jake, the Poet); Joe Spinell (Cop); Rochelle Oliver (Abortionist); Gui Adrisano (Marco); Carole Manferdini (Southern

Mike Kellin and Shelley Winters in *Next Stop, Greenwich Village* (1976).

Girl); Jeff Goldblum (Clyde, the Actor); Rutanya Alda (Party Guest).

No, Neil Simon did not write this comedy which Pauline Kael (*5001 Nights at the Movies*, 1991) rated a "wonderful autobiographical lyric satire. . . . With a tip-top cast. . . ." Despite stock characterizations and sometimes trite situations, Paul Mazursky's nostalgic coming-of-age story had a joyful brashness and should have been more popular than it was. Among the Village people that the awakening hero discovers in 1950s New York City bohemia is a black homosexual poet, a role played with excessive zest by Antonio Fargas, who made a speciality of such parts (i.e., *Car Wash*, 1976, q.v.).

In 1953 Brooklyn, 22-year-old Jewish Larry Lapinsky (Lenny Baker) breaks free of his overly possessive mother (Shelley Winters) and moves to Greenwich Village, determined to become an actor. Before long, he has become a neighborhood regular, dating Sarah (Ellen Greene), consoling the suicidal Anita (Lois Smith), exchanging news with compassionate Connie (Dori Brenner) and indulging the excessive would-be poet Bernstein (Antonio Fargas), and the Method actor, Clyde (Jeff Goldblum). Between acting classes, Larry works at a natural food store and copes with repeated surprise visits from his doting mother and henpecked father (Mike Kellin). When Sarah becomes pregnant and vetoes the idea of marriage, another of their group, Robert (Christopher Walken) the playwright, helps Larry arrange for an abortion. After making a successful screen test with a film studio, Larry learns that Sarah and Robert have slept together. Meanwhile, Anita kills herself, signally the end of their Village clique. Before embarking for Hollywood, Larry visits his family in Brooklyn.

Vincent Canby weighed this "second-rate memoir": "*Next Stop, Greenwich Village* isn't aggressively awful. It is inept but mostly it's just commonplace. Its white bread trying to pass as rye." As to the cast, Canby, noted the presence of "a young black man improbably named Bernstein (Antonio Fargas), who also doubles as the homosexual." In contrast, *Variety* cited the comedy's "wonderful humanity and credibility," deciding it was "a very beautiful motion picture." Especially admiring of Shelley Winters' broad characterization, the trade paper reported on the supporting cast ("a group of arresting people"): "Dori Brenner, the type girl who hides her sensitives in kookiness; Antonio Fargas, the gay equivalent of Brenner's character. . . ." Geoff Brown (British *Monthly Film Bulletin*) judged, "Most of the comedy elements are reserved for subsidiary scenes and characters, and are distressingly traditional in tone. . . . Mazursky has managed throughout to stifle all the film's potential virtues."

In the gathering together of the beatnik types for *Next Stop, Greenwich Village*, Antonio Fargas makes a strong if stock impression as a 1950s-style triple minority (black, gay, poet). He is the prancing outcast who hides his depression (he admits to having been "brutalized physically and mentally" over the years) beneath his flamboyancy, and spends much of his time picking up and losing tricks. As Vito Russo (*The Celluloid Closet*, 1987) notes, "[Filmmaker Paul] Mazursky so good at evoking the period that we understand in some measure how gays like Bernstein coped with their self-hatred in the 1950s and survived because they found a tolerant pocket of civilization to inhabit."

165. The Night of the Iguana

(Metro-Goldwyn-Mayer, 1964), 125 min. Not rated.

Producer, Ray Stark; associate producer, Alexander Whitelaw; director, John Huston; based on the play by Tennessee Williams; screenplay, Anthony Veiller, Huston; art director, Stephen Grimes; costumes, Dorothy Jeakins; makeup, Jack Obringer, Eric Allwright; music/music director, Benjamin Frankel; associate director, Emilio Fernandez; sound, Basil Fenton-Smith; camera, Gabriel Figueroa; editor, Ralph Kemplen.

Cast: Richard Burton (Reverend T. Lawrence Shannon); Ava Gardner (Maxine Faulk); Deborah Kerr (Hannah Jelkes); Sue Lyon (Charlotte Goodall); James Ward (Hank Prosner); Grayson Hall (Judith Fellowes); Cyril Delevanti (Noono); Mary Boylan (Miss Peebles); Gladys Hill (Miss Dexter); Billie Matticks (Miss Throxton); Emilio Fernandez (Barkeeper); Eloise Hardt, Thelda Victor, Betty Proctor, Dorothy Vance, Liz Rubey, Bernice Starr, Barbara Joyce (Teachers); Roberto Leyva (Pedro); C. G. Kim (Chang); Fidelmar Duran (Pepe).

When Tennessee Williams's provocative, but talky *The Night of the Iguana* played on Broadway in 1961, the show's main attraction had been the return to Broadway of Bette Davis as the vulgar, randy hotel keeper, Maxine Faulk. When John Huston filmed the portentous property in 1964 in Mexico, the highlight of the on-location shooting had been the paparazzi's overzealous reportage of exactly how Elizabeth Taylor, *not* in the film, was getting along with Ava Gardner, who *was* in the movie as co-star to Taylor's husband, Richard Burton. When released, a highlight of the movie was Grayson Hall's strong performance as the frustrated, righteous spinster schoolteacher, who has a yen for one of her young charges (Sue Lyon), but buries it from others and herself beneath her straightlaced religious primness. As one observer notes ironically of the dykish teacher, "Miss Fellowes is a very moral person. If she ever found out the truth about herself, it would destroy her." Hall received a Best Supporting Actress nomination for her forceful portrayal of the latent lesbian, losing the Oscar to Lila Kedrova (*Zorba the Greek*).

As a tour guide for Blake Tours, defrocked clergyman Reverend T. Lawrence Shannon (Richard Burton) is a disillusioned drunkard. His current assignment is to shepherd a flock of lady schoolteachers through the countryside. The tourists are headed by self-righteous Judith Fellowes. The youngest on the tour bus is

Richard Burton, Cyril Delevanti, Deborah Kerr and Ava Gardner in *The Night of the Iguana* (1964).

eighteen-year-old, promiscuous Charlotte Goodall (Sue Lyon). She is drawn to Shannon and goes to his hotel room one night. The two are caught by Judith who is upset primarily because of her own craving for Charlotte. The jealous Fellowes threatens to have Shannon fired. Hoping to let the matter simmer down, Shannon leads the bus to the crumbling Coste Verde hotel. The establishment is owned by Maxine Faulk (Ava Gardner), Shannon's long-standing friend. She is now a widow and makes it known she would like Shannon to take the place of her former husband.

Hannah Jelkes (Deborah Kerr), an impoverished itinerant sketch artist and her 97-year-old grandfather, the poet Nonno (Cyril Delevanti), arrive at the hotel. Subsequently, Hank Prosner (Skip Ward), the young tour driver, repairs the bus, easily gaining Charlotte's interest, and takes off with the group. Shannon is beside himself, now at his wits' end over the botch he has made of his life and of "man's inhumanity to God." Hannah comforts him and the understanding Maxine steps aside. However, after Nonno finishes a new poem, he dies. Hannah insists on leaving the hotel alone. Shannon and Maxine remain at the ramshackled Coste Verde.

Time magazine applauded, "A picture that excites the sense, persuades the mind, and even occasionally speaks to the spirit —one of the best movies ever made from a Tennessee Williams' play." *Newsweek* agreed that it was "that fine rarity, an improvement on the play." Bosley Crowther (*New York Times*) had misgivings: "it has difficulty in communicating precisely what it is that is so barren and poignant about the people it brings to a tourist hotel . . . [It] fails to generate the sympathy and the personal compassion that might make their suffering meaningful. . . . Grayson Hall is incredibly frantic as the chaperone of the voracious girl [Lyon]. . . ." Eleanor Keen (*Chicago Sun-Times*), who gave the movie three stars, found the movie full of "a great deal of talk" but agreed "The performances are strong and fascinating. . . . Miss Lyon is overmatched with a cast of this caliber, but Grayson Hall is excellent." Keen noted decorously: "A great deal of importance has been added to the chaperone's role, but it remains one-faceted."

The Night of the Iguana grossed a relatively strong $4,324,950 in distributors' domestic film rentals. Besides Hall's Oscar nomination, the movie received an Academy Award bid for its Cinematography: Black-and-White, but lost to *Zorba the Greek*. During the decade, Hollywood would continue to explore the repressed lesbian in *7 Women* (1965) and *Rachel, Rachel* (1968), qq.v., two additional case studies of unhappy women who have buried their sexual desires in their work and religion. (Unlike the co-heroine of *The Children's Hour*, 1962. q.v., who dies for coming out of the closet, these unfulfilled homosexuals are left to brood in their private misery, apparently the then current punishment that Hollywood and society meted out to them for being different. In *7 Women*, Sue Lyon was again the catalyst for the suppressed longings of the spinster older woman (Margaret Leighton).

166. No Exit (Zenith International Film Corp., 1962), 85 min. Not rated. (a.k.a.: *Sinners Go to Hell*)

Producers, Fernando Ayala, Hector Olivera; associate producers, Julio Kaufman, James G. Zea; director, Tad Danielewski; based on the play *Huis Clos* by Jean-Paul Sartre; screenplay, George Tabori; art director, Mario Vanarelli; costumes, Horace Lannes; makeup, Aida Fernandez; music, Vladimir Ussachevsky; assistant directors, Esteban Etcheverrito, Ricardo Becher; sound, Jose Feijoo; camera, Ricardo Younis; supervising editor, Carl Lerner.

Cast: Viveca Lindfors (Inez); Rita Gam (Estelle); Morgan Sterne (Garcin); Ben Piazza (Camarero); Susano Mayo (Florence); Orlando Sacha (Gomez); Manuel Roson); Mirtha Miller (Carmencita); Miguel A. Irate (Robert); Elsa Dorian (Shirley); Mario Horna (Albert); Carlos Brown (Roger Delaney III).

In this dated (even at the time of release) existentialist drama, lesbianism is equated with cowardice and infanticide.

Three disparate individuals find themselves trapped together in a hotel room. They are journalist Garcin (Morgan Sterne), upper class society woman Estelle (Rita Gam) and Inez (Viveca Lindfors), a lesbian. Unable to avoid one another, each of the trio takes turns matching up with one another, hoping to outwit the others. Before long, the shameful nature of each hypocritical party is revealed. The so-called heroic reporter was actually executed for being a coward. Estelle had been hiding her nymphomaniac nature, that she had mercenarily chosen a wealthy husband, that she had disposed of her unwanted son and, in the process, drove her ruined husband to killing himself. As for the intense Inez, it is discovered that she committed suicide, guilt-ridden over having seduced a married partner who, in turn, had killed herself. In an outburst of hate, Estelle stabs Inez who has unsuccessfully tried to seduce her. However, the paper knife is far from deadly. At last, the three realize they are doomed to eternal hell together, from which there is no exit. The realization prompts them into a nervous fit of laughter, then into deadly silence.

Bosley Crowther (*New York Times*) warned that the screen adaptation, expanded by more than thirty minutes from the play by using flashbacks to establish the hateful characters acts of deceit, "reveals nothing more about the characters than is spewed out by them on the stage." For Crowther, "the whole thing is so antiseptic and is directed so stagily by Mr. Danielewski that it is visually monotonous on the screen." *Variety* confessed, "it is largely a static play on film . . . [basically] confined to the one room, and there's not much that can be done about it. . . . Miss Lindfors plays the lesbo with earnest conviction, never trying to justify her abnormality."

Based on the one-act drama *Huis clos* (1944) by French playwright Jean-Paul Sartre, *No Exit* was filmed in English in Buenos Aires, Argentina. The screenplay was by Lindfors's husband,George Tabori. It was the first of several lesbian roles the actress would play on screen: *Sylvia* (1965), *Puzzle of a Downfall Child* (1970), *Marilyn: the Untold Story* (1980), qq.v.

167. No Way to Treat a Lady

(Paramount, 1968), color, 108 min. Not rated.

Producer, Sol C. Siegel; director, Jack Smight; based on the novel by Wililam Goldman; screenplay, John Gay; art directors, Hal Pereira, George Jenkins; set decorator, Jenkins; costumes, Theoni V. Aldredge; makeup, Robert O'Bradovich; music, Stanley Myers; song, Myers and Andrew Belling; assistant director, Terence Nelson; sound, William Nallan, Charles Grenzbach; camera, Jack Priestley; editor, Archie Marshek.

Cast: Rod Steiger (Christopher Gill); Lee Remick (Kate Palmer); George Segal (Morris Brummel); Eileen Heckart (Mrs. Brummel); Murray Hamilton (Inspector Haines); Michael Dunn (Mr. Kupperman); Martine Bartlett (Alma Mulloy); Barbara Baxley (Belle Poppie); Irene Dailey (Mrs. Fitts); Doris Roberts (Sylvia Poppie); Ruth White (Mrs. Himmel); Val Bisoglio (Detective Monaghan); David Doyle (Lieutenant Dawson); Kim August (Sadie); Joey Faye (Superintendent); Patricia Ripley (Woman); Jay Sidney (Medical Examiner); Don Blair (Reporter); Tom Ahearne (Father O'Brien); Richard Nicholls (Man in Sardi's); R. Bernard (Indignant Man); John Gerstad (Dr. Shaffer); Bill Fort (Staff Editor); Zvee Scooler (Old Man); Eddie Philips (News Vendor); John Dutra (Man with Dog); Burr Smidt (Detective Sergeant); Linda Candy (Teenage Girl); Jim Dukas (Police Artist); Don Koll (Detective); Vincent Sardi, J. Molinski (Themselves); Bob O'Connell, Tony Major, Glen Kezer (Officers); Al Nesor, Sam Coppola, Louis Baisle (Customers).

In the same year that Tony Curtis was *The Boston Strangler*, q.v., Rod Steiger, who had played the mother-obsessed Mr. Joyboy in *The Loved One* (1965), q.v., played another mama's boy in the wicked black comedy, *No Way to Treat a Lady*. It was a tour-de-force permitting Steiger to romp (or chomp) through several different disguises—including one in drag—as the unmarried theatre producer whose love-hate for his deceased actress mother leads him onto a murderous rampage. While never being explicit, the movie builds up a composite of the killer's character traits to suggest that he is gay. Besides being middle-aged and single, he is fastidious, artistic and overly sensitive. (Moving along a different tangent, the movie draws a parallel and a contrast between the egalitarian strangler and the nebishy cop on the case, who is also mother-dominated and single, but very heterosexual.)

In New York City, several middle-aged, drab women are strangled, the work of a serial killer. The resourceful killer, anxious to share his exploits with an interested party, develops a rapport with New York Police Department homicide detective Morris Brummel (George Segal), relishing their conversations concerning his recent victims. This notoriety by association makes Morris a buffoon to his peers and a joke to his dominating Jewish mother (Eileen Heckart). While investigating the crime spree, the unmarried Brummel meets Kate Palmer (Lee Remick), a witness to the first murder. Morris and Kate begin dating and she proves a match for the overpowering Mrs. Brummel. Meanwhile, the psychotic theatre producer/manager Christopher Gill (Rod Steiger) chides Brummel for not solving the case, and tantalizingly confides, "I promise not to be a bad boy again." But he always is and the murders continue, even to his attempting to eliminate Kate. In the climax, the police detective pursues Christopher to

George Segal and Lee Remick in *No Way to Treat a Lady* (1968).

the deserted theatre where he has a penthouse and, in the showdown, shoots Gill dead.

Vincent Canby (*New York Times*) concluded, "Although *No Way to Treat a Lady* has the shape of a conventional suspense tale, the film is at its most entertaining—and, in fact, is only acceptable—as a series of macabre, sometimes broadly funny confrontations of caricatures . . . John Gay's script . . . makes nothing much of this Oedipean hang-up common to both cat and mouse, nor does it offer more than the sketchiest motivations for anything that happens." Canby did concede, "Mr. Steiger gives a beautifully uninhibited performance as a hammy, Mom-haunted Broadway producer, . . ." Lee Beaupre (*Variety*) was much more enthusiastic of this New York City-filmed caper: "Paramount has a winner in this entertaining suspense film neatly laced with mordant

humor," but observed, "Stronger, more appropriate direction could have pushed the film into the category of minor classic. . . . Steiger obviously relishes the multiple aspect of his part, and audiences should equally relish his droll impersonations of an Irish priest, German handyman, Jewish cop, middle-aged woman, Italian waiter and homosexual hairdresser."

While not a major box-office success, *No Way to Treat a Lady* made a decent return on its production costs.

168. Norman . . . Is That You?
(Metro-Goldwyn-Mayer/United Artists, 1976), color, 91 min. PG-rated.

Producer; George Schlatter; associate producers, Albert J. Simon, S. Bryan Hickox; director, Schlatter; based on the play by Ron Clark, Sam Bobrick; screenplay, Clark, Bobrick, Schlatter; art director, Stephen M. Berger; set decorator, Fred R. Price; costumes, Michael Travis; music, William Goldstein; songs, Goldstein and Ron Miller; assistant directors, William J. Hole Jr., Tom Foulkes, Albert Shepard; sound, Tom Ancell, William McCaughey, Bill Hawley, Hal Belcher; camera, Gayne Rescher; editor, George Folsey Jr.

Cast: Redd Foxx (Ben Chambers): Pearl Bailey (Beatrice Chambers); Dennis Dugan (Garson Hobart); Michael Warren (Norman Chambers); Tamara Dobson (Audrey); Vernee Watson (Melody); Jayne Meadows (Mrs. Adele Hobart); George Furth, Barbara Sharma (Bookstore Clerks); Sergio Aragones, Sosimo Hernandez (Desk Clerks); Wayland Flowers (Larry Davenport); Allan Drake (Cab Driver).

"It is not clear . . . whether the gay community or the nongay community will find more to be exasperated about in *Norman*. Every straight community stereotype about gay life is trotted out to humorous effect . . . and while the movie makes a rather arch plea for tolerance, you detect the old business of having your cake and making fun of it, too." (Charles Champlin, *Los Angeles Times*)

On Broadway, *Norman . . . Is That You?* (1970) ran for only twelve performances. Its theme of two battling parents learning and then accepting that their son is gay did not appeal to theatergoers. (Ironically, over the years, the broad comedy would become a perennial favorite in stock productions.) As a Hollywood film, to accommodate its stars, Redd Foxx and Pearl Bailey, the roles of the parents were switched from Jewish to black, while their son's lover remained white. .

Baffled Ben Chambers (Redd Foxx), who operates a dry-cleaning establishment in Arizona, arrives unexpectedly in Los Angeles, intent on getting sympathy from his son, Norman (Michael Warren). He has just found out that his brother has been having an affair with his wife, Beatrice (Pearl Bailey). Ben's quandary accelerates when he discovers that Norman is living with a man, Garson Hobart (Dennis Dugan). Determined to save his son from ruination, he arranges for a hooker, Audrey (Tamara Dobson), to "make a man" of Norman. When the embarrassed and an-

gered Norman walks out, a non-plussed Ben goes to bed with Audrey himself. Later, the disinclined Norman is seduced by his friend, Melody (Vernee Watson). While this is happening, good-natured Garson suggests his dominating widowed mother (Audrey Meadows) as a date for Ben. Still later, Ben rehires Audrey , this time to woo Garson away from Norman.

By now, Beatrice's Mexican fling with her brother-in-law has run its unproductive course. She shows up at Norman's apartment, wanting his sympathy. As Ben and Beatrice battle back and forth, Norman announces that he has joined the Navy to escape the clutches of his meddlesome dad. His action leads the Chambers to reconcile and they hire Garson to work in their dry-cleaning establishment, convinced it will lead Norman back to the fold.

Richard Eder (*New York Times*) did not find much merit in this slapped together PG-rated production: "It is a series of bad jokes about homosexuality, strung upon trite situation comedy and collapsing into what is meant to be an uplifting message about people being allowed to do their own things." John Pym (British *Monthly Film Bulletin*) found that the movie's fault lay in George Schlatter's "stage-bound direction" and "the constraints placed on an energetic cast by a static plot which steadfastly fails to surprise."

Not wanting to offend anyone, *Norman . . . Is That You?* not so subtly played it both ways in presenting its fence-straddling point of view with its cop-out ending that has the butch gay hero going on to an undefined straight future, while the enlightened parents embrace their mincing in-law.

Norman. . . Is That You? was originally rated R, but after an appeal, it was changed to PG. The movie was "condemmed" by the National Catholic Film Office and found offensive by the National Council of Churches for "its tawdry, flippant and insensitiv treatment of both heterosexual and homosexual love."

Tamara Dobson and Redd Foxx in *Norman . . . Is That You?* **(1976).**

169. Ode to Billy Joe (Warner Bros., 1976), color, 105 min. PG-rated.

Producers, Max Baer, Roger Camras; associate producer, Mark Sussman; director, Baer; based on the song by Bobbie Gentry; screenplay, Herman Raucher; art director, Philip Jefferies; set decorator, Harry Gordon; makeup, Marvin Westmore; music, Michel Legrand; songs: Gentry; Alan and Marilyn Bergman; assistant director, Anthony Brand; stunt coordinator, Beau Gibson; sound, Darin Knight; special effects, Gene Grigg; camera, Michel Hugo; second unit camera, Robert Jessup, Lyn Lockwood; editor, Frank E. Morriss.

Cast: Robby Benson (Billy Joe McAllister); Glynnis O'Connor (Bobbie Lee Hartley); Joan Hotchkis (Anna "Mama" Hartley); Sandy McPeak (Glen "Papa" Hartley); James Best (Dewey Barksdale); Terence Goodman (James Hartley); Beck Brown (Becky Thompson); Simpson Hemphill (Brother Taylor); Ed Shelnut (Coleman Stroud); Eddie Tair (Tom Hargitay); William Hallberg (Dan McAllister); Frannye Capelle (Belinda Wiggs); Rebecca Jernigan (Mrs. Thompson); Ann Martin (Mrs. Hunicutt); Will Long (Trooper Bosh); John Roper (Trooper Ned); Pat Purcell, Jim Westerfield (Alabama Boys); Jack Capelle (Alabama Driver); Al Scott (Master of Ceremonies).

For several years after singer Bobbie Gentry wrote her hit song "Ode to Billie Joe" (1967), people wondered about the lyrics in which Billy Joe and his girlfriend throw something (what?) off the Tallahatchie Bridge and the fact that the next day he kills himself (why?) by jumping off the same bridge. Gentry would say later, "The song is sort of a study in unconscious cruelty . . . what was thrown off the bridge really isn't that important." However, moviemakers felt differently. Their decision led to this 1976 feature which grossed $11.6 million in distributors' domestic film rentals. The movie's soundtrack featured Bobbie Gentry performing a new version of the title song.

In the spring of 1953 in Chickasaw County, Mississippi, fifteen-year-old Bobbie Lee Hartley (Glynnis O'Connor) finds herself the object of romantic interest of two-years-older Billy Joe McAllister (Robby Benson), who works at the local saw mill owned by Dewey Barksdale (James Best). Bobbie's parents, particularly her church deacon father (Sandy McPeak) insist she is too young to date. Nevertheless, the smitten teenagers meet secretly and fall in love. Subsequently, after a rowdy party at the lumber mill, Billy Joe vanishes for a few days. Bobbie Lee comes across him in the woods. The very upset young man refuses to explain his absence. Instead he tells her to meet him at the Tallahatchie Bridge at sunset. She arrives and he takes her good-luck doll (named Benjamin) and tosses it into the water. Later, after failing in their fumbled attempts to make love, he explains that he had sex with a man after the party. ("It's an offendment against nature," he says. "I don't know how I could have done it. I swear. I don't know how I could be wanting you and do that!") He refuses to say whom the other party is.

The next day, Billy Joe's body is found floating in the river, not far from the doll. Everyone in town assumes that the youth killed himself because he had made Bobbie Lee pregnant. As a result the shamed McAllisters leave town and Mr. Hartley is removed as a church deacon. Leaving town to have her "abortion," (and preserve Billy Joe's reputation) she comes across a remorseful Dewey Barksdale. He confesses that it was he who seduced Billy Joe. When he offers to tell the authorities, she convinces him not to and, instead, to leave town. ("We can't have people believing Billy Joe McAllister jumped off a bridge cause of a man, can we?") She says the least they can do for Billy Joe is to keep his legend alive. As Dewey prepares to drive her to the bus station, she admits, "I'll be back before long. I'm only fifteen. What do I know of the world?"

While generally positive in his appraisal, Richard Eder (*New York Times*) found flaws: "Sometimes it is cute where it's supposed to be funny, and sometimes it is soft where it's supposed to be lush. . . . [The film's] virtue lies in the setting-out of the two characters—Billy Joe and a girl named Bobby—their timid and then more demanding courtship. . . .Its failure comes when Mr. Baer tries to stuff these two, with all their liveliness and appeal, into the song, and invents an answer to the mystery that is grotesquely out of keeping. . . . Robby Benson . . . manages his boisterous, wooly-headed role with great charm." In contrast, *Variety* found the picture "a superbly sensitive period romantic tragedy. . . . James Best also shares major acting honors in the role of Benson's employer, who precipitates the climax. The ultimate events are painted in the grays of the real world. . . . This is no shoddy exploitation ripoff picture. . . . Nor is it goopy sentimentality."

Because *Ode to Billy Joe* was deliberately set in the quaint backwoods country of the 1950s South, it was assumed that 1970s moviegoers would accept the movie's pre-Gay Liberation concepts. They include Billy Joe's passive (?) deed being a one-time thing (Dewey confirms this notion with "I tried to tell him it would probably never happen again"), that his "sin against God" has to be cleansed by his killing himself, and that his memory (as a stud who supposedly impregnates his underage girlfriend) should be preserved by a lie. It was a very mixed message for audiences.

The very atmospheric *Ode to Billy Joe* was filmed on location in the Mississippi delta country.

170. Once Bitten (Samuel Goldwyn Co., 1985), color, 97 min. PG-13-rated.

Executive producer, Samuel Goldwyn Jr.; producers, Dimitri Villard, Robby Wald, Frank E. Hildebrand; associate producer, Russell Thacher; director, Howard Storm; story, Villard; screenplay, David Hines, Jeffrey Hause, Jonathan Roberts; production designer, Gene Rudolf; costumes, Jill Ohanneson, Harold O'Neal; makeup, Steve Laporte; choreographers, Joanne Divito, Randy Grazio; assistant directors, Gene Sultan, Nicholas Batchelor, Robert Altshuler; stunt coordinator, Jim Winburn; sound, Mark Ulano; special effects, Court Wizard; camera, Adam Greenberg; editor, Marc Grossman.

Cast: Lauren Hutton (Countess); Jim Carrey (Mark Kendall); Karen Kopins (Robin Pierce); Cleavon Little (Sebastian); Thomas Ballatore (Jamie); Skip Lackey (Russ); Jeb Adams (World War I Ace Vampire); Joseph Brutsman (Confederate Vampire); Stuart Charno (Cabin Boy Vampire); Robi Klein (Flowerchild Vampire); Glen Mauro, Gay Mauro (Twin Vampires); Carey More (Moll Flanders Vampire); Peter Elbling (Bookseller); Richard Schaal (Mr. Kendall); Peggy Pope (Mrs. Kendall); Anna Mathias (Daphne); Kate Zentall (Tanya); Laura Urstein (Darlene); Megan Mullally (Suzette); Garry Goodrow (Wino); Dan Barrows (Harry); Alan McRae (Man in Drag); Philip Linton (Boy in Shower); Don Richey (Bouncer); Operlene Barley (Lunch Counter Lady); Dominick Brascia (Young Man Buying Ice Cream); Nancy Hunter (Woman Shopper in Unisex Store); Anthony Storm, Casey Storm (Kids); Rainbow Shalom, Kimberlye Gold, Nancy Scher, Kelly Salloum, Maria Vidal (High School Band).

Joseph Gelmis (*Newsday*) efficiently and satirically summarized this "numbing, enervating" blend of teenage sex romp and horror motif: "Take a 400-year-old female vampire [Lauren Hutton], her gay retainer [Cleavon Little] and assorted hangers-on. House them in a Hollywood mansion. Choose for her latest victim a high school senior [Jim Carrey] whose only protection against becoming a vampire himself is to lose his virginity. Assign the teenager a girl friend [Karen Kopins] who will do anything to save him from a fate worse than death."

Rex Reed (*New York Post*) chided, "Just when you thought intelligence, good taste and box-office boredom had finished off the lethargic, inept monsters of *Transylvania 6-5000* [1985], along comes *Once Bitten*, a dreadfully dull teenager-vampire epic. . . . Bring garlic." *Variety* thought the production was "too timid to make its premise interesting. . . . Rather than injecting new life into the tired teen genre, the vampire material merely sinks to the commonplace." The trade paper thought Lauren Hutton was "upstaged by the stylized elegance of her modern mansion. . . . [However] As her vampire valet, Cleavon Little is the only thing worth watching as he glides through the house. Even here the filmmakers were too meek to explore the amusing possibilities of a gay vampire."

Looking for cheap laughs, this mindless comedy pokes fun at anything within range, frequently its gay subjects. Cleavon Little camps it up as the swishy, lisping bloodsucker. This pop-eyed, mincing minion likes to hide in his mistress's wardrobe closet, leading to such witty repartee as:

Countess: Out of the closet.

Sebastian: I came out of the closet centuries ago.

In a far more homophobic vein, and one which earned enduring notoriety as such, there is a sequence when two of the hero's buddies (Thomas Ballatore, Skip Lackey) poke around the school shower room hoping to determine if their pal has fang marks on any part of his body, which would prove he is lost to vampirism. When they are discovered peeping at their nude peers, there is general Pandemonium:

Friend #1: This is the suckiest thing that could ever happen. The whole school thinks we're gay.

Friend #2: Don't be such a twerp. Our past histories speak for themselves. No one is going to think we're gay.

Friend #1: [Resignedly] This is it. We might as well move in together and get his and his towels.

Flaws, warts and all, *Once Bitten*, nevertheless, earned $4,415,284 in distributors' domestic film rentals.

171. Only When I Laugh (Columbia, 1981), color, 120 min. R-rated. (British release title: *It Hurts Only When I Laugh*)

Producers, Roger M. Rothstein, Neil Simon; director, Glenn Jordan; based on the play *The Gingerbread Lady* by Simon; screenplay, Simon; production designer, Albert Brenner; art director, David Haber; set decorator, Marvin March; costumes, Ann Roth; makeup, Tom Case; music, David Shire; assistant directors, Bill Beasley, Jim Van Wyck; sound, Tommy

Overton, Les Lazarowitz; camera, David M. Walsh; editor, John Wright.

Cast: Marsha Mason (Georgia Hines); Kristy McNichol (Polly); James Coco (Jimmy Perino); Joan Hackett (Toby Landau); David Dukes (David Lowe); John Bennett Perry (Lou, the Actor); Guy Boyd (Man); Ed Moore (Dr. Bob Komack); Byron Webster (Tom); Peter Coffield (Mr. Tarloff); Mark Schubb (Adam Kasabian); Ellen LaGamba (Receptionist); Venida Evans (Nurse Garcia); Nancy Nagler (Heidi); Dan Monahan (Jason); Michael Ross (Paul); Tom Ormeny (Kyle); Ken Weisbrath (Waiter); Henry Olek (George, the Director); Jane Atkins (Doreen); Kevin Bacon (Don); Ron Levine (Gary); Rebecca Stanley (Denise Summers); Nick LaPadula (Bartender); Phillip Lindsay (Super); Birdie Hale (Super's Wife); Wayne Framson (Father); Jon Vargas (Manuel).

Almost entirely rewriting his quasi-flop Broadway play, *The Gingerbread Lady* (1970), into *Only When I Laugh*, Neil Simon uses trademark wisecracks and one-liners to delineate his New York actress heroine, a recovering alcoholic. Among her circle of close friends is loyal Jimmy Perino (James Coco), a gay actor, who admits that "Next to sex, dishing with the girls is the best thing I know," but sighs about his failed career after 22-years of trying ("Do you know what it feels like to be turned down for a hemorrhoid commercial?"). Reflecting a truism of twentieth century American society that has become a cliche (or visa versa), the homosexual Jimmy Perino is the heroine's best pal in *Only When I Laugh* (a point made much of in the movie and in the reviews). Since sex never gets in the way of their friendship, he is her ideal male companion, bolstered by the fact that he is better organized, more sensitive and has a greater sense of style than most of her women acquaintances. The fact that he needs this larger-than-life woman to fill the voids in his life is a subtext of his characterization. James Coco handled his role so adroitly that he received a Best Supporting Actor's Oscar nomination.

Having dried out at a Long Island clinic for twelve weeks, Georgia Hines (Marsha

James Coco and Marsha Mason in *Only When I Laugh* (1981).

Mason) returns to her walk-up New York apartment, shaky about facing life sober. Her friends include perpetually unemployed actor Jimmy Perino (James Coco) and fortyish, insistently chic Toby Landau (Joan Hackett). Fearful of taking on responsibilities, Georgia hesitates when her 17-year-old daughter, Polly (Kristy McNichol), begs to come stay with her, rather than remain with her dad. Georgia finally agrees to her request—reluctantly. Meanwhile, a former boyfriend, playwright David Lowe (David Dukes), offers Georgia the starring role in his new Broadway comedy, *Only When I Laugh*, which deals with their highly-charged past life together. Pressures mount as Georgia meets David's young girlfriend (Rebecca Stanley), helps Toby deal with her husband walking out on her on her birthday, consoles Jimmy who has lost a coveted tiny role in an off-off-off Broadway play, and tries to be a real mother to her adolescent daughter.

Yielding to temptation, Georgia's one sip of champagne leads to another and, before long, the tipsy woman is rude to impressionable Polly and her new boyfriend (Mark Schubb). This incident causes the embarrassed Georgia to stalk out of her friend's apartment, get into a bar brawl, and, in a burst of self-pity, to reject her daughter's efforts to be caring for her. In fact, Georgia demands that Polly return to her dad. However, plain-talking Jimmy and Toby force Georgia to deal with truths. Thereafter, she meet her ex-husband for lunch, so they can decide—jointly and responsibly—on their daughter's future.

Kevin Thomas (*Los Angeles Times*) admitted that accepting Neil Simon's witty one-liners as conversation is an acquired taste, especially in an essentially serious drama. "At times the repartee pings and pongs relentlessly, but it does give way to people we can care about. And, of course, Neil Simon can be very, very funny." In assessing the movie's structure, Thomas observed of the Mason-Hackett-Coco triumvirate: "While Coco is just as caring of Mason as Hackett is, he subconsciously reinforces Mason's dependency, as she herself comes to realize, . . ." For Alex Keneas (*Newsday*), "Well, you either 'relate' to Simon or you don't. . . . Mason, Coco and Hackett are all plausible vehicles for Simon's fast and cynical New York Jewish/show-biz repartee." However, Keneas argued, "But these longtime friends through thick and, now, crisis thin, are only partly flesh and blood. Why? Because they never touch one another's lesions."

More favorable was David Ansen (Newsweek) who judged, "[Director Glenn] Jordan gives both the audience and his excellent cast room to breathe and neatly keeps things just off the brink of overbearing melodrama. . . .Coco seems more relaxed on screen than usual—he's a sad-sack charmer—and Hackett makes her comic foil surprisingly human."

Only When I Laugh earned three Academy Award nominations: Best Actress (Marsha Mason; Katharine Hepburn won for *On Golden Pond*); Best Supporting Actor (James Coco; John Gielgud won for *Arthur*); Best Supporting Actress (Joan Hackett; Maureen Stapleton—who ironically had played the lead in *The Gingerbread Lady* on Broadway—won for *Reds*). *Only When I Laugh* grossed $12,507,141 in distributors' domestic film rentals. Jimmy Coco would play a far less obviously stated gay friend-of-the-heroine in Elizabeth Taylor's TV movie, *There Must Be a Pony* (1986). George Carlin would perform a siilar role as the gay next-door neighbor in *The Prince of Tides* (1991).

172. Our Sons (ABC-TV, May 19, 1991), color, 100 min. Not rated.

Executive producers, Robert Greenwald, Carla Singer; co-executive producer, William Hanley; producer, Philip Kleinbart; co-producer, Micki Dickoff; supervising producer/director, John Erman; suggested by the documentary *Too Little, Too Late* by Dickoff; teleplay, Hanley; production designer, James Hulsey; set decorator, Lisa Smithline; costumes, Van Broughton Ramsey; makeup, George Masters, Ricki Sharp; special character makeup, Michele Burke Winter; music, John Morris; assistant directors, Yudi Bennett, Debra Kent; sound, Bo Harwood; camera, Tony Imi; editor, Robert Florio.

Cast: Julie Andrews (Audrey Grant); Ann-Margret (Luanne Barnes); Hugh Grant (James Brant); Zeljko Ivanek (Donald Barnes); Tony Roberts (Harry); Hal England (Charly); Loyla Ramas (Patient's Wife); Annabelle Weenick (Nurse); Lisa Blake Richards (Female Bar Patron); Essex Smith (Trailer Park Manager); Frank Whiteman (George); Elizabeth Austin (Sally); George Whiteman (Male Bar Patron).

"Everything has happened since Martin Sheen and Hal Holbrook played masculine gay lovers 19 years ago in ABC's ground-breaking, *That Certain Summer* [q.v.]. Everything and nothing. . . . Although nearly two decades have passed— with AIDS having become an international scourge in the '80s—TV still fears gay-related themes as a lethal minefield to be tiptoed through only at great fiscal risk." (Howard Rosenberg, *Los Angeles Times*)

With two such high-profile stars as Julie Andrews and Ann-Margret as its bankable stars, there was much anticipation concerning this highly-touted TV movie, the first prime-time feature film since *An Early Frost* (1985), q.v. to deal head-on with the subject of homosexuality and AIDS—putting to one side the biography TV dramas on *Liberace* (1988) and *Rock Hudson* (1990), qq.v. Unfortunately, the well-intentioned drama proved to be contrived, shallow, predictable and safe. Some viewers were so disaffected that Julie Andrews's expensively tailored wardrobe and Ann-Margret's bizarrely teased blonde wig received more attention than the production itself.

Supercharged San Diego businessperson Audrey Grant (Julie Andrews) is a hands-on, successful executive. However, as a single (divorced) mother, she practices avoidance with her grown-up

Ann-Margret
Julie Andrews

Before
you can
accept
a
son's
death,
you
must
accept
his life.

ABC Sunday Night Movie   9:00 PM

Advertisement for *Our Sons* (1991).

son, James (Hugh Grant), whom she has known for years is homosexual and who now lives with his lover, Donald (Zeljko Ivanek). James breaks Audrey out of her complacency by asking her to fly to Fayetteville, Arkansas not only to tell Donald's mother, Luanne (Ann-Margret), that her son is dying, but to convince her to come see Donald in the hospital before it is too late. The problem with persuading Luanne, James says, is that "This is a woman for whom homosexuality is an offense against God, man and nature."

Elitist Audrey arrives at barmaid Luanne's trailer park in an airport limousine and bullies the single woman into returning to California with her. En route, the two very different women, discover that, despite contrasting outward reactions in dealing with their sons' homosexuality, each loves her child very much. Presently, Donald—thrown out of the family home at sixteen when his parents found out he was gay—is more afraid of being rejected again by Luanne than of dying. The reunion is not easy for either party. Pushed onward by Audrey and the example of James's loving care of Donald, Luanne breaks through her anger (at Donald not being "normal") and her prejudices (against "one of them" whom God has punished with AIDS). Later, with Luanne, Audrey and James nearby, Donald dies peacefully at home. After a memorial service, Luanne takes his son's body back to Arkansas for burial. Meanwhile, the ordeal has forced Audrey to break her self-absorption to admit her years of pent-up pain about James being gay. (She realizes, at last, "It's not a question of liking or disliking, but accepting. . . .") At the end, James, no longer diffident about his future well-being, promises to be AIDS-tested.

Miles Beller (*Hollywood Reporter*) found, "There's an inclination toward easy pathos to this telefilm . . . sentimentality arising from blatant bathos rather than from fine articulated characterizations. . . . While Andrews and Ann-Margret go about their jobs with praiseworthy finesse, not even their performances can triumph over *Our Sons'* overwrought manner." *Daily Variety* found, "the telefilm works through chunks of two-role scenes . . . to build its case against homophobia and against ignorance over AIDS. . . .all is correctly written, but an emotional wallop is lacking. Grant acts movingly in his scenes with Ivanek, whose makeup is crushingly realistic; Ivanek wins sympathy with his acceptance of the finality of his situation—and his caring for James." For Howard Rosenberg (*Los Angeles Times*) "*Our Sons* is a creative failure, so rigidly predictable that its earnest message about the dread of AIDS is minimized. . . . [It] plays peekaboo with AIDS, nervously approaching it from around a corner as if not to freak out advertisers or offend conservative media watchdogs that wield economic boycotts like spiked clubs. . . . Of the two actresses, only Ann-Margret is able to free herself from the movies manacles and perform in a way that touches you. Andrews sort of goes along for the elegant limo ride."

Based on Micki Dickoff's 1987 documentary (*Too Little, Too Late*) *Our Sons* was dedicated "to the memory of 108,731 people in the U.S. who have died of complications form AIDS."

173. Outrageous! (Cinema 5, 1977), color, 100 min. R-rated.

Producers, William Marshall, Hendrick J. Van Der Kolk; associate producer, Peter O'Brian; director, Richard Benner; based on the story "Making It" by Margaret Gibson; screenplay, Benner; art director, Karen Bromley; set director, Bruce Calnan; costumes, Michael Daniels; makeup, Shonagh Jabour; music, Paul Hoffert; song, Hoffert and Brenda Hoffert; assistant directors, John Ryan, Barbara Laffey; sound, Doug Ganton; camera, James B. Kelly; editor, George Appleby.

Cast: Craig Russell (Robin Turner); Hollis McLaren (Liza Connors); Richard Easley (Perry); Allan Moyle (Martin); David McIlwraith (Bob); Gerry Salzberg (Jason); Andree Pelletier (Anne); Helen Shaver (Jo); Martha Gibson (Nurse Carr); Helen Hughes (Mrs. Connors); Jonah Royston (Dr. Beddoes): Richard Moffatt (Stewart); David Woito (Hustler); Rusty Ryan (Jimmy); Jackie Loren (Herself); Michael Daniels (Performer in Gold); Michel (Performer in Pink); Trevor Bryan (Miss Montego Bay); Mike Ironside (Drunk); Rene Fortier (Manatee D.J.); Maxine Miller (Peggy O'Brien); and: Brent Savoy.

"When I was fourteen, I looked in the mirror and said, 'Admit it, Robin, you're different.' A few years later, I looked again and said. 'Robin, you're a typical screaming hairdresser.' . . . Somehow I got through all the days and all the jobs, never really happy but somehow got by. [Now] I blew off all the lids. All the good looking boys see is a drag queen." (Spoken by the character Robin Turner in *Outrageous!*)

Schizophrenic Liza Connors (Hollis McLaren) disappears from an Ontario Hospital where she has been a (voluntary) patient for several years, and shows up at the Toronto apartment of her long-time friend Robin Turner (Craig Russell), a hairdresser. The visit turns into a permanent situation with Robin easing Liza through her nightmarish fears. In turn, Liza, along with Martin (Allan Moyle), another drop-out patient pal of her's, convince Robin to follow his dream of a show business career. They urge him to enter an amateur drag contest which he wins. He soon becomes a regular attraction at local gay bars and quits his beauty salon job. Meanwhile, Liza, who became pregnant from a one-night affair with a taxi driver (Richard Moffatt), is determined to have her baby. Robin goes to New York where he is befriended by a cabbie, Bob (David McIlwraith), who becomes his agent, and his female impressionist career blossoms at the Jack Rabbit Club. Learning that Liza has lost her baby and has become severely depressed again, Robin brings Liza to New York where, he insists, she will fit right in—just another neurotic among the eight million there.

Janet Maslin (*New York Times*) found structural faults within *Outrageous!* with its parallel stories of two outsiders (a gay man and a schizophrenic). "Unfortunately, the movie winds up exploiting them in an insidious and very unpleasant way. Robin and Liza seem to define themselves through their ability to shock or at least unsettle those around them. . . . It could be argued that *Outrageous!* . . . presents a no-holds-barred look at a certain stratum of homosexual culture and is thus noteworthy for its verisimilitude. . . . [However, it] unwittingly enforces stereotypes as dangerous as those favored by Anita Bryant. . . . Craig Russell and Hollis McLaren are more than convincing as Robin and Liza, but they're a little hard to watch. . . ."

In contrast, *Variety* enthused, "It's the best film made up to now on drag shows, the gay world, and the trials and tribulations of the homosexual. But it's a human story of a relationship. . . . The dialogue between these misfits carries the pic with refreshing ease from start to finish."

Other than its rough production edges, *Outrageous!* is an strong showcase for the talents of female impersonator Craig Russell, who, in the course of this drama, performs remarkable interpretations of Tallulah Bankhead, Bette Davis, Judy Garland, Peggy Lee, Ella Fitzgerald, Mae West, et al. Much has been made, over the years, about the insensitivity of comparing a gay person to a "crazy', but that owes more to the movie's literary origin than to negativism. (*Outrageous!* was based on a story, "Making It," by a schizophrenic [Margaret Gibson] who had once shared a Toronto apartment with a hairdresser [Craig Russell].) *Outrageous!* has a refreshing optimism. As the burgeoning Robin notes of his beauty shop customers: "These women here live life like it's a can of coke and are afraid to drink it too fast or it'll all be gone. Life isn't a can of coke." It sets the tone for the movie, a tragicomedy with a marvelous, offbeat sense of humor. In its time, *Outrageous!* was considered rather daring and "right on" in its portrayals.

Made on a $165,000 budget in/around Toronto, Canada, *Outrageous!* was shot in 16mm and blown up to 35mm. A decade later, director/writer Richard Benner reunited with Craig Russell and Hollis McLaren for *Too Outrageous*, q.v.

174. P.J. (Universal, 1968), color, 109 min. Not rated. (British release title: *New Face in Hell*)

Producer, Edward J. Montagne; director, John Guillerin; story Philip Reisman Jr., Montagne; screenplay, Reisman; art directors, Alexander Golitzen, Walter M. Simonds; set decorators, John McCarthy, Robert Priestly; costumes, Jean Louis; makeup, Bud Westmore; music, Neal Hefti; song, Percy Faith and Reisman; assistant directors, Phil Bowles, Skip Cosper; sound, Waldon O. Watson, Lyle Cain; matte supervisor, Albert Whitlock; camera, Loyal Griggs; editor, Sam E. Waxman.

Cast: George Peppard (P. J. Detweiler); Raymond Burr (William Orbison); Gayle Hunnicutt (Maureen Preble); Brock Peters (Police Chief Waterpark); Wilfrid Hyde-White (Billings-Browne); Jason Evers (Jason Grenoble); Coleen Gray (Betty Orbison); Susan Saint James (Linette Orbison); Severn Darden (Shelton Quell); H. Jane Van Duser (Elinor Silene); George Furth (Sonny Silene); Barbara Dana (Lita); Herbert Edelman (Charlie); John Qualen (Poppa); Bert Freed (Police Lieutenant); Ken Lynch (Thorson); Jim Boles (Landlord's Agent); Arte Johnson (Jackie); King Charles MacNiles (Calypso Singer); Don Haggerty (Ape); Kay Farrington (Mrs. Thorson); Lennie Bremen (Greavy).

As a hard-boiled detective drama, *P.J.* was not very good, nor was fast-aging George Peppard very resourceful as its down-at-the-heels private eye. What makes this film relevant to this book is a sequence set in a New York gay bar in which the bruiser hero tackles (successfully, of course) some two-dozen leather-outfitted homosexuals. The bar scene was as much Hollywood fantasyland as the one used in Otto Preminger's *Advise and Consent* (1962) or Frank Sinatra's *The Detective* (1968), qq.v. However, the scene indicated once again that the American movie industry was beginning to come out of the closet regarding a once forbidden topic—homosexuality. Unfortunately, the mainstream images *P.J.* projected regarding the gay minority were prejudicial and stereotypical.

In New York City, P. J. Detweiler (George Peppard), a broke private investigator accepts a demeaning assignment as bodyguard to Maureen Preble (Gayle Hunnicutt), the girlfriend of tycoon William Orbison (Raymond Burr). Later, to protect Maureen from further attempts on her life, Orbison takes her, his wife (Susan Saint James), Detweiler and others to his private Bahamas island retreat. There, P.J. kills Orbison's partner, Jason Grenoble (Jason Evers), in self-defense. The detective begins to realize that he had been set-up by Orbison and Maureen to get rid of Jason. Pursuing his employer back to New York City, Detweiler has a showdown with the two culprits, with the latter killing each other in a shootout. The jaded P.J. now is ready for a new case.

Vincent Canby (*New York Times*) granted that "the dialogue is rough and amusing" and that director John Guillermin "keeps it all moving so swiftly there is not much time to worry about motivations." Noting the recent changes in the production code regarding "sex and society's seamier side" Canby wondered why *P.J.* ended being so "soft and marshmallowy." "This is despite the fact that there are in *P.J.* lines of dialogue and bedroom episodes, plus one nightmare scene in a homosexual bar, that might likely have turned [Humphrey] Bogart himself into a Puritan." *Variety* summarized, "If it's violence you want, you get it; if it's a story that holds water, you don't." As to the cast, the trade paper thought Peppard "handles himself well" and that Raymond Burr "returns to his old film forte of bad guy and does it convincingly."

During the course of stomping stolidly through *P.J.*, George Peppard generates most of his expression through arching an eyebrow now and again. He is the homophobic gumshoe who refuses to shake hands with Shelton Kewell (Severn Darden), Maureen's house employee, who appears too sissy to the detective what with his outre look (his cigarette holder, etc.) and slinky walk. When P. J. asks her why she has such a peculiar (i.e. gay) servant, she replies offhandedly, "He isn't much, but he sleeps in." To which, the wisecracking Detweiler snaps, "Where, at the bottom of the garden?" Later, when the case leads the private eye to the Gay Caballero Bar— a dark, gloomy place full of men wearing gold earrings, he gets an immediate response when he archly asks several starring patrons, "Any of you tomboys know a guy named Shelton Kwell?" This leads to a one-against-all brawl in which Detweiler is the easy victor. He emerges from the scrape almost unscathed, except for a bleeding nose and a few fingernail scratches on his face, the latter the present of unmanly combattants.

P.J., completed in March 1967, was not released until a year later.

175. Papillon (Allied Artists, 1973), color, 150 min. PG-rated.

Executive producer, Ted Richmond; producers, Robert Dorfman, Franklin J. Schaffner; associate producer, Robert O. Kaplan; director, Schaffner; based on the novel by Henri Carriere; screenplay, Dalton Trumbo, Lorenzo Semple, Jr.; production designer, Anthony Masters; art director, Jack Maxsted; set decorator, Hugh Scaife; costumes, Anthony Powell; makeup, Charles Schram; music, Jerry Goldsmith; assistant directors, Jose Lopez Rodero, Juan Lopez Rodero; stunt coordinator, Joe Canutt; sound, Deek Ball; special effects, Alex Weldon; camera, Fred Koenekamp; editor, Robert Swink.

Cast: Steve McQueen (Papillon [Henri Charriere]); Dustin Hoffman (Louis Dega); Victor Jory (Indian Chief); Don Gordon (Julot); Anthony Zerbe (Toussaint, the Leper Colony Chief); Robert Deman (Maturette); Woodrow Parfrey (Clusoit); Bill Mumy (Lariot); George Coulouris (Dr. Chatal); Ratna Assan (Zoraima); William Smithers (Warden Barrot); Gregory Sierra (Antonio); Barbara Morrison (Mother Superior); Ellen Moss (Nun); Don Hammer (Butterfly Trader); Dalton Trumbo (Commandant); Val Avery (Pascal); Victor [Vic] Tayback (Sergeant); Dar Robinson (Mc-

Queen's Cliff Stunt); Mills Watson (Guard); Ron Soble (Santini); E.J. Andre (Old Con); Richard Angarola (Commandant); Jack Denbo (Classification Officer); Len Lesser (Guard); John Quade (Masked Breton); Fred Sadoff (Deputy Warden); Allen Jaffe (Turnkey); Liam Dunn (Old Trustee); Anne Byrne Hoffman (Mrs. Dega).

Over the decades, several motion pictures have dealt with the infamous Devil's Island penal colony, but none so expansively as *Papillon*, a $13 million production starring Steve McQueen and Dustin Hoffman. The film was based on the bestseller (1969) by Henri Charriere, who had spent several hellish years in that French Guiana prison compound. Among the many prisoners depicted in this oversized movie is handsome young Maturette, a homosexual trustee, who has gained special privileges because of his fraternizing with the guards.

In 1931 France, Papillon (Steve McQueen), a safecracker, is wrongly sentenced to a life term at Devil's Island, even though he is innocent of killing a small-time pimp. Aboard ship to the dreaded compound, he meets Louis Dega (Dustin Hoffman) a forger/swindler rumored to have a stash of money with him. Before they reach their destination, Papillon saves Dega from a murderous convict. At the prison, Papillon and Dega survive the regimen under the strict warden (William Smithers). However, the non-conforming Papillon spends most of the next few years in solitary confinement for various attempted prison breaks. Released to the prison infirmary, Papillon once again devises a new escape plan. This time his scheme calls for joining with a homosexual trustee/orderly, Maturette (Robert Deman), and an older prisoner, Clusiot (Woodrow Parfrey).

At first, Dega, who has a relatively (!) comfortable existence at the prison, refuses to participate in the breakout attempt. However, after Clusiot is killed by a guard, Dega is dragged into the flight. They sail in a small boat for Colombia.

Once there, they are stopped by an army patrol squad, with only Papillon escaping to the jungle. But later he is also captured and spends years in solitary confinement back at Devil's Island. When released, the much aged, Papillon becomes a prison colonist on the island where he encounters Dega busily tending a nearby plot of land. Still unbroken after all these years, Papillon hatches a new break-out plan, but Dega refuses to join him. As Papillon disappears over the horizon, Dega looks on wistfully. A postscript advises that Papillon lived out the rest of his life as a free man, and that he outlasted the prison at Devil's Island.

While admiring *Papillon*'s breathtaking visuals and admitting that it "is the escapist movie we used to go see," Vincent Canby (*New York Times*) decided that the movie "fills the screen with information designed to convince us that because the setting is real, so must be the people in it. . . . [The] screenplay . . . defines its characters less in terms of what they feel or think than in terms of extravagant incidents and superhuman heroics." As to the cast, Canby thought McQueen was "as all-American as a Rover Boy" and that Hoffman "is fun to watch as an intelligent character as written." The reviewer then noted of the supporting cast: "There are dozens of the characters in the story, all more or less obligatory to a Devil's Island adventure . . . the perverted trustee (in other films he's sometimes presented as a male nurse). For Richard Combs (British *Monthly Film Bulletin*), "what is missing is any of the book's anger at the outrageous hypocrisy, injustice and inhumanity of the system. . . ."

Despite its mixed reviews *Papillon* earned $22,500,000 in distributors' domestic film rentals. It was Oscar-nominated for Best Original Dramatic Score, but lost the Academy Award to *The Way We Were*. *Papillon* was originally rated R for its excessive violence, but upon appeal, the classification was changed to PG (parental guidance suggested). Dalton

Trumbo, the once blacklisted writer who scripted *Papillon*, has an unbilled role in the picture as the commandant at the film's opening. The word "papillon" in French means butterfly. The prisoner/hero of this movie was known by this nickname because of the butterfly tattoo on his chest.

Beating *Papillon* into distribution by a few months was *I Escaped from Devil's Island*, q.v., a rip-off low-budget picture geared to take advantage of the pre-release publicity generated by the other. It too featured a homosexual convict among the storyline's escapees.

176. **Parting Glances** (Cinecom, 1986), color, 90 mins. Not rated.

Executive producer, Paul A. Kaplan; producers, Yoram Mandel, Arthur Silverman; associate producers, Nancy Greenstein, Victoria Westhead; director/screenplay, Bill Sherwood; production designer, John Loggia; art directors, Daniel Haughey, Mark Sweeney; set decorator, Anne Mitchell; costumes, Sylvia Heisel; makeup, Franco; assistant directors, Mandel, Tony Jacobs; sound, Scott Breindel, Timothy Martyn; camera, Jacek Laskus; editor, Sherwood.

Cast: Richard Ganoung (Michael); John Bolger (Robert); Steve Buscemi (Nick); Adam Nathan (Peter); Kathy Kinney (Joan); Patrick Tull (Cecil); Yolande Bava (Betty); Richard Wall (Douglas); Jim Selfe (Douglas's Sidekick); Kristin Moneagle (Sarah); John Siemens (Dave); Bob Kohrherr (Sam); Theodore Ganger (Klaus); Nada (Liselotte); Patrick Ragland (Ex-Seminarian); Cam Brainard (Ricky); Daniel Haughey (Commendatore, the Ghost); Sylvia Hartowicz (Chris, the Little Girl); Hanna Hartowicz (Chris's Mother); Nicholas Hill (Cab Driver); Lee Greenstein (Lady at Record Store); Jordan McLean (Boy at Record Store); Lori Tirgrath (Customer at Record Store); Elaine Swayneson (Jamaican Woman at Party); Markus Lawson (African Man at Party); David Lines (Bearded Man in Suit at Party); Gardiner Kendall, Victor Rivers (Hearing-Impaired Men at Disco); Michael Medeiros (Tall Muscleman in Pool Dream); Eric Miller (Brawny Muscleman in Pool Dream); Al Hughes (Jogging Muscleman in Pool Dream).

"Most gay movies . . . are dehumanizing clinical pornography. The handful of serious gay films that do open in art houses are simplistic problem dramas . . . . *Parting Glances* is something else. It takes for granted the right of its consenting adults to live as they please and pictures them— some of them, anyway—as individuals rather than sexual stereotypes." (Joseph Gelmis, *Newsday*)

Parting Glances is an extremely effective low-budget romantic drama, an unpretentious insider's look at the intertwining relationships of three gay men and their assorted friends. It is neither preachy, apologetic, gooey nor affected. It simply delineates the pressurized modern world in which homosexual love not only encompasses the unexpected twists of any (straight or gay) relationship, but has the added weight of being part of a subculture in which AIDS has become a deadly reality and also has reawakened homophobia.

In New York City, Michael (Richard Ganoung), a publications editor, deals with several crises: his long-term boyfriend, Robert (John Bolger), a print journalist, is going to Africa for an extended period; his best friend and former lover, Nick (Steve Buscemi), a musician, is dying of AIDS. Michael and Robert are guests at a farewell party given by Cecil (Patrick Tull), Robert's bisexual boss, and his wife, Betty (Yolande Bava). Returning home, Robert tells Michael that he requested the overseas assignment, needing time to sort out their stagnant relationship and also in order not to have to deal with Nick's dying. Later, Robert, Michael and Nick attend a party given by Joan (Kathy Kinney), a mutual friend. While there, Michael overhears Robert explaining to another acquaintance (Kristin Moneagle) his true feelings about Michael's ties to Nick. This conversation forces Michael to realize that he has always loved Nick more than Robert. The next morning, Robert departs for the airport, while Nick phones Michael from Fire Island to say he can no longer cope with life—and then hangs up. Meanwhile, Robert, deciding at the last minute not to go abroad, returns home.

They reconcile and Michael flies out to Fire Island where he finds Nick meditating by the seashore.

Janet Maslin (*New York Times*) granted the film had a "lively style and a handsome look" but found its "tone is flippant, and its sense of character entirely superficial. . . . Most of . . . [it] functions as a parade of homosexual stereotypes, . . ." Of the cast, Maslin best liked (real-life comedian) Steve Buscemi, whose Nick "is the most unsentimental and original figure here. Mr. Buscemi has a powerfully anarchic presence, particularly beside the relative complacency of the others. . . ." David Denby (*New York*) conceded "*Parting Glances* is infinitely preferable to such Hollywood drivel as *Making Love* [1982, q.v], but as much as I admire the decency of its attitudes, I wish it were more exciting and not so desperately self-conscious." More appreciative was Michael Wilmington (*Los Angeles Times*), who explained, "The qualities one likes best . . . are its immaculate, flashing wit, its easy grace and the nimble but compassionate way it deals with a potentially explosive subject. . . ."

The extremely economically-made *Parting Glances* was a first-time feature for filmmaker Bill Sherwood. The successful film showed just how far moviemakers had come in reflecting the new sensibility about/by gays.

177. Partners (Paramount, 1982), color, 98 min. R-rated.

Executive producer, Francis Veber; producer, Aaron Russo; associate producer, Mitchell L. Gamson; director, James Burrows; screenplay, Veber; production designer, Richard Sylbert; set decorator, George Gaines; costumes, Wayne Finkelman; makeup, John Morin, Hallie Smith-Simmons; music, Georges Delerue; orchestrator, Jack Hayes; assistant directors, Thomas Lofaro, David Valdes; stunt coordinator, Ralph Garrett; sound, Pat Mitchell; camera, Victor J. Kemper; editor, Danford B. Greene.

Cast: Ryan O'Neal (Detective Sergeant Benson); John Hurt (Fred Kerwin); Kenneth McMillan (Captian Wilkens); Robyn Douglass

(Jill); Jay Robinson (Halderstam); Denise Galik (Clara); Joseph R. Sicari (Walter); Michael McGuire (Monroe); Rick Jason (Douglas); James Remar (Edward K. Petersen); Jennifer Ashley (Secretary); Darrell Larson (Al); Tony March (Second Aide); Seamon Glass (Gillis); Steve Reisch (Counter Boy); Carl Kraines (First Aide); Bob Ozman (Detective); Carol Willard (Officer); Iris Alhanti (Jogger); Bob Bigelow (Man on Balcony); John Garber (Body Builder); Sherrie Lessard (Telephone Operator); Ed McCready (Doorman); Jackie Millines (Photo Assistant); Ray Sanders (Muscle Man); Luis Torres (Pablo); Gene Ross, Douglas Bruce, Bill Cross, Craig Shreeve, Gregory L. Hodal (Cops).

". . . [*Partners*] is a very unfunny American movie whose idea of a homosexual is someone who drives a pink volkswagen. . . . *Partners* brings back the good old days when homosexuals were portrayed as swishy fruits, leering queens and pathetic spinsters. . . ." (David Ansen, *Newsweek*)

The (un)intentionally offensive *Partners* was scripted by French writer Francis Veber, who had co-written the French movie comedy hit, *La Cage Aux Folles* (1978). The R-rated movie was panned by critics for being muddled, dull and pandering to stereotypes; it was protested by gay groups for being full of homophobic-based caricatures. It was released in the same year as *Making Love* and *Victor/ Victoria*, qq.v., all part of mainstream Hollywood's efforts to capitalize on gay awareness in the pre-AIDS era.

In Los Angeles, an amused police Captain Wilkins (Kenneth McMillan) assigns two disparate cops to special duty. Macho chauvinist Sergeant Benson (Ryan O'Neal) and wimpy, gay departmental clerk Fred Kerwin (John Hurt) are ordered to move into a West Hollywood apartment together, posing as a gay couple. Their mission is to investigate the killing of a gay man named Davis. Once established undercover, they learn that Davis had a boyfriend, Walter (Joseph R. Sicari). An unwilling Benson courts him and learns that Davis—like another victim, Clyde

Thompson—had posed for a porno magazine. Next, Benson gains access to the publication's photographer, Jill (Robyn Douglass), on the pretext of being a model. Later investigation leads Benson to realize that Jill was involved with Edward K. Petersen (James Remar), Clyde's former boyfriend, in a blackmail scheme. Due to Kerwin's bungling, the set-up to catch Petersen fails and the man is later found dead. After Jill is murdered by one of her blackmailed victims, Douglas (Rick Jason), the latter traps Benson and admits that he also killed Davis and Peterson. He notes that it was Jill who had eliminated Thompson. At this juncture, Fred arrives. While saving his partner, he is badly wounded and Douglas dies. Benson tells Kerwin that when he recovers they will live together, which gives the man a will to live. The sadistic Wilkins promises to hold Benson to that promise.

Vincent Canby (*New York Times*), who found *Partners* a "one joke" affair, observed that the co-stars "often look more foolish than their characters are supposed to feel. . . . Mr. Hurt . . . has an especially unhappy time, being required to behave so ineffectually that he confirms all of the most blatant stereotypes about limp-wristedness. . . ." For Kevin Thomas (*Los Angeles Times*), "*Partners* is not so homophobic as it is merely ignorant and clumsy. But as such, it is thuddingly offensive. It means to send up sexual stereotypes . . . but it's so crass and heavy-handed that all it does is get the same old cheap laughs from them. . . ."

One of the minority who found the movie a "superior comedy" was Bill Kaufman (*Newsday*) who reasoned, "Hollywood, now apparently keenly aware of audience sensitivities, has handled the once-taboo subject of the gay milieu adroitly." One of *Partners*' minor subthemes explored briefly and crudely has the womanizing cop hero realizing what it is like to be visually dissected and pawed (when he is cruised by gay characters mistaking him for a possible conquest).

Partners might have been a breakthrough in gay-themed cinema. Instead it became, in the words of Rex Reed (*New York Post*) "Hollywood's latest crime against humanity in general and homosexuals in particular. . . . [This] sleazy, superficial film implies that gay cops cannot be trusted to work with straight cops because they might fall in love with them."

178. The Pawnbroker (Landau Releasing Orgnaization, 1965), 114 min.

Executive producer, Worthington Miner; producers, Roger Lewis, Philip Langner; associate producer, Joseph Manduke; director, Sidney Lumet; based on the novel by Edward Lewis Wallant; screenplay, David Friedkin, Morton Fine; art director, Richard Sylbert; set decorator, Jack Flaherty; costumes, Anna Hill Johnstone; makeup, Bill Herman; music, Quincy Jones; assistant director, Dan Eriksen; camera, Boris Kaufman; editor, Ralph Rosenblum.

Cast: Rod Steiger (Sol Nazerman); Geraldine Fitzgerald (Marilyn Birchfield); Brock Peters (Rodriguez); Jaime Sanchez (Jesus Ortiz) Thelma Oliver (Ortiz's Girlfriend); Marketa Kimbrell (Tessie); Baruch Lumet (Mendel); Juano Hernandez (Mr. Smith); Linda Geiser (Ruth); Nancy R. Pollock (Bertha); Raymond St. Jacques (Tangee); John McCurry (Buck); Charles Dierkop (Robionson); Eusebia Cosme (Mrs. Ortiz); Warren Finnerty (Savarese); Jack Ader (Morton); E. M. Margolese (Papa); Marianne Kanter (Joan); Ed Morehouse (Robinson); Marc Alexander (Rubin).

The independently-produced *The Pawnbroker* was certainly one of the grimmest studies of contemporary New York, featuring a powerful performance by Rod Steiger in a strongly symbolic story full of flashbacks. He plays a tormented Jewish pawnbroker in New York City who cannot forgive himself or others that he is alive while his family died in the Holocaust of World War II. Among the ironies of the pawnbroker's numbed existence is that his business is financed with dirty money earned by a black vice lord. The latter, as it turns out, happens to have a white male lover.

Sol Nazerman (Rod Steiger) operates a rundown pawnshop in Spanish Harlem, with Puerto Rican Jesus Ortiz (Jaime Sanchez) as his eager assistant. Haunted by the nightmare of his family and friends dying in the Nazi concentration camps, Sol is emotionally detached from, above all, his customers, let alone the well-meaning Jesus or Marilyn Birchfield (Geraldine Fitzgerald), a local social worker who takes a personal interest in him. The uncommunicative Nazerman is shocked to learn that his backer, Rodriguez (Brock Peters), operates a prostitution ring, among other illegal enterprises. (It reminds Sol all too vividly of his wife being raped before his eyes by German officers.) When Sol confronts Rodriquez, the latter makes him admit that he really was not that naive about the source of the money. As his painful life becomes more unbearable, Nazerman reacts bitterly to his optimistic Puerto Rican helper. As a result, the disillusioned Ortiz joins in a scheme to rob the pawnshop. Ironically, while Sol welcomes death and taunts the robbers by refusing to give them his money, it is Jesus Ortiz who steps in the path of the gun aimed at Nazerman. Horrified by his helper's death and his own survival—again—Nazerman slams his hand down on the sharp receipt spindle. In agonizing pain, he runs out into the street.

Bosley Crowther (*New York Times*) highly praised *The Pawnbroker* as a "dark and haunting drama" of "the shabbiness of man—of the misused, debilitated hero, as well as those among whom he lives." As to the superior ensemble, besides Steiger, Crowther found that "Others of the cast are likewise striking . . . [including] Brock Peters as a brutal Harlem crime boss. . . ." The British *Monthly Film Bulletin* decided that, "The trouble [with *The Pawnbroker*] is that not only does the film fail to throw light on any of . . . [its stated moral] problems, it actually ends on a note that can only be construed as negative and ambiguous. . . . [The] film abounds with cinematic and dramatic tricks forcing home a point with a facile contrast: the white suits and the all-white luxury apartment of the Negro racketeer. . . .."

With its stark messages of human responsibility, it was easy for viewers to overlook the sexual orientation of the self-made black vice lord. In a few quick unobtrusive moments, *The Pawnbroker* presents the man's blond-hair, Caucasian boyfriend. In one sequence, the live-in secretary/companion is shown seated at the dining room table next to his "master" who is talking on the phone. Later, there is the scene in which Nazerman confronts Rodriguez. As the two elder men verbally lash out at one another in Rodriguez's high tech apartment living room, the kept man silently opens the front door and walks upstairs. Very soon thereafter, Rodriguez, upon dismissing Sol, smugly follows up the stairs after his sex partner. *Newsday* obliquely referred to this character as Rodriguez's "white underling."

Rod Steiger was nominated for a Best Actor Academy Award for *The Pawnbroker*, but lost the Oscar to Lee Marvin (*Cat Ballou*).

179. Penitentiary (Jerry Gross, 1979), color, 99 min. R-rated.

Producer, Jamaa Fanaka; co-producers, Alicia Dhanifu, Al Shepard; associate producers, Irving Parham, Leon Isaac Kennedy, Lynette Stansell; director/screenplay, Fanaka; art director, Adel Mazen; set decorator, Beverly Green Etheredge; costumes, Debra Bradford, Deirdre Naughton; makeup, Gregory Lewis; music, Frank Gaye; song, Mark Gaillard and the Slim and Trim Band; assistant directors, Jovon Gilloham, Yance Hamlett, Sergio Mimms; stunt coordinator/second unit director, John Sherrod; sound, Ed White; camera, Marty Ollstein; additional camera, Stephen Posey; editor, Betsy Blankett.

Cast: Leon Isaac Kennedy (Martel "Too Sweet" Gordone); Thommy Pollard (Eugene T. Lawson); Hazek Spears (Linda); Donovan Womack (Jesse Amos); Floyd Chatman (Hezzikia "Seldom Seen" Jackson); Wilbur "Hi-Fi" White (Sweet Pea); Gloria Delaney (Peaches); Badja Djola ("Half Dead" Johnson); Chuck Mitchell (Lieutenant Arnsworth); Cepheus Jaxon (Poindexter); Dwaine Fobbs ("Lying"

Latney Winborn); Ernest Wilson ("Cheese"); Will Richardson (Magilla Gorilla); Elijah Mitchell, Darrell Harris, Lonnie Kirtz (Nuts); Tony Andrea (Moon); Ray Wolfe ("A" Block Night Guard); Charles Young ("Tough Tony," Manager and Referee); Michael Melvin, Steve Eddy (Bikers); Bill Murry ("Rappin'" Larry); Terri Hayden (Counter Lady); Herman Cole (Cook); Carl Erwin (Sam Cunningham); Irving Parham ("A" Block Day Guard); Warren Bryant (Gay Boxing Spectator); Lorri Gay (Second Girl in Rest Room); Thomas Earl Stiratt ("Wolf"); Walter Gordon (Second Male in Rest Room); Joaquin Leal (Rubin); David Carter, Hassan Abdul-Ali, Marcus Guttierrez (Guards); Zee Howard (Female Lieutenant); Cardella Demilo, Onia Fenee, Deloris Figueroa, Ann Hutcherson, Gwynn Pineda, Irene Stokes, Beverly Wallace (Female Guard); Renee Armanlin, Zeola Gaye, Brenda Joy Griffin, Shelli Hughes, Sarah Jaxon, Jackie Shaw, Irene Terrell, Barbara Torres, Lisa Visco (Female Inmates); William Bey, Robert Wayne Cornelius, Shawn Davis, Quitman Gates, Dominic Giusto, Johnny Jones, Casey J. Littlejohn, Sam Olden, Tony Rapisarda, Tyrone S.B. Thompson, Edgardo Williams, Roderic Williams (Male Inmates).

See summary under *Penitentiary III*.

180. Penitentiary III (Cannon, 1987) color, 91 min. R-rated.

Producers, Jamaa Fanaka, Leon Isaac Kennedy; associate producer, Ernest Johnson; director/screenplay, James Fanaka; production designer, Marshall Toomey; art director, Craig Freitag; set decorator, Beverly Etheredge; costumes, Marie Burrell Fanaka; makeup/special effects, Mike Spatola; assistant directors, Brent Sellstrom, Pat Kirck; music, Garry Schyman; second unit director, John Sherrod; sound, Oliver Moss; camera, Marty Ollstein; second unit camera, Joseph W. Calloway; editors, Alain Jakubowicz, Ed Harker.

Cast: Leon Isaac Kennedy (Martel "Too Sweet" Gordone); Anthony Geary (Serenghetti); Steven Antin (Roscoe); Ric Mancini (Warden); Marie Burrell Fanaka (Chelsea Remington); Raymond "The Haiti Kid" Kessler (Midnight Thud Jessup); Rick Zumwalkt (Joshua); Magic Schwarz (Hugo); Jim Bailey (Cleopatra); Big Bull Bates (Simp); Big Yank (Rock); Bert Williams (Tim Shoah); Mark Kemble (Rufus McClay); Jack Rader (Fred); Madison Campudoni (El Cid); Mike Payne (Jess); Drew

Bundini Brown (Sugg); Ty Randolph (Sugar); J. J. Johnson, Earl Garnes (Announcers); Jim Phillips (Suited Gentleman); Faith Minton, Marcella Ross, Ray Hollitt (Female Boxer); Danny Trejo (See Veer); Mary O'Connor, Cardella Demilo (Female Guards); "Dr. De" Ron Demps (Referee).

The *Penitentiary* series (1979, 1982, 1987), which owes a great deal to Sylvester Stallone's *Rocky* movies, were all directed by Jamaa Fanaka and each starred Leon Isaac Kennedy. The *Penitentiary* entries are fanciful motion pictures, raw and full of the energy and flavor so associated with the 1970s black action film cycle. However, this trio of action movies progressed from the crude to the absurd, and from the underbudgeted to the overindulged. The first and third installments each make a statement about homosexuality behind bars, tying this theme to overtones of racism.

In *Penitentiary* (1979), black hitchhiker Martel Gordone (Leon Isaac Kennedy) is sent to prison on an unjustified homicide charge (it was a case of self-defense). Once inside "the big house," his fondness for candy earns him the nickname "Too Sweet." In Martel's oppressive cell block, Jesse Amos (Donovan Womack) is the tough boss and his prime henchman is "Half Dead" Johnson (Badja Djola). Later, Too Sweet rescues Jesse's sexually harassed cellmate, Eugene T. Lawson (Thommy Pollard), from being sodomized. This action leads to Gordone and Jesse battling it out, and, as a result, Martel is shipped off to solitary confinement. Still later, they are permitted to settle their differences in the prison boxing tournament.

Too Sweet is coached by veteran convict Hezzikia "Seldom Seen" Jackson (Floyd Chatman), a former boxing trainer. Martel wins the championship match. Later, the disgruntled Amos and Johnson attempt revenge on Gordone for his victory. When Lawson helps Martel, he is killed. As a result, the vengeful Too Sweet fights Amos in another match. He wins

again, leading to his release from the prison.

Kevin Thomas (*Los Angeles Times*) judged, "Filled with vividly drawn larger-than-life characters and loaded with action, *Penitentiary* bursts with energy and emotion. It's operating in the best, bravura sense. . . . Fanaka creates a world of overwhelming sexual tension and constant danger. . . ." Martyn Auty (British *Monthly Film Bulletin*) offered, "What makes *Penitentiary* an even more debased experience is that the prison's all-black population is made to embody every racist stereotype. . . . [Too Sweet's] final victory is nothing more than a corrupt evasion of corrupt justice, made possible by the subjugation of fellow blacks already brutalised within a redneck-run prison. For all its posturing, this is a film that ideologically enslaves blacks."

Within *Penitentiary*, the facility is depicted as overcrowded, bursting with racial tension, full of corruption on both sides of the bars, and the sexually-deprived men venting their frustrations in mayhem, murder and homosexual rape. (This latter element reflects a new maturity in Hollywood, compared to the 1930s and 1940s Warner Bros. prison melodramas where the likes of James Cagney, George Raft and Humphrey Bogart wallowed in brutal but sexually chaste prison situations.) In adapting to his vicious environment, *Penitentiary*'s hero not only defends his space and self-respect, but his sexual honor as well. He snarls to a meek brother, "Don't nobody have to be nobody's property!" Before the movie ends, he has become a seasoned survivor who fights in and out of the ring to keep on living.

Made on an estimated cost of $250,000, *Penitentiary* grossed $13,120,235 in ticket sales. It led to the disappointing *Penitentiary II* (1982), made on a $1 million budget and offering a cameo by Mr. T. Too Sweet (Leon Isaac Kennedy) is sent back into prison where he battles Jesse "The Bull" Amos (Donovan Womack) in the ring. The overproduced derivative sequel lacked the bite of the original not only in the ring but in the prison sequences (a minor aspect of the movie).

In 1987, Jamaa Fanaka and Leon Isaac Kennedy, seemingly unable to duplicate their *Penitentiary* success in other areas, made *Penitentiary III*, budgeted at $2 million. This third installment of the Martel Gordone cycle led *Variety* to ponder "Are cartoons and professional wrestling matches fun? If you answer yes to the second question then this movie definitely is for you."

Prisoner Serenghetti (Anthony Geary) is a bigwig both behind bars and outside, thanks to his network of underworld contacts. He needs Too Sweet (Leon Isaac Kennedy) back in prison to use in an upcoming jailhouse match on which he intends to make heavy bets. Thus, he has Gordone drugged during a boxing match causing the fighter to pummel his ring opponent to death. Now imprisoned on a manslaughter charge, Too Sweet is quickly drawn into the conflict between the rival boxing teams sponsored, on the one hand by the warden (Ric Mancini) and, on the other, controlled by Serenghetti. Gordone survives a battle with one of Serenghetti's thugs, the Midnight Thud (Raymond "The Haiti Kid" Kessler), a murderous midget boxer convict. Later, Too Sweet and Midnight Thud become pals and when Gordone is maneuvered into fighting again, Midnight Thud instructs him in martial arts skills. In the big match, Gordone is victorious and Serenghetti's reign is finally broken.

The excessive *Penitentiary III* earned mixed critical response. Duayne Byrge (*Hollywood Reporter*) observed, "While *Penitentiary III* is sensibly roped off into a tight strong ring—good guys vs. bad guy in the championship bout—there's a bevy of weird and bizarre between-story-round stuff that spruces up the formula. . . . *Penitentiary III* is a lean and mean entertainment." Jonathan Gold (*LA Weekly*) judged, "Jamaa Fanaka brings us yet another poorly shot, abysmally lighted and thoroughly entertaining trip through his surrealistic pen, where S & M guards hang out in medieval dungeons and nasty mobmen run the joint from their plushy appointed cells. The picture isn't good, but it sure is fun. . . ."

One of the more bizarre aspects of the quite weird *Penitentiary III* is the (cardboard) characterization of megalomanic homosexual kingpin, Serenghetti, an albino who resides in splendor. The casual viewer might wonder what the incarcerated prison boss is doing with a handmaiden girlfriend in his elaborate cell suite. A closer check (of the credits) reveals that "Cleopatra" is played by famed female impressionist Jim Bailey. Whether on purpose, or because of last-minute editing, his role is almost nonexistent. He parades through the picture in several striking drag outfits but says very little. Even in its abbreviated form, his appearances says a good deal about sexual role playing behind bars, something that would have been unheard of in earlier Hollywood films.

Penitentiary III was not a box-office champion, not only because of internal artistic problems, but because its distributor was in corporate disorder.

181. A Perfect Couple (Twentieth Century-Fox, 1979), color, 110 min. PG-rated.

Executive producer, Tommy Thompson; producer, Robert Altman; associate producers, Robert Eggenweiler, Scott Bushnell; director, Altman; screenplay, Altman, Allan Nicholls; art director, Leon Erickson; costumes, Beth Alexander, Anna Vilms; makeup, Tom Tuttle; music, Nicholls; songs: Tony Berg and Ted Neeley; Berg, Neeley and Nicholls; Nicholls, B. G. Gibson, Berg; Berg and Nicholls; Tomi-Lee Bradley, Berg, Nicholls and Neeley; Cliff DeYoung and Berg; Nichols; Nicholls and Otis Stephens; Tom Pierson and Nicholls; assistant directors, Thompson, Bill Cosentino; sound, Robert Gravenor, Don Merritt, Dave Palmer; camera, Edmond L. Koons; editor, Tony Lombardo.

Cast: Paul Dooley (Alex Theodopoulos); Marta Heflin (Sheila Shea); Titos Vandis (Panos

Theodopoulos); Belita Moreno (Eleousa Theodopoulos); Henry Gibson (Fred Bott); Dimitra Arliss (Athena); Allan Nicholls (Dana #115); Ann Ryerson (Skye #147, a Veterinarian); Poppy Lagos (Melpomeni Bott); Dennis Franz (Costa); Margery Bond (Wilma); Mona Golabek (Mona); Terry Wills (Ben); Susan Blakeman (Penelope Bott); Melanie Bishop (Star); Fred Bier, Jette Seear (The Imperfect Couple); Tom Pierson (Conductor for Los Angeles Philharmonic Orchestra); Mona Golabek (Piano Solist); *Keepin 'Em Off the Streets*: Ted Neeley (Teddy); Heather MacRae (Mary); Tomi-Lee Bradley (Sydney-Ray); Steven Sharp (Bobbi); Tony Berg (Lead Guitar and Musical Director); Craig Doerge (Keyboards); Jeff Eyrich (Bass Guitar); David Luell (Saxophone); Butch Sanford (Guitar); Art Wood (Drums); Renn Wood (Guest Appearance).

Paul Dooley and Marta Heflin, who were among the ensemble cast of Robert Altman's *A Wedding* (1978), had the leads in *A Perfect Couple*, dealing with two unlikely candidates for romantic bliss meeting through a video dating service. Among the characters parading through the very imperfect *A Perfect Couple* are members of the musical group, which include Mary (Heather MacRae) and Syndey-Ray (Tomi-Lee Bradley), a contented lesbian couple, and the gay Bobbie (Steven Sharp).

Middle-aged Alex Theodopoulos (Dooley) comes from a tradition-bound Greek family which adores classical music, Sheila Shea (Heflin) is younger and a singer with a pop group. What both Los Angeleans share in common, besides their mutual attraction, is the tight social unit each endures at home. His well-to-do family lives by old world values ruled by a strong-willed reactionary patriarch (Titos Vandis); she shares quarters above a warehouse with her musician group (Keepin' 'Em off the Streets), headed by a strict disciplinarian (Ted Neeley). Neither side approves of the interloper, and whenever Alex or Sheila are at the other's place there is never any privacy. Later, when Alex's cellist-playing sister (Belita Moreno) dies of heart failure while breaking away from

parental control, the tragedy is a sufficient catalyst to push Alex into doing his own thing and establishing a permanent relationship with Sheila.

Janet Maslin (*New York Times*), disappointed by this mundane film, had to search hard to find its few virtues: "when it isn't bending over backward to accommodate the songs, the film has some sweet, funny moments." As to the repeated, intrusive musical interludes, Maslin confided, "By the time it's over, the thing you may wish most fervent about Keepin' 'Em Off the Streets is that Mr. Altman hadn't decided to." In its end-of-review explanation of the film's PG-rating, the *Times* noted, "It includes one love scene, no violence, and a few mild mentions of homosexuality." For *Variety*, A Perfect Couple "reaffirms both Altman's intelligence and his inaccessibility. . . . Altman is attempting something much more ambitious than just a love story . . . He and co-scripter Allan Nicholls have tried to integrate the musical score to a degree that it becomes another character. . . . That attempt proves the downfall of *Perfect Couple*. . . ." In contrast, Tom Milne (British *Monthly Film Bulletin*) decided, "The trouble with the film, ultimately, is that its winsome Marty aspect steadily gains the upper hand, leaving Keepin' 'Em Off the Streets and their superbly staged numbers out on a limb which merits much more attention."

182. Personal Best (Warner Bros., 1982), color, 124 min. R-rated.

Executive producer, David Geffen; producer, Robert Towne; associate producer, Peter Peyton; director/screenplay, Towne; production designer, Ron Hobbs; set decorator, Rick Simpson; costumes, Linda Henrikson, Ron Heilman; makeup, Christina Smith, Karl Silvera; music, Jack Nitzsche, Jill Fraser; assistant directors, Jerry Grandy, Bill Beasley; special effects, Dale Newkirk; sound, Ben Sobin; camera, Michael Chapman, Allan Gornick Jr.; supervising editor, Ned Humphreys; editors, Jere Huggins, Jacqueline Cambas, Walt Mulconery.

Cast: Mariel Hemingway (Chris Cahill); Scott Glenn (Terry Tingloff); Patrice Donnelly (Tory Skinner); Kenny Moore (Denny Stites); Jim Moody (Roscoe Travis); Kari Gosswiller (Penny Brill); Jodi Anderson (Nadia "Pooch" Anderson); Maren Seidler (Tanya); Martha Watson (Sheila); Emily Dole (Maureen); Pam Spencer (Jan); Deby LaPlante (Trish); Mitzi McMillin (Laura); Jan Glotzer (Karen); Jan Van Reenen (Yelovitch); Allan Feuerbach (Zenk); Jane Frederick (Fern Wadkins); Cindy Gilbert (Charlene Benveniste); Marlene Harmon (Pam Burnside); Linda Waltman (Debbie Floyd); Cindy Banks (Kim Stone); Milan Tiff (Willie Lee); Earl Bell (Randy Van Zile); Larry Pennell (Rick Cahill); Luana Anders (Rita Cahill); George de la Pena (Raoul); Robert Paten (Colin Sales); Margaret Ellison (Nellie Bowdeen); Charlie Jones, Frank Shorter (TV Announcers); Jim Tracy (Duane); Janet Hake (Waitress); Sharon Brazell (Hostess); Chuck Debus (Coach); Gregory Clayton (Trainer); David Edington (Waiter); Robert Horn (Water Polo Coach); Christopher Vargas (Water Polo Player); Wendell Ray (PA Announcer); Richard Martini (Meet Manager); Len Dawson (Announcer); Clim Jackson, John Smith (Men's Team Members); Anna Biller, Susan Brownell, Desiree Gauthier, Sharon Hatfield, Linda Highower, Joan Russell, Themis Zambrzycki (Women's Team Members); Dr. Leroy R. Perry Jr. (Chiropractor).

"Male or female, how do you compete with a body you have already surrendered to your opponent?" (Advertisement for *Personal Best*)

Not since *A Different Story* (1978) and *Making Love* (1982), qq.v., had a Hollywood mainstream gay-themed movie been considered such a cop-out on so many levels: (1) the graphic exploitation of lesbian love in a gratuitous, chauvinistic way; (2) suggesting that gay women, far more than men, allow, romance and lust to affect their professional judgment; (3) having the lesbian woman lead character go straight after having a cure-all heterosexual romance. These criticisms become even more valid after the release of *Lianna* (1983) and *Desert Hearts* (1985), qq.v., two far superior studies of women defining their love for other women.

In 1976, at the Olympic trials, Pentathlete Tory Skinner (Patrice Donnelly) is intrigued when she meets younger Chris Cahill (Mariel Hemingway), a hurdler discouraged by her mediocre performance. They spend the evening together, getting high, arm-wrestling and making love. Terry Tingloff (Scott Glenn), Tory's demanding trainer is persuaded by her to coach Chris. His successful work leads to her running at the World Student Games (1978) in Colombia. Tory fares badly in the competition, while Chris does well. Thereafter, Terry suggests that Chris now train for the Pentathlon, which the latter is reluctant to do because she would have to compete against Tory. At first hurt and threatened by her lover's rivalry, Tory makes a suggestion to help Chris. Accidentally, this advice causes Chris to injure her knee, and she is convinced that Tory sabotaged her deliberately. Angered, Chris spends the night with Tingloff. Later, she and water polo player Denny Stites (Kenny Moore) become lovers. In 1980, at the Olympic tryouts in Oregon, Chris and Tory meet for the first time in quite a while. In the final track event, Chris helps her one-time friend by psyching out Tory's chief rival (Cindy Gilbert). As a result, Chris and Tory both qualify for the Olympic squad.

Time (Richard Schickel) summarized this as a film that "may finally disarm everyone with its full-frontal naturalness, its unsmirking bawdiness, its obvious liking for athletes as people, and its refusal (most of the time) to poeticize sport." Vincent Canby (*New York Times*) reported that first-time director Robert Towne "is a talented man with a certain weakness. You might even call it a guilty pleasure. . . . He especially loves . . . [women's] pelvic regions, which he photographs as frequently as possible in close-up. . . . He's also fond of the feet and muscled calves of women athletes, which he photographs in close-ups. . . . Mr. Towne's one solid achievement as a director is the quality of the performances he has obtained from the

Patrice Donnelly, Jodi Anderson and Mariel Hemingway in *Personal Best* (1982).

members of his cast only two of whom, Miss Hemingway and Scott Glenn, are professional actors.' Alex Keneas (*Newsday*) judged that *Personal Best* is "easier to admire for its technical proficiency than for the bill of fare. . . . [It] fails to involve us in its fixation. As dramatic feat, it's less fleet than flat."

Despite a saturation advertising campaign, *Personal Best* did not appeal to a wide audience and earned less than $4 million in distributors' domestic film rentals, suffering the identical fate as the same year's *Making Love*.

183. Petulia (Warner Bros-Seven Arts, 1968), color, 105 min. R-rated.

Executive producer, Denis O'Dell; producer, Raymond Wagner; director, Richard Lester; based on the novel *Me and the Arch Kook Petulia* by John Haase; adaptor, Barbara Turner; screenplay, Lawrence B. Marcus; production designer, Tony Walton; art director, Dean Tavoularis; set decorator, Audrey Blasdel; costumes, Walton; makeup, Gus Norin; music/music conductor, John Barry; assistant director,

John Bloss; sound, Francis E. Stahl; camera, Nicholas Roeg; editor, Anthony Gibbs.

Cast: Julie Christie (Petulia Danner); George C. Scott (Dr. Archie Bollen); Richard Chamberlain (David Danner); Arthur Hill (Barney); Shirley Knight (Polo); Pippa Scott (May); Kathleen Widdoes (Wilma); Roger Bowen (Warren); Richard Dysart (Motel Receptionist); Ruth Kobart, Ellen Geer (Nuns); Lou Gilbert (Mr. Howard); Nate Esformes (Mr. Mendoza); Maria Val (Mrs. Mendoza); Vincent Arias (Oliver); Eric Weiss (Michael Bollen); Kevin Cooper (Stevie Bollen); Joseph Cotten (Mr. Danner); Austin Pendleton (Intern); Barbara Colby (Patient); Rene Auberjonois (Salesman); Josephine Nichols (Neighbor); De Ann Mears (Nurse); and: The Grateful Dead, Big Brother and the Holding Company, The Ace Trucking Company, The Committee, Members of the American Conservatory Theatre.

"These characters may have had special resonance in their day, but now they seem about as relevant as a black-light poster. Luckily, though, the stylistic innovations of the movie continue to be as jarring and witty as ever. . . . If only all this style had

Richard Chamberlain and Julie Christie *in Petulia* (1968).

more content at its core." (Jim Farber, *Video Review*)

In San Francisco, young Petulia Danner (Julie Christie), bored with her six-month marriage to moody David (Richard Chamberlain), becomes intrigued with middle-aged, divorced Dr. Archie Bollen (George C. Scott). Impetuous Petulia entices the randy Bollen in a one moment, and in the next she refuses to go through with their motel rendezvous. The next morning, she whimsically steals a tuba which she carts to Archie's apartment. Despite and because of her kookiness, rather stuffy Bollen is bemused sufficiently to pursue their relationship. He rejects a reconciliation with his ex-wife (Shirley Knight) and breaks off with his mistress (Pippa Scott). Later, when David beats Petulia up, Bollen pressures her to press charges, but she mysteriously refuses and David's wealthy father (Joseph Cotten) hushes up the matter. A year passes. Archie encounters his lost love at the hospital's maternity ward. This time, he asks her to start a real relationship. She agrees, but he suddenly finds that he cannot go through with it. After they say their goodbye, she is taken into the delivery room, all the while calling his name.

Renata Adler (*New York Times*) decided "*Petulia* is a strange, lovely, nervous little film, very jaggedly cut . . . so that the parts don't quite match. . . ." *Variety* judged this an "excellent contemporary romantic drama" in which the "plot kernel is just a springboard for the style in which the story is told. Sometimes the result is pretentious, sometimes not . . . Of particular, lingering interest . . . is the relationshp between Miss Christie and hubby Chamberlain. Latter, playing an emasculated pretty boy, is very good in projecting the logical personality of a gutless immature man, . . ." The British *Monthly Film Bulletin* found, "Richard Lester's choice of San Francisco . . . as the setting for his 'sad love story' is not simply a baroque piece of window dressing. His film is principally about people's inability to make contact with one another . . . and the touristic attractions of the swinging city . . . are indications of the reasons for this failure."

After his long run (1961–66) as the wholesome humanistic "Dr. Kildare," Richard Chamberlain's appearance as the sadistic, father-dominated David in *Petulia* caused quite a stir. At the time, most viewers focused on David's brutal nature, conveyed by a smirk and a mean look suddenly clouding his pretty boy features. What was left ambiguously subtle in *Petulia* was petulant David's strong attraction to men, ranging from toying with the young Mexican waif (Vincent Arias) Pe-

tulia finds in Tiajuna to his interest in the two handsome helpers working on his yacht. At one juncture in this mod film, Petulia says pointedly to her father-in-law, "You can tell David he can come out of the cupboard." With minimium exposition, director Lester has captured the essence of this highly frustrated bisexual, a brooding Adonis at peace in neither sexual camp.

There would be no question about the sexual persuasion of Richard Chamberlain's character in the British-made *The Music Lovers* (1971), in which he played the famed Russian composer, Peter Tchakovsky, a closeted, but well-known, homosexual.

184. Play It As It Lays (Universal, 1972), color, 99min. R-rated.

Producers, Frank Perry, Dominick Dunne; director, Perry; based on the novel by Joan Didion; screenplay, Didion, John Gregory Dunne; production designer, Pato Guzman; costumes, Joel Schumacher, Halston, Gustave Tassell; makeup, Byron Poindexter; songs, McKendree Spring; assistant director, Edward Teets; camera, Jordan Croneweth; editor, Sidney Katz.

Cast: Tuesday Weld (Maria Wyeth); Anthony Perkins (B. Z.); Tammy Grimes (Helene); Adam Roarke (Carter Lang); Ruth Ford (Carlotta): Eddie Firestone (Benny Austin); Diana Ewing (Susannah); Paul Lambert (Larry Kulik); Chuck McCann (Abortionist's Assistant); Severn Darden (Hypnotist); Tony Young (Johnny Waters); Richard Anderson (Les Goodwin); Elizabeth Claman (The Chickie); Mitzi Hoag (Patsy); Roger Ewing (Nelson); Richard Ryal (Apartment Manager); Tyne Daly (Journalist); Mike Edwards (B. Z.'s Lover); John Finnegan (Frank); Tracy Morgan (Jeanelle); Darlene Conley (Kate's Nurse); Arthur Knight (Himself); Albert Johnson (Himself); Alan Warnick (TV Panelist).

Play It As It Lays was one of several Hollywood films—including *Valley of the Dolls* (1967), *Funny Lady* (1975) and *Only When I Laugh* (1981), qq.v.—to depict a gay man as the best pal and (sometimes) emotional support of a despairing, high-powered female entertainer. It is a somber, but pretentious and meandering excursion into life's "real" meaning, using sick contemporary Hollywood as its metaphoric frame of reference. Anthony Perkins—everyone's favorite on-screen neurotic—was cast in *Play It As It Lays* as the suicidal and homosexual film producer, B. Z., whose domineering, wealthy mother (Ruth Ford) pays Helena (Tammy Grimes) to remain his wife, all for the sake of appearances.

At age thirty, Maria (Tuesday Weld) finds life a catastrophe, leading to a nervous breakdown. Her agonies include the fact that her self-absorbed new breed film director husband, Carter (Adam Rourke), has no time for her, their daughter is hopelessly retarded, her parents, from whom she has been long estranged, have recently died, and she has had an abortion as a result of one of many one-night affairs. And now with everything crushing in on her, Maria's best friend—and Carter's movie producer—decides that life is meaningless. Having reached this zero point, B. Z. takes an overdose of sleeping pills with a chaser of vodka and dies in Maria's arms. However, spunky Maria refuses to abandon hope. When asked why she bothers to go on, she replies, "Why not?"

Vincent Canby (*New York Times*) saw several major problems in the translation of Joan Didion's well-received novel to the screen: "Mr. Perry and his screenwriters have found no visual equivalent to Miss Didion's prose. . . . The eye is dazzled in all the wrong ways . . . We never have much time to get inside Maria's mind. . . ." *Variety* more kindly noted that this pessimistic drama "requires spectator 'effort' on action and character development. . . . Perkins looks maturely boyish as the rootless young film director, supplying the only note of compassion in the film—a futile sentiment in a gentle cynic who eventually takes his life in a well-stage suicide sequence" The trade paper's analysis of Perkins's role, of course, missed the point of his character.

To be noted in the film's cast/character credits was the listing of actor Mike Ed-

wards as "B. Z.'s Lover." This credit demonstrated that, in some ways, Hollywood had certainly changed. However, in deciding that the homosexual neurotic should die and the mentally disintegrating heterosexual should live, this aimless movie proved that the motion picture industry was still projecting the same old discriminatory message on screen.

185. Poison (Zeitgeist Films, 1991), color, 85 min.

Executive producers, James Schamus, Brian Greenbaum; producer, Christine Vachon; associate producer, Lauren Zalaznick; director/screenplay, Todd Haynes; production designer, Sarah Stollman; art director, Charles Plummer; set designer, John Hansen; costumes, Jessica Haston; music, James Bennett; assistant director, Vachon; sound, Neil Danzier, Reilly Steele; camera, (color) Maryse Alberti, (black and white) Barry Ellsworth; editors, James Lyons, Haynes.

Cast: *Hero*: Edith Meeks (Felicia Beacon); Millie White (Millie Sklar); Buck Smith (Gregory Lazar); Anne Giotta (Evelyn McAlpert); Lydia Lafleur (Sylvia Manning); Ian Nemser (Sea White); Rob LaBelle (Jay Wete); Evan Dunsky (Dr. MacArthur); Marina Lutz (Hazel Lampercht); Barry Cassidy (Officer Rilt); Richard Anthony (Edward Comascho); Angela M. Schreiber (Florence Giddons); Justin Silverstein (Jake); Chris Singh (Chris); Edward Allen (Fred Beacon); Carlos Jimenez (Jose); *Horror*: Larry Maxwell (Dr. Graves); Susan Norman (Nancy Olsen); Al Quaqliata (Deputy Hansen); Michelle Sullivan (Prostitute); Parlan McGaw (Newscaster); Frank O'Donnell (Old Doctor); Charles Cavalier (Cop); Kyle deCamp, Aimee Scheff (Neighbors); Jessica Lorraine Traverson (Nurses); Phil W. Petrie (Doctor); Richard Hansen (Narrator); Bruce Cook (Dr. Strick); Chris Henricks (Sleazy Man); *Homo*: Scott Renderer (John Broom); James Lyons (Jack Bolton); John R. Lombardi (Rass); Tony Pemberton (Young John Broom); Andrew Harpending (Young Jack Bolton); Tony Gigante (Inspector); Douglas F. Gibson (Van Roven); Damien Garcia (Chanci); Lee Simpson (Miss Tim); Joey Grant (Jamoke); Gary Ray (Canon); David Danford (Basco); Jason Bauer (Doran); Ken Scatz (Preacher); Maurice Clapisson, Matthew Ebert (Guards); Shawn Wilson (John Brook, at Age Six).

Suggested by three works (*Our Lady of the Flowers*, *Miracle of the Rose*, *Thief's Journal*) of French writer Jean Genet, the tri-part *Poison* won the Grand Jury prize for best dramatic feature at the 1991 Sundance Film Festival in Park City, Utah. *Variety* rated it "a conceptually bold, stylistically audacious first feature" by underground filmmaker Todd Haynes. The trade paper added, "Haynes has put together a provocative look at societal outcasts and twisted behavior that can be read in ways both artistic and political."

"Hero," a fantasy allegory conceived in a documentary style, has a seven-year old boy murdering his father after discovering his mother sleeping with the gardener, and the boy then flying off with her. In "Horror," suggesting the format of 1950s science fiction movies and interweaving contemporary concern with the deadly AIDS virus, earnest Dr. Graves (Larry Maxwell) discovers the source of mankind's sexual drive. After drinking the potion, the young scientist becomes a ferocious monster, eventually jumping to his death. The third episode, "Homo," is set in a sordid 1940s French prison where a toughened convict (Scott Renderer) obsessively stalks a new inmate (James Lyons), whom he knew years before. Together, they talk about their gay sex fantasies, smoke cigarettes, have sex and reminisce. Eventually, all the talk leads to an attempted prison break and the newcomer's death.

Variety cautioned, "'Homo' . . . will throw more than a few unsuspecting viewers. A mood of seething, violent homoeroticism permeates . . . in an episode spiked with multiple glimpses of rear-entry intercourse and one of genital fondling." Michael Wilmington (*Los Angeles Times*) rated *Poison* "an arty, literary, socially conscious movie. . . . The prison scenes in *Poison* unspool like a swanky gay fantasy, washed in romantic blue light, populated by blue-clad convicts. . . . These scenes [including the "sexual initiation or degradation"] aren't real at all. They're deliberately imbued with erotic fantasy. And that may be more disturbing, for some audiences, than explicit sex. . . . None of the sexual scenes in *Poison*—and there aren't many—are free of suggestions of pain or fear. . . . [It is] clear that the 'poison' of the title is, partially society's attitudes towards the three 'deviant' characters—whom it beats up, imprisons, hunts down."

Poison, funded by the National Endowment for the Arts, proved controversial with overzealous watchdog citizen organizations who objected that a government organization supported a movie so "pornographic" and so pro-homosexual.

186. Poison Ivy (New Line Cinema, 1992), color, 89 min. R-rated.

Executive producers, Melissa Goddard, Peter Morgan; line producer, Rick Nathanson; associate producer, Jana Marx; director, Katt Shea Ruben; screenplay, Katt Shea Ruben, Andy Ruben; production designer, Virginia Lee; art director, Hayden Yates; set decorator, Michele Munoz; costumes, Ellen Gross; makeup, Debbie Zoller; music, Aaron Davies; choreographer, Ted Lynn; assistant director, J. B. Rogers; sound, Bill Robbins; camera, Phedon Papmichael; editor, Gina Mittleman.

Cast: Drew Barrymore (Ivy); Sara Gilbert (Sylvie Cooper); Tom Skerritt (Darryl Cooper); Cheryl Ladd (Georgie Cooper); Alan Stock (Bob); Jeanne Sakata (Isabelle); E. J. Moore (Kid); J. B. Quon (Another Kid); Leonardo Dicaprio (1st Guy); Michael Goldner (Man in Car); Charley Hayward (Tiny); Tim Winters (Old Man); Billy Charles Kane (James); Tony Ervolina (Man on Screen); Mary Gordon Murray (Doctor); Julie Jay (Nurse Behind Desk); Charla Sampsel (Orderly); Angel Broadhurst (Death Rocker); Randall Caldwell (Truck Driver); Tom Ruben (Roofer); Lisa Passero (Lisa); Lawrence Levy (Jeff); Sandy Roth Ruben (Estelle); Warren Burton (Max).

Borrowing heavily from the premise of the Italian-made *Teorema* (1968) and *Something for Everyone* (1970), q.v., this uninspired feature traded heavily on the cast pairing of Drew Barrymore, the one-time child star of *E.T.* (1982) who had had an often controversial off-screen life, with

Sara Gilbert, one of the daughters from the TV sitcom "Roseanne" (1988—).

Decidedly outgoing Ivy (Drew Barrymore) easily wins the friendship of her introverted, intellectual high school classmate, Sylvie Cooper (Sara Gilbert). Soon thereafter, the manipulative Ivy takes up residence with Sylvie and her wealthy parents, Darryl (Tom Skerritt), a recovering alcoholic who is a conservative TV commentator, and Georgie (Cheryl Ladd), an emphysema sufferer. Before long, the cunning Ivy is in full control of the Hollywood Hills home, using her allures to temp each member of the dysfunctional household, including the pet dog. Darryl, lusting after the provocative Ivy, returns to drinking, the withdrawn Sylvie discovers she has strong emotional/sexual feelings for her controlling girlfriend, etc. Eventually, everything spirals out of control.

Todd McCarthy (*Daily Variety*) rated the exploitive *Poison Ivy* a "laughably bad meller" full of contrived incidents which appear "as just ludicrous and bad rather than tantalizing or exciting." As to the inept acting, McCarthy weighed, "Unfortunate thesps take it all very seriously." Ella Taylor (*LA Weekly*) concluded, "Like *Basic Instinct*, *Poison Ivy* works from a two-bit psychology of childhood trauma that has cheap emotion pouring out of everyone—all the time. . . . The problem with *Poison Ivy* . . . is that it has nothing to propose, no idea to add to a very overworked story about women warped into evil because they have no family." *Entertainment Weekly* gave *Poison Ivy* a "C," explaining, "It's an arty exploitation thriller, all sleek, machinelike surface." For David Kronke (*Los Angeles Daily News*), "the film isn't good enough to fulfill or justify the promise of its lurid premise. More disappointingly, it isn't bad enough to dismiss as bad camp fun."

187. Prison Girls (United Producers, 1973), color, 94 min. R-rated.

Producers, Nicholas J. Grippo, Burton C. Gershfield; director, Thomas DeSimone; screenplay, Lee Walters; art director, Robinson Royce; music supervisor, Christopher Huston; assistant director, Gershfield; sound, William Kaplan; camera, Gerhard Hentschel; supervising editor, Ron Ashcroft; editor, Paul Young.

Cast: With: Robin Whitting, Angie Monet, Tracy Handufss, Maria Arrold, Liz Wolfe, Linde Melissa, Dorothy Dick, Jamie McKenna, Carol Peters, Claire Bow, Donna Sutter, Ushie Digard, Susan Landis, Bolivia Tierman, Lois Darst, Ilona Lakes, Susan Sterling, Joni Johnston, Lisa Ashbury, Jason Williams, Howard Alexander, Lee Blackmore, John Barnum, Chesley Noone, L. D. Dicksman, Rick Loots, Arnie Renfro, Steve Wilete, Brent Blasell.

Filmed with the gimmick of 3-D cinematography which required the viewers to wear special Polaroid glasses, the story of this soft-core porno entry opens at the Santa Helena Women's Correction Center. There six model prisoners are given a weekend pass. It is hoped their furlough will help them adjust to their upcoming paroles. One, a prostitute, returns to her former pimp and comes under his power again, while another enjoys a sexual romp with her husband. A third, Joyce, visits with her brother-in-law, only to have a gang of bikers break into his place and force him to rape her. As for Toni, she dates a rich acquaintance only to find that Gert, her lesbian jailmate, is invited to party with them, which leads to a sexual threesome. As for Cindy, she is shot by the police when her boyfriend insists she leave the country with him. The five survivors return to jail.

A. H. Weiler (*New York Times*) was amused with *Prison Girls* which "vividly illustrates this observer's conviction that soft-core pornography can't be much of a help either to serious penology or dedicated thrill-seeker."

188. The Private Files of J. Edgar Hoover (American International, 1978), color, 112 min. PG-rated.

Producer, Larry Cohen; associate producers, Arthur Mandelberg, Peter Sabiston; director/screenplay, Cohen; production designer, Cathy Davis; set decorator, Carolyn Loewenstein;

Broderick Crawford in *The Private Files of J. Edgar Hoover* **(1977).**

costumes, Lewis Friedman; makeup, Rifka Gold, Josephine Cianella; music, Miklos Rozsa; assistant director, Reid Freeman; sound, Robert Gheraldini, Jane Landis; camera, Paul Glickman; editor, Christopher Lebenzon.

Cast: Broderick Crawford (J. Edgar Hoover); Jose Ferrer (Lionel McCoy); Michael Parks (Robert F. Kennedy); Ronee Blakley (Carrie DeWitt); Celeste Holm (Florence Hollister); Rip Torn (Dwight Webb); Michael Sacks (Melvin Purvis); Dan Dailey (Clyde Tolson); Raymond St. Jacques (Martin Luther King Jr.); Andrew Duggan (Lyndon B. Johnson); John Marley (Dave Hindley); Howard DaSilva (Franklin D. Roosevelt); June Havoc (Hoover's Mother); James Wainwright (Young Hoover); Lloyd Nolan (Attorney General Stone); Ellen Barber (FBI Secretary); Lloyd Gough (Walter Winchell); Brad Dexter (Alvin Karpas); Jennifer Lee (Ethel Brunette); George Plimpton (Quentin Reynolds); Jack Cassidy (Damon Runyon); William Jordan (John F. Kennedy); Henderson Forsythe (Harry Suydam); George

D. Wallace (Senator Joseph McCarthy); Art Lund (Benchley); Mary Alice Moore (Miss Bryant); Dan Resin (President's Advisor); Brooks Morton (Earl Warren); Richard Dixon (President Nixon); James Dukas (Frank, the Waiter); Ron Faber (Hijacker); Margo Lynn Curtis, Tanya Roberts (Stewardesses); Larry Pines (Kelly); John Stefano (Harry); Gordon Zimmerman (Lepke); Marty Lee (Media Man).

In real life J. Edgar Hoover (1895–1972) was a crime fighter who held sway as director of the U.S. Federal Bureau of Investigation (FBI) for nearly fifty years (1924–72), using unorthodox methods to retain tight control over the Bureau through several presidencies. Publicly, Hoover, who never married, was a confirmed moral prude, but privately, he was reputed to have had a very closeted sex life.

In the made-for-cable movie, *J. Edgar*

Hoover (1987), starring Treat Williams, much is made of the square-jawed, obsessive law enforcer not having time for sexual pursuits. (He jokes, "I really think the reason I never married is God made a woman like Eleanor Roosevelt.") In contrast, in *The Private Files of J. Edgar Hoover*, made by quirky Larry Cohen and featuring a veteran cast, much is made by indirection of Hoover's sexual leanings. An episode in this helter-skelter chronicle finds tough Washington, D.C. columnist Dave Hindley (John Marley) making allegations that Hoover is having a homosexual relationship with his long-time companion, Clyde Tolson (Dan Dailey). Hindley tells his editor, "Let's bring it out in the open. If Hoover wants to deny he's a fag, you'll give him plenty of space, won't ya?" This results in a shouting matching between Hindley and Hoover (Broderick Crawford). However, thereafter the matter is dropped to focus on more enticing matters: John F. Kennedy's assassination, Hoover bargaining with Lyndon Johnson to avoid mandatory retirement, and, after J. Edgar's death, Clyde Tolson rescuing certain documents from being shredded by the chief's staff to be passed on—so it is suggested—to those opposed to the Richard M. Nixon regime.

Regarding *The Private Files of J. Edgar Hoover*, Paul Taylor (British *Monthly Film Bulletin*) noted ironically "that a portrait of America's arch-conservative should emerge as arguably the most radical Hollywood genre film in years." *Variety* was more reactive, insisting, "Matching the picture's sleazy sensationalism in story is its sleazy sensationalistic look and sound. This may be the motion picture industry's first historical horror story." But, the trade paper admitted, "As Hoover, the jowly [Broderick] Crawford turns in a fine performance. . . . However, the remainder of the performances . . . are grotesque attempts to mimic well known public officials." Dan Dailey looked totally bewildered by his passive role as the Chief's amiable, subjugated companion.

189. The Private Life of Sherlock Holmes (United Artists, 1970), color, 125 min. GP-rated.

Producer, Billy Wilder; associate producer, I. A. L. Diamond; director, Wilder; based on the characters created by Sir Arthur Conan Doyle; screenplay, Wilder, Diamond; production designer, Alexander Trauner; art director, Tony Inglis; set decorator, Harry Cordwell; costumes, Julie Harris; makeup, Ernest Gassner; music, Miklos Rozsa; choreographer/ballet advisor, David Blair; sound, J. W. N. Daniel, Dudley Messenger, Gordon K. McCallum; special effects, Wally Veevers, Cliff Richardson; camera, Christopher Challis; editor, Ernest Walter.

Cast: Robert Stephens (Sherlock Holmes); Colin Blakely (Dr. John H. Watson); Irene Handl (Mrs. Hudson); Stanley Holloway (1st Gravedigger); Christopher Lee (Mycroft Holmes); Genevieve Page (Gabrielle Valladon); Clive Revill (Rogozhin); Tamara Toumanova (Petrova); George Benson (Inspector Lestrade); Catherine Lacey (Old Lady); Mollie Maureen (Queen Victoria); Peter Madden (Von Tirpitz); Robert Cawdron (Hotel Manager); Michael Elwyn (Cassidy); Michael Balfour (Cabby); Frank Thornton (Porter); James Copeland (Guide); Alex McCrindle (Baggage Man); Kenneth Benda (Minister); Graham Armitage (Wiggins); Eric Francis (2nd Gravedigger); John Garrie, Godfrey James (Carters); Ina De La Haye (Petrova's Maid); Ismet Hassan, Charlie Young Atom, Teddy Kiss Atom, Willie Shearer (Submarine Crew); Daphne Riggs (Lady-in-Waiting); John Gatrell (Equerry); Martin Carroll, John Scott (Scientists); Philip Anthony (Lieutenant Commander); Philip Ross (McKellar); Annette Kerr (Secretary); Kynaston Reeves (Old Man); Anne Blake (Madame); Marilyn Head, Anna Matisse, Wendy Lingham, Penny Brahms, Sheena Hunter (Girls); Tina Spooner, Judy Spooner (Twins); and: David Kossoff, Paul Stassino, Paul Hansard.

Several actors have portrayed Sherlock Holmes on camera, but none gained the recognition or identification that Basil Rathbone did with the role in the late 1930s and early 1940s. In 1970, ace director Billy Wilder sought to puncture the overstuffed legend of the renown crime solver with his expensively-produced *The*

Private Life of Sherlock Holmes, filmed in England. Not only does this lengthy shaggy dog tale present the Deerstalker as capable of deductive misjudgment, but he is a pompous soul who relies on cocaine injections and may or may not be homosexual.

In the opening preamble set in 1890s London, London, Sherlock Holmes (Robert Stephens) claims to be tired of living up to the fantasies created in Watson's (Colin Blakely) published journals. Thereafter, the aristocratic sleuth accepts an invitation to attend a performance of *Swan Lake* and, after the show, to meet with Petrova (Tamara Toumanova), the prima ballerina of the visiting Russian ballet. She quickly lets it be known that she craves to have a child, but wants the father to be as intellectually superior as she is beautiful and graceful. She has selected Holmes as the likely candidate. He politely declines, but she insists. Trying to dissuade her, he suggests that, like Tchaikovsky, he does not find women "his glass of tea." When she insist he "come to the point," he states "Watson and I have been bachelors for several years. . . ." The shocked woman asks, "Dr. Watson? . . . He is your glass of tea?" A diffident Holmes retorts, "If you want to get picturesque about it."

News of this revelation quickly spreads backstage, and Watson, much the ladies' man, finds himself the object of titters and the sudden object of interest by limp-wristed dancers. Back at 221B Baker Street, the agitated Watson, insisting he can easily prove his own healthy reputation with the ladies, blusters: "I must beg you to forgive the presumption and ask you straightforwardly. Have there been women in your life?" After a tantalizing pause, Holmes responds, "The answer is yes., Watson. I *will* forgive your presumption." The question in point—Holmes's sexual persuasion—is never answered in the movie. The remainder of the film focuses on a case involving Gabrielle Valladon (Genevieve Page), a double agent, and the legendary Loch Ness monster.

Vincent Canby (*New York Times*) was pleased by "Billy Wilder's mostly comic charming, psycho-sexual analysis" and pointed out that "sex" is the main focus of this excursion. "To put it bluntly, and profanely were Holmes and Dr. Watson . . . lovers? . . . I suspect that only Billy Wilder would have the nerve to raise such a question, and then to dispatch it in a movie that is gentle enough to become the Thanksgiving holiday attraction at the [Radio City] Music Hall." Canby goes on to say that no, Sherlock and Dr. John were not gay, but "Wilder's Holmes . . . can't help but be amused at the terror the idea arouses in the very conventional Dr. Watson. . . ." The *Motion Picture Exhibitor* warned that the movie "has a curious coldness which might thwart audience involvement. . . .it never captures that brandy, coffee and cigars English club atmosphere which so enthralled viewers of the 30s and 40s."

The Private Life of Sherlock Holmes was a major box-office disappointment. Its multi-layered, satirical treatment of homosexuality was one of the film's more successful gambits. It should be noted that, in cutting the release print from a 3½ to a 2 hour running time, several introductory sequences showing Holmes being betrayed by women were deleted. Thus, the Russian ballerina scene takes on more weight than it should, and the viewer is led astray by such surviving lines as Holmes's "Actually, I don't dislike women, I merely distrust them . . . the twinkle in the eye . . . the arsenic in the soup. . . ."

190. The Producers (Embassy, 1968), color, 88 min. Not rated.

Presenter, Joseph E. Levine; producer, Sidney Glazier; associate producer, Jack Grossberg; director/screenplay, Mel Brooks; art director, Charles Rosen; set decorator, James Dalton; costumes, Gene Coffin; makeup, Irving Buchman; music/music conductor, John Morris; songs; Norman Blagman and Herb Hartig; Brooks; assistant directors, Michael Hertzberg, Martin Danzig; sound, Alan Heim; camera, Joseph Coffey; editor, Ralph Rosenblum.

Cast: Zero Mostel (Max Bialystock); Gene Wilder (Leo Bloom); Dick Shawn (Lorenzo St. Du Bois); Kenneth Mars (Franz Liebkind); Estelle Winwood ("Hold Me, Touch Me" Old Lady); Christopher Hewett (Roger De Bris); Andreas Voutsinas (Carmen Giya); Lee Meredith (Ulla); Renee Taylor (Eva Braun); Michael Davis (Production Tenor); John Zoller (*New York Times* Critic); Madlyn Cates (Woman at Window); Frank Campanella (Bartender); Arthur Rubin, Zale Kessler, Bernie Allen, Rusty Blitz, Anthony Gardell (Auditioning Hitlers); Mary Love, Amelia Barleon, Nell Harrison, Elsie Kirk (Old Ladies); Barney Martin (German Officer in Play); Diana Eden (Showgirl); Tucker Smith, David Evans (Lead Dancers); Josip Elic (Violinist); William Hickey (Drunk in Theatre Bar).

For many moviegoers, *The Producers* is director Mel Brooks's finest screen creation; it won an Academy Award for Brooks (Best Screenplay Written Directly for the Screen). The vulgar comedy has a wonderfully daffy premise. A sleazy Broadway producer sells backers 25,000 percent interest in his new show—*Springtime for Hitler*, a musical based on the life and loves of Der Fuhrer!—hoping the production will flop, so he can keep the profits unnoticed by his backers. The movie provides a marvelous showcase for the oversized talents of Zero Mostel as the seedy, crooked showman and Gene Wilder as his timid and very neurotic accountant. Together, they take Broadway by storm, but, eventually, end in jail, where they con their fellow inmates by selling them (oversubscribed) shares in a new show, *Prisoners of Love*. En route to the big house, the undynamic duo meet a procession of eccentrics, ranging from several randy old ladies whom Mostel courts for their bank accounts, to Franz Liebkind (Kenneth Mars), the diehard Nazi author of the Hitler show, and burned-out hippie Lorenzo St. Du Bois (Dick Shawn), who stars in the tasteless production. Not least of all is Roger De Bris (Christopher Hewitt), a talentless director who is an outrageous gay leather queen/transvestite. A surprised Renata Adler (*New York Times*) admitted the frequently disjointed *The Producers* "is a violently mixed bag. Some of it is shoddy and gross and cruel; the rest is funny in an entirely unexpected way." Among the comedy's highlights, Adler cited a scene involving Carmen Giya (Andreas Voutsinas), Roger's live-in lover and the producers: "There is a lovely conversation with the director's roommate, played . . . as a prancing young person in black slacks, black turtleneck, beads, and a beard curled up in front like the toe of a dancing slipper." *Variety* labeled the film a "Pie-in-the-face farce." However, Tom Milne (British *Monthly Film Bulletin*) was not amused: "by the time the actors . . . have finished . . . strenuously mugging and throwing themselves around to prove that it is funny, it isn't very any more. Over and over again promising ideas are killed off, either by over-exposure (the visit to the transvestite director degenerates into a tiresome anthology of camp mannerisms) or by bad timing. . . ."

Besides Brooks's screenplay for *The Producers* winning an Oscar, the movie received an Academy Award nomination for Best Supporting Actor (Gene Wilder; Jack Albertson won for *The Subject Was Roses*).

191. Protocol (Columbia, 1984), color, 95 min. PG-rated.

Executive producer, Goldie Hawn; producer, Anthea Sylbert; associate producer, Lewis J. Rackmil; director, Herbert Ross; story, Charles Shyer, Nancy Meyers, Harvey Miller; screenplay, Buck Henry; production designer, Bill Malley; art directors, Tracy Bousman, Enrico Fiorentini; set decorators, Chuck Pierce, Mary Olivia Swanson; costumes, Wayne A. Finkelman; makeup, Thomas Case, Frank Griffin; music, Basil Poledouris; assistant directors, John Kretchmer, Dennis Maguire, Mark Radcliffe, L. Andrew Stone; second unit director, Jimmy Devis; stunt coordinator, Max Kleven; sound, Al Overton Jr., Dan Wallin, Karen Wilson; special effects, Phil Cory; camera, William A. Fraker; editors, Paul Hirsch, Lynzee Klingman.

Cast: Goldie Hawn (Sunny Davis); Chris

Zero Mostel, Lee Meredith and Gene Wilder in *The Producers* (1968).

Sarandon (Michael Ransome); Richard Romanus (Emir of Ohtar); Andre Gregor (Nawaf Al Kabeer); Gail Strickland (Mrs. St. John); Cliff DeYoung (Hilley); Keith Szarabajka (Crowe); Ed Begley Jr. (Hasser); James Staley (Vice-President Merck); Kenneth Mars (Lou); Jean Smart (Ella); Maria O'Brien (Donna): Joel Brooks (Ben); Grainger Hines (Jerry); Kenneth McMillan (Senator Norris); Richard Hamilton (Mr. Davis); Mary Carver (Mrs. Davis); Jack Ross Obney (Jimmy); Kathleen York (Charmaine); Georganne LaPiere (Bobbie); Pamela Myers (Gloria); Joe George (Bartender); Tom Spratle (Grandpa); Dortha Duckworth (Grandma); Sally Thorner, Jeanne Mori, Elizabeth Anderson (TV Newspersons); Archie Hahn, George D. Wallace, Julie Hampton, Thom Sharp, Paul Willson, Holly Roberts (TV Commentators); Lyman Ward (Senator Kenworthy); Joe Lambie (Doctor); Daphne Maxwell (Helene); Michael Zand (Assassin); Cece Cole (Jimmy's Girl); Roger Til (Belgium Ambassador); Marcella Saint-Amant (Belgium Ambassador's Wife); Ellen Tobie (Mrs. St. John's Secretary); John Ratzenberger (Grover House); Alice O'Connor (Mother of America); A. S. Csaky (Sunny's Cousin); Ken Gibbel (Husky Biker); Ken Hill (Man in Green Jacket); Albert Leong, Peter Pan (Cooks); Robert Donovan, Amanda Bearse (Soap Opera Actors); Marcie Barkin, Deborah Dutch, Lorraine Fields (Safari Girls).

"The first hour of *Protocol* is so much fun, and the Goldie Hawn character is such an engaging original, that at first I couldn't believe they were going to throw away all that work by going for a standard Hollywood ending. . . ." (Roger Ebert, *Movie Home Companion*, 1986)

The mores of Hollywood movies and the public at large had come a long way in the years between *Advise and Consent* (1962), q.v., and *Protocol* (1984). Now a character in *Protocol* could wise-crack,

"Men in D.C. are all married, gay or work for the government." Now, the comedy's heroine, a daffy blonde cocktail waitress named Sunny Davis (Goldie Hawn), could share a house with two gay roomies (Joel Brooks, Grainger Hines) and carry on a legitimate conversation with them. When the movie falls apart in the final portion, director Herbert Ross frantically works in a barroom brawl, one with more disparate types than any Hollywood movie has a right to include, ranging from S & M leather queens, bikers, hookers, Japanese tourists, Near East dignitaries, etc.

When Sunny Davis (Goldie Hawn), a waitress at Lou's Safari Bar in Washington, D.C. accidentally saves the Emir of Ohtar (Richard Romanus) from being assassinated, she becomes a media darling. Scheming White house aides have naive Sunny join the Department of Protocol, intending that Sunny be offered to the grateful Emir as one of his wives in exchange for a favorable treaty. Once in Ohtar, the natives rebel and a scandal ensues, but at the end of the inevitable Congressional investigation, a now politically-aware Sunny is found innocent. She marries a former governmental aide (Chris Sarandon) and win an election to become a Congressman from her home state of Oregon.

Vincent Canby (*New York Times*) alerted his readers: "the whole projects begins to look a bit overcalculated, not just to protect the star but to beautify her . . . [With] the exception of Andre Gregory, who plays a cockeyed Arab guru . . . nobody is allowed to come anywhere near the point where the star-producer might be upstaged." Candy noted as one of the movie's "better moments" the bar brawl involving "a a gang of leather-clad motorcyclists, plus some happy homosexuals who are friends of Sunny." *Variety* was more to the point, "Goldie Hawn's insistence on Saying Something Important takes a lot of the zip out of *Protocol*. . . ." Kim Newman (British *Monthly Film Bulletin*) pointed out that, "*Protocol* merely flirts with political issues such as government accountability, so that the only question worth pondering in the end is why Goldie Hawn emerged from *Laugh-In* as a movie star, and not Judy Carne, JoAnn Worley, Ruth Buzzi or Chelsea Brown."

Despite the feeling that *Protocol* was a contrived distillation of *Mr. Smith Goes to Washington* (1939) and *Born Yesterday* (1950), the comedy grossed $14.2 million in distributors' domestic film rentals.

192. Puzzle of a Downfall Child

(Universal, 1970), color, 104 min. R-rated.

Presenter, Jennings Lang; producer, John Foreman; associate producer, Frank Cafey; director, Jerry Schatzberg; story, Schatzberg, Adrien Joyce [Carl Eastman]; screenplay, Joyce; art director, Richard Bianchi; set decorator, Hubert J. Oates; costumes, Terry Leong; makeup, Richard Philippe; assistant directors, Robert P. Schneider, Martin E. Miller; sound, William Gramaglia; camera, Adam Holender; editor, Evan Lottman.

Cast: Faye Dunaway (Lou Andreas Sand); Barry Primus (Aaron Reinhardt); Viveca Lindfors (Pauline Galba); Barry Morse (Dr. Galba); Roy Scheider (Mark); Ruth Jackson (Barbara Casey); John Heffernan (Dr. Sherman); Sydney Walker (Psychiatrist); Clark Burckhalter (Davy Bright); Shirley Rich (Peggy McCavage); Emerick Bronson (Falco); Joe George (1st Man in Bar); John Eames (1st Doctor); Harry Lee (Mr. Wong); Jane Halleran (Joan); Susan Willis (Neighbor); Barbara Carrera (T. J. Brady); Sam Schacht (George).

". . . the title is enough to warn one that this is going to be literary in the worst way. Once the movie gets started and it turns out to be about a movie being planned about the anguished life of a high-fashion model . . . it's hard to know what's worse —that she calls herself Lou Andreas Sand or that her real name is Emily." (Pauline Kael, *The New Yorker*)

Everything about this slow, boring stinker wreaks of pretentiousness. The "important" story is framed by photographer Aaron Reinhardt (Barry Primus) visiting Lou Andreas Sand (Faye Dunaway) at her lonely Long Island beach house. There, the former top fashion model

Viveca Lindfors and Faye Dunaway in *Puzzle of a Downfall Child* **(1970).**

agrees to let him tape record her reminiscences about her past for his projected movie. As the narrative flashes back and forth, the reality of Lou's escapades are contrasted with the fantasy of her more chaste recollections. Among the people resurrected from her past are fashion photographer Pauline Galba (Viveca Lindfors), who ignores her weak-willed husband (Barry Morse) to satisfy her craving for Lou. In turn, Pauline battles besmitten Mark (Roy Scheider), a Madison Avenue advertising executive, who wants to marry Lou. The latter, unable to commit to a relationship, breaks off with him. Later, as Lou's career fails, she turns to drink and drugs to calm her anxieties, and following a nervous breakdown, she retreats to her beach cottage. Back in the present, Lou insists she is pulling herself together. As Aaron leaves she asks him why, after their

long close relationship, they were never lovers. He replies they once were.

Roger Greenspun (*New York Times*) found merit to this tale of alienation: "despite some lapses and many excesses, [it] is very good indeed. . . . An excellent photographer, he [director Jerry Schatzberg] is also full of ideas about photography— and in this the director and his subject and their world most wonderfully combine." In contrast, Richard Combs (British *Monthly Film Bulletin*) argued that this movie was "a primer catalogue of sexual and other confusions that fails to add up to a whole personalty, or to one genuine note of anguish." *Variety* criticized the movie for its "somewhat dated cinema-verite chic—time-disjointing storytelling, abstract visuals, plus truth-and-illusion ambiguities . . ." However, the trade paper reacted favorably to some of the cast,

Viveca Lindfors in particular, "deliberately deglamorized. . . . Miss Lindfors remains capable of grabbing audience attention and holding it until she is ready to let go."

Viveca Lindfors, who had played a lesbian in *No Exit* (1962), q.v., would play the same sort of role again in *Sylvia* (1965) and *Marilyn: The Untold Story* (1980), qq.v.

193. Q & A (Tri-Star, 1990), color, 134 min. R-rated.

Executive producer, Patrick Wachsberger; producers, Arnon Milchan, Burtt Harris; associate producer, Lilith A. Jacobs; director, Sidney Lumet; based on the novel by Judge Edwin Torres; screenplay, Lumet; production designer, Philip Rosenberg; art director, Beth Kuhn; set decorator, Gary Brink; costumes, Ann Roth, Neil Spisak; makeup, Joe Cranzano; music, Ruben Blades; assistant director, Harris; sound, Chris Newman, Dennis Maitland II, Mike Farrow; camera, Andrzej Bartkowiak; editor, Richard Cirincione.

Cast: Nick Nolte (Lieutenant Mike Brennan); Timothy Hutton (Al Reilly); Armand Assante (Bobby Texador); Patrick O'Neal (Kevin Quinn); Lee Richardson (Leo Bloomenfeld); Luis Guzman (Luis Valentin); Charles Dutton (Sam Chapman); Jenny Lumet (Nancy Bosch); Paul Calderon (Roger Montalvo); International Chrysis (Jose Malpica); Dominick Chianese (Larry Pesch); Leonard Cimino (Nick Petrone); Fyvush Finkel (Preston Pearlstein); Gustavo Brens (Alfonse Segal); Martin E. Brens (Armand Segal); Maurice Schell (Detective Zucker); Tommy A. Ford (Lubin); John Capodice (Hank Mastroangelo); Frederick Rolf (District Attorney); Hal Lehrman (Alshul); Gloria Irizarry (Mrs. Bosch); Brian Neill (Sylvester/Sophia); Susan Mitchell (Flo); Drew Eliot (Magnus); Frank Raiter (Seabury), Harry Madsen (Tony Vasquez); Jerry Ciauri (Bruno Valli); George Kodisch (Inspector Flynn); Burtt Harris (Phil); Michael A. Joseph (Pimp); Cynthia O'Neal (Agnes Quinn); Victor Colicchio ("After Hours" Avarado); Anibal Lleras, Jose Rafel Arango ("After Hours" Patron); David Dill (Bartender); Alex Ruiz (Danny); Richard Solchik (Phillie); Edward Rogers III (Jose's Apartment Detective); Junior Perez (Captain of *Nancy*); Peter Gumeny (Guard); Edward Rowan (Ed); Danny Darrow (Phone Investigator); Jose Collazo (Fisherman).

Many of Sidney Lumet's feature films are placed in New York City (*The Pawnbroker*, 1965, *The Group*, 1966, *The Anderson Tapes*, 1970, *Dog Day Afternoon*, 1973, *Garbo Talks*, 1984, qq.v.) and have a subordinate theme and/or characters who are gays. Several of Lumet's best motion pictures have dealt with corruption within the New York police department (*Serpico*, 1973, *Prince of the City*, 1981). *Q & A*, Lumet's most ambitious production in several years, deals with both. With high-charged performances by Nick Nolte and Armand Assante, and its emphatic theme of dishonesty and racism in the NYPD, it was assumed *Q & A* would be a crowd-pleaser. Instead, it grossed only $5 million in distributors' domestic film rentals. Tom Milne (British *Monthly Film Bulletin*) put his finger on the film's major fault: "Instead of following up the implications . . . [of bigotry and corruption in the police force], the script opts for a string of action sequences . . . [that] belong in any old TV cop series. . . ." It did not help matters that the movie's hero was played so weakly by Timothy Hutton, or that its anti-hero (Nolte's role), an Irish cop, was such an unsympathetic rule-bender who despises all minorities, including several drag queens whom he pressures as stool pigeons and whom he (un)consciously craves as sex partners.

Veteran New York City cop, beer-bellied Lieutenant Mike Brennan (Nick Nolte), forces a scum-bum, Tony Vasquez (Harry Madsen), into a showdown and kills him. Then, using his standard tactics, he bulldozes witnesses into agreeing that his murder of the Latino was in self-defense. Meanwhile, Al Reilly (Timothy Hutton), an idealistic, eager beaver assistant District Attorney), investigates the case. His superior officer, Kevin Quinn (Patrick O'Neal), assures him that Brennan's actions were legitimate and that the follow-up is merely a formality.

However, the situation becomes complicated. One of the witnesses to the shooting was Bobby Texador (Armand Assante) whose live-in girlfriend, Nancy Bosch (Jenny Lumet), was Al's girlfriend until he broke off the relationship upon discovering that her father was black. As the evidence mounts, the disillusioned Al realizes that Brennan's racist brutality led to the killing and that Quinn is hiding the facts. Encouraged by Leo Bloomfield (Lee Richardson), his departmental mentor, Reilly doggedly pursues the clues. The chase leads to Puerto Rico where Texador has gone with Nancy and transvestite performer Roger Montalvo (Paul Calderon). However, Montalvo is there because he has been terrorized by Brennan into setting up Vasquez to be murdered. (Brennan had been systematically wiping out a youth gang, whose only surviving members had been Texador and Vasquez. The members of the gang had once witnessed a killing by the present-day D.A. Quinn who had, in turn, over the years blackmailed Mike into being his hit man.).

In the showdown, Brennan kills both Texador and Montalvo, but later dies resisting arrest. Because the case would cause a major police scandal, it is hushed up. As for Quinn, he has left his position to run for governor. Bloomfield wryly assures the amazed Reilly that it is an election Quinn can never win.

Variety championed, "Sidney Lumet grabs a tiger by the tail with *Q & A*, a hard-hitting thriller. . . . Bravura thesping by Nick Nolte. . . . [This film dares] to expose a dark, twisted underworld with homosexuals and transsexuals integrated into the plot. Nolte's character persecuting minorities is given a universal application as he manhandles the transvestite hooker played by Brian Neill, the gay key witness played by Paul Calderon and Calderon's she-male friend essayed by International Chrysis, all deeply affecting as victims." Roger Ebert (*Movie Home Companion*, 1991) rated the film four stars, reasoning "Lumet has made a lot of other movies

about tough big-city types . . . but this is the one where he taps into the vibrating awareness of race which is almost always there when strangers of different races encounter each other in situations where one has authority and another doesn't. . . . It is fascinating the way this movie works so well as a police thriller on one level, while on other levels it probes feeling we may keep secret even from ourselves."

194. Queen Christina (Metro-Goldwyn-Mayer, 1933), 97 min. Not rated.

Producer, Walter Wanger; director, Rouben Mamoulian; story, Salka Viertel, Margaret Levin; screenplay, H. M. Harwood, Viertel; dialogue, S. N. Behrman; art directors, Alexander Touboff, Edwin B. Willis; costumes, Adrian; music, Herbert Stothart; sound, Douglas Shearer; camera, William Daniels; editor, Blanche Sewell.

Cast: Greta Garbo (Queen Christina); John Gilbert (Don Antonio De la Prada); Ian Keith (Magnus); Lewis Stone (Chancellor Oxenstierna); Elizabeth Young (Countess Ebba Sparre); Sir C. Aubrey Smith (Aage); Reginald Owen (Prince Charles); Georges Renavent (French Ambassador); Gustav von Seyffertitz (General); David Torrence (Archbishop); Ferdinand Munier (Innkeeper); Akim Tamiroff (Pedro); Cora Sue Collins (Christina, as a Child); Edward Norris (Count Jacob); Lawrence Grant, Barbara Barondess (Bits); Paul Hurst (Swedish Soldier); Edward Gargan (Fellow Drinker); Wade Boteler (Rabble Rouser); Fred Kohler (Member of the Court); Dick Alexander (Peasant in Crowd); Major Sam Harris (Nobleman).

It was no accident that Greta Garbo starred in *Queen Christina*, a screen biography of Sweden's intriguing Queen Christina (1626–1689), who insisted she would die "not an old maid, but a bachelor." (According to legend, Christina abdicated her throne rather than suffer through a royal marriage). In real life, the ruler was a short, mannish monarch who relished smutty stories and enjoyed the favors of her lady-in-waiting. Thus, there were many reasons why Garbo felt an affinity for her fellow Swede. Therefore, when the actress's good friend, Salka Viertel, sug-

Greta Garbo and John Gilbert in *Queen Christina* **(1933).**

gested Greta star in a screen story about this unique Queen, the legend agreed. Garbo insisted that one-time matinee idol, John Gilbert, her frequent co-star in silent films, be cast as her leading man.

In 1933, the Hollywood movie industry's production code office would certainly not condone a factual depiction of the monarch's unusual lifestyle. However, enough suggestions appear on screen to give a full flavor of this exceedingly mannish ruler (tempered and feminized on camera by Garbo's striking beauty). Within this MGM feature, Garbo's Queen Christina stomps around in man's clothing (leading to a plot conceit in which she shares a bedroom at an inn with the Spanish Ambassador), has a faithful valet (C. Aubrey Smith) rather than a chambermaid, and takes her oaths of allegiance to Sweden as the new *king*.

Queen Christina's sexual orientation is made clear in Garbo's few scenes with her lady-in-waiting, Countess Ebba Sparre (Elizabeth Young). In one, the young Ebba rushes breathlessly into Christina's chambers, anxious to spend time with her majesty. Christina and she embrace and kiss fully on the lips. Ebba bemoans the fact that her dear one is so preoccupied with court work. "You're surrounded by musty old paper and musty old men and I can't get near you." To console the pouting lady-in-waiting, Christina promises that they will go away to the country soon for a few days together. Later, Ebba falls prey to court intrigue and her friendship with Christina suffers. The distraught Ebba confesses to her loved one, "Since I've lost your favor, I've not slept." Thereafter, feeling betrayed by her relationship with Ebba (who later announces her intention to marry a man), Christina begins an affair with Don Antonio (John Gilbert), the Spanish Ambassador, leading to yet another bizarre episode in the film. Don Antonio first mistakes the mannishly dressed Christina for a page boy and then amusedly agrees to share a room with this stranger who attracts him so much. (To appease the censors, as the two undress in the bedroom, the Ambassador insists he had a hunch that his new friend was a she all the time.)

Within *Queen Christina*, the new ruler (Greta Garbo) of seventeenth century Sweden rejects the amorous advances of Magnus (Ian Keith) and inveigles her way out of her court-arranged marriage to Prince Charles (Reginald Owen), the hero of the Swedish army. Later, having shared several days together with Don Antonio (John Gilbert), the Spanish Ambassador, at a snowbound inn, both are distraught to learn the other's true identity at her court. It develops that Don Antonio has come to Sweden to arrange a marriage between she and the King of Spain. Later, the jealous Magnus arouses the people against this Catholic foreigner who has won Christina's heart. To protect Don Antonio, Christina sends him away and then abdicates the throne. When he dies in a duel with Magnus, she embarks on a ship bound for Spain with her lover's casket, never to return.

Bedazzled by her performance, several contemporary critics (intentionally?) missed the point of Garbo's complex characterization. In discussing the premises of this "easy flowing romance," Mordaunt Hall (*New York Times*) noted, "When Christina was born one is informed that her father Gustavus Adolphus regretted that she was not a boy. He persuaded her as a child to wear knickerbockers and it can be assumed that Oxenstierna, Chancellor of Sweden, insisted that she continue dressing as a boy after she was crowned Queen. This penchant for male attire is the result of a beguiling incident. . . ." *Variety* faulted the film for being "slow and ofttimes stilted," citing the episode in which she mistaken for a "flip Nordic

youth," and went on to observe that "The background is an obviously romantic admixture of history and fiction. . . .."

In 1974, Liv Ullmann would star as the seventeenth century Swedish ex-monarch who journeys to Rome to convert to Catholicism in the British-made *The Abdication*.

195. Queens Logic (New Line Cinema, 1991), color, 136 min. R-rated.

Executive producers, Taylor Hackford, Stuart Benjamin; producers, Stuart Oken, Russ Smith; associate producers, Patricia Churchill, Tony Spiridakis; director, Steve Rash; story, Joseph W. Savino; screenplay, Spiridakis; production designer, Edward Pisoni; art director, Okowita; set decorator, Marcie Dale; costumes, Linda Bass; music, Joe Jackson; assistant directors, Joel Tuber, Martha Elean; sound, Thomas Brandau; camera, Amir Mokri; editor, Patrick Kennedy.

Cast: Kevin Bacon (Dennis); Linda Fiorentino (Carla); John Malkovich (Eliot); Joe Mantegna (Al); Ken Olin (Ray); Tony Spiridakis (Vinny); Chloe Webb (Patricia); Tom Waits (Monte); Jamie Lee Curtis (Grace); Michael Zelniker (Marty); Kelly Bishop (Maria); Terry Kinney (Jeremy); Ed Marinaro (Jack).

"I'm just a poor repressed homosexual from the boroughs who needs to get laid." (The character Eliot in *Queens Logic*)

Queens Logic asks the age-old question "Can one go home again?" This question is more complicated here as several of the characters have been emotionally stagnating in their old neighborhood all their lives. One (John Malkovich) of them in this buddy-buddy film is a balding, lonely bachelor, a very masculine homosexual who will not sacrifice his self-integrity to play the usual mating games.

Five friends in their thirties, all former roommates from the 1970s, reunite in Queens, New York. The reason for this meeting is that one of them, Ken (Ray), an idealistic artist, has agreed finally to marry his live-in girlfriend, Patricia (Chloe Webb), a beautician. His cousin, the swaggering macho Al (Joe Mantegna), who operates a fish market, is having

John Malkovich in *Queens Logic* (1991).

domestic problems with his wife Carla (Linda Fiorentino). Al's younger brother, Vinny (Tony Spiridakis), an aspiring actor, wonders if life as a randy bachelor on his own is so great after all. Then, there is dour Eliot (John Malkovich), a homosexual who works at the fish market with Al. Dennis (Kevin Bacon), a struggling trumpeter who hates his meager existence in Hollywood, has flown in for the occasion and soon wishes he had remained in his home turf. During the course of the few days leading up to Ray and Patricia's on-again, off-again nuptials, each character re-examines his life, wondering what happened to the glorious dreams of his/her youth.

Eliot has more than his share of problems. He admits:

"I am a homosexual who cannot relate to gay men . . . their role-playing, their affectations. . . .This makes it impossible for me to break through and talk to the men, not the homosexuals. I refuse to give up anything that makes me a man, to make them feeling safe. . . . I'm not a threat. I know who I am. I am going to be stronger than that. And besides, I haven't met anybody yet."

At Ray's engagement party, the morose Eliot gets to know Marty (Michael Zelniker), a professional piano player who lives in the neighborhood. Finally, having found someone he can relate to intellectually, emotionally and sexually, Eliot impetuously agrees to move into the city with his new-found friend.

Michael Wilmington (*Los Angeles Times*) decided, "*Queens Logic* should be funny, pungent, poignant, but somehow it keeps turning strident and sentimental." For Wilmington, "Eliot is the movie's most curious, and revealing, character; a homosexual who is both celibate and something of a homophobe, he seems to simultaneously subvert and reaffirm all the male-bonding cliches." Tom Jacobs (*Los Angeles Daily News*) pointed out, "The most original character is probably Eliot . . . [who] has a subdued demeanor and a large lament. . . . Here's a man who, in every respect but his sexuality blends in beautifully with the fun-loving, unpretentious community of Queens. The problem is the only other gay men he knows live in Manhattan, and he cannot stand their life-style or snobbish attitude. So he remains alone. . . .Now there's a character we've

never seen before in a film. His presence provides some idea of the uncliched nature of Tony Spiridakis'' screenplay." Dennis Fischer (*Drama-Logue*) decided, "Queens is one of the noisiest and most boisterous neighborhoods in New York, but director Steve Rash does not provide much of a sense of place. . . . .. Malkovich is quite good playing a troubled soul who prefers to stand by his friends. . . ."

Because it was too contrived and derivative, *Queens Logic* earned less than $1 million in distributors' domestic film rentals. One of the picture's highlights is a cameo by Jamie Lee Curtis as a well-to-do woman who finds herself invited to the engagement party.

196. A Question of Love (NBC-TV, November 26, 1978), color, 100 min. Not rated.

Producers, William E. Blinn, Jerry Thorpe; associate producer, Michael A. Hoey; director, Thorpe; teleplay, Blinn; art director, Stephen Berger; set decorator, Warren Welsh; costumes, Bernie Pollack, Denita Del Signore; makeup, Mel Berns Jr.; music, Billy Goldenberg; assistant directors, Tom Foulkes, Lorraine Senna; sound, William Randall; camera, Charles G. Arnold; editor, Byron Chudnow.

Cast: Gena Rowlands (Linda Ray Guettner); Jane Alexander (Barbara Moreland); Ned Beatty (Dwayne Stabler); Clu Gulager (Mike Guettner); Bonnie Bedelia (Joan Saltzman); James Sutorius (Richard Freeman); Keith Mitchell (Billy Guettner); Josh Albee (David Guettner); Jocelyn Brando (Mrs. Hunnicutt); Gwen Arner (Dr. Tippit); John Harkins (Dr. Berwick); Nancy McKeon (Susan Moreland); S. John Launer (The Judge); and: Philip Sterling, Donald Hotton, Michael C. Gwynne, Ned Wilson, Susan Batson, Macon McCalman, Ruth Silveira.

"What me and Barbara got is . . . we just care for each other. It' s just as simple as that. . . . I know a lot of people think that it's wrong. I know a lot of people say that two homosexuals can't really care for each other for a long time. I don't know about anybody else. I just know about Barbara and me and it's not that way with us. I don't think it'll ever be." (Spoken by the

THE STORY OF A MOTHER'S FIGHT TO KEEP HER CHILD
They want to take Linda Rae Guettner's son away from her.
Not because she isn't a wonderful mother.
Not because she's divorced...
Linda Rae is in love with another woman.

GENA ROWLANDS
JANE ALEXANDER
A QUESTION
OF LOVE

ABC SUNDAY NIGHT MOVIE 9:00 PM 7 8
A WORLD TELEVISION PREMIERE
THIS PROGRAM DEALS WITH CHILD CUSTODY RIGHTS OF A GAY PARENT

Advertisement for *A Question of Love* (1978).

character Linda Ray Guettner in *A Question of Love*)

The pathfinding telefeature, *That Certain Summer* (1972), q.v., set the way for later TV dramas dealing with homosexuality, including *A Question of Love*, which focuses on two female lovers struggling to maintain their mutual love and self-respect in an atmosphere of bigotry. What makes this fact-based drama exceptional, above and beyond its strong acting, is its straight-forward presentation of the subjects' lifestyles. This virtue is exemplified in an opening sequence between the recently-divorced mother, Linda (Gena Rowlands), and her teenaged son, David (Josh Albee):

David: Are you a lesbian?

Barbara: I'll answer that question if you're sure you want me too.

David: [Nods yes.]

Barbara: Yes I am. I am a lesbian.

Having divorced her airline mechanic husband, Mike (Clu Gulager), Linda Ray Guettner (Gena Rowlands), a nurse, and her two sons—teenager David (Josh Albee) and the younger Billy (Keith Mitchell)—move into the house owned by her lover, Barbara Moreland (Jane Alexander), a bank employee. One weekend, while staying with his dad, David tells his father about Linda's relationship with Barbara. As a consequence, Mike sues Linda for custody of his sons. Barbara remains supportive through the emotional and expensive ordeal, but Linda's mother, Mrs. Hunnicutt (Jocelyn Brando), is antagonistic when the news of her daughter's lifestyle is made public. Filled with anger, guilt and embarrassment, she demands opf her daughter, "What kind of mother raises a pervert for a daughter?" Loving her mother despite hcr bigotry, Linda can only reply, "Some things just happen."

Meanwhile, the tension of the pending court case affects Linda's relationship with Barbara, with the former blurting out, "I wish to hell I'd never met you. . . . Those boys are everything to me." In the courtroom, the prosecuting attorney (Ned Beatty) does his best to embarrass the defendant, coyly asking, "Do you think this is the age of the homosexual?" Despite the fact that Mike has an irresponsible case history (a drunken driving charge, having once broken Linda's nose, getting the daughter of a co-worker pregnant and then arranging for her abortion), the court finds in his favor of Mike. Now Linda must explain to young Billy why he cannot remain with her over the Christmas holidays but with his brother go, to live at his father's house, the latter having recently remarried. By now, Linda and her mother have patched up their differences, as have Linda and Barbara. Linda resolves to appeal the court's decision.

Daily Variety applauded, "Bill Blinn's screenplay intelligently articulates the delicate theme, and it is smartly directed by Jerry Thorpe. Earl Davis (*Hollywood Reporter*) affirmed, "[Gena] Rowlands' performance of contained, seething emotion is superlative—rich, deep and remarkable. [Jane] Alexander's role is a little too reactionary and passive for her immense gifts, but she supports in sturdy fashion."

Unlike *Lianna* (1983), *Desert Hearts* (1985) and *My Two Loves* (1986), qq.v., *A Question of Love* is not concerned with a woman's discovery and acceptance of her true sexual feelings. The protagonist here has already found herself. Instead, in having to make public her gayness, she must deal with overlapping and often conflicting needs and requirements of being both a woman and a mother, which, in turn, also affects her professional standing as a nurse.

197. **Rachel, Rachel** (Warner Bros.—Seven Arts, 1968), color, 101 min. Not rated.

Producer, Paul Newman; associate producer, Arthur S. Newman Jr., Harrison Starr; director, Newman; based on the novel *A Jest of God* by Margaret Laurence; screenplay, Stewart Stern; art director, Robert Gundlach; set decorator, Richard Merrell; costumes, Domingo Rodriguez; makeup, Bob Philippe; music/music conductor, Jerome Moross; song, Moross and

Stern; assistant directors, Alan Hopkins, Robert Koster; sound, Jack Jacobsen; camera, Gayne Rescher; editor, Dede Allen.

Cast: Joanne Woodward (Rachel Cameron); James Olson (Nick Kazlik); Kate Harrington (Mrs. Cameron); Estelle Parsons (Calla Mackie); Geraldine Fitzgerald (Reverend Wood); Donald Moffat (Niall Cameron); Terry Kiser (Preacher); Frank Corsaro (Hector Jonas); Bernard Barrow (Leighton Siddley); Nell Potts (Rachel, as a Child); Shawn Campbell (James); Violet Dunn (Verla); Izzy Singer (Lee Shabab); Tod Engle (Nick, as a Child); Bruno Engl (Bartender); and: Beatrice Pons, Dorothea Duckworth, Simm Landres, Connie Robinson, Sylvia Shipman, Larry Fredericks, Wendell MacNeal.

Thanks to Joanne Woodward's resilient performance, *Rachel, Rachel*, is a fascinating if somewhat uneven account of a woman coming out of a shell imposed by her long-standing fears of experiencing life. While her now-liberated character goes on to a new future, her equally lonesome spinster teacher pal, Calla Mackie (Estelle Parsons), remains behind. The latter represses her lesbian desires by fanatically "leanin' on the Lord" and burying her painful frustrations in flighty behavior. Weighed down by conservative mores, the tiny town and her religious upbringing, Calla only comes out of the closet briefly—ironically aroused by the fervor of a evangelical revivalist meeting. She is as surprised by her impulsive act as the heroine is upset. This revealing segment of *Rachel, Rachel* showed a small, but significant, advance on how Hollywood treated the standard repressed celluloid spinster, even from those films of a few years earlier (i.e. *The Night of the Iguana*, 1964, *7 Women*, 1966, qq.v).

In a small New England town, plain 35-year-old Rachel Cameron (Joanne Woodward), who has never really grown up emotionally, is convinced her life is getting worse. The spinster teacher lives with her whining mother (Kate Harrington) over the funeral parlor that her father once owned. When she is not tending her mother's excessive demands, she cares for an endless procession of school children.

Another unmarried teacher, Calla Mackie (Estelle Parsons), a born-again Christian, invites her to attend a revival meeting. Urged to release her pent-up emotions by a visiting preacher (Terry Kiser), Rachel is upset to discover her long-repressed feelings of hostility and her need for companionship. When Calla tries to calm her, and in the process makes brief sexual overtures to her with kisses, Rachel is shocked and repulsed. Later, wanting somehow to change her life, Rachel encourages attentions from Nick Kazlik (James Olson), a former high school friend who is visiting town briefly. When she takes the situation too seriously, he bows out. Afterwards, Rachel thinks she is pregnant and decides to leave town and have her child. Calla helps her find a teaching position in Oregon. Even after discovering she is not pregnant (it was a cyst easily removed by minor surgery), Rachel, with her unwilling mother in tow, embarks on her new life, wondering what the future holds for her.

Renata Adler (*New York Times*) decided this movie was "a little sappy at moments, but the best written, most seriously acted American movie in a long time. . . . Miss Woodward . . . [is] extraordinary good. . . . Among many carefully thought-out scenes, including one brief, quasi Lesbian encounter between Miss Woodward and Miss Parsons that is a little to heavy for what the film prepares one to accept, there is a scene in which Miss Parsons delivers a note of apology to her friend by night. The scene is deft, soppy and funny. So is most of the film." *Variety* was less impressed; "Offbeat film moves too slowly to an upbeat, ironic climax, via modern cinematic styles which induce lethargy. . . . Miss Parsons' character makes a Lesbian pass at Miss Woodward, a pitiable and somewhat touching plot point which, once introduced, is handled crudely in later resolution. Jan Dawson (British *Monthly Film Bulletin*) found much merit in Paul Newman's directorial debut: "Not only is small town life painstakingly observed . . . but the town itself is shown caught in the same stage of transition as Rachel herself, pulled between two generations." Of the supporting performances, Dawson approved of Parsons's as "the woman whose life reflects a more extroverted image of Rachel's own."

Rachel, Rachel grossed $6.1 million in distributors' domestic film rentals. It was nominated for four Academy Awards: Best Picture (*Oliver!* won); Best Actress (Joanne Woodward; both Barbra Streisand for *Funny Girl* and Katharine Hepburn for *The Lion in Winter* won); Best Supporting Actress (Estelle Parsons; Ruth Gordon won for *Rosemary's Baby*); Best Screenplay—Based on Material from Another Medium (*The Lion in Winter* won);

The low-budget *Rachel Rachel* was filmed on location in Bethel, Danbury and Georgetown, Connecticut. Nell Potts, Joanne Woodward's daughter by Paul Newman, appears as the young Rachel.

198. A Rage in Harlem (Miramax,

1991), color, 108 min. R-rated.

Executive producers, Nick Powell, William Horberg, Terry Glinwood, Harvey Weinstein, Bob Weinstein; producers, Stephen Woolley, Kerry Boyle; co-producers, Forest Whitaker, John Nicolella; line producer, Thomas A. Razzano; director, Bill Duke; based on the novel by Chester Himes; screenplay, John Toles-Bey, Bobby Crawford; production designer, Steve Legler; art director, Nina Ruscio; set decorator, K. C. Fox; costumes, Nile Samples; makeup, Matiki Anoff; music, Elmer Bernstein; songs, Bernstein, Jonathan Paley, Jeff Vincent, Jimmy Scott and Andy Paley; Andy Paley and Richard Penniman; assistant directors, Warren D. Gray, Brian Whitley; second unit director/stunt coordinator, Julius le Flore; sound, Paul Cote; camera, Toyomichi Kurita; second unit camera, Phillip Alan Waters; editor, Curtiss Clayton.

Cast: Forest Whitaker (Jackson); Gregory Hines (Goldy); Robin Givens (Imabelle); Zakes Mokae (Big Kathy); Danny Glover (Easy Money); Badja Djola (Slim); John Toles-Bey (Jodie); Ron Taylor (Teena); Samm-Art Williams (Hank); Stack Pierce (Coffin Ed Johnson); George Wallace (Grave Digger Jones); Willard E. Pugh (Claude X); Helen Martin (Mrs. Canfield); Wendell Pierce (Louis); T. K. Carter (Smitty); Leonard Jackson (Mr. Clay); Reynaldo Rey (Blind Man); Clebert Ford (Porter); John Seitz (Lester Bunton); Jack Beatty (Sheriff); Birdie M. Hale, Olivette Miller-Briggs (Domestics); Beatrice Wind (Clerk); John W. Hardy (Reverend Gaines); Antonia Dotson (Female Mourner); Ernest Perry Jr. (Junkie); James Spinks (Bartender); Cornelus Staford (Weasel); Tracy A. Saylor (Skanky Whore); Jesse James Turnblow (Will Kill); James Copeland (Jailer); Jonathan Booker (Doorman); Kevin Rutven (Bus Driver); William L. Schwarber (Goon); Tasha O'Bryant (Minna); Arthur Burghardt (Bo); Eugene Robinson Jr. (Pug); Kipp Cochran (Cop); Robert Woods Jr. (Henchman); Screamin' Jay Hawkins (Himself).

In *Cotton Comes to Harlem* (1970) and *Come Back, Charleston Blue* (1972), Raymond St. Jacques and Godfrey Cambridge had cavorted as the irrepressible Coffin Ed Johnson and Grave Digger Jones, two flavorful Harlem policemen. Those raucous if crude pictures had been made at the height of Hollywood's black action movie cycle and both of them, especially the first, had been artistic and commercial successes. Two decades later, it was decided to repeat the period mixture as before, but the magic was missing from this adaptation of a Chester Himes detective novel. Moreover, magnetic Coffin Ed and Grave Digger were reduced to subordinate characters in the tame, sanitized proceedings, which included the bulky, drag queen bordello manager, Big Kathy.

Daily Variety explained the picture's inherent problems: "Director Bill Duke has brought a stylish sheen to *A Rage in Harlem*, but his mixing of comedy and violence . . . is uncertain. Many viewers will be turned off by the excessive bloodshed, but the fine cast keeps it watchable. . . . [The] humor too often turns ugly. . . ."

In 1956, Mississippi, Slim (Badja Djola) leads a black gang which has stolen a cache of gold ore. During the excitement of a police raid, Slim's mistress, double-crossing Imabelle (Robin Givens) escapes with the ore and heads for Harlem in New

York City where she knows of a fence, Easy Money (Danny Glover) who can convert her hot merchandise into cash. In Harlem, she takes advantage of naive, ultra-religious undertaker's assistant, Jackson (Forest Whitaker). Later, Slim arrives and convinces Imabelle to help him rob Jackson of his life's savings. The latter, getting into deep trouble and debt to match wits with his opponents, persuades his crooked stepbrother, Goldy (Gregory Hines), to help him get out of his troubles. In the see-sawing battle for control of the ore, Goldy's transvestite pal, Big Kathy (Zakes Mokae), a brothel madam, is murdered. By the time the sexy Imabelle leaves town, she has saved Jackson's life, Goldy has a percentage of the coveted ore, and Jackson has jumped on the train to join his gold-digging sweetheart who is returning to Mississippi.

Eric Mankin (*LA Reader*) assessed of this blend of romance and comedy, "A surprisingly assured and sexually comic performance from Robin Givens and a strong supporting cast . . . are ample compensation for the shortcomings in this somewhat pallid adaptation." John Powers (*LA Weekly*) admitted that director Duke "lacks the panache that could charge this murderous farce with the rage the title promises. What Duke does best is handle actors. . . .and this picture's worth seeing simply for its vibrant character work: Zakes Mokae's beatific transvestite, Big Kathy; John Toes-Bey's saucy, knife-happy Jodie; and especially Badja Djola's menacing Slim. . . ."

A Rage in Harlem, with location work in Cincinnati to duplicate 1950s Harlem, grossed a modest $4.2 million in distributors' domestic film rentals. A highlight of the movie is Screamin' Jay Hawkins seen performing at the Undertakers' Ball.

199. Rebel Without a Cause

(Warner Bros., 1955), color, 111 min. Not rated.

Producer, David Weisbart; director, Nicholas Ray; inspired by the story, "The Blind Run" by Dr. Robert M. Lindner; screen story idea, Ray; adaptor, Irving Shulman; screenplay, Stewart Stern; production designer, William Wallace; art director, Malcolm Bert; set decorator, William Wallace; costumes, Moss Mabry; makeup, Gordon Bau; music, Leonard Rosenman; assistant directors, Don Page, Robert Farfan; sound, Stanley Jones; camera, Ernest Haller; editor, William Ziegler.

Cast: James Dean (Jim Stark); Natalie Wood (Judy); Sal Mineo (Plato [John Crawford]); Jim Backus (Frank Stark); Ann Doran (Mrs. Stark); Corey Allen (Buzz); William Hopper (Judy's Father); Rochelle Hudson (Judy's Mother); Virginia Brissac (Jim's Grandma); Nick Adams (Moose); Jack Simmons (Cookie); Dennis Hopper (Goon); Marietta Canty (Plato's Maid); Jack Grinnage (Chick); Beverly Long (Helen); Steffi Sidney (Mil); Frank Mazzola (Crunch); Tom Bernard (Harry); Clifford Morris (Cliff); Ian Wolfe (Planetarium Lecturer); Edward Platt (Ray); Robert Foulk (Gene); Jimmy Baird (Beau); Dick Wessel (Guide); Nelson Leigh (Sergeant); Dorothy Abbott (Nurse); Louise Lane (Woman Officer); House Peters (Officer); Gus Schilling (Attendant); Bruce Noonan (Monitor); Almira Sessions (Old Lady Teacher); Peter Miller (Hoodlum); Paul Bryar (Desk Sergeant); Paul Birch (Police Chief); Robert B. Williams (Ed, Moose's Father); David McMahon's (Crunch's Father).

Rebel Without a Cause was the watershed movie which made James Dean, in his second starring screen role, an icon of the teenage set. (Sadly, however, by the time *Rebel* was released, Dean had died in a car accident.) This film, as well as the same year's *Blackboard Jungle*, showed Hollywood focusing more squarely on the problems of growing up in mid-1950s America when so many values and traditions had been shattered. That teens from decent homes, such as the trio featured in this picture, could get into so much trouble and cause themselves and others so much pain astounded adults. Conversely, the movie seemed authentic to younger viewers who were dealing with their own problems of alienation. Orbiting in the shadow of the story's young lovers (James Dean, Natalie Wood) was moody, ultra-sensitive Plato, a baby-faced, precocious outsider who tapes a picture of Alan Ladd inside his locker door. It is he who attaches himself to the handsome Rebel (Dean), as much out of suppressed sexual longing as for their shared anti-establishment outlook on life. (In one scene, Plato wanting to be close to his new pal asks, "Hey want to come home with me? . . . We could talk and in the morning we could have breakfast. . . .") In typical Hollywood fashion, it is Plato the misfit who dies.

Three teenagers, each having problems with their neglectful parents at home, become friends when they are arrested by the police for different reasons. Jim Stark (James Dean), a newcomer to town, had been found drunk and disorderly; Judy (Natalie Wood) had been picked up for wandering the streets after 1 A.M.; sixteen-year-old Plato (Sal Mineo), whose parents have separated and who is being raised by a black maid (Marietta Canty), has been detained for having shot several puppies. As a result of their time together at the police station, Jim and Plato, the ostracized different one, become high school pals, while Jim pursues Judy, the girlfriend of the head of the school gang, Buzz (Corey Allen). In order to settle their feud over Judy, Jim and Buzz embark on a dangerous "chicken run" car race near a high cliff. The race ends in Buzz's accidental death.

Later, Jim and Judy disappear into a deserted mansion to make love. When Plato learn that Buzz's gang intends to get revenge on Jim, he rushes to warn his friends, but the punks follow him there. Plato uses his father's gun and kills one of the attackers. The gun shots bring the police. Jim attempts to calm down the distraught Plato who starts to surrender. However, one of the nervous cops misunderstands Plato's sudden move and shoots him dead. As the crowd disperses, Jim and Judy leave the scene with their parents, the latter now, hopefully, more understanding of their "rebellious" offsprings.

Bosley Crowther (*New York Times*) agreed that *Rebel Without a Cause* "is a

picture to make the hair stand on end. . . . But convincing or not in motivations, this tale of tempestuous kids and their weird way of conducting their social relations is tense with explosive incidents. . . . There is . . . a pictorial slickness about the whole thing in color and CinemaScope that battles at times with the realism in the direction of Nicholas Ray." *Variety* rated the film "exciting, suspenseful and provocative, if also occasionally far-fetched." In approving of the performances, the trade paper described that Sal Mineo "stands out on performance and is an important value in the film." The conservative *Harrison's Reports* rated the picture "An unpleasant but visually gripping juvenile delinquency melodrama . . . frequently brutal and shocking. . . . [It] does not present the problem [of juvenile delinquency] with powerful drama impact, nor does it effectively suggest how the problem might be combatted."

Studying *Rebel Without a Cause* in retrospect, Vito Russo (*The Celluloid Closet*, 1987) found comparisons between Sal Mineo's Plato and Tom Robinson Lee of *Tea and Sympathy* (1956), q.v.: "Plato is the mama's boy, brought up by a smothering maid in the absence of his father. In his adoration of James Dean, he seeks a father more than a lover. But because Dean returns his feelings so blatantly, sparks fly." As to the camaraderie of the film's teen gang, Russo notes "*Rebel Without a Cause* pleads a redefinition of manhood in the same way that *Tea and Sympathy* one year later would plead tolerance for 'shy but normal' young men whose behavior sets them apart from the pact."

Rebel without a Cause grossed a sizeable $4.6 million in distributors' domestic film rentals. It received two Academy Award nominations: Best Supporting Actor (Sal Mineo; Jack Lemmon won for *Mister Roberts*); Best Supporting Actress (Natalie Wood; Jo Van Fleet won for *East of Eden*).

200. Reflections in a Golden Eye

(Warner Bros., 1967), color, 109 min. Not rated.

Producer, Ray Stark; associate producer, C. O. Erickson; director, John Huston; based on the novel by Carson McCullers; screenplay, Chapman Mortimer; production designer, Stephen Grimes; art director, Bruno Avesani; set decorators, William Kiernan, Joe Chevalier; costumes, Dorothy Jeakins; makeup, Frank Larue, Phil Rhodes, Amato Garbini; music, Toshiro Mayuzumi; assistant director, Vana Caruso; sound, Basil Fenton-Smith, John Cox; special effects, Augie Lohman; camera, Aldo Tonti, (uncredited) Oswald Morris; editor, Russell Lloyd.

Cast: Elizabeth Taylor (Leonora Penderton); Marlon Brando (Major Weldon Penderton); Brian Keith (Lieutenant Colonel Morris Langdon); Julie Harris (Alison Langdon); Zorro David (Anacleto); Gordon Mitchell (Stables Sergeant); Irvin Dugan (Captain Weincheck); Fay Sparks (Susie); Robert Forster (Private Williams); Douglas Star (Dr. Burgess); Al Mulock (Old Soldier); Ted Beniades (Sergeant); John Callaghan (Soldier).

"Hell hath no homicidal fury like a homosexual scorned. . . . The shame of it is that this conclusion is so anticlimactic and banal, because there is so much in the picture that seems to be leading to—certainly prepares us to expect—much more." (Bosley Crowther, *New York Times*)

Carson McCullers's 1941 novel received a most eccentric, disturbing and odd screen adaptation. It foreshadowed by a year *The Sergeant* (1968), q.v., which also dealt with a military man suppressing his homosexuality in the confines of service life, which leads to tragedy. In *Reflections*, Marlon Brando's married officer, on the surface going through the paces of his orderly military/domestic life, can barely represses his longing for the handsome private he stalks so relentlessly. In his inability to deal with his gay feelings, his greatest fear is to become a freak, like the extremely effeminate, strange houseboy, Anacleto, At the end, the Major's latent homosexuality explodes, leading him to homicide. It was strong, baffling drama for 1960s Hollywood.

In 1948 Georgia, Major Weldon Penderton (Marlon Brando) and his willful wife, Leonora (Elizabeth Taylor), live on an Army post. While the finicky Major is a martinet with his men, at home he is treated badly by his contemptuous wife. Dissatisfied with their sexual life, she has a rather open affair with Lieutenant Colonel Morris Langdon (Brian Keith). Langdon's wife, Alison (Julie Harris) is a house-bound psychotic who has lost touch with reality after the death of their deformed baby (leading her to mutilate her breasts). Barely aware of her husband, her constant companion is her sissy houseboy, Anacleto (Zorro David). Meanwhile, Leonora, an expert horsewoman, allows the handsome, young, but withdrawn Private Williams (Robert Forster) to tend the Pendertons's stables and care for her favorite stallion, Firebird. The frustrated Williams frequently sneaks into the Penderton home at night to study the sleeping Leonora and to play with her lingerie.

One day, the prissy Weldon observes Williams riding naked in the forest, unleashing the Major's lust for the man. Meanwhile, Alison suffers another nervous breakdown—brought on by observing Williams's fetish ritual at the Pendertons—and her husband puts her in a private sanitarium. There she dies conveniently of a heart attack and the fey Anacleto disappears. One evening, Williams, who has been teasing the obsessed Weldon for some time, returns to the Pendertons. On this rainy night, the major spies him and believes he has come to be with him. When Weldon observes the private entering Leonora's room, he takes his service revolver and kills him.

Judith Crist (NBC-TV's "Today Show") announced: "*Reflections in a Golden Eye* has one possible virtue: it will send you right back to Carson McCuller's book (hopefully to read it), because one can't imagine that her perceptive novel had nothing more to offer than nutty people and pseudo pornography." *Variety* critiqued, "Instead of building to what could

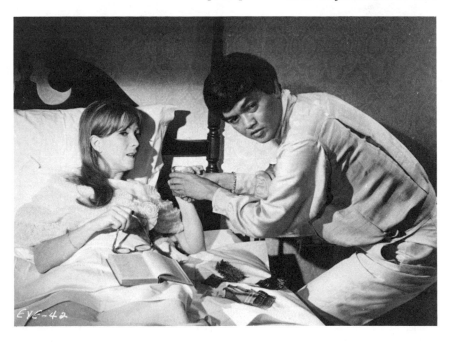

Julie Harris and Zorro David in *Reflections in a Golden Eye* (1967).

have been a literate exposition of latent homosexuality, film is more accurately a succession of scenes thrown to individual players . . . The most outstanding and satisfying performance is that of Brian Keith. . . . Forster, making his film debut . . . cannot be evaluated fairly, for his part is practically silent. Huston's direction of players is erratic, although his visual sense is intact."

Originally, Montgomery Clift was to have played opposite Elizabeth Taylor as her husband, the major. However, he died two months before production began. When Richard Burton and then Lee Marvin refused the assignment of the repressed homosexual, Marlon Brando accepted the role. To appease Taylor, the movie was shot on sound stages in Rome, with location work at Mitchell Air Field in Long Island. As an artistic gimmick, when the movie was released originally, prints were treated specially to give the color a washed-out, sepia-toned look. For later distribution, the movie used full Technicolor. The Catholic Church gave the movie a C (condemned) rating.

201. **Reform School Girl** (American International, 1957), 71 min. Not rated.

Executive producer, James H. Nicholson; producers, Robert J. Gurney Jr., Samuel Z. Arkoff; director/screenplay, Edward Bernds; art director, Don Ament; music, Ronald Stein; camera, Floyd Crosby; editor, Richard C. Meyer.

Cast: Gloria Castillo (Donna Price); Ross Ford (David Lindsay); Edward Byrnes (Vince); Ralph Reed (Jackie); Jan Englund (Ruth); Yvette Vickers (Roxy); Helen Wallace (Mrs. Trimble); Donna Jo Gribble (Cathy); Luana Anders (Josie); Diana Darrin (Mona); Nesdon Booth (Deetz); Wayne Taylor (Gary); Sharon Lee (Blonde); Jack Kruschen (Mr. Horvath); Linda Rivera (Elena); Elaine Sinclair (Midge): Dorothy Crehan (Matron); Claire Carleton (Mrs. Horvath); Lillian Powell (Mrs. Patton); Sally Kellerman (Reform School Girl).

". . . .my first film was also my worst. It was called *Reform School Girl. . . .* My ex-boyfriend, Edd 'Kookie' Byrnes, was one of the stars. I played the school dyke and carried a tool case. When I came on the screen, everybody in the theater laughed. I didn't work for three years after that." (Sally Kellerman, actress)

Seventeen-year-old Donna Price (Gloria Castillo) finds herself on a joy ride with reckless Vince (Edward Byrnes) and, before long, a pedestrian is killed. He forces Donna to take the blame and she is dispatched to a young women's correctional facility where the impressionable teenager is nearly overwhelmed by her situation. Meanwhile, paranoid Vince has his real girlfriend, Josie (Luana Anders), sent to the same institution to make sure that Donna does not squeal. The tough Josie quickly incites several of the tougher young inmates to help terrorize Donna. Their harassment leads to a rumble where Donna stabs another inmate in self-defense. Before she can be sent to the State Prison for Women, the truth about the fight is discovered and she is released.

Variety labeled this a "Cheapie for the adolescent trade. . . . For the prurient-minded, there's much leg display, and for the immature audiences, there's a plaintive adolescent philosophy about non-squealing.

Hackneyed in its plot with only minimum character development, the film hid, from all but the most discerning viewer, that the tough prison babes depicted shared more than room space in *Reform School Girl*. However, no one, including the censors, seemed to mind that such cliched, representational types were portrayed.

202. Reform School Girls (New World Pictures, 1986), color, 94 min. R-rated.

Executive producers, Gregory Hinton, Leo Angelos; producer, Jack Cummins; director/screenplay, Tom DeSimone; production designer, Becky Block; set decorator, Tom Talbert; music, Martin Schwartz; sound, Steve Nelson; camera, Howard Wexler; editor, Michael Spence.

Cast: Linda Carol (Jenny); Wendy O. Williams (Charlie); Pat Ast (Head Matron Edna); Sybil Danning (Warden Sutter); Charlotte McGinnis (Dr. Norton); Sherri Stoner (Lisa); Denise Gordy (Claudia); Laurie Schwartz (Nicky); Tiffany Helm (Fish); Darcy DeMoss (Knox).

Tom DeSimone had directed earlier several women-behind-bars entries, including *Prison Girls* (1973), q.v., and the popular European-made *The Concrete Jungle* (1982), q.v. Wendy O. Williams, the shapely lead singer of the punk rock group The Plasmatics, was cast in the satirical *Reform School Girls* as the butchest of the teenage inmates.

Jenny (Linda Carol), innocent about life, finds herself behind bars at the Pridemore Reform School. There, the virginal miss must cope with the dishonest, obsessively religious Warden Sutter (Sybil Danning), who brandishes a rifle, and the tough, sadistic head guard, Edna (Pat Ast), who claims "The name of the game is power, girls." In addition, Jenny must endure dormitory life with such aggressive types as the leather-clad, rugged Charlie (Wendy O. Williams). The latter is the cell block bully who insists "I'm all the stud you need!" Jenny's only friend inside the institution is traumatized Lisa (Sherri Stoner), a casualty of the brutal penal system.

Definitely not made to please reviewers but to tease viewers as an exploitation of exploitation movies, the R-rated *Reform School Girls* won no plaudits for its intentionally cliched trip through prison hell. Patrick Goldstein (*Los Angeles Times*) found, "*Girls* is far too feeble to qualify as a raunchy prison parody. . . . [The] predominantly female cast seems to have been chosen more for their profiles than their personalities. . . . [It] is so witless that its funniest line comes from the ad campaign, 'So young . . . so bad . . . so what?' So what, indeed." Leo Seligsohn (*Newsday*) argued, "In the old days, it was simply called trash. These days, it's called a spoof. . . . Under the guise of mocking yesteryear's junk genre, the film is a mega-garbage scam that mocks its audience. . . . Trading on bad acting, shrieking, flesh and sadism . . . it's spoof-proof."

In contrast, *Variety* was amused and teasingly noted, *"Reform School Girls* don't have it so bad. For one thing, they don't have to wear uniforms—or much else for that matter. they talk dirty, play dirty and are allowed to take long, long showers. They can even earn special privileges from the head matron for consenting to various requests."

203. Riot (Paramount, 1969), color, 97 min. R-rated.

Producer, William Castle; associate producer, Dona Holloway; director, Buzz Kulik; based on the novel *The Riot* by Frank Elli; screenplay, James Poe; production designer/art director, Paul Sylbert; makeup, Charles Blackman; music, Christopher Komeda; songs, Komeda and Robert Wells; Johnnie Lee Willis, Deacon Anderson and Blackman; assistant director, Danny McCauley; sound, John Wilkinson, Clem Portman; camera, Robert Hauser; editor, Edwin H. Bryant.

Cast: Jim Brown (Cully Briston); Gene Hackman (Red Fletcher); Ben Caruthers (Joe Surefoot); Mike Kellin (Bugsy); Gerald S. O'Loughlin (Grossman); Clifford David ("Big Mary" Sheldon); Bill Walker (Jake); Ricky Summers ("Gertie"); Michael Byron (Murray); Jerry Thompson (Deputy Warden Fisk); M. Gerri, John Neiderhauser (Homosexuals); Frank A. Eyman (The Warden); and: Lee Joe Barta, Jack Baxter, Barry Bruce, Earl Donald Christenson, Bobby Favors, Danny Flores, Ralph Gipson, Herman Gorablenkow, Frances D. Gray, Earl Henderson, Charles E. Hart, Thomas B. Ingles, Kenneth Kelly, Baqui Montes, Dwight Palmer, Jess Pina, Levi Robertson, Jack Story, Clair Sullivan, John Targett, Louis Taylor, Thomas Weldon, Trent Wood, Don Ramone-Wooton, Duane Edward Young.

Hollywood had a long history of depicting and exploiting the injustices of the penal system and its brutal inhumanity toward convicts. Such films as *The Big House* (1930), *The Last Mile* (1932), *I Am a Fugitive from a Chain Gang* (1932), *Brute Force* (1947) and *Riot in Cell Block 11* (1954) remain landmarks. *Riot* went several steps further. Not only did it exploit murderous racial discrimination behind bars, but it was also one of the first American prison movies to openly delineate homosexuality behind bars. Subtlety had no place in *Riot* and the depiction of gay activities in the facility was geared to shock, titillate and amuse.

Black convict Cully Briston (Jim Brown) is sent to the isolation tank, where he is pulled into a riot engineered by hot-headed Red Fletcher (Gene Hackman). Once they grab several guards as hostage, the instigators soon control a good part of the 1,200-convict penitentiary. The calculating Fletcher pretends that the uprising is based on a checklist of grievances. However, he is merely stalling for time so he can break out through a tunnel shaft that extends beyond the concrete walls. Meanwhile, the unsuspecting Deputy Warden Fisk (Jerry Thompson), also stalling for time, negotiates with Fletcher and his crew. During a party given by the rioters, in which one cell block area is turned over to sexual activities with the gay men in drag, several stool pigeon convicts are sentenced to death by a kangaroo court. By now, the Warden (Frank A. Eyman) has returned from his vacation and sets about regaining order. At the same time, Red and eleven others, including Briston, have reached the tunnel. However, when they work their way outside, they are greeted by machine-gun fire and gas grenade explosions. Briston, Fletcher and the crazed Joe Surefoot (Ben Carruthers) have gas masks, and they reach the base of a guard tower. After Surefoot murders a guard, he attempts to knife Briston. However, Fletcher stops him, and Fletcher and Surefoot struggle to the death. Briston alone escapes.

Vincent Canby (*New York Times*) who found the film small-focused but well-paced, observed, "[Director Buzz] Kulik employs just about every obligatory scene in the old con vs. keeper confrontation, including a few variations. At the height of the riot, there is a gaudily photographed bacchanal on what is known as 'queen's row." *Variety* summarized, "Exploitation scripting, okay direction." The trade paper took note of "Salty dialog, an overdone homosexual incident, and vivid knife-slashing battles." Acknowledging Jim Brown's "immensely strong screen presence" and deciding that Gene Hackman "gives the best performance," *Variety* reported that several of the supporting cast were "excellent" including "Clifford David (as a masculine-looking homosexual medical attendant)."

Riot was filmed on location at Arizona State Penitentiary with prison warden Frank A. Eyman and hundreds of inmates/personnel joining in the moviemaking. The picture was adapted from the 1967 book by ex-convict Frank Elli, based on a real life incident at a Minnesota prison.

204. The Ritz (Warner Bros., 1976), color, 90 min. R-rated.

Producer, Denis O'Dell; director, Richard Lester; based on the play by Terrence McNally; production designer, Phillip Harrison; costumes, Vangie Harrison; makeup, Paul Rabiger; music/music director/arranger; Ken Thorne; assistant director, Dusty Symonds; sound, Roy Charman, Gerry Humphreys; special effects, Colin Chilvers; camera, Paul Wilson; editor, John Bloom.

Cast: Jack Weston (Gaetano Proclo); Rita Moreno (Googie Gomez); Jerry Stiller (Carmine Vespucci); Kaye Ballard (Vivian Proclo); F. Murray Abraham (Chris); Paul B. Price (Claude Perkins); Treat Williams (Michael Brick); John Everson (Tiger); Christopher J. Brown (Duff); Dave King (Abe Lefkowitz); Bessie Love (Maurine); Tony DeSantis (Sheldon Farenthold); Ben Aris (Patron with Bicycle); Peter Butterworth (Patron in Chaps); Ronnie Brody (Small Patron); Hal Gallili (Patron with Cigar); John Ratzenberger, Chris Harris (Patrons); George Coulouris (Old Man Vespucci); Leon Greene (Musclebound Patron); Freddie Earle (Disgruntled Patron); Hugh Fraser (Disc Jockey); Bart Allison (Old Priest); Samantha Weysom (Gilda Proclo); Richard Holmes (Pianist).

"Depending on where one's taste lies *The Ritz* is either esoteric farce for the urban cosmopolite, or else one long tasteless and anachronistic Fiftyish 'gay' joke." (*Variety*)

Even in pre–AIDS 1976, it was a daring notion to make a *major* motion picture comedy set in a gay bath house. *The Ritz* was based on a Broadway farce (1975) which had run for nearly a year, with Rita Moreno winning a Tony Award for Best Supporting Actress in a play. Moreno, along with the original cast's Jack Weston, Jerry Stiller, F. Murray Abraham, Paul B. Price et al, filmed the screen version in England. What had seemed frantic and funny on stage, lost a great deal in the movie translation. Nevertheless, the film had its moments, especially in Moreno's campy song number and when three of the bath house patrons perform an Andrews Sisters routine.

A dying old man, Vespucci (George Coulouris,) demands that his son, Carmine (Jerry Stiller), kill his detested son-in-law, Gaetano Proclo (Jack Weston), who runs a street-cleaning business in Cleveland. Pudgy Gaetano, in New York with his wife, Vivian (Kaye Ballard), to pay respects to Papa Vespucci, hides out at a Manhattan gay bath house. There, Claude Perkins (Paul B. Price), an old Army buddy who is a chubby chaser, spots Gaetano and propositions him continuously. Meanwhile, two of the club's attendants (John Everson, Christopher J. Brown), hoping to pacify volatile Puerto Rican entertainer Googie Gomez (Rita Moreno), who is scheduled to perform poolside at the facility, convince her that Proclo is actually a Broadway producer come to catch her showcase. Meanwhile. Carmine has hired a private detective, Michael Brick (Treat Williams), to keep an eye on Proclo. When Carmine shows up at the baths, he thinks Chris (F. Murray Abraham), a patron anxious for a man at any cost, is Brick. In the meantime, Brick, who has never seen his employer, mistakes Proclo for Carmine. Before long,

Vivian appears, searching for Gaetano. She is present when the gun-wielding Carmine traps her husband by the pool. At that moment, she learns from the firm's bookkeeper (Bessie Love) that the Vespucci family owns the bath house. Upon threatening Carmine to give this information to a rival Mafia faction, she successfully gets Carmine to drop the contract on her husband. The Proclos leave the bath house, while Carmine, who earlier in the mayhem ends up dressed as a woman, is carted off the premises by policemen.

Richard Eder (*New York Times*) observed, "if the farce suffers mainly from wearing lead shoes, the homosexual gimmick suffers from something more serious." According to Eder, "To have a tolerance, or even an acceptance of homosexuality doesn't rule out having an underlying physical distaste for it. Inevitably perhaps, the camera . . . shoves up too close—for most of us, I think—too much pale flesh organized around unshared intentions." On the plus side, Eder applauded "the jokes" and "the lineup of weird characters" but decided "The acting is often more energetic than funny. . . ." For John Pym (British *Monthly Film Bulletin*), the movie version "seems a badly stage-managed farce," "the multiple sets fail to create any sense of the bath-house as a single madcap unit and [director Richard] Lester has in several instances sacrificed fast takes for slow-burning reactions and overblown effects. . . ."

Without a doubt, Rita Moreno stole the show as the third-rate entertainer with the fractured English ("my career ees no yook"). She does a terrific (and deliberately terrible) medley of "Everything's Coming Up Roses" and "Begin the Beguine." This segment even surpasses the hilarious secene of three of the patrons (Weston, Abraham, Price) in drag camping to the Andrews Sisters's "Three Gay Caballeros." After a spell, Treat Williams's heterosexual detective—with a high-pitched voice and a low intelligence —wears thin, as does Kaye Ballard's

burlesque of a highly-emotional Italian woman.

With its specialized theme, *The Ritz* did not prove to be big box-office at all.

205. Rock Hudson (ABC-TV, January 8, 1990), color, 100 min. Not rated.

Executive producers, Frank Konigsberg, Larry Santisky; producers, Renee Palyo, Diana Kerew; supervising producers, Ilene Amy Berg, Dennis Turner; associate producer, Jayne Bieber; director, John Icholla; based on the book *My Husband, Rock Hudson* by Phyllis Gates; teleplay, Dennis Turner; production designer, Richard Sherman; set decorator, Michael Warga; costumes, Jodi Tillen; makeup, Allan Apone; music, Paul Chihara; assistant directors, Herb Gains, Chiatra Mojtabai; sound, Walt Martin; camera, Tom Sigel; editor, Peter Parasheles.

Cast: Thomas Ian Griffith (Rock Hudson); Andrew Robinson (Henry Willson); Diane Ladd (Kay Fitzgerald); Daphne Ashbrook (Phyllis Gates); William R. Moses (Marc Christian); Thom Matthews (Tim Murphy); Michael Ensign (Mark Miller); Jocelyn O'Brien (Sally); Don Galloway (John Frankenheimer); Matthieu Carriere (French Doctor); Diana Behrens (Doris Day); Larry Dobkin (Raoul Walsh); Jean Kasem (Madge); George Christy (Reporter); John Shepard (Captain in *Fighter Squadron* scene); Francis Guinan (Carl); Rhoda Gemighani (TV Producer); Julie Tesh (May); Mary Ellen Trainor (Talent Agent); Joie Magidow (Sophie); Arlene Banas (Host); Tom Fuccello (American Doctor); Wu Ping (Hospital Doctor); Katsy Chappel (Nurse); Annick Romain (French Woman); Tom Alexander (Sean); Peter Radon (Master of Ceremonies); David Sage (Harold Rhoden); Tom McGreevey (Judge); Peter Neptune, Dana James, Tom Miller, Mary Hales (Reporters).

A major problem with programming "daring" topics on prime-time network TV is the potential of alienating cautious advertisers. They fear sponsoring unorthodox storylines because their action might incite conservative consumers to boycott their products. As such, ABC-TV lost a good deal of revenue when it aired *Rock Hudson*, because the TV movie featured the still-taboo subject of homosexuality in depicting the late legend's life.

The legend belonged
to everyone.
The secret was
his alone.

ROCK HUDSON

ABC MONDAY NIGHT MOVIE 9 PM abc 7 8

Advertisement for *Rock Hudson* (1990).

Ironically, the presentation of Hudson's gay lifestyle was so timidly and tepidly handled that the only indecent aspects of this production were the teleplay, direction and acting.

As became generally known only after he contracted full-blown AIDS in his last two years, handsome screen star Rock Hudson (1925–1985), had led a dual existence for decades. On screen, he played the movie stud; away from the camera, he was a practicing homosexual who had several long-term relationships. His last was with Marc Christian, who after Hudson's death, filed a hefty lawsuit against the estate and several other individuals. Christian accused Hudson of acting irresponsibly in failing to disclose his fatal, transmittable illness to him, his lover. After a later court ruling in favor of Christian and seeveral filed appeals, the parties settled the case privately out of court in 1991.

Because the telefilm was based on the book by Hudson's only wife, Phyllis Gates, and several of the people depicted were still alive, the telefeature was overly subjective and very circumspect in its delineation. It also carried the caveat "composite characters and resequencing of events have been used for dramatic purposes."

The narrative opens in 1988, three years after the death of Rock Hudson (Thomas Ian Griffith), with Marc Christian (William R. Moses) in a Los Angeles court testifying that by not disclosing he had AIDS, "Rock Hudson did a bad thing. He was not a bad man." The chronicle flashes back to post World War II Hollywood. Would-be actor Roy Fitzgerald comes to the attention of agent Henry Willson (Andrew Robinson), who not only changes his name, finds him screen work (and a contract at Universal International Pictures), but also monitors the hunk's personal life. The pressures of keeping his gay life hidden from the public leads to the break-up of Hudson's relationship with young Tim Murphy (Thom Matthews). It is the latter who says prophetically, "You're so damned scared of being queer you're going to spend your whole damn life denying who and what you are."

Wanting to be acceptable to his mainstream audience, superstar Rock talks himself into marrying Willson's secretary, Phyllis Gates (Daphne Ashbrook). However, it is a short-lasting union, especially after he admits there have been other men since they were married. Later, Hudson fires the possessive Willson as his agent/watchdog, while his accepting mother (Diana Ladd) and his good friend/administrative associate, Mark Miller (Michael Ensign), remain the two constants in his life. In the early 1980s, Hudson builds a relationship with much younger Marc Christian. Still later, Rock learns he has AIDS, but decides not to tell Marc. When his condition worsens, Hudson quietly seeks treatment in Paris, but abandons that to return to the U.S. to costar for a season on TV's "Dynasty." Finally, the truth is made known. Hudson finds irony in the situation. (He admits he spent a life believing "If it ever came out I was gay it would kill me. . . . And look, it has.") The movie concludes with the notation: "Rock Hudson's death focused worldwide attention on AIDS and the need for research and education to combat the deadly disease."

David Hiltbrand (*People*) rated *Rock Hudson* a D⁺ and labeled it a "stilted docudrama" that was "spectacularly superficial." Hiltbrand judged: "Other than a startlingly heightened presentation of homosexual seduction, the movie is a fizzle. . . . Thomas Ian Griffith . . . brings an endearing vulnerability to the role in his early scenes. But that performance trails off sharply. . . . Andrew Robinson, who starred in the network's infinitely better biopic of Liberace [q.v.] last year, is fine as Henry Willson. . . ." *TV Guide* which described this vehicle as "a candid portrait," rated it two out of four stars. Fran Wood (*New York Daily News*) warned, "It isn't often that we see a television movie with the degree of sleaziness found in . . .

[*Rock Hudson*] but, then again, it isn't often that network television airs movies aimed only at our most prurient and voyeuristic interests. . . . It contains scenes which will make you cringe with embarrassment, and its attempts at portraying sexual play between adult males are both sophomoric and distasteful. . . . . There also isn't much of a performance anywhere in this movie."

The fact that the uncharismatic Griffith looked so little like Hudson was only heightened by the TV movie's use of actual movie posters and authentic newsreel clips of the real Hudson. Downplaying the controversial nature of his Marc Christian's lifestyle, William R. Moses provided a very humanistic portrayal, as did Diana Ladd in her assignment as Hudson's confidant and den queen mother.

Because of the poor audience ratings— only 24%—ABC's *Rock Hudson* received, rival NBC-TV cancelled plans to present a four-hour movie largely based on Sara Davidson's biography written with the ailing Hudson. The miniseries was to have been based on Carmen Culver's teleplay and to be co-produced by Stan Margulies and Ken Kaufman.

206. The Roman Spring of Mrs. Stone (Warner Bros., 1961), color, 104 min. (a.k.a.: *The Widow and the Gigolo*)

Producer, Louis De Rochemont; associate producer, Lothar Wolff; director, Jose Quintero; based on the novel by Tennessee Williams; screenplay, Gavin Lambert; additional dialogue, Jan Read; production designer, Roger Furse; art director, Herbert Smith; set decorator, John Jarvis; Miss Leigh's gowns, Pierre Balmain; costumes, Bumble Dawson; makeup, Bob Lawrence; music, Richard Addinsell; song, Paddy Robert and Addinsell; assistant directors, Peter Yates, Jake Wright, Tony Wallis; sound, Cecil Mason; camera, Harry Waxman; supervising editor, Ralph Kemplen.

Cast: Vivien Leigh (Karen Stone); Warren Beatty (Paolo di Leo); Lotte Lenya (Countess Magda Terribili-Gonzales); Coral Browne (Meg); Jill St. John (Barbara Bingham); Jeremy Spencer (Young Man); Stella Bonheur (Mrs.

Jamison-Walker); Josephine Brown (Lucia); Peter Dyneley (L. Greener); Carl Jaffe (Baron); Harold Kasket (Tailor); Viola Keats (Julia); Cleo Laine (Singer); Bessie Love (Bunny); Elspeth March (Mrs. Barrow); Henry McCarthy (C. Kennedy); Warren Mitchell (Giorgio); John Phillips (Tom Stone); Paul Stassino (Renaldo, the Barber); Ernest Thesiger (Stefano); Mavis Villiers (Mrs. Coogan); Thelma D'Aguiar (Mita, the Maid).

"Decadence itself can be quite fascinating, and especially when the decadents are such beautiful people as Vivien Leigh and Warren Beatty." (Arthur Knight, *The Saturday Review*)

The 1950s and 1960s saw Hollywood producing screen versions of several Tennessee Williams's works, including *Cat on a Hot Tin Roof* (1958), *Suddenly, Last Summer* (1959) and *The Night of the Iguana* (1964), qq.v. These films were based on Broadway plays, while *The Roman Spring of Mrs. Stone* derived from Williams's 1950 novella. What they all shared in common was their author's sometimes direct, but more often, oblique depictions of homosexuality. These dramatic pieces reflected his era's majority assumption that such a minority lifestyle was unnatural and decadent and the related reaction by repressed homosexuals of the day that their "shameful" sexual feelings better remain closeted. Because Williams was such an acclaimed, commercial artist, a pre-liberated Hollywood dared to adapt his works to the screen. That his literary work contained "deviant" themes could be handled by emasculating the point (as in the case of *Cat on a Hot Tin Roof*) or beclouding the issue in arty symbolism (as in *The Roman Spring of Mrs. Stone*). Just like the male hooker character in *American Gigolo* (1980), q.v., there are indications in *Roman Spring* that Warren Beatty's handsome, narcissistic Paolo had had sexual liaisons with men over the years. As for Lotte Lenya's waspish Countess from Budapest, her characterization is just a more refined cousin to the nononsense lesbian she would portray in the British-made James Bond adventure, *From Russia with Love* (1963).

Middle-aged, stage star Karen Stone (Vivien Leigh) abandons her craft after a disastrous pre-Broadway play tryout. While en route to Rome for an Italian vacation, her husband (John Phillips), dies of a heart attack. However, she remains in the Eternal City. Through a bitchy procuress, Countess Magda Terribili-Gonzales (Lotte Lenya), Karen meets a young Italian gigolo, Paolo di Leo (Warren Beatty). They become lovers, with Karen insuring his attention through expensive gifts. However, Paolo needs cash to share with the greedy Countess. Thus, the latter vengefully introduces Paolo to a young Hollywood movie star, Barbara Bingham (Jill St. John), with whom he then has an affair. The rejected Mrs. Stone returns to her apartment, noting the attractive stranger (Jeremy Spencer) who has been following her silently for weeks. As the movie ends, she tosses him a key to her apartment.

Bosley Crowther (*New York Times*) admitted of Vivien Leigh, who had won an Oscar for appearing in the movie of Tennessee Williams's *A Streetcar Named Desire* (1951): "As beautiful, chic and accomplished as Vivien Leigh obviously is . . . she cannot do much with the banalities in *The Roman Spring of Mrs. Stone.* . . ." Furthermore, Crowther had unkind words for co-star Warren Beatty who was "hopelessly out of his element as a patent-leather ladies' man in Rome. His manners remind one of a freshman trying to put on airs at a college prom, his accent recalls Don Ameche's all-purpose Italian Spanish one." (British *Monthly Film Bulletin*) decided, "A certain vicarious enjoyment can be gained from any film which revels as openly as this one does in vice, lust, loneliness and debasement. . . . Warren Beatty is serviceable as the sullen young gigolo, considering that the part is so ambiguous." *Variety* predicted (rightly) that the movie would be "for some tough sledding, principally because of the un-

happy, unsavory characters dealt with . . . with whom an audience will have enormous difficulties establishing compassion, let alone identification."

207. **Rope** (Warner Bros., 1948), color, 80 min. Not rated.

Producers, Sidney Bernstein, Alfred Hitchcock; director, Hitchcock; based on the play *Rope's End* by Patrick Hamilton; adaptor, Hume Cronyn; screenplay, Arthur Laurents, (uncredited) Ben Hecht; art director, Perry Ferguson; set decorators, Emile Kuri, Howard Bristol; costumes, Adrian; makeup, Perc Westmore; music, Leo F. Forbstein, (uncredited) David Buttolph; camera, Joseph Valentine, William V. Skall; editor, William H. Ziegler.

Cast: James Stewart (Rupert Cadell); John Dall (Shaw Brandon); Farley Granger (Philip); Joan Chandler (Janet Walker); Sir Cedric Hardwicke (Mr. Kentley); Constance Collier (Mrs. Atwater); Edith Evanson (Mrs. Wilson, the Governess); Douglas Dick (Kenneth Lawrence); Dick Hogan (David Kentley).

Often, Alfred Hitchcock was intrigued by the technical challenges of filmmaking, such as the use of 3-D cinematography in *Dial M for Murder* (1954). Earlier, in *Rope*, he undertook to expand traditional dramatic intensity by (1) having the movie's storyline action exactly parallel the film's running time; (2) limiting the story's locales essentially to the three rooms of the two young men's apartment; (3) establishing long, unedited takes for scenes to match the length of a reel of film. For *Rope*, he used Patrick Hamilton's British play, *Rope's End*, a narrative of two handsome, pampered men who share their elegant lives together and, on a whim, murder a prep school classmate. The play/movie's unstated parallel to the infamous 1920s Chicago murderers, Leopold and Loeb—two rich young lovers who killed for the thrill of outsmarting the law and proving their intellectual/moral superiority —was obvious.

As a bonding experience and to substantiate their disregard for all laws, aggressive Shaw Brandon (John Dall) and passive Philip (Farley Granger) murder their acquaintance, David Kentley (Dick Hogan) and stash his body in a large chest in the living room of Shaw's apartment. Their rationale for killing Kentley ("a perfect victim for a perfect murder") was that he was an inconsequential weakling of no particular consequence. To prolong the thrill of their "perfect crime," the two pretentious men have invited several guests to a cocktail party, including the boy's father, Mr. Kentley (Sir Cedric Hardwicke), the boy's fiancee, Janet Walker (Joan Chandler), the boy's aunt, Mrs. Atwater (Constance Collier), the boy's rival, Kenneth Lawrence (Douglas Dick), and Rupert Cadell (James Stewart). The latter, now a publisher, had been all three boys' housemaster in prep school. During the get-together, the emotionally-charged Shaw delights in speculating on why David has not appeared at the party. In contrast, Philip is suffering badly under the strain. Before long, Cadell, who recalls many Nietzchean philosophical discussions with his hosts on the subject of good and evil, has a hunch they know full well why Kentley has not appeared. After the guests leave, Rupert returns, just as Shaw and Philip are about to dispose of the corpse. In the ensuing cat-and-mouse game, the perceptive Rupert uncovers the body. Revolted by their smug disregard of law and life, he summons the police, while Shaw fixes a drink and Philip plays the piano.

Bosley Crowther (*New York Times*) was unimpressed by Hitchcock's cinematic juggling: "apart from the tedium of waiting for someone to open that chest . . . the unpunctuated flow of image becomes quite monotonous. And the effort of application of a story of meager range becomes intense. . . .. The use of Technicolor makes for realism in contrasting hues, but maybe the mood of this story would have come over better in black-and-white." Of the cast, the *Times* noted, "John Dall does a hard, aggressive job of making this unpleasant fellow supremely contemptible, and Farley Granger is tangibly wretched as the less ecstatic one. James Stewart is strangely limp and mopish as the old friend. . . ."

Harrison's Reports, who referred to the focal figures as "two intellectual but degenerate undergraduates," rated the movie "An exceptionally fine psychological thriller," but wondered "whether or not it will prove to be a popular picture . . . for as entertainment it has a morbid quality that has seldom, if ever, been surpassed on the screen. . . ."

Rope was not a hit with audiences. Not only was its presentation overly static, but there was no one with whom the moviegoer could empathize. If Dall and Granger seemed stiff in their performances, a very uncomfortable, miscast Stewart (perhaps realizing the film's underlying homoerotic texture?) was totally flat. One can only imagine Charles Laughton or even Ray Milland in the role. (Originally, Cary Grant was scheduled for the teacher and Montgomery Clift was wanted to play one of the murderers; both refused the assignments as too image-shattering.) The movie's few minutes of liveliness were provided by veteran Constance Collier.

The Leopold-Loeb case would be the fictionalized subject of *Compulsion* (1959) and the direct basis of *Swoon* (1992), qq.v. Alfred Hitchcock would return to homoerotica again—and far more directly—in *Strangers on a Train* (1951), q.v., starring Robert Walker and Farley Granger.

208. The Rose (Twentieth Century-Fox, 1979), color, 134 min. R-rated.

Executive producer, Tony Ray; producers, Marvin Worth, Aaron Russo; director, Mark Rydell; story, Bill Kerby; screenplay, Kerby, Bo Goldman; production designer, Richard MacDonald; art director, Jim Schoppe; set decorator, Bruce Weintraub; costumes, Theoni V. Aldredge; makeup, Jeff Angell; music arranger/music supervisor, Paul A. Rothchild; assistant directors, Larry Franco, Chris Soldo; sound, Jim Webb, Chris McLaughlin; camera, Vilmos Zsigmond; editors, Robert L. Wolfe; C. Timothy O'Meara.

Cast: Bette Midler (Rose); Alan Bates (Rudge); Frederic Forrest (Houston Dyer);

Harry Dean Stanton (Billy Ray); Barry Primus
(Dennis); David Keith (Mal); Sandra McCabe
(Sarah Willingham); Will Hare (Mr. Leonard);
Rudy Bond (Monty); Don Calfa (Don Frank);
James Keane (Dealer); Doris Roberts (Rose's
Mother); Sandy Ward (Rose's Father); Michael
Greer (Emcee); Claude Sacha, Michael St. Lau-
rent, Sylvester, Pearl Heart (Female Impersona-
tors); Butch Ellis (Waiter); Richard Dioguardi,
Luke Andreas, Seamon Glass (Truckers); John
Dennis Johnston (Milledge); Jonathan Banks
(Television Promoter); Jack O'Leary (Short
Order Cook); Harry Northup (Skinny Guy);
Cherei Latimer (Secretary); Pat Corley (Police
Chief); Dennis Erdman (Billy Ray's Kid);
Hugh Gillin (Guard); Joyce Roth (Airport
Waitress); Frank Speiser (Reporter at Rose's
House); Annie McGuire (Don Frank's Wife);
Hildy Brooks (Waitress in Diner); Jack Starrett
(Dee); Victor Argo (Lockerman); Kelly Boyd
(Blonde Girl in Leonard's); Cyndi Gottfried
(Redhaired Girl in Leonard's); L. D. Frazier
(Nightclub Doorman); Lawrence Guardino
(Cop at Police Station); Constance Cawlfield,
Dimo Condos, Lorrie Davis, David Garfield,
Kathryn Grody, Jack Hollander, Sandra Seacat,
Chip Zien, Ted Harris (Reporters); Phil Rubin-
stein (Pot Belly); Charlie McCarthy (Cop in
Luxor Baths); Danny Weiss, Steve Hunter,
Robbie Louis Buchanan, Jerome Noel Jumon-
ville, Norton Buffalo, Mark Leonard, Mark
Underwood, Pentti Glan (The Rose Band).

In *The Rose*, how much the lead character does or does not resemble the late Janis
Joplin is unimportant. What is crucial is
that Bette Midler—once the Queen of
Camp—provides a riveting performance
as a top rock entertainer who "can't
drudge up the sincerity anymore." In *The
Rose* she presents a devastatingly powerful portrayal of a rock star destroyed by
self-doubts, substance abuse, career pressures and the parasites surrounding her.
Within this very downbeat film, the self-
destructing Rose (Bette Midler) is pursued
by and pursues men, seeking distractions
in order to recharge her dwindling energies. While on tour in Memphis, she has a
brief re-encounter with Sarah Willingham
(Sandra McCabe), a youngish woman
with whom Rose once shared confidences
and love.

It is a tender sequence in which, after a
concert, the two women friends reunite
and reminisce. In the process, Sarah
washes Rose's hair. Sarah admits to missing Rose very much and kisses her, while
Rose, absorbed in thoughts of her new
boyfriend, Houston Dyer (Frederic Forrest), can only talk of this latest man who
"doesn't care who I am." As Sarah admits,
"I'm jealous of you Rose. I want what you
have." The two women hug, rock back
and forth, cry and kiss. Suddenly, Rose's
boyfriend appears, shocked and subconsciously envious of the intimacy he sees
and which he has never had with her.
"Why? Why?" he asks as he slaps her. In
truth, Rose does not know.

A far lighter moment occurs earlier in
the film when Rose visits one of her old
haunts, a trashy New York City nightclub
where female impersonators provide the
musical/comedy entertainment. The emcee (Michael Greer), an old friend of Rose
(who used to live above the club), is croak-
ing "I've Written a Letter to Daddy"
a la Bette Davis and rattling off "in"
jokes. Baffled by this gay-hip atmosphere,
Rose's naive stud, Houston, blurts out:
"Weirdsville. Reminds me of a dream I
had once in the Philippines." Meanwhile,
the drag show accelerates, with performers imitating the standards icons—Diana
Ross, Barbra Streisand, Mae West. Then
one emerges as Rose. In a wry moment,
the real and fake Rose (which is which?)
dish each other with joyful sarcasm and,
then, perform a duet. It was a joyous case
of art imitating life, for the Divine Miss M
(Bette Midler) had long been a favorite
of gay audiences, having made successful early appearances at the Continental
Baths, a Manhattan gay bath house.

Variety enthused, "*The Rose* should do
for Bette Midler what *Lady Sings the
Blues* did for Diana Ross seven years ago;
establish her as a first-rate dramatic actress, as well as a potent songstress. . . .
The Rose is a supreme Midler vehicle, one
that should turn on an entirely new audience for her." Jack Kroll (*Newsweek*) en-

Tom Berenger in *Rustlers' Rhapsody* (1985).

dorsed, "Bette Midler's performance is an event to be experienced—a fevered, fearless portrait of a tormented, gifted, sexy child-woman who sang her heart out until it exploded."

The Rose grossed $19.1 million in distributors' domestic film rentals. It received four Academy Award nominations: Best Actress (Bette Midler; Sally Field won for *Norma Rae*); Best Supporting Actor (Frederic Forrest; Melvyn Douglas won for *Being There*); Best Sound (*Apocalypse Now* won); Best Film Editing (*All That Jazz* won). Midler had two hit singles from the movie's soundtrack: "When a Man Loves a Woman" and "The Rose."

209. Rustlers' Rhapsody (Paramount, 1985), color, 88 min. PG-rated.

Executive producer, Jose Vicuna; producer David Giler; associate producers, Michael Green, Herve Hacherel; director/screenplay, Hugh Wilson; production designer, Gil Par-

rondo; art director, Raul Paton; set decorator, Julian Mateos; costumes, Wayne Finkelman; makeup, Cristobal Criado; music, Steve Doriff; songs: Doriff and Milton Brown; Snuff Garrett; Nancy Masters; assistant directors, Michael Green, Luis Gomez Valdivieso, Roberto Parra; stunt coordinator, Jose Luis Chinchilla; sound, David Lee; special effects, Antonio Parra; camera, Jose Luis Alcanine; supervising editor, John Victor Smith; editors, Zack Steenberg, Colin Wilson.

Cast: Tom Berenger (Rex O'Herlian); G. W. Bailey (Peter); Marilu Henner (Miss Tracy); Fernando Rey (Railroad Colonel); Andy Griffith (Colonel Ticonderoga); Sela Ward (Colonel Ticonderoga's Daughter); Brant Van Hoffman (Jim); Christopher Malcolm (Jud); Manuel Pereiro, Paul Maxwell (Sheepherders); Jim Carter (Blackie); Margarita Calahorra (Sheepherder's Wife); Billy J. Mitchell (Town Doctor); Patrick Wayne (Bob Barber); John Orchard (Town Sheriff); Emilio Linder (Sheepherder in Saloon); Alan Larson (Bartender); Thomas Abbott (Saloon Owner); Elmer Modlin (Real Estate Broker) Juan Miguel Manrique (Town Boy); Dennis Vaughan (Minister); Eduardo

Garcia, Ignacio Carreno, Alicia F. Cavada, Jose Sacristan, Tabare Carballo, Solier Fagundez, George Bullock, Roman Ariznavaretta, Jorge Brito, Eugenio Serrano, Miguel Garcia, Francisco Gomez, Basilio Escudero, Gabriel Laguna, Camilio Vila, Hal Burton (Stunt Players).

Occasionally, as in *Callaway Went Thataway* (1951) or *Blazing Saddles* (1974), Hollywood creates a solid spoof of the all-but-gone Western genre. More usually, as in *Hearts of the West* (1975) or *Rustlers' Rhapsody*, both featuring Andy Griffith, the efforts to satirize the cliches are more leaden than light. Regarding *Rustlers' Rhapsody*, Rex Reed (*New York Post*) exploded, "This cornball send-up of the old Saturday afternoon cowboy epics . . . hasn't got a brain in its saddlebags big enough to raise it above the level of a sophomoric stupor." According to Leo Seligsohn (*Newsday*), "As spoofs go, this one doesn't quite make it to the end of the trail."

Singing cowboy star Rex O'Herlian (Tom Berenger), once the king of B Westerns in the 1930s and 1940s, finds himself in a new "real-life" adventure. Riding into a frontier town (that looks like every other frontier town), O'Herlian, in full regalia and move makeup, makes a strange impression on the locals, including Blackie (Jim Carter) who observes,'You look like one of those fellas that is attracted to other men." Thereafter, Rex finds the cattle baron (Andy Griffith) is linked with the railroad colonel (Fernando Rey) in their mutual war against the encroaching sheepherders. Handsome Rex, who is coveted by a randy dance hall girl (Marilu Henner) and the colonel's over-sexed daughter (Sela Ward), finds himself in the middle of the range war. He is aided in the good fight by the town's reform drunk (G. W. Bailey), who becomes O'Herlian's sidekick. All ends satisfactorily, with Rex riding off to the next town for the next adventure and. . . .

A major premise of *Rustlers' Rhapsody* insists that Rex, the epitome of a clean-living cowboy, with his multi-gallon white hat, designer duds, silver-tipped boots, etc. may just not be all man. This suggestive hint leads his rival, Bob Barber (Patrick Wayne), to ponder whether milk-sipping Rex, who never cusses, is really "confident in his heterosexuality." This accusation so bothers the virginal hero that he immediately abandons the company of his palomino horse Wildfire to bed the brassy dance hall queen and the colonel's hot-blooded daughter. The film's emphasis on this premise led David Edelstein (*Village Voice*) to wonder, "Is this why [director/scenarist Hugh] Wilson revived a long-gone archetype—to speculate on his masculinity? Or does he think he's celebrating a bygone era when men could be decent and virginal and still be men? He doesn't seem to know what he's doing, but he sure loves those homo jokes."

One of the film's few champions was Kevin Thomas (*Los Angeles Times*) who approved of its "confident and relaxed" satire, the caliber of "the film's throwaway gags" and "its great on-target look."

Rustlers' Rhapsody, a commercial bust, was filmed in Almeria, Spain on a period set used in the 1960s by Spaghetti Western filmmaker Sergio Leone. On the soundtrack, Rex Allen Jr. sings "Last of the Silver Screen Cowboys." For the record, the usually accomplished Tom Berenger makes a valiant effort to overcome the bum jokes and anemic satire, but the script defeats him.

210. Saint Jack (New World Pictures, 1979), color, 112 min. R-rated.

Executive producers, Hugh M. Hefner, Edward L. Rissien; producer, Roger Corman; associate producer, George Morfogen; director, Peter Bogdanovich; based on the novel by Paul Theroux; screenplay, Bogdanovich, Howard Sackler, Theroux; art director, David Ng; set decorator, Lucius Wong, Richard Chew; costumes, Lorita Ong, Louise Walker; makeup, Graham Freeborn; sound, Jean-Pierre Ruh; assistant directors, Denys Granier-Deferre, Tjacn Tan Leng Teck; camera, Robby Muller; editor, William Carruth.

Cast: Ben Gazzara (Jack Flowers); Denholm Elliott (William Leigh); James Villiers (Frogget); Joss Ackland (Yardley); Rodney Bewes (Smale); Mark Kingston (Yates); Lisa Lu (Mrs. Yates); Monika Subramaniam (Monika); Judy Lim (Judy); George Lazenby (Senator); Peter Bogdanovich (Eddie Schuman); Joseph Noel (Gopi); Ong Kian Bee (Hing); Tan Yan Meng (Little Hing); Andrew Chua (Andrew, the Taxi Driver); Ken Wolinski (Australian Businessman); Peter Tay (Mike); Osman Zailani (Bob); Elizabeth Ang (Shirley); S. M. Sim (Mr. Tan); Peter Pang, Ronald Ng, Seow Teow Keng (Triad Gang); Charles M. Longbottom (Stanley [George Milton]); Sonny Ng (Sonny); Bridgit Ng (Bridgit); Lily Ang (Lily); Diana Voon (Mammy); Oggi (Djamilia); Colonel L. T. Firbank (Colonel Gunstone); Elsie Quah (Esther); Nancy Koh, Dorene Kiong (Esther's Cronies): Bill Snorgrass (Floyd); Kitty Ooi (Wong May); Salem Sanwan (Yusof); H. J. Zaccheus (Ganapathy, the Gatekeeper); Len Burke (Australian Customer); Leith Masavage (Marvin); P. Ganesan (Raffles Bellboy); K. M. Goh (Triad Tattooist); Brian Leonard (Harmonium Player); Patrick Waterman (Minister).

On one hand, Roger Ebert (*Movie Home Companion*, 1991) rated *Saint Jack* four stars:

"Sometimes a character in a movie inhabits his world so freely, so easily, that he creates it for us as well. Ben Gazzara does that . . . as an American exile in Singapore who finds himself employed at the trade of pimp. . . . One of the joys of this movie is seeing how cleanly and surely [director Peter] Bogdanovich employs the two levels of his plot. . . . Bogdanovich, assisted by a superb script and art direction, shows us Jack Flowers's world so confidently—and because Ben Gazzara makes Jack so special."

On the other hand: Ralph Novak and Peter Travers (*People Magazine Guide to Movies on Video*, 1987) decided:

". . . the movie tells, haltingly, of an American in Singapore who runs a whorehouse against brutal Chinese competition. The movie is largely incoherent and amateurishly shot and acted. Ben Gazzara . . . is so wooden he's absolutely unsympathetic, as are most of the other characters.

Worse, whole scenes seem to have been shot out of focus."

Intentionally or not, the unsentimental *Saint Jack* is a moody, murky and muddled film, bolstered more by Denholm Elliott's performance as the desperate Englishman who dies of a heart attack than by Gazarra's detached interpretation of the cigar-chomping, seemingly glib pimp. Within the plot, Jack Flowers (Ben Gazzara), anxious to leave his cesspool existence in Singapore, is told he can earn $250,000 *if* he provides incriminating evidence against a homosexual U.S. Senator (George Lazenby) due in town on a visit. Having taken the photographs of the Congressman dallying with a Chinese boy at his hotel, Jack suddenly has a pang of moral conscience and destroys the blackmailing material.

To be noted in this box-office misfire is filmmaker Bogdanovich's appearance as Eddie Schuman. He is the opportunistic American who gives Jack several opportunities to make easy, as well as immoral and illegal, dollars at the cost of his dignity. The gay senator was played by George Lazenby, once the screen's James Bond (*On Her Majesty's Secret Service*, 1969).

211. Salome (Allied Producers and Distributors, 1923), 5,595. Not rated.

Director, Charles Bryant; based on the play by Oscar Wilde; screenplay, Peter M. Winters [Natacha Rambova]; set designer/costumes, Rambova; music arranger, Ulderico Marcelli; camera, Charles Van Enger.

Cast: Alla Nazimova (Salome); Rose Dione (Herodias); Mitchell Lewis (Herod); Nigel De Brulier (Jokaanan); Earl Schenck (Young Syrian); Arthur Jamsine (Page); Frederic Peters (Naaman, the Executioner); Louis Dumar (Tigellinus).

An assortment of actresses have played the alluring Biblical seductress Salome in the American cinema: Theda Bara (1918), Diana Allen (1923), Rita Hayworth (1953) and Brigid Bazlen (1961). None provided such an unusual interpretation as did Russian-born Alla Nazimova (1879–

1945), who produced and starred, at the age of 44, in this rarified silent production. It was based loosely on Oscar Wilde's 1894 play with sets inspired by Aubrey Beardsley's drawings, and filmed on two sets of one large sound stage. Natasha Rambova, its costume and set designer, as well as adaptor (and some film historians insist director) was then the wife of Rudolph Valentino. She was also reputed to be Madame Nazimova's lover, and the assembled cast has always been rumored/ touted to have been all-gay. (In Ken Russell's *Valentino*, 1977, q.v., Nazimova [Leslie Caron] is asked by a reporter, "Is it true that Rudolph Valentino refused to be in your all-homosexual production of *Salome?*") All these reasons combine to overlay the starkly theatrical and fantastic *Salome*—with its half-nude dancing men servants—with a decidedly gay flavor. In the pruned-down version of *Salome* that was released, several explicit scenes of "depravitiy and immorality" (according to the New York censor board and others) were deleted, including one suggesting a sexual relationship between two soldiers.

In ancient Judea, when the heretical prophet, Jokaanan (Nigel De Brulier), rejects her advances ("Let me kiss your mouth," she implores; "Never! Daughter of Babylon! Daughter of Sodom! Never!"), Salome seeks revenge. She performs a tantalizing dance for her stepfather, Herod (Mitchell Lewis), on condition that he grant her Jokaanan's head on a silver platter. Granting her evil request, the lustful Herod quickly has a change-of-heart after observing Salome kissing the severed head. He has the temptress killed.

Harrison's Reports deplored, "It is heart-breaking for one to see so much money wasted on stories that could never in the world make a good picture. . . ." *Variety* assessed, " 'Nazimova in Facial Expressions'; with Salome as the background, would have been much better billing for the picture . . . Salome as a picture is going to please a few who are Nazimova devotees, a few that like higher art in all its

form perversions, and then its box office value will end. . . ." In contrast, the *New York Times* insisted, "The eye looks upon it and finds it good . . . the picture appeals at once as a work of free imagination." However, the *Times* observed, "Mme. Nazimova's Salome is satisfactory oto the censors . . . but can an approved Salome be interesting, can she be a genuinely dramatic figure. . . ."

This cinematic oddity did much to destroy Nazimova's career and fortune.

212. **Saturday Night at the Baths**

(Mammouth, 1975), color, 86 min. R-rated.

Producers, David Buckley, Steve Ostrow; director, Buckley; screenplay, Buckley, Franklin Khedouri; camera, Ralf Bode; editors, Jackie Raynal, Suzanne Fenn.

Cast: Ellen Sheppard (Tracy); Robert Aberdeen (Michael); Don Scotti (Himself); Steve Ostrow (Steve); Caleb Stone (Judy Garland); J. C. Gaynor (Shirley Bassey); Toyia (Diana Ross); and: Janie Olivor, Phillip Ownes, R. Douglas Brautigham, Paul J. Ott, Paul Vanase, Lawrence Smith, Pedro Valentino.

"Though some may call it gay propaganda, pic is a surprisingly sincere, sometimes naive attempt. . . ." (Addison Verrill, *Variety*)

Set at the Continental Baths, New York City's (in)famous gay bath house, this low-budget feature was co-produced by Steve Ostrow, the club's owner who plays himself in this independent release. The film's director, David Buckley, was a founder of the countercultural *Screw* magazine along with his brother Jim, whose Mammoth Films released this picture.

Briefly told, Tracy (Ellen Sheppard) chides her piano player boyfriend, Michael (Robert Aberdeen) for being so uptight. She urges him to loosen up his stereotypical responses, especially regarding gays. Prompted by her words, he gets himself hired at the Continental Baths one Saturday night as a pianist where he finds himself attracted to the facility's friendly manager, Steve (Steve Ostrow). The two have sex, and the now-liberated

Al Pacino and Gene Hackman in *Scarecrow* (1973).

Michael returns to continue his relationship with Tracy.

Variety, which championed the picture, noted its dim commercial outlook: "Gays may take offense at one sequence which utilizes the worst examples of homosexual stereotypes. . . . Straight males will avoid it and . . . few femmes would take a lover or husband to a film which urges him to try boys for a change." In contrast, A. H. Weiler (*New York Times*) found the movie "slightly steamy and enervating" and some of the sexual coupling "raunchily explicit." Weiler dismissed the film as essentially inconsequential.

A highlight of *Saturday Night at the Baths*, whose heterosexual and homosexual scenes are non-exploitive, is the cabaret scenes at the Continental where female impersonators cavort as Shirley Bassey, Judy Garland, Carmen Miranda and Diana Ross. While this minor feature—which some viewers found condescending—was in limited release, on Broadway Terrence

McNally's farce, *The Ritz*, set at a thinly-disguised Continental Baths, was having a hit run. Later, that play would be transformed into a middling 1976 feature film, q.v., which was certainly more amusing but not as real or empathetic as this trend-breaking entry.

213. Scarecrow (Warner Bros., 1973), color, 112 min. R-rated.

Producer, Robert M. Sherman; director, Jerry Schatzberg; screenplay, Garry Michael White; production designer, Al Brenner; costumes, Jo Ynocencio; makeup, Frank Griffin; music, Fred Myrow; assistant directors, Tom Shaw, Charles Bonniwell; sound, Barry Thomas, Victor Goode; special effects, Candy Flanagin; camera, Vilmos Zsigmond; editor, Evan Lottman.

Cast: Gene Hackman (Max); Al Pacino (Lion [Francis Lionel DelBouchi]); Dorothy Tristan (Coley); Ann Wedgeworth (Frenchy); Richard Lynch (Jack Riley); Eileen Brennan (Darlene); Penny Allen (Annie); Richard Hackman (Mickey); Al Cingolani (Skipper); Rutanya Alda (Woman in Camper).

Gene Hackman has always been a major source of acting energy on screen. In this little-remembered, metaphoric buddy picture, he is teamed with Al Pacino, who thankfully provides a restrained performance (compared to his role the same year in *Serpico*). Together they depict a strange duo who embark on a leisurely odyssey of self-discovery and growing friendship. One of their several escapades crossing America lands them in jail and brings the more inarticulate one (Pacino) face-to-face with an aggressive homosexual (Richard Lynch). On one level, the segment is gratuitous local color; on another, it was a way for American filmmakers in the 1970s to demonstrate that the bonding male leads were merely platonic pals—and nothing more!

In northern California, Lion (Al Pacino), after five years in the Navy, is hitchhiking to Detroit, intent on confronting his ex-wife (Penny Allen) and seeing their child. The bespectacled, cigar-smoking Max (Gene Hackman) has just served six years in San Quentin prison. With savings earned during his jail stretch, he intends to open a car-wash business in Pittsburgh. These two unlikely souls join forces on the road, with hot-tempered Max forever getting them into trouble, while laid-back Lion insists that humor is a better weapon than anger. The two of them stop in Denver to visit Max's sister, Coley (Dorothy Tristan). Loosening his emotional rigidity, Max now agrees to start his car wash in Denver. While celebrating, the two men get drunk and end being sentenced to a month on a prison farm. There, Max becomes more sullen and withdrawn, while the baffled Lion turns to the friendship of a knowing trustee, Jack Riley (Richard Lynch). The latter attempts to persuade the naive Lion to have sex with him ("How about giving old Riley a little relief here"), leading Lion to fight back—to his and Riley's amazement. Seeing his badly-beaten pal, Max pulls out of his shell. Later, when opportunity permits, he beats up Jack. Subsequently, the two men reach

Denver where Annie, whom Lion had deserted, lies to him on the phone, insisting their child was still-born. A short while later, Lion goes into emotional shock and must be hospitalized. Max promises his catatonic friend that he will stand by him and use his cherished savings to speed along his friend's recovery.

Vincent Canby (*New York Times*) decided, "For most of *Scarecrow*—for as long as the movie doesn't intrude on their essential aimlessness . . . [Max and Lion] are two marvelously realized characters. . . . It all goes decisively wrong when . . . [director and scripter] decide to saddle the pair with a poetic vision that suddenly makes everything needlessly phony. . . ." *Variety* rated this "a periodically interesting but ultimately unsatisfying character study . . . Gene Hackman is excellent . . . but Al Pacino is shot down by the script which never provides him with much beyond freaky second banana status. . . ." For Richard Combs (British *Monthly Film Bulletin*), "*Scarecrow* turns up some striking images of the American landscape. . . . Jerry Schatzberg's direction . . . floats airily over the surfaces. *Scenes-a-faire* are created with monotonous regularity; particularly so for the lurid climaxes of the homosexual assault on Lion in prison and his final breakdown. . . ."

214. Score (Audubon Films, 1973), color, 89 min. R-rated.

Producer, Radley Metzger; associate producer, Ava Leighton; director, Metzger; based on the play by Jerry Douglas; screenplay, Douglas; camera, Franjo Vodopivee; editor, Doris Toumarkine.

Cast: Claire Wilbur (Elvira); Calvin [Cal] Culver (Eddie); Lynn Lowery (Betsy); Gerald Grant (Jack); Carl Parker (Mike).

"Puzzlement for the trade will be the response of the straight male audience to the gay sex scenes . . . Newly liberated femme audiences may well turn-on to it all. . . ." (Addison Verrill, *Variety*)

Radley Metzger, who had tantalized audiences with softcore porno entries such as *Carmen, Baby* (1967) and *Camille 2000* (1969), was forever pushing the limits of the latest U.S. Supreme Court obscenity rulings. Hoping to appeal to more mainstream audiences, he turned to this "sophisticated" comedy based on a 1970 off-Broadway play. Claire Wilbur had appeared in the original stage version, while model/actor Cal Culver was best known as Casey Donovan, star of gay porno flicks. In order to save costs, Metzger shot this offbeat feature in Yugoslavia.

Can a liberated, swinging couple, Elvira (Claire Wilbur) and Jack (Gerald Grant) persuade young newlyweds Eddie (Calvin Culver) and Betsy (Lynn Lowry) to try bed swapping—man-to-man and woman-to-woman? The answer in 89 minutes is yes, complete with arty but graphic nudity and softcore porno coupling as well as the timely arrival of an obliging, handy repairman (Carl Parker).

Variety found Wilbur "arch as Dracula's daughter," Culver "overly coy," Lowry "better" and Grant "quite good." Robert H. Rimmer (*The X-Rated Video Guide*, 1986) enthused, "The bisexual seduction scenes are cleverly intercut. After a bisexual night . . . monogamous innocence is replaced by 'It doesn't matter who you love just so long as you love.' Excellent erotic filmmaking by a master of the art."

For the record, this was probably the first mainstream American film to tout, by example, that amyl nitrate was indeed an aphrodisiac.

215. The Sergeant (Warner Bros., 1968), color, 108 min. R-rated

Executive producer, Robert Wise; producer, Richard Goldstone; director, John Flynn; based on the novel by Dennis Murphy; screenplay, Murphy; production designer, Willy Holt; art director, Marc Frederix; makeup, Michel Dereulle; music, Michel Magne; assistant director, Louis Pitzele; sound, Julien Coutellier; camera, Henri Persin; editor, Francoise Diot.

Cast: Rod Steiger (Master Sergeant Albert Callan); John Phillip Law (Private First Class Tom Swanson); Ludmila Mikael (Solange);

Frank Latimore (Captain Loring); Elliott Sullivan (Pop Heneken); Ronald Rubin (Corporal Cowley); Philip Roye (Aldous Brown); Jerry Brouer (Sergeant Komski); Memphis Slim (Nightclub Singer); Gabriel Gascond (Solange's Brother-in-Law).

". . . the point of view has been shifted to a kind of dramatic no-man's land between the private and the sergeant. The movie has become the story of the sergeant's self-discovery, ending in the defeat and suicide that once were so obligatory in popular, homosexual literature. . . ." (Vincent Canby, *New York Times*)

One could easily understand why Academy Award winner Rod Steiger would be attracted to *The Sergeant*. It was an acting challenge, like the multiple roles of *No Way to Treat a Lady* (1968), q.v., that appealed to his professionalism. Following in the wake of the unsuccessful *Reflections in a Golden Eye* (1967), q.v., which had a similar storyline, it was strange that *The Sergeant* should have been considered commercially viable. However, Hollywood was intrigued with exploring/exploiting its new liberalism—especially in the transition period between the waning industry production code of the mid-1960s and the late 1968 inauguration of a new industry classification/rating system. Like *Reflections*, *The Sergeant* dealt with a repressed military man thrown into constant contact professionally with handsome young men. Unable to deal with the threatening situation, he implodes finally and kills himself. It was an old-fashioned approach to the subject of "unnatural love" and "strange attractions," but then, the movie's book original had been written in far more repressive 1958.

In 1952, career soldier Master Sergeant Albert Callan (Rod Steiger), who showed bravery during World War II combat, is assigned to peace-time duty at a petroleum supply depot in France. The punctilious, super-organized Callan soon diverts control from weak-willed Captain Loring (Frank Latimore) to himself and imposes

John Phillip Law, Rod Steiger and Ludmila Mikael in *The Sergeant* **(1968).**

strict control over the antagonistic men. Meanwhile, Callan, who was once married, has become (sub)consciously attracted to handsome, very straight and very naive Private First Class Tom Swanson (John Phillip Law). Wanting him close by, he makes Swanson his orderly room clerk. When the latter wants to spend time with his French girlfriend, Solange (Ludmila Mikael), the jealous Callan refuses to give him passes. Swanson interprets this to be the result of the Sergeant's loneliness and spends a lot of his free time with his superior officer. Only after Callan drives Solange off does Swanson realize the underlying basis of Callan's motives. He becomes openly defiant. Unable to deal with the situation, Callan becomes drunk and publicly tries to kiss the repulsed young man. The next day, Loring relieves Callan of duties. The following day, the sergeant takes a rife from the company arsenal and

marches into a nearby woods and shoots himself.

Vincent Canby (*New York Times*) was put off: "Although Steiger is too good an actor to camp it up, he comes on with all the subtlety of a drag queen—unctuous, mean, commanding, pathetic—in his courtship of the private. . . . As played by John Phillip Law, the private also is remarkably dense and—when not being dense—he is so hostile that it would seem the sergeant would have to be psychotic to run after him with such boozy abandon. . . . . As directed by John Flynn . . . [*The Sergeant*] is a film busy with obvious symbols, a beer bottle handled as if it were a phallus, fondled guns and the like." Canby also pointed out, "In the context of today's liberated movie-making—with, among other things, Coral Browne nibbling on Susannah York in *The Killing of Sister George* [q.v.]—this study of repressed homosexuality seems almost quaint. It also is basically confused." On the other hand, *Variety*, which rated *The Sergeant* "moving" and full of "sensitivity," found a greater theme to the entry: "To say that this is a story about a homosexual is like claiming that an iceberg floats completely on the surface of water. To be sure, three is a near-climactic kiss forcibly emplanted by Steiger on Law; its plot motivation is perfect, its handling tasteful. The pic is about a situation far worse than physical-act homosexuality; a total, pervading enslavement of one person to another."

In retrospect, Vito Russo (*The Celluloid Closet*, 1987) concluded, "Neither *The Sergeant* nor *Reflections in a Golden Eye* offers the possibility of homosexual relationships; they deal only in sexually motivated manipulations . . . most of it unconscious and unexplored. The result is caricature. . . ." In each case, the gay character is killing what he sees as the source of his homosexuality. Both films insist that there is no option, no way out for these doomed people."

Location scenes for *The Sergeant* were shot in France. The opening battlefield prologue, set in 1944 France, was shot in black-and-white.

216. Sergeant Matlovich Vs. the U.S. Air Force (NBC-TV, August 21, 1978), color, 100 min. Not rated.

Executive producer, Thomas W. Moore; producer, Paul Leaf; associate producer, Jean Anne Moore; director, Leaf; teleplay, John McGreevey; art director, Bill Sully; set decorator, Ned Parsons; costumes, Ronald A. Dawson, Bernadene Mann; makeup, Doug Kelly; music, Teo Macero; assistant director, Stuart Fleming; sound, Alan Bernard; camera, Mario Tosi; editor, Thomas Stanford.

Cast: Brad Dourif (Sergeant Leonard P. Matlovich); Frank Converse (Captain Larsen Jaenicke); William Daniels (Father Veller); Stephen Elliott (Mat's Father); Rue McClanahan (Mat's Mother); David Spielberg (David Addlestone); Mitch Ryan (Lieutenant Colonel Applegate); Barra Grant (Susan Hewman); Alfred Ryder (Colonel Grand); David Ogden Stiers (G-2 Captain); Marc Singer (Jason); Donald Moffat (Colonel Benton); Ellen Holly (Amy); Harrison Page (Josh); William Bogert (Major Holloway); Edward Gallardo (Diego); Charles H. Gray (Colonel McLean); Harv Selsby (Airman); Rick Goldman (Sergeant Dunn); Shaka Cumbuka (Airman Jones); Tom Ormeny (Sergeant Marsh); Ron McIlwain (Captain Marsh); Bill Dearth (Timmons); Stuart Dillon (Needham); Jack Bender (Allcott); Roy West (Teenage Girl's Father); Jean Moore (Jean); Lawrence Howard (1st Airman); Gavan O'Herlihy (Art Stinson); Jane Ralston (Teenage Girl); David Ralston (1st Soldier); Steven Anderson (Reeber); Otto Felix (2nd Soldier); Sunya Moina (Tall Black Woman); Michael Fuller (Dr. John William Money); Birgit Winslow (Birgit); David Milton (Joe Green); and: Bill Duke, Arnold Soboloff, Sandy Ward, Alice Hirson, William Wintersole, James E. Brodhead, Robert Burgos, Jack Stuaffer, Sal Viscuso, Barney McFadden.

This ardent made-for-television movie was promoted as "A very private matter, a very public affair." It dealt with the U.S. military's staunch view (still held at present) that homosexuals are unfit material for service in the armed forces, a discriminatory situation well-known but "accepted" almost unconditionally before this real-life case exposed the matter to media dissection. (It was all the more embarrassing to the military because Matlovich had served three tours of duty in Vietnam, had won the Purple Heart, Bronze Star, etc.)

What made this TV production acceptable in the see-sawing liberality of the 1970s were its basis on a recent real-life case and its two-fold ending. The telefilm concludes with the uncloseted Matlovich being given a general discharge from the U.S. Air Force (a reality which pleased the moral majority). However, the movie notes in a postscript that its subject is currently living in the Washington, D.C. area and is involved in local politics and various civil rights issues (which made Matlovich a quasi-role model for gays).

In the mid-1970s, Sergeant Leonard P. Matlovich (Brad Dourif) is about to be discharged (dishonorably) from the U.S. Air Force for admitting that he is homosexual. Despite great pressures from every avenue, including his own self-doubts, he contests the ruling, wanting to remain in the service. With his attorneys (Frank Converse, David Spielberg, Barra Grant) he contends the validity and legality of the military's theories that a gay military person creates "the possibility of security breaches based on blackmail" and that "the vast majority of Air Force members today would not have the necessary respect for or confidence in a military member known to be a homosexual."

Through a series of flashbacks, Matlovich recalls his strong Catholic upbringing and his inability to explain to his parents (Stephen Elliott, Rue McClanahan) his barely suppressed homosexual longings. To prove his masculinity and to follow in the path of his career military father, he joins the toughest branch of the Air Force and proves his bravery on the battlefields of the Vietnam War. There his best friends are a very heterosexual serviceman (Marc Singer) and kindly Father Veller (William Daniels). When Leonard can no longer hide his growing awareness of his true sexual orientation, he is rebuffed by former friends and military counselors (David Ogden Stier). Finally unable to maintain a hypocritical posture of condoning discrimination against gays ("I had to live with myself as a human being"), he writes a letter in March 1975 challenging the Air Force regulations.

With its jumpy continuity (suggesting several editing chops), *Sergeant Matlovich Vs. the U.S. Air Force* relies on its strong subject matter to carry its dramatic weight. Brad Dourff is earnest in his sincere characterization. However, his angst —authentic and appropriate—does not make for good drama, nor do the unshaded performances of several of the supporting cast; especially Rue McClanahan and Stephen Elliott as his parents, and David Ogden Stiers and Alfred Ryder as bigoted military men. As his buddy, muscular

Marc Singer seems more anxious to be a virile leading man than to shade his performance into one of confusion and fear that his best pal is "that way." As a very talky, educational essay, this telefeature is fine; as entertainment it is dull. Completed in 1977, this controversial TV movie, which has no sexually explicit scenes, was not aired until August 1978.

Daily Variety decided, "Sluggish-moving, superficial drama which has little emotional impact. . . . It's over-loaded with arguments pro and con, but woefully weak on good, solid dramatics. . . . Brad Dourif limns the sergeant with too much restraint." Earl Davis (*Hollywood Reporter*) concurred, "what seriously undermines the evident earnestness of the project is its timidity—you can't tackle certain subjects with an overall air of politeness. . . ."

It should be noted that this movie included the then recently-accepted theory— by some of society at large and psychiatric associations in particular—that homosexuality should no longer be regarded as a mental disease, but rather, considered as an alternative lifestyle.

217. 7 Women (Metro-Goldwyn-Mayer, 1966), color, 87 min. Not rated.

Producer, Bernard Smith; director, John Ford; based on the story "Chinese Finale" by Norah Lofts; screenplay, Janet Green, John McCormick; art directors, George W. Davis, Eddie Imazu; set decorators, Henry Grace, Jack Mills; costumes, Walter Plunkett; makeup, William Tuttle; music, Elmer Bernstein; assistant director, Wingate Smith; sound, Phil Mitchell; special camera effects, J. McMillan Johnson; camera, Joseph La Shelle; editor, Otho S. Lovering.

Cast: Anne Bancroft (Dr. D. R. Cartwright); Sue Lyon (Emma Clark); Margaret Leighton (Agatha Andrews); Flora Robson (Miss Binns); Mildred Dunnock (Jane Argent); Betty Field (Florrie Pether); Anna Lee (Mrs. Russell); Eddie Albert (Charles Pether); Mike Mazurki (Tunga Khan); Woody Strode (Lean Warrior); Jane Chang (Miss Ling); Hans William Lee (Kim); H. W. Gim (Coolie); Irene Tsu (Chinese Girl).

**Anne Bancroft, Sue Lyon, Mildred Dunnock, Margaret Leighton, Eddie Albert
and Betty Field in *7 Women* (1965).**

In cinema history, this mongrel production has two significances: (1) it was John Ford's final theatrical feature and (2) veteran actress Patricia Neal suffered (and survived) several massive strokes during production and was replaced by Anne Bancroft. Beyond that and cinema tastes to one side, the movie proved to be melodramatic claptrap, filled with overwrought bad performances, distracting sound stage outdoor sets, and unremarkable filmmaking. As Pauline Kael (*The New Yorker*) explained, "This picture is more absurd than the deliberate spoof movies, because each cliche character and situation is played in apparent earnest; it's almost deadpan farce." One of the movie's most shrill performances is provided by Margaret Leighton as the middle-aged repressed lesbian who yearns not so subtly for nubile, young Sue Lyon, the latter an in-

ept actress who had played the archetypal nymphette in *Lolita* (1962) and had tempted both sexes in *The Night of the Iguana* (1964), q.v.

In 1935 Mongolia near the Chinese border, a warlord, Tunga Khan (Mike Mazurki) terrorizes the populace. In the midst of the war-torn area is an American mission run by Agatha Andrews (Margaret Leighton), a prim and pseudo-pious spinster. Her staff includes the elder, fawning Jane Argent (Mildred Dunnock), the pregnant, fluttery Florrie Pether (Betty Field) with her hen-pecked teacher husband (Eddie Albert) and young Emma Clark (Sue Lyon). Into their shaky midst comes the new replacement, the cynical Dr. D. R. Cartwright (Anne Bancroft). Her direct methods irritate Agatha, especially when Emma starts admiring this too self-sufficient newcomer. (Agatha chides her charge, "Emma, I've devoted myself to you. I've tried to teach you, to guide you, and you repay me by losing your faith.")

After the Chinese soldiers flee the area, Tunga Khan and his ravaging troops occupy the mission. Cartwright convinces the lustful Tunga to let her deliver Florrie's baby and then offers herself to the tyrant in exchange for the others' safe departure. Once the missionaries have left—with only the antagonistic Agatha not appreciating the sacrifice involved—the doctor slips poison into the drinks she prepares for the warlord and herself.

Howard Thompson (*New York Times*) reported that *7 Women* "gets off to a graphic, arresting start (with some ripe Elmer Bernstein music) [and] tapers off to a stark, bony melodrama of female hysteria and mayhem." *Variety* observed, "It's the theme itself that militates against any more than passing interest. . . ."

Cut from 93 to 87 minutes, *7 Women*, after bad initial word-of-mouth was dumped onto the double-bill marketplace, paired with Rita Hayworth's *The Money Trap*.

218. The Shadow Box (ABC-TV, December 28, 1980), color, 100 min. Not rated.

Producers, Jill Marti, Susan Kendall Newman; director, Paul Newman; based on the play by Michael Cristofer; teleplay, Cristofer; art director, Tom H. John; set decorator, Bill Harp; costumes, Bob Harris Jr., Marie Brown; makeup, Barbara Guedel; music, Henry Mancini; assistant directors, Mel Howard, Alice West; sound, Larry Jost; camera, Adam Holender; editor, Allan Jacobs.

Cast: Joanne Woodward (Beverly); Christopher Plummer (Brian); Valerie Harper (Maggie); James Broderick (Joe); Sylvia Sidney (Felicity Thomas); Melinda Dillon (Agnes); Ben Masters (Mark); Curtiss Marlowe (Steve); John Considine (Interviewer).

The Shadow Box is one of a number of movie projects in which Joanne Woodward has either co-starred with her husband, Paul Newman, or been directed by him. Like their earlier *Rachel, Rachel*

(1968), q.v., and her *Summer Wishes, Winter Dreams* (1973), q.v., homosexual characters play a part in the proceedings. On stage, *The Shadow Box* (1977) had earned its author, Michael Cristofer, both a Tony Award and a Pulitzer Prize. Sadly, what had been touching live drama became detached filmed theatre as a made-for-television movie.

Among several terminal cancer patients at a hospice retreat in California, an interviewer (John Considine) talks with three invalids to analyze their state of mind about their pending deaths. Meanwhile, the trio, who each has a private cottage, has visiting relatives and loved ones with whom to deal. New Jerseyite Joe (James Broderick) must make his wife (Valerie Harper) accept his forthcoming death. He hopes to instill a lasting belief in their son (Curtiss Marlowe) that his dad truly loved him. Cynical, elderly Felicity Thomas (Sylvia Sidney) has a no-nonsense attitude about her fate. However, the wheelchair-bound victim fantasizes about the virtues of a non-present daughter (who actually has abandoned her), instead of appreciating her other child. The latter is the tolerant, but shrinking violet, offspring (Melinda Dillon), who has endured the nagging Felicity for years.

The third subject of the inteview is middle-aged Brian (Christopher Plummer), a writer being tended by his younger lover, Mark (Ben Masters). Suddenly, Brian's alcoholic ex-wife, Beverly (Joanne Woodward) arrives at the facility. Outspoken to a fault, the sophisticated lady hides her concern for Brian under a mask of callous extroversion. "Just think of me as your average tramp," she announces to the perplexed Mark. Then, taking a closer look at her replacement, she tells the uncomfortable man: "You don't look like a faggot. I was expecting one of those clones from Christopher Street." Adapting to her offensive defenses, he retorts, "You'll get used to me. Just think of me as your average pervert." Later, she jibes, "Does he pay you by the month or by how much you put out?" Beverly and Mark eventually relax their vicious sparring, but they cannot forego their roles as (friendly) rivals for Brian's attentions.

Finally, Beverly accepts that Brian is better off having the sensitive Mark as his death bed companion and she resignedly leaves. Before she goes, she cautions the teary-eyed Mark, "One favor you owe him. Don't hurt him. Don't hurt him with your hopes."

Daily Variety rated this production "a rich, engrossing telefilm. . . . [Christopher] Plummer is startling convincing as the supposedly ecstatic man frightened inside. . . . [Ben] Masters' Mark is a shrewd portrayal, solid and well defined. . . ." In contrast, Gail Williams (*Hollywood Reporter*) noted, "[Paul] Newman's direction too often concentrates on the physical and psychic distance between the characters, rather than moving in for revealing close-ups that could have maximized the trenchant impact of the superb acting he evinces."

Interestingly, as written, what gives the Christopher Plummer segment its bite and tenderness is not the interaction between the outwardly calm but inwardly frightened Mark and Brian. Rather, it is the coming-to-terms of their mutual situation by procrastinator Beverly and responsible Brian, both of whom share a love for a man fast moving beyond their reach. For a refreshing change in Hollywood filmmaking, homosexuality is treated here as a human situation not a condition "demanding" exploitation or moralization.

The Shadow Box was filmed at the Salvation Army Camp in Calabasas, California. The TV movie received several Emmy Award nominations: Best Director, Outstanding Drama Special and Best Drama Special Teleplay. One of the producers of this telefilm was Newman's daughter Susan from his first marriage.

219. Sheila Levine Is Dead and Living in New York (Paramount, 1975), color, 113 min. PG-rated.

Producer, Harry Korshak; director, Sidney J. Furie; based on the novel by Gail Parent; screenplay, Kenny Solms; production designer, Fernando Carrere; set decorator, Reg Allen; costumes, Ronald Talsky; music, Michel Legrand; songs: Leo Robin and Ralph Rainger; Hal David and Leon Carr; assistant directors, Gene Marum, Barry R. Steinberg; sound, James Stewart, Ron Cogswell; camera, Donald M. Morgan; editor, Argyle Nelson.

Cast: Jeannie Berlin (Sheila Levine); Roy Scheider (Sam Stoneman); Rebecca Dianna Smith (Kate); Janet Brandt (Bernice); Sid Melton (Manny); Charles Woolf (Wally); Leda Rogers (Agatha); Jack Bernardi (Uncle Herm); Allen Secher (Rabbi); Talley Parker (Rochelle); Jon Miller (Norman); Noble Willingham (Principal); Richard Rasof (Attendant); Evelyn Russell (Miss Burke); Don Carrara (Harold); Sharon Martin Goldman (Melissa); Karen Anders (Aunt Min); Craig Littler (Steve); Sandy Helberg (Artist); John Morgan Evans (Conductor); Charles Walker (Engineer); Charles Arthur (Clerk); Cecilia McBride, Susan Waugh (Typists); Erin Fleming (Girl); Lyle Moraine (Pianist); Sandra Golden, Victor Raphael (Performers).

Frequently, no one is more prejudiced than a recently liberated minority now merging into mainstream society. Such a real-life situation crept (accidentally?) into the misguided *Sheila Levine Is Dead and Living in New York*. This romantic drama was based on Gail Parent's popular novel (1975) which she co-adapted to the screen. Filled with "comedy" overtones, the movie traces the transformation of klutsy Jewish Sheila Levine (Jeannie Berlin), who moves to tough New York City, into a liberated feminist/career woman. In the process, she nabs the hip doctor (Roy Scheider) she has craved since their first meeting in a single's bar.

Lacking charisma, Sheila is attracted to opposites as friends. She rooms with good-looking Kate (Rebecca Dianna Smith), a relatively affluent swinger who leads the good life. Meanwhile, clumsy Sheila plods along at her job (a children's recording company), slowly gaining a sense of self as a woman and an individual. (Her eventual growth leads to career

**Jeannie Berlin and Roy Scheider in *Sheila Levine Is Dead and Living in New York*
(1975).**

success and the interest and capture of the previously disinterested boyfriend.) In moving from being a put-upon outsider to successful, but disparging, member of the majority, Sheila becomes thoughtless and callous in her reaction to the attentions of a co-tenant in her apartment building. Agatha (Leda Rogers) is a lesbian who takes a fancy to Sheila, giving her wistful looks in the hallway and elevators. Uncomfortable with the situation, Sheila impetuously decides to mar her roommate's perfect life—all at Agatha's expense. She informs the gay woman that beautiful Kate is the one she should be focusing on, especially since she has a yen for lesbians. (This is not true, just Sheila being mean, especially at Agatha's expense.)

Vincent Canby (*New York Times*) was annoyed with the screen adaptation which turned the heroine "into a tired Jewish joke. This Sheila is so aggressively naive and dumb . . . that it's quite impossible to believe that even her family could stand her. . . . Watching Sheila schlep from one arbitrary disaster to another in the course of the movie is not funny and it's not moving. It is mere exploitation." A far kinder *Variety* labeled this entry "a very appealing bittersweet romantic drama with comedy . . . Jeannie Berlin's title role performance is outstanding." In passing judgment on the supporting cast, the trade paper stated, "But Leda Rogers is stuck in an awkward role as a neighbor lesbian with a hanker for Berlin; this is the sort of forced caricature-character that ruins a lot of films."

Sheila Levine Is Dead and Living in New York was a box-office misfire, remembered in retrospect only for its satirical, sarcastic title. Three years later, the subject of a non-beautiful Jewish girl in Manhattan finding her self-worth was far better handled in *Girlfriends*, q.v. This movie also presented the heroine with a lesbian acquaintance with whom she must deal (which she does in a far kinder manner). Like *Sheila Levine*, *Girlfriends* employed the gay woman to emphasize the point that its protagonist was not herself lesbian and that her woman-to-woman friendships were strictly platonic.

220. Short Eyes (Paramount, 1977), color, 104 min. R-rated. (a.k.a.: *Slammer*)

Executive producer, Marvin Stuart; producer, Lewis Harris; associate producers, Walker Stuart, Martin Hirsh; director, Robert M. Young; based on the play by Miguel Pinero; screenplay, Pinero; production designer, Joe Babas; set decorator, Pat Prather; costumes, Paul Martino; music, Curtis Mayfield; songs: Mayfield; H.P. Denenberg and Martin Hirsch; assistant director, Robert Colesberry; sound, Bill Daly; camera, Peter Sova; additional camera, Bob Kaylor, Eddie Marritz; editor, Edward Beyer.

Cast: Bruce Davison (Clark Davis); Jose Perez (Juan); Nathan George (Ice); Don Blakely (El Raheem [Johnson]); Shawn Elliott (Paco); Tito Goya (Cupcakes [Julius Micado]); Joe Carberry (Longshore [Charly Murphy]); Kenny Steward (Omar); Bob Maroff (Mr. Nett, the Keeper); Keith Davis (Mr. Brown, the Keeper); Miguel Pinero (Go Go); Willie Hernandez (Cha Cha); Tony De Benedetto (Tony); Bob O'Connell (Captain Allard); Mark Margolis (Mr. Morrison); Richard Matamoros (Gomez); Curtis Mayfield (Pappy); Freddie Fender (Johnny); Harry Baker, Bob Balhatchet, Brodie Barr, Sam Barton, Thommie Blackwell, Richard Robinson Brown, Johnny Barnes, Ted Butler, Yusef Bulos, Carlos Corrasso, George Cox, Richard De Fabees, Nick De Marini, Shelley Desai, Orlando Dole, Charles Douglass, Juan Feliciano, Ernie Fierron, Fred Greene, Luis Guzman, Eddie Earl Hatch, Gerald Jaffe, Donald C. Hawkes, Lee Jines, Sherman Jones, Gordon Keys, Ruben Luciano, Leroy Lessane, Jose Machado, Pedro O'Campo, Ruben Ortiz, Edwin Perez, Rodney Rincon, Joseph Rosario, Ramon Rodriguez, Ronald Salley, Richard Spore, Joe Terra, Roy Thomas, Alberto Vasquez, Andre Waters (Inmates).

With the added realism brought to jailhouse movies by *Riot* (1969), q.v., and to a far lesser extent by *Fortune and Men's Eyes* (1971), q.v., most new Hollywood penitentiary dramas added racial unrest and (forced) homosexual encounters to their plotlines. The stark *Short Eyes* is one of the most naturalistic prison dramas in American moviemaking, portraying realistically the workings and pecking orders of prison society. It is based on the 1974 play by Miguel Pinero, which won the New York Drama Critics Circle Award for Best American Play.

In "The Tombs," the run-down New York City male-prisoner detention center, there is much racial tension. A new prisoner, Clark Davis (Bruce Davison), is introduced into the overcrowded, dirty cell block. Before long, through the grapevine, everyone knows that Davis has been charged with child molestation and is awaiting sentencing. Clark is branded "short eyes" (the nickname given to such despised criminals by their peers). Frightened by his surroundings and the hatred of his fellow convicts, Clark thinks he has found a sympathetic listener in the Puerto Rican, Juan (Jose Perez). He pours out his history of child abuse. His confessions disgust Juan, who, nevertheless, warns Davis to have himself transferred immediately to protective custody if he hopes to survive. Meanwhile, among the other population, the forceful Puerto Rican Paco (Shawn Elliott) attempts to rape the young Cupcakes (Tito Goya), the cell block's pretty boy.

When it appears that Davis may escape prosecution through a technicality, the block's convict council decides his fate. The men seize Clark and one of them cuts Davis's throat. Later, Captain Allard (Bob O'Connell) announces that officially Davis's death will be listed as a suicide, and then he casually mentions that Clark was innocent of the charge made against him. Finally, the once-naive Cupcakes is released on bail, and is told by a streetwise prison pal to forget all about Davis's murder.

The critics were impressed by this brutal drama, filmed within the actual inner city holding jail. Vincent Canby (*New York Times*) pointed out, "the theatrical origins contribute to the claustrophobic atmosphere that is essential to the point of *Short Eyes*, which is about a kind of overcrowding that is the physical equivalent to emotional desperation. There's no way out." *Variety* rated the production "a bold, direct, powerful, often brutal no-holds-barred slice of prison life. It is not a pretty or romantic sight. . . . There is never a doubt that the mostly black and Puerto Rican inmates . . . are criminals, prone to reveling in their past behavior." John Pym (British *Monthly Film Bulletin*) judged that the movie "has a ring of authoritative truth which, for all the film's faults, one cannot ignore. . . . The film's black moral—that in order to retain their sanity, the inmates have to find a scapegoat, someone whom they can persecute— seems in the end in no way commonplace. . . . The faults of the film derive mainly from Pinero's need to underline his moral."

Because of its heightened realism— in which all the prisoners seem to be either homosexual, racist, or generally embittered—and the lack of relief action (i.e. escapes) the very talky *Short Eyes* proved too harrowing to be successful at the box-office. To be noted in the film is playwright/scenarist Miguel Pinero's appearance as Go Go. Respected musician Curtis Mayfield (who wrote the movie's soundtrack score) plays the bespectacled Pappy, while another musician, Freddy Fender, is on hand as Johnny.

221. Sidney Shorr: A Girl's Best Friend (NBC-TV, October 5, 1981), color, 100 min. Not rated.

Producer, George Eckstein; associate producer, Maria Padilla; director, Russ Mayberry; story, Marilyn Cantor Baker; teleplay, Oliver Hailey; art director, Frank Swig; costumes, Bobbie Mannix; makeup, Norman Page; music, Billy Goldenberg; assistant directors, John Anderson, Debra Michaelson; sound, Richard Raguse; camera, Charles G. Arnold; editor, Jim Benson.

Cast: Tony Randall (Sidney Shorr); Lorna Patterson (Laurie Morgan); David Huffman (Jimmy); Kaleena Kiff (Patti Greta); Ann Weldon (Judge Wilcox); John Lupton (Frank); Tom Villard (Eric); Betty Carvalho (Nurse); Tom Ficello (Reese); Daniel Grace (Waiter); Martin Rudy (Mallory).

In "The Odd Couple" (1970–75), Tony Randall had played prim fussbudget Felix Unger to Jack Klugman's sloppy Oscar Madison. The plotline of that TV sitcom stressed repeatedly that these two divorced New Yorkers were quite heterosexual, sharing an apartment only out of economic necessity and convenience. Tony Randall's TV movie *Sidney Shorr: A Girl's Best Friend*, the pilot for his series "Love, Sidney" (1981–83), had quite the reverse premise. Here his character is again compulsively meticulous and excessively proficient in domestic science. However, the added twist is that Sidney is homosexual and the TV movie, in its own coy ways, makes no bones about it. Since this property aired in the pre-AIDS period, it was considered a cute, innovative concept.

The telefeature opens with gloomy New Yorker Sidney Shorr meeting adrift Laurie Morgan (Lorna Patterson), a would-be actress from Wyoming. It is a rainy night and Sidney, a middle-aged art illustrator, invites her to stay over at his eight-room apartment. Appreciative but suspicious of this kind bachelor man, Laurie puzzles out the situation (not yet realizing the implications of the framed photograph of a handsome young man):

Laurie: Don't . . . ah . . . get any ideas.

Sidney: [Bemused] Me? You don't have to worry about me.

Laurie: I'm not worrying about you. I'm asking about you.

Sidney: You don't have to worry.

Laurie: Oh. . . . I get it. . . . Oh, that's good.

Thus having established its premise that Sidney is gay and still grieving for his dead lover, the plot has Laurie move in, the first woman Sidney has lived with since his deceased domineering mother shared the flat. From there, the movie concerns itself with a labored account of Laurie both sprucing up the dreary apartment and her benefactor's life, thus giving Shorr a new reason for living (but not cause enough to find a new boyfriend). Meanwhile, she dates—usually the wrong man—and finds herself pregnant. With Sidney's encouragement, she has the child and Sidney becomes the baby girl's nanny. Five years pass, and Laurie is now a successful soap opera actress—playing a lesbian home wrecker—and falls in love with her director, Jimmy (David Huffman). When Jimmy is offered a better assignment in Los Angeles, he wants Laurie and her daughter (Kaleena Kiff) to go with him. Maternalistic Sidney feels rejected and institutes a custody hearing. The judge (Ann Weldon) decides in Laurie's and Jimmy's favor, explaining delicately that the child has a "right to a family life with a normal father." All ends happily (!), however, when it is agreed that Sidney will visit his friends frequently in California, and that each summer the beloved youngster will come stay with Uncle Sidney for a month.

Reviewing the telefilm/pilot, *Daily Variety* reported, "Much has been made in print about the character's homosexuality but it is a minor point in the film— seemingly a device to assure the viewer that hanky-panky with Patterson in not on his mind. A certain neurotic possessiveness in the character did not automatically endear him to viewers." As to Randall's performance, the trade paper decided, "Randall, on occasion, was a trifle too mannered for complete believability, although his scenes with [Kaleena] Kiff had genuine warmth."

Oliver Hailey received an Emmy Award nomination for his teleplay, based on a story by Marilyn Cantor Baker, the daughter of famed comedian, Eddie Cantor. When the TV series, "Love, Sidney" premiered on October 28, 1981, Swoosie Kurtz had inherited the role of Laurie, while her daughter was still played by Ka-

leena Kiff. In the teleseries which lasted for two seasons on NBC-TV, a smart viewer might infer that bachelor Sidney was gay, but the scripts never stated that Shorr was homosexual. In fact, his character seemed to have been neutralized almost totally.

222. Silkwood (Twentieth Century-Fox, 1983), color, 131 min. R-rated.

Executive producers, Buzz Hirsch, Larry Cano; producers, Mike Nichols, Michael Hausman; associate producers, Joel Tuber, Tom Stovall; director, Nichols; screenplay, Nora Ephron, Alice Arlen; production designer, Patrizia Von Brandenstein; art director, Richard Janes; set decorators, Derek Hill, Dennis Peeples; costumes, Ann Roth; music, Georges Delerue; assistant directors, Michael Hausman, Tuber; sound, Larry Jost; camera, Miroslav Ondricek; editor, Sam O'Steen.

Cast: Meryl Streep (Karen Silkwood); Kurt Russell (Drew Stephens); Cher (Dolly Pelliker); Craig T. Nelson (Winston); Diana Scarwid (Angela); Fred Ward (Morgan); Ron Silver (Paul Stone); Charles Hallahan (Earl Lapin); Josef Sommer (Max Richter); Sudie Bond (Thelma Rice); Henderson Forsythe (Quincy Bissell); E. Katherine Kerr (Gilda Schultz); David Strathairn (Wesley); Bruce McGill (Mace Hurley); J. C. Quinn (Curtis Schultz); Kent Broadhurst (Carl); Richard Hamilton (Georgie); Les Lannom (Jimmy); M. Emmet Walsh (Walt Yarborough); Graham Jarvis (Union Meeting Doctor); Ray Baker (Pete Dawson); Bill Cobbs (Man in Lunchroom); Norm Colvin (Zachary); Haskell Kraver (Ham); Kathie Dean (Stewardess); Gary Grubbs (Randy Fox); Susan McDaniel, Tana Hensley, Anthony Fernandez (Karen's Children); Betty Harper (May Bissell); Tess Harper (Linda Dawson); Anthony Heald (2nd Union Meeting Doctor); Nancy Hopton, Betty King (Nurses); Dan Lindsey (Man at Fence); John Martin (Man with Flashlight); Will Patton (Joe); Vern Porter (Bill Charlton); Christopher Saylors (Buddy); Don Slaton (Man in Moonsuit); James Rebhorn, Michael Bond, Tom Stovall (Los Alamos Doctor).

Inspired by *Norma Rae* (1979) and *The China Syndrome* (1979), *Silkwood* used the real-life case of Karen Silkwood (1946–1974) as a basis for its fictional adaptation. The movie proved to be a grip-

Cher in *Silkwood* (1983).

ping drama, as it portrays a worker's life-and-death struggle to make corporate America and, in turn, the government care about death-threatening working conditions in the work environment. In the midst of this heady drama, a subplot dealt with the straight heroine's lesbian roommate, played nonchalantly and effectively by Cher.

In a small Oklahoma town during the

early 1970s, Karen Silkwood (Meryl Streep), whose children by a prior relationship live with their father in Texas, is employed at the Kerr-McGee plutonium processing plant. There, her flippant manner causes problems with management. She shares a house with two fellow workers: her lover, Drew Stephens (Kurt Russell), and the lesbian Dolly Pelliker (Cher). One day on the job Karen is exposed to radiation, but testing results indicate the dosage was within "acceptable" limits. Later, she is transferred to another department of the company where she discovers her sexually harassing boss (Craig T. Nelson) is readjusting equipment designed to find improperly processed nuclear reactor fuel rods. As her awareness of worker rights and plant dangers grows, she joins in union activities. As such, she is among the group testifying in Washington D.C. in front of the Atomic Energy Commission. During this trip, she starts an affair with labor organizer, Paul Stone (Ron Silver). Although the relationship does not last, Drew, already angry at her union activities, moves out.

The employees vote in the union at the plant and Karen is viewed increasingly with suspicion by the plant's management. She is the victim of additional contamination scares, including one in which her house is stripped clean. By now, she is convinced that she is being deliberately poisoned by angered plant executives. She, Drew (with whom she has reconciled) and Dolly (who may or may not have been forced into revealing Karen's investigations to the company) go to Los Alamos for medical examinations. There, they are told their radiation levels are still "acceptable. On her way to meet a *New York Times* reporter to discuss the X-ray tampering episode at Kerr-McGee, Karen dies in a mysterious road accident—one that is never resolved.

David Denby (*New York* magazine) felt that "The filmmakers have created an entire way of life, first establishing the milieu and the characters and then letting the story grow out of it. . . . And Cher is right, too, as the joking, melancholy lesbian, Dolly. . . . She's very touching as a lonely woman who tags along with a sexually entranced couple." *Variety* agreed, "Cher also has some wonderful moments, none better than in an intense argument scene with Streep which turns into a lovely reconciliation. Diana Scarwid is low-keyed but still outrageous as Cher's lover, and the quartet's domestic trials provide some welcome comic relief to the otherwise heavy drama."

According to Sheila Benson (*Los Angeles Times*), "As a nuclear-age horror story, *Silkwood* is both haunting and deeply disturbing." but it "fails in its most crucial obligation as gripping drama or first-rate storytelling. . . . [The] film's most real performance is not Streep's . . . but Cher's, touching and funny as Karen's longing, lonely lesbian roommate. Wide-ranging and accurate as Cher's performance is, we're never allowed to get close to it or to her, not emotionally, nor even by way of close-ups." On the negative side were comments by Richard Schickel (*Time*): "rarely has the desperation to square inspiration myth with provable, nonlibelous reportage been more apparent. And rarely has the failure to do so been more dismaying."

Putting to one side the film's rationale for making the lesbian character the heroine's possible betrayerd, *Silkwood*'s depiction of Dolly Pelliker is very refreshing, casual and non-exploitive of her alternative lifestyle. This depiction is greatly buoyed by Cher's understated performance as affection-hungry Dolly. In her relatively brief scenes, Cher makes a mark with her naturalness: schlepping around in oversized sweat shirts and scruffy jeans, putting up with her dull-witted mortuary beautician friend (Diana Scarwid), and admitting to missing Karen's boyfriend more than Karen does.

Silkwood grossed $17,825,000 in distributors' domestic film rentals. It received five Academy Award nominations:

Best Actress (Meryl Streep; Shirley Mac-Laine won for *Terms of Endearment*); Best Supporting Actress (Cher; Linda Hunt won for *The Year of Living Dangerously*); Director (James L. Brooks won for *Terms of Endearment*); Best Screenplay, Written Directly for the Screen (*Tender Mercies* won); Best Editing (*The Right Stuff* won).

223. Slammer Girls (Lightning Pictures, 1987), color, 80 min. R-rated. (a.k.a.: *The Big Slammer*)

Producer, Chuck Vincent; associate producer, Jeanne O'Grady; director, Vincent; screenplay, Craig Horrall, Vincent, Rick Marx, Larue Watts; additional dialogue, Watts; costumes, Eddie Heath; makeup, Eva Polyka; music, Ian Shaw, Kai Joffe; assistant directors, Bill Slobodian, John Weidner; camera, Larry Revne; editor, Marc Ubell [Chuck Vincent].

Cast: Devon Jenkin (Melody Campbell); Jeff Eagle (Raquel [Harry Wiener]); Jane Hamilton [Veronica Hart] (Miss Crabapples); Ron Sullivan [Henri Pachard] (Governor Caldwell); Tally Brittany [Chanel] (Candy Treat); Darcy Nychols (Tank); Stasia Micula (Mosquito); Sharon Cain (Rita); Beth Broderick (Abigail); Sharon Kelly (Professor); Kim Kafkaloff (Ginny); Philip Campanaro (Gary); Michael Hentzman (Russell); Louis Bonanno (Cabby); Jane Dorskey (Jailer); Sheila Schick (Susan); Peter Rado (Sergeant Santini); Captain Haggerty (Sally); David Reingold (Aide); Bill Slobodian (Priest); Scott Baker (Doctor); John Boyd (Conductor); Frank Manceso (Cop); Marla Machent (Hooker); Donna Davidge (Cauliflower); Joel Nagle (Orderly); Beatrice Lynn (Potato); Carol Ford (Druggie Con); Chris McNami (Obese Con); Isabelle Cullinen (Lonely Con); Jacklyn Sydney (Tough Con); Larry Catanzano (Laundry Supervisor); Dave Mazzeo (Reporter); Lloyd T. Williams, Ron Chalon, Jay Lanno, Andy Kristie (Guards); Adam Fried, Joe Prichard (Laundry Men); Sara Warrington (Little Girl); Sheryl Marshall, Scarlet Smith, Carol Cross (Shower Girls); Steve Lazaroff, Rick Kessler, Michael Knight, Gary Zelman, Joel Von Ornsteiner, Todd Green (Guards).

Variety judged the R-rated, satirical *Slammer Girls* "silly rather than funny." This softcore porno farce is occasionally amusing, but often just boring. Compared to the chauvinistic movies it hopes to sati-rize, there is comparatively scant nudity or raunchy details—just enough to keep some viewers awake.

Shortly after Jackson Caldwell (Ron Sullivan) becomes the new state governor, he is shot by a mysterious blonde woman. After a police dragnet, the prime suspect, the virginal Melody Campbell (Devon Jenkin), is captured by the law on her wedding night. She is found guilty and sentenced to twenty years in the slammer. The prison's recently-appointed administrator announces to the media, "Miss Campbell will get no special privileges while I'm warden. She will be brutally abused like all the other prisoners!"

The scared Melody is inducted into the dormitory bullpen, full of toughies, weirdos, and life's burn-outs. "Welcome to death's door," says one hospitable inmate. Before long, the innocent Melody is dragged by her peers to the showers, the favorite recreational activity for the convicts. Meanwhile, reporter Harry Weiner (Jeff Eagle) goes undercover as a convict named Raquel, intent on discovering if and why Melody shot the Governor. Melody survives brutal treatment by the sadistic Miss Crabapples (Jane Hamilton), the head matron. Later, the abused Melody, who has been in and out of solitary several times, joins in a prison breakout, which also includes Harry/Raquel. However, Melody is caught and when brought before the Governor, confesses she did shoot him—she is his illegitimate daughter whom he abandoned years ago. Now that everything is resolved, Melody and Harry marry at the prison and plan to co-author a book about her prison experiences.

Ignoring the strained humor, faulty satire and atrocious acting of this film, there are some moments of inspired lunacy within *Slammer Girls'* satire of prison genre conventions. For example, whenever there is a dull moment on the cell block, one of the inmates is sure to pipe up, "Let's go to the showers. Let's go to the showers."

Made in 1985, *Slammer Girls* did not

find release until 1987. Some of the cast were recruited from softcore porno filmmaking: e.g. Jane Hamilton and Ron Sullivan.

224. **Some Call It Loving** (CineGlobe, 1973), color, 103 min. R-rated.

Producer, James B. Harris; associate producer, Ramzi Thomas; director, Harris; based on the story "Sleeping Beauty" by John Collier; screenplay, Harris; costumes, Jax; music/music director, Richard Hazard; camera, Mario Tosi; editor, Paul Jasiukonis.

Cast: Zalman King (Robert); Carol White (Scarlett); Tisa Farrow (Jennifer); Richard Pryor (Jeff); Veronica Anderson (Angelika); Logan Ramsey (Doctor); Brandy Herred (Cheerleader); Ed Rue (Mortician); Pat Priest (Nurse); Joseph DeMeo (Bartender).

This oblique independent movie is a reworking of "The Sleeping Beauty" story, with its story set in California. As updated and enshrouded in romantic metaphors, the picture finds the idealistic Robert (Zalman King), a jazz saxophonist, coming across a sleeping young woman, Jennifer (Tisa Farrow), at a carnival sideshow. He purchases her and then awakens her, bringing her back to the spacious mansion where he lives. There, its owner, Scarlett (Carol White), is erotically aroused by the newcomer while continuing her ambiguous relationship with Robert. (Scarlett also has a hankering for Angelica [Veronica Anderson], the house maid.) Meandering into the complex situation, is Robert's dying friend, Jeff (Richard Pryor), high on drink and drugs. Eventually, the brooding Robert takes the again comatose Jennifer back to a carnival where he puts her back on display for the curious. Was it all a dream, and if so, his or hers?

A. H. Weiler (*New York Times*) had little patience with this "rambling, contemporary fable that is merely pretentious." He observed of the cast, that Zalman King "cannot be faulted for appearing confused most of the time" and that Carol White is "slightly imperious and sexy as the seductress" and Tisa Farrow "is pretty, but essentially juvenile, as the innocent,

awakened beauty." *Variety* remained undecided, noting, "Some may call it obtuse and quirky and others insightful." As to the players, the trade paper found "Carol White sharply omnipresent as the lesbo or bisexual head of the house."

225. **Some of My Best Friends Are . . .** (American International, 1971), color, 109 min. R-rated. (a.k.a.: *The Bar*)

Executive producer, Joseph Rhodes; producers, Marty Richards, John Lauricella; director/screenplay, Mervyn Nelson; art director, Ray Menard; set decorators, Nino Nocellino, Frank Schoem; costumes, Andy Greenhut; makeup, Gudron Holt; music, Gordon Rose; assistant directors, Steve Marshall, Elliott Tuckerman; sound, Robert Colbert; camera, Tony Mitchell; editors, Angelo Ross, Richard Cadenas.

Cast: Alan Dellay (Pete Thomas); Nick Denoia (Phil); Tom Bade (Tanny); David Baker (Clint); Paul Blake (Kenny); Gary Campbell (Terry Nabour); Carleton Carpenter (Miss Untouchable); Robert Christian (Eric); Candy Darling (Karen/Harry); Jeff David (Leo); Dan Drake (Lloyd); David Drew (Howard Wilkins); Jim Enzel (Gable); Tommy Fiorello (Ernie); Fannie Flagg (Helen); Joe George (Al); Gil Gerard (Scott); Uva Harden (Michel); Rue McClanahan (Lita Joyce); Hector Martinez (Jose); Peg Murray (Mrs. Nabour); Dick O'Neil (Tim Holland); Larry Reed (Louis Barone); Gary Sandy (Jim Paine); Lou Steele (Barrett Hartman); Clifton Steere (Giggling Gertie); Sylvia Sims (Sadie); Joe Taylor (Nebraska); Ben Yaffee (Marvin Hocker); and: Rita Bennett, Mona Crawford, Mary Love, Alisson Russo, Karolyn Russo, Bill Tarman, Seymour Weinstein.

"An evening with the homos; well-made for the trade." (*Variety*)

Christmas Eve at Manhattan's Blue Jay Bar, a gay establishment owned by an organized crime syndicate which exploits its customers. As the help finish decorating the club, various customers arrive. Among them are commercial artist Terry Nabour (Gary Campbell), who is starting an affair with Scott (Gil Gerard), an airline pilot; married man Barrett Hartman (Lou Steele), who has his Swiss ski instructor

Ben Yaffee, Uva Harden, Lou Steele and Gary Sandy in *Some of My Best Friends Are. . .* **(1971).**

lover, Michel (Uva Harden), in tow; Howard Wilkins (David Drew), a very repressed church accompanist; a seemingly shy spinster Karen (Candy Darling), who is really Harry, a transvestite; and the elegant, aging Miss Untouchable (Carleton Carpenter), who lives in a cynical, private dream world. As the hectic evening proceeds, many of the patrons and employees undergo several crises. Terry's mother (Peg Murray) arrives and tells her offspring that, as a gay man, he is no longer welcome at home, which pushes him actively into a relationship with Scott. Sadie (Sylvia Sims), the club hostess/cook, proves that beneath her tough talk she is sentimental ("You boys make me feel just like a queen"). Aging Lita Joyce (Rue McClanahan), a bitchy fag hag, barges into the premises, furious that Scott could drop her for another man. A love-hungry waiter (Nick De Noia), despairing of finding his Prince Charming, is cheered up by the patrons who chant "We Believe in Fairies." Nebraska (Joe Taylor), a newcomer in town, finds romance at the bar. Karen/Harry is beaten up in the men's room by a tough hustler (Gary Sandy) who insists he has gay sex only for the money. Meanwhile, Barrett, who has been debating whether he should leave his wife, wavers back and forth. He leaves the Blue Jay, but then changes his mind. However, by now the bar has closed for the night. When last seen, the depressed Michel (who insists "Facing death does not take courage. Two men facing a life together does") has gotten maudlinly drunk and sunk to the floor in a stupor.

Vincent Canby (*New York Times*), who described this film as "a very sad gay movie," decided that the director/scenarist Mervyn Nelson "shares with his characters not only a large amount of boozy self-pity, but also the sort of romanticism that permits characters to define themselves—without irony—in the cliches of old-fashioned Hollywood soap opera." Canby observed, "Not all the performances are bad, but I find it curious that the only decent performances are given by women."

John Russell Taylor (British *Monthly Film Bulletin*) advised, "Possibly *Some of My Best Friends Are* . . . is seriously meant as a contribution to human understanding of the homosexual's problems (it has, somewhat alarmingly, been taken as such by some rather distinguished American critics). But whatever its intentions, it comes over as so ludicrously inadequate that it looks most like a belated and ineffectual attempt to climb on to the Gay Lib band wagon without actually alienating anyone else. . . . In comparison, even *Boys in the Band* looks like a masterpiece of subtlety and deep thought. And anyway, it was a lot more fun."

Within the period 1970–1971, Hollywood released *The Boys in the Band*, *Fortunes and Men's Eyes* and *Some of My Friends* Are . . . *Boys* and *Friends*, in particular, sought to examine/exploit gay stereotypes, which even by then were dated cliches (as was the expression which begat the film's title). As Vito Russo (*The Celluloid Closet*, 1987) noted in retrospect, "much of the fascination of . . . [*Friends* resides] in the portrait it paints of the classic pre-liberation bar scene. . . . Yet the film never makes concrete connections between self-hatred, political oppression and apathy." Russo concluded that *Friends* shows that "Gay life on the town turns out to be a bunch of disenfranchised losers huddled around a blowtorch for the warmth and holiday spirit they cannot get from the families who have forsaken them. The film is epic tack."

Some of My Best Friends Are . . . was filmed at New York City's Zodiac Bar. Ironically, ex-MGM star, Carleton Carpenter, the one name in the cast, had scarcely any dialogue (beyond the word "Noel"). To be noted among the players is Fannie Flagg as the wistful hat check girl; she later wrote the novel on which *Fried Green Tomatoes* (1991), q.v., was based.

226. Something for Everyone

(National General Pictures), color, 1970. R-rated. (a.k.a.: *The Rook*. British release title: *Black Flowers for the Bride*)

Producer, John P. Flaxman; director, Harold Prince; based on the novel *The Cook* by Harry Kressing; screenplay, Hugh Wheeler; art director, Otto Pischinger; set decorator, Herta Pischinger; costumes, Florence Klotz; makeup, Raimund Stangl; music, John Kander; assistant director, Eberhard Schroder; sound, John Strauss; camera, Walter Lassally; editor, Ralph Rosenblum.

Cast: Angela Lansbury (Countess Herthe von Ornstein); Michael York (Conrad Ludwig); Anthony Corlan (Heluth von Ornstein); Heidelinde Weis (Annaliese Pleschke); Eva-Maria Meineke (Mrs. Pleschke); John Gill (Mr. Pleschke); Jane Carr (Lotte von Ornstein); Despo (Bobby); Wolfried Lier (Klaus); Walter Janssen (Father Georg); Klaus Havenstein (Rudolph); Enzi Fuchs (Waitress); Erland Erlandson (Schoenfeld); Hans Possenbacher (Carl); Hilde Weisner (Princess Palamir); Hela Gruel (Cook); Marius Aicher (Scullery Boy); Mogens von Gadow (Station Master); James F. Hurley (General); Ernst Zeigler (Elderly Man); and: Erik Jelde.

Based on a 1965 novel, *Something for Everyone* is a dark black comedy steeped in traditional middle-European sophisticated attitudes towards unorthodox lifestyles. Directed in an overly leisurely manner by Broadway's Hal Prince, the movie proved too rarified for American consumption outside of urban centers. What viewers found most shocking in the storyline was not the depiction of grasping duplicity and murder, but that the manipulative lead figure was bisexual.

While bicycling through the Bavarian Alps, young, handsome Conrad Ludwig (Michael York) takes notes of Castle Ornstein. The social climber is anxious to become a household member and share in its impressive lifestyle. Ludwig thinks nothing of killing the footman, Rudolph (Klaus Havenstein)—pushing him in front of a train—in order to take his place at the castle. There he hopes to ingratiate himself with the Countess Herthe von Ornstein (Angela Lansbury), not knowing that

Angela Lansbury and Michael York in *Something for Everyone* **(1970).**

she is financially shaky. In turn, Conrad
sets about seducing each member of the
peculiar household. When the butler,
Klaus (Wolfried Lier) observes a liaison
between Conrad and Helmuth (Anthony
Corlan), the Countess's son, he threatens
to tell the young man's mother. Ludwig
retaliates by denouncing the butler as a
Neo-Nazi, and the man is forced to leave
town. Later, Conrad arranges for passive
Helmuth to wed Annaliese (Heidelinde
Weis), the offspring of rich Americans, as

a mean of restoring the von Ornstein fortune. After the union, Annaliese finds her husband and Ludwig embracing. To silence her, Conrad kills her and her family in a contrived car accident. However, Lotte (Jane Carr), the Countess's plump daughter, witnesses this maneuver. As a result, she forces Conrad to marry her, ending his hopes of wooing the Countess.

T. E. Kalem (*Time*) was put off by this narrative of "sadistic mayhem" in which "decadence functions as a backdrop to a silly operetta." Larry Cohen (*Hollywood Reporter*) was more favorably inclined to this film full of a'devastating, throat-cutting sense of humor. . . . In a part that necessitates . . . an almost mystical sexual charisma, Michael York is properly charming and sinister. . . . Anthony Corlan is also exceptionally good as the tormented homosexual son; it is a brooding, delicate interpretation of considerable sensitivity and shouldn't be overlooked next to Miss Carr's hysterically threatening presence." *Variety* had mixed feelings about this "offbeat tale of horror," deciding that Angela Lansbury's "from-the-start Bette Davis approach eventually helps turn the film into camp." As to York, the trade paper assessed that his "bearing and acting, though somewhat limited, herein fits the part like a glove."

Location work for *Something for Everyone* was accomplished in Fussen, Bavaria and Saltzburg, Austria. York would play another bisexual in *Cabaret* (1972), q.v. To a far lesser effect, the theme of the grasping bisexual manipulator would be replayed by Drew Barrymore in *Poison Ivy* (1992), q.v.

227. Spartacus (Universal, 1960), color, 196 min. Not rated.

Executive producer, Kirk Douglas; producer, Edward Lewis; directors, Stanley Kubrick, (uncredited) Anthony Mann; based on the novel by Howard Fast; screenplay, Dalton Trumbo; production designer, Alexander Golitzen; art director, Eric Orbom; set decorators, Russell A. Gausman, Julia Heron; costumes, Bill Thomas, J. Arlington Valles; makeup, Bud Westmore; music, Alex North; assistant director, Marshall Green; sound, Waldon O. Watson, Joe Lapis, Murray Spivack, Ronald Pierce; camera, Russell Metty; additional camera, Clifford Stine; editor, Robert Lawrence.

Cast: Kirk Douglas (Spartacus); Laurence Olivier (Marcus Licinius Crassus); Tony Curtis (Antoninus); Jean Simmons (Varinia); Charles Laughton (Gracchus); Peter Ustinov (Lentulus Batiatus); John Gavin (Julius Caesar); Nina Foch (Helena Glabrus); Herbert Lom (Tigranes); John Ireland (Crixus); John Dall (Glabrus); Charles McGraw (Marcellus); Joanna Barnes (Claudia Marius); Woody Strode (Draba); Harold J. Stone (David); Peter Brocco (Ramon); Paul Lambert (Gannicus); Bob Wilke (Guard Captain); Nick Dennis (Dionysius); John Hoyt (Caius, a Roman Officer); Frederick Worlock (Laelius); Dayton Lummis (Symmachus); Lili Valenty (Old Crone); Jill Jarmyn (Julia); Jo Summers, Autumn Russell, Kay Stewart, Lynda Williams, Louise Vincent (Slave Girls); James Griffith (Otho); Joe Haworth (Marius); Dale Van Sickel (Trainer); Vinton Haworth (Metallius); Carleton Young (Herald); Hallene Hill (Beggar Woman); Paul Burns (Fimbria); Leonard Penn (Garrison Officer); Harry Harvey Jr., Eddie Parker, Herold Perkins (Slave Leaders); Dick Crockett, Harvey Parry, Rod Normond, Larry Perron, Carey Loftin (Guards); Bob Morgan, Reg Parton, Tom Steele, Aaron Saxon, Wally Rose (Gladiators); Ken Terrell, Boyd "Red" Morgan (Ad Libs); Otto Malde (Roman General); Bub Burns, Seamon Glass, George Robotham, Stubby Kruger (Pirates); Chuck Courtney, Russ Saunders, Valley Keene, Tap Canutt, Joe Canutt, Wayne Van Horn, Brad Harris, Jerry Brown, Chuck Hayward, Buff Brady, Cliff Lyons, Rube Schaffer (Soldiers); Ted de Corsia, Arthur Batanides, Robert Stevenson (Legionnaires); Terence de Marney (Major Domo).

When first released in 1960, *Spartacus* was heralded as a vivid spectacle. Its saga of a Thracian slave (Kirk Douglas) who spurs a massive revolt in first century B.C. among the slaves against their Roman masters, was pronounced more intelligent than the multi Oscar-winning *Ben-Hur* (1959), q.v., then the benchmark of Hollywood Biblical epics. At the time, it was considered daring to allow Dalton Trumbo, blacklisted during the film indus-

Tony Curtis and Laurence Olivier in *Spartacus* (1960).

try's 1950s anti-Communist witch hunt, to use his real name in the movie's credits. Made on a $12 million budget, *Spartacus* grossed $10.3 in just distributors' domestic film rentals. It won four Academy Awards: Best Supporting Actor (Peter Ustinov); Best Cinematography—Color; Best Art Direction—Set Decoration: Color; Best Costumes: Color. It was nominated for two additional Oscars: Best Scoring of a Dramatic or Comedy Picture (*Exodus* won); Best Editing (*The Apartment* won).

In the flurry of original distribution, little was mentioned about a pivotal scene cut from release prints of *Spartacus*. This scene provided the rationale for why Marcus Crassus (Laurence Olivier), a Roman patrician and grasping politician, had such a fascination for his poet slave, Antoninus (Tony Curtis). In addition, it explained why the latter disappears suddenly from the storyline (later turning up at the war camp of Spartacus the gladiator), and why Marcus Crassus is thereafter so

vengeful against his former slave, pitting Antoninus against Spartacus in a gladiatorial bout, and decreeing the winner (which turns out to be Spartacus) shall be crucified. The deleted footage showed the epicene Marcus Crassus bathing with his handsome new slave servant on hand to give him a back massage. Their discussion was about tastes, on the surface, of foods, but, on a deeper level, really of sexual proclivities:

Marcus: Do you eat oysters?

Antoninus: When I have them, master.

Marcus: Do you eat snails?

Antoninus: No, master.

Marcus: Do you consider the eating of oysters to be moral and the eating of snails immoral?

Antoninus: No, master.

Marcus: Of course not. It is all a matter of taste.

Antoninus: Yes, master.

Marcus: And taste is not the same as appetite and, therefore, not a question of morals is it?

Antoninus: It could be argued so, master.

Marcus: . . . my noble Antoninus, my taste includes both snails and oysters.

Before Marcus, who now gazes outward towards Rome, can complete his thesis on the need for everyone to be loyal to the Eternal City and its noble leaders—even to self-abasement—Antoninus has disappeared. He had caught his master's drift and wanted no part of a literal master-and-slave relationship.

While assembling the 1960 release print, deletions were made to appease industry censors, especially the Legion of Decency which threatened to condemn the picture if changes were not made. Thus some of the gorier gladiator combat footage, as well as more graphics bits of battlefield carnage, etc. were excised as well as the highly-controversial sexual discussion between Marcus Crassus and Antoninus. Then in 1990, when Robert A. Harris et al restored *Spartacus* to its original print quality and running time (adding about ten minutes), it was deemed imperative for authenticity to include the oysters-and-snails-footage. Because the soundtrack to that sequence had not survived, it was necessary to re-dub the lines. Tony Curtis did his lines, while Anthony Hocking was hired to repeat the dialogue of Laurence Olivier who had died in 1989.

Entertainment Weekly rated the restored version (for theatrical and later home video release) an A-, noting: "what counts isn't so much the addition of two or three meekly risque scenes as the stupendous new 70mm print that's been unveiled for the occasion. The images now have a golden, surreal majesty." F. X. Feeney (*Movieline*) decided "The seductive bath scene between Olivier and the young slave played by Tony Curtis, seen here in the prime of his blue-eyed beauty, is a vital counterpoint to the love story unfolding between Spartacus and the slave girl Varinia (Jean Simmons); without, Crassus' later attempt to have Varinia all to himself feels false and melodramatic—we lose all concrete sense that his hatred of Spartacus conceals a fierce attraction."

228. Stir Crazy (Columbia, 1980), color, 111 min. R-rated.

Executive producer, Melville Tucker; producer, Hannah Weinstein; associate producer, Francois deMenil; director, Sidney Poitier; screenplay, Bruce Jay Friedman; production designer, Alfred Sweeney; costumes, Patricia Edwards; makeup, Richard Cobos; music, Tom Scott; songs, Michael Masser and Randy Goodrum; Scott and Rob Preston; choreographer, Scott Salmon; assistant directors, Daniel J. McCauley, Joseph Moore, Don Wilkerson; stunt coordinator, Mickey Gilbert; sound, Glenn Anderson; camera, Fred Schuler; editor, Harry Keller.

Cast: Gene Wilder (Skip Donahue); Richard Pryor (Harry Monroe); Georg Stanford Brown (Rory Schultebrand); JoBeth Williams (Meredith); Miguel Angel Suarez (Jesus Ramirez); Craig T. Nelson (Deputy Ward Wilson); Barry Corbin (Warden Walter Beatty); Charles Weldon (Blade); Nicholas Coster (Warden Henry Sampson); Joel Brooks (Len Garber); Jonathan Banks (Jack Graham); Erland Van Lidth De Jeude (Grossberger); Lee Purcell (Susan); Karmin Murcelo (Theresa Ramirez); Franklyn Ajaye (Young Man in Hospital); Estelle Omens (Mrs. R.H. Broache); Cedrick Hardman (Big Mean); Henry Kingi (Ramopn); Pamela Poitier (Cook's Helper); Alvin Ing (Korean Doctor); Joseph Massengale (Ceasar Geronimo); Herman Poppe (Alex); Luis Avalos (Chico); Esther Sutherland (Sissie); James Oscar Lee (Kicker); Rod McCary (Minister); Claudia Cron (Joy); Bill Bailey (Announcer); Donna Benz (Nancy); Grand Bush (Big Mean's Sidekick); Thomas Moore (Judge): Donna Hansen (Mrs. Sampson); Gwen Van Dam (Mrs. Beatty); Herb Armstrong (County Jail Guard); Herbert Hirschman (Man at Dinner Party); Don Circle (Bank Teller); Kenneth Menard (Repairman); Billy Beck (Flycatching Prisoner); Lewis Van Bergen (Guard).

Gene Wilder and Richard Pryor had enjoyed great success with *Silver Streak* (1977), leading them to reunite for this prison genre spoof, directed by Sidney Poitier. Wacky, illogical and excessive, it poked fun at the conventions of big house dramas, including homosexuality behind bars.

Gene Wilder, Richard Pryor and Gene Earle in *Stir Crazy* (1980).

Aspiring actor Harry Monroe (Richard Pryor) and determined playwright Skip Donahue (Gene Wilder) lose their jobs. The two abandon New York City to try their professional luck in California. En route, they stop in a small town where they become involved innocently in a bank robbery and are sentenced to 125 years in jail. Once at Glenboro State Prison, the duo must adapt to the rough inmates in their cell block: ranging from dominating Jack Graham (Jonathan Banks), to homosexual Rory Schultebrand (Georg Stanford Brown) and to oversized mass murderer, Grossberger (Erland Van Lidth de Jeude).

Because Skip demonstrates a skill in riding the mechanical bull owned by Warden Beatty (Barry Corbin), he is entered in the intra-prison rodeo competition. Harry, Rory and the enterprising Jesus Ramirez (Miguel Angel Suarez) manage to become part of Skip's rodeo crew, leading to their escape. While making good their getaway, Skip and Harry learn that the actual bank robbers have been caught.

Many of the standard prison conventions are lampooned in hit-or-miss style within the film, including newcomers' fear of being raped. There are several scenes in the comedy of Pryor and Wilder "coping" with the very gay inmate (Georg Stanford Brown), who has a yen for Pryor.

David Ansen (*Newsweek*) found *Stir Crazy* "only intermittently funny" blaming scripter Bruce Jay Friedman: "he's trying for a formula film and can't land on the right formula. Is it a buddy movie, a caper comedy, a parody of prison films, an urban-cowboy neo-Western, a New York vs. Sun Belt comedy?" David Denby (*New York*), unimpressed with the "disappointingly routine slastick" found one highlight, "Walking down a row of cells filled with tough blacks cons, Pryor, terrified of sexual assault, says to Wilder, 'Gotta get bad,' and he pulls shoulders up and eases the rest of his body into a snaky, loose-hipped con's walk. As Wilder falls into a spastic white man's imitation of him, the movie achieves its one original moment." John Coleman (*New Statesman*) in approving of many of the cast's performances, noted that George Stanford Brown was "excellent . . . as an amiably importuante gay inmate" and particularly liked the cell scene in which the mass murderer sings "Down in the Valley" while Pryor casually helps Brown wind his wool.

The unsubtle *Stir Crazy* earned $58,364,420 in distributors' domestic film rentals.

229. The Strange One (Columbia, 1957), 100 min. Not rated. (British release title: *End As a Man*)

Producer, Sam Spiegel; director, Jack Garfein; based on the novel and play *End As a Man* by Calder Willingham; screenplay, Willingham; art director, Joseph C. Wright; costumes, Willis A. Hanchett; makeup, Robert E. Jiras; music/music director, Kenyon Hopkins; assistant directors, Arthur Steckler, Jack Grossberg; sound, Edward Johnstone; camera, Burnett Guffey; additional camera, Clifford Poland; editor, Sidney Katz.

Cast: Ben Gazzara (Jocko De Paris); Pat Hingle (Harold Knoble); [Peter] Mark Richman (Cadet Colonel Corger); Arthur Storch (Simmons); Paul E. Richards (Cockroach [Perrin McKee]); Larry Gates (Major Avery); Clifton James (Colonel Ramey); Geoffrey Horne (Georgie Avery); James Olson (Roger B. Gatt); Julie Wilson (Rosebud); George Peppard (Robert Marquales).

"*The Strange One* offers a somewhat different story of life in a military academy in that it has homosexual overtones. . . . Although nothing offensive is shown, two of the characters, mainly through dialogue, make their homosexual tendencies clear." (*Harrison's Reports*)

Calder Willingham adapted his novel *End as a Man* (1947) into a Broadway play (1953) which ran for 137 performances. Several of the cast (Ben Gazzara, Pat Hingle, Paul E. Richards, [Peter] Mark Richman) and its director (Jack Garfein) repeated their assignments for this low-budget screen version. Although its depiction of homosexuality at a southern military academy is merely suggested, the industry's production code office required approximately three minutes of footage be cut.

Even coming two years after the tentative and distorted *Tea and Sympathy*, q.v., it was amazing that this controversial movie was made at all. However, in the wake of the Senator McCarthy Communist witch hunt, many filmmakers in Hollywood were anxiously making amends by producing such motion pictures as this which (in)directly suggested the dangers of accusing a man falsely (here of being drunk) on circumstantial evidence.

At a southern military college, sadistic upperclassman Jocko De Paris (Ben Gazzara) and his buddy, Harold Knoble (Pat Hingle), force two freshmen—Robert Marquales (George Peppard) and Simmons (Arthur Storch)—to go along with a crooked poker game to dupe the dim-witted football player, Roger Gatt (James Olson). When the victim becomes angered at his losses, Jocko goads him into beating up Simmons. The ruckus is overheard by Georgie Avery (Geoffrey Horne), a sophomore and the son of Major Avery (Larry Gates), the school's chief officer. Georgie reports the incident, but when Major Avery investigates, he finds nothing amiss. No sooner does Avery leave the dormitory, then the game proceeds. This time Georgie investigates himself, breaking into the room. He is beaten unconscious by Jocko, liquor is forced down his throat, and he is dumped outside on the quadrangle. He is found the following morning, surrounded by several whiskey bottles. Although Major Avery suspects the truth, he has no evidence to support him. Therefore, he must expel Georgie for being intoxicated.

To make sure none of his stooges betray him, the twisted De Paris compromises

George Peppard and Arthur Storch in *The Strange One* (1957).

each one of them in turn. Meanwhile, Avery interrogates the snide Jocko who, in turn, goads the officer into slapping him. The arrogant de Paris plans to use this incident to get Avery removed from office. Marquales now realizes the personal nature of Jocko's scheme—to gain revenge on the Major for once having publicly disciplined him. Marquales makes the truth known to the cadet leaders who hold a kangaroo court. The now whimpering Jocko is found guilty and his peers—in Ku Klux Klan style—force him to leave the academy.

Bosley Crowther (*New York Times*) was disturbed that the movie missed the point of the book/play original: i.e. "that brutalization and corruption of young men were ironically fostered and shielded by the 'code of honor' in existence at a Southern military school." Crowther noted "the suggestion of a homosexual angle, so strong in the play, is very cautiously hinted here." The *Times* felt that Gazzara provides "a tantalizing picture of devilish cleverness and of impudence and arrogance that make the blood run cold. . . ." *Variety* found Gazzara's performance "Irritatingly realistic" and that Arthur Storch "deftly handles the part of a less virile student. He's a freshman who cringes under taunts of upper classmen, balks at washing in a community shower for obvious reasons and has no interest in the opposite sex."

In this sadomasochistic study, there is no one stranger than the brutal Jocko De Paris, who frequently parades about in his underwear and a military hat while puffing on a cigarette from a cigarette holder. He takes relish in pummeling fellow students with verbal and physical intimidation, thriving on his coterie of fawning stooges. Among his admirers is the equally bizarre Cockroach (Paul E. Richards), an oddball, who frequently struts around wearing a shower cap. He has an overt crush on his idol, Jocko, who, in turns, calls him "queer as a $3 bill." (One of the excised scenes from *The Strange One* featured Cockroach lovingly polishing Jocko's sword; the sexual symbolism was too strong for the censors to permit. Another sequence has the lovesick Cockroach telling De Paris to get rid of the hooker he is with and come be with him. Cockroach's words are bleeped.) Later, in the movie, the toadying Cockroach admits that he is proud to be different (i.e. gay) and that he is an artist who is writing an autobiographical novel—the very homoerotic *Nightboy*—much of it centered around his hero, Jocko.

Time magazine noted of the daring *The Strange One* that viewers will "learn what goes on inside a sadist—mostly repressed homosexuality." Even with this tentative step forward, Hollywood was coming of age, reflecting changes in public mores.

230. Strangers on a Train (Warner Bros., 1951), 101 min. Not rated.

Producer/director, Alfred Hitchcock; based on the novel by Patricia Highsmith; adaptor, Whitfield Cook; screenplay, Raymond Chandler, Czenzi Ormonde; art director, Ted Haworth; set decorator, George James Hopkins; costumes, Leah Rhodes; makeup, Gordon Bau; music, Dimitri Tiomkin; sound Dolph Thomas; special effects, H. F. Koenekamp; camera, Robert Burks; editor, William H. Ziegler.

Cast: Farley Granger (Guy Haines); Ruth Roman (Anne Morton); Robert Walker (Bruno Antony); Leo G. Carroll (Senator Morton); Patricia Hitchcock (Barbara Morton); Laura Elliott (Miriam Joyce Haines); Marion Lorne (Mrs. Antony); Jonathan Hale (Mr. Antony); Howard St. John (Captain Turley); John Brown (Professor Collins); Norma Varden (Mrs. Cunningham); Robert Gist (Leslie Hennessey); John Doucette (Hammond); Howard Washington (Waiter); Dick Wessell (Baggage Man); Edward Clark (Mr. Hargreaves); Al Hill ("Ring the Gong" Concessionaire); Leonard Carey (Butler); Edna Holland (Mrs. Joyce); Dick Ryan (Minister); Tommy Farrell, Rolland Morris (Miriam's Boy Friends); Louis Lettieri (Boy); Murray Alper (Boatman); John Butler (Blind Man); Roy Engle, Joel Allen (Policemen); Eddie Hearn (Sergeant Campbell); Mary Alan Hokanson (Secretary); Janet Stewart,

Shirley Tegge (Girls); Georges Renavent (Mon. Darville); Odette Myrtil (Mme. Darville); Charles Meredith (Judge Dolan); Minna Phillips, Monya Andre (Dowagers): Laura Treadwell (Mrs. Anderson); J. Louis Johnson (Butler); Sam Flint, Ralph Moody (Men); Joe Warfield (Seedy Man); Harry Hines (Man under Merry-Go-Round); Alfred Hitchcock (Man Boarding Train with Bass Fiddle).

Just as Alfred Hitchcock's *Rope* (1948), q.v., had dealt with an attempted perfect murder, so did *Strangers on a Train*. Both also dealt with homosexual relationships: in *Rope* it was actual but only implied in the presentation, whereas in *Strangers* it was wish fulfillment on the part of the sociopathic sissy for the handsome young tennis player and was far more explicitly suggested. Whereas *Rope* was structurally efficient and dull, *Strangers* was more subtle and complex in its locale and story intricacy and far more spellbinding. Ironically, at the time of release, this classic suspense yarn was considered only moderately interesting by many reviewers.

In the club car aboard a Washington, D.C. to Manhattan train, neurotic, pampered Bruno Antony (Robert Walker) spots famous tennis player Guy Haines (Farley Granger). The two men talk and, before long, Bruno admits to knowing a great deal about Guy. For example, he is aware that Haines is anxious to divorce his wife, Miriam (Laura Elliott,) so he can marry Anne (Ruth Roman), the daughter of U.S. Senator Morton (Leo G. Carroll). Half-jokingly, Bruno suggests that Guy murder Antony's despised father (Jonathan Hale) and that, in return, Bruno will kill Miriam. He reasons that since neither has an apparent motive to murder the other, they will never be implicated— hence a perfect crime. Haines is flabbergasted by this wacky offer and quickly parts company with the disturbed Bruno. The latter takes the cigarette lighter which Haines leaves behind.

Later, Bruno goes to Haines' home town where he strangles Miriam at an amusement park. Next, he contacts the

Advertisement for *Strangers on a Train* **(1951).**

shocked Haines, demanding that he keep his part of the bargain or else. Subsequently, Bruno gate-crashes a cocktail party given by Senator Morton. While demonstrating the ease of murdering anyone—using a dowager guest (Norma Varden) as his subject—he notes the resemblance between Morton's observing younger daughter, Barbara (Patricia Hitchcock) and Miriam. Antony becomes so entranced with the similarity that he almost kills the helpless party guest. This event leads precocious Barbara into deducing that Antony killed Guy's estranged wife. Later, Bruno alerts Guy that he intends to leave Haines's cigarette lighter at the murder scene to implicate him. Pursued by surveillance policemen who count him as a major suspect, Guy rushes to the amusement park with the assistance of Anne and Barbara. As Guy and Bruno fight on the merry-go-round, the cops begin shooting at them, causing the operator's death. The ride goes out of control and Bruno is fatally injured. The police arrest Guy as his wife's killer. However, when they locate Guy's lighter in Bruno's pocket, Guy's innocence is finally established.

Bosley Crowther (*New York Times*) was not especially entertained by the film's premise in which the "story just does not stand." Furthermore, the critical Crowther observed, "Robert Walker as the diabolic villain is a caricature of silken suavity and Farley Granger plays the terrified catspaw (as he did in *Rope*) as though he were constantly swallowing his tongue." On the other hand, *Variety* ranked the film a "gripping, palm-sweating piece of suspense. . . . Story offers a fresh situation for murder. . . .. Granger is excellent as the harassed young man innocently involved in murder. Miss Roman's role . . . is a switch for her, and she makes it warmly effective. Walker's role has extreme color, and he projects it deftly."

In retrospect, Vito Russo (*The Celluloid Closet*, 1987) scrutinized the film: "[Robert] Walker's choice was particularly exciting in terms of the plot. The tension

it created between his malignantly fey Bruno and Granger's golly gee tennis player, Guy Haines, heightened the bizarre nature of their pact. . . . Bruno's homosexuality emerged in terms that would be used increasingly throughout the Fifties to define gays as aliens. His coldness, his perverse imagination and an edge of elitist superiority made him an extension of the sophisticated but deadly sissy played by Clifton Webb in *Laura* [1944], Peter Lorre in *The Maltese Falcon* [1941, q.v.] and Martin Landau in *North by Northwest* [1959]."

Strangers on a Train would be remade to little effect as the programmer, *Once You Kiss a Stranger* (1969). Carol Lynley inherited the Robert Walker role, Paul Burke was a drunken golf pro, Philip Carey was Burke's sports rival and Whit Bissell appeared as Lynley's detested psychiatrist.

231. Streamers (United Artists Classics, 1983), color, 118 min. R-rated.

Executive producers, Robert Michael Geisler, John Roberdeau; producers, Robert Altman, Nick J. Mileti; associate producer, Scott Bushnell; director, Robert Altman; based on the play by David Rabe; screenplay, Rabe; production designer, Wolf Kroeger; art director, Steve Altman; set decorator, Robert Brown; costumes, Scott Bushnell; makeup, Bill Edwards; assistant directors, Allan Nicholls, Ned Dowd; sound, John Pritchett; camera, Pierre Mignot; editor, Norman Smith.

Cast: Matthew Modine (William "Billy" Wilson); Michael Wright (Carlyle); Mitchell Lichtenstein (Richard "Richie" Douglas); David Alan Grier (Roger Hicks); Guy Boyd (Sergeant First Class Rooney); George Dzundza (Sergeant Cokes); Albert Macklin (Martin); B.J. Cleveland (Private First Class Bush); Bill Allen (Lieutenant Townsend); Paul Lazar (Military Popice Lieutenant); Phil Ward (Military Police Sergeant Kilick); Terry McIlvain (Orderly); Todd Savell (Military Police Sergeant Savio); Mark Fickert (Dr. Banes); Dustye Winniford (Staff Sergeant); Robert S. Reed (Military Police).

David Rabe's *Streamers* (1976), won the New York Drama Critics Best Play

Mitchell Lichtenstein and Michael Wright in *Streamers* (1983).

award. On the surface the play dealt with fledgling servicemen, training to be parachutists in the Vietnam conflict. The symbolic "streamers" (i.e. men whose chutes do not open on the drop down) refers to every individual rushing to his/her destiny, whatever it may be and however it may be reached. Another theme of this stark drama is an examination of homosexuality and homophobia. Thus, it is deliberately set within a claustrophobic Army barracks, in a contradictory military atmosphere which fosters intense emotional camaraderie, but not of a physical sort.

In 1965, at the training camp of the 83rd Airborne Division, recruits nervously prepare to be shipped to Vietnam. In the program, three soldiers are alone in the barracks: Billy (Matthew Modine), a thoughtful but restless recruit; Roger (Alan Grier), an easy-going young black man; and the fey Richie (Mitchell Lichteinstein), a preening gay youth. Another member, Martin (Albert Macklin), whom

the nellie Richie has fussed over, has cut his wrists in a suicide attempt, and is later discharged. Meanwhile, another soldier, the neurotic Carlyle (Michael Wright), hearing there is another black on the post, comes to Roger's barracks, angry that his own unit is full of white men and restless about army life in general. The two supervising sergeants, the beer-bellied Cokes (George Dzundza) and Rooney (Guy Boyd), spend much of their time drunk, playing cards, and airily lecturing the recruits about the excitement of combat.

Prompted by Richie's taunting, Billy tells a story about a pal he once had who used to put down gays until he himself became homosexual, leading Richie to theorize later that Billy was talking about himself. Carlyle remains in the barracks that night, having passed out. The next day, he taunts the others about their easy life, including having Richie available to satisfy their physical needs. Roger and Carlyle go to town on a pass, with Billy joining them to get back at the flirtatious Richie. When they return, Richie provokes Carlyle with witty put-downs, leading the latter to claim Richie as his property. When Billy refuses to leave the barrack so Carlyle can have Richie, the two scuffle and Billy is stabbed fatally. The inebriated Rooney appears, and he too is knifed to death. After the ruckus is sorted out, Cokes returns, looking for Rooney. Richie admits to the Sergeant that he is gay. The latter, in a philosophical bent (he is dying of leukemia), admits he is no longer as much a bigot and "There are a lot of things worse to be in the world."

Jack Kroll (*Newsweek*) approved of Altman's "chillingly filmed" production in which "A U.S. barracks becomes a microcosm of social tension that blows up in the pressurized crucible of Army life. . . . The nonstar cast is tremendous, especially Wright as the soldier who triggers a civil war within this troubled Army of a troubled society." For Judith Crist (*Saturday Review*), "The stage roots are evident, but Altman has turned both the dramatic speeches and the claustrophobic set to his advantage, letting the actors . . . rule the screen. The result is an engrossing and harrowing film."

In contrast, Alex Keneas (*Newsday*) warned, "On stage *Streamers* . . . .generated an edgy energy and menace. Altman's *Streamers* is curiously, disappointing flat. . . . Although as an ensemble the actors are very good, *Streamers* is visually lethargic, as Altman's camera autocratically forbids the eye to roam from talking heads." A disappointed Michael Feingold (*Village Voice*) observed, "If you've taken Altman seriously as an artist of some technical originality and some range of imagination, you're likely to wonder where it's gone. . . . The stagy dubiousness and contradictions of Rabe's original script . . . are made more glaring by the film's dogged realism."

In retrospect, Vito Russo (*The Celluloid Closet*, 1987) emphasized, "Unfortunately, Altman directs Mitchell Lich-

tenstein to play the homosexual character as such a flaming, sophisticated queen that the question of whether or not he is really homosexual, essential to the drama, doesn't exist. . . . Straight men aren't threatened by a flamboyant faggot because they know they aren't like that; they're threatened by a guy who's just like they are who turns out to be queer."

Streamers was not a box-office success.

232. Suddenly, Last Summer

(Columbia, 1959), 114 min. Not rated.

Producer, Sam Spiegel; director, Joseph L. Mankiewicz; based on the play by Tennessee Williams; screenplay, Gore Vidal, Williams; production designer, Oliver Messel; art director, William Kellner; set decorator, Scott Slimon; costumes, Messel, Jean Louis, Norman Hartnell, Joan Ellacott; makeup, David Aylott; music, Boxton Orr, Malcolm Arnold; assistant director, Bluey Hill; special effects, Tom Howard; camera, Jack Hildyard; editors, Thomas G. Stanford, William W. Hornbeck.

Cast: Elizabeth Taylor (Catherine Holly): Montgomery Clift (Dr. John Cukrowicz); Katharine Hepburn (Mrs. Violet Venable); Albert Dekker (Dr. Hockstader); Mercedes McCambridge (Mrs. Holly); Gary Raymond (George Holly); Mavis Villiers (Mrs. Foxhill); Patricia Marmont (Nurse Benson); Joan Young (Sister Felicity); Maria Britneva (Lucy); Sheila Robbins (Dr. Hockstader's Secretary); David Cameron (Young Blond Intern); Roberta Woolley (Patient).

"*Suddenly, Last Summer* goes further than anyone has previously cared, I won't say dared, to go. It will be almost certainly so alien to most audiences I doubt they will be able to show it much sympathy, not because it is poorly done, but rather because of its essentially poetic strength." (Paul V. Beckley, *New York Herald-Tribune*)

Contrary to this film, there are no known cannibalistic homosexuals lurking in the seaside resorts of Spain. But literal-minded moviegoers of 1959 might not agree. Expanded from a long-one act off-Broadway play (1958) by Tennessee Williams, this movie opened up the play's two character monologues from a single set-

Advertisement for *Suddenly, Last Summer* (1959).

ting to encompass flashbacks, sanitarium scenes, additional players, etc. Buried within its high-toned speeches and stylized performances—mannered Katharine Hepburn, shrill Elizabeth Taylor, dazed Montgomery Clift—was an unsympathetic narrative of suffocating mother love. In lengthy exposition, the film told of how the woman's pampered, homosexual offspring was (figuratively) devoured by his former prey—handsome and impecunious young men.

Earlier in the 1950s, two of Williams's Broadway hits—*A Streetcar Named De-*

sire (1951) and *Cat on a Hot Tin Roof* (1958), q.v.,—had reached the Hollywood screen with their homosexual references withdrawn. Now, some two years before the film industry's production code would permit the discussion/presentation of themes dealing with homosexuality, Williams's about-face, anti-gay study was allowed under special code office dispensation. In fact, when released, the Catholic Church's Legion of Decency, after demanding certain cuts be made, gave the movie a special classification, explaining, "Since the film illustrates the horrors of such a lifestyle, it can be considered moral in theme even though it deals with sexual perversion."

In New Orleans, respected psychiatrist Dr. John Cukrowicz (Montgomery Clift) is informed by his superior, Dr. Hockstader (Albert Dekker), that if John accedes to demanding and wealthy, Mrs. Violet Venable (Katharine Hepburn), their under-endowed psychiatric asylum, Lion's View, will receive a $1 million bequest. Visiting the eccentric widowed Mrs. Venable at her ostenstatious home—with its exotic gardens—Cukrowicz learns that his mission is to perform a lobotomy on Catherine Holly (Elizabeth Taylor), the daughter of Violet's sister-in-law, Mrs. Holly (Mercedes McCambridge). Upon examining the hospitalized Catherine, the psychiatrist is convinced she is more sane than her outlandish aunt and more coherent than her fawning, mercenary mother. Balancing the value of helping many patients via Mrs. Venable's grant versus the damage to be done Catherine, John arranges a final confrontation in Mrs. Venable's garden. There, in a highly-charged confession induced by truth serum, Catherine reveals the sordid truth.

For years, Mrs. Venable had ignored her husband (now deceased) in favor of their handsome, intellectual son, Sebastian. When the boy grew of a certain age, she accompanied him on annual global excursions, making available to the shy young man the male companionship he so

craved. When she grew too old to attract men, Sebastian's beautiful cousin, Catherine, had been substituted. Then last summer, the jaded, aging Sebastian, now finding it difficult to gain his pleasures, began to frequent a public beach. Catherine would wear a form-fitting bathing suit to help attract the males. One day, the starving urchins had turned on Sebastian and killed him. (Catherine shrieks, "They seemed to devour him!") By this point, the horrible reality has caused Mrs. Venable's mind to snap. As she is led inside, she imagines John to be her dead son and that they are together in the past, as before.

Bosley Crowther (*New York Times*) acknowledged "There's no doubt that a great deal of the feeling of dank corruption that ran through the play has been lost or pitifully diluted by a tactful screening of the words." However, he concluded the movie was ruined NOT because "the true nature of the most-talked-of-character could not be tagged (he was obviously a homosexual, as well as a sadist of some sort, in the play)," but because of the adaptation's "tedious talking and a terminal showdown that is irritatingly obscure." *Harrison's Reports* rated the film the "diseased product of the mind of Tennessee Williams" and that it was a mystery why anyone "ever bothered with it in the first place."

In contrast, Alton Cook (*New York World-Telegram*) complimented the movie: "The play might have remained vague without the clarifying influence of three profound performances. . . ." Arthur Knight (*Saturday Review*) felt "Mankiewicz, particularly in his telling of the flashback to 'last summer,' with Miss Taylor's face superimposed over the dread events, has given vivid, cinematic life to facets of Williams' play."

With its star cast and its controversial, adult nature, *Suddenly, Last Summer*, lensed in black-and-white on London sound stages, grossed a strong $6,375,000 in distributors' domestic film rentals. It received three Academy Award nominations: Best Actress (Katharine Hepburn and Elizabeth Taylor; Simone Signoret won for *Room at the Top*); Best Art Direction—Set Decoration: Black-and-White (*The Diary of Anne Frank* won).

The advertising campaign for *Suddenly, Last Summer* cagily exploited a photograph of the shapely Elizabeth Taylor in her clinging white bathing suit. It became the movie's most identifiable and remembered image. As for the character of the "depraved" Sebastian Venable, only viewed in partial shots during flashback scenes, he had become a near-invisible figure, which is how the Hollywood majority and the public of the day seemed to view the gay minority.

233. Summer Wishes, Winter Dreams (Columbia, 1973), color, 88 min. PG-rated.

Executive producer, Phil Feldman; producer, Jack Brodsky; director, Gilbert Cates; screenplay, Stewart Stern; production designer, Peter Dohanos; set decorator, Philip Smith; makeup, Fern Buckner, Bill Lodge; music, Johnny Mandell; assistant directors, Michael Hertzberg, Neil Machlis, Ted Tester; sound, Jack C. Jacobsen; camera, Gerald Hirschfeld; editor, Sidney Katz.

Cast: Joanne Woodward (Rita Walden); Martin Balsam (Harry Walden); Sylvia Sidney (Rita's Mother); Dori Brenner (Anna); Win Forman (Fred Goody); Tresa Hughes (Betty Goody); Peter Marklin (Joel); Ron Rickards (Bobby Walden); Charlotte Oberley (Waitress); Minerva Pious (Mrs. Bimberg); Helen Ludlam (Grandmother); Grant Code (Grandfather); Sol Frieden (Mr. Goldblatt); Gaetano Lisi (Student in Theatre); Nancy Andrews (Mrs. Pat Hungerford); Lee Jackson (Carl Hurlbutt); David Thomas (Chauffeur); Marian Swan (Nurse); Dennis Wayne (Dancer in Dream).

It is no accident that during the course of *Summer Wishes, Winter Dreams*, two characters attend an art house screening of Ingmar Bergman's *Wild Strawberries* (1957). For, like that classic Swedish movie, this earnest but plodding feature intends to show individuals looking back on their lives and regretting past decisions. One of the choices haunting the un-happy female lead is having pushed her son out of her life because he is homosexual.

On the surface, chic, fortyish Rita Walden (Joanne Woodward) has everything a woman could desire: a comfortable upscale life in Manhattan, a devoted husband, Harry (Martin Balsam), who is a successful ophthalmologist and two children who are grown and moved away. However, Rita is troubled. She disagrees with the permissive, but practical way her daughter Anna (Dori Brenner) is raising her baby. She is bothered that she no longer hears from her son Bobby (Ron Rickards), now living in Amsterdam and whom she is convinced is homosexual. Having emotionally castrated her loyal husband, she is displeased with his non-responsiveness to her worries. And her mother (Sylvia Sidney), with whom she has always felt detached, reminds her too much of what she has become with her own offsprings.

When her mother dies, Rita copes badly with the decision to sell the family's old farm, which she associates with a more carefree part of her life. Insisting that Bobby must be consulted, she convinces Harry to fly to Europe where he can also attend a ophthalmology convention. In London, the nightmare-plagued Rita has an emotional crisis, brought on by Bobby's failure to contact her. Harry insists they go on to France so he can revisit his days of World War II glory/trauma. As he explores familiar sights, Harry undergoes a catharsis. Finally sensing what her husband used to be, and what she and he have become, Rita reconciles with him. She now admits that Bobby, living with a lover in Holland, was driven away by her intolerance. While he will not see her now, perhaps, she hopes someday he will want to communicate with the new Rita.

Nora Sayre (*New York Times*) pinpointed the movie's structural problem: "Miss Woodward has been directed to win the [Academy Award] sweepstakes. Misery floods the screen. yet, it's very hard to believe that the kind of vigorous, sinewy character she evokes could feel so perpetually defeated. . . . since she acts as if she had been drinking Drano, the moments of vulnerability just aren't convincing. . . ." *Variety* underlined that the movie misfired in underlining its "basic theme of middle-aged American emptiness. . . . The more the film captures the tedium the more the picture drags. . . . Each time director Gilbert Cates reaches . . . a high point and handles it successfully, he chooses, however, to back off and start over again." The trade paper acknowledged, "Performances by Woodward, Balsam and Sidney (her first pic in 17 years) are first-rate. . . ."

Even for 1973, the film's handling of homosexuality (the alienation of a gay child by homophobic, guilt-ridden parents) is too quaint. For example, while in the movie theatre watching *Wild Strawberry*, Rita suddenly flashes back to an image of her once bursting into her son's bedroom, where he (ambivalently surprised and/or smirking) is being bewitched by a muscular, pirouetting ballet dancer (Dennis Wayne). Such antiquated Freudian claptrap as this scene portrays is reminiscent of the dream sequences out of *Spellbound* (1945). Later, when Harry forces Rita to confront the truth about their son's roommate, he old-fashionedly mentions "It's what those people call a lover . . . like that kid he brought home before." The stunned Rita retorts in a manner inconsistent with her usually hip, self-sufficient personality: "You said that was a phase." Even in still repressive 1970s America, this handling of gayness was out-of-touch with reality.

Demographically geared to older audiences, *Summer Wishes, Winter Dreams*, with its location filming in Europe, was not a commercial success. However, it won two Academy Award nominations: Best Actress (Joanne Woodward; Glenda Jackson won for *A Touch of Class*); Best Supporting Actress (Sylvia Sidney; Tatum O'Neal won for *Paper Moon*).

234. Swashbuckler (Universal, 1976), color, 101 min. PG-rated. (British release title: *The Scarlet Buccaneer*)

Executive producer, Elliott Kastner; producer, Jennings Lang; associate producer, William S. Gilmore Jr.; director, James Goldstone; story, Paul Wheeler; screenplay, Jeffrey Bloom; production designer, John Lloyd; set decorator, Hal Gausman; costumes, Burton Miller; choreographer, Geoffrey Holder; music, John Addison; assistant directors, Peter Bogart, Wayne Farlow; stunt coordinators, Buddy Van Horn, Victor Paul; sound, Don Johnson, Robert Hoyt; special effects, Frank Brendel; camera, Philip Lathrop; editor, Edward A. Biery.

Cast: Robert Shaw (Ned Lynch); James Earl Jones (Nick Debrett); Peter Boyle (Lord James Durant); Genevieve Bujold (Jane Barnet); Beau Bridges (Major Folly); Geoffrey Holder (Cudjo); Avery Schreiber (Polanski); Tom Clancy (Mr. Moonbeam); Anjelica Huston (Woman of Dark Visage); Bernard Behrens (Sir James Barnet); Dorothy Tristan (Alice); Mark Baker (Lute Player); Kip Niven (Willard Culverwell); Tom Fitzsimmons (Corporal); Louisa Horton (Lady Barnet); Sid Haig (Bald Pirate); Robert Ruth (Bearded Pirate); Robert Morgan (Peglegged Pirate); Jon Cedar (Pirate Gun Captain); Diana Chesney (Landlady); Manuel De Pina (Barnet Servant); Tom Lacy (Chaplain); Alfie Wise (Sailor); Harry Basch (Banana Man); Lee Pulford, Alyscia Maxwell, Isobel Estorick, Mary Margaret Amato, Lisa Moore, Lisa Daniels, Catana Tully, Erika Carlson (Pirates' Ladies); Pepe Serna, Ron Joseph, Miguel Godreau, Avind Harum, Chester Hayes, Eduardo Reyna Juarez, Eleanor McCoy, Adele Yoshioka, Victoria Aly (Street Entertainers); Brenda Venus, Victoria Ann Berry, Rutanya Alda, Kathryn Reynolds, Mitch Davis, Earl Maynard (Bath Attendants).

What seemed like a good idea, a satirical send-up of the bawdy pirate genre, emerged as a heavy-handed, tasteless mishmash, complete with a fey dastardly villain (Peter Boyle) who has a sadistic young lover. Nothing worked in this lethargic-venture. *Variety* analyzed, "There's no sincerity in *Swashbuckler*. There's not even a consistent approach. This tacky pastepot job can't make up its mind whether it is serious, tongue-in-cheek, satirical slapstick, burlesque, parody or travesty. . . ."

In the year 1718, at Kingston on the island of Jamaica, Lord Durant (Peter Boyle) is the self-indulgent acting Governor full of dastardly schemes. However, all his planning, to be executed by the bumbling Major Folly (Beau Bridges), comes unstuck because of the pirate Ned Lynch (Robert Shaw). After the swashbuckler rescues Nick Debrett (James Earl Jones) from being hung, the two grab as booty the confiscated fortunes of Sir James Barnet (Bernard Behrens), the deposed Chief Justice. Thereafter, Barnet's daughter, Jane (Genevieve Bujold) finds herself accidentally teamed with Ned and Nick in fleeing the British troops. Once safe, Jane convinces Ned to help remove the corrupt Durant from office. Thereafter, Jane is captured and brought to Durant's headquarters, which leads to the pirate and his forces storming the fort stronghold. Folly and his inept men cannot stop the invasion. In the climatic sword fight between Lynch and Durant, the latter is projected out a window and tumbles into the carriage waiting for his getaway. Left in charge, Ned and Jane pursue their romance.

Vincent Canby (*New York Times*), admitting a fondness for traditional pirate fare, judged, "the movie is such a mess you might suspect it was tacked together by nearsighted seamstresses. . . . Worse, though, is a plot that is skimpy of incident, acted by people who have been most miscast." Regarding the picture's PG rating (altered to remove its R rating), the *Times* printed, "I suppose [it is due to] . . . a couple of scenes in a busy whorehouse and the dopey reference to the governor's homosexuality, which this mindless film equates with political corruption." The annoyed Ray Loynd (*Los Angeles Herald-Examiner*) exclaimed, "The prince of darkness here, Boyle, and his delicate lute player friend . . . are characters on a kinky cruise all their own. Who said this movie wasn't camp? It is funny as the castle walls come tumbling down to find them bathing and playing. . . .Boyle's ornate marble tub."

One of the many misfires in *Swashbuckler* was its parody of the Walter Slezak-type blackguard (a la *Sinbad the Sailor*, 1947; *The Pirate*, 1948). In an attempt to take the parody as far as the permissive 1970s would allow, one of the villain's portrayed "degenerate" characteristics was his blatant homosexuality. The effeminate Durant is the type who has a crew of semi-nude black men tending to his every whimsical need (pedicures, manicures, etc.). For a lover, he has an angelic-faced lute player (Mark Baker). As it develops, this acting governor has a penchant for sado-masochism and his kept boyfriend is well versed in the habit of attaching mechanical metal fingers (with sharp points) to do his master's bidding. Later in the proceedings, the lute player fatally impales himself on the mechanical claws. Hollywood was still portraying villains as sociopaths whose deviancy was confirmed by their homosexuality.

235. Switch (Warner Bros., 1991), color, 103 min. R-rated.

Producer, Tony Adams; associate producer, Trish Caroselli Rintels; director/screenplay, Blake Edwards; production designer, Rodger Maus; art director, Sandy Getzler; set decorator, John Franco Jr.; costumes, Ellen Mirojnick; makeup, Larry Abbott; music, Henry Mancini; assistant directors, David C. Anderson, Matthew Dunne, Katy Garretson; stunt coordinator, Joe Dunne; sound, Jerry Jost, Robert Fernandez; camera, Dick Bush; editor, Robert Pergament.

Cast: Ellen Barkin (Amanda Brooks); Jimmy Smits (Walter Stone); JoBeth Williams (Margo Brofman); Lorraine Bracco (Sheila Faxton); Tony Roberts (Arnold Freidkin); Perry King (Steve Brooks); Bruce Martyn Payne (The Devil); Lysette Anthony (Liz); Victoria Mahoney (Felicia); Basil Hoffman (Higgins); Catherine Keener (Steve's Secretary); Kevin Kilner (Dan Jones); David Wohl (Attorney Caldwell); James Harper (Lieutenant Laster); John Lafayette (Sergeant Phillips); Jim J. Bullock (The Psychic); Diane Chesney (Mrs. Wetherspoon); Joe Flood (Mac, the Guard); Emma Walton (Fur Protester); Louis Eppolito (Al, the Guard); Yvette Freeman (Mae, the Maid); Dennis Paladino (Duke); Tea Leoni

Ellen Barkin and Lorraine Bracco in *Switch* (1991).

(Dream Girl); Rick Aiello (Wiseguy at Duke's); F. William Parker (Barber); Ben Hargian (Minister); David Gale (Doctor); Jessie Jones (Arnold's Secretary); Savant Tanney (Judge Harcrow); Virginia Morris (Assistant District Attorney); Robert Clotworthy (Baliff); Patricia Clipper (Girl in Elevator); Robert Elias (Photographer); Michelle Wong (Photo Assistant); Marti Muller (Woman Client); Lily Mariye (Nurse); Karen Medka (Saleswoman); Tracy Lambert, Taunie Vernon (Store Models); Michael Badalucco (Hard Hat); Faith Minton (Nancy, the Bouncer); Rebecca Wood, Linda Dona (Gay Club Patrons); Helene Apothaker (Gay Club Waitress); Richard Provost, Linda Gary (Voices of God); Molly Okuneff (Little Girl).

Taking a leaf from the frolicsome *Turnabout* (1940) and the lumbering *Goodbye, Charlie* (1964), among others, Blake Edwards created this heavy-handed sex farce. The film vulgarly trashes the potential premise of what might occur when a chauvinistic male dies and returns to Earth as the opposite sex. Edwards never resolves whether the sex transformation leaves the now-female protagonist heterosexual when she/he is lusted after by men. In addition, in order to insure that all types of sexual orientation are uniformly badly treated, Edwards introduces an ill-handled lesbian situation.

Ladykiller advertising executive Steve Brooks (Perry King) is murdered by a trio of disgruntled past conquests: Margo Brofman (JoBeth Williams), Liz (Lysette Anthony) and Felicia (Victoria Mahoney). He awakens in hell to be told by the Devil (Bruce Martyn Payne) that he can return to life and go on to Heaven IF he find a woman on Earth who will really like him. To explain reemerging on Earth as a woman (a complication devised by the devilish head of Hell), Steve pretends to be his half-sister Amanda (Ellen Barkin), insisting that Steve has gone off to Europe. Amanda confronts Margo and blackmails her into helping Steve/Amanda pull off the gambit. While searching for a woman who liked Steve, Amanda is befriended by Steve's pal, Walter Stone (Jimmy Smits).

Meanwhile, taking over Steve's Madison Avenue chores, lecherous Amanda woos a major client, cosmetic corporation head, Sheila Faxton (Lorraine Bracco), who turns out to be a lesbian. With Steve's typical lack of scruples, Amanda flirts with Sheila in order to gain the contract, but stops short of consummating the relationship. Subsequently, Amanda (who is asleep and thereafter does not remember the episode) and Walter have sex. Then, Steve's body is discovered and Amanda is declared insane and institutionalized when she insists that she is Steve. Thereafter, the locked-up Amanda and Walter marry and the pregnant Amanda expires in childbirth. Before dying, she realizes her little girl loves her. Now safely in Heaven, Amanda ponders whether she will (or want to) be a female or male angel.

Owen Gieberman (*Entertainment Weekly*) rated *Switch* a C−, explaining, "What's disappointing—and, indeed, rather bizarre—about *Switch* is that Edwards shows almost no interest in a woman's experience outside of..well, the clothes. . . . He [Edwards] stages several queasy homoerotic (or is it autoerotic?) encounters—queasy because the scenes are so unresolved, so coyly vague. . . ." *Variety* panned the film: "*Switch* is a fainthearted sex comedy. . . . Things look like they will shift into high gear when Amanda meets . . . a lesbian. . . . Unfortunately, pic chickens out from this point on, to a dismaying end. Uptight when the moment of truth arrives with Bracco, Amanda literally passes out in the bedroom and never pursues a woman again. . . . Ellen Barkin is clearly game for anything the director wants her to do . . . but mugs and overdoes the grimacing and macho posturing. Smits and Bracco are smooth enough. . . ." Eric Mankin (*Los Angeles Reader*) felt that "Whatever its short comings, *Switch* is funny, but acknowledged, "*Switch* doesn't begin to have the depth or the finished perfection of, say (to take a film on the same subject), *Tootsie* [1982]."

Switch sat on the shelf for several months, but, when released finally, grossed $7 million in distributors' domestic film rentals. In no way, was the leaden *Switch* in the same class as Blake Edwards's earlier *10* (1979) and *Victor/Victoria* (1982), qq.v.

236. Swoon (New Line Cinema, 1992), 90 min. Not-rated.

Executive producers, Lauren Zalaznick, James Schamus; producer, Christine Vachon; line producer, Zalaznick; associate producer, Peter Wentworth; director/screenplay, Tom Kalin; collaborating writer, Hilton Als; production designer, Therese Deprez; costumes, Jessica Huston; makeup, Jim Crawford; music, James Bennett; assistant director, Vachon; sound, Neil Danziger, Tom Paul; camera, Ellen Kuras; editor, Kalin.

Cast: Daniel Schlachet (Richard Loeb); Craig Chester (Nathan Leopold Jr.); Ron Vawter (State's Attorney Crowe); Michael Kirby (Detective Savage); Michael Stumm (Dr. Bowman); Vala Z. Crabla (Germaine Reinhardt).

Both Alfred Hitchcock's *Rope* (1948) and *Compulsion* (1959), qq.v., had dealt to one degree or another with the notorious case ("the crime of the century") of highly intellectual and well-to-do Richard Loeb and Nathan Leopold Jr. In 1924 Chicago, they had committed a random, coldblooded murder of a youngster to prove their intellectual/moral superiority. In both earlier movies, it was strongly suggested (in every way possible, given the time of release) that the two young men were gay and were lovers. That underlying theme behind the murder was brought out blatantly in *Swoon*, shot in fourteen days on an exceedingly low budget in New York state on 16mm black-and-white film blow up to 35mm. The key roles were played by Daniel Schlachet (as the dominant Richard Loeb) and Craig Chester (as the subservient Nathan Leopold Jr.), with the script utilizing primary source materials (courtroom testimony, etc.) to attain its verisimilitude of these two law students so absorbed in their Nietzchean nihilistic philosophy.

Todd McCarthy (*Daily Variety*) commented on filmmaker Tom Kalin's unique approach to the familiar subject matter: "Kalin extends this conception of apartness [i.e. intellectual superiority] to their homosexuality, essentially equating gayness with outlaw status in a hostile society. . . . Leopold and Loeb commit the ultimate offense by murdering a child, surely the most fundamental symbol of the straight world. This reading of the case history is what makes the film provocative. . . . Other notable aspect is the picture's look, and Ellen Kuras' cinematography in particular." McCarthy faulted the director's over use of anachronistic devices to grab the viewer's attention, the switch to a sudden documentary style in the final portion of the film, and extraneous segments flaunting "some gaudy 'girls.' " Aesthetically, McCarthy concluded, "In any conventional sense, *Swoon* is arid . . . and, given the passion the two characters feel for each other, sapped of life."

Duane Byrge (*Hollywood Reporter*) admitted that "*Swoon* is a real eye-opener, detailing the crime as the climax of a master-slave homosexual love relationship." However, Byrge pointed out, the movie "is not, of course, everyone's cup of tea. Even those sophisticated enough to appreciate the film's full-frontal psychology may find its aesthetics tediously precious." . . .

Ellen Kuras's cinematography for *Swoon* won an award at the 1992 Sundance Film Festival at Park City, Utah. Two (Christine Vachon and Lauren Zalaznick) of *Swoon*'s producers, had done similar chores on the gay-themed *Poison* (1991), q.v. *Swoon*, originally rated R by the Motion Picture Association of America's Classification & Rating Administration, surrendered its categorization and was released unrated.

237. Sylvia (Paramount, 1965), 115 min. Not rated.

Producer, Martin Poll; associate producer, Shirley Mellner; assistant producer, Steve Shagan; director, Gordon Douglas; based on the novel by E. V. Cunningham; screenplay, Sydney Boehm; art directors, Hal Pereira, Roland Anderson; set decorators, Sam Comer, Arthur Krams; costumes, Edith Head; makeup, Wally Westmore; music, Walter Scharf; song, Paul Francis Webster and David Raksin; assistant directors, Dick Moder, James Rosenberger; sound, Harry Lindgren, John Wilkinson; process camera, Farciot Edouart; camera, Joseph Ruttenberg; editor, Frank Bracht.

Cast: Carroll Baker (Sylvia West [Karoki]); George Maharis (Alan Macklin); Joanne Dru (Jane Phillips); Peter Lawford (Frederick Summers); Viveca Lindfors (Irma Olanski); Edmond O'Brien (Oscar Stewart); Aldo Ray (Jonas Karoki); Ann Sothern (Mrs. Gracie Argona); Lloyd Bochner (Bruce Stamford III); Paul Gilbert (Lola Diamond); Nancy Kovack (Big Shirley); Paul Wexler (Peter Memel); Jay Novello (Father Gonzales); Connie Gilchrist (Molly Banter); Alan Carney (Gus); Shirley O'Hara (Mrs. Karoki); Anthony Caruso (Muscles [Wilbur]); Gene Lyons (Gavin Cullen); Val Avery (Pudgey Smith); Manuel Padilla (Pancho Goodman); Majel Barrett (Anne, the Bookstore Clerk); and: Bob Random.

Indulgently padded to 115 minutes and filled with "name" players, *Sylvia* was another showcasing vehicle for reemerged 1950s star, Carrol Baker. To hedge their bets on this lurid expose of "Who is Sylvia?," Paramount filmed it in economical black-and-white. Among the veteran supporting cast was Viveca Lindfors as the middle-aged librarian who gets misty-eyed at the mere recollection of tantalizing Sylvia. Her brief scenes were directed ambiguously and cautiously (it still being the prim 1960s). However, considering the movie's overall tawdry tone, that Lindfors had gained great attention playing a lesbian in *No Exit* (1962), q.v., and the implication that the sexually abused young heroine seeks love anywhere and anyhow she can get it, it is not stretching reality to categorize Lindfors's character as gay.

Los Angeles millionaire Frederick Summers (Peter Lawford) hires young private investigator Alan Macklin (George Maharis) to investigate the background of his mysterious fiancee, Sylvia (Carroll Baker). The trail leads Macklin back to Pittsburgh and to librarian Irma Olanski

Viveca Lindfors and George Maharis in *Sylvia* (1964).

(Viveca Lindfors) who remembers Sylvia fondly as a shy child with an attraction for literature and for aesthetics. Later, the sleuth uncovers that Sylvia was ravaged by her stepfather (Aldo Ray), drawn into prostitution in Mexico by a phony missionary (Paul Wexler), and taken to New York City by a married salesman (Edmond O'Brien). Macklin traces Sylvia's path thereafter from Manhattan penny arcade cashier, (Ann Sothern). From chic, married Jane Phillips (Joanne Dru), Alan learns that Sylvia returned to being a hooker for Lola Diamond (Paul Gilbert), a transvestite club owner/madam, who boasted a stable of expensive call girls.

With the payoff from a sadistic client (Lloyd Bochner), Sylvia had quit the trade and relocated to California where she wrote poetry. Back in California, Alan meets the elusive Sylvia and admits he has fallen in love with her. Since Summers—now knowing Sylvia's background—has broken their engagement—she is free to marry the detective.

Bosley Crowther (*New York Times*) rejected *Sylvia* as a "hopelessly cheap and mawkish tale." For Crowther, "Miss Baker is as lifeless as a stick, and the script by Sydney Boehm is a collection of all the cliches of bordello literature. . . . Viveca Lindfors casts a ray of credibility through the role of a poor librarian." The British *Monthly Film Bulletin* observed, "the film is almost excessively discreet about its heroine's scarlet path. . . . Carroll Baker, too long miscast as an embryonic Jean Harlow, calls expertly on reserves of quiet scorn and—quite an achievement—even dignity. Certainly she holds her own with an uncommonly strong supporting cast; Viveca Lindfors, electrifying as a middle-aged librarian guardian angel. . . ."

238. The Tamarind Seed (Avco Embassy, 1974), color, 123 min. PG-rated.

Producer, Ken Wales; associate producer, Johnny Goodman; director, Blake Edwards; based on the novel by Evelyn Anthony; screenplay, Edwards; art director, Harry Pottle; music/music director, John Barry; song, Barry and Don Black; assistant director, Derek Cracknell; sound, John Bramall, Gordon McCallum; camera, Freddie Young; editor, Ernest Walter.

Cast: Julie Andrews (Judith Farrow); Omar Sharif (Feodor Sverdlov); Anthony Quayle (Jack Loder); Daniel [Dan] O'Herlihy (Fergus Stephenson); Sylvia Syms (Margaret Stephenson); Oscar Homolka (General Golitsyn); Bryan Marshall (George MacLeod); David Baron (Richard Paterson); Celia Bannerman (Rachael Paterson); Roger Dann (Colonel Moreau); Sharon Duce (Sandy Mitchell); George Mikell (Major Sukalov); Kate O'Mara (Anna Skriabina); Constantin de Goguel (Dimitri Memenov); John Sullivan, Terence Plummer, Leslie Crawford (KGB Agents); Alexei Jaw-dokimov (Igor Kalinin); Janet Henfry (Embassy Section Head).

The Tamarind Seed boasted a plush mounting and a high-toned cast. However, it was far too genteel, naive and antiquated to succeed in the mid-1970s marketplace, already oversaturated with actionful, violent espionage thrillers. Despite its deliberately convoluted, cynically ironic plotline dealing with the cold war, it proved that gorgeous cinematography and nice trappings cannot save a dull movie. Moreover, the inclusion of a homosexual villain did nothing to add needed tension to this cotton candy meeting of "Darling Lili" and "Dr. Zhivago."

In Barbados, idealistic widow Judith Farrow (Julie Andrews), a British Home Office employee on holiday, meets worldly Feodor Sverdlov (Omar Sharif), a Russian military attache assigned to the Paris embassy. This oddly-matched couple begin an affair, which causes grave concern to both sides of the Iron Curtain. Back in Paris, Fergus Stephenson (Daniel O'Herlihy) has Judith's background checked out. Upon her return to England, Judith is told to drop her relationship with Sverdlov. Nevertheless, she continues her romance with the handsome Russian. Later, through international diplomatic connections, Feodor learns it is no longer safe for him to return to his homeland and he seeks asylum in England. He agrees to reveal the identity of a top British spy working for the Russians, if he is given safe passage to Canada. At this juncture, Margaret Stephenson (Sylvia Sims), who has long known her husband Fergus is a secret homosexual, discovers that he is the spy in question. Nevertheless, she remains loyal to him. Meanwhile, Judith and Feodor return to Barbados, hoping to divert their trackers. There, they barely survive an attack by Russian undercover agents. As for Stephenson, he is about to be trapped by his country's spy force.

Vincent Canby (*New York Times*) was taken aback by this "staggering sobersided romantic foolishness" which seemed absorbed "in the chastity of its heroine." After sympathizing with the stars, Canby acknowledged, "The supporting performances are not at all bad . . . [including] Dan O'Herlihy (as the British minister in Paris) and Sylvia Sims as his unhappy wife." Richard Combs (British *Monthly Film Bulletin*) found that filmmaker Blake Edwards could not overcome the usual conventions of the genre and that "The null romantic pairing of Julie Andrews and Omar Sharif also renders the plot particularly unconvincing. . . ." On the plus side, Combs cited, "Edwards does at least manage a few convincingly tough and ambivalent sketches, in particular the unmasking of the sleek English diplomat as the master spy. . . ."

The Tamarind Seed, which debuted at Radio City Music Hall, was a critical and financial dud.

239. Tea and Sympathy (Metro-Goldwyn-Mayer, 1956), color, 122 min. Not rated.

Producer, Pandro S. Berman; director, Vincente Minnelli; based on the play by Robert Anderson; screenplay, Anderson; art directors, William A. Horning, Edward Carfagno; set decorators, Edwin B. Willis, Keogh Gleason; costumes, Helen Rose; makeup, William Tuttle; music, Adolph Deutsch; assistant director, Joel Freeman; sound supervisor, Dr. Wesley C. Miller; camera, John Alton; editor, Ferris Webster.

Cast: Deborah Kerr (Laura Reynolds); John Kerr (Tom Robinson Lee); Leif Erickson (Bill Reynolds); Edward Andrews (Herb Lee); Darryl Hickman (Al); Norma Crane (Ellie Martin); Dean Jones (Ollie); Jacqueline de Wit (Lilly Sears); Tom Laughlin (Ralph); Ralph Votrian (Steve); Steven Terrell (Phil); Kip King (Ted); Jimmy Hayes (Henry); Richard Tyler (Roger); Don Burnett (Vic); Mary Alan Hokanson (Mary Williams); Ron Kennedy (Dick); Peter Miller (Pete); Bob Alexander (Pat); Michael Monroe (Earl); Byron Kane (Umpire); Paul Bryar (Alex); Harry Harvey Jr., Bobby Ellis (Boys); Saul Gorss, Dale Van Sickel (Burly Men); Peter Leeds (Headmaster at Bonfire); Del Erickson (Ferdie).

"Years from now, when you talk about this, and you will, be kind." (Spoken by Laura Reynolds to Tom Robinson Lee in *Tea and Sympathy*)

Robert Anderson's *Tea and Sympathy* (1953) shocked Broadway audiences for 712 performances with its sensitive account of a school master's wife showing affection to a confused young student accused of homosexuality by his peers. Eager to translate this hit show to the screen, MGM hired its three Broadway stars (Deborah Kerr, John Kerr and Leif Erickson) to repeat their roles. To appease Hollywood censors and conventional-minded moviegoers, the studio softened the play's themes in several ways: (1) a framing device was added to emphasize that the youth is "straightened out" by his "normal" sexual experience with a compassionate woman and that he becomes a typical married heterosexual; (2) there was nothing more to the boy's alleged homosexuality than fellow students misunderstanding his oversensitivity (caused by a broken home life as a child), excessive romantic idealism (he does become a writer) and tremendous clumsiness at sports (he is equally awkward at dancing or courting women of any type); (3) the school master's homoerotic camaraderie with his students on the sports field does not exist; (4) the schoolmaster's persecution of the sensitive student is not out of fear that he may have homosexual tendencies himself, but from an intolerance of the youth's refusal to be one of the boys and for his nonopolizing too much of the time and interest of the housemaster's wife.

What emerged in the filmed *Tea and Sympathy* may have been weak tea (as adapted by the playwright himself). However, it was a pathbreaking step in the American film industry's slow coming to terms with presenting aspects of homosexuality overtly on screen. Unfortunately, this movie helped to perpetuate myths that U.S. filmmakers would use in the years to come as rules in treating alternate life-

Leif Erickson and Deborah Kerr in *Tea and Sympathy* (1956).

styles on screen: (1) gayness is not a sexual orientation but the manifestation of stereotypical warning signs (an unmanly walk, overt interest in domestic science, a preference for the arts over sports, etc.); (2) heterosexual copulation will immediately cure a gay man of his ailment; (3) shunning homosexuals is healthy, for gayness could infect the majority lifestyle adversely; (4) homophobia is an understandable male revulsion at a sick minority, ruling out any possibility that the detractors might actually question their own masculinity.

Tom Robinson Lee (John Kerr), now a successful, married writer with children, returns to the private Chilton School for his tenth anniversary. He thinks back to his senior year at this New England prep school. At that time, he was housed in the dormitory house supervised by macho Bill Reynolds (Leif Erickson), an instructor/

athletic coach, and his wife of a year, cultured Laura (Deborah Kerr). Bright, caring Tom roomed with sympathetic, all-American Al (Darryl Hickman). However, Lee was the butt of jokes by his classmates, including Ralph (Tom Laughlin) and Ollie (Dean Jones). They could not accept him because he was too dreamy, idealistic, and inept at sports or chasing women. To them, he was "sister boy." Never having gotten over her first husband's untimely death, Laura is disillusioned already with her marriage to gruff, insensitive Bill, and takes pity on Tom, another outsider. She discusses the matter with Bill, who reminds her that she must only provide her charges with "tea and sympathy."

Laura overhears the bewildered Tom making a date with promiscuous Ellie Martin (Norma Crane), a deed that could get him expelled, but one which also could give him an improved status with his classmates. She tries to stop him from going. However, he keeps the rendezvous, but it is a fiasco. (Revolted by the thought of cheap sex, he gets drunk, upon which Ellie throws him out, and he is caught by school authorities). At this point, shunned by Reynolds, his father (Edward Andrews) and his schoolmates, the confused boy attempts suicide. Deeply sympathetic to his plight, Laura gives herself to Tom, hoping it will restore his perspective. Thereafter, she and Reynolds separate.

Back in the present, Tom, seeing the broken Bill who still teaches at Chilton and reading an old letter from Laura to him, realizes now all the sacrifices she made on his behalf.

William K. Zinsser (*New York Herald-Tribune*) approved of the translation to screen as having been made "in good taste. . . . Its emphasis has been changed slightly, but the spirit of the play remains intact. . . . After all it never was a story about homosexuals. It is a story about bullies." Bosley Crowther (*New York Times*), more concerned with the movie's handling of the wife's indiscretion than with the boy's confusion about his sexual lifestyle, observed, "Mr. Anderson has toned down a few of the more unpleasant words. The most shocking epithet tossed freely at the hero is 'sister-boy.' And some of the more outspoken comments exchanged between husband and wife have been reduced to innuendos, rather than candid words. . . . Throughout, Mr. Kerr's performance of the lad is incredibly sure. . . . Miss Kerr. . . .reveals as the housemaster's wife one of the most genuine and tender female characters we have seen on the screen. . . ."

Variety noted: "The housemaster part, played with muscle-flexing exhibitionism by Leif Erickson, has lost some of its meaning, in the tone-down. On the stage his efforts at being 'manly' carried the suggestion that, indeed, he was trying to compensate a fear of a homo trend in his own makeup. The suggestion is di-

luted. . . ." *Time* magazine suggested that "obviously the American public isn't old enough to know that there is such a thing as homosexuality."

240. Tell Me That You Love Me, Junie Moon (Paramount, 1970), color, 112 min. GP-rated.

Producer, Otto Preminger; associate producer, Nat Rudich; director, Preminger; based on the novel by Marjorie Kellogg; screenplay, Kellogg; production designer, Lyle Wheeler; set decorator, Morris Hoffman; costumes, Ronald Talsky, Phyllis Garr, Halston; makeup, Charles Schram; music, Philip Springer; music director, Thomas Z. Shepard; assistant director, Norman Cook; camera, Boris Kaufman; editor, Henry Berman, Dean O. Ball.

Cast: Liza Minnelli (Junie Moon); Ken Howard (Arthur); Robert Moore (Warren); James Coco (Mario); Kay Thompson (Miss Gregory); Fred Williamson (Beach Boy); Ben Piazza (Jesse); Emily Yancy (Solana); Leonard Frey (Guiles); Clarisse Taylor (Minnie); James Beard (Sidney Wyner); Julie Bovasso (Ramona); Gina Collens (Lila); Barbara Logan (Mother Moon); Nancy Marchand (Nurse Oxford); Lynn Milgrim (Nurse Holt); Ric O. Feldman (Joebee); James D. Pasternak (Artist); Angelique Pettyjohn (Melissa); Anne Revere (Miss Farber); Elaine Shore (Mrs. Wyner); Guy Sorel (Dr. Gaines); Wayne Tippett (Dr. Miller); Pete Seeger, Pacific Gas & Electric (Themselves); and: Ulla Bomser, Cynthia Korman, Anne Larson.

Despite an unappealing title, a trio of highly neurotic leading characters, and Otto Preminger's heavy-handed direction, *Tell Me That You Love Me, Junie Moon* is frequently an affecting drama, thanks to a sterling cast, especially Liza Minnelli. One of the drama's less sturdy elements was its theory that a homosexual can be "cured" of his gayness overnight—literally—by sleeping with a woman.

As a result of her demented boyfriend (Ben Piazza) pouring battery acid on her face, the once-pert Junie Moon (Liza Minnelli) copes with both physical and emotional scars. In the hospital, she makes two friends: Arthur (Ken Howard), a slightly retarded epileptic, whose ailment

Robert Moore in *Tell Me That You Love Me, Junie Moon* (1970).

led to his being raised in foster homes; and Warren (Robert Morse), a paraplegic gay man raised by one of his mother's friends, the homosexual Guiles (Leonard Frey), who, in turn, is a paraplegic due to a gunshot wound he received on a hunting trip while trying to seduce his then companion. When the three loners, Junie, Ar-

thur and Warren, leave the hospital, they share a rundown cottage rented from the wealthy, eccentric Miss Gregory (Kay Thompson). At first, Junie finds the timid Arthur a job at a fish market run by Mario (James Coco). Later, Mario dismisses Arthur when he receives an anonymous phone call from a malicious neighbor falsely insisting his employee is a homosexual. Nevertheless, because he is falling in love with Junie, Mario lends the trio money to vacation at a seaside resort. Once there, the wheelchair-bound Warren is carried about by handsome, muscular Beach Boy (Fred Williamson), an employee who soon attracts his attention. However, it is Beach Boy's girlfriend, Solana (Emily Yancy) who seduces Warren. The next morning, a joyful Warren insists he is a new man, no longer gay (and insists he will never fuss around the kitchen again making brownie). Meanwhile, Arthur admits to Junie that he loves her, but she is suspicious of all men. Finally, they make love. The next day, Arthur's health deteriorates and before they can return to their cottage, he dies in Junie's arms. The only mourners at his funeral are Junie, the Mario and Warren.

Like most of the critical reaction, *Variety* was disaffected by this offbeat film, insisting that director Otto Preminger gave the film "a somewhat bland mounting" causing it to "miss the poetics inherent in the tale. He has managed to avoid overt sentimentalism but also the more profound. . . . [Picture] is riddled with good intentions but also dramatic ambivalence. . . ." As to the cast, the trade paper decided, "Miss Minnelli is her quirky, hurt but game self with Moore worrying about his role but not truly finding the mixture of queer spite and strength it needs." David McGillivray (British *Monthly Film Bulletin*) thought "Otto Preminger, presumably crusading for both the mentally and physically handicapped in one fell swoop, sheds precious little light on their problems in this love-conquers-all story. . . . Junie Moon is full of wisecracks, strange smart-Aleck dialogue and the most peculiar flashbacks. (Warren, reared by an effeminate photographer—Leonard Frey . . . recalls his youth in a series of low-comic vignettes. . . . The jokes and the tricks are obviously intended to lighten the load but the whole thing is impossible to take seriously anyway. . .).".

Tell Me That You Love Me, Junie Moon failed quickly at the box-office. It was filmed partially on location in Massachusetts and at Sequoia National Park and Shelter Island, California.

241. 10 (Warner Bros., 1979), color, 122 min. R-rated.

Producers, Blake Edwards, Tony Adams; director/screenplay, Blake Edwards; production designer, Rodger Maus; set decorators, Reg Allen, Jack Stevens; costumes, Pat Edwards; makeup, Byron Roylance, Ben Nye II; music, Henry Mancini; song, Carol Bayer Sager and Robert Wells; assistant directors, Mickey McCardle, Nick Marck, Karen Murray; stunt coordinator, Dick Crockett; sound Bruce Bisenz; special effects, Fred Cramer; camera, Frank Stanley; editor, Ralph E. Winters.

Cast: Dudley Moore (George Webber); Julie Andrews (Samantha "Sam" Taylor); Bo Derek (Jenny); Robert Webber (Hugh Fallon); Dee Wallace (Mary Lewis); Sam Jones (David); Brian Dennehy (Bartender); Max Showalter (Reverend); Rad Daly (Josh); Nedra Volz (Mrs. Kissel); James Noble (Fred Miles); Virginia Kiser (Ethel Miles); John Hawker (Covington); Deborah Rush (Dental Assistant); Don Calfa (Neighbor); Walter George Alton (Larry); Annette Martin (Redhead); John Hancock (Dr. Croce); Lorry Goldman (TV Director); Arthur Rosenberg (Pharmacist); Mari Gorman (Waitress); Marcy Hanson (Blonde); Senilo Tanney (Hotel Manager); Kitty De Carlo (Customer); Bill Lucking (1st Officer); Owen Sullivan (2nd Officer); Debbie White (Reservation Clerk); Laurence Carr (Airline Passenger); Camila Ashland (Nanny); Burke Byrnes, Doug Sheehan (Cops); J. Victor Lopez, Jon Linton (Beachboys); John Chappell (Man on Beach); Art Kassul (Large Man); Julie Alter, Jeannetta Arnette, Gail Bowman, Michael Champion, Lisa Chess, S. Colombatto, Lynn Farrell, Yolanda Galardo, Adam Anderson, Adrian Aron, Sheila Cassidy, Gregory Chase, Ellen Clark, Antonia Ellis, Vivian Farren, Sharri Zak (Party Guests).

Blake Edwards's *10* hit the right audience pulse. This hilarious farce, a sleeper hit, was blessed with an easily-identifiable narrative of a neurotic man relentlessly pursuing his dream woman only to discover, after ensnaring her, that he was happier with his illusion. It offered the disarming Dudley Moore at his idiosyncratic best and provided a marvelous showcase for the strikingly beautiful Bo Derek. This hit comedy (grossing $37 million in distributors' domestic film rentals) created several fads: rating dates on a 1–10 scale, making love to a recording of "Bolero," and Bo Derek sightings. Just like Julie Andrews's understated performance as Moore's (im)patient love, Robert Webber provided a well-shaded characterization as Moore's song-writing partner. His character is a middle-age gay man who pursues his own parallel illusions (handsome young men), fully knowing—as Moore's character belatedly discovers—that such fantasies never have satisfactory finales.

In Los Angeles, popular song composer George Webber (Dudley Moore) celebrates his 42nd birthday. Despite the presence of his loving singer girlfriend, Samantha "Sam" Taylor (Julie Andrews), fidgety George has the middle-age blues. Driving along one day he is captivated by a beautiful bride-to-be, Jenny (Bo Derek), whom he spots in her limousine. He is enraptured by this fantasy lady whom he chases to her wedding—which he disrupts when stung by a bee. Thereafter, the frustrated George is belligerent with Sam and argumentative with his partner, Hugh Fallon (Robert Webber), the latter having found domestic bliss with his latest beach-boy lover (Walter George Alton). Unable to forget Jenny, Webber tracks her whereabouts to a Mexican resort where she and her husband, David (Sam Jones), are honeymooning. Having argued with Sam before impetuously darting after his lady love, George alternates his time in Mexico between trying to apologize to Sam on the phone and, variously, attempting to get close to his obsession. Finally, he succeeds when, one day, he saves David from being swept away on his surfboard. The grateful Jenny goes to bed with George, but he realizes that he is turned off by her permissive sexual attitudes. Back in Los Angeles, he and Sam reconcile.

Vincent Canby (*New York Times*) was captivated by the "frequently hilarious" *10* in which "noses are meant to be stung, heads to have hangovers, and beautiful women to be pursued at any cost. . . . The movie belongs very much to Mr. Moore, who manages to be funny without ever having to appear stupid. . . ." *Variety* confirmed, "*10* is a shrewdly observed and beautifully executed comedy of manners and morals. Covering much the same geography and some of the same concerns as *Shampoo* [1975] with a similar serio-comic approach, film offers more than enough laughs and titillation to please mass audiences. . . ." Comparing the structural importance of Sam and George to the hero's life, the trade paper acknowledged, "A less central but more successful contrast to Moore's obsessive behavior is seen in Robert Webber's unhappy gay relationship with a macho beach bum. Both men are scrambling to hold onto youth and beauty in their different ways, neither with satisfactory results. . . . Webber is superbly understated."

There is a great resonance in the scenes between gay Hugh Fallon and his straight music writing partner, George. Hugh is wryly humorous about George's male menopause, insisting that his friend is one of the world's greatest "Anglo-Saxon heterosexual bores." As Hugh acknowledges, "I could analyze you a lot better than that expensive shrink. The trouble is, you'd come out gay and I couldn't do that to Sam." When the unhappy, somewhat homophobic George becomes jealous of Hugh's currently happy domestic situation, he complains about Hugh's hunky young boyfriend: "Doesn't he do anything except swim and jog on the beach?." An amused but self-aware Hugh responds, "Oh yes, he makes me happy, so I let him swim and jog on the beach." Later, reflecting the uneasy basis of his fantasy chasing, Hugh snips at Larry, his kept companion: "Please bring all the receipts. George thinks you take advantage of me." Larry retorts, "Well I suppose I do, but then nobody's perfect." Still later, after Hugh and

Larry have broken up and the latter has departed for Europe, the sadder-but-wiser Hugh admits wistfully, "due to some foolish pride on my part, I don't think I'll take him back." Here is a man who knows himself well. To date, Hugh Fallon is one of the most fully realized and sympathetic portrayals of a gay person in the American cinema.

10 received an Oscar nomination for Best Original Song: "Song from *10* (Its Easy to Say)," but lost to *Norma Rae*'s "It Goes Like It Goes."

242. That Certain Summer

(ABC-TV, November 1, 1972), color, 73 min. Not rated.

Producers, Richard Levinson, William Link; director, Lamont Johnson; teleplay, Levinson, Link; art director, William D. DeCinces; music, Gil Melle; camera, Vilis Paenieks; editor, Edward M. Abroms.

Cast: Hal Holbrook (Doug Salter); Martin Sheen (Gary McClain); Joe Don Baker (Phil Bonner); Marlyn Mason (Laureen Hyatt); Scott Jacoby (Nick Salter); Hope Lange (Janet Salter); James McEachin (Mr. Early, the Conductor); Jan Shepard (Jody Bonner); Clarke Gordon (Artist); Carolyn Bueno (Mrs. Michele); Patti Steele (Woman); Myron Natwick (Man at Party).

"A lot of people, most people I guess, think it's wrong. They say it's a sickness, that it's something that has to be cured. I don't know. I do know that it isn't easy. If I had a choice, it isn't something I'd pick for myself." (Doug Salter to his son in *That Certain Summer*)

In the early 1970s, American feature films were just starting to explore the once-taboo topic of homosexuality, with such entries as *The Boys in the Band* (1970), *Fortune and Men's Eyes* (1971) and *Some of My Best Friends Are . . .* (1971), qq.v. It was natural for U.S. network television to want to deal also with such controversial, topical material. A 1972 episode of the TV sitcom "All in the Family," had arch bigot Archie Bunker coping with the new knowledge that a drinking buddy, a former football player

friend, was gay. In February 1972, CBS-TV dealt obliquely with male-to-male sex behind bars in the TV movie, *The Glass House*, q.v.

Then came the made-for-television movie, *That Certain Summer*. It was produced and written by Richard Levinson and Warren Link, the creators of "Columbo" among other innovative TV fare. In this acclaimed telefilm drama, boasting a prestigious cast, they dealt directly with the subject of homosexuality. To appease network policy watchers (which included staff psychiatrists), the scripters were told, according to a later interview given by Levinson, "somewhere in the script we had to introduce a character . . . who would give voice to prevailing public opinion. . . .[F]inally we decided to have the homosexual himself, rather than some bigot imposed on the story, tell his son the harsh truth, that some people think homosexuality is a sickness—some people do—and that if he had his choice, he wouldn't be a homosexual. We justified this in our minds by feeling that in a racist and bigoted society, it is simply more comfortable being rich, white and straight than poor, black or gay."

Doug (Hal Holbrook) and Janet Salter (Hope Lange) are divorced. One summer weekend when their fourteen-year-old son, Nick (Scott Jacoby), comes from his mother's place in Los Angeles to Sausalito to stay with his father, he is upset to find his father preoccupied with a young companion, Gary McClain (Martin Sheen). Finally, realizing he must confront reality, Doug takes a chance on telling Nick why he and Janet split up, explaining that he is gay and that Gary is his lover. Nick is hurt, angry and confused, and runs away. Eventually, a truce is reached between son and father.

Daily Variety reported, "Film, bound to stir up some televiewers, still grabs hold as characters struggle to solve age-old problem. . . . The film is courageous in taking on a challenging subject; not backing off." Steve H. Scheurer (*Movies on TV and Videocassette*, 1991), in retrospect, rated it 3½ stars, complimenting the "tasteful and honest" script.

For *That Certain Summer*, Scott Jacoby won a Best Supporting Actor Emmy, while Hal Holbrook and Hope Lange received Best Actor/Actress nominations. Lamont Johnson won the Directors Guild of America Award for his handling of the telefilm. Thirteen years later, Martin Sheen would play a father initially intolerant of his son's homosexuality in *Consenting Adult* (1985), q.v.

That Certain Summer, which found adherents and detractors on both sides of the pro- and anti-gay issue, paved the way for future TV shows dealing with gay characters, whether in episodes of sitcoms ("Maude," "Rhoda" or "Mary Hartman, Mary Hartman"), full dramas ("Family, "Kojak" "Medical Center") or such TV movies as *Cage without a Key* (1975), *Alexander: The Other Side of Dawn* (1977), *Sergeant Matlovich Vs. the U.S. Air Force* (1978) or *A Question of Love* (1978), qq.v.

243. There Was a Crooked Man

(Warner Bros., 1970), color, 126 min. R-rated.

Executive producer, C. O. Erickson; producer/director, Joseph L. Mankiewicz; based on the story "Prison Story" by David Newman, Robert Benton; screenplay, Newman, Benton; art director, Edward Carrere; set decorator, Keogh Gleason; costumes, Anna Hill Johnstone; makeup, Perc Westmore; music, Charles Strouse; song, Strouse, Lee Adams; stunt coordinator, Roger Creed; assistant directors, Don Kranze, Bill Green, Chris Seitz; sound, Al Overton Jr., George Hause; special effects, John Barton; camera, Harry Stradling Jr.; editor, Gene Milford.

Cast: Kirk Douglas (Paris Pitman Jr.); Henry Fonda (Sheriff Woodward Lopeman); Hume Cronyn (Dudley Whinner); Warren Oates (Floyd Moon); Burgess Meredith (The Missouri Kid); John Randolph (Cyrus McNutt); Arthur O'Connell (Mr. Lomax); Martin Gabel (Warden Francis E. Le Goff); Michael Blodgett (Coy Cavendish); Claudia McNeil (Goldie, the Madam); Alan Hale Jr. (Tobaccy Watkins); Victor French (Whiskey); Lee Grant (Mrs.

Bullard); C. K. Yang (Ah-Ping Woo); Pamela Hensley (Edwina); Bert Freed (Skinner); Barbara Rhoades (Miss Jessie Brundidge); J. Edward McKinley (Governor); Dora Merende (Churchgoer); Gene Evans (Colonel Wolff); Jeanne Cooper (Prostitute); and: Bart Burns, Ann Doran, Byron Foulger, Karl Lukas, Larry D. Mann, Paul Newlan, Paul Prokop.

The darkly-satirical *There Was a Crooked Man*, a very offbeat Western, portrays the baser nature of men from both sides of the law. Set in a rugged prison in the 1880s, this R-rated feature depicts tough prisoners being controlled by tougher jailers, who are more determined and more corrupt. Among the prisoners in this wry narrative are a bickering middle-age gay couple—whom one character calls the "daisies"—and a handsome young stud, the latter the object of lust by a bullish guard. These characterizations, as well as the male and female nudity in the film, were filmmaker Joseph L. Mankiewicz's way of taking advantage of the newly liberalized industry production code.

Paris Pitman Jr. (Kirk Douglas) hides $500,000 grabbed in a bank robbery in a snake-infested hole. Later, Paris, the only crook to survive the heist, is captured by steadfast Sheriff Woodward Lopeman (Henry Fonda) and sentenced to ten years at the Arizona Prison. The new group of prisoners arriving at the ramshackle penitentiary includes: chip-on-his-shoulder Paris; handsome young Coy Cavendish (Michael Blodgett), who killed a man in a pool hall fight; aging scam artists Cyrus McNutt (John Randolph) and Dudley Whinner (Hume Cronyn), who are incessantly arguing lovers. The braggart Pitman shares a crowded, dank cell with McNutt, Whinner, Cavendish, the murderer Ah-Ping Woo (C.K. Yang), the excitable Floyd Moon (Warren Oates) and an old-timer, the Missouri Kid (Burgess Meredith). Later, the greedy Warden Le Goff (Martin Gabel) suggests to Pitman that, if will share the money with him, Le Goff will permit him to escape. However, before Paris's breakout can occur, the warden is murdered by Ah-Ping. A new warden is appointed, who turns out to be Pitman's nemesis—Woodward Lopeman. The liberal Lopeman begins a new regime at the prison, except for Pitman whom he intends to whip into conformity. Meanwhile, Coy, working on the rock piles, is propositioned by the lustful Skinner (Bert Freed), an offer he rejects, leading to more abuse from this sadistic guard.

Eventually, the incorrigible Pitman engineers an escape, allowing three of his fellow convicts to die—including Floyd and Coy—before he flees. Lopeman pursues Pitman who is trying to retrieve his money cache. While doing so, he is bitten by a rattlesnake and dies. Lopeman arrives on the scene, packs the corpse on the back of a horse and escorts it back to the prison. Then, he rides off to Mexico, his saddlebag packed with the stolen bounty. A closing title card reads, "And he lives happily ever after."

Pauline Kael (*The New Yorker*) responded negatively to this cynical narrative: "This example of commercialized black-comedy nihilism sees to have been written by an evil 2-year old, and it has been directed in the Grand Rapids style of filmmaking. . . . There's nobody to root for but Kirk Douglas, a red-haired, jokester-killer." Vincent Canby (*New York Times*) decided, "One of the movie's bothersome idiosyncrasies is that it wants to utilize its myths and to work against them. Thus, the film, which begins as a broad satire, turns into fairly straight melodrama involving prison riots and such things, before ending on a note of gentle cynicism. . . ." *Variety* complained that it "has a crooked plot that is neither comedy nor convincing drama. . . . It is the type of action drama in which neither the actors nor director appear to believe the script or characters. . . . The territorial prison . . . set . . . looks like a set . . . and [nothing] suspends the basic disbelief. As to the cast, the trade paper reported, "Hume Cronyn and John Randolph play a bickering old homosexual couple with a flair and touching humor that is the best thing in the film."

In retrospect, Bernard F. Dick (*Joseph L. Mankiewicz*, 1983), who found much of worth in *There Was a Crooked Man*, noted:

"While the Dudley-Cyrus relationship exists in prison films (although it is more common in a women's prison movie like *Caged* [1950, q.v.], it is more characteristic of the Western where men are often forced into male/female roles. In *Red River* (1948), Walter Brennan functions as a kind of wife-cook to John Wayne, when Wayne finds a surrogate son in Montgomery Clift, Brennan shifts his affection to an Indian, assuming the dominant or masculine role and treating the Indian like a squaw."

244. These Three (United Artists, 1936), 93 min. Not rated.

Producer, Samuel Goldwyn; director, William Wyler; based on the play *The Children's Hour* by Lillian Hellman; screenplay, Hellman; art director, Richard Day; costumes, Omar Kiam; music, Alfred Newman; assistant director, Walter Mayo; sound, Frank Maher; camera, Gregg Toland; editor, Daniel Mandell.

Cast: Miriam Hopkins (Martha Dobie); Merle Oberon (Karen Wright); Joel McCrea (Dr. Joseph Cardin); Catherine Doucet (Mrs. Lily Mortar); Alma Kruger (Mrs. Tilford); Bonita Granville (Mary Tilford); Marcia Mae Jones (Rosalie Wells); Carmencita Johnson (Evelyn); Mary Ann Durkin (Joyce Walton); Margaret Hamilton (Agatha); Mary Louise Cooper (Helen Burton); Walter Brennan (Taxi Driver); and: Frank McGlynn, Anya Taranda, Jerry Larkin.

Self-willed, independent producer Samuel Goldwyn insisted on spending $50,000 to purchase the screen rights to Lillian Hellman's hit Broadway show, *The Children's Hour* (1934). When told by shocked associates that this was a colossal waste of money, since the industry production code would forbid him to produce a picture dealing with lesbians, the filmmaker shrugged and replied, "That's Okay. We'll make them Americans!"

Before the filming of this highly controversial story of lives ruined by a spiteful little girl's rumor that her school mistresses are lesbians could begin, Hollywood's newly-structured Hayes Office demanded that (1) Goldwyn not use the title *The Children's Hour* for his production, (2) the publicity for the picture not refer to Lillian Hellman's work by name or inference, and (3) the theme not deal with two women suspected of "unnatural love." Goldwyn overcome these obstacles through the help of Lillian Hellman, who altered her story to deal NOT with the repercussions of suspected gay love, but of the ramifications of marital infidelity.

In a small New England town, Martha Dobie (Miriam Hopkins) and Karen Wright (Merle Oberon) open a private girls' school in an old house. Both young women fall in love with handsome Dr. Joseph Cardin (Joel McCrea), although it is Karen who becomes engaged to Cardin, while Martha keeps her love for the physician a secret. When Martha dismisses Mrs. Lily Mortar (Catherine Doucet), one of the teachers, for being a harsh influence on the students, the latter insists to Martha that she is being spiteful because Lily knows that Martha loves Cardin. This is overheard by a student (Marcia Mae Jones) who passes on the misinformation to her spoiled brat classmate, Mary Tilford (Bonita Granville). To get even with her teachers for reprimanding her for misdeeds, Mary tells her doting grandmother, Mrs. Tilford (Alma Kruger), an embellished malicious lie about Karen and Cardin having an affair. Soon, the school is devoid of pupils. Mrs. Tilford is sued for libel, but Martha and Karen lose their case. Eventually, the truth is revealed and an apologetic Mrs. Tilford explains the facts to Karen, who has become increasingly uncertain of whether or not Martha and Joseph had a hidden relationship. A sadden Martha leaves town and Karen goes to Vienna, where Cardin is furthering his medical studies. The two lovers are reunited.

Frank S. Nugent (*New York Times*) thought "Miss Hellman's job of literary carpentry is little short of brilliant" but admitted, "There may be some dissatisfied comments from those who saw the play, for *These Three* lacks the biting, bitter tragedy of *The Children's Hour*. It chooses (or the censors chose for it) to ignore any implications of an abnormal relationship between the two women school teachers . . . and it progresses to what must be considered a happy and romantic ending." A pleased Abel Green (*Variety*) rated *These Three* "A thoroughly fine cinematic transmutation. . . . Stripped of its unsavory original theme . . . the film version is an even more appealing presentation for popular consumption. . . . *These Three* is ultra in every department."

Having learned its lesson with the landmark *The Children's Hour*, Hollywood abandoned adapting any more Broadway plays dealing with "forbidden" love until the mid-1950s. Then, to appease the still vigilent censors, it distorted *Tea and Sympathy* (1956), diluted *The Strange One* (1957), and badly botched *Cat on a Hot Tin Roof* (1958), qq.v. As for *The Children's Hour*, it would be remade by William Wyler in 1961, q.v. However, by then changing mores had reduced much of its shock value, and, if that were not enough, Wyler turned out a plodding, still timid version of Hellman's strong drama.

245. They Only Kill Their Masters (Metro-Goldwyn-Mayer, 1972), color, 97 min. PG-rated.

Producer, William Belasco; associate producer, Barry Mendelson; director, James Goldstone; screenplay, Lane Slate; art director, Lawrence G. Paull; set decorator, Philip Abramson; costumes, Arnold M. Lipin; makeup, Charles Schram; music, Perry Botkin Jr.; assistant director, Wes McAfee; dog trainer, Karl Miller; sound, Al Overton Jr., Harry W. Tetrick; camera, Michael Hugo; editor, Edward A. Biery.

Cast: James Garner (Police Chief Abel Marsh); Katharine Ross (Kate); Hal Holbrook (Dr. Watkins, the Veterinarian); Harry Guardino (Captain Streeter, the Sheriff); June Allyson (Mrs. Watkins); Christopher Connelly

(John, the Cop); Tom Ewell (Walter, the Cop); Peter Lawford (Lee Campbell); Edmund O'Brien (George, the Liquor Store Owner); Arthur O'Connell (Ernie, the Cafeteria Owner); Ann Rutherford (Gloria, the Police Secretary); Art Metrano (Malcolm); Harry Basch (Mayor); Jenifer Shaw (Diana); Jason Wingreen (Mallory); Robert Nichols (Doctor); Norma Connolly (Mrs. DeCamp); David Westberg (State Trooper); Lee Pulford (Jenny Campbell); Roy Applegate (Harry); Alma Lenor Beltran (Rosa); and: Murphy the Dog.

The once glamorous Metro-Goldwyn-Mayer had fallen on hard ways by the time of this programmer, as had most of its cast. This tidy whodunit provides an excursion into nostalgia (including filming on the still standing sets from the Andy Hardy movie series). It also provides a storyline jolt, casting squeaky-clean June Allyson as a lesbian murderess.

The gossipy California coastal town of Eden Landings is atwitter when the body of divorcee Jenny Campbell (Lee Pulford) washes ashore. Everyone assumes that her Doberman pinscher—found standing near the corpse—was the cause of her badly-mauled body. However, congenial Police Chief Abel Marsh (James Garner), just back from vacation, is not so sure. He orders an autopsy. The post mortem discloses that the victim died in fresh water and that she was pregnant. Marsh soon finds himself adopting the "killer" dog (to prevent it being destroyed) and romancing Kate (Katharine Ross), the comely assistant to the local vet, Dr Watkins (Hal Holbrook). The mystery becomes more complicated when the deceased's ex-husband (Peter Lawford) is found murdered, and then Jenny's beach house is burned to the ground. The investigation leads to Dr. Watkins, who is shot by the Sheriff's deputies when he tries to kill Abel. However, by then, it is clear that he was protecting his jealous wife (June Allyson), who is responsible for the murder spree. As Mrs. Watkins explains succinctly about Jenny: "She was a bitch. She wouldn't let it be the two of us. . . . Then she wouldn't let it be three [including Dr. Watkins]. She got pregnant. There was nothing left. Nothing left of him, nor of me. I had no choice."

Howard Thompson (*New York Times*) approved of this unpretentious crime yarn in which "a bright, plucky policeman tools around a rather humdrum little community confronting some bright but cagey characters who seem as real as he does. . . . The treatment extends through the denouement, opening a nasty, sexual can of worms with telling restraint." He admired the cast, adding, "And let's not forget a brief, unorthodox appearance by June Allyson, who does beautifully." Brenda Davies (British *Monthly Film Bulletin*) agreed. "Director James Goldstone's evocation of atmosphere recalls *In the Heat of the Night* [1967]. . . . Dialogue and characterisation are especially sharp, and both are helped by a cast of splendid old professionals. . . ."

246. To Be or Not to Be (Twentieth Century-Fox, 1983), color, 108 min. PG-rated.

Executive producer, Howard Jeffrey; producer, Mel Brooks; associate producer, Irene Waltzer; director, Alan Johnson; based on the screenplay by Edwin Justus Mayer; new screenplay, Thomas Meehan, Ronny Graham; production designer, Terence Marsh; art director, J. Dennis Washington; set decorators, Craig Edgar, Joseph E. Hubbard; costumes, Albert Wolsky; music, John Morris; choreographer, Charlene Painter; assistant directors, Ross G. Brown, Pamela Eilerson; sound, Gene S. Cantamessa; camera, Gerald Hirschfeld; editor, Alan Balsam.

Cast: Mel Brooks (Frederick Bronski); Anne Bancroft (Anna Bronski); Tim Matheson (Lieutenant Andre Sobinski); Charles Durning (Colonel Erhardt); Jose Ferrer (Professor Siletski); Christopher Lloyd (Captain Schultz); James Haake (Sasha Kinski); Scamp (Mutki); George Gaynes (Ravitch); George Wyner (Ratkowski); Jack Riley (Dobish); Lewis J. Stadlen (Lupinski); Ronny Graham (Sondheim); Estelle Reiner (Gruba); Zale Kessler (Bieler); Earl Boen (Dr. Boyarski); Ivor Barry (General Hobbs); William Glover (Major Cunningham); John Francis (British Intelligence Aide); Raymond Skipp (RAF Flight Sergeant); Marley

Sims (Rifka); Larry Rosenberg (Rifka's Husband); Max Brooks (Rifka's Son); Henry Kaiser (Gestapo Officer); Henry Brandon (Nazi Officer); Milt Jamin (Gestapo Soldier); George Caldwell (Gestapo Guard); Wolf Muser (Desk Sergeant); Lee E. Stevens (2nd Nazi Officer); Foy Goldman (Adolph Hitler); Robert Goldberg (Hitler Adjutant); John McKinney (Elite Guard Officer); Eda Reiss Merin (Frightened Jewish Woman); Manny Kleinmuntz (Husband of Jewish Woman); Phil Adams (Airport Sentry); Curt Lowens (Airport Officer); Ron Diamond (Pub Bartender); Gillian Eaton (Pub Usherette); Terence Marsh (Startled British Officer); Leeyan Granger, Sandra Gray, Lainie Manning, Antonette Yuskis, Clare Culhane, Stephanie Wingate (Ladies); Robin Haynes, Ron Kuhlman, John Otrin, Blane Savage, Joey Sheck (Polish Fliers); Scott Beach (Narrator); and: Dieter Curt, Howard Goodwin, Paul Ratliff, Ian Bruce, John Frayer, Edward J. Heim, Spencer Henderson, George Jayne, Bill K. Richards, Neil J. Schwartz, Tucker Smith, Ted Sprague.

In the midst of World War II, Ernst Lubitsch produced a sharp black comedy, *To Be Or Not to Be* (1942), starring Jack Benny and Carole Lombard. Although it was handled with wit and elan, the satire dealt with subjects—Adolph Hilter, rampaging Nazis, Jewish persecution—too close to audiences' hearts for much humor to be found in the film's situations. Moreover, before the picture debuted, its leading lady had died in a tragic plane crash. The movie never recovered at the boxoffice from its problems. Forty-one years later, ace prankster Mel Brooks thought it would be a safe movie to remake, casting his wife, Anne Bancroft, in the Lombard role, and hiring Alan Johnson, who choreographed "Springtime for Hitler" for *The Producers* (1968), q.v., as director. To provide added twist and dimension, Brooks incorporated the character Sasha as Bancroft's gay dresser. Sasha must not only cope with an ignoble love life, but he is also increasingly at peril because of Hitler's determination to round up all homosexuals and send them to the death camps.

In 1939, as Poland is about to be drawn into World War II, stars Anna Bronski (Anne Bancroft) and her husband, Frederick (Mel Brooks) are performing on stage in Warsaw. Frustated by her egotistical husband, she is flattered to receive attention from handsome pilot Lieutenant Andre Sobinski (Tim Matheson). Later, after the German invasion, Andre flees to England where he learns that freedomfighting Professor Siletski (Jose Ferrer), another expatriate, is actually a German spy returning to Warsaw to break down the Polish underground. Andre sneaks back into Warsaw and, with the help of the Bronskis, acquires a list of Siletski's targets. When Siletski is killed, Frederick impersonates him and matches wits with the ruthless German Colonel Erhardt (Charles Durning) who, it develops, has a yen for Anna. During a command performance for the visiting Hitler (Foy Goldman), the Bronskis and their troupe outsmart the storm troopers and sneak a group of Jewish fugitives—who have been hiding in the theatre's basement—to safety. Andrew flies them all to England.

Kevin Thomas (*Los Angeles Times*) was unmoved by the production: "The reworking of a classic was probably doomed from the start. . . ." He missed the "Lubtisch touch" and observed that "we know far more than was known in 1942 of the full extent of the Nazi evil." He thought Brooks and Bancroft could not "rise about their material" and that Charles Durning "is far superior to the rest of the picture. As to James Haaka as Anna's gay dresser, Thomas cited, "the gutsy, whiplash wit and confident charisma that Haaka brings to his Gypsy persona [on the club stage] have been straitjacketed in a stereotypic sissy role. The misuse of Haake is as good as example as any of what's gone wrong with the film." Rex Reed (*New York Post*) rated the remake "a borscht-belt Polish joke" and observed there was "something smarmy in updated jokes about homosexuals wearing pink triangles and Jews wearing yellow stars that I found offensive."

In contrat, David Ansen (*Newsweek*)

insisted, "because the copy is so entertaining in its own right, it seems more a tribute than ripoff." He acknowledged, "the most significant addition in the new script . . . is an acknowledgment of how the Nazis persecuted homosexuals." Vincent Canby (*New York Times*), rating the remake "smashingly funny," pointed out, "Mr. Brooks's uncontrollable urge to carry bad taste so far that it might possibly become redeeming is evident from time to time, as in a line referring to contributions to theater by Jews, gypsies and homosexuals. As if to make amends he turns Anna's faithful dresser . . . into a swishily courageous homosexual, who wears his pink triangle with pride. . . . These [including the trouper who recites Shylock's soliloguy] are not among the film's great inspirations."

With its mixed critical reception, *To Be or Not to Be* grossed a modest $6 million iin distributors' domestic film rentals.

247. To Live and Die in L.A.
(Metro-Goldwyn-Mayer/United Artists, 1985), color, 116 min. R-rated.

Excecutive producer, Samuel Schulman; producer, Irving H. Levin; co-producer, Bud Smith; director William Friedkin; based on the novel by Gerald Petievich; screenplay, Friedkin, Petievich; production designer, Lilly Kilvert; art director, Buddy Cone; set decorator, Cricket Rowland; costumes, Linda Bass; makuep, Jefferson Dawn; music, Wang Chung; assistant directors, Charles Meyers, Bob Roe; stunt coordinators, Pat E. Johnson, Buddy Joe Hooker; sound, Jean-Louis DuCarme, Rodger Pardee; camera, Robby Muller; second unit camera, Robert Yeoman; supervising editor, Bud Smith; editor, Scott Smith.

Cast: William L. Petersen (Richard Chance); Willem Dafoe (Eric Masters); John Pankow (John Vukovich); Debra Feuer (Bianca Torres); John Turturro (Carl Cody); Darlanne Fluegel (Ruth Lanier); Dean Stockwell (Bob Grimes); Steve James (Jeff Rice); Robert Downey (Thomas Bateman); Michael Greene (Jim Hart); Christopher Allport (Max Waxman); Jack Hoard (Jack); Val DeVargas (Judge Filo Cedillo); Dwier Brown (Doctor); Michael Chong (Thomas Ling); Jackelyn Giroux (Claudia Leith); Michael Zand (Terrorist); Bobby Bass, Dar Allen Robinson (FBI Agents); Anne Betancourt (Nurse); Katherine M. Louie (Ticket Agent); Edward Harrell (Airport Guard); Gilbert Espionoza (Ultro's Bartender); John Petievich, Zarko Petievich, Rick Dalton, Richard L. Lane, Jack Cota (Agents); Shirley J. White (Airline Passengers); Gerald H. Brownlee (Visiting Room Guard); David M. DuFriend (Tower Guard); Ruben Garcia (Ruben, An Inmate); Joe Duran (Prison Guard); Buford McClerkins, Gregg Dandridge (Prison Assailants); Donny Williams, Earnest Hart Jr. (Rice's Friend); Thomas F. Duffy (2nd Suspect); Gerry Petievich (Special Agent); Mark Gash (Mark Gash); Pat McGroaty (Criminal); Brian Bradley (Tourist); Ojane Leaves (Serena); Cherise Bate, Jane Leaves, Michael W. Higgins, Chris Lattanzi, Shaun Earl (Dancers).

Director William Friedkin went through several professional peaks and valleys after his well-received *The French Connection* (1972). He sought to recapture some of his past glory in the hard-hitting *To Live and Die in L.A.,* which focused on corruption on both sides of the law in smoggy Los Angeles. The movie's astonishing car chase—going the wrong way!!—on an L.A. freeway was its thrilling high spot. However, there were several other virtues to this generally overlooked feature. It had an engaging group of performers (including Willem Dafoe, William L. Peterson, Dean Stockwell and Darlanne Fluegel), benefitted from overall fast pacing, and boasted an assortment of plot twists to maintain viewer interest. Among this feature's subordinate, but well-etched, characters was Bianca Torres (Debra Feuer), an attractive bisexual moll. Her role in the proceedings was geared to make the movie more cynical and hip, as well as provide an out-of-the-norm extension to the portrayed criminal netherworld.

To Live and Die in L.A. focuses on the battle of wits and nerve between U.S. Secret agent Richard Chance (William L. Petersen) and his ace counterfeiter opponent, Eric Masters (Willem Dafoe). In their see-sawing battle for the upper hand, several people die, including the two main foes. Chance's partner, John Vukovich (John Pankow) survives the ordeal, but, in the process, sacrifices his professional standards for expediency and survival. Others caught in the ongoing battle are crooked attorney Bob Grimes (Dean Stockwell); police informant Ruth Lanier (Darlanne Fluegel), who lives with Chance and whose stool pigeon services are inherited by Vukovich, and Bianca Torres (Debra Feuer). The latter would as soon couple sexually with her jealous stripper girlfriend, Serena (Ojane Leaves), as be with the hot-tempered forger, Eric Masters. As the surviving characters go their separate ways, the ambitious Bianca asks Grimes, the veteran underworld mouthpiece, why he associates with such scum. He replies coolly that, just like her, he is in it for the money.

Variety panned the film: "*To Live and Die in L.A.* looks like a rich man's 'Miami Vice.'. . . . As usual, the people in a Friedkin film are living intensely under high pressure situations that rarely let up. . . . Friedkin keeps dialog to a minimum, but what conversation there is proves wildly overloaded with streetwise obscenities. . . . Everyone here seems capable of deception and moral duplicity, and then proceeds to live up to those expectations." In contrast, Roger Ebert (*Movie Home Companion*, 1991) gave the thriller four stars, applauding the celebrated freeway chase set piece, as well as the film's cast and added "The film isn't just about cops and robbers, but about two systems of doing business, and how one of the systems finds a way to change itself in order to defeat the other. That's interesting. So is the chase."

Richard Combs (British *Monthly Film Bulletin*) observed of Friedkin, who had directed *The Boys in the Band* (1970) and *Cruising* (1980), qq.v., that in this new entry "Love-hate relationships abound between Secret Service man Richard Chance, his partners and his counterfeiting adversary, but it is only because Friedkin makes this seem so homoerotic in visual impact that the film becomes homophobic in implicitly denying it. (*Cruising*, of course, was already much more explicit on both counts)."

In a marketplace overcrowded with big action pictures, *To Live and Die in L.A.* proved to be a box-office disappointment, grossing only $6,593,342 in distributors' domestic film rentals.

248. Tony Rome (Twentieth Century-Fox, 1967), color, 110 min. Not rated.

Producer, Aaron Rosenberg; director, Gordon Douglas; based on the novel *Miami Mayhem* by Marvin H. Albert; screenplay, Richard Breen; art directors, Jack Martin Smith, James Roth; set decorator, Walter M. Scott, Warren Welch; costumes, Moss Mabry, Elinor Simmons, Malcolm Starr; makeup, Ben Nye; music/music director, Billy May; songs: Lee Hazelwood, May and Randy Newman; assistant director, Richard Lang; action sequence director, Buzz Henry; sound, Howard Warren, David Dockendorf; camera, Joseph Biroc; editor, Robert Simpson.

Cast: Frank Sinatra (Tony Rome); Jill St. John (Ann Archer); Richard Conte (Lieutenant Dave Santini); Sue Lyon (Diana Kosterman Pines); Gena Rowlands (Rita Neilson Kosterman); Simon Oakland (Rudolph Kosterman); Jeffrey Lynn (Adam Boyd); Lloyd Bochner (Vic Rood); Robert J. Wilke (Ralph Turpin); Virginia Vincent (Sally Bullock); Joan Shawlee (Fat Candy); Richard Krisher (Donald Pines); Lloyd Gough (Jules Langley); Babe Hart (Oscar); Templeton Fox (Mrs. Schuyler); Rocky Graziano (Packy); Elizabeth Fraser (Irma); Shecky Greene (Catleg); Jeanne Cooper (Lorna); Harry Davis (Ruyter); Stanley Ralph Ross (Sam Boyd); Buzz Henry (Nimmo [Joe Thurman]); Deanna Lund (Georgia McKay); Michael Romanoff (Sal, Matire d'Hotel); Tiffany Bolling (Photo Girl); Joe E. Ross (Bartender); Jilly Rizzo (Card Player).

With *Tony Rome*, Frank Sinatra entered into a new phase of his lengthy Hollywood screen career. Here, he played a hard-boiled private eye, a guy with a leering eye for flashy broads, a smart-ass quip for anyone upstaging him and a right hook for troublesome tough guys. Most deadly of all, he had an intolerant and condescending sneer for those whose lifestyle was not as "normal," healthy and all-American as his. This group included a lesbian stripper and a homosexual drug dealer.

In Miami, when drunken newlywed Diana Pines (Sue Lyon) is found unconscious at a motel, Ralph Turpin (Robert J. Wilke), who works there, hires his ex-partner, private detective Tony Rome (Frank Sinatra), to take her home. Her father, construction millionaire Rudolph Kosterman (Simon Oakland), hires Rome to find out what his daughter has been doing. In handling the case—with and without the help of his police detective pal (Richard Conte)—Tony survives the onslaught of assorted hoodlums, including Nimmo (Buzz Henry) and Catleg (Shecky Greene), and eventually finds Turpin dead in his office. He has to kill two other hoods (Lloyd Gough, Babe Hart) before he makes a connection between Nimmo and Rita (Gena Rowlands), the second Mrs. Kosterman. The search to find Nimmo takes him to the Flora Dora Club where he tails stripper Georgia McKay (Deanna Lund), a lesbian, and drug pusher, Vic Rood (Lloyd Bochner), a gay man. Eventually, Rome discovers that Rita, still legally wed to Nimmo, had been blackmailed into selling her jewelry (and substituting paste) to pay off her nemesis, and that Diana's stepfather (Jeffrey Lynn) wanted to kill Kosterman so his daughter, Diana, would inherit the fortune. In the showdown, Nimmo is killed, while Boyd and Catleg are arrested. Rita and Kosterman reaffirm their love and agree to provide for Diana's mother. As for Rome, who has been pursued intermittently by a shapely divorcee (Jill St. John), he returns to the comfort of his houseboat in Biscayne Bay and his ring-a-ding-ding life.

Bosley Crowther (*New York Times*), who found Sinatra and the film synthetically derivative of old Humphrey Bogart movies, decided, "For those who like their screen detective recognizable and raw, and their mystery melodramas seamy and colloquial, this thing with Mr. Sinatra should satisfy their taste. It is brassy, trashy, vulgar and Miama Beach colorful. . . . All in all, there's enough demonstration of social vlgarity, degeneracy and crime in the course of this vivid melodrama to satisfy the most lurid tourist taste. . . ." *Variety*, which responded well to the caper, observed, "By fadeout, few will particularly care about the mystery angle, for the eye and ear is bedazzled with vignette. . . ."

While the scene between no-nonsense Tony and the drug pusher (Lloyd Bochner) is almost non-descript, except for the movie's concept of how a well-heeled homosexual decorates his apartment, the sequence in which the detective follow Georgia McKay (Deanna Lund) back to the Starcrest Trailer Park is something else. Tony burst in on Georgia conversing with her drunken, hefty lover, Irene (Elizabeth Fraser). Initially attracted to the shapely stripper, he is contemptuous now that he has discovered she swings the wrong way and that he is in "the wrong ball park." He is disgusted as the weepy Irene slobbers over her "baby" and telling the stupified Rome "She shouldn't be traipsing around at this hour with me." As the overly-possessive Irene gets on Georgia nerves, the attractive partner snarls, "Lose a few pounds and shut up." Irene responds by slugging her mate. Then the two women make up and start hugging and kissing. Having had enough, the private eye snaps flippantly, "You want the lights on or off." They don't hear him and he decides, "Ah . . . they're better off."

In the next year's *The Detective*, q.v., set in New York, Sinatra would play a world-weary police detective, who rides herd on the sleazy underbelly of the big city. That movie also includes an excursion into the gay ghetto and features homosexual "deviants" who commit murders. Sinatra was giving mainstream audiences what he thought they wanted. Also in 1968, he made a sequel to *Tony Rome* called *Lady in Cement*.

249. Too Much Sun (New Line Cinema, 1990), color, 100 min. R-rated.

Executive producers, Seymour Morganstern, Al Schwartz; producer, Lisa M. Hansen; co-producers, Joe Bilella, Jon Stuckmeyer; associate producer, Catalaine Knell; director, Robert Downey; story, Schwartz; screenplay, Downey, Laura Ernst; production designer, Shawn Hausman; set decorator, Jeff Cazanov; costumes, Margaret A. Schnaidt; Dennis Bansmer; assistant director, David Householter; stunt coordinator/second unit director, Spiro Razatos; sound, Charles Kelly, David Brownlow; camera, Robert Yoeman; editor, Joseph D'Augustine.

Cast: Robert Downey Jr. (Reed Richmond); Eric Idle (Sonny Rivers); Andrea Martin (Bitsy Rivers); Jim Haynie (Father Seamus Kelly); Laura Ernst (Susan Connor); Leo Rossi (George Bianco); Ralph Maccio (Frank Della Rocco Jr.); Howard Duff (O. M. Rivers); Jennifer Rubin (Gracia): Lara Harris (Sister Ursula); James Hong (Frank Rocco Sr.); Melissa Jenkins (Nurse).

"And who do you think a jury will believe, a homosexual, a lesbian or a man of God?" (Spoken by a priest character in *Too Much Sun*)

Robert Downey had gained fame as the counterculture director of such irreverent, low-budget movies as *Putney Swope* (1968), *Pound* (1970) and *Greaser's Palace* (1972). However, the iconoclast was at a low creative ebb when he turned out this bottom-of-the barrel "comedy" featuring his son, Robert Downey Jr.

In Los Angeles, dying multi-millionaire O. M. Rivers (Howard Duff) is under the influence of am ambitious priest, Father Seamus Kelly (Jim Haynie). The grasping man of cloth convinces him to insert a clause in his will that, unless one of his two children has a child within the next year, all Rivers's money goes to the church. The problem, as everyone knows, is that both Sonny (Eric Idle) and Bitsy (Andrea Martin) are gay, firmly attached to their respective partners, George (Leo Rossi) and Susan (Laura Ernst). Not wanting to lose the family fortune to the conniving Kelly, Sonny concocts a scheme to get Susan impregnated so they can pro-

duce the needed heir. This proves a fiasco, however, as does a later coupling aboard a yacht between him and a prostitute (Jennifer Rubin). Meanwhile, the gloating Father Seamus and his devious helper, Sister Ursula (Lara Harris), contemplate their pending good fortune. However, it is discovered that Sonny, in a drunken moment years ago, had a brief fling with a Spanish woman, which produced a son, Reed (Robert Downey Jr.). Similarly, Bitsy, at her sweet sixteen party, had sex with the valet (James Hong), which produced Frank Jr. (Ralph Macchio). Reed and Frank Jr., both struggling real estate agents, appear together on the scene to claim the inheritance. All's well that ends well, to quote a well-known playwright.

Daily Variety sighed, "There's too little fun in *Too Much Sun* which is a shame because it has a promising premise and a great cast that turns on the heat but gets lost in the mirages of a wandering script. . . ." Kevin Thomas (*Los Angeles Times*) judged that this movie "is intended as hip social farce, but comes off as something that might have been made by a band of thumb-nosing high school students" For Thomas, "the problem is not that Downey is trying to treat gays and lesbians with humor but that he is so uninspired in his attempt to generate laughter. (Yes, he can't resist the near-impossible; an AIDS joke). . . . [The movie] lays waste to its large, gifted and game cast. . . ."

Too Much Sun is a dumb film to be avoided, and did little business at the box-office.

250. Too Outrageous! (Spectrafilm, 1987), color, 105 min. R-rated.

Producer, Roy Krost; director/screenplay, Dick Benner; art director, Andris Hausmanis; set decorators, Liz Calderhead, Marlene Graham; costumes, Alisa Alexander; makeup, Inge Klaudi; assistant directors, Tony Thatcher, David Till, Reid Dunlop; stunt coordinator, Shane Cardwell; sound, Daniel Latour; camera, Fred Guthe; editor, George Appleby.

Cast: Craig Russell (Robin Turner); Hollis McLaren (Liza Connors); David McIlwraith

(Bob); Ron White (Luke); Lynne Cormack (Betty Treisman); Michael J. Reynolds (Lee Sturges); Timothy Jenkins (Rothchild); Paul Eves (Tony Sparks); Frank Pellegrino (Manuel); Norma Dell'Agnese (Homeless Lady); Norman Duttweiler (Man in Drag in New York); Kent Staines (Snotty Waiter); Rusty Ryan (Jack Rabbit Club Bartender); Doug Millar (Audience Member); Kate Davis (Betty's Receptionist); Doug Paulson, George Hevenor (Executives); Jimmy James (Phil the Waiter/ Marilyn Monroe Impersonator); Barry Flatman (Phil Kennedy, the Talk Show Host); Ray Paisley (Chuck, the Bartender); Raymond Accolas (French Director); Francois Klanfer (French Announcer); Linda Goranson (Hospital Receptionist); Doug Inear (TV Emcee).

Craig Russell had made a strong impact with the cult hit *Outrageous!* (1977), q.v., as well as his later performances of female impersonations in clubs and on television. After a badly-received Carnegie Hall concert (1980) he vanished into Germany for several years. In 1987, *Outrageous!* director Richard Benner—who had also directed *Happy Birthday, Gemini*, 1980, q.v.—reunited Russell and his co-stars, Hollis McLaren and David McIlwraith for *Too Outrageous*. However, by then, a great deal had happened. Harvey Fierstein, in his hit play *Torch Song Trilogy* (1982), q.v., had stolen a lot of Russell's thunder as a newer, sharper version of a flip-talking gay comedian. Moreover, the outbreak of the AIDS epidemic had drastically altered the gay scene. Additionally, by the time of *Too Outrageous!*, Russell was less plucky and less spontaneous (this was a retread, after all). Finally, he had tougher on-camera competition in interpreting female living legends. above all, by cast member Jimmy James who did a smashing impersonation of Marilyn Monroe.

In the follow-up story, Robin Turner (Craig Russell) has been performing his drag act successfully at the Jack Rabbit Club for several years. He rooms with Liza Connors (Hollis McLaren), whose schizophrenia has been stabilized through drugs and by her therapeutic writing. They share an apartment with Robin's manager, Bob (David McIlwraith) and the latter's lover, Luke (Ron White), who is Turner's accompanist. Then, high-powered agent Betty Treisman (Lynne Cormack) enters the scene, convinced that she can make Robin a mainstream star, by sanitizing him into "Canada's Comic Illusionist." For a while, as they try the act out in Toronto, the dream comes true. As a bonus, Robin finds a hunky lover, a singer, Tony Sparks (Paul Eves), and Liza enjoys a romance with handsome Manuel (Frank Pellegrino). Before long, both Robin and Liza have to reassess their relationships. By the finale, they have reaffirmed the true value of Bob and Luke and returned to humbler horizons.

Jami Bernard (*New York Post*) rated *Too Outrageous!* "a benign comedy" which is "full of good intentions. But not nearly outrageous enough." Lynn Darling (*Newsday*) regarded the sequel "an awkward but winning froth of a movie in a minor key." She observed that, "Director/writer Dick Benner apparently has himself discovered the down side of success and stuffed his sequel full of bitter but overdrawn lessons. Forget most of that stuff and concentrate instead on the friendship between Robin and Liza. . . ." Michael Musto (*Village Voice*) found that Russell "does have the rare drag-queen courage to use his own voice rather than lip synch. . . ." For Musto, the picture "ultimately wins out with its relentless sincerity, its glorification of outcasts, and humanization of types most contemporary filmgoers would rather not deal with."

Too Outrageous! did marginal box-office business in its limited theatrical release. A sad footnote to the picture is that both Craig Russell and Richard Benner died of AIDS in 1990.

251. **Torch Song Trilogy** (New Line Cinema, 1988), color, 122 min. R-rated.

Executive producer, Ronald K. Fierstein; producer, Howard Gottfried; associate producer, Marie Cantin; director, Paul Bogart;

based on the play by Harvey Fierstein; screenplay, Fierstein; production designer, Richard Hoover; set decorator, Michael Warga; costumes, Colleen Atwood; makeup, Christa Reusch; music, Peter Matz; choreographer, Scott Salmon; assistant directors, Dennis McGuire, Peter Bogart; sound, Steve Nelson; camera, Mikael Salomon; editor, Nicholas C. Smith.

Cast: Anne Bancroft (Ma); Matthew Broderick (Alan); Harvey Fierstein (Arnold); Brian Kerwin (Ed); Karen Young (Laurel); Eddie Castrodad (David); Ken Page (Murray); Charles Pierce (Bertha Venation); Axel Vera (Marina Del Rey); Benji Schulman (Young Arnold); Nick Montgomery, Robert Neary (Chorus Boys); Kim Clark, Stephanie Penn (Female Bar Patrons); Geoffrey Harding (Man with Lighter); Lawrence Lott (Steve); Michael Bond (Bar Patron); Michael Warga (Bartender); Phil Sky (Man in Back Room); Lorry Goldman (Phil, Arnold's Brother); Edgar Small (Jack, Arnold's Father); Harriet C. Leider (Maitre d'); Paul Joynt, Mitch David Carter (Club Hecklers); Bob Minor (Gregory); Byron Deen (Roz); John Beckman (1st Cab Driver); Rabbi Elliott T. Spar (Rabbi); Alva Chinn (Photographer); Gregory Gilbert (Hustler); John Norman, Mark Zeisler (Thugs); Peter MacKenzie (1st Young Man) Peter Nevargic (2nd Young Man); Ted Hook (Old Man); Niall Gartlan (Boy in Fight); Catherine Blue, John Brnaga (Teachers); Tracey Bogart (Secretary at School); Alan Fudge (Dr. Fisher); Frits de Kneght (2nd Cab Driver).

"My biggest problem is being young and beautiful. It's my biggest problem because I've never been young and beautiful. Oh, I've been beautiful. God knows, I've been young. But never have the twain met." (The character Arnold in *Torch Song Trilogy*)

When Harvey Fierstein first mounted *Torch Song Trilogy* as a unified three-act play off Broadway in 1982, the three-hour-plus comedy/drama was hailed as a highly creative outpouring of the new Gay Pride era. It was a work filled, at heart, with traditional family values and a quest for self-respect, and an entertaining thesis to demonstrate that there was more to homosexuality than sexual pursuits. As a result of *Trilogy*, Fierstein went on to win several prizes, become a nationally-

known talent and to appear on screen in such films as *Garbo Talks* (1984), q.v. with Anne Bancroft. Meanwhile, AIDS, little known in the early 1980s, escalated into a global catastrophe. By the time *Torch Song Trilogy* was adapted belatedly for the screen, AIDS had made such a devastating impact that the movie was forced to confine its action to a specific period (1971–1981) so its characters could function as Fierstein had conceived them originally and not have to deal with the disease's impact on the gay lifestyle. Moreover, by 1988, the once pudgy, bawdy Fierstein had become part of the Establishment. All these factors had their toll in lessening the quality of the screen version of *Torch Song Trilogy*. The movie emerged in 1988 as a sometimes funny, sometimes contrived, curiosity piece geared for mainstream audiences. And, wonderful as she often can be, Anne Bancroft, as Ma, was NO Estelle Getty, the latter having brilliantly originated the role of Ma in the 1982 stage production.

In 1971 New York City, Arnold (Harvey Fierstein), performs as the drag act Virginia Hamm in a gay club. At the Stud Bar, he meets school teacher Ed (Brian Kerwin) and they start a relationship of sorts. Self-deprecating Arnold is blissful until he discovers that the very handsome Ed is dating a woman. They break off their relationship, leaving Arnold more depressed than usual. Six months later, the teacher asks Arnold for another chance.

At Christmastime in 1973, Arnold is still performing on stage. He is heckled by a trio of young drunks, one of whom, Alan (Matthew Broderick), passes out. Arnold takes him to his apartment to recuperate. The following evening, Alan, a model who has spent much of his recent years hustling, begins to appreciate Arnold's genuine kindness. He pursues the amazed Arnold and eventually the couple share an apartment. Several years later, Arnold's father (Edgar Small) dies. Arnold and Alan spend a weekend in the country with Ed and his girlfriend, Laurel (Karen

Young), where Ed, still in doubt about how straight or gay he really is, seduces Alan. Back in New York, and soon to become foster parents to teenager David (Eddie Castrodad), Arnold and Alan move to a new apartment in Greenwich Village. While out shopping for a celebration dinner, Alan intervenes when a gang is beating up a gay man. In the ensuing fight, he is clubbed to death.

In the spring of 1980, Arnold, who has never gotten over Alan, is busy raising David. Ed, who has broken off with his wife, has moved in with Alan, and is sleeping on the living-room couch. Arnold's domineering mother (Anne Bancroft) arrives from Florida for a stay. She knows all about her son, but NOT about Ed, Alan or David. As mother and son visit the cemetery where Arnold's father and Alan are buried, resentments stored over many years surface. Arnold's mother begins to shout that she wishes he had never been born. When Arnold goes on a drinking binge, he is rescued by Ed, who now admits he has come to terms with his gayness. He again asks for another chance with Arnold. The next morning, Arnold and his mother reconcile, before she leaves to go back to Florida.

Kevin Thomas (*Los Angeles Times*) admitted, "just about any venturesome approach would have been preferable to the lethally glossy, totally conventional Hollywood treatment that *Torch Song Trilogy* has been given. . . . [It] has had the life steamrolled right out of it, leaving it seeming terribly dated, hopelessly synthetic and without an ounce of style." Of the cast, Thomas said, "in close-up Fierstein's mugging seems more self-indulgent than brave and endearing." As to Kerwin (who played Ed on stage) and Broderick (who was seen as David in the stage version): "Kerwin . . . is more persuasive than Broderick . . . who simply seems self-conscious. . . ." As to Bancroft, she "has done these ethnic types so often as to be tiresome. . . .."

Elliott Stein (*Village Voice*) reported,

"Alas, Anne Bancroft is a disaster; Sylvia Miles would have been better. . . . The drag acts are delightful, but teasingly fleet. Charles Pierce is seen for a moment onstage with Arnold as a drag called Bertha Venation, 'doing' Bette Davis. The film could have done with a bit less of Mrs. Beckoff and a bit more Bertha." Lynn Darling (*Newsday*) was kinder: "Fierstein, of course, is the heart and soul of this movie, and he is immensely winning, with his foghorn voice and pained smiling eyes that accept the inevitability of a great deal of foolishness n the pursuit of love. . . . Like the play . . . [the movie is] a bit of a fairy tale that seeks to reassure those who would believe otherwise that pain and happiness find their targets equally in all of us. This time around though, the hard-won happy endings seem all the more ephemeral, all the more valiant, huddled as they are under the wave about to come crashing down."

Sadly, on film *Torch Song Trilogy* had lost its impertinent flavor, uniqueness and importance. Compared to such recent movies as *Parting Glances* (1986) and *Longtime Companion* (1990), qq.v., *Torch Song Trilogy* ended up being a disaffecting museum piece. Costing $7 million to make, it grossed only $2.5 million during its domestic release.

252. Trackdown: Finding the Goodbar Killer (CBS-TV, October 15, 1983), color, 100 min. Not rated.

Producers, Sonny Grosso, Larry Jacobson; associate producers, Benjamin Gruberg, Mimi Bohbot; director, Bill Persky; teleplay, Albert Ruben; art director, Michael Molly; costumes, Lee Austin; akeup, Carla White, Mike Maggi; music, Stephen Lawrence; assistant directors, Peter Guliano, Deborah L. Marrs; sound, Michael Scott Goldbaum; camera, Fred Murphy; editor, Norman Gay.

Cast: George Segal (Detective John Grafton); Shelley Hack (Logan Gay); Alan North (Lieutenant Walter Belden); Barton Heyman (Alan Cahill); Steve Allie Collura (Steve Miscelli); Shannon Presby (John Charles Turner); Jean DeBaer (Betty Grafton); Tracy Pollan

(Eileen Grafton); Bo Rucker (Trick Johnson); Marek Johnson (Mary Alice Nolan); Mike Miller (Assistant District Attorney); William Kiehl (Arthur, Cahill's Attorney); Joe Spinell (Escobar, the Doorman); John Christopher Jones (Artist); Christina-Avis Krauss (Vanessa Blustein); Dick Latessa (Puliese); Stephen Mendillo (Sergeant Reed); Marvin Scott (TV Reporter); Frank Licato (Second Policeman); Dustyn Taylor (Mrs. Turner); John Randolph Jones (Flanagan); Jo Ana Joseph (Woman with Artist); John Fitzgerald (Proprietor); Ray Martucci (Policeman); Joe Lisi, Thomas Moore, John Ring, Dominic Accardi, John Lafferty, John Scott, Buddy Short (Detectives); Peter Kowanko (Michael Nolan); Francine Dumont (Police Officer); Frank Simpson (Duty Officer); Ed Miller (Hostrup); Martin Starkand (Woman's Date); Ken Larson (Sonny); Hubert Kelly (Informant); Jim Desmond (Reporter); Richard DuBois, Richard Portnow (Bartenders); Tom Degidon (Second Reporter); and; Harry Madsen, Frank Patton.

One of the more notorious murders in the early 1970s was the killing of a Manhattan school teacher (Marek Johnson) on New Year's Day of 1972. It led to Judith Rossner's acclaimed novel, *Looking for Mr. Goodbar* (1975), and to a popular movie (1977), q.v. In turn, this well-done telefeature focuses on the hunt for the bisexual murderer, played in the 1977 movie by Tom Berenger. What gives this made-for-television film its specific quality is not the emphasis on the police detective's determined manhunt or his troubled domestic life. Rather, it is the sad relationship between the young killer and his faithful older lover. The latter is unwilling to accept the horrible deed his boyfriend has committed. The homicide detective investigating the case is surprisingly—given the past history of Hollywood movies—unprejudiced against the gay accomplice—showing empathy for this lovesick victim who, like himself, cannot keep his domestic life running smoothly.

In New York City, the police are summoned to apartment #8E at 633 West 72nd Street where they find the knifed body of a young school teacher. Detective John Grafton (George Segal) of the city's Homicide Task Force is assigned the case. The diligent policeman pursues the clues, while coping with marital discord at home. His wife (Jean DeBaer) insists that he is paying insufficient attention to her and to their daughter (Tracy Pollan) who leaves for college in the fall. In tracing the leads, Grafton meets attractive Logan Gay (Shelley Hack), a friend of the deceased. She not only helps him with the case, but develops a romantic attachment to him. Meanwhile, middle-aged Alan Cahill (Barton Heyman) is in a state of denial. On New Year's Eve he and his handsome young kept boyfriend, John Charles Turner (Shannon Presby), have had another of their fights. The latter had insisted, once again, that he had had enough of Cahill's suffocating attention and was heading for Florida to see a girlfriend. Thereafter, Turner had disappeared for several hours. When he returned to the apartment, he was in a panic, insisting he had killed a teacher, a woman he picked up in a single's bar. Emotionally subservient Cahill refuses to believe this latest "lie," but pampers Turner by giving him money to leave town. By dogged pursuit, Grafton locates the numbed Cahill and convinces him to betray his loved one. When Turner telephones Cahill from Indianapolis—where he has gone to hide out—his former lover leads him into a police trap. With the case solved, the repentant Grafton makes amends with his wife and daughter.

A postscript to the movie details that, subsequent to a visit to his prison cell by Alan Cahill in New York, John Charles Turner had hanged himself. At the exact moment he was buried in Indiana, Turner's son was stillborn in a Florida hospital. As for Alan Cahill, he died of asphyxiation in a fire in his Manhattan apartment.

Gail Williams (*Hollywood Reporter*) rated this TV follow-up "an unsatisfying—and somewhat distasteful—production" and thought the inclusion of the policeman's private life "never amounts to more

Advertisement for *Trackdown: Finding the Goodbar Killer* (1983).

than padding." *Daily Variety* complained, "Albert Ruben's script has been inflated with Segal's private world; instead of enriching the story by filling out his character. . . ." In retrospect, Leonard Maltin (*TV Movie and Video Guide*, 1991) found "Segal is wonderfully average as the plodding cop."

Shot on location in New York City, this film was the TV movie debut of George Segal. Before it aired, author Judith Rossner brought court action to prevent its screening, insisting that this "unauthorized" narrative would dilute the potential of the sequel to *Looking for Mr. Goodbar* she was planning (but which has never happened). Thus, a declaimer was added to the TV movie, disassociating it from Rossner and/or her novel.

253. Trash (Cinema V Distributing, 1970), color, 103 min. X-rated.

Presenter/producer, Andy Warhol; director/screenplay, Paul Morrissey; song, Joe Saggarino; sound, Jed Johnson; camera, Morrissey; editor, Johnson.

Cast: Joe Dallesandro (Joe); Holly Woodlawn (Holly); Jane Forth (Jane); Michael Sklar (Welfare Investigator); Geri Miller (Go-Go Dancer); Andrea Feldman (Rich Girl); Johnny Putnam (Boy from Yonkers); Bruce Pecheur (Jane's Husband); Diane Podlewski (Holly's Sister); Bob Dallesandro (Boy on Street).

As in *Flesh* (1968), q.v., also directed by Paul Morrissey for Andy Warhol's film Factory, the X-rated *Trash* continues the misadventures of bisexual Joe (Joe Dallesandro). He is the New York City hustler whose charismatic street toughness and ambivalence to life turns on both sexes. Whereas in *Flesh* he had been horny and virile, in *Trash* he has become impotent due to his drug dependency. His live-in girlfriend in this atmospheric street odyssey is played by transvestite personality Holly Woodlawn. On its own, the presence of Holly—with the sex of her character left ambiguous—adds a homoerotic overtone to the bizarre, if lethargic, proceedings.

Heavy-duty junkie Joe (Joe Dallesandro) and his keeper, Holly (Holly Woodlawn), subsist in a basement apartment on New York's Lower East side. Joe's heroin addiction has left him impotent. Restless as ever, he visits Geri (Geri Miller), once his girlfriend and now a go-go dancer. Later, he talks with wealthy Andrea (Andrea Feldman), frantic to score in order to get some LSD. Nagged by Holly to bring home some money, he robs an uptown apartment, but is interrupted in the process by Jane (Jane Forth), the newlywed tenant. She takes a liking to Joe and gives the lice-infected robber a bath. Meanwhile, her husband (Bruce Pecheur) returned. He is initially turned on by Joe being with Jane, but later tosses the naked Joe out on the street, where the intruder collapses from a drug overdose. Back at his apartment, Holly's pregnant sister (Diane Podlewski) appears but is thrown out when she tries to seduce Joe. A welfare worker (Michael Sklar) arrives to investigate his clients' status, since Holly has filed a claim that she is expecting. The ruse is uncovered and the investigator departs, leaving Joe and Holly, once again, alone.

Vincent Canby (*New York Times*) admitted: "*Trash* is alive, but like the people in it, it continually parodies itself, and thus it represents a kind of dead end in filmmaking." Addison Verrill (*Variety*) approved of this "slick, commercial and very nude anti-drug feature." He noted, "The Dallesandro resume of ample endowments has not included much mention of acting ability, but here he displays both a forceful screen presence and ease in front of the camera. . . . His efforts are matched frame by frame by . . . Holly Woodlawn, a bourbon-voiced transvestite (though few may guess it). . . ."

Trash was shot in 16mm and blown up to 35mm. Released by Cinema V, *Trash* helped Andy Warhol-Paul Morrissey's film products emerge from its underground status to mainstream film fare.

254. Uptight (Paramount, 1968), color, 104 min. M-rated.

Producer, Jules Dassin; associate producer,

Joe Dallesandro and Jane Forth in *Trash* (1970).

Jim DiGangi; director, Dassin; suggested by the novel *The Informer* by Liam O'Flaherty; screenplay, Dassin, Ruby Dee, Julian Mayfield; production designer, Alexandre Trauner; art director, Phillip Bennett; set decorator, Ray Moyer; costumes, Theoni V. Aldredge; makeup, Bob Sidell, Bob Morley; music/music conductor, Booker T. Jones; assistant directors, Martin Horstein, William McGary, Reuben Watt; sound, Terry Kellum, David Forrest; camera, Boris Kaufman; editor, Robert Lawrence.

Cast: Raymond St. Jacques (B. G.); Ruby Dee (Laurie); Frank Silvera (Kyle); Roscoe Lee Browne (Clarence); Julian Mayfield (Tank Williams); Janet MacLachlan (Jeannie); Ji-Tu Cumbuka (Rick); Max Julien (Johnny); John Wesley Rodgers (Larry)); Richard Anthony Williams (Corbin); Robert DuQui (Speaker); James McEachin (Mello); Michael Baseleon (Claude); Juanita Moore (Johnny's Mother); Vernett Allan (Ralph); Ketty Lester (Alma); Errol Jaye (Mr. Oakley); and: Leon Bibb, Isabelle Cooley, Alice Childress, David Moody, Kirk Kirksey, Van Kirksey, Mello Alexandria.

The 1960s had seen significant changes in both governmental and public attitudes towards discriminated-against blacks. But the slow progress of civil rights legislation led to continual racial unrest. This social upheaval prompted Hollywood to capitalize on it with *Uptight*, the initial Hollywood studio feature to focus on contemporary black revolutionaries. *Uptight* was a thinly-veiled updating of John Ford's *The Informer* (1935), adapted uneasily to the black idiom. Cast in the role of a police informer was Roscoe Lee Browne. *Variety* highlighted, "Now to make this character a heavy, it is necessary to establish that Browne's character is a homosexual. A point made all too obvious. Being a man who lives by his own dubious standards is not enough, since all the characters do. So, in a forced gambit to find something objectionable, the scripters have made him an elegant fag."

In April 1968 Cleveland, a few days after the assassination of Dr. Martin Luther King Jr., the city is overwhelmed by black rioters. Meanwhile, Johnny Wells (Max Julien), Rick (Ji-Tu Cumbuka) and Larry (John Wesley Rodgers) rob an ammunition arsenal. Their compatriot, Tank Williams (Julian Mayfield), was drunk and did not participate in the heist, which messed up the plans and lead to a watchman being shot during the getaway. Because of his negligence, black militant leaders B.G. (Raymond St. Jacques) and Corbin (Richard Anthony Williams) drop Williams from their revolutionary group. Later, a dapper police informer, Clarence (Roscoe Lee Browne), alerts Williams that he can earn $12,000 for information leading to Wells's capture and that he also will see to it that Tank's police record is magically erased. Then too, Tank's girlfriend (Ruby Dee) begs him to get them some money so she can stop hustling on the streets. Williams eventually tells the police where to find Wells, leading to the latter's death in a police manhunt. Thereafter, the betrayer is hunted down and shot by Larry and Rick.

Vincent Canby (*New York Times*) admitted "None of this really works, but *Uptight* is such an intense and furious movie that it's impossible not to take it seriously. . . . [The movie] doesn't pack much drama, principally, I think, because the subsidiary characters all are more interesting than Tank." *Variety* was put off by this hybrid adaptation. "Besides bestowing undue nobility to black militants, it also succeeds in displaying a series of all-black, modern-day character stereotypes. . . ." An unenthused Jan Dawson (British *Monthly Film Bulletin*) pointed out the film's structural flaw, "With the informer himself robbed of any moral stature, his dilemma is reduced to an abstraction, particularly since the characters between whom he is buffeted back and forth all seem specially selected to represent one of the choices open to him (the violent revolutionary, the politically ambitious integrationist, the stool pigeon who—for emphasis—is homosexual and quotes Shakespeare). Donald Bogle (*Blacks in American Films and Television*, 1986) observed of *Uptight*: "audiences never see a heated black/white confrontation. In fact, if the movie made any statement at all, it was that blacks were effectual mainly at wiping out one of their own."

Uptight, with location filming in Cleveland, was also released in a cut-down 94 minute version. For Jules Dassin, who had left the United States in the midst of the anti-Communist witch hunt of the 1950s, it was his first American-made feature in almost two decades.

255. Valentino (United Artists, 1977), color, 132 min. R-rated.

Producers, Irwin Winkler, Robert Chartoff; director, Ken Russell; based on the story "Valentino, an Intimate Expose of the Sheik" by Brad Steiger, Chaw Mank; screenplay, Ken Russell, Mardik Martin; art directors, Philip Harrison, Malcolm Middleton; set decorator, Ian Whittaker; costumes, Shirley Russell; makeup, Peter Robb-King; music, Ferde Grofe, Stanley Black; song, Ken Russell; choreographer, Gillian Gregory; assistant director, Jonathan Benson; sound, John Mitchell; camera, Peter Suschitsky; editor, Stuart Baird.

Cast: Rudolf Nureyev (Rudolph Valentino); Leslie Caron (Alla Nazimova); Michelle Phillips (Natasha Rambova); Carol Kane ("Fatty's" Girl); Felicity Kendal (June Mathis); Seymour Cassel (George Ullman); Peter Vaughan (Rory O'Neil); Huntz Hall (Jesse Lasky); David De Keyser (Joseph Schenck); Alfred Marks (Richard Rowland); Anton Diffring (Baron Long); Jennie Lindon (Agnes Ayres); William Hootkins ("Fatty"); Bill McKinney (Jail Cop); Don Fellows (George Melford); John Justin (Sidney Olcott); Linda Thorson (Billie Streeter); June Bolton (Bianca De Saulles); Penny Milford (Lorna Sinclair); Dudley Sutton (Willie); Robin Brent Clarke (Jack De Saulles); Anthony Dowell (Vaslav Nijinsky); James Berwick (Fight Referee); Marcell Markham (Hooker); Leland Palmer (Majorie Tain); John Alderson (Cop); Hal Galili (Harry Fischbeck); Percy Herbert (Studio Guard); Nicolette Marvin (Marshal Lee); Mark Baker (Assistant Director); Mildred Shay (Old Lady); Lindsay Kemp (Mortician); John Ratzenberger, Norman Cancer, Robert O'Neil (Newshounds); Christine Carlson (Tango Dancer).

On screen, several actors had impersonated Rudolph Valentino (1895—1926), the charismatic Italian-born, Hollywood silent film star. They included Anthony Dexter (*Valentino*, 1951), Franco Nero (*The Legend of Valentino*, 1975) and Matt Collins in Gene Wilder's spoof, *The*

Jennie Linden and Rudolf Nureyev in *Valentino* (1977).

World's Greatest Lover (1977). However, no casting of the Latin Lover was more offbeat than having Russian ballet legend Rudolf Nureyev portray the enigmatic Italian-born movie icon. With Ken Russell directing, it was assumed that the movie would explore the long-held contention that this "pink powder puff" actor—as his detractors called him—was homosexual or at least bisexual.

During the course of Russell's typically excessive movie, nearly all the characters have a chance to impugn Valentino's manhood. In the picture, this comes to a fore when a reporter rushes up to Alla Nazimova (Leslie Caron), herself a silent picture star and known to be a lesbian. He asks, "Is it true that Rudolph Valentino refused to be in your all-homosexual production of *Salome*? [1923]. Accepting the thrust of his gibe, but not offended, she retorts, "He was not available at the time!" This is basically as close as Russell's film

gets to settling the issue of Valentino's sexual persuasion.

In 1926, in New York City, several personalities attend Rudolph Valentino's funeral, each recalling their association with the late celebrity. The depiction of his life starts with the immigrant's arrival in New York City in 1915, where he soon becomes a gigolo and taxi dancer. After a disastrous affair with Bianca De Saulles (June Bolton), a gangster's wife, he comes to Los Angeles, where he drifts into moviemaking. By 1921, he is given the lead in the epic, *The Four Horsemen of the Apocalypse*. His success there leads to his appearance opposite Alla Nazimova (Leslie Caron) in her *Camille* that year and to the beginning of an affair with her confidante/lover, Natasha Rambova (Michelle Phillips). The dominating Natasha, a set designer, author, and director on her own, marries the subservient Rudolph. As his career improves, she attempts to gain more control over his professional activities. Her meddling and their personal incompatibilities lead to their break up. After a boxing match with a newspaperman (Peter Vaughan), who has contested the star's masculinity, Valentino collapses and later dies.

Expecting something "viscerally offensive" from Russell's *Valentino*, Janet Maslin (*New York Times*) was let down, except for a key scene midway through the biography. There, the celebrity is confined to a crowded cell (on a bigamy charge), not given bathroom privileges, and mauled by his slimy cellmates. For Maslin: "The most intriguing thing about Valentino, as he appears here, is his old-world notion of manly honor. . . . The best parts of the film are those that pit Valentino against Hollywood. . . ." Regarding the cast, Maslin acknowledged Nureyev's gracefulness and malleability, but cited the problem of his "uncertain accent" and his "trouble delivering snappy patter with much conviction." For the *Times*, "Michelle Phillips was "suitably steely-eyed" but sounded "even less authentic" while Caron "copes admirably with the script's strangeness by reading her lines more peculiarly than is necessary, shouting and waving her arms all the while." Pauline Kael (*The New Yorker*) thought that "By attaching the names of actual people to his sadomasochistic fantasies, the director . . . gives the picture a nasty inside-joke appeal. The only redeeming element is Rudolf Nureyev in the title role; he doesn't evoke Valentino, but from time to time he has a captivating, very funny temperament of his own."

Shot in England and Spain, *Valentino* was not a success. Peculiar and unreal as it is, no one can totally fault a production which hires ex-Bowery Boys stalwart, Huntz Hall, to play a grasping film mogul.

256. Valley of the Dolls (Twentieth Century-Fox, 1967), color, 123 minutes. GP-rated.

Producer, David Weisbart; director, Mark Robson; based on the novel by Jacqueline Susann; screenplay, Helen Deutsch, Dorothy Kingsley; art directors, Jack Martin Smith, Richard Day; set decorators, Walter M. Scott, Raphael Bretton; costumes, Travilla; makeup, Ben Nye; music/music director, Johnny Williams; songs, Andre Previn and Dory Previn; choreographer, Robert Sidney; assistant directors, Eli Dunn, Richard Lang; sound, Don J. Bassman, David Dockendorf; special camera effects, L. B. Abbott, Art Cruickshank, Emil Kosa Jr.; camera, William H. Daniels; editor, Dorothy Spencer.

Cast: Barbara Parkins (Anne Welles); Patty Duke (Neely O'Hara); Paul Burke (Lyon Burke); Sharon Tate (Jennifer North); Susan Hayward (Helen Lawson); Tony Scotti (Tony Polar); Martin Milner (Mel Anderson); Charles Drake (Kevin Gilmore); Alexander Davion (Ted Casablanca); Lee Grant (Miriam); Naomi Stevens (Miss Steinberg); Robert H. Harris (Henry Bellamy); Jacqueline Susann (Reporter); Robert Viharo (Director); Mikel Angel (Man in Hotel Room); Barry Cahill (Man in Bar); Richard Angarola (Claude Chardot); Joey Bishop (Master of Ceremonies at Telethon); George Jessel (Master of Ceremnies at Grammy Awards); Judith Lowry (Aunt Amy); Jeanne Gerson (Neely's Maid); Linda Peck, Pat Becker, Corinna Tsopei (Telephone Girls); Robert Street (Choreographer); Robert Gibbons (Desk Clerk at Lawrenceville Hotel); Leona Powers (Woman at Martha Washington Hotel); Barry O'Hara (Assistant Stage Manager); Norman Burton (Neely's Hollywood Director); Margot Stevenson (Anne's Mother); Jonathan Hawke (Sanitarium Doctor); Marvin Hamlisch (Pianist); Billy Beck (Man Sleeping in Movie House); Dorothy Neumann, Charlotte Knight (Neely's Maids); Robert McCord (Bartender at New York Theatre); Peggy Rea (Neely's Voice Coach); Gertrude Flynn (Ladies Room Attendant).

A year after the publication of Jacqueline Susann's voyeuristic delight of life, love and drugs among the Hollywood and New York show business set, the bestseller was transferred to the screen. What had been glossy soap opera in print became childish tripe on screen, dragged down by its inept leading ladies: shrill Patty Duke, leaden Barbara Parkins and mushy Sharon Tate. On the plus side the

Susan Hayward in *Valley of the Dolls* (1967).

film boasted a bravura performance by Susan Hayward—replacing Judy Garland—as a Ethel Merman-like Broadway stage queen. In addition, it had gorgeous cinematography and several bouncy songs by Andre and Dory Previn. The movie's title theme, sung on the soundtrack by Dionne Warwick, became a big selling single record.

Anne Welles (Barbara Parkins) abandons New England for a career in New York City. As a theatrical law firm secretary, she works for handsome Lyon Burke (Paul Burke) and is present when Broadway superstar Helen Lawson (Susan Hayward) fires multi-talented newcomer, Neely O'Hara (Patty Duke) from a forthcoming musical. Thereafter, Lyon negotiates Neely's career on TV which, eventually, launches her successful Hollywood movie career. Meanwhile, gorgeous but untalented Jennifer North (Sharon Tate) marries club singer Tony Polar (Tony Scotti), despite the objections of his sister/manager, Miriam (Lee Grant).

After Lyon refuses to marry Anne, he drops his law practice to return to writing, while Anne stars in several TV commercials. Neely has two failed marriages: publicist Mel Anderson (Martin Milner) and successful fashion designer/costumer Ted Casablanca (Alex Davion). The latter, a bisexual man, revenges her mistreatment of him by fooling around with a woman. Not coping well on her own, Neely turns increasingly to drugs and alcohol, entering her own "valley of the dolls" with Seconals. Deciding to dry out, she enters a clinic where Tony is dying of an incurable disease. As for Jennifer, she has been starring in softcore porno films in Europe to pay her husband's medical bills. Upon discovering she has breast cancer, and fearing a mastectomy, she commits suicide with an overdose of sleeping pills. Neely attempts a Broadway comeback, but collapses in the theatre's alleyway prior to her performance, and her understudy proves sensational on stage. Lyon locates Anne back in New England, where she has kicked her pill dependency. She politely refuses his marriage offer, preferring to build a more stable, simpler life in her home town.

Bosley Crowther (*New York Times*) warned, "It's an unbelievably hackneyed and mawkish mishmash of backstage plots. . . . It's every bit as phony and old-fashioned as anything Lana Turner ever did. . . ." Compared to the poor showing of the remaining cast, Crowther applauded the presence of veteran Susan Hayward: "Her aging musical comedy celebrity is the one remotely plausible character in the film." *Variety* summarized, "Talky sudsy version of the book. Handsome production, otherwise dull." In detailing the "stock characters out of pulp fiction," the trade paper listed "allegedly homosexual dress designer Alex Davion [as Ted Casablanca] (whose scene involves some strictly heterosexual dalliance). . . ." British *Monthly Film Bulletin* panned the film: "Think of a showbiz cliche and *Valley of the Dolls* has it. . . . Mark Robson directs so as to give every hoary situation a break. . . ."

Valley of the Dolls grossed an enormous $20 million in distributors' domestic film rentals. It led Twentieth Century-Fox to produce what turned out NOT to be a sequel, *Beyond the Valley of the Dolls* (1970), q.v. In 1981, there appeared the TV movie, *Jacqueline Susann's Valley of the Dolls*, an update of the story, with Steve Inwood as Teddi Casablanca.

During the course of *Valley of the Dolls*, while powerful movie star Neely is mistreating everyone around her, including husband #1, Mel, she sets her sights on handsome Ted Casablanca. Jealousy causes meek Mel to turn bitchy. "You sure are spending a lot of time with that fag." "He's not a fag!" she shrieks, insisting "And I am just the dame who can prove it!" True to her word, she divorces Mel and later marries the "queer" who is actually bisexual.

Like the earlier *Inside Daisy Clover* (1965) and the later *The Legend of Lylah Clare* (1968), *Myra Breckinridge* (1970), *Beyond the Valley of the Dolls* (1970) and *Play It as It Lays* (1972), qq.v., *Valley of the Dolls* was an example of how Hollywood delighted in focusing on the reality of the movie industry populated with a high percentage of gay talent. In most cases in the 1960s and 1970s, the industry chose to depict these homosexuals and lesbians as the expendable play toys of powerful female superstars.

257. Vendetta (Concorde, 1986), color, 88 min. R-rated. (a.k.a.: *Angels Behind Bars*)

Producers, Jeff Begun, Ken Solomon, Ken Dalton; associate producers, Richard Harrison, Greg Hinton; director, Bruce Logan; screenplay, Emil Farkas, Sion Maskell, Laura Cavestani, John Adams; art director, Chris Clarens; set decorator, Timothy Ford; costumes, Meg Mayer; assistant directors, Elliott Rosenblatt, Katherine Palmer-Collins; stunt coordinator, Farkas; special effects, John Hartigan; sound, Dennis Carr; camera, Robert New; second unit camera, Bryan Greenberg; editor, Glen Morgan.

Cast: Greg Bradford (Joe-Bob); Holly Butler (Movie Star); Karen Chase (Laurie Collins [Cusack]); Lisa Clarson (Bobo); Roberta Collins (Miss Dice); Pilar Delano (Inmate); Joshua Brooks, J. W. Fails (Parking Attendants); Eugene Robert Glazer (David Greene); Will Hare (Judge Waters); Cynthia Harrison (Debra); Hoke Howell (Deputy Curly); Lisa Hullano (China); Ginger Johnson (Dakota); Kelita Kelly (Sandy); Marta Kober (Sylvia); Jack Kosslyn (Warden Haines); Dixie Lee (Rosie); Linda Lightfoot (Wanda); Charles Joseph Martin (Willis); Sandy Martin (Kay Butler) Durga McBroom (Willow); Adzine Melliti (Gino); Michelle Newkirk (Bonnie Cusack); Dave Nicolson (District Attorney); Carol Porter (Candy); Joanelle Nadine Romero (Elena); Tracette St. Julian (Celebrity Take-Off); Ken Shriner (Steve Nelson); Ken Solomon (Coroner); Gamy L. Taylor (Judge Stivers); Marianne Taylor (Star); Marshall Teague (Paul); Topaze (Disc Jockey); Mark Von Zech (Randy); Carol Porter, Kathleen Stevens, Lynell Carter, Patti Burdo, Patrice Davis, Shawni Davis (Girls in Shower); Joshua Brooks, J. W. Fails (Parking Attendants). Pleasant Gehman, Rose Flores, Kerry O'Brian, Marsky Reins, Boom Boom Dixon (Screamin' Sirens).

"Considering the genre, most of the cast turn in very credible performances, even if they don't look much like prisoners . . . There is also a lot less flesh exposed here than in most other women prisoner films, but that which is shown looks seamy, not sexy." (*Variety*)

To satisfy the continuing interest in women-behind-bars movies, Concorde produced *Vendetta*, and heightened the voyeuristic delights by adding elements of slasher films.

Bonnie Cusack (Michelle Newkirk) shoots her date in self defense when he attempts to rape her. At Duran Correctional Institute, this "fresh meat" is indoc-

trinated into the prison community by being attacked by women inmates in the showers. Before long, her plea to be let alone earns her the hatred of lesbian drug dealer Kay Butler (Sandy Martin), who has the newcomer tossed over an upper story cell block tier. Her movie stunt player sister, Laurie (Karen Chase), wants revenge and engineers her own sentencing to Duran to seek out the culprit(s). One by one she kills those responsible for Bonnie's untimely end, her last prey being Kay. However, as the two women square off for the finale, Miss Dice (Roberta Collins), the warden, intervenes, and shoots the lunging Kay. Freed from prison, the now-at-peace Laurie drives off with her boyfriend (Marshall Teague).

Variety pointed out, "The only light moments—not to be confused with humorous ones—are those with [Sandy] Martin, the lesbian who plays the butch bit to the hilt. . . . As the prison's chief bully and main supplier of heroin, when she walks into a scene, she takes over." Jay Robert Nash and Stanley Ralph Ross (*The Motion Picture Guide Annual*, 1988) observed: "Of course, all the obligatory scenes are there: long showers, rapist guards, brutal beatings, and more showers; plus, this prison allows conjugal visits, so we can have more sex . . . [These] films are as seedy as come. . . ." *The Phantom's Ultimate Video Guide* (1989) rated *Vendetta* two out of four diamonds, printing, "Highlights include the Screamin' Sirens' heartfelt rendition of 'Love Slave,' a spirited Prince impersonation performed in reverse drag. . . ."

258. A Very Natural Thing (New Line Cinema, 1974), color, 80 min. R-rated.

Producer, Christopher Larkin; associate producer, Leslie Rodgers; director, Larkin; screenplay, Larkin, Joseph Coencas; music, Bert Lucarelli, Gordon Gottlieb, The Musemorphoses; camera, C. H. Douglass; editor, Terry Manning.

Cast: Robert Joel (David); Curt Gareth (Mark); Bo White (Jason); Jay Pierce (Alan); Barnaby Rudge (Hughey); Marilyn Meyers

(Valerie); A. Bailey Chapin (Minister); Robert Grillo (Edgar); Kurt Brandt (Charles); George Diaz (Miguel); Deborah Trowbridge (Jason's Ex-Wife); Jesse Trowbridge (Jason's Child); Michael Kell, Sheila Rock, Linda Weita (Boating Family).

"The idea for a film about gay relationships and gay liberation themes came out of my own personal reaction, on the one hand, to the mindless, sex-obsessed image of the homosexual prevalent in gay porno films and, on the other hand, to the debasing caricatures and slurs about gay people and gay life coming out of the vast majority of commercially oriented films." (Program notes by Christopher Larkin for *A Very Natural Thing*)

Compared to *The Boys in the Band* (1970), *Fortune and Men's Eyes* (1971) and especially *Some of My Best Friends Are . . .* (1971), qq.v., which were essentially straights viewing gays from the heterosexual point of view, *A Very Natural Thing* was a very liberating feature film for the early 1970s. Its auteur was an ex-monk, Christopher Larkin, who hoped to reflect the actual point of view of contemporary gay men seeking to define themselves in their own terms rather than by traditional heterosexual role models. While his film, during its first half, intends to parody such overly romantic (heterosexual) films as *Love Story* (1970) it becomes so over-indulgently romantic itself during the second half, that it turns off the very audience to which it is trying to appeal.

Young ex-monk David (Robert Joel), having accepted he is gay, but not yet having the chance to explore its ramifications, moves to New York City where he teaches school. He aims to find liberation and, at the same time, hopes to meet a long-term mate. His first choice, the cynical Ivy League graduate, Mark (Curt Gareth), an insurance salesman, is a short-lasting affair in which David discovers Mark is too independent and too insecure for compatibility. The disillusioned David moves out eventually. Turning from monogamy,

to promiscuity, he explores all the gay haunts. At a gay pride rally in Washington Square Park, he meets Jason (Bo White), a photographer who stills retains emotional attachments to his ex-wife (Deborah Trowbridge) and their child (Jess Trowbridge). With Jason's help, David begins to mesh his idealism with his craving to be a liberated gay man.

Variety's Addison Verrill judged "pic is a veritable guidebook to the local gay subculture, from the rambles of Fire Island to the steam baths. . . . Pic's major flaw lies in its concentration on a main character, David . . . so whining, humorless and constantly demanding that audience sympathy goes . . . [elsewhere]. . . ." The *New York Post* judged *A Very Natural Thing* "an argument rather than an entertainment." Reviewer Judith Crist was highly critical of the film, writing, "If the gay lib movement wants its own mediocre movie preachment—here it is." A. H. Weiler (*New York Times*) admitted that the movie "is sensitive and realistic in its approach" but "is not especially moving. The succession of ecstasies, tiffs, quarrels and searchings for meanings are, despite the essential honesty, the stuff of standard, not unusual, drama."

259. Victor/Victoria (Metro-Goldwyn-Mayer/United Artists, 1982), color, 133 min. PG-rated.

Producers, Blake Edwards, Tony Adams; associate producer, Gerald T. Nutting, director, Edwards; based on the film *Victor Und Viktoria* by Rheinhold Schunzel, Hans Hoemburg; screenplay, Edwards; production designer, Rodger Maus; art directors, Tim Hutchinson, William Craig Smith; set decorator, Harry Cordwell; costumes, Patricia Norris; music, Henry Mancini; songs: Mancini and Leslie Bricusse; choreographer, Paddy Stone; assistant directors, Richard Hoult, Peter Kohn, Paul Tivers; stunt coordinator, Joe Dunne; sound, Roy Charman; camera, Dick Bush; editor, Ralph E. Winters.

Cast: Julie Andrews (Count Victor Grazinski/Victoria Grant); James Garner (King Marchan); Robert Preston (Carroll "Toddy" Todd); Lesley Ann Warren (Norma); Alex Karras (Squash);

James Garner, Julie Andrews and Robert Preston in a publicity pose for
Victor/Victoria **(1982).**

John Rhys-Davies (Andre Cassell); Graham Stark (Waiter); Peter Arne (Labisse); Sherloque Tanney (Bovin); Michael Robbins (Hotel Manager); Norman Chancer (Sal); David Grant (Restaurant Manager); Maria Charles (Madame President); Malcolm Jamieson (Richard); John Cassady (Juke); Mike Tezcan (Clam); Christopher Good (Stage Manager); Matyelock Gibbs (Cassell's Receptionist); Jay Benedict (Guy Langois); Olivier Pierre (Langois's Companion); Martin Rayner (Concierge); George Silver (Fat Man with Eclair); Joanna Dickens (Large Lady in Restaurant); Terence Skelton (Deviant Husband); Ina Skriver (Simone Kallisto); Stuart Turton (Boy Friend to Actress); Geoffrey Beevers (Police Inspector); Sam Williams, Simon Chandler (Chorus Boys); Neil Cunningham (Nightclub Master of Ceremonies); Vivienne Chandler (Chambermaid); Bill Monks (LeClou); Perry Davey (Balancing Man); Elizabeth Vaughan (Opera Singer); Paddy Ward (Photographer); Tim Stern (Desk Clerk).

". . . for the most part the movie is the kind of 'pure entertainment' that Hollywood supposedly isn't turning out anymore. A 'pure' movie about homosexuals and female impersonators? Certainly, at least in the sense that its intent is to amuse, nothing more or less." (Robert Asahina, *New Leader*)

Based on a 1933 German film, *Victor/Victoria*, takes up the comic mantle where Billy Wilder's *Some Like It Hot* (1959), with Tony Curtis and Jack Lemmon, left off, and puts into useful perspective the French film comedy success, *La Cage Au Folles* (1978). Like the mega hit *Tootsie*—released in the same year as *Victor/Victoria*—the leading character of Blake Edwards's comedy is not gay, merely cross-dressing to gain employment. On the other hand, Robert Preston's character in *Victor/Victoria*, an aging Parisian club performer, most certainly is and it is his zestful presence that gives the movie its much-needed burst of energy and farcical tone. As John Coleman (*New Statesman*) reacted—a bit strongly—the film "would be an unmitigated disaster were it not for two minutes' mugging from Graham Stark as a French waiter and the brave buoyancy of Robert Preston as a homosexual cabaret artiste. Julie Andrews walks through the witless role of a woman pretending to be a man who does a nightclub act as a woman. . . . Leslie Bricusse writes some more frightful songs, and I say to hell with it."

In 1934 Paris, struggling songstress Victoria Grant (Julie Andrews), auditions unsuccessfully at the Chez Lui, an established gay nightclub. The headlining act at the club is Carroll "Toddy" Todd (Robert Preston), a flamboyant homosexual. That evening, the impulsive Toddy, angered by the thoughtlessness of his young unfaithful boyfriend, Richard (Malcolm Jamieson), insults the kept man, which leads to a club brawl. The result is that Toddy is fired. Now broke, he comes across the down-and-out Victoria at a bistro. She suggests a gambit for getting them free meals. This leads to another public brawl and, with no place to go, Victoria returns with Toddy to his flat to recuperate. In the morning, when she substitutes one of Richard's suits for her drenched clothing, Toddy is inspired to pass her off as a man performing in drag. As Count Victor Grazinski, Victoria becomes a club hit at the Chez Lui and her career is bolstered by an impresario, Andre Cassell (John Rhys-Davies).

Now a Parisian sensation, the Count comes to the attention of footloose Chicago businessman King Marchan (James Garner). Rather quickly, he has a hunch that he/she is a she and he flirts with her, causing King's moll, Norma (Leslie Ann Warren), to become jealous. Before long, King—who now knows that Victor is Victoria—is in love with her, and she with him. However, she will not give up her stage act. Meanwhile, thinking his boss has come out of the closet by dating Victor, King's bodyguard, Squash (Alex Karras), admits he is gay. By now, the angered Norma has alerted Marchan's less-than-savory Chicago business associates that King is acting very queer indeed. They arrive in Paris to see for themselves. Victoria now tells everyone the truth—except for her employer, Labisse (Peter Arne), the arrogant manager of Chez Lui. He is suspicious that he is a she and has had a detective following her. The ruse is saved when Toddy takes over Victoria's stage act and, as always, is a big hit.

Vincent Canby (*New York Times*) observed: "Although *Victor/Victoria* preaches tolerance and understanding of homosexuality, and though it uses the word 'gay' in a way that I doubt was much used in 1934 Paris, even in the demimonde portrayed in this film, the roots and comedy are as ancient as the use of masks and disguises in the theatre." Canby enthused, "*Victor/Victoria* combines the sweetness of

Darling Lili [1970] with the unbridled hilarity of *S.O.B.* [1981], but without that comedy's bitterness. It is an unqualified hit. . . . As happens in farce, everyone falls in love with everyone else, and because this is a liberated farce, the possible combinations are more than doubled—they're squared. . . ." For Sheila Benson (*Los Angeles Times*), "By the film's close, more people have popped out of closets than in a French farce, but the prevailing winds are warmer and more kindly than in any Blake Edwards film so far. His homosexual characters are firm in their own minds about their sexuality and at peace right where they are. That alone makes Preston's Toddy light years away from Robert Webber's character in *10* [1979, q.v.]."

David Denby (*New York*), who rated *Victor/Victoria* a "genial, low-intensity farce," pointed out "Edwards makes sweet-tempered jokes about all this [plotline] confusion—the spinning of sexual identities in the gay world delights him because it introduces a note of irresistible craziness into life. . . . Homosexuals don't frighten Edwards, but any whiff of decadence certainly does. The studio-built Paris streets are handsome and evocative, but the gay cabarets lack atmosphere, and whatever period flavor the movie has is destroyed when the actors open their mouths and speak the overexplicit jargon of the 1980s—'relationship,' 'gay,' even 'alterative life-style—rather than the coded and barbed homosexual idiom of the day."

Victor/Victoria grossed $10,490,315 in distributors' domestic film rentals. It won an Academy Award for Best Original Score. It received six additional Oscar nominations: Best Actress (Julie Andrews; Meryl Streep won for *Sophie's Choice*); Best Supporting Actor (Robert Preston; Louis Gossett Jr. won for *An Officer and a Gentleman*); Best Supporting Actress (Lesley Ann Warren; Jessica Lange won for *Tootsie*); Best Screenplay Based on Material from Another Medium):

Missing won); Best Art Direction—Set Decoration: (*Gandhi* won); Best Costumes (*Gandhi* won).

In mid-1992, work began anew on the long-discussed Broadway musical adaptation of *Victor/Victoria*, with music by Henry Mancini, lyrics by Leslie Bricusse and book by Blake Edwards. Julie Andrews was still being asked to repeat her screen role for the stage version.

260. A View from the Bridge
(Continental Distributing, 1962), 110 min. Not rated.

Producer, Paul Graetz; director, Sidney Lumet; based on the play by Arthur Miller; screenplay, Norman Rosten; art director, Jacques Saulnier; music, Maurice Le Roux; assistant director, Dossia Mage; sound, Jo de Bretagne; camera, Michel Kelber; editor, Francoise Javet.

Cast: Raf Vallone (Eddie Carbone); Jean Sorel (Rodolpho); Maureen Stapleton (Beatrice Carbone); Carol Lawrence (Catherine); Raymond Pellegrin (Marco); Morris Canovsky (Mr. Alfieri); Harvey Lembeck (Mike); Mickey Knox (Louis); Vincent Gardenia (Lipari); Frank Campanella (Longshoreman).

Arthur Miller's long one-act play, *A View from the Bridge*, appeared on Broadway in 1955 to mixed reviews and closed after 149 performances. The drama focused on Eddie Carbone, a virile Brooklyn stevedore, who harbors repressed desires for his beautiful young niece. When she becomes involved romantically with an Italian immigrant, the longshoreman is driven to jealous extremes. To break up the romance, he suggests that the young Sicilian is homosexual. When this ploy fails, he reports the newcomer to immigration authorities, leading to the final tragedy. A pivotal point within the play occurs when Carbone (played by Van Heflin) kisses the Sicilian (enacted by Richard Davalos) on the lips, insisting, "That's what you are!" Heflin would comment later, "That kiss always got gasps from the audience. We got away with it, I suppose, because neither of us looked effeminate."

The 1962 film version followed the same basic storyline. Macho Italian-

Raf Vallone and Carol Lawrence in *A View from the Bridge* **(1962).**

American longshoreman Eddie Carbone (Raf Vallone), despite the presence of his loyal wife (Maureen Stapleton), is desperately attracted to his eighteen-year-old niece, Catherine (Carol Lawrence). Rodolpho (Jean Sorel) and Marco (Raymond Pellegrin), two of Bea's Sicilian cousins, arrive in New York illegally, and are housed at Eddie's. The young Rodolfo and Catherine soon fall in love, leading the crazed Eddie to brand Rodolpho an opportunist. When his condemnation fails, he accuses the innocent young man of being gay—kissing him on the lips to prove his theory. Later, the distraught Eddie betrays the two brothers and they are taken away by immigration authorities. Rodolpho is released because of his pending marriage to Catherine. While Marco is out on bail, he taunts Carbone in front of his family and neighbors. The scorned Eddie kills himself by burying a cargo hook into his own chest.

Bosley Crowther (*New York Times*) enthused, "Mr. Lumet has drenched the drama in a proletarian atmosphere so absolute and authentic that actuality seems to pulsate on the screen. . . . The one great obstruction to the drama—and a fatal obstruction it becomes—is the slowly evolving demonstration that the principal character is a boor. . . . [Lumet] has got some remarkable good people to play it compellingly. . . . Jean Sorel, a handsome French actor, plays the nephew a bit too solemnly. . . ." *Variety* critiqued, "There is a tendency to be theatrical in hewing close to a series of dramatic incidents. . . . The photographic reality removes the Greek tragedy envelope of the play. . . . [Lumet's] handling of the big [kissing] scene with the docker and his niece's suitor is right and tactful."

The ambitious but commercially unsuccessful *A View from the Bridge,* made abroad to avoid U.S. censorship and for economic reasons, would be the first instance in modern cinema of male-to-male kissing on screen. .

Location scenes for this American co-production were shot in Brooklyn, with sound stage work accomplished in Paris. The movie was distributed in Italy as *Uno sguardo dal ponte* and in France as *Vu du pont.* In 1965, Arthur Miller revamped/improved his play a great deal and it opened off-Broadway (with Robert Duvall, Jon Voight, Susan Anspach) for a 780-performance run.

261. Walk on the Wild Side (Columbia, 1962), 114 min. Not rated.

Producer, Charles K. Feldman; associate producer, Joseph Lebworth; director, Edward Dmytryk; based on the novel *A Walk on the Wild Side* by Nelson Algren; screenplay, John Fante, Edmund Morris; production designer, Richard Sylbert; set decorator, William Kiernan; costumes, Charles Le Maire; makeup, Ben Lane; music, Elmer Bernstein; songs, Mack David and Bernstein; assistant director, Floyd Joyer; sound, George Cooper; camera, Joseph MacDonald; editor, Harry Gerstad.

Cast: Laurence Harvey (Dove Linkhorn); Capucine (Hallie Gerard); Jane Fonda (Kitty Twist); Anne Baxter (Teresina Vidaverri); Barbara Stanwyck (Jo Courtney); Joanna Moore (Miss Precious); Richard Rust (Oliver); Karl Swenson (Schmidt); Donald Barry (Dockery); Juanita Moore (Mama); John Anderson (Preacher); Ken Lynch (Frank Bonto); Todd Armstrong (Lieutenant Omar Stroud); Kathryn Card (Landlady); Lillian Bronson (Amy Gerard); Adrienne Marden (Eva Gerard); Sherry O'Neil (Reba); John Bryant (Spence); Paul Maxey (Auctioneer); Virginia Holden, Barbara Hines, Elaine Martone, Pat Tiernan, Florence Wyatt (Doll's House Girls).

Hallie Gerard: I want to sit and drink with a man, not with you.
Jo Courtney: You're being perverse!" (Characters in *Walk on the Wild Side*)

Anxious to take advantage of Hollywood's liberalized production code regarding homosexuality, the major studios hurried several features into production dealing with the formerly taboo topic: *Advise and Consent, The Children's Hour,* qq.v., and *Walk on the Wild Side.* Based on Nelson Algren's racy novel, *Walk on the Wide Side* (1956), unfortunately, evolved as unintentional high camp. Shot cheaply in black-and-white, it abounded with miscast players performing inadequately or stiffly from embarrassment. A succession of five script writers worked on this major misfire. Unlike the victim of *The Children's Hour* who is branded a lesbian and kills herself for the shame the lie and her own thoughts caused, in *Walk on the Wild Side,* the lesbian is one in actuality. Her sexual orientation is shown as just another manifestation of her corruption (as a preying brothel madame). Her characterization would be a type that Hollywood would perpetuate for decades.

In the 1930s penniless Texas farmer Dove Linkhorn (Laurence Harvey) goes to Louisiana to find his sweetheart, Hallie Gerard (Capucine). Along the way, he meets slatternly Kitty Twist (Jane Fonda), a tantalizing young woman and Teresina Vidaverri (Anne Baxter), a sexually-starved Mexican widow who operates a small cafe. Eventually, the idealistic Dove finds Hallie at the Doll's House, a ritzy bordello in New Orleans's French Quarter. Although she is being kept there in fine style by tough Jo Courtney (Barbara Stanwyck), the lesbian madam, Linkhorn hopes to woo her back. When Jo realizes Hallie may slip out of her grasp, she has her thugs beat up Dove. Now an employee of the Doll's House, Kitty finds the battered Linkhorn and brings him to Teresina's. Kitty tells Hallie where Link is, which prompts her to rush to his side. The unyielding Jo, accompanied by her bodyguard Oliver (Richard Rust), follows her loved one. In the showdown, Oliver aims at Dove but accidentally shoots Hallie who dies in Link's arms.

Bosley Crowther (*New York Times*) announced, "It is incredible that anything as foolish would be made in this day and age. . . . It's as naughty as a cornsilk cigarette. . . . There is ever so slight a suggestion that the prostitute . . . is admired by the madame of the bordello. . . . But that this is any more than the admiration of an employer for a highly productive employee is a thing that only the most susceptible to press-agentry might suspect." The *Times* reviewer found Capucine "crystalline and icy," European-born Laurence Harvey as a Texan "barely one-dimensional" and silver-haired Barbara Stanwyck "like something out of moth balls as the madame."

An unimpressed British *Monthly Film Bulletin* had little tolerance for this "shop-soiled melodrama" in which the "dialogue is equally risible. . . . Since the film obviously prides itself on calling a spade a spade, it is ironic . . . [that the director and cast react] to their materials as

if they were up to their waists in a quagmire."

To be noted is that an alternative ending was filmed, but discarded. This ending had Jo's amputee husband (Karl Swenson) beating Dove and then murdering Hallie. The movie's theme song (by Elmer Bernstein and Mack David) was Oscar-nominated, but lost to *Days of Wine and Roses*.

262. **Where the Day Takes You**

(Cinetel Films, 1992), color, 92 min. R-rated.

Executive producers, Lisa M. Hansen, Marc Rocco; co-executive producer, Don McKeon; co-producer, Phil McKeon; director, Rocco; screenplay, Michael Hitchcock, Kurt Voss, Rocco; production designer, Kirk Petrucelli; set decorator, Greg Grande; assistant director, Scott Javine; sound, Bill Fiege; camera, King Baggot; editor, Russell Livingstone.

Cast: Dermot Mulroney (King); Lara Flynn Boyle (Heather); Balthazar Getty (Little J); Sean Astin (Greg); James LeGros (Crasher); Ricki Lake (Brenda); Kyle MacLachlan (Ted); Peter Dobson (Tommy Ray); Stephen Tobolowsky (Charles); Will Smith (Manny); Adam Baldwin (Black); Laura San Giacomo (Interviewer); Christian Slater (Social Worker).

A decade after *Angel* (1982) and its two sequels, qq.v., examined the microcosm of Hollywood, California street life, Marc Rocco directed this venture, filled with an intriguing cast. The 21-year-old King (Dermot Mulroney), recently paroled from jail, returns to his tinseltown haunts. He keeps together his flock of panhandling strays, who live under the Hollywood Freeway by an embankment they call the "Hole." Among his followers are the drugged out Greg (Sean Astin), a runaway from middle-class suburbia; the gun-carrying Little J (Balthazar Getty); chunky Brenda (Ricki Lake); the Texan Crasher (James LeGros); and a newcomer from Chicago, the shapely Heather (Lara Flynn Boyle). The homeless youths soon get into deep trouble with the law on a variety of charges (drug pushing, prostitution, car parts theft, etc.).

Amy Dawes (*Daily Variety*) admitted that the picture "inevitably winds up giving the runaway's life the kind of romantic-tragic scope that appeals to troubled teens. . . . [A] couple as attractive as Mulroney and Boyle still makes running like wolves look a lot more fun than high school. . . . On the other hand, she praised Rocco who "shapes some very fine performances, particularly from Mulroney, Boyle and Getty, while Steve Tobolowsky turns in a memorably chilly perf as a wealthy gay man who pays Getty for titillation."

263. Where's Poppa? (United Artists, 1970), color, 85 min. R-rated.

Producers, Jerry Tokofsky, Marvin Worth; director, Carl Reiner; based on the novel by Robert Klane; screenplay, Klane; art director, Warren Clymer; set decorator, Herbert Mulligan; costumes, Albert Wolsky; music, Jack Elliott; songs, Elliott and Norman Gimbel; second unit director, Burtt Harris; assistant director, Norman Cohen; sound, Dennis Maitland; camera, Jack Priestley; editors, Bud Molin, Chic Ciccolini.

Cast: George Segal (Gordon Hocheiser); Ruth Gordon (Mrs. Hocheiser); Trish Van Devere (Louise Callan); Ron Leibman (Sidney Hocheiser); Rae Allen (Gladys Hocheiser); Vincent Gardenia (Coach Williams); Joe Keys Jr. (Gang Leader); Alice Drummond (Woman in Elevator); Tom Atkins (Policeman in Apartment); Florence Tarlow (Miss Morgiani); Jane Hoffman, Helen Martin (Job Applicants); Barnard Hughes (Colonel Hendriks); Paul Sorvino (Owner of "Gus & Grace's Home"); William Le Massena (Judge); Michael McGuire (Army Lawyer); Rob Reiner (Roger); Israel Lang (Muthafucka); Garrett Morris (Garrett); Arnold Williams (Arnold); Buddy Butler (Buddy); Martha Greenhouse (Owner of Happy Time Farms); Jack Manning (Lawyer for Memphis Maulers); John Gilliar (Policeman in Courthouse); Rehn Scofield (Bailiff); John McCurry (Policeman in Jail Cell); April Geleta (Taxi Lady); Edward Brooks (Sheldon Hocheiser); W. Benson Terry (Cab Driver); Fuddles (Shoeshine Man).

Where's Poppa? is one of the daffiest comedies to emerge out of the 1970s Hollywood, and is now regarded as a cult classic. Not surprisingly, it was directed by Carl Reiner, who has always had a strong attraction for such irreverent farce. Once a viewer accepts the premise of the Jewish schlemiel being ruled by a whacked-out elderly mother—by comparison, Sophia of TV's "Golden Girls" is conservatively sane—then anything is believable in this crazed outing. One of the movie's other conceits has the jerk's brother, hen-pecked by a demanding wife, accidentally raping a male cop in Central Park while dressed in a gorilla suit he borrowed from his brother after his clothes were stolen earlier by park muggers. Not only is the molested policeman not upset, but he sends his assaulter roses and a thank-you note "for a wonderful evening" after the fact. To further complicate matters, the enthused lawman wants the guy's name and phone number! Taken as an example of Reiner's and the scriptwriter's outrageous humor, it is a goofy but fun premise; not the crude homophobic joke perceived by some viewers.

Poor, put-upon New Yorker Gordon Hocheiser (George Segal)! He is modest attorney dutifully caring for his aged, widowed mother (Ruth Gordon). she is a semi-senile eccentric who thrives on corn flakes laced with coca cola and thinks nothing of pulling down her son's trousers in front of his latest date to kiss his tush. He is still a bachelor because she manages to chase away any young woman who comes into his life. Gordon has attempted everything to solve the situation, even trying to frighten his mama to death. Meanwhile, he hires a new nurse, Louise (Trish Van Devere,) to care for her. When Gordon falls in love with the new nurse, he fears his mother will drive her away. Thus, he begs his married brother, Sidney (Ron Leibman), to take over responsibility for their parent. However, the latter cannot, for his wife (Rae Allen) will not permit it. In the course of rushing back and forth across Central Park one night—attempting to answer Gordon's calls for help—park muggers force Sidney into a situation of molesting an undercover vice cop in drag. Subsequently, the frazzled

George Segal, Ruth Gordon and Ron Leibman in *Where's Poppa?* (1970)

Gordon and no-longer tolerant Louise drop mama off at a nursing home and flee.

Roger Greenspun (*New York Times*) had mixed feelings about this movie, but acknowledged that it "deals with an exceptionally viable mixture of local jokes and black comedy that works as well as it does because everybody in the film possesses either enough good humor or outrageous imagination. . . ." *Variety* assessed, "Many . . . will be offended by this black comedy. . . . Many others will feel it only hurts when you laugh, and that director Carl Reiner . . . has pulled off one of the most outrageous and funniest comedies this year. . . ." In contrast, Stefan Kanfer (*Time*) was not much amused by Reiner's efforts: "His film is but a single joke, and the punch line is the commonplace twelve-letter obscenity."

Once the viewer accepts the rape as having happened (although the moviemakers make it deliberately unreal by having Sidney never remove any of his gorilla costume during the attack), the premise takes on its own reality. Thereafter, there is something wackily touching about the wife-dominated Sidney being moved by his victim's interest in him. "Long stem roses," he sighs. "I never got flowers from anyone. Such a nice man. A real human being." Clutching his bouquet of flowers, Sidney is teary-eyed at this rare display of sensitivity from a fellow New Yorker. Now, his only concern is: "Gordy, do you think I should leave my phone number?"

264. White Trash (Fred Baker Film & Video Company, 1992), color, 85 min.

Producer/director, Fred Baker; based on the play by Mel Clay; screenplay, Clay; art director, Steve Nelson; costumes, Rikki Roberts; music, Baker; assistant director, Niva Ruschell; sound/camera, Baker; editor, Robert Simpson.

Cast: John Hartman (Casino); Sean Christiansen (John [Rio]); Periel Marr (Rotten Rita); Wheaton James (Percy); Jack Betts (CC's Father); Winnie Thexton (CC's Sister); Brian Patrick (CC).

White Trash was shot on a $46,000 budget using a Hi-8 video camera, with the footage blown up to 35mm for theatrical screenings. The script hopes to be up-to-date in its language (profuse profanity and all the meandering buzz-words of teenage culture), but ends up sounding awkward and amateurish.

Three teenagers, Casino (John Hartman), John (Sean Christiansen) and Rotten Rita (Periel Marr) share a seedy Hollywood apartment. All three hustle—the two guys targeting West Hollywood gays —to support their drug habits. The trio are gloomy because their best friend, the handsome CC (Brian Patrick), another hustler, has just died of AIDS. CC had been a casual lover of Rita, and she is pregnant with his baby. Obviously, she is wondering whether she and the child-to-be have contracted CC's AIDS. Needing courage to attend their friend's funeral that day, they phone a pimp (Wheaton James) to get drugs to help them through the ordeal. The boys offer him the girl as payment, to which she reluctantly agrees. At this point CC's father (Jack Betts) and sister (Winnie Thexton), middle-class conservatives from New Jersey, arrive. After the funeral the father insists on getting to know his friends. One of the drugged-out hustlers seduces the sister, while the straight-laced father reveals an attraction to the free-wheeling lives of his son's friends. At the end, the father offers Rita the opportunity for a more normal life back on the East Coast.

Joseph McBride (*Daily Variety*) rated *White Trash* "An astringent corrective to the fairy-tale view of Hollywood street life. . . . Acting is on the semi-amateurish and mannered side, but effective nonetheless." Amy Waldman (*LA Weekly*) decided the moviemakers' "project is small-scale and even smaller-minded. . . . [What]

little plot *White Trash* possesses is told, rather than enacted by unskilled actors reciting hopelessly cliched lines." Kevin Thomas (*Los Angeles Times*) faulted the dialogue, "the more they [the characters] talk the less interesting they become, which makes us wonder why we should be concerned about their fates. . . . CC's friends all look far too healthy and wholesome for their hard lifestyles, indeed, they are too good-looking to have to work the streets."

265. Who Killed Teddy Bear?

(Magna Pictures Distribution, 1965), 90 min. Not rated.

Presenter, Marshall Naify; producer, Everett Rosenthal; director, Joseph Cates; story, Arnold Drake; screenplay, Leon Tokatyan, Drake; art director, Hank Aldrich; music/music conductor, Charlie Calello; assistant director, Sidney Kupferschmid; sound, Charles Federmack; camera, Joseph Brun; editor, Angelo Ross.

Cast: Sal Mineo (Lawrence); Juliet Prowse (Norah); Jan Murray (Bill Madden); Elaine Stritch (Billie); and: Margo Bennett, Dan Travanty, Diane Moore, Frank Campanella, Bruce Glover, Tom Aldredge, Rex Everhart, Alex Fisher, Stanley Beck, Casey Townsend.

Like the later *Who Killed Mary What'er Name?* (1971), *Who Killed Teddy Bear?* is a low-budget murder thriller filmed in New York City. Among the offbeat cast is resourceful Elaine Stritch as the lesbian disco boss. She is the tough-talking woman who keeps a watchful/lustful eye over her employee, Juliet Prowse.

When Norah (Juliet Prowse), who works at a trendy Manhattan discotheque, receives disturbingly obscene phone calls, she reports the matter to the police. Vice squad detective Bill Madden (Jan Murray) takes on the case, but becomes so obtrusive that Norah suspects he is the villain. (Actually, he has empathy for Norah, because his own wife was murdered years before by a sex maniac.) Meanwhile, good-natured Norah innocently befriends Lawrence (Sal Mineo), a club busboy, not realizing he is the perpetrator of the calls. For protection, Norah moves in with Bill and his daughter. The psychotic Lawrence tracks Norah to her new digs, voyeuristically watching her through his binoculars. One night, her boss Billie escorts Norah home, with her own agenda in mind. Nothing happens and she leaves, only to be raped and murdered by the agitated Lawrence, who mistakes her for Norah. Later, the busboy becomes bolder with Norah at the disco, letting slip that he is the disturbed caller. While fleeing, he is killed by the police.

Variety rated this an "Exploitation entry for sex market. . . . with "the action, designed strictly for shock appeal . . . Some of the footage . . . including young pervert's emotions as he dreams of his quest and his indecent murmurings as he continually telephones her, is ultra frank. . . ." As to the cast, which featured ex-teenage star Sal Mineo in a turnabout role, the trade paper reported that Elaine Stritch "delivers well in a sharp-tongued role."

This little-seen feature creates a tense atmosphere all of its own and is worth viewing for Sal Mineo's adept performance as the deeply disturbed tormentor.

266. Wild in the Streets (American International, 1968), color, 97 min. Not rated.

Executive producer, Burt Topper; producers, James H. Nicholson, Samuel Z. Arkoff; associate producer, William J. Immerman; director, Barry Shear; based on the story "The Day It All Happened, Baby" by Robert Thom; screenplay, Thom; art director, Paul Sylos; set decorator, Harry Reif; costumes, Richard Bruno; makeup, Fred Williams; music, Les Baxter; songs, Barry Mann and Cynthia Well; assistant directors, Chuck Colean, Lew Borzage; sound, Al Overton; camera, Richard Moore; editors, Fred Feitshans, Eve Newman.

Cast: Shelley Winters (Mrs. Flatow); Christopher Jones (Max Frost [Max Flatow Jr.]) Diane Varsi (Sally LeRoy); Ed Begley (Senator Albright); Hal Holbrook (John Fergus); Millie Perkins (Mary Fergus); Richard Pryor (Stanley X); Bert Freed (Max Jacob Flatow Sr.); Kevin Coughlin (Billy Cage); Larry Bishop (The Hook [Abraham Saltine]); May Ishihara (Fuji Ellie); Michael Margotta (Jimmy Fergus); Don Wyndham (Joseph Fergus); Kellie Flanagan

(Young Mary Fergus); Salli Sachse (Hippie Mother); Paul Frees (Narrator); Walter Winchell, Melvin Belli, Kenneth Banghart, Louis Lomax, Dick Clark, Jack Latham, Pamela Mason, Allan J. Moll, Army Archerd, Gene Shacove (Themselves).

It was considered quite a coup that this exploitation feature (made at a cost of $1 million) grossed $6.5 million in distributors' domestic film rentals and that it received an Oscar nomination for Best Editing (*Bullitt* won). There were several marketable aspects to this unusual picture: (1) the movie's satirical premise that people over thirty should be placed in retirement camps, (2) the outrageous campiness of Shelley Winters's shrill performance, and (3) the presence of heartthrob Christopher Jones. Little attention was paid by most to the fact that one of the hero's brain trust was gay. This plot premise was added to create additional shock value to this "with-it" feature.

Upset with his dominating mother (Shelley Winters) and his passive dad (Bert Freed), fifteen-year-old troublemaker Max Flatow (Christopher Jones) leaves home, using his drug-pushing money to make his getaway. Seven years pass. Now known as Max Frost, he is a multi-millionaire rock entertainer living in the lap of luxury in Beverly Hills. His entourage includes freaked-out girlfriend Sally LeRoy (Diane Varsi), former child prodigy/business manager Billy Cage (Kevin Coughlin) and Stanley X (Richard Pryor), a black militant. Meanwhile, California congressman John Fergus (Hal Holbrook) campaigns for the U.S. Senate, running on a youth ticket. He persuades Max to perform at a rally. There Max flippantly suggests the voting age should be lowered to fourteen. This notion receives widespread support from the flower children younger set. Max manipulates Sally's election to the Senate, and, after lacing the Senators' water with LSD, gets a vote passed removing an age requirement to hold office. Thereafter, Max—"a leader of men and little girls"— wins the election to become U.S. Presi-

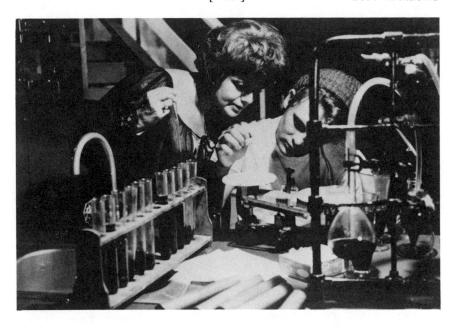

Shelley Winters and Chris Jones in *Wild in the Streets* **(1968).**

dent. Once in office, he sends all those over thirty-five—including his shrieking mother—to retirement camps where they are drugged with hallucinogens. At the end, reflecting the shape of things to come, Max annoys two seven-year-old boys by accidentally killing their pet crawfish. The angered youths agree to one day get rid of everyone over ten.

Renata Adler (*New York Times*) pegged *Wild in the Streets* "an instant classic . . . for the drive-ins in summertime. . . ." Adler was particularly taken with Shelley Winters's "wonderful exaggeration." *Variety* described the effort as "An often chilling political science fiction drama, with comedy" and that "Good writing and direction enhance the impact." In describing the cast, the trade journal mentioned "Kevin Coughlin, as a 15-year-old tax whiz and legal ace, also a teenage faggot. . . ."

As Billy Cage, the youngest graduate from Yale Law School, Kevin Coughlin's character has a 186 I.Q. He is a flashy dresser, a guitarist, and, most importantly to Max's cause, a crackerjack financial adviser. Pointing up Billy's alternative sexual lifestyle, are two brief scenes. In one, Cage says ruefully to his much-coveted, sexy leader, "Make it with girls only, huh? Some kind of crazy throwback." Frost replies, You're groovy, but you're outnumbered." A later scene at the mansion has Billy and the drugged-out Sally discussing the handsome, soon-to-be-duped Senator Fergus:

Sally: I wonder if I could get him?
Billy: I wonder if I could get him?
Sally: Isn't he too old for you?
Billy: [Wistfully] Isn't Max enough for you?

267. Windows (United Artists, 1980), color, 96 min. R-rated.

Producer, Michael Lobell; associate producer, John Nicholella; director, Gordon Willis; screenplay, Barry Siegel; production designer, Melvin Bourne; art director, Richard Fuhrman; set decorator, Les Bloom; costumes, Clifford Capone; makeup, Irving Bruckman; music, Ennio Morricone; assistant directors, Robert Colesbery, Lon Fusaro; sound, Christopher Newman; camera, Willis; editor, Barry Malkin.

Cast: Talia Shire (Emily Hollander); Joseph Cortese (Detective Bob Luffrono); Elizabeth Ashley (Andrea Glassen); Kay Medford (Ida Marx); Michael Gorri (Sam Marx); Russell Horton (Steven Hollander); Michael Lipton (Dr. Marin); Rick Petrucelli (Obecny) Ron Ryan (Detective Swid); Linda Gillin (Policewoman); Tony Di Benedetto (Nick); Bryce Bond (Voiceover); Ken Chapin (Renting Agent); Marty Greene (Ira); Bill Handy (Desk Officer); Robert Hodge (Desk Sergeant); Kyle Scott Jackson (Detective); Pat McNamara (Doorman); Gerry Vichi (Ben); Oliver (Jennifer, the Cat).

"*Windows* exists only in the perverted fantasies of men who hate lesbians so much they will concoct any idiocy in order to slander them." (David Denby, *New York*)

Gordon Willis, the acclaimed cinematographer for *Klute* (1971), two of *The Godfather* films (1972, 1974) and various Woody Allen features, made a peculiar directorial debut with *Windows*. It was a slasher feature that generated a great deal of controversy over its subject matter—a jealous lesbian gone murderously berserk in New York City. Gay and lesbian groups protested vehemently over its distorted depiction which equated homosexuality with sociopaths. However, when all was said and done, *Windows* proved to be its own worst enemy. It was crudely structured, suffered from underdeveloped character motivation and was badly acted.

Already timid and nervous, mousey workingwoman Emily Hollander (Talia Shire) is nearly raped at knife-point in her Brooklyn Heights apartment by a cab driver. Her attacker tape records her perilous ordeal. Thereafter, Emily suffers from a stuttering complex in moments of danger. Detective Bob Luffrono (Joseph Cortese) of the 12th Precinct, who investigates the case, takes more than a pro-

fessional interest in Emily. Meanwhile, poet Andrea Glassen (Elizabeth Ashley), Emily's chic, rich friend and neighbor begins spying on her through a powerful telescope, especially after Emily moves to a new apartment. It develops that the sleek Andrea is a lesbian with a disturbing fixation on her straight woman pal. It is later discovered that Andrea had hired the taxi driver to torment Emily (on two different occasions) so she could listen to the "erotic" tape recordings, adding to her voyeuristic delights of spying on Emily. Pushed out of hiding by the police dragnet, the obsessed Andrea is willing to kill the terrorized Emily at the climax. With a mere phone call, simpering, naive Emily is lured to Andrea's hideaway (with the viewer supposed to be in suspense whether the heroine will be raped, murdered or both.) However, the police rescue Emily in time. As Luffrono leads the traumatized Emily to safety, the shocked victim murmurs, "She kept telling me all night she loved me." He replies, "Well, in her dumb way, she did."

In critiquing this "*Rear Windows* for bigots," Dean Billanti (*Films in Review*) explained, "Director Gordon Willis tries every sleazy trick imaginable to establish Ashley as a big, bad lesbian, including the old chestnut about animals perceiving evil before humans—Shire's cat throws a fit when Ashley attempts to pick it up . . ." Joseph Gelmis (*Newsday*) insisted, "*Windows* isn't worth looking into . . . The level of the dialogue is moronic. . . . Elizabeth Ashley's crazed closet lesbian is so ridiculous that she evokes more guffaws than suspense when she goes on a rampage." David Ansen (*Newsweek*) insisted, "*Windows* is utterly ineffective as a thriller because the audience knows what's up practically from the start. . . . One hasn't a clue why Ashley is so tormented, why this rich, attractive woman doesn't have other girlfriends, or why she chooses Shire as the object of her amour. . . ."

Windows, filmed in New York City, would be cut to 87 minutes to remove its more blatantly offensive scenes of violence, sexual voyeurism, etc. to allow its rating to be switched from R to PG. This change still did not help this cinematic mess at the box-office. Colorful character actress Kay Medford was wasted in a gratuitous role as Shire's perplexed new neighbor. After *Windows*, Gordon Willis returned to what he did best—cinematography.

268. Without a Trace (Twentieth Century-Fox, 1983), color, 121 min. PG-rated.

Producer, Stanley R. Jaffe; associate producer, Alice Shure; director, Jaffe; based on the novel *Still Missing* by Beth Gutcheon; screenplay, Gutcheon; production designer, Paul Sylbert; art director, Gregory Bolton; set decorator, Alan Hicks; costumes, Gloria Gresham; makeup, Irv Buchman, Vince Callaghan, Allen Weisinger; music, Jack Nitzsche; assistant directors, Terry Donnelly, Robert E. Warren; sound, Jack C. Jacobson; camera, John Bailey; editor, Cynthia Scheider.

Cast: Kate Nelligan (Susan Selky); Judd Hirsch (Detective Al Menetti); David Dukes (Graham Selky); Stockard Channing (Jocelyn Norris); Jacqueline Brookes (Margaret Mayo); Keith McDermott (Phillippe Lucienne [Patrick Sullivan]); Kathleen Widdoes (Ms. Hauser); Daniel Bryan Corkill (Alex Selky); Cheryl Giannini (Pat Menetti); David Sion (Eugene Menetti); William Duell (Polygraph Operator); Joan McMonagle (Vivienne Grant); Louise Stubbs (Malvina Robbins); Deborah Carlson (Naomi Blum); Charles Brown (Sachs); Sheila M. Coonan (Anna); Peter Brash (Mr. Garrett); L. Scott Caldwell (Janet Smith); Ellen Barber (Martina); Theodore Sorel (Dr. Mandlebaum); Sam J. Coppola (Schoyer); Elaine Bromka (Production Assistant); Roger Kozo (Makeup Man); Caroline Aaron (Makeup Woman); Lee Sandman (Coffee Shop Owner); Fred Coffi (Officer Coffin); Marissa Ryan (Justine Norris); Dan Lauria (Baker); Donny Burke (Ward): Stephanie Ann Levy (Marcia Menetti) Peggy Woody, Kathrin King Segal (Girls on Movie Line): Marcella Lowery (Sergeant Rocco); Luke Sickle (Jank); Jane Cecil (Mrs. Applegate); Todd Winters (Technician); Timothy Minor (Soundman); Lynn Cohen (Woman with Dog); Kymbra Callaghan (Hairdresser); Ronald Barber (Guard); Carlotta A. DeVaughn (Correction Officer); Robert Ott Boyle, Joseph

M. Costa, Richmond Hoxie, Elizabeth Lathram, Terrance K. O'Quinn, Angela Pietropinto, Tory Wood (Parents); Don Amendolia, Tony Devon, Thomas Kopache, Lou Leccese, Mark McGovern, Steve Mendillo, Bob Scarantino, Martin Shakar, Bill Smitrovich (Police); Ashby Adams, Hy R. Agens, MacKenzie Allen, Peter Burnell, Bruce Carr, Maria Cellari, Gregory Chase, Paul Collins, Ken Cory, William Fowler, Edmund Genest, Roxanne Gregory, Gracie Harrison, Richmond Hoxie, W. H. Macy, Freda Foh Shen, James Storm, Brenda Thomas, Allan Weeks, Hattie Winston (Reporters); Phyllis Haynes, Mary Ellen McPhillips (Hosts of "Straight Talk" Show); Tom Dunn, Sara Lee Kessler (TV News Announcers); Edward O. Downes, Hugh Weisgall, Joe Mandelbaum (Guests on "Straight Talk" Show).

Despite Kate Nelligan's strong performance and the elaborate production values with its New York locations, *Without a Trace* is very antiseptic. This is especially disconcerting because, at first glance, the picture would seem to be an affecting tearjerker—about a mother refusing to abandon hope that her kidnapped little boy is still alive. (The movie, and the novel it was based on, was suggested by the 1979 actual case of six-year-old Etan Patz who permanently vanished on his way to school from his Soho, Manhattan home.) Part of the problem with *Without a Trace* is its too mechanical set-up of hints about the pending kidnapping. In addition, overly-dramatic Nelligan fails to include much vulnerability or warmth in her characterization. There are also several story-line missteps, one occurs midway through the thriller. At that point, a recurring character—the woman's occasional apartment cleaner (Keith McDermott)—is suddenly considered a suspect because (1) he is homosexual and (2) he has been seen associating with teenage hustlers known to be involved with sado-masochism.

On its own, this plotline is a change from the old Hollywood where, as in *The Boston Strangler* (1968), q.v., the gay character would be an immediate suspect. However, the lifestyle-tolerant *Without a*

Trace, does a quick about-face. The police detective (Judd Hirsch), doggedly sensitive and conscientious up to now, suddenly reveals himself to be very bigoted about the gay suspect. Glad to have the case "solved," he does no further checking to determine that the man's criminal record in college occurred only because his lover's angered parents filed a sodomy charge against him (but not against their son). The law man has no lab test performed to find out whose blood is on the remnant of the missing boy's underwear located in Philippe's possession. (Philippe claims he grabbed the clothing from a rag pile to stem the blood when he cut his finger cleaning at her house.). Then when the case is really solved—because the mother heeds a "crank" caller from Connecticut claiming to have seen the child— the movie totally ignores any apology to the wrongfully-accused suspect.

Jack Kroll (*Newsweek*), fascinated with portions of the movie, faulted it for being "about too many things, none of them explained satisfactorily." He added that "The movie lives mainly in its solid, honest performances. . . ." Linda Gross (*Los Angeles Times*) thought it "an absorbing but flawed film" but disliked the ending which "comes out of nowhere and is overplayed." Rex Reed (*New York Post*) had little patience with the film's "too many false leads, red herrings and unprofessional police procedures that don't wash." On the other hand, Reed approved of the cast, including the supporting players: "especially Keith McDermott, as the cleaning man who gets dragged through a shocking miscarriage of justice because he happens to be gay."

Without a Trace grossed an underwhelming $4.3 million in distributors' domestic film rentals.

269. Women's Prison (Columbia, 1955), 80 min. Not rated.

Producer, Bryan Foy; director, Lewis Seiler; story, Jack DeWitt; screenplay, Crane Wilbur, DeWitt; art director, Gary Odell; set decorator, Louis Diage; music director, Mischa Bakaleinikoff; assistant director, Carter De Haven Jr.; sound, George Cooper; camera, Lester H. White; editor, Henry Batista.

Cast: Ida Lupino (Amelia Van Zant); Jan Sterling (Brenda Martin); Cleo Moore (Mae); Audrey Totter (Joan Burton); Phyllis Thaxter (Helene Jensen); Howard Duff (Dr. Clark); Warren Stevens (Glen Burton); Barry Kelley (Warden Blackburn); Gertrude Michael (Sturgess); Vivian Marshall (Dottie); Ross Elliott (Don Jensen); Mae Clarke (Saunders); Adelle August (Grace); Don C. Harvey (Captain Tierney); Edna Holland (Sarah); Lynne Millan (Carl); Juanita Moore (Polyclinic Jones); Mira McKinney (Burke); Mary Newton (Enright); Diane DeLaire (Head Nurse); Jana Mason (Josie); Lorna Thayer (Deputy Sheriff Green); Murray Alper (Mug); Ruth Vann, Mary Lou Devore (Girl Patients); Eddie Foy III (Warden's Secretary).

Producer Bryan Foy and director Lewis Seiler were old hands at prison melodramas when they turned out Columbia's *Women's Prison*. This programmer was somewhat similar to Warner Bros.'s far superior *Caged* (1950), q.v. Like the Hope Emerson character in *Caged*, *Women's Prison* featured a stern female head guard, who thrived on a harsh atmosphere and by the subservient women under her domination. With all the clues provided by Ida Lupino's performance there was little doubt of Amelia Van Zant being a (repressed) lesbian.

Bewildered housewife Helene Jensen (Phyllis Thaxter) is sentenced to prison for vehicular manslaughter. Once behind bars, the frightened woman is tormented by the institution's sadistic, frigid head guard, Amelia Van Zant (Ida Lupino). The latter, frustrated by a loveless existence, bitterly resents any of her charges who have the least bit of romance in their humdrum lives. (She insists, "I know these women, all of them and only a strong mind can control them!") Several inmates— including Brenda Martin (Jan Sterling), Mae (Cleo Moore) and Joan Burton (Audrey Totter)—support Helene against the tyrannical Amelia, as does kindly prison physician, Dr. Clark (Howard Duff), who refers to Van Zant as a "borderline psychopath."

One day, Glen Burton (Warren Stevens), a prisoner in the men's section, sneaks into the women's quarters to be with his wife Joan. When, as a result, Joan becomes pregnant, the penitentiary's warden, Blackburn (Barry Kelley), fears repercussions from the prison board. In turn, Blackburn threatens Amelia with losing her post, if she doesn't discover how Glen snuck through security. Amelia interrogates Joan and, when the prisoner will not confess, she beats her severely. Joan has a miscarriage and dies. The enraged convicts revolt and hold Amelia hostage. In the showdown, the traumatized Van Zant becomes a raving maniac and is led away. Dr. Clark assures the calmed inmates that reforms will be instituted at once. Meanwhile, Helene wins her freedom.

Variety admitted, "At times the melodrama runs a bit heavy. . . . . While femme players . . . are far from glamorous in the drab prison garb, they register well in their respective assignments." A.H. Weiler (*New York Times*), agreed that the moviemakers had done a workmanlike job, but that "it's scarcely a riot or a revelation. . . ."

In retrospect, Jerry Vermilye in *Ida Lupino* (1977) cited, "*Women's Prison*, with its cardboard characters and predictable plot turns, was merely cheap sensationalism, though briskly directed by Lewis Seiler. In Lupino's capable hands, frigid Amelia Van Zant, who takes out her frustrations on the female inmates, becomes a truly hateful villainess, without any redeeming features." Jim Morton, in his essay "Women in Prison Films" for *Re/Search: Incredibly Strange* Films (1986), judged that Ida Lupino "spectacularly played" her assignment as the vicious guard matron and that her role "remains the definitive performance for all WIP [women in prison] films to follow." On the other hand, there are those

critics who regard Lupino's strident performance—with its heavy lesbian overtones—as semi-camp, just like her similar going-crazy sequence in *They Drive By Night* (1940).

Ida Lupino would play a comparable sadistic role in the TV movie, *Women in Chains* (1972).

270. Won Ton Ton, the Dog Who Saved Hollywood (Paramount, 1976), color, 92 min. PG-rated.

Producers, David V. Picker, Arnold Schulman, Michael Winner; associate producer, Tim Zinnemann; director, Winner; screenplay, Schulman, Cy Howard; art director, Ward Preston; set decorator, Ned Parsons; makeup, Philip Rhodes; music, Neal Hefti; assistant directors, Charles Okun, Arne Schmidt; sound, Bob Post; camera, Richard H. Kline; editor, Bernard Gribble.

Cast: Bruce Dern (Grayson Potchuck); Madeline Kahn (Estie Del Ruth); Art Carney (J. J. Fromberg); Phil Silvers (Murray Fromberg); Teri Garr (Fluffy Peters); Ron Leibman (Rudy Montague); Dennis Morgan (Tour Guide); Shecky Greene (Tourist); Phil Leeds, Cliff Norton (Dog Catchers): Romo Vincent (Short Order Cook); Sterling Holloway (Old Man on Bus); William Demarest (Studio Gatekeeper) Virginia Mayo (Miss Battley); Henny Youngman (Manny Farber); Rory Calhoun (Philip Hart); Billy Barty (Assistant Director); Henry Wilcoxon (Silent Film Director); Ricardo Montalban (Silent Film Star); Jackie Coogan (Stagehand #1); Aldo Ray (Stubby Stebbins); Ethel Merman (Hedda Parsons); Yvonne De Carlo (Cleaning Woman); Joan Blondell (Landlady); Andy Devine (Priest in Dog Pound); Broderick Crawford (Special Effects Man); Richard Arlen (Silent Film Star #2); Jack LaRue (Silent Film Villain); Dorothy Lamour (Visiting Film Star); Nancy Walker (Mrs. Fromberg); Gloria DeHaven (President's Girl #1); Louis Nye (Radio Interviewer); Johnny Weissmuller (Stagehand #2); Stepin Fetchit (Dancing Butler); Ken Murray (Souvenir Salesman); Rudy Vallee (Autograph Hound); George Jessel (Awards Announcer); Rhonda Fleming (Rhoda Flaming); Ann Miller (President's Girl #2); Dean Stockwell (Paul Lavell); Dick Haymes (James Crawford); Tab Hunter (David Hamilton); Robert Alda (Richard Entwhistle); Fritz Feld (Rudy's Butler); Janet Blair (President's Girl #3); Den-

Ron Leibman, Fritz Feld and Madeline Kahn in *Won Ton Ton, The Dog Who Saved Hollywood* **(1976).**

nis Day (Singing Telegraph Man); Mike Mazurki (Studio Guard); The Ritz Brothers (Cleaning Women); Jesse White (Rudy's Agent); Carmel Myers, Jack Carter (Journalists); Victor Mature (Nick); Barbara Nichols (Nick's Girl); Army Archerd (Premiere Master of Ceremonies); Fernando Lamos (Premiere Male Star); Zsa Zsa Gabor (Premiere Female Star); Cyd Charisse (President's Girl #4); Huntz Hall (Moving Man); Doodles Weaver (Man in Mexican Film); Edgar Bergen (Professor Quicksand); Morey Amsterdam, Eddie Foy Jr. (Custard Pie Stars); Peter Lawford (Slapstick Star); Patricia Morison, Guy Madison (Stars at Screening); Regis Toomey (Burlesque Stagehand); Alice Faye (Secretary at Gate); Ann Rutherford (Grayson's Studio Secretary); Milton Berle (Blind Man); John Carradine (Drunk); Keye Luke (Kitchen Cook); Walter Pidgeon (Grayson's Butler); William Benedict (Man on Bus); Dorothy Gulliver (Old Woman on Bus); Eli Mintz (Tailor); Edward Ashley (2nd Butler); Kres Mersky (Girl in Arab Film); Jane Connell (Waitress); Jack Bernardi (Fluffy's Escort); Pedro Gonzales-Gonzales (Mexican Projectionist); Eddie Le Veque (Prostitute's Customer): Ronny Graham (Mark Bennett); James R. Brodhead (Priest); Augustus Von Schumacher (Won Ton Ton, the Dog).

Won Ton Ton deserves a minor acknowledgment for rounding up so many veteran movie personalities for one picture. It is just unfortunate that no one thought of providing a proper showcase for this aging but talented assemblage. Unlike Mel Brooks's *Silent Movie* (1976), *Won Ton Ton*'s spoof of 1920s Hollywood and the rise to stardom of canine star Rin Tin Tin was a box-office turkey. One of its "satirical" premises was to have a sheik movie hero (styled after Rudolph Valentino) be gay. Like most everything else in this lumbering nostalgic excursion, the hypothesis was executed too broadly and too repeatedly to make an impact.

In 1920s Hollywood, J. J. Fromberg (Art Carney), the head of New Era Studios, is desperate for a fresh box-office attraction. Tour guide Grayson Potchuck (Bruce Dern), an aspiring studio executive, convinces Fromberg to make an Alsatian dog—recently escaped from the pound and more recently the rescuer of would-be film actress Estie del Ruth (Madeline Kahn)—the lot's new star. Potchuck directs Won Ton Ton in several hit movies and he and Estie move into a lush mansion. One day, the frustrated aspiring actress meets Rudy Montague (Ron Leibman), a movie matinee idol, at a picture palace. He has gone to the screening in his favorite disguise—as a woman. Unduly flattered by the awed Estie, the narcissistic dunce hires her to star with he and Won Ton Ton in a new movie (*Custer the Brave*), supposed to provide Rudy with a new screen image. However, the movie is a bomb and Fromberg fires everyone involved in the production. Nevertheless, Estie's unintentional comedy in *Custer* leads to her being hired as a slapstick performer and she becomes a screen sensation. Meanwhile, she and Grayson marry, but Won Ton Ton disappears. However, one day he returns. Fearing that success could ruin the animal's life twice, Estie refuses to acknowledge that this dog is indeed the former canine luminary.

Richard Eder (*New York Times*) alerted, "What saves the movie, a jumble of good jokes and bad . . . is Madeline Kahn. . . . The movie itself is an untidy, sometimes pleasant mess. . . ." *Variety* sized up the effort as a "Clumsy silent film era comedy" which "leaves no stone unturned in straining for broad, low laughs in the worst possible way. . . . [Ron] Leibman appears a travesty on Valentino, an offscreen drag queen who makes a flop film with the dog." John Pym (British *Monthly Film Bulletin*) warned, "Michael Winner does not have Mel Brooks' frenzied gift for marshalling this sort of material; and, to make matters worse, the script attains a level of parody no higher than Ron Leibman's mincing cari-

cature of Valentino, embellished with little more than the standard mannerisms of the familiar theatrical queen."

271. Young Man with a Horn

(Warner Bros., 1950), 112 min. Not rated.

Producer, Jerry Wald; director, Michael Curtiz; based on the novel by Dorothy Baker; screenplay, Carl Foreman, Edmund H. North; art director, Edward Carrere; set decorator, William Wallace; costumes, Milo Anderson; makeup, Perc Westmore; music director, Ray Heindorf; song: Sammy Cahn and Heindorf; second unit/montage director, David C. Gardner; sound, Everett A. Brown; camera, Ted McCord; editor, Alan Crosland Jr.

Cast: Kirk Douglas (Rick Martin); Lauren Bacall (Amy North); Doris Day (Jo Jordan); Hoagy Carmichael (Willie "Smoke" Willoughby); Harry James (Offcamera Trumpeter); Juano Hernandez (Art Hazzard); Jerome Cowan (Phil Morrison); Mary Beth Hughes (Marge Martin); Nestor Paiva (Louis Galba); Orley Lindgren (Rick Martin, as a Boy); Walter Reed (Jack Chandler, the Bartender); Jack Kruschen (Cab Driver); Alex Gerry (Dr. Weaver); Jack Shea (Male Nurse): James Griffith (Walt); Dean Reisner (Joe); Everett Glass (Man Leading Song); Dave Dunbar (Alcoholic Bum); Robert O'Neill (Bum); Paul E. Burns (Pawnbroker); Julius Wechter (Boy Drummer); Ivor James (Boy Banjoist); Larry Rio (Owner); Hugh Charles, Sid Kane (Men); Vivian Mallah, Lorna Jordan, Lewell Enge (Molls); Bridget Brown (Girl); Dan Seymour (Mike); Paul Dubov (Maxie); Keye Luke (Ramundo); Frank Cady (Hotel Clerk); Murray Leonard (Bartender); Hugh Murray (Doctor); Dick Cogan (Interne); Katharine Kurasch (Miss Carson); Burk Symon (2nd Pawnbroker).

"Centering around the rise and downfall of an outstanding trumpet player, *Young Man with a Horn* is a compelling drama, best suited for adult audiences. . . . Lauren Bacall, as the sophisticated neurotic [Kirk] Douglas marries, overacts the part badly." (*Harrison's Reports*)

Based on Dorothy Jordan's novel (1943), a thinly-veiled account of jazz great Bix Beiderbecke (1903–1931), *Young Man with a Horn* was diluted and distorted into a typical 1950s Warner Bros. drama. Kirk Douglas (with the great Harry James providing the actual off-camera trumpet playing) was his dimpled, intense self. Doris Day was at her usual buyont self—either smiling or being tearful, and wonderfully refreshing in her vocal interludes. On the other hand, Lauren Bacall was glum and nervous, not her usual straight-forward, independent self. She was cast as the rich dilettante who marries the trumpeter on a whim, but finds he is no substitute for what intrigues her most—other women. Since Hollywood was not yet about to call a lesbian a lesbian on screen, her sexual inclinations were left to suggestions, wistful looks, and double entendre dialogue, passed off as the rambling of a selfish erratic woman.

Through flashback, piano player Smoke Willoughby (Hoagy Carmichael) recalls how young Rick Martin (Kirk Douglas) is first attracted to music and how he learns to play the trumpet from a great black jazz musician, Art Hazzard (Juano Hernandez). By age twenty, Rick is performing with a dance orchestra on the road, becoming pals with pianist Smoke and group vocalist, Jo Jordan (Doris Day). Because Martin is so driven by his music, which he insists must be played his way (i.e. with integrity and innovation), he and Jo break up. Later, she becomes a headliner and maneuvers the down-on-his luck Martin into joining a bland big band, led by Phil Morrison (Jerome Cowan). Meanwhile, Rick remains friends with Hazzard, whose own career is declining.

Another of Jo's many friends is socialite Amy North (Lauren Bacall), who has dabbled recklessly in several careers from pre-medical to interior decorator to pilot. The meeting of Amy and Rick leads to marriage, which, in turn, leads to disaster. She tires of him, finding more diversion with a new woman friend. Rick and Amy fight and she leaves. Distraught at losing Amy and having abandoned his music, Rick turns to drink. He ends in a alcoholic ward at Bellevue Hospital where he is later found by Smoke and Jo. With their encouragement, he regains his health and re-

turns to his beloved music, content to have finally found that elusive wonderful trumpet note Hazzard always told him existed.

Time magazine warned, "[The movie] which starts out to adapt the best-selling story of a jazz musician's integrity, winds up badly in need of some integrity of its own." Thomas M. Pryor (*New York Times*) found *Young Man with a Horn* to be "a pedestrian story that is overly-long and frequently stumbles over its eloquently meaningless dialogue. . . . [But] the banalities of the script are quite effectively glossed over in the slick pictorial smoothness . . . and the exciting quality of the score. . . . Lauren Bacall has the role of the confused, mentally sick wife. It is a heavy, disagreeable part that would tax the ability of a more accomplished actress. . . ."

To suggest to filmgoers what Amy North really is, she is frequently outfitted in severe, mannish outfits. Rick Martin notes the masculine quality to her voice: "I love the sound of your voice. . . . The wonderful rough spots." With typical Hollywood instant psychological analysis, the script has Amy admit she hated her doctor father, but loved her mother (the reverse of the norm!). When Martin attempts to kiss her, she pulls away, explaining (?) "It's not you. . . . Stay away. It's my last warning. Only people who respect themselves can ever love fully, freely. I don't happen to respect myself." Even good-natured Jo Jordan cautions Rick about Amy, "She's a strange girl and you've never known anyone like her before . . . Way inside she's all mixed up." When Amy is about to leave the obsessed Rick, she confesses, "I was off the track for a while." Then she adds sadistically, "Maybe I'll go to Europe. . . . I met a girl the other day, an artist. Maybe we'll go to Paris together." If all this is not enough, the few scenes of Amy and her new friend, Miss Carson (Katharine Kurasch), confirms Amy's preference for women. Miss Carson, with her mannish severe face (and thick eyebrows), hangs on Amy's arm, courting her new friend with, "I'm dying to see the rest of your sketches. We'll have dinner out and go back to my place." Finally comprehending what he has refused to accept before, the disgusted Rick Martin scorns Amy for rejecting him for another woman. He calls her a "Big flash on the outside, but nothing inside."

Having titillated the filmgoer with this oblique depiction of a lesbian, *Young Man with a Horn* ends on a conventionally approved attitude. Rick spits as her: "You're a sick girl, Amy. You'd better see a doctor!"

272. Zorro, the Gay Blade (Twentieth Century-Fox, 1981), color, 93 min. PG-rated.

Producers, George Hamilton, C. O. Erickson; associate producers, Don Moriarty, Greg Alt; director, Peter Medak; based on the character created by Johnston M. McCulley; story, Hal Dresner, Alt, Moriarty, Bob Randall; screenplay, Dresner; production designer, Herman A. Blumenthal; art director, Adrian Gorton; costumes, Gloria Gresham; makeup, William Tuttle; music/music director, Ian Frazer; choreographer, Alex Romero; assistant directors, Daniel J. McCauley, Joseph Paul Moore, Steve McEveety; stunt coordinator, Victor Paul; sound, Larry Jost, Dan Wallin; special effects, Allen L. Hall; camera, John A. Alonzo; editor, Hillary Jane Kranze.

Cast: George Hamilton (Don Diego Vega/Bunny Wigglesworth); Lauren Hutton (Charlotte Taylor Wilson); Brenda Vaccaro (Florinda); Ron Leibman (Esteban) Donovan Scott (Paco); James Booth (Velasquez); Helen Burns (Consuela); Clive Revill (Garcia); Carolyn Seymour (Dolores); Eduardo Noriega (Don Francisco); Jorge Russek (Don Fernando); Eduardo Alcarez (Don Jose); Carlos Bravo (Luis); Roberto Dumont (Ferraro); Jorge Bolioi (Pablito); Dick Balduzzi (Old Man); Ana Eliza, Perez Bolanos (Granddaughter); Francisco Mauri (Guard); Julia Colman (Martinez); Francisco Morayta (Ramirez); Pilar Pellicer (Francisco's Wife); Owen Lee (Sergeant); Gustavo Ganem (Barman); Armando Duarte (Soldier); Norm Blankenship (Whipping Master); Frank Welker (Narrator).

"*Zorro, the Gay Blade* is reasonably entertaining for the first half hour, buoyed by George Hamilton's outlandish accent and some clever gags. Then the title character arrives on the scene, and the satire sinks into clumsy parody and petty homosexual-baiting. Such movies are pernicious. How many children will wander into this PG-rated comedy and be assaulted by its smarmy stereotypes and limp-wrist humor?" (David Sterritt, *Christian Science Monitor*)

Having satirized the vampire genre with the profitable *Love at First Bite* (1979), super suntanned George Hamilton turned to the Zorro legend, creating a heavy-handed send-up that was "dedicated to Rouben Mamoulian and the other great filmmakers whose past gives us our future." The film, set in old California, opens with an off-screen narrator alerting the audience to the pattern of humor in the film. "To the people he was a hero who would live forever in their hearts. To the landowners, however, he was a pain in the ass." So begins this childish reinterpretation of *The Mark of Zorro*, which once had been a marvelous swashbuckling showcase for Douglas Fairbanks Sr. (1920) and Tyrone Power (1940).

In 1840, dapper Don Diego Vega (George Hamilton) returns home to Los Angeles to discover that his father has died while out riding. Power-hungry Esteban (Ron Leibman), Diego's childhood friend, is now the tyrannical Alcalde and is married to Florinda (Brenda Vaccaro), whom Diego and Esteban courted as youths. Opening a secreted black coffin, Vega learns that his father was once the legendary Zorro. A letter urges Diego or his twin brother, Ramon (George Hamilton), to take over the cape, mask and sword and champion the poor peasants. However, Vega soon breaks his ankle and must rely on Ramon, who has turned up on leave from the British Navy, now using the name of Bunny Wigglesworth. (Bunny chirps, "They say the Navy makes men. Well I'm living proof they made me.") With Diego and Bunny alternating as the elusive, high-spirited Zorro, the locals cheer the masked man's return, while a hysterical Esteban vows to unmask this bothersome cavalier. Meanwhile, a comely feminist from Boston, Charlotte Taylor Wilson (Lauren Hutton), deduces that the Masked Zorros and the twin brothers may be two of the same. Later, Esteban imprisons Charlotte, hoping to lure Zorro into a trap that will reveal his identity. Vega rides to the rescue to prevent her from dying in front of the firing squad. At that very moment, Bunny, who had left to return to his Naval duties, rides onto the scene, as a gold-lame outfitted Zorro. On screen, flashes "Z End."

Sheila Benson (*Los Angeles Times*) admitted, "so much is funny, so much sweetly, maniacally innocent about George Hamilton's performance(s) . . . that you find yourself wishing passionately that the rest of the film matches it . . . It sags badly, veers out of control, then swings back again to reward you with a delicious piece of silliness." David Denby (*New York*) enthused, "The movie revives one of the pleasantly silly tricks of forties comedy—the star, playing two roles." Less entertained was Alex Keneas (*News-*

day): "As Zorro, Hamilton keeps flashing a polyurethane smile and basking in the legend. . . . Mostly he sounds like a Steve Martin Chicano who is having problems projecting his accent. As if to compensate, Leibman declaims the tyrannical Alcalde in megadecibels."

In retrospect, Vito Russo (*The Celluloid Closet*, 1987), never one to overlook a potentially inferred anti-gay slur, was amused in a positive way by *Zorro, the Gay Blade*. He reasoned: "Sequences that could have easily been offensive . . . are gently humorous. There is no cruel edge to the humor, which more often than not sends up people's ideas about gay stereotypes instead of using them to wound. . . . Bunny [Wigglesworth] is an asexual sissy who presents no threat but, like Robert Preston's Toddy in *Victor/ Victoria* [1982, q.v.], he possesses style, defiance and freedom, traits almost always denied such characters."

Made on a tight budget—even the crowd scenes are sparse!—*Zorro, the Gay Blade* grossed a substantial $5.1 million in distributors' domestic film rentals.

INDEX

References are to entry number, not pages.